Local Government Finance:

The Challenges of the 21st Century

Second Global Report on Decentralization
and Local Democracy

GOLD II
2010

United Cities and Local Governments
Cités et Gouvernements Locaux Unis
Ciudades y Gobiernos Locales Unidos

Edward Elgar
Cheltenham, UK • Northampton, MA, USA

United Cities and Local Governments
Cités et Gouvernements Locaux Unis
Ciudades y Gobiernos Locales Unidos
Avinyó 15
08002 Barcelona
www.cities-localgovernments.org

Design and Layout   MIA BCN
Proofreader   Vivian Yela
Illustrations and graphics   Gérard Fagot

CONTENTS

Published by
Edward Elgar Publishing Limited
The Lypiatts
15 Lansdown Road
Cheltenham
Glos GL50 2JA
UK

Edward Elgar Publishing, Inc.
William Pratt House
9 Dewey Court
Northampton
Massachusetts 01060
USA

A catalogue record for this book
is available from the British Library

Library of Congress Control Number: 2011936418

MIX
Paper from responsible sources
FSC® C018575

ISBN978 0 85793 976 0 (cased)

Printed and bound by MPG Books Group, UK

FOREWORD

Bertrand Delanoë
Mayor of Paris, France
President of UCLG

The 2nd Global Report on Decentralization and Local Democracy, that I have the pleasure to present you with, is dedicated to local finance. It confirms the growing role of local governments in all regions of the world. It equally demonstrates the important imbalances that can exist in the sharing of resources and responsibilities between national and local governments. These imbalances have only been worsened with the impact of the global financial and economic crisis.

Thus, everywhere in the world, local authorities have more and more responsibilities in service provision, the putting into practice of social policy, environmental management, and local development. They ensure between two thirds to a half of the public investment in OECD countries as well as in certain emerging nations –China, South Africa and Brazil.

However, if the responsibilities of local government are growing, the share of funds available to ensure these responsibilities is often inadequate, in particular in developing countries. This issue is made worse by the low level of autonomy local governments have with regard to financial management in the majority of regions.

Without autonomy and resources local democracy is crippled. Its advances, which include the free election of local representatives in the majority of countries, remain precarious and can generate a profound disillusionment which threatens to ricochet back and fissure its own democratic foundation.

This divide between responsibilities and the sharing of resources specifically impacts the attainment of the Millennium Development Goals (MDGs). In fact, it is in sub-Saharan Africa and in the least advanced countries of Asia, where the means of local governments are the weakest, that the attainment of the MDGs is lagging the most. If local governments in the European Union spend nearly 3,250 € a year per inhabitant to meet the needs of their citizens, in sub-Saharan Africa and certain countries of Asia only 24 € per inhabitant is available, and significantly less in the poorest countries.

The 2nd Global Report demonstrates that the financing of urban and local development is one of the weak links of development aid policies. With accelerating urbanization the current level of available financing does not allow for a response to the existing and ongoing "urbanization of poverty".

Our world organization, United Cities and Local Governments, has estimated that 200 billion USD is needed annually, over the next 25 years, for investment in cities of developing countries to ensure that the most marginalized communities receive essential services in order to reduce poverty and slum development.

For developed countries, the Report equally signals the constraints on local finance in responding to structural changes –aging populations, migratory fluctuations, reductions in energy use and CO_2 emissions, and risk prevention. But above all, it signals against the tendency to unload on local governments where they are not directly responsible, a disproportionate weight of budgetary and financial deficits through the assigning of new responsibilities without the necessary funding.

I can only support the conclusions of this Report on the need to establish new political regulations between central and local governments in each country, as well as at the world level. A strengthened dialogue between the different levels of government is therefore indispensable so as to ensure a better sharing of means and competencies, a better balance between democracy and solidarity, two pillars on which the future of our countries, cities and populations is balanced, two principles based in the cardinal notions of justice and responsibility.

Bertrand Delanoë

EDITORIAL PROJECT

Publishers

- **Director:** Elisabeth Gateau, Secretary General, UCLG
- **Deputy Director:** Alberto Laplaine Guimarãis, Deputy Secretary General, UCLG
- **Principal Adviser:** Emilia Sáiz, Chief of Staff, Director of Statutory Issues and Institutional Relations, UCLG
- **Coordination:** Edgardo Bilsky, Director of Programmes and Research, UCLG
- **Coordination Assistant:** Claire Frost, Project Officer, UCLG
- **Support team from UCLG:** Dominique Arrestat, Pere Ballester, Mohamed Boussraoui, Jean-Baptiste Buffet, Sandra Climent, Alexis Demko, Sara Hoeflich, Ricardo Martínez, Mónica Mora, Carole Morillon, Thibaut Nancy, Natalène Poisson, Marie-Laure Roa, Maya Sawmy, Elisabeth Silva, Renske Steenbergen
- **Interns:** Justine Delefortrie, Eugénie Monasterio, Elsa Payan

Steering Committee

UCLG Regional and Metropolitan Sections

- Don Borut, Secretary General, UCLG North America
- Jean-Pierre Elong Mbassi, Secretary General, UCLG Africa
- Josep Roig, Secretary General, Metropolis
- Rassikh Sagitov, Secretary General, UCLG Euro-Asia
- Guillermo Tapia, Secretary General, FLACMA, UCLG Latin America
- Frédéric Vallier, Secretary General, Council of European Municipalities and Regions (CEMR), UCLG Europe
- Peter Woods, Secretary General, UCLG Asia Pacific
- Selahattin Yildirim, Former Secretary General, UCLG Middle East & Western Asia

Experts Coordination

- Jorge Martínez-Vázquez, Regents Professor of Economics and Director of International Studies, Andrew Young School of Policy Studies, Georgia State University, U.S.A.
- Paul Smoke, Professor of Public Finance and Planning and Director of International Programs, New York University / Robert F. Wagner Graduate School of Public Service, U.S.A.

Principal Partners

- William Cobbett, Manager, Cities Alliance
- Àngel Cortadelles i Bacaria, Director General of International Relations, Generalitat de Catalunya, Spain
- Sandrine Delibiot, Director of International Relations and Marketing, Public and Wholesale Banking, Dexia Bank
- Antoni Fogué, President of the Diputación de Barcelona and of the UCLG Committee on Decentralization and Local Self-Government, Spain
- Nathalie Le Denmat, Director of Local Governments and Urban Development, French Development Agency – Agence Française de Développement (AFD), France

Regional Advisers

- Sandra Ceciarini, Director of Citizenship and International Cooperation, CEMR
- Rudi Hauter, Associate to the Secretary General, UCLG Asia Pacific
- Christopher Hoene, Director of Research, National League of Cities, U.S.A.
- Souleymane Maiga, Chief of Staff, UCLG Africa
- Néstor Vega, Academic Coordinator, FLACMA, UCLG Latin America
- Cenk Tikiz, General Coordinator, UCLG Middle East & Western Asia

ACKNOWLEDGMENTS

Main authors by chapters

Introduction

- Jorge Martínez-Vázquez, Andrew Young School of Policy Studies, Georgia State University, U.S.A.
- Paul Smoke, New York University / Robert F. Wagner Graduate School of Public Service, U.S.A.

Africa

- François Yatta, Independent Researcher, Niger
- François Vaillancourt, Université de Montréal, Canada

Asia Pacific

- Blane D. Lewis, Lee Kuan Yew School of Public Policy, National University of Singapore, Singapore
- Bob Searle, Independent Consultant and former head of Australia's Grants Commission, Australia

Eurasia

- Natalia Golovanova, Center for Fiscal Policy (Moscow), Russia
- Galina Kurlyandskaya, Center for Fiscal Policy (Moscow), Russia

Europe

- Luiz de Mello, Economics Department, Organisation for Economic Co-operation and Development (OECD)

Latin America

- Jorge Martínez-Vázquez

Middle East & Western Asia

- Mehmet Tosun, University of Nevada, U.S.A.

North America

- William F. Fox, University of Tennessee, U.S.A.
- Enid Slack, University of Toronto, Canada

Financing Metropolitan Areas

- Roy Bahl, Andrew Young School of Policy Studies, Georgia State University, U.S.A.

Conclusions

- Jorge Martínez-Vázquez
- Paul Smoke

Other Contributors

All UCLG sections, the *Partenariat pour le Développement Municipal* (PDM) based in Cotonou, Benin for West and Central Africa and the *Municipal Development Partnership* (MDP) based in Harare, Zimbabwe for East and Southern Africa collaborated in the collection of data and information.

Special acknowledgments for financial and advisory support

Generalitat de Catalunya

Diputació de Barcelona

Agence Française de Développement (AFD)

Cities Alliance

DEXIA Group

1. Introduction

Jorge Martínez-Vázquez,
Georgia State University, USA

Paul Smoke,
New York University, USA

Local governments around the world today play a key role in facilitating development and improving living standards. As more robust governance mechanisms are adopted and civil society develops even where they have historically been weak, local governments have grown to operate in an increasingly open and responsive manner. Today they are considered by many central governments to be important partners in dealing with a range of public policy issues and functions, including building more efficient and equitable social service systems and providing significant portions of key infrastructure that supports economic development and improves the quality of life.

The road to this point, however, has been far from smooth or easy, and many challenges to effective local governments persist to various degrees. Decentralization has been uneven and has faced major obstacles. In many countries intergovernmental systems remain problematic in various respects, and local governments are not adequately equipped to perform their functions well and to become more effective partners of higher level governments in meeting pressing common goals.

This report builds on the 2008 First Global Report on Decentralization and Local Democracy (GOLD I), which provides a broad based overview of local government systems around the world. GOLD II focuses on a specific aspect of decentralization —the fiscal architecture and performance of local governments. This topic was chosen for GOLD II because fiscal architecture is fundamental to ensuring that local governments can deliver public services and function successfully in meeting other essential responsibilities.

Increasing fiscal decentralization (measured as the subnational share of total national public expenditures) has been a global trend in recent decades. There are, however, significant variations across and within regions. Local budgets account on average for 25 percent of public expenditures in the European Union, for example, but less than 5 percent in many developing countries. If fiscal decentralization is evaluated in terms of expenditure and revenue autonomy, there has been progress, but it has been uneven across countries and generally less robust on the revenue side. Global experiences also demonstrate that intergovernmental fiscal relations are not fixed —they tend to evolve with social, political, economic, demographic and technological forces that affect the overall role of the public sector.

GOLD II takes the pulse of the current state of the local public finances around the world with the main goal of identifying and analyzing the principal challenges that local governments face in providing public services more efficiently and equitably. The report also offers concrete recommendations for priority policy reforms regionally and globally.

Why is Local Government Finance Important?

The potential importance of local government finance is based on two main pillars. The core rationale is that local governments are well positioned to improve how public resources are used and the extent to which diverse citizen needs are satisfied. The second justification is the role that local governments could potentially play in dealing with several significant contemporary global challenges that broadly, although differentially, affect virtually all countries.

The Core Rationale

The conventional case for decentralization is grounded on two basic propositions. The first is that local governments are closer to the people than the central governments, and they have superior access to local information that allows them to respond better to the needs of citizens. The second is that they face stronger incentives to perform well on local matters than the central government, so that they are in a better position to derive the most from public resources at their disposal and are more likely to seek innovative means of doing so. These two propositions are related: access to local information and incentives to use it well must work synergistically to produce better results.

Although the value of local governments in this regard is well recognized, and there is some supporting if uneven empirical evidence, there are caveats. Close collaboration and innovative institutional arrangements are needed between local governments and higher levels of government to provide services that involve economies of scale or affect multiple local governments.

Equally important, the validity of the two basic propositions regarding the benefits of local governments depends on meeting fundamental requirements. At a minimum, there must be sufficient autonomous local government powers and resources, satisfactory local technical and managerial capacity, and adequate incentives (electoral and beyond) for local governments to be held accountable to their constituents and to behave in a fiscally responsible manner. Central governments can play a role in helping local governments to meet these requirements, but this requires time and ongoing support in countries where they are not in place. Thus, appropiate implementation —the sequencing and pace—of intergovernmental fiscal reforms is just as important as sound design.

Global Challenges and the Role of Local Governments

In addition to the general desirability of decentralization if appropriately designed and implemented, a number of specific and interrelated global trends present great challenges to individual countries and the broader international community and reinforce the potentially important role of local governments. First, the world is facing multiple environmental and resource crises, such as global warming, energy shortages and food security concerns, which have emerged prominently in domestic and global policy circles in recent years. These crises individually and collectively impact local governments in very specific ways, but local governments may also be in a strong position to help respond to them.

Second, increasing urbanization (see Figure 1.1), which exacerbates the crises mentioned above and generates great public service needs, is a pervasive global trend, especially in developing countries. A majority of the world's residents now live in urban areas, and the share is expected to exceed 60 percent by 2030.[1] According to the United Nations (UN), 95 percent of the urban growth in the next two decades is expected to be in Asia, Africa and to a lesser extent in Latin America, and it will be focused in small and medium sized cities. Rapid urban growth also implies an increasing urbanization of poverty. If current trends persist, one out of five persons will live in urban slums by 2030. The struggle to meet the Millennium Development Goals and advance the global fight against poverty may be won or lost primarily in the urban areas of developing countries. Increasing urbanization also creates a need for innovative mechanisms to govern and serve metropolitan areas that are growing in size, complexity and number. Developing sound intergovernmental relations and an appropriate fiscal architecture in metropolitan areas present daunting challenges because many different governments and public enterprises are typically involved in service provision in

1. *United Nations Department of Economic and Social Affairs Population Division*

Figure 1.1: Expected Urban Growth Between 2002-2015

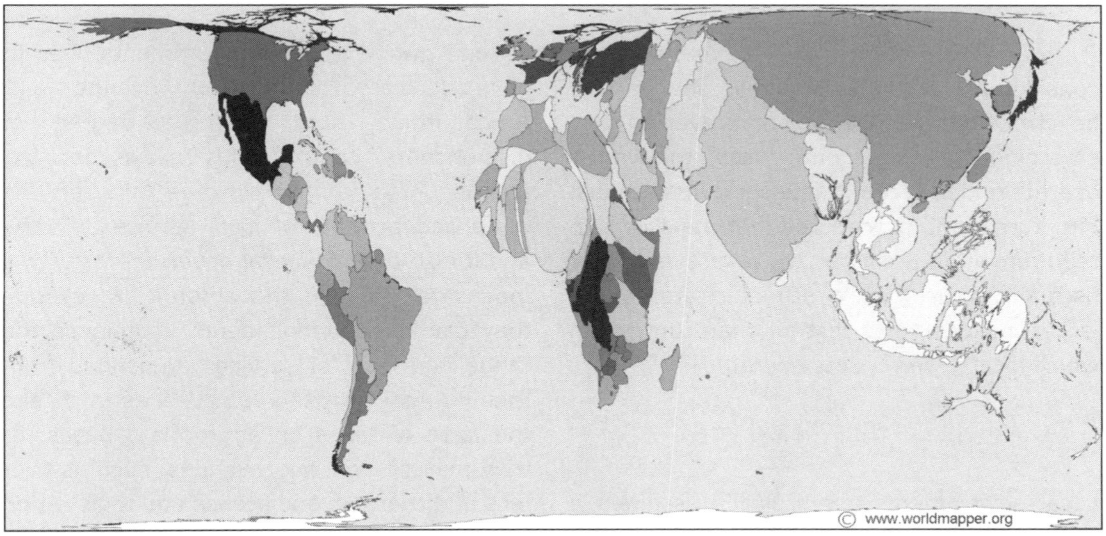

Note: Territory size shows the proportion of all extra people that will start living in urban areas between 2002 and 2015, in each territory.

Source: World Mapper; City Growth (2005)

a metropolitan area. Despite the challenges, some analysts believe that local governments can play an important role in meeting the demands of urbanization and metropolitan governance.

Third, many countries around the globe face a considerable backlog of infrastructure demands and anticipate the emergence of new ones, in great part because of urbanisation. Addressing the challenges of urbanization and the growth of large metropolitan areas lacking adequate basic infrastructure will require substantial investments in the coming decades, often in sectors for which local governments have major responsibility. According to one estimate, investment in infrastructure and basic services in the order of 200 billion USD annually will be required over the next 25 years to meet these shortfalls.[2] The demand will be greatest in developing countries, but advanced industrialized countries must also invest to deal with their aging populations and infrastructure. Special local investments in resilient infrastructure will be needed in many countries that face a growing risk of natural disasters.

Finally, the global financial and economic crisis that began in 2008 is deeper than anything experienced since WWII in terms of employment, income, and financial wealth losses.[3] The crisis has distressed practically all central governments around the world and it has affected most local governments in some ways as well. At the same time, there is considerable diversity in how local governments across different countries have fared. While some local governments have seen their funding cut and all types of expenditures reduced, others have actually experienced a growth in funding and have increased certain types of expenditures. In some countries, local governments may be able to play a significant role in mitigating the effects of the global financial crisis.

2. *World Bank (2005) estimated the investment needs in public infrastructure in developing countries, amounting to 600 billion USD per year over the next 25 five years. However, these figures include all public infrastructures, whether national (energy, communications and information technology, transport; water and sanitation, etc.) or urban (local roads, local water supply, and sanitation, waste disposals, schools, street lightning...).(World Bank. 2005. "Infrastructure and the World Bank: A progress report", The World Bank). The UCLG Committee on Local Finance estimated one third of this amount, i.e. 0.4 percent of World GDP, needs to be channeled to urban infrastructure (UCLG. 2007.* UCLG Policy Paper on Local Finance, *UCLG)*

3. *UCLG, The Impact of the Crisis on Local Governments. (UCLG. 2009.* "China", The Impact of the Global Crisis on Local Government. *UCLG).*

The Structure and Requirements of Local Government Finance Systems

If local governments are to realize their considerable potential in public service and help to effectively deal with prevailing and emerging challenges and crises, they must operate under a legal framework, institutional structures, and procedures that meet certain requirements. Some of these are explicitly fiscal in nature, while others relate to the larger political and institutional context in which local governments operate.

Core Elements of the Fiscal System

Local governments are typically assigned a range of service delivery and other key functions by constitutional or legal provisions. It is generally accepted that these functions should be appropriate in terms of their relevance for localities and their suitability for local implementation. There is also general agreement that clarity of functional assignment is important to ensure that local governments and their constituents have a consistent understanding of local responsibilities. Sufficient expenditure autonomy is considered critical so local governments can respond to local needs.

Local governments also need access to funds to discharge their functions and to meet evolving expectations of their constituents. Central governments have a comparative advantage in revenue generation, so a major portion of local resources is often derived from shared taxes and intergovernmental transfers. Transfers can be unconditional or conditional, and they may be used for recurrent and capital spending. Transfers should be funded by a stable and predictable pool of resources and allocated by appropriate criteria or formulae. The balance between conditional and unconditional transfers may vary in different contexts, but some unrestricted resources allow local governments to exercise the autonomy that is central to their own comparative advantage in service delivery.

Beyond transfers, local governments need to have dedicated sources of revenue over which they must have a degree of discretionary control. This allows for the creation of a tangible linkage between the costs and benefits of local service delivery, and it also provides local governments with a means to increase the amount of revenue they can raise independently to finance the range and level of services demanded from them. Local own-source revenues may take the form of taxes on appropriate bases, or they may be non-tax revenues, such as user fees and charges, and license and registration fees, among others.

Finally, as intergovernmental fiscal systems mature, local governments need to have adequate access to infrastructure finance. Some development spending can be funded with transfers, but eventually local governments, particularly in urban areas, need access to the capital market, whether directly or, in less advanced systems, through intermediary institutions with some government involvement. Local borrowing, however, needs to be governed by a suitable framework and adequate fiscal responsibility safeguards.

Non-Fiscal System Requirements

The focus of this report is on finance, but other aspects of intergovernmental systems covered in GOLD I are critical to ensuring effective local governments. As noted above, accountability is central to attaining the potential benefits of decentralization. This is often framed as the political dimension of decentralization, and the mainstream "gold standard" for accountability is regular democratic elections. Not all countries have or want free and competitive local elections, however, and other mechanisms that allow for citizen engagement with local governments —public access to information, feedback, and complaint mechanisms, etc.— can improve accountability. Moreover, local elections alone are a rather blunt accountability instrument, and non-electoral mechanisms can play a critical role in enhancing local accountability even where elections are well established.

Institutional dimensions of decentralization are also extremely important. Local governments need appropriate organizational structures, well-defined systems and procedures for managing public resources, and suitable frameworks and mechanisms for engaging with other levels of government, private sector firms and nongovernmental actors. Moreover, local governments must possess or be able to develop the capacity needed to properly operate within the institutional framework.

Although these political and institutional aspects of local government systems were covered in GOLD I and are not given primary attention in this report, their role in making fiscal decentralization effective cannot be over-stated. Without adequate accountability mechanisms, appropriate operational systems and sufficient capacity, autonomous local fiscal powers can lead to problematic rather than productive outcomes.

The Global Reality of Local Government Finance Systems

Some countries have long had robust local finance systems with strong development of the components outlined above, and many others have taken steps to develop systems in recent years. At the same time, all countries —from the most advanced industrial to the most fragile developing— face various challenges illustrated throughout GOLD II. Some challenges are related to weak system development and capacity constraints, particularly in developing countries, or more generally to resource shortfalls. Other challenges are external to the finance system but affect demands placed on it and the way it functions.

System Challenges and Dilemmas

Many elements of local finance systems outlined above do not exist, are incomplete, or have been implemented inconsistently with the underlying framework, particularly in developing countries. Fiscal frameworks range from well to poorly designed (relative to normative principles and contextual realities) in terms of revenue and expenditure assignments, correspondence between revenues and expenditures, transfers, subnational borrowing frameworks, etc. More broadly, overall constitutional and legal frameworks for local government (with respect to legal status, political mechanisms, empowerment, administrative and staffing structures, etc.) range from being well developed to barely having begun.

A common problem with fiscal systems is insufficient clarity in the assignment of local government expenditure responsibilities. Even where responsibilities are reasonably well defined in more advanced systems, expenditure challenges may be created by unfunded mandates from higher level governments and the lack of well developed methodologies and practices to translate expenditure assignment responsibilities into quantifiable resource needs. Degrees of autonomy in expenditure decisions also vary widely.

An overarching challenge with service provision in a multi-level government system is which functions should be undertaken at each level and how levels should interact, including the metropolitan governance issues outlined above. These are tough decisions since there is a common trade-off between fiscal viability at higher levels and political connectivity at lower levels. In struggling to achieve a balance, countries must consider the benefits and pitfalls of amalgamation versus division, as well as the potential value of creating mechanisms to bridge jurisdictional fragmentation, such as the use of special districts and/or frameworks for voluntary joint initiatives across local governments.

Progress has been made in developing tax sharing and intergovernmental transfers, but problems persist. Transfers may be inadequately or unreliably funded, and the criteria used to allocate resources may be unclearly specified or inappropriate. Despite growing fiscal disparities across localities in much of the world, few countries use genuine equalization grants to increase parity in access to basic services across communities, some of which have low revenue capacity or high spending needs due to demographics or other factors beyond their control. Where equalization grants exist, they may be poorly funded or undermine incentives for local tax efforts or expenditure efficiency. Many countries also struggle with the right balance between unconditional grants, which promote autonomy, and conditional grants, which ensure attention to national priorities.

Challenges to local revenue generation are particularly pervasive. Although there is more agreement about the need for strong expenditure autonomy than there is for revenue autonomy, some discretion is seen as necessary to promote local accountability. Even where taxes that are widely considered to be appropriate local sources, such as the property tax, are allowed, they may not be well used. The property tax is a difficult and expensive tax to administer and tends to be especially unpopular among taxpayers. Even when it is relatively well administered, its revenue potential may be limited, and other productive revenue sources have often not been assigned to local governments.

Only a few countries in more developed regions have robust systems of local government development finance. Many countries implement capital conditional grant programs and local governments dedicate a large share of resources to financing investments, but the longer-term response to the needs outlined above must include enhancing responsible access to credit for local governments. Some countries have successfully operated financial intermediaries for local governments, but this approach has faced challenges and has been undermined by political pressures in many cases.

These challenges to developing robust local finance systems, and in some countries poor local government performance, have led to instances of backtracking on decentralization. Since the publication of GOLD I there has been an emerging recentralization trend in some countries around the world. Disappointing performance in emerging systems, however, may result from expecting too much too quickly from nascent local governments and failing to adequately support building their capacity to fulfill the roles expected of them.

External Challenges

A number of major phenomena outlined earlier —natural resource crises (environmental, energy, food security), urbanization, infrastructure shortfalls, and the global financial crisis— were framed as problems that local governments could contribute to alleviating. At the same time, it is important to recognize that they also pose considerable challenges to local governments. Dealing with them effectively will require more resources, greater technical expertise, and considerable ability to negotiate complex issues with a range of interested parties with varying degrees of power. Thus, the extent to which local governments could take action to respond to these serious global threats to development depends on the extent to which they are properly equipped and supported to do so.

In this regard, it is important to note that some central governments seem not to understand their own critical role in providing an environment conducive to local government action intended to meet these challenges. On the contrary, the tendency towards recentralization in some countries seems to have been exacerbated by the response to the world financial and economic crisis. Central governments in a number of African, Latin American, and Eurasian countries have adopted policies of unilaterally interrupting the disbursement of revenue sharing and other transfers. In other cases, central governments have increased control over funding allocations or mandates over how local governments must spend resources.

The Diversity of Experience

Although local government finance is important in many countries and some basic commonalities and challenges as outlined above can be identified, it is important to keep in mind that there are also important differences across regions and countries. As reported in GOLD I, there is great variation around the world in how local governments are structured and empowered. GOLD II demonstrates in more detail that there is also extraordinary variety in how the fiscal architecture of local government is organized and performs both across different regions and among countries within each region.

Historical roots and trajectories have a lot to do with how local government systems are structured and the roles they play. In much of Latin America, for example, the influence of centralized colonial regimes can be seen, particularly on fiscal matters. At the same time, some large countries, such as Argentina and Brazil, have long traditions of provincial governance, and local governments have, with various interruptions, been more important in Latin America than in other non-OECD regions. In the Middle East and Western Asia, the strong influence of the Ottoman Empire can be seen in still heavily centralized systems, fiscal and beyond, that prevail throughout countries in the region.

A number of regions exhibit considerable intraregional variation. Although centralized systems have dominated the Asia-Pacific region, diversity is evident. Some countries were colonized by Britain (e.g. India and Malaysia) and others by France (e.g. Cambodia and Vietnam), with a few outlier influences (e.g. Spain/U.S. in the Philippines and the Netherlands in Indonesia). Some countries, such as China and Thailand, were never colonized for extended periods. Their systems draw on their own as well as borrowed traditions. Australia and New Zealand differ from other Asia-Pacific countries in that both were British colonies where descendants of colonists stayed and co-existed with indigenous people, institutionalizing but adapting colonial governance conventions. These various influences have resulted in a great variety of local government structures and fiscal systems in the region.

The countries in Eurasia started in fundamentally similar positions with the same initial system of administration and fiscal architectures inherited from the former Soviet Union, but they have opted to reorganize their local governance systems quite differently. In the Africa region, there is a stark contrast between the centralized local administration traditions of former French colonies in West and Central Africa and the strong local government traditions left by the British in East and Southern Africa, although the latter were often weakened in the post colonial period. There has been considerable effort to decentralize and strengthen local governments across the region, and in many countries there is now a mixture of the local administration and local government traditions.

In Europe, many countries show rich decentralization experiences with strong institutional underpinnings, but the systems vary considerably and face significant policy challenges. In North America, Canadian and U.S. local governments play an important role in the public sector, but they are creatures of intermediate governments (provinces or states) rather than the national government. This leads to internal diversity since each province/state has separate local government legislation, a situation which also occurs in some other countries in other regions, such as Argentina, Australia and India. In the U.S., there is a particularly complex local government structure with thousands of counties, and tens of thousands of sub-county general-purpose governments and special-purpose districts.

These governance traditions across regions, of course, have been subject to evolving political and economic forces over the years that have resulted in many changes to the systems, including to the fiscal architecture. At the same time, the influence of these traditions persists in both obvious and subtle ways. In moving forward with future reforms, it is important to be aware of the nature and strength of this influence and what it implies for the pursuit of viable and sustainable local government finance reforms.

Summary of the GOLD II Mission and Organization of the Report

It is not too dramatic to state that local government finance systems around the world are currently at a crossroads. Efforts to decentralize and more fully empower local governments have been prominent, but they have encountered a variety of challenges, both relatively universal and fairly specific to particular regions and countries. The overall situation has been exacerbated by the emergence of a number of prominent and consequential crises –environmental, economic, and financial– in recent years.

Times of crisis present an opportunity to reflect on how local government finance systems work and how they can be improved. There is, of course, the possibility of overreacting during crises and making shortsighted and ultimately problematic decisions, both small and large, for the sake of getting through difficult times. Such opportunistic reforms may alleviate immediate problems but are likely to ultimately undermine the ability of local governments to meet their responsibilities in effective and sustainable ways.

Moving forward with the reform of local government finance requires systematic analysis of the positive and negative aspects of current intergovernmental systems, as well as careful consideration of how local governments can be empowered and supported to play a more productive role. This introduction has broadly outlined some of the key issues and options that need to be considered on this front. The rest of this report considers these issues and options more deeply at the regional and global levels.

The following chapters focus on specific UCLG regions: Africa (Chapter 2), Asia-Pacific (Chapter 3), Eurasia (Chapter 4), Europe (Chapter 5), Latin America (Chapter 6),

Middle East and Western Asia (Chapter 7) and North America (Chapter 8). Each of these chapters reviews the local government finance systems in the target region and the contexts in which they are operating. The chapters outline intergovernmental systems, with a focus on describing and analyzing the fiscal aspects. Positive and problematic features of local government finance are summarized, and specific opportunities and challenges are highlighted. Finally, each regional chapter closes with a summary of the main issues and regional specific policy recommendations and issues for further investigation.

It is important to note that the regions covered in these chapters vary in terms of the number of countries included and the level and quality of information available. Thus, some chapters cover a greater proportion of countries than others, and in some cases more attention was given to countries for which better information was available.

Following the regional chapters, Chapter 9 focuses on the special circumstances and challenges of Metropolitan Areas across regions. Finally, the report concludes with an overall summary of key findings in Chapter 10. The final chapter also provides general advice for broad-based policy reforms and future work needed to more fully understand local government finance and to develop and support more detailed reforms both globally and in specifications and countries.

2. Africa

François Yatta,
Independent Researcher, Niger

François Vaillancourt,
Université de Montréal, Canada

The majority of African countries have made progress with decentralization in recent years, particularly at the policy and political level. As indicated in the GOLD I report, local governments today are an important part of the institutional landscape. They are taking on more and more responsibilities and their actions have progressively become an increasingly important part of the day-to-day lives of citizens. Reforms to reinforce local governments continue to be undertaken and are expected in a number of different countries; such as strengthening their financial resources and gaining freedom in raising and using these resources.

However, countries have progressed at different rates and rarely has the path been linear. In Gabon, for example, the decentralization process began in 1996, but transfer of responsibilities did not begin until 2009. In many countries this process is also facing difficulties. Globally, the share of public expenditure managed by local government remains low. The implementation of decentralization policies is half hearted and certain national governments are taking steps backward. In Mali and Burkina Faso, the principle of the simultaneous transfer of responsibilities and resources, was recently questioned. In Uganda, the management of local personnel has been recentralized and the status of the capital city has been modified in order to create a metropolitan authority, whose governing body is appointed by the central government. In Malawi and Togo, local elections have been suspended for long periods and centrally appointed officials manage local governments (the practice since 1999 in Malawi). In some countries, the share of the revenues of local government coming from national resources has decreased in recent years (Benin, Côte d'Ivoire, Mali, Senegal, Tanzania, Togo and Uganda).

The African continent is currently faced with rapid urbanisation rates (3.2 percent per year on average for the period of 2005-2010, UNFPA 2007). However the development of a large metropolis and medium size cities is accompanied, to varying degrees, by serious service deficits and slum expansion. In 2007, the United Nations estimated that 72 percent of the urban population of sub-Saharan Africa lived in slums (ibid). Improving the quality of life for these populations, and specifically improving access to basic services is indispensable to ensure economic development and to reinforce social and political stability. These challenges must be met by local authorities, working hand in hand with national leaders across Africa.

To respond to this challenge, local authorities need appropriate and sufficient resources and responsibilities. In this chapter, the situation of local finances is examined for a sample of African countries, including Algeria, Cameroon, Kenya, Mauritania, Morocco, South Africa, Zambia and Zimbabwe. The chapter is divided into five main sections: the macroeconomic context; the description of local financial systems; an analysis of the main problems of fiscal decentralization; the impact of the 2008-2009 financial crisis and finally recommendations for improving the financial circumstances of local governments in Africa.[1]

Macroeconomic and Financial Framework of Fiscal Decentralization

Fiscal decentralization in Africa, like anywhere else in the world, is strongly conditioned by the macroeconomic and financial situation of countries. The overall low level of public spending has a direct negative impact on the funding of local management and on fiscal decentralization.

Africa has seen renewed high growth in the last decade; an average GDP growth rate of around 5.5 percent in recent years, with a reduction to 2 percent in 2009 due to the economic and financial crisis. According to the

1. *The Africa chapter of the GOLD II report draws primarily on data from 24 countries collected by UCLG, completed with data from recent research and publications.*

African Development Bank[2], this growth –prior to the world financial crisis— was mainly due to the increase in oil exports and the oil price shock that pushed up the growth rates of oil-producing countries like Angola, Nigeria, Sudan, and Chad. Nevertheless, non-oil producing countries have also experienced high median growth rates.

The economic recovery, however, continues to be tenuous. Development and structural growth is extremely vulnerable to natural and external shocks over which African countries have no control. In addition, Africa is struggling to increase its share of international trade. Just before the implementation of the structural adjustment programs, designed to bring Africa in line with the rest of the world, 12 percent of world trade was from the African region. This figure slipped to 9 percent in the 1990s, and is likely lower at present.

In addition, the region continues to suffer from poverty. Recent projections suggest the poverty rate in Africa will exceed 38 percent in 2015, which is significantly higher than the 22.3 percent Millennium Development Goals (MDGs) target. To achieve the MDGs goal of halving poverty by 2015, the continent needs to increase and sustain annual growth at between 7 percent and 8 percent.

Fiscal decentralization is suffering from the difficult financial situation most African countries are in today. Although revenue generation by African countries has been gradually improving since the early 2000s, following four decades of stagnation, the future outlook is not bright. Trade liberalization has had a direct impact on public finances, especially on tax revenues.[3]

Even with the completion of fiscal transition, as countries move to less reliance on trade taxes and more reliance on internally generated revenue, analysts are questioning whether the expected incomes from an extended implementation of the value added tax (VAT) can replace reductions in customs duties. The possible revenue loss would impact public spending and consequently social programs, especially in health and education. In Congo, for example, the simulated loss of customs revenue from application of the Economic Partnership Agreement (EPA) with the European Union is equivalent to total public expenditure on education.[4]

This change in public finances has occurred along with the further deterioration of fiscal balances.[5] Despite their success in mobilizing resources, African countries are struggling to cover their primary expenditure, as well as their contribution to investment and the interest expenses of domestic and foreign debt. In three regional groups out of five (Central Africa, West Africa and North Africa) the average fiscal balance has moved from deficit to surplus since 2005 as a result of better management of public finances and taxation. The improved situation in North Africa was due to oil-exporting countries with higher oil prices and increased production. These countries posted a surplus budget balance of approximately 5 percent of GDP. However, countries such as Egypt, Sudan, and Tunisia have seen their deficits increase. The budget position of Central Africa improved as a result of the recovery of its principal economy, Cameroon, and the oil revenue from Gabon, Congo, and Equatorial Guinea. In West Africa, the reported improvement corresponds to the implementation of macroeconomic reforms, even if the surplus is due to Nigeria's oil resources. In the other two regions (East and Austral Africa), a recovery seems to be taking more time.

Local Governments Structures and Local Financial System in Africa

In this broader context, local finance systems have received growing interest across Africa. In West and Central Africa piloting mechanisms

2. *African Development Bank (AfDB), Development Centre of the Organisation for Economic Co-Operation and Development, and United Nations Economic Commission for Africa: African Economic Outlook.*
3. *Free trade agreements have generated major consequences: At the bilateral level, under partnership agreements between African-Caribbean-Pacific countries and the European Union, removal of duties on imports would reduce total tax revenues in the Gambia and Cape Verde by 20 percent and in Ghana, Rwanda, Mauritius and Senegal by 11 percent. In the West African Economic and Monetary Union (WAEMU), gradual removal of customs duties on intra-community trade has had serious consequences. Between 1 July 1996 and 30 September 2006, member States were paid an amount equal to 143 billion USD as compensation. Lastly, global trade liberalization has sharply reduced customs duties. These are the foundation of public finance in Africa, accounting for an average of 14.7 percent of tax revenues in West Africa –from 5 percent for Nigeria to 34 percent for the Gambia (Busse et al, 2004) – and 16.4 percent in Central African countries –from 2.4 percent Equatorial Guinea to 24 percent for the Democratic Republic of the Congo. Customs revenues for certain countries were often as high as 30 percent in the early 2000s.*
4. *Source: Beyond Economic Partnership Agreements in Africa. Laurence Hinkle, Mombert Hoppe and Richard Newfarmer*
5. *African Development Bank (AfDB), Development Centre of the Organisation for Economic Co-Operation and Development (OECD) and the United Nations Economic Commission for Africa: African Economic Outlook.*

for decentralization and local finance have been created or reactivated recently, for example: the National Committee of Local Finance (CONAFIL) in Benin and Côte D'Ivoire; and the National Council on Decentralization and Inter-Ministerial Committee on Local Services in Cameroon (2010); and the Burkina Faso's National Decentralization Conference in 2010 which focused on financing decentralization. In 2009, Gabon initiated transfer of responsibilities 14 years after the first decentralization laws were passed. In Mauritania, a new law for local government is being studied. The project would introduce regions as a new unit of local governance and expand local government roles. However, in Mali, the law promising that transfers of responsibility would be accompanied with corresponding financial resources was revised.

In South Africa, the process of local finance modernisation has been underway since 2003, with the *Municipal Finance Management Act*, which revised budgetary and accounting processes, the internal auditing and control system, and the procurement and bidding processes. In other countries of Southern and Eastern Africa, it should also be noted, that the processes of legislative and constitutional reform are underway. In Kenya, reforms approved in August 2010 include: a constitutional status for local governments (counties), direct election of mayors and the executive and giving them control over municipal budgets, as well as clarification of the functions and resources of local governments, and an assignment of 15 percent of the national revenues. However the future of existing local authorities in urban areas remain unclear. In Uganda, a new program of financial management and transparency (*Financial Management and Accountability Programme* – FINMAP) has been in place for the last 3 years to strengthen the fiscal decentralization strategy (FDS). In 2010, Zambia approved their *Plan for Decentralisation Implementation* and restructuring of the system of transfers to make fund allocation more transparent and predictable. In Malawi, the Parliament made plans to reduce the number of wards in 2010. The government has also created a national commission on local finance and increased between 2004 and 2010 the sectors transferred to local governments from three to seven (initially agriculture, education and health; now also forests, water and environment, and gender equality).

In North Africa, where decentralization is advancing more slowly, some important reforms are underway. In Morocco, the reform of the *"Charte Communale"* increased the flexibility of the fiscal and accounting controls constraining local government, reduced the veto power of central over local government and increased local responsibilities. A multi-year program is also being introduced to strengthen local government autonomy in pricing local services and to formalize the agreement between public decision makers and centrally appointed accountants, including management control indicators fixed within the contract. The King recently announced that both the role and autonomy of regions would be reformed. In Algeria, the government is preparing a municipal code that would give local governments more flexibility to manage their budgets and revenues in the future. It also proposes both solidarity funds to support equalization and systems of citizen consultation (local referendums).

The following section deepens the discussion of five important aspects of fiscal decentralization: State structure and territorial organisation, local government responsibilities and expenditures, revenues, transfers, and access to loans.

States and Territorial Organisation

There are five federal countries in Africa: Comoros, Ethiopia, Nigeria, Sudan and Tanzania (Tanzania is more of a bipartite

Table 2.1: Number of Decentralised Entities by Level - Population Indicators for 27 African Countries, 2008

Country	Local level	Intermediate level 1	Intermediate level 2	Average local population (in thousands)	Population of capital (in thousands)	% urban population	Total country population (in thousands)
Algeria	1541	48 wilayas [1]		21	2,947	65	34,178
Benin	77			120	223.5	41	8,792
Burkina Faso	351	45 provinces	13 regions	43	1,475	20	15,746
Cameroon	360 municipalities and 14 cities				1,248	57	18,879
Côte d'Ivoire	718 municipalities and 2 districts (Abidjan and Yamoussoukro)	56 departments	19 regions	20	3,802	49	20,617
Egypt	4641 villages and 220 towns	433 centres	29 governorates[1]	15	11,100	43	83,083
Ethiopia	556 woredas	68	9 + 2 city regions	153	4,585	17	85,237
Gabon	52	49 departments		29	540,818	85	1,515
Ghana	138			169	1,661 (2001)	50	23,382
Kenya	175 (1 city, 44 municipalities and 130 rural councils)	47 counties[2]		218	3,100	22	39,003
Malawi	40 (28 rural districts, 8 urban towns and 4 cities)			330	732	19	14,269
Mali	703	49 circles	8 regions + District of Bamako	18	1,494	32	12,700
Mauritania	216			14	673	41	3,200
Morocco	1503 (221 urban and 1282 rural)		16 regions	21	627	56	34,859
Mozambique	43			477	1,099	37	21,669
Namibia	54	13 regions		33	251	37	2,109
Niger	265	36	8	55	215	16	15,306
Nigeria	774		36 states + federal district of Abuja	115	778.5	48	149,229
Rwanda	31 (30 districts and Kigali city)			310	800	18	10,473
Senegal	543	14 regions		29	2,604	42	13,712
South Africa (SA)	226 local municipalities	8 metro, 44 municipal districts	9 provinces	172	2,345	61	49,052
Tanzania	25 cities, 97 rural districts (108 townships and 10571 villages)				2,456	25	41,049
Togo	354 municipalities	30 prefectures	5 regions	19	1452	42	6,020
Tunisia	264		24 governates	39	992	67	10,486
Uganda	1010 divisions, sub-counties and towns	97 districts and municipalities		30	1,533	13	32,370
Zambia	72 districts (4 cities, 14 municipalities and 54 districts)			35	3,000	35	11,863
Zimbabwe	90			129	1572	37	11,393

Source: Compilation by authors, national data collected by UCLG provided by the local government associations. Only governance levels with a directly or indirectly elected council or assembly are listed here. For the data on population: City Population (national population: 2009 estimations, urban population: 2008 estimations). Togo: planned under new legislation

1. The Executive, the Wali or Governors, are nominated by the Central Government.

2. As specified in 2010 Constitution.

confederation). South Africa and the Democratic Republic of the Congo (DRC) are quasi-federal States. Other countries are unitary States. Table 2.1 presents an overview of the data on the territorial organisation of the countries analysed in this chapter.

Great diversity can be observed in territorial organization, as far as tiers and range of local authorities are concerned. This diversity complicates comparison across countries. Since 2005, an increase in the number of local governments has occurred in some African countries (Burkina Faso, Côte d'Ivoire, Ghana, Kenya, Mozambique and Uganda).

Responsibilities and Expenditure

Overall, African local governments have limited spending autonomy. The division of responsibilities and expenditure between local authorities and central governments is often unclear. The responsibilities of local governments are written into the constitution or the laws of most of the African countries analyzed, except for Tunisia and Niger, but there is a huge divergence between *de jure* and *de facto* practice. This is the case, for example, in Côte d'Ivoire, Egypt, Ethiopia, Rwanda, and Algeria. The responsibilities granted to local government are often shared among several local levels and the state.

In all countries, the higher levels of government (region/provinces or centre) exert a controlling power over local government. This is exercised through budget rules and circulars that specify the various percentages to use when preparing the budget (for example, not more than 50 percent on payroll expenses or the earmarking of at least 40 percent of a specific transfer for investment). Higher levels may also have veto power during budget review.

Budgetary controls, both prior to and post approval, are not uncommon. Budget approval is often dependent on legal compliance with mandates on revenues, expenditures, and budget balance. Local governments in countries such as Ghana, Gabon, Egypt, Tunisia, Rwanda, and Zambia are strictly controlled by higher levels, with reviews of the budget structure as well as component budget lines. For countries like Kenya, Uganda, and Burkina Faso, the reviews concern only the budget structure. In Malawi, South Africa, Tanzania, and Algeria they focus principally on budget lines. In Morocco, the recent organisational reforms of local finance (2009) and local accounting (2010) have reduced veto powers. In Senegal, the individual decisions taken by local governments are not submitted for prior approval to a higher authority.

Finally, the timeframes for budget approvals can be long in many countries. In Francophone West Africa, for example, Mali and Niger, legal approval timeframes are generally exceeded, because it takes so long for the oversight authority to provide comments.

Another indicator of the autonomy of local governments is whether or not they are free to hire and dismiss personnel. Only about a third of the countries analyzed give their local governments full control over these decisions: Benin, Gabon, Ethiopia, Mozambique, Morocco, Rwanda, Tanzania and South Africa. In Ghana, Mali, Malawi and Algeria, decisions to hire and dismiss local-level staff are taken jointly by central and local government. For all other countries, local employees are either hired after approval of or directly by the central government, as is the case in both Egypt and Tunisia. In Zambia local governments have full control over the management of their staff (including salaries), but central government can interfere in these processes. In Malawi and Kenya, local authorities can hire and fire their subordinate staff, whereas only the central government can appoint professional staff. In some countries, such as Mauritania, the authority to hire staff is used as a pre-election vote-catching technique, which increases the wage bill (Yahya Ould Kebd, 2010).

The procedure for assigning powers and responsibilities to local governments varies from one country to another. Most countries transfer specific blocks of responsibility (e.g. South Africa and Morocco), while countries like Niger and Cameroon grant general powers and responsibilities to local governments. Some countries, such as Tanzania, provide a detailed list of mandatory and optional functions.

There are three groups of expenditure responsibility in the countries analyzed here. The first group of basic tasks common to all countries comprises of the maintenance of small equipment, roads, street lighting, waste collection, recreational activities (culture, leisure, and sports), as well as urban and residential planning. The second group includes preschool and primary school education and basic health services, as well as transport and environmental protection. These occur in Algeria, Benin, Guinea, Morocco, Namibia, Niger and Zambia or in some municipalities (large urban municipalities in Kenya, for example, or regional administrative centres). In a few countries, such as South Africa, Uganda and Zimbabwe, the third more advanced functions, including the promotion of local economic development and employment, energy distribution, police and security, and secondary education may also be assigned.

The sharing of powers and responsibilities among the various levels is very common in countries such as Mali, Tanzania, Zambia and Zimbabwe. For example, local governments are generally responsible only for maintenance of school infrastructure. Scheduling, investment, and staff salaries are managed by different ministries. Other factors of note include:

- Responsibility for water and electricity remains significantly different between Anglophone and Francophone countries. In South Africa and Ghana, water boards or companies often provide them; in Francophone countries they are more likely governed under a national enterprise. In Kenya, former municipal enterprises have recently formed regional groups.

- In countries with several subnational levels, the correct scale for service delivery is under debate. For example, in Côte d'Ivoire and South Africa, the search for economies of scale and externalities has led lawmakers to assign some services such as the distribution of water and the production of energy to higher decentralized levels and/or the State.

- Concerns for redistribution and social equity have led lawmakers in most countries to give central government control over such areas as welfare and housing. For other countries, these are assigned to and shared between the central and local levels. In Côte D'Ivoire, for example, social assistance is a municipal responsibility.

Given the common divergence between *de jure* and *de facto* functional assignment, it is helpful to use other indicators of decentralization. Figure 2.1 examines the ratio of local to total public expenditures.[6] The (non-weighted) average for all countries analyzed is 8.3 percent, but the differences between countries are important. The highest ratio (17-23 percent) is in Uganda, Rwanda, and South Africa. However, the ratio in most countries (16 countries) is lower than 10 percent, or even under 5 percent (11 countries). In other words, the contribution of African local

6. *Local public expenditure includes the intermediate level (governorate, region, department, etc.). The data comes from records compiled by UCLG and completed by data from other works and studies.*

Figure 2.1. Local Expenditure Share of Total Public Expenditure in 23 African countries, 2007

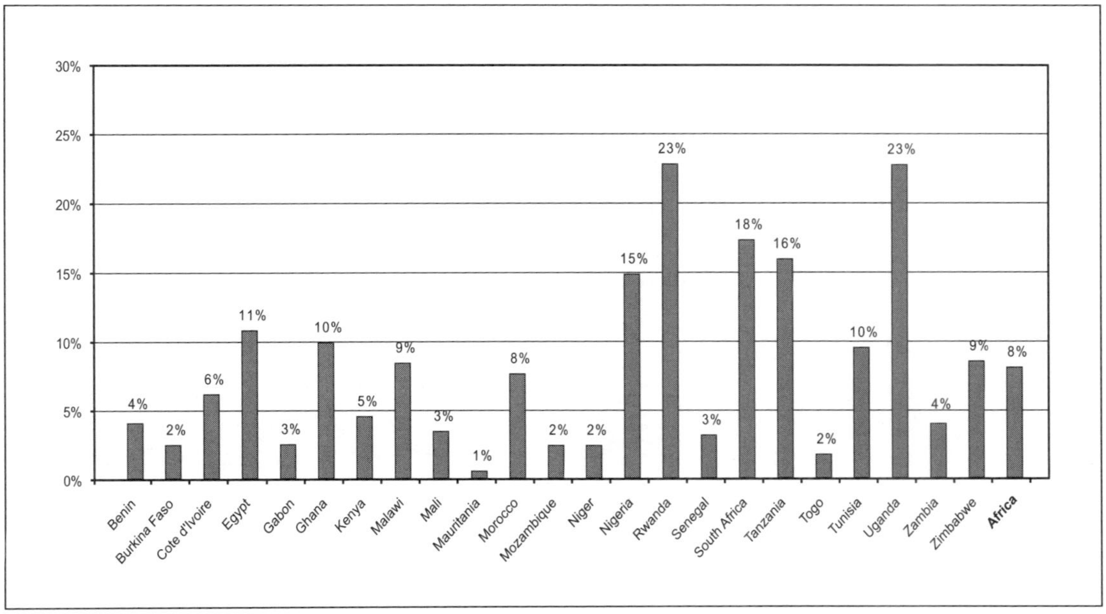

Source: Calculation by authors with country data collected by UCLG and completed by data from other studies (see bibliography).

Figure 2.2. The Weight of Local Authorities in Total Public Revenue, Africa, 23 countries, 2007

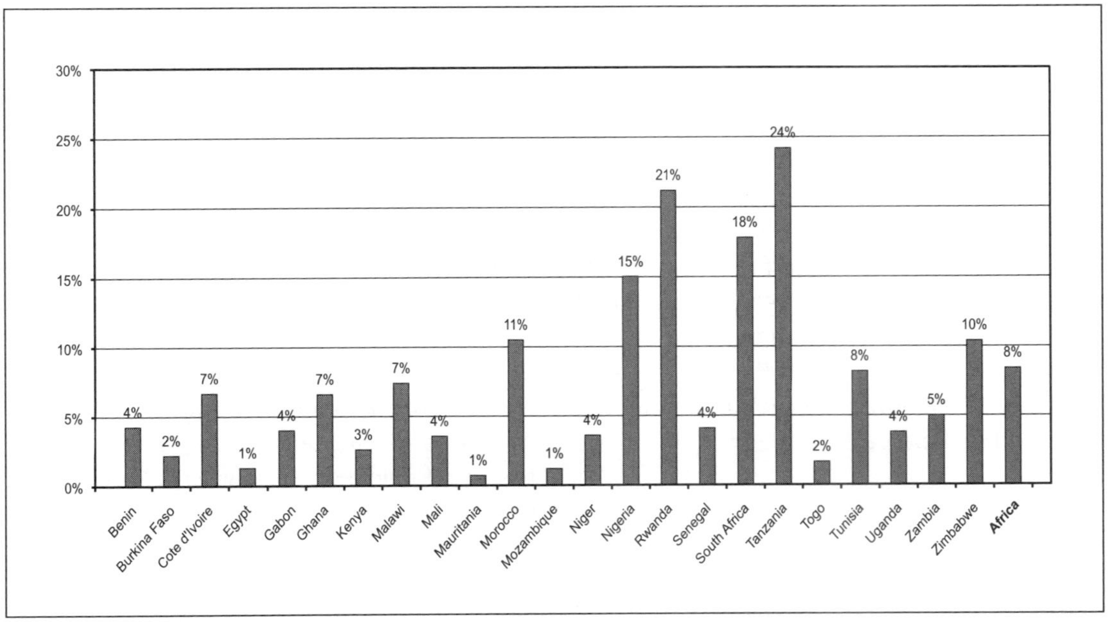

Source: Calculation by authors with national country data collected by UCLG and completed by data from other works and studies (see bibliography).

Figure 2.3: Structure of Local Revenues, Africa, 15 countries, 2007

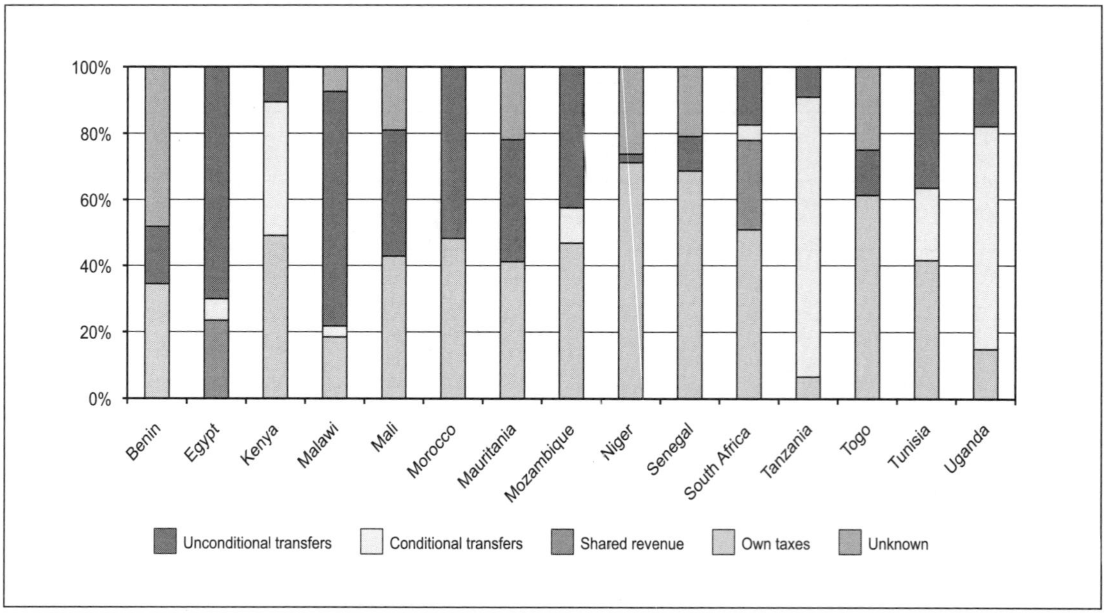

Source: Calculation by authors with national country data collected by UCLG and completed by data from other works and studies.

authorities to public expenditure is generally far below that of those in Europe (where the average is 25 percent), and this does not even consider the level of autonomy exercised in making these expenditures.

Total Resources and Own-Source Resources

In Africa, there has been less decentralization of revenues than expenditures. Figure 2.2 reports the local share of total government revenues for 23 countries. In the majority of countries (17), local government revenues represent less than 10 percent of public revenue and in 13 countries, less than 5 percent. Only Tanzania and Rwanda exceeds 20 percent, followed by South Africa and Nigeria (15-18 percent).

The numbers in Figure 2.2 include autonomous revenue as well intergovernmental transfers. Figure 2.3 breaks down local revenues into sources, showing that in the majority of countries, about half of local government revenues come from intergovernmental transfers while the other half come from local taxes. However, the situation differs substantially across countries. In some cases transfers provide the bulk of local revenues, 85-90+ percent in extreme cases like Tanzania and Uganda. In Egypt, local governments fully depend on shared taxes and transfers.

On the other side there are countries where taxes, fees, and charges dominate local budgets: Niger, Senegal and Togo, followed by South Africa. Here own revenues provide approximately two thirds of local revenue. South Africa falls in this range, if shared taxes are included. However in some countries (Niger and Togo for example), the predominance of own revenue is not necessarily a sign of autonomy. Morocco and Kenya fall slightly below a 50/50 split in their balance between own revenue and transfers, and below this are Mauritania, Tunisia, Mozambique, and Malawi.

Figure 2.4: Autonomy indicator, Africa, 14 countries, 2007

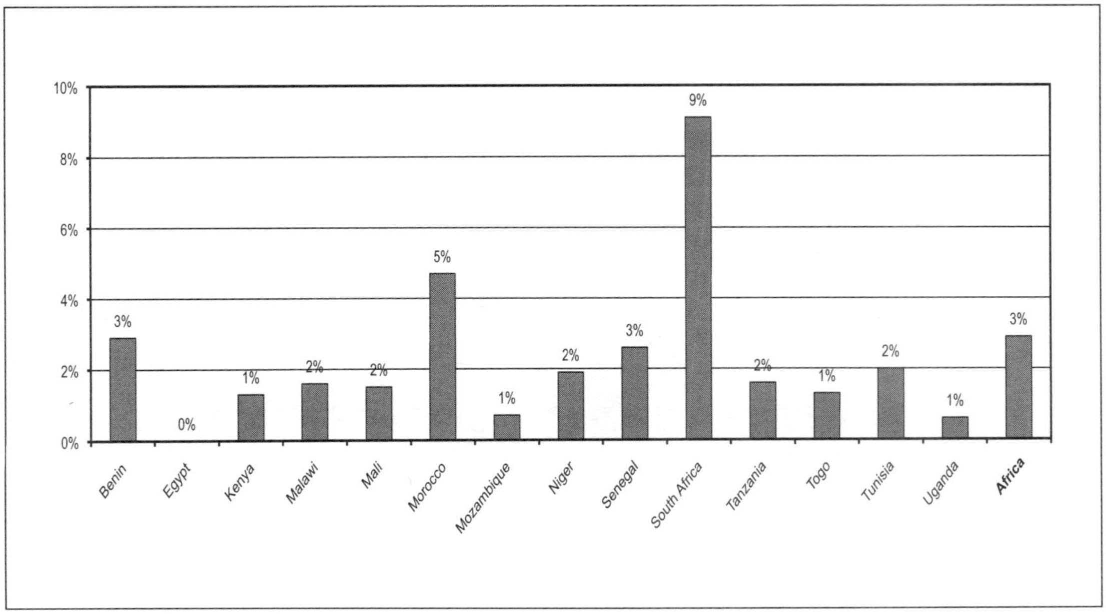

Source: Calculation by authors with national country data collected by UCLG and completed by data from other works and studies (see bibliography).

Own source incomes for the majority of local governments come from a limited number of taxes, charges, and duties. Many countries generate incomes from local services, but these are often insufficient to cover costs. Principal sources include: property tax (both built and non-built land), residential tax, licenses and various charges (for business, markets, construction permits, bars, gambling, shows, advertising, hotels) and service fees (water, sanitation, waste collection). Vehicle taxes exist in certain countries (Zimbabwe), but they are often shared with the center (Algeria, Côte D'Ivoire, Egypt, Morocco). Local governments in few countries may levy business taxes (Algeria, Morocco, Tunisia, Togo) or non-petroleum resource extraction (mining, forestry) shares with the central governments of Morocco, Tanzania, and Gabon.

More unusual are taxes on the informal sector (Burkina Faso). The participation of local governments in personal revenue tax is limited, but sometimes they are included in shared taxes, over which local governments have no control, or transfers (Gabon, Morocco, Kenya). This is also the case for shared portions of the VAT (Algeria, Egypt, Morocco, Nigeria, Senegal and Togo) and portions of the tax on the production or export of petrol in the principal production countries (Algeria, Cameroon, Côte D'Ivoire, Egypt and Nigeria).

Even where fiscal bases are already limited, the central government may weaken them further. Zambia, for example, abolished the tax on agriculture (crop levies) in 2009. Uganda suspended the graduated personal tax, the main local revenue source, in 2005. Tanzania has also eliminated local taxes and reduced tax rates, and Mozambique cut tax rates by 30 percent. On the other hand, Morocco has assigned a share of the VAT, as well as the management of various taxes to local and regional governments. Some are shared between the different levels (for

Table 2.2: Taxation Power of Local Governments for 22 African countries, 2008

Country	Rate	Basis	Tax collection	Fees collection	Veto of central government
Algeria	No	No	No	No	Yes
Benin	Yes	No	No	No	No
Burkina Faso	Yes	No	No	Yes	
Cameroon	Yes	No	No	Yes	Yes
Côte D'Ivoire	Yes	No	No	Yes	Yes
Egypt	No	No	No	No	Yes
Ethiopia	Yes	Yes	Yes	Yes	No
Gabon	No	No	No	Yes	No
Ghana	Yes	No	No	Yes	Yes
Kenya	Yes	Yes	Yes	Yes	Yes
Malawi	Yes	No	Yes	Yes	No
Mali	Yes	No	No	Yes	No
Mozambique	No	No	Yes	Yes (Private)	No
Niger	Yes	No	No	Yes	No
Rwanda	Yes	No	Yes	Yes	Yes
Senegal	Yes	No	No	Yes	Yes
South Africa	Yes	Yes	Yes	Yes	Yes
Tanzania	Yes	Yes	Yes	Yes	Yes
Tunisia	No	No	No	No	Yes
Uganda	Yes	No	Yes	Yes	Yes
Zambia	No	No	Yes	Yes	Yes
Zimbabwe	Yes	Yes	Yes	Yes	Yes

Source: Compilation by authors, from data collected at national level by UCLG and from other studies (see bibliography).

example: 5 percent of local service taxes for regional governments and 95 percent to the city).

As noted above, however, the relative importance of own revenue in local budgets is not an indicator of financial autonomy if sub-national entities have little or no power to determine the tax base, fix tax rates or collect taxes. Figure 2.4 presents a weighted indicator of autonomy: the ratio of the own revenues of local governments to total public revenue. It was obtained by multiplying the size of the local sector (Figure 2.2) by the share of local taxes and fees (Figure 2.3). This indicator enables us to consider the impact of financial autonomy depending on the size of the activity covered by this autonomy. It shows that the country with the highest level of fiscal decentralization is South Africa.

This national measure, however, does not show the significant differences within each country among the various types of local governments, and between local governments of the same type. As a rule, decentralized, intermediary tiers in non-federal countries –provinces, regions or departments– depend more on transfers than municipalities. This is partly because they were created more recently and the main local tax bases were already taken by municipalities. Rural (or small) municipalities are also usually more dependent on transfers than larger urban municipalities.[7] This is because the rural areas have less economic activity and the taxation of rural properties, is problematic or even prohibited.

This analysis of local resources must also be considered within the legislative and regulatory framework of local taxes. In most African countries, regulations on decentralization and/or constitutions define a scope of specific resources for local governments. The legislative and regulatory documents governing decentralization define the conditions for exercising power by local governments with respect to taxation and resource collection.

Table 2.2 reviews the power of the various countries to raise taxes. It describes whether or not local governments are free to set tax rates or change the base of some taxes. It also specifies whether local governments collect local taxes and fees. Lastly, the table indicates whether higher-tier authorities have the right to control or veto local governments budgets.

Fiscal autonomy ranges from local government having full authority without any central veto on local resources at one extreme, as in Ethiopia, to a situation in which the centre can veto local revenues and/or budgetary decisions, as in Egypt. Between extremes, local governments in countries like Uganda and Gabon cannot create new taxes or fix tax bases, but they have significant authority to collect revenue without higher interference. Mozambique is interesting because its local governments have no authority to create taxes or define bases, but have great latitude in collection, and local governments in this country have innovated to involve the private sector in tax collection.[8] In Tunisia, tax collection is, in principle, under the jurisdiction of the centre but some sixty local authorities actually carry out their own tax collection (Ben Letaieff, 2010).

There are important distinctions between Francophone and Anglophone countries as shown in Figures 2.5 and 2.6. In the former, local governments have no power to raise taxes. Parliamentarians and the central government change local tax bases

Figure 2.5: Own Tax Process: Model for Francophone Africa

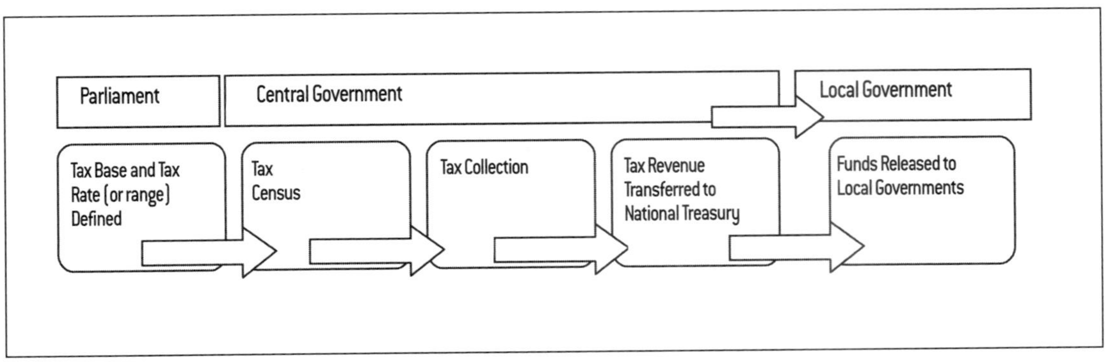

7. *In Mali, the share of revenues obtained from transfers is 36 percent for all municipalities. This figure ranges from 68 percent for those with fewer municipalities of less than 10,000 inhabitants to 43 percent for those with municipalities of 20 to 50,000 inhabitants and 16 percent for Bamako. The intermediate level of government (cercles) receives 42 percent of its funding from transfers, while 52 percent, of regional government funding is made up of transfers. In the same vein, in Burkina Faso, transfers account for 29 percent of municipal revenues as a whole, but 67 percent of revenues for municipalities with a population less than 20,000 inhabitants and 18 percent for those with populations of more than 100,000. They also account for 47 percent of the funding of regions. In Mozambique transfers account for 70 percent of the incomes of rural local government incomes, but less than 40 percent for large cities. In South Africa, medium size cities collect 44 percent of the revenues collected by large cities, while rural local governments cannot even reach 5 percent of this figure.*

8. *"Privatization of market tax collection has been widely promoted in East Africa but was found to be rather complex and risky. Based on unrealistic fiscal potential analysis lump sum agreements might lead to an either inappropriate profit of the private tax collector or a high loss for the district. Profit margins for private collectors were found to be mostly inadequate, resulting in no significant increase, but occasional decrease in public revenues. Monitoring for districts is apparently difficult" (Niña Boschmann, 2009, p. 9)*

Box 2.1: Local/Shared Taxes and Local Government in Nigeria

In Nigeria, three dimensions of local revenue include: power over local tax, responsibility of tax collection, and who benefits from taxes. A tax can be determined at the federal or federated state level, collected by federal, state, or local governments and spent by any level. Several examples illustrate: (1) Capital gains tax is set at the federal level, collected jointly by the federal government and states and spent by states; (2) VAT is set by the federal government, collected by the federal government and federated states and spent by the federal government, federated states and local governments; (3) television and radio licences are set by the federal government, but collected and spent by local governments; (4) property tax is set at the federated state level, but collected and spent by local governments. In all cases, local governments collect their taxes and fees, even if they are set by federal or state governments.

Source: Akindele S. T. and OLaopa (2002): Fiscal federalism and local government finance in Nigeria. Republic of Nigeria and Olisa Agbakoba SAN & Hilary Ogbonna (2004): Local Government Administration and Development in Nigeria – A Capacity Building Manual by the Human Rights Law Service HURILAWS

and rates. In some countries, local governments have the right to define the tax rate. For example, in Côte d'Ivoire local governments can change rates for business tax, licences and residence tax. In Benin, local governments can fix property tax rates within the range of 4 percent to 8 percent that has been determined by Parliament. In Senegal, local authorities have the power to determine in certain cases the basis for the revenues of public properties or services. They have the power of the "additional cent", a surcharge that can be established by deliberation. This allows local authorities to charge levies at the local level.

In Anglophone influenced countries, such as Tanzania and Zimbabwe, local councils have more room to set local taxes or change tax rates (Figure 2.6). In some cases, such powers are closely monitored by the central government before or after municipal council adoption. For example, in Kenya, all changes in property tax rates must be approved by the Minister for Local Government. In South

Figure 2.6: Own Tax Process: Model for Anglophone Africa

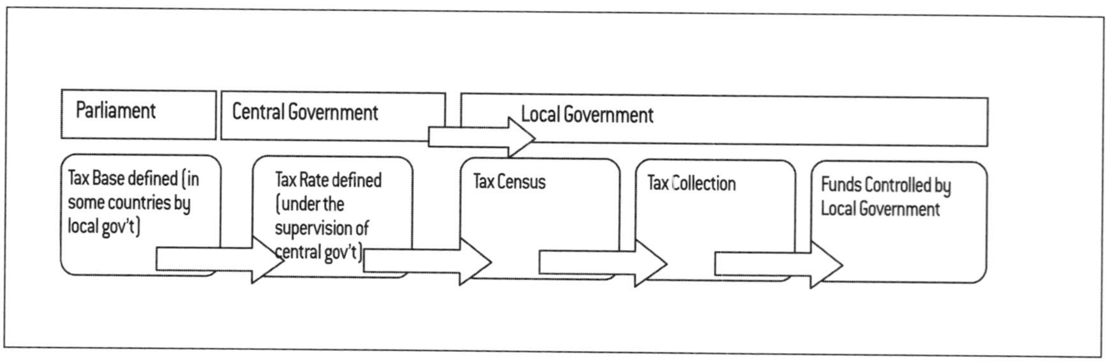

Box 2.2: An Example of the Importance of Municipal Taxes Collection: The case of Burkina Faso and Morocco

In a Francophone context characterised by the principle of the unity of the state treasury (*unicité de caisse*), it is useful to compare the proportions of local revenues managed by the municipal revenue collection agency and the Treasury. This distinction also covers the tax register, the tax bases and fees determined by local governments.

In Burkina Faso, on average, 43 percent of local government revenues were collected by municipal collection agencies in 2004. Thus, local governments in Burkina Faso have real control over nearly half their tax and fees revenues. The 57 percent of local revenue from local taxes determined by law consists of resources that are not controlled by local governments.

Overall, the smaller municipalities have greater room for decision making. About 20 local governments control nearly 50 percent of revenues, with six of them controlling more than 80 percent. Major towns like Ouagadougou directly collect 37 percent of revenues, which means that a large proportion of their local revenue is managed by central authorities. This is due to the structure of the economic activity in areas dominated by a large modern sector.

In Morocco, the revenues managed and levied by local authorities are becoming more important than revenues managed by the State on their behalf. Taxes and receipts, service products and property revenues account for 49 percent of local revenues compared to 42 percent for revenues managed by the State; the remaining 9 percent correspond to the transferred revenues.

Source: Calculations by the authors based on data from local governments in Burkina Faso and Morocco.

Africa, property tax rates are set by local governments within bounds.

With respect to local fees and non-tax revenue, local government, in both Anglophone and Francophone countries have a bit more flexibility. In most Francophone countries, the National Assembly decides which fees can be levied, but local governments have the power to change tax rates. For example, in Ghana, daily variations can be seen in market access fees, slaughterhouse fees, food for impounded animals, etc. Unlike with tax revenue, local governments are responsible for collection and can even set up municipal fees collection management boards under certain conditions and up to a certain amount.

Non-fiscal resources can be significant. In Morocco, for example, revenues from services (8 percent) and assets (17 percent) make up a quarter of local government incomes. In West Africa, incomes from services and use of public properties yielded nearly 20 percent of local incomes from 2004 to 2007.[9] In South Africa revenues from services (water, sanitation, and electricity) are responsible for nearly half of the income of local governments (around 44 percent in metropolitan and

9. *Source: Partenariat pour le Développement Municipal (PDM).*

medium size cities, but less than 10 percent in small cities and rural areas). Such revenues, however, are limited in the majority of African countries.

Another issue is the management of the tax collection process, which remains extremely centralized in Francophone countries. Deconcentrated departments conduct the tax censuses to estimate the local tax base. This is recorded on the roll by tax authorities, who issue tax assessments and collect these local taxes. The deconcentrated departments, Treasury Department and/or Revenue Department, transfer the revenues to the National Treasury. After this, revenue collection information is released to local authorities. Although local governments are formally excluded from tax collection, in some countries they assist with certain activities, such as the distribution of tax notices (labour and fuel, for example).

In the Anglophone countries, centralization is less significant. Local governments themselves are the main agents of the tax collection process. Generally, local governments collect their taxes and fees, even if central or state governments determine the amounts. For example, in Kenya, local governments are in charge of updating the assessment roll (for which they can use the services of private companies), determining the rates of taxes to pay (subject to central review), collecting taxes and following up outstanding payments.

In some English-speaking countries, the tax process entails major costs for local authorities, especially for collection. In Tanzania, for example, the cost of administering local taxes can reach 80 percent of yields and can exceed 100 percent in some districts. Zimbabwe experiences the same problem aforementioned. In these countries, negotiations are under way to "contract" central assistance in local tax collection; in Tanzania, this will be done for a fixed period of time by the Tanzanian Revenue Authority. In French-speaking Africa, local authorities are seeking some role in revenue collection. These different tendencies reflect the diversity of central-local fiscal relations across the continent. A balance must be found to ensure an appropriate role and better collaboration between both actors in the management of local finance.

In countries with a French administrative tradition, local authorities are usually legally prohibited from opening private bank accounts, although this is becoming more common in a growing number of countries. The public treasury is the bank of the public sector and local authorities are obliged to deposit their liquid funds in it. This compulsory deposit function is reinforced by the fact that the treasury collects both national and local taxes. In Cameroon, local governments were allowed to hold accounts in commercial banks until 2010, but they must now use the treasury system. In Anglophone countries, municipalities are often free to open accounts and keep their funds in the banks of their choice.

State Transfers to Local Government

The systems of transfer to local authorities vary tremendously across the African region. A number of characteristics are noteworthy.

- *The significant use of conditional transfers in the majority of countries.* In South Africa only one transfer in fifteen is unconditional, (the Equitable Share grant). This situation undermines local government's autonomy, as the priorities of sectoral ministries prevail. In Burkina Faso, on the other hand, only one in four transfers to local government is conditional (the global grant for equipment which must be spent on investment).

- *The use of formulas to distribute national funds to local governments*. Some formulas are simple while others are more complex. The Equitable Share in South Africa, for example, has four different components (base service; institutional capacity; equalization; correction and stabilisation). For basic services for example there are levels of support: one full grant for poor households relying on municipal services and a second partial grant for households not yet relying on municipal networks. The simplest formulas are based on population, and often of geographic size, urban or rural nature of the local government and level of poverty.

The analysis of intergovernmental transfers must answer two questions: 1) How is the total amount transferred to be set? 2) How is it transferred? In the countries of Africa there are diverse answers to these questions. For the first question, the total amount to be transferred is determined using one of the three following methods:

- *A fixed percentage*, either of total central revenue or of revenue from one or more specific taxes, assigned either from budgeted or collected revenues. In Ghana, for example, 7.5 percent of national revenues has been dedicated to transfers since 2008, while 2 percent of five taxes is dedicated to transfers in Côte d'Ivoire. In Morocco, 30 percent of the VAT funds transfers, while in Kenya 5 percent of the personal and corporate income tax goes into the Local Authority Transfer Fund. Senegal by law has established that the Decentralization Endowment Funds receives 3.5 percent of the total VAT income.

- *A fixed amount* determined yearly, as with any other national budget allocation, with or without consulting local governments. This is the case in Benin or Tunisia, where fixed annual amounts were set in the 1990s, but each year since has seen a reduction, not only in the nominal amount of the transfer, but also its relative significance in municipal revenues.

- *A variable amount determined by a formula* (a percentage of the recipient's expenditures or an amount depending on population characteristics: age, education, etc.). An example of this can be seen in South Africa's Equalization Grants, where the amount is determined using the number of poor households among other indicators.

Each alternative has its advantages and disadvantages. For example, the central government can become disinterested in the collection of a tax if it retains only a small percentage. A fixed percentage enables local governments to project the amount of transfers and therefore manage revenues better. Annual determination of transfer amounts, on the other hand, reduces their predictability to local governments, although it allows for better adaptation to changing needs. Thus, if the center transfers functions, it can ensure their finance by increasing transfers. Also, funding budget deficits encourages local government wastage, even when administrative controls are in place, as the experience in Morocco, until 1996, demonstrates.

For the second question on transfer mechanisms, there are two main dimensions: equalization and conditionalities. The first, aims at guaranteeing a minimum level of government services across the country by ensuring that all local governments have adequate revenues. The second aims at ensuring that the behaviour of local governments, usually in terms of spending, aligns better with the priorities of the central government.

Equalization formulas are widely used. A simple indicator such as population size or

Box 2.3: Using "origin base" or "derivation" as a Rule for Shared Tax Transfers

Several countries use the derivation principle to share resources with local governments and to structure the sharing of national taxation revenues based on the place of collection.

In Nigeria, VAT is distributed to local governments based on the following criteria: 50 percent of VAT is shared among local governments -30 percent by population and 20 percent by origin of collection (derivation)-. Also, of the 13 percent of oil extraction resources due to the central government, 30 percent is returned to the local level based on derivation.

In the Democratic Republic of Congo (DRC), the Constitution provides a derivation principle which allocates 40 percent of national taxes collected in their territory, to provinces.

In Gabon, the national government transfers a percentage of personal income tax based on what local authority collected it. The distribution is as follows 25 percent to cities, 7 percent to the equalization funds of cities and 68 percent to the State. For intermediate tiers (departments), the distribution is: 65 percent to local government, 7 percent to equalization funds and 28 percent to the central government.

In Senegal, the principle of derivation is used to return the following percentages of nationally collected taxes: 59 percent of the vehicle tax; 50 percent of the surplus value of real estate; 60 percent of the Unique Global Contribution; 60 percent of court imposed fines on the territory of cities and rural local governments.

The derivation principle can be useful if it is applied to taxes paid by the residents of the territory that benefit from them and are not exported. This works for the individual income tax but not taxation on imports (VAT for imported goods, customs tariff). Indeed, this taxation is often collected in a few specific locations (international airport, harbour, capital city, border town) and is then paid by consumers nationally via its inclusion in the price of products. This is why a derivation revenue sharing formula was replaced by one based on population in Cameroon. The derivation revenue sharing formula was considered to be giving undue revenues to Douala (Cameroon's main harbour).

Source: Yatta François (2009): La décentralisation fiscale en Afrique; enjeux et perspectives Karthala, p. 324 and UCLG country profiles.

target size, is often used (Burkina Faso, Malawi, and Mozambique), but more complex formulas are also used (South Africa). Conditional grants are paid, if the recipient meets a number of criteria (submission of a budget, financial accounts, etc.), or must be spent according to certain criteria (minimum percent on investments, in a specific sector, etc.) or with some percentage financed by local revenues. Equalization transfers give

Box 2.4: An Effort at Transparency and Objectivity: Transfers in Kenya and Malawi

In Kenya, the Local Authorities Transfer Fund (LATF) was started in 1998 to improve public services, the management of local finance, and the reduction of local governments' debt. LATF is funded by 5 percent of the national income tax. The amount mobilised by the fund increased from 12.9 million USD (1999) to 121.8 million USD (2009). It is redistributed between 175 local governments on the basis of a fixed amount per local authority. Sixty percent of the total is based on population and the remainder based on urban population (increasing with it). Some criteria must be followed to benefit from the LATF: (1) spend a maximum of 45 percent of the total budget on staff and (2) devote at least 65 percent LATF transfer to the investment budget. Until 2010, withdrawals were based on the following rule: 60 percent of the allocated amount is released if the council submits its budget to the LATF committee; the additional 40 percent is released if the council submits its public accounts, a revenue enhancement plan, and a service delivery plan to the LATF committee.

In Malawi, the National Local Government Finance Committee (NLGFC) is in charge of supporting local authorities in preparation of their budgets and the distribution of national grants to local authorities. Two thirds of these grants are distributed to urban authorities according to the following formula: 50 percent of the amount equally distributed between local authorities, 30 percent on the basis of the population, 13 percent to local authorities affected by drought on the basis of their population and 7 percent to the less developed cities according to their population. The remaining third of the national amount of the grant is exclusively reserved to rural local authorities, of which 30 percent is equally shared between local authorities and 70 percent is shared according to 4 factors: population, surface, illiteracy, and infant mortality. The District Assemblies must submit their draft budget 90 days before the beginning of the fiscal year.

Source: Ministry of Local Government (2004) Status Report overview of the status of decentralization 1993 – 2004 and F. Yatta (2009) and Jamie Boex, Randson Mwadiwa, R. Kampanje (2001): Malawi Intergovernmental Fiscal Transfers Study. Final Report. Government of Malawi, UNCDF, UNDP. Lilongwe and Atlanta, April 2001.

local governments more autonomy than conditional transfers—they are usually unconditional.

There are many examples in Africa to illustrate different types of transfers (see Annex 2.2). For example, in Algeria and Benin, the purpose of transfers is to ensure fiscal balance, so they cover the differences between expenditure and revenues. This, however, can discourage local revenue efforts and encourage unnecessary spending. Other systems can increase some types of spending, for example, salary costs. The fear of counterproductive effects often leads central governments to impose various forms of control (for example on recruitment), thereby reducing the autonomy of municipalities in decision-making.

A well-designed transfer system should promote municipal autonomy both directly (in the transfer parameters) and indirectly (in the legal and regulatory environment). It may also be appropriate for transfers to have incentive effects on local revenues, for example, to reward efforts at tax roll registration or local tax collection. Such transfers must not be linked to revenues as is the case in Tunisia, or in Ghana, with the District Assemblies Common Fund (DACF). Transfers may also try to facilitate efficient expenditure management, for example, by increasing school attendance rates. Some transfers reward compliance with administrative requirements (budget, development plan, etc.). For example, in Madagascar meeting such conditions allows access to the Local Development Fund and in Ghana, it gives access to and distribution of the Assembly's District Development Facility (DDF). In Zambia the central government is developing a new formula-based transfer system to make the financing of local government more predictable and transparent, which will include performance incentives.

Borrowing by Local Governments

Access for African local governments to debt and financial markets is limited. Even in the cases where legislation authorises access, the financial situation of local authorities and the limited development of financial systems, makes access difficult.

The table below (Table 2.3) presents the principles that govern the access of local governments for borrowing by country. In some countries, such as Kenya and Tunisia, the amount of the loan is restricted. In other countries, such as Malawi, debt service levels are taken into account; the supervisory authority cannot approve a loan beyond a given debt service threshold. In most

Table 2.3: Conditions of Access to Loans to the Local Governments of 16 African countries

Indicator Used	Financial Market	Specialized Financial Institution
Amount	Kenya Rwanda Tunisia	Kenya Morocco Rwanda Tunisia
Debt service	Malawi	Morocco Mozambique
Total resource threshold	Benin Burkina Faso Côte d'Ivoire Egypt Gabon Mali Niger Senegal Togo Uganda	Benin Burkina Faso Côte D'Ivoire Egypt Gabon Mali Morocco Niger Senegal Togo

Source: Compiled by the authors

countries, such as Burkina Faso, supervisory authorities use the criteria of a threshold of local government's own resources to ensure that they can pay back loans. Morocco assesses multiple factors: the amount of the loan, debt service, and the resource threshold.

Access to loans, however, is generally not direct. In most African countries, a financial intermediary manages funds earmarked for local governments. The lending systems for local governments use a wide range of instruments. There are currently 11 financial institutions for local authorities in Africa: Development Bank of Southern Africa (DBSA), Infrastructure Corporation Limited (INCA) in South Africa, National Agency for Local Government Investment in Mali (*Agence Nationale d'Investissement des Collectivités territoriales*-ANICT), Municipal Development Fund (*Fonds de Développement Communal*-FDC) in Rwanda, Loan and Support Fund for Local Authorities in Tunisia (*Caisse de Prêts et de Soutien aux collectivités locales*-CPSCL), Special Council Support Fund (*Fonds d'Équipement et d'Intervention Intercommunal*-FEICOM) in Cameroon, Loan Fund for Local Authorities (*Caisse de Prêts aux Collectivités Territoriales*-CPCT) in Niger, Municipal Development Agency (*Agence de Développement Municipal*-ADM) in Senegal, Loan Fund for Local Authorities (*Fonds de Prêt aux Collectivités Locales*-FPCL) in Côte d'Ivoire, Council Support Fund (*Fonds d'Equipement Communal*-FEC) in Morocco and Development Fund for Local Authorities (DFLA) in Malawi. Some institutions are more active than others due to lack of funds.

Three of these financial institutions are more or less specialized as intermediary institutions; that were created for the purpose of funding local authorities. They are the Development Bank of Southern Africa (DBSA), the Infrastructure Finance Corporation Limited[10] (INCA) in South Africa, and the Municipal Infrastructure Finance Fund (FEC) in Morocco. Both the INCA and DBSA draw their resources from financial markets and lend to local authorities in the same way as a classic bank. Unlike South African banking institutions, the FEC in Morocco borrow from the financial market, the government, and from various development partners who provide support for decentralization and/or local development.

Several other institutions are financially autonomous agencies with an administrative status: the National Agency for Local Government Investment in Mali, the Municipal Development Fund in Rwanda, the Special Council Support Fund in Cameroon, the Loan Fund for Local Authorities of Niger and the Loan and Transfer Fund for Local Authorities of Tunisia.

Lastly, there are some agencies created in the 1990s, through international cooperation projects such as the Municipal Development Agency in Senegal and the Loan Fund for Local Authorities in Côte d'Ivoire and the Development Fund for Local Authorities in Malawi. These agencies are sustained by government resources and international support.

The functions of specialized lending systems are diverse and varied, ranging from their essential role of lenders to grants and institutional support (Table 2.4). Few loan systems accept to serve as guarantees for loans taken out with other institutions. In general, the absence of this function is explained by the fact that no financial institution on the marketplace lends to local authorities. It is sometimes also explained by the fact that central government wishes to steer borrowing by local governments towards a single institution.

Aside from Zimbabwe, which is a special case[11], South Africa represents the most significant regional experience. In South Africa, two-thirds of loans taken out by local

10. INCA was created in 1996 by a consortium of public and private institutions, in particular the First National Bank of South Africa, a few South African insurance companies and financial institutions and four international partners: Proparco, a subsidiary of Agence Française de Développement (AFD), Dexia international and two German and British financial institutions. The four international partners sit on the board of directors of the INCA.

Table 2.4: Loan System Services Provided to Local Authorities

	Grants	Loans	Interest subsidy	Guarantee	Institutional support
Tunisia (CPSCL)	X	X	X		X
Morocco (FEC)		X			X
Senegal (ADM)	X	X	X		X
Rwanda (FDC)		X		X	
South Africa (DBSA)		X			X
Côte D'Ivoire (FPCT)		X			
South Africa (INCA)		X			
Cameroon (FEICOM)	X	X			X
Niger (FPCT)		X			
Mali (ANICT)	X			X	X
Malawi		X			

Source: François Paul Yatta (2009). "La décentralisation fiscale en Afrique: Enjeux et perspectives", "Economie et Développement" Collection, éditions Karthala and the UCLG country profiles.

governments come from long-term market loans. Already in the mid-1990s, South African local governments were using long-term loans for capital investments in water, electricity, roads, education and other municipal services. The relatively sound finances of local governments and the widespread belief that the government would bail out those in trouble, enabled local governments, especially white ones, to access loans through bank loans and municipal bonds. Bank loans are the most common form as only the richest local governments can access resources from municipal bonds. These were predominantly made up of the local governments that currently make up the city of Johannesburg. Lastly, it must be remembered that municipal bonds barely made up 1 percent of central government bonds.

In Francophone Africa, Douala implemented one of the rare experiences of bond issuance for the capital market. In 2005, the city raised around 19 million dollars from the new stock market, the Douala Stock Exchange. The Regional Stock Exchange (BRVM) of Abidjan is in theory an opportunity for local authorities in West Africa to access financial markets. This stock exchange, which was established under the West African Economic and Monetary Union (WAEMU), is governed by the Regional Savings and Capital Market Board (CREPMF) and has been operational since 1988. In principle, the market is open to all public (government and administrations) or private (listed and unlisted companies) entities. In practice, however, for the moment, no local government has been able to access a BRVM loan as the central governments refuse to provide approval, a pre-condition of all BRVM loans.

In spite of the limited access to borrowing, it remains possible to observe problems of local authority debt. In Algeria, for example, problems of budget management brought on structural deficits that the government is attempting to get under control. In 2007 approximately 980

11. The offering was mainly made up of insurance companies, pension funds and Post Office Savings Bank reserves. In the 1990s, the central government required insurance companies and other market participants to keep a percentage of their holdings in bonds issued by the central government, para-state organisations and municipalities. As finance institutions (pension funds, Post Office Savings Bank, etc.) were practically obliged to buy them, these bonds had low interest rates, making them a veritable windfall for all bond issuers. Analysts admit that the municipal bond market in Zimbabwe is actually a "false" market that is unsustainable. There are two main reasons for this, the required authorisation of ministries in charge of local governments and finances and the State guarantee, and prescriptions from central government with respect to the financial market. We will therefore only discuss the case of South Africa.

Box 2.5: The Relationship between Decentralization and Deconcentration

A comparison of selected East Africa countries, Kenya, Malawi, Tanzania, Uganda and Zambia reveals different models. Kenya has a deconcentration bias characterized by the simultaneous presence of both a local government and deconcentrated administration. Districts and county councils, for example, cover the same territory. A centrally appointed district commissioner heads the district while the county is headed by a clerk (appointed by central but officially accountable to the elected country councils). Consequently, there is very strong control and there are often cases of conflicts of tasks between local governments' officials and deconcentrated services. Conversely, Uganda has a low level of deconcentration (even if the latest tendencies are towards recentralization). In this country, there are no deconcentrated agencies that compete with local government departments. Local governments are therefore in a stronger position, although central directives in recent years have to some extent made them executing agents of national policy. Tanzania is between the two extremes. In this country, deconcentration means the transformation of a position of central control to a position of assistance and facilitation of local governments.

This competition between deconcentrated departments and local governments can even result in resource wastage. In Zambia the decentralization process begun in 2002 generated a parallel deconcentration of certain sectors to the district level, notably education and health. This brought a duplication of human and financial resources and a multiplication of conflicts. In Malawi, ministries implement deconcentrated activities that duplicate local government activities, including in health services, environmental and forest management, road maintenance, farming and irrigation. Business permits to private entrepreneurs are issued both by the Ministry of Trade and Industry and local authorities. However, this duplication does not translate into a better level of service provision.

Source: JICA (2006) Local Level service Delivery, Decentralization and good governance : A comparative study of Uganda, Kenya and Tanzania: education, health and agriculture sectors; Jamie Boex et al (2001) : Malawi Intergovernmental Fiscal transfer; F. Yatta (2009)

local governments were in deficit; in 2008 this number has increased to nearly 1,200. Through the complementary finance law passed in 2008 the government erased 22.3 billion DZD in local government debt and measures were taken to reduce future deficits. In 2010, the number of local governments in debt dropped to 400. In Kenya the government has conditioned local government access to the LATF grant on progressive debt reduction.

Main Issues of Fiscal Decentralization in Africa

In this section, we will analyze the main problems linked to territorial organization, expenditure, total and own resources, transfers and local debt.

Territorial Organisation

Territorial organisation has a direct effect on the decentralization process and the effectiveness of responsibility transfers to local government. The manner in which decentralization and deconcentration are superimposed and how they relate to each other—independent, complementary or duplicative— has an important impact on how transferred responsibilities are taken in charge by local governments and in consequence on their budgets.

In the last ten years, there have been a series of reforms in several African countries that have created intermediate levels of governance between central government and municipalities (Burkina Faso, Côte D'Ivoire, Gabon, Mali, Morocco, Senegal, Togo and soon Mauritania). In Kenya, the new constitution approved by referendum in August 2010 will transform the 47 counties into an intermediate level of government, assuming the existing local authorities remain in place (they will in the short term). Mali has three local government levels: communes, circles (the equivalent of departments or provinces) and regions. In Senegal the regions, cities, and rural local governments coexist. Madagascar, a country that has been fully divided into local authorities since independence, has been oscillating between regions and provinces as the intermediate level from one constitution to another.

There is an ongoing debate about the relevance of the various levels and the availability of the resources to support them. A cost-benefit analysis of these choices must take into account their impact not only on public services and on the representation of regions in national decision-making, but also on internal tensions between regional groups.

Expenditure Control of Local Authorities

There is commonly a lack of clarity in the sharing of responsibilities between the central government and local governments. Decentralization laws often do not provide sufficient detail on the sharing of responsibilities and even clear laws may not be accompanied by modifications to contradictory sectoral laws and policies, as can be seen in Benin, Zambia and Tunisia. For example, if decentralization laws transfer responsibilities for education or transportation to local governments but sectoral laws remain unchanged, the stage is set for conflict between deconcentrated agencies which, for various reasons (prestige, tradition, human and financial resources) do not wish to give up mandates, and local governments who wish to take up their new functions. Since the deconcentrated services are often more equipped to act, in contrast to the local governments that are often lacking financial and human resources, decentralization is considerably slowed[12].

This confusion regarding the division of tasks may be aggravated by international donors. New development aid modalities – budgetary aid and sector wide support – often favour the recentralization of sectoral policies – such as education, health, water and sanitation, among others – through the concentration of financial means in the ministries, without taking the new responsibilities of local governments into consideration. In Mauritania, for example, only 4 percent of the investments realized in cities that fell under the responsibilities of local government were devolved and included in local budgets.[13] Thus, in practice and contrary to the legislation, local governments are deprived of these tasks and their corresponding resources, which significantly reduce fiscal decentralization. In addition, donors tend to introduce parallel aid mechanisms that do not support and may undermine government institutions. Several donors develop alternative interventions with communities, social and professional associations, non-governmental organisations (NGOs), traditional chiefs, etc.

12. *Reforms are currently expected in a number of countries, notably in Kenya and Zimbabwe where development of a decentralization plan (Decentralization Implementation Plan and National Decentralization Policy) will permit the clarification of responsibilities between the different levels of government.*

13. *See Yahya Ould Kebd (2010).*

Box 2.6: Omnipresent Central Government Control: the example of Tanzania

In Tanzania, the Office of the Prime Minister in charge of Regional Administration and Local Government, which replaced the Ministry of Regional Administration and Local Government, exercises a tight control on the fiscal power of local governments.

In spite of the decentralization policy, both the Office of the Prime Minister and the Ministry of Finance (MoF) continue to exercise a great deal of influence on the fiscal activities of local governments through regional secretariats. The Office of the Prime Minister provides guidelines and budget standards and audits local governments to ensure that they comply with these standards. It monitors local budgets and provides the technical capacity required and technical training. However, local governments do not have a great deal of leeway due to central government restrictions implemented through the conditional grants that are used to finance nearly all local government expenditure.

It is obvious that the promotion of decentralization by deconcentration is a difficult task. Even ten years on, the central government continues to take part in nearly every aspect of the fiscal activity of local governments.

Source: Odd-Helge Fjeldstad (2001) Fiscal decentralization in Tanzania: For better or for worse?; Jameson Boex and Jorge Martinez-Vazquez (2005) Local Government Finance Reform in Developing Countries: The Case of Tanzania

The transfer to local government of new responsibilities, without the corresponding human or financial resources (unfunded mandates) creates difficulties similar to those generated by imprecise laws. In Uganda, for example, new laws on territorial organisations (Land Act) and on education have created new districts without financial resources, and needed human resources and salaries are not assured. In South Africa and Zambia the local authorities have also experienced recent cases of functional transfers without the corresponding resources (in the domain of local economic development, tourism and library creation). In Zimbabwe local government received a grant to cover the transfer of education responsibilities in the 1990s, but this was progressively reduced and finally eliminated.

Inappropriate transfers of powers and responsibilities to local governments continue to be problematic. This is the case, for example, of countries like Mozambique and Malawi where social security and public housing are financed by local authorities, often under shared jurisdiction. Local governments generally do not have the financial resources required to set up redistribution policies at the local level. Given the financial and economic disparities between local governments, these services can be harmonised only at the national level, if some level of equity is to be maintained among the various territories.

Another set of problems concerns the level of autonomy local governments have to define their spending priorities and in some countries to control their own resources. The control exercised by central government on budget decisions weakens local authorities. As noted earlier, in the various countries, the draft budget or budget proposal voted-in by the municipal council is submitted for the approval of higher authorities, such as the local representative of the national authority (prefect, governor, etc.) and/or ministries (Interior, Local Government, Finance, etc.) In this case, the local authority must wait for review by these higher authorities before final budget approval.

There may also be budget controls to ensure adherence to national policies, both before and after local budget approval. In the event of a disagreement between the local government and the national authority, the final decision typically favours the latter. In Francophone countries, if the deliberations of the municipal council do not take the review of the higher authority into account, the latter can declare the budget unenforceable.

The "unified treasury" principle dominant in the Francophone countries also weakens the local authority control over revenues. As previously explained the centre can require local governments to use their resources for central priorities, creating accounting problems and reductions in available resources for local authorities.

Own Resources of Local Government

The financial difficulties associated with poverty afflicting African countries partly explain why they have problems transferring sufficient resources to local government. In Africa the tax ratio as a proportion of GDP reached 27.4 percent in 2007. For middle income countries (18 countries), the tax ratio as a proportion of GDP varies between 25 percent and 34 percent that is to say levels that are comparable with similar countries of other continents. But for low income countries the tax ratio as a proportion of GDP is lower than 15 percent (32 countries) (OECD, AfDB and UNECA, 2010) This low level of taxation, for the majority of countries, explains why the State was only able to partially cover the demand of public services in many areas even before the implementation of decentralization. The decentralization of responsibilities did not lead to a relevant transfer of resources because there were no resources to transfer, either at the central or at local level.

As noted in the first section, fiscal decentralization is currently suffering, in most countries, from an incomplete fiscal transition. Custom duties are on the decline in most African countries, driven by regional integration and globalisation, and Governments are hesitant to share their resources, as currently they do not have a replacement tax that is as easy to collect and has the same returns as customs duties.

Even if local governments could identify citizen priorities and reflect them in local budgets approved by the supervisory authorities, they have very few resources for meeting the needs of their residents. Why is this so?

- Local governments have limited revenue generation powers.

- Central governments see local government resources as expendable and the burden of fiscal adjustments often falls on them. There are many examples of this practice, which reduces the predictability of local funding. Controls exerted over tax collection and the practices of "unified treasury" systems also limit the level of local governments control over their resources, receiving only partial information on tax collection in their communities.

- Local tax administration, particularly for the property tax, requires significant technical skill and is affected by the magnitude of informal urban settlements. As noted in the introduction, 72 percent of the sub-Saharan populations live in slums. In this context, land registers are difficult to establish and even more difficult to update.

- Other issues relate to the methods used to calculate property tax. In general, urban

Box 2.7: Collaboration Between Central Governments and Municipal Services in the Management of the Fiscal Chain: the example of Côte d'Ivoire.

To significantly improve the tax recovery rate (33 percent), decree No. 97-35 of 22 January 1997, strengthened by law No. 2003-489 of 26 December 2003, regulates the collaboration between the central role in local tax collection and municipal services. This includes the identification of taxpayers of property tax, patents, licences and comprehensive taxes, the keeping of files and their quarterly update (creation, editing and discontinuation of activities by the taxpayer), the acquisition of all the elements necessary for the setting up of roles and the control of recovery (distribution of warnings).

Teams were created in each municipality for tax collection. The were composed as follows:

- Local employees (the number of agents dedicated to this depends on the extent of the municipality and its fiscal potential);
- Treasury employees (those responsible for municipal revenues); National Fiscal Department employees, (responsible for property tax revenues).

All the above-mentioned operations are carried out by these teams.

Source: PDM (2002) and Yao Charles Kouassi (2010).

development and resulting increases in property value, are not well taken into account. In Tanzania, for example, the law establishes two modalities for setting property values for local taxation: the market value and the replacement cost. But the notion of property in Tanzania is limited to the right of use, which converts property into a non commercial good. Given the non-existence of a property market, the method to evaluate property tax relies on the value of the replacement costs of structures. The second constraint is linked to delays in re-evaluation of the tax base: in Morocco, a decree has established a revaluation period, every three years a maximum and a minimum value is set for the square meter reference price; in Ghana, the period for this re-evaluation should be five years but in reality is between 10 and 15 years. When you add the lack of land titles for the great majority of properties, it is fair to say that, land management issues are insufficiently accounted for when examining local finance issues. It is an area that deserves to be investigated as a possible lever of local resource mobilization.

- The lack of qualified human resources in local government in the majority of countries, and in particular in small local governments and rural areas, does not allow local governments to take on the management of local taxes. This constraint isolates local governments from tax management, most notably in Francophone countries, or leads local governments in Anglophone countries to delegate this

Box 2.8: Examples of the Assessment of the Cost of Transferred Powers and Responsibilities: Cameroon and Senegal

Cameroon is one of the few countries to carry out work to assess the cost of transferred responsibilities. Two studies commissioned by the department in charge of decentralization show that the current cost of the traditional mandates of municipalities stands at FCFA 36.2 billion while the cost of the transferred tasks can been estimated at FCFA 115 billion (base 2000) or between FCFA 190 and 200 billion (updated in 2005).

In Senegal, the decentralization process has transferred nine responsibilities to local government: environment and natural resource management, health, social welfare, youth, sports and recreation, culture, education, planning, land use planning, town planning and housing. The government has decided to delegate to local government the sums that used to be earmarked for these nine responsibilities when they were provided by central government, representing an annual amount of approximately FCFA 6 billion (USD 8.5 million).

Source: F. Yatta (2009); and the Economic Commission for Africa (2004): Renforcer la gestion financière locale et la décentralisation fiscale en Afrique : Etat des lieux et proposition d'un plan d'action.

collection to national agencies (for example in Zimbabwe) or the private sector (Kenya, Mozambique).

- Finally, one of the structural constraints that goes against the efforts of local governments to mobilize their own revenues is often linked to the lack of trust on the part of the population. Problems of corruption exposed in certain countries sometimes also affect the local level where, due to proximity these bad practices are directly felt by residents. Even if measures have been taken to improve the situation, African local governments still have to convince their citizens that they are able to design and implement local policies, improve the quality of local expenditure and deliver adequate services to them.

Transfers

Transfers represent around 50 percent of the funding of local governments, and even more in many African countries. They make up the difference between the cost of transferred powers and responsibilities, own revenues from local taxes and other sources, and they also offset differences in development and resource bases between local governments. A review of mechanisms of transfer to local governments in Africa reveals the following problems.

- Fiscal decentralization suffers from a lack of knowledge about the cost of the transferred responsibilities. Solving this problem is even more difficult when functions are not clearly defined.

- Needs-oriented funding solutions are in some cases based on the expenditure funding packages that existed before decentralization, as is the case in Burkina Faso with the payment of civil servants' salaries. This means that local governments who were in advantageous positions before decentralization (capital town with a proximity to power, national-level civil servants who enjoy

Box 2.9: Transfers that Never Arrive at Destination!

In African countries, the government does not always pay the monies due to local government, which often represent very significant amounts.

For example, in Ghana one of the four payments planned under the District Assemblies Common Fund (DACF) for 2009 was delayed, presumably to be paid in 2010. This represents 25 percent of the scheduled amount and approximately 20 percent of the total revenue of Ghanaian local governments.

In Côte d'Ivoire, Decree No. 98-05 of 14 January 1998 established the current expenditure block grant (*Dotation Globale de Fonctionnement* - DGF). This grant is written into the budget law each year on the basis of 2 percent of selected tax revenues collected during the two years preceding grant payment. The levies include tax on business profits, taxes on salaries, domestic value added tax and service tax. In practice, the total amount of grants has been below 10 billion FCFA, well below 2 percent of the included taxes.

In Gabon, the government does not transfer the legally specified share of national taxes (business tax, tax on the revenue from securities, income tax from liberal professions, VAT) to local governments. This requires implementation decrees that have never been issued.

In Cameroon, the budget law for the 2004 fiscal year applied 50 percent of the municipal share of the VAT as a contribution to the national efforts under the Heavily Indebted Poor Countries Initiative (HIPC). This diversion was supposed to stop at the end of the 2004 fiscal year, but it continued until the end of the 2009 fiscal year.

In Malawi decentralization policy recommends the transfer of 5 percent of the net national revenues to local governments via unconditional grants, but the government has never transferred more than 2 percent.

Source: F. Yatta (2009) ; Gérard Gagnon (2002): Le financement du développement local; Un état des lieux en Afrique de l'Ouest, Eléments de comparaison Ghana-UEMOA; contributions from the workshops organized in Rabat, 7 May 2010.

local services, member of the ruling group, etc.) will continue to be advantaged. This is also the case in Gabon. For example, the financing of primary school teachers, benefits local governments who already have schools, while financing based on the number of school-going age children takes into account present and not past needs. If decentralization is implemented by changing gradually from the first mode of financing to the second, it is essential to make sure that local governments can raise the necessary funds.

Some formulas cover the difference between revenues and expenditures. In 1996, Morocco replaced this type of formula with an equalization mechanism.

This was done as the first method discouraged tax effort, promoted unnecessary spending and created a dysfunctional situation. The use of this type of budget balancing transfer should be discouraged.

- Irregularity and unpredictability of transfers is also a problem. Agreed upon transfers never arrive (fully) at their intended destination despite having been voted in Parliament and written in the budget law. In Tanzania, for example, the formulas that exist to calculate the transfers are simply not applied. In these situations, local governments find themselves without the necessary resources to implement public services. There is a risk of this situation becoming more widespread during tax transition and even worse with the global economic crisis creating general challenges for public finance.

- An even more serious problem occurs when countries step back from good principles on which their transfers are based. In several countries (Burkina Faso, Mali), the policy documents on decentralization establish the principle of simultaneity between the transfer of responsibilities and the transfer of resource, but the difficulties in implementing this principle has resulted in the postponement of transfers.

Borrowing Capacity

Despite the high urbanisation rate and the increase in the demand for public investments, the use of debt by local governments is very limited, even where permitted by legislation. Only a few large local governments have access to borrowing. The debts taken out by local government are often short-term loans (credit facilities) with retail banks and in many countries they are used primarily to ease cash flow strains.

- Weak demand from local governments is a main reason for the under-development of the local credit market. The small share of local governments in public finance and the limited local revenue system observed in most countries increases risks and the price of credit.

- Local government access to the financial market remains very limited even in countries where there is a developed and efficient financial market.

- Specialized finance institutions have yielded mixed results:

  - Loans end up going only to local governments with institutional development sufficient for them to meet loan requirements (application preparation, financial assessment of the project, etc.).

  - The activity of specialized finance institutions has not succeeded in establishing a culture of borrowing and repayment, which has often been undermined by the existence of several other sources of "more easily obtainable" funding, such as government subsidies and grants from donor agencies. Loans from international donor agencies are generally cheaper than other sources regardless of the country's macroeconomic and financial position. The situation has been made more complex with the recent development of sub-sovereign loans at interest rates ranging between 0.75 percent and 6 percent granted by international donors to some African cities, such as Ouagadougou and Dakar. Although this is desirable in principle, it needs to be

Box 2.10: Financing: towards endogenous solutions

The FinAfricaCities programme, co-financed by the AFD and Cities Alliance is currently examining how to finance investments in Sub-Saharan cities. These cities will have approximately 340 million additional inhabitants over the next twenty years, requiring investments of approximately 45 billion USD a year.

For this investment to occur, local governments must increase their relative share in the financing of local investments for two reasons. The first is that national budgets will focus on increasing expenditure on their own core functions. Secondly, current trends seem to indicate that development aid will not be able to play a much larger role than it does today.

The increasing need for investment implies a significant change in the scale and volume of financing. In the end, both the modalities of urban financing and the financial system will need to be changed. The on-going changes in the African economies may indicate that now is the time for a progressive evolution towards endogenous solutions.

The ideal endogenous solution is financing in local currency, supported by resources coming from local savings. These savings are gathered by financial institutions and banks of the continent on the one hand and the financial markets on the other. The creation of specialized institutions for local governments on the Pan-African level or at the regional level is neither necessary nor appropriate, given the number of development banks already in existence across the continent. On the other hand, the efficiency of the systems will be supported by the development of structures such as local investment funds like those recently created in China, India, and South-East Asia.

The second endogenous solution, which is almost universally used, is financing via land development and investment. The reluctance of African governments to engage in this process for a variety of reasons is currently untenable given the needs. The implementation of this solution supposes the existence of specialized operators to service local governments. The institutional positioning of these operators is very important. Partnerships between the public and private sectors allow a better distribution of risks across projects. They therefore seem well adapted to the African situation if their decision making autonomy is guaranteed.

Information facilitated by Thierry Paulais/FinAfricaCities/Cities Alliance.

coordinated with the financial market in order not to affect its development.

- In some countries, specialized finance institutions have been a major factor in the increase in the debt of local governments often with serious problems of repayment. For example, in Tunisia, more than half of the country's municipalities have overextended themselves after 10 years of intervention on the part of the Loan and

Support Fund for Local Authorities (CPSCL).

- In South Africa, the Development Bank of Southern Africa (DBSA) and Infrastructure Finance Corporation Limited (INCA) seem to have turned away from local governments because of the risks involved. Such difficulties have led to the closing of some of these finance institutions (CPCT in Niger and FDC in Rwanda) and the restructuring of many others (DBSA in South Africa, FPCL in Côte d'Ivoire and CPSCL in Tunisia). In general, recovery problems arise because of the failure of local governments to budget the debt service, the refusal by some elected representatives to honour commitments of predecessors, politically motivated government bailouts of delinquent local governments, and lax policies of the specialised finance institutions.

There is a need to learn from these lessons and to review the role and institutional format of specialised finance institutions in order to ensure greater management autonomy and transparency and to extend access to borrowing to local governments beyond major towns.

The Global Financial and Economic Crisis

In 2009, the impact of the financial crisis translated into a reduction of growth in the majority of the economies of the region; the GDP growth rate dropped from 5.6% in 2008 to 2.5% in 2009. All countries were affected, especially those with intermediate incomes and those oil exporter countries that were more integrated into the global economy. Local governments were also affected.

According to international organisations, while the recovery began in Africa during the first trimester of 2010, only a moderate improvement in the growth rate is forcast (4%). The losses in employment that have touched millions of households, will have long term effects, most notably on human development. This will have implications for meeting the Millennium Development Goals (MDGs).

The financial crisis also reduced the transfer of funds from expatriate workers. After having reached approximately 41 billion in 2008[14], it is estimated that with the crisis, there has been a reduction of 6.6% in 2009. For some communities, this has had serious impacts as these remittances not only finance a major part of local economic activity, but also sustain household spending.

Another feared effect of the crisis concerns official development assistance. Is unlikely to receive the additional resources foreseen in Gleneagles, largely due to the reduced contributions of certain European donors important for Africa (OECD, 2010). Reductions in ODA in 2007 already affected numerous local investment programs.

Even if it is too early to have quantified evidence of the impact on local governments, they will be affected given the existing low level of local resources. To support the economy during the economic downturn, two thirds of regional countries have cut their public spending: in balancing their budgets they will be forced to make difficult choices. Local governments will most likely suffer significant funding reductions, as was the case in a number of countries in 2009.

The impact of the crisis on local revenues will in all likelihood be more important in 2010 due to the behaviour of the principal revenues of local governments, especially land and property tax. In many African countries, local taxes are paid only when necessary, for

14. Source: African Centre for Gender and Social Development (2009), African Perspectives on the Global Economic and Financial crisis, including the impact on health.

example when the taxpayer needs a permit to build or sell property. The social impact of the economic downturn will limit new constructions and transactions, and subsequently reduce revenues.

Investment and credit constraints have already led to the closure of some businesses and the curbing of the creation of new companies. This has affected and will continue to affect the flow of resources of local governments derived from local taxes.

On the whole, we are witnessing the effects of a double edged sword, with a sharp increase in the demand for social expenditure for the poor as a result of the crisis within the real economy on the one hand, and a significant drop in own resources of local authorities on the other.

Conclusion and Recommendations (presented by UCLG Africa)

The decentralization process observed in Africa over the last two decades has had an important impact. It has contributed to a deepening democracy and improving governance in many African countries that were in search of legitimacy. Its objective has also been, naturally, the improving of service delivery and the quality of life for citizens. However, as discussed in previous sections, local governments in Africa are faced with serious funding problems that hamper the implementation of their responsibilities.

In the light of these problems, the following six proposals aim at reinforcing financial decentralization and making public commitments in favour of decentralization more credible. These proposals should also contribute to the creation of a necessary political dialogue between the main stakeholders concerned (governments, local governments, political parties, civil society, NGOs, etc.):

1) A necessity: the strengthening of the role of local governments in public expenditure to increase the credibility of decentralization.

Decentralization will be perceived as an unrealisable dream if the transfer of responsibilities to local governments does not contribute to improving citizens' quality of life due to local elected officials not having the resources to meet the responsibilities assigned to them by law. The implementation of the principle of subsidiarity dictates that local governments carry out, through the responsibilities devolved to them, a significant share of public expenditure. The first reasonable objective would be to double African local governments' share in public expenditure over the next five years. In a 10-15 year horizon, local governments should be able to reach the world average (around 20-25 percent) of public expenditure implemented by local governments.

To ensure that this goal is met and to facilitate their lobbying of national stakeholders such as the central government, Parliament and development partners, national associations of local governments must have at their disposal precise indicators to estimate their share in the public expenditure and follow its evolution. This is only possible through the implementation and strengthening of a method for institutionalizing standardized and systematic study and analysis of local governments' accounts.

2) An emergency: clarification of responsibilities between the different levels of government and estimation of the cost of decentralized responsibilities.

A recurrent observation in Africa is that the sharing of responsibilities between the different levels of government lacks precision and that the transfer of responsibilities to local governments has not gone hand in hand with a simultaneous transfer of financial resources to implement them. There are numerous laws that have been waiting for years to be applied or that have been too quickly ratified without defining the means of their implementation, and without their harmonisation with the existing laws and regulations. Maintaining a central veto power which strips local governments of their substance and autonomy, barely having taken on their new responsibilities, clouds the vision of decentralization in the field.

In fact, most local governments and their associations call for greater clarity as to their responsibilities and the means they should receive to assume them. An urgent priority in this regard is the launching of a systematic evaluation of the cost of transferred responsibilities by examining, ministry by ministry, the budget allocated when these were direct central responsibilities. This objective evaluation of the cost of transferred responsibilities should also take into account their territorial dimension, which would allow for a better understanding of their coverage and the cost of transfer. Given that each ministry cannot solve the problem of transferring the corresponding resources in isolation, a possible solution would be to establish a specific fund for the transfer of responsibilities, jointly managed by the ministry responsible for local governments and by the national local government association. This fund would house all resources for transferred responsibilities and could eventually also include additional resources assigned in accordance with the development of political will to advance the decentralization process. Planning and programming transfers of responsibilities would allow transfers to be adapted, along with the necessary technical resources, according to the national budget capacities to support them financially and effectively.

3) A priority: reinforcing the financial resources and autonomy of local governments.

Giving more room in financial matters for local governments is one of the objectives of fiscal decentralization. As shown in the previous sections, local taxes are the main source of revenues for local governments. This includes local fees and own taxes and the fees and taxes shared with the centre.

To improve local government control of and the efficiency of local tax systems, they should take part in the tax process, both in identifying the tax base and in collecting fees and taxes. In the countries where the administrative culture assigns the identification of taxpayers and the collection of fees and taxes to the national level, a first improvement could be to establish performance contracts between the centre and the local authorities in order to identify taxpayers and collect local taxes.

It is also equally advisable that areas of shared national taxes be discussed with the national local government association before the adoption of the annual budget law, and that this law should undergo a transparent design process. This would help avoid unexpected situations, such as the 2009 Budget Law withdrawal in Benin, of the industrial tools and licence tax base (*outillage industriel de l'assiette de la patente*) which had a considerable negative impact on the revenues of local authorities. During this dialogue, local authorities should pay particular attention to the taxes applied to economic activity and to land and property, and to the possible sharing with local governments, taxes on personal and corporate income, as is done in other continents.

As far as economic activity is concerned, the main questions to be discussed concern the sharing of the value added tax (VAT) and of the taxation of informal sector activities. With regard to this point, it would undoubtedly be useful if national local government associations take the initiative to set up specialized committees on these topics and present proposals, rather than waiting for the government to come up with unilateral solutions. This recommendation is even more applicable with regard to the informal sector: local authorities are best positioned to identify and control the operators in this sector and negotiate with them both the tax level that seems appropriate and how to identify the corresponding taxpayers.

The efficiency of land and property taxes depends on knowledge of the tax base. To benefit from this knowledge, it is necessary to have tools such as a land register, addresses or cadastral database, the creation and management of which often remain beyond the current capacities of most African local authorities, in particular those of medium and small towns and rural centres. For this reason it is important to discuss with the national government the possibility of technical support for the creation and management of a geographical information system that will allow the identification of the use, appropriation and exploitation of land and natural resources. This support should also include the creation of technical teams guaranteeing the updating and management of this system. The creation of these kinds of instruments must also benefit from decentralized cooperation programmes. This project must be a priority as it is decisive for the creation of a mortgage market whose current non-existence represents a significant liability for the development of a dynamic, efficient land and property market within Africa's municipalities.

In order to effectively mobilize revenue, local authorities need to have a good knowledge of local fiscal potential and of the best way of mobilizing it. If there is one field in which local authorities have to emphasize their added value, it is precisely in their ability to improve the collection of taxes and fees which will contribute to improving their service provision to citizens, while justifying the financial legitimacy of decentralization policies, which in theory, should provide an increased ability to act, drawn from their stronger public approval.

Local officials must firmly commit to mobilizing local resources as this is the only sustainable way of reinforcing local authorities' financial autonomy. In addition to mobilizing own resources, they should also run campaigns on general fiscal awareness in order to inform citizens on the good use made of local resources. This is why local budgetary reforms, in particular performance reporting to populations and central governments, the improvement of local public expenditure, and the tradition of internal audits all play an important part in reinforcing the legitimacy of local authorities to their citizens and in improving civic fiscal behaviour.

The effort local authorities make towards financial autonomy must not be undermined by central budgetary management or unified treasuries. For this reason it is necessary to progressively relax controls on budgeting and replace them with legal controls and increased transparency. It is also necessary to seriously consider the relaxing or even abandoning of unified treasury systems in countries that include local governments in them. If this is to occur, local governments must adhere to stricter financial management processes and increase the regularity of reporting to their constituents and the central authorities. Adopting instruments such as the participatory budgeting could help in this process.

4) A major request: better defined rules for transferring financial resources from central governments to local authorities.

Given the important share of transfers within local budgets, it is necessary to make the rules that govern the organization of these transfers as transparent and legible as possible, in order to ensure the traceability of transfers for the State, as well as predictability for local authorities.

The dialogue on the organization of financial transfers from the State to local authorities must be based in the most precise information available on the amounts and origins of funds, as well as the modalities of allocation (equalization transfers or conditional transfers). This information should be transmitted to each municipality and made public in an official document such as an official bulletin to facilitate civil society debate. This dialogue would be even more fruitful if it were organized within a framework of equally consultative partnership, These could follow the pattern used in the national committees on local finances created in some States –in particular within the West African Economic and Monetary Union (UEMOA)–, in which representatives from the Finances Ministry, the Ministry in charge of local governments, and the national association of local authorities are brought together. It would be advisable that such frameworks also include representatives from the Parliament, from economic stakeholders and from civil society. They could also, if necessary, be open to representatives from development partners.

Transfers should, to the greatest extent possible, be predictable. For this reason it is advisable in the context of Africa to set a minimum level of public resources that must be transferred by the State to local authorities every year, and to ensure that these follow an objective formula negotiated between the two parties. Such a formula should take into account the need to encourage local authorities involved in local economic development, as well as the need to address equity and equalization between local authorities with different economic levels and/or facilities.

5) A necessity that cannot be ignored: encouraging access of local authorities to loans and financial markets.

Although most States' legislations allow local authorities the ability to borrow from financial establishments or to access financial markets, in reality this ability is only used by a very limited number of African local authorities. The often drastic conditions imposed on local authorities when attempting to access loans provides a first explanation of this state of affairs. A second reason is the lack of adaptation of the financial tools and requirements that local authorities must use and meet to access credit. Thirdly, there is a certain level of ignorance both nationally and on the part of local authorities both of the potential offered by the financial market and of the true debt capacities of local authorities.

Nevertheless, the tremendous need for infrastructures and facilities in African local authorities is obvious, and cannot be met only with the mobilization of local authorities' savings or even with the mobilization of State resources. It is necessary that local authorities have access to loans and financial markets to meet the challenges raised by the continent's rapid urban growth.

Delegating some local public services to private operators is a first method that many local authorities are currently using to respond to the challenges of urban growth. This approach is particularly useful for the commercial services, where the income from their operation generally justifies the investment.

In order for local governments to access institutional financing from the financial market, they must have clear books of account and improve their local governance to be able to inspire the confidence of financial operators. However it should also be the responsibility of the State to promote instruments that could facilitate local authorities' access to loans. The development of financial institutions specialized in granting loans to local authorities or in the intermediation for local authorities' access to the financial market is a first step, provided that the work of these institutions is better evaluated.

The almost complete absence of African local authorities from the bond market is also a sign of the poor development of African financial markets and, undoubtedly of the lack of preparation on the part of African central and local authorities to access potential revenue source that could easily be exploited if developed. This difficulty could be caused by the problem mostly medium and small local authorities have in establishing acceptable applications for funds. The idea of a mutualisation of demands, along with technical support organized in the framework of a development fund for cities, as suggested by the World Organization of Metropolises (METROPOLIS), is worth studying. A study should be launched across Africa to analyze the conditions for making this proposal a reality within the context of the continent. Launching this reflection is a priority agenda for United Cities and Local Governments Africa (UCLGA).

The improvement and harmonization of budgetary and accounting procedures of local authorities is a pre-condition for accessing loan. These procedures do indeed vary greatly between local authorities both within the same country and between local authorities from different countries. In addition to this external and internal heterogeneity, there are several constrains which remain important: local accounting which is poorly adapted to decentralization, non-consolidation of the expenditures within municipal budgets, lack of built capital, etc. This work will increase the transparency of local accounts, an essential element for developing a sustainable financial market.

6) A pressing need: strengthening human resources for African local authorities, in particular in the field of management and financial engineering.

This strengthening typically comes from what local authorities can do themselves, via programmes and projects of decentralized cooperation, both at the national level and at the continental/international level. The local government associations must learn from each other to improve negotiation procedures with national government and the follow-up of budget negotiations at the parliamentary level. These exchanges can contribute to the modernization of local financial systems so as to facilitate in the long-term the access to financial markets and promote citizen participation in budgetary decisions at the local level. One of the first tasks will be strengthening the capacity of local governments and their associations to regularly follow and analyse, in each country, their finances and financing.

The idea of creating a fund that would encourage the strengthening of capacities via the exchange of staff and experts was suggested by the participants of the latest AfriCities Summit held in December 2009 in Marrakech. UCLGA is currently studying the best way to implement this proposal as quickly as possible with the support of all partners wishing to participate.

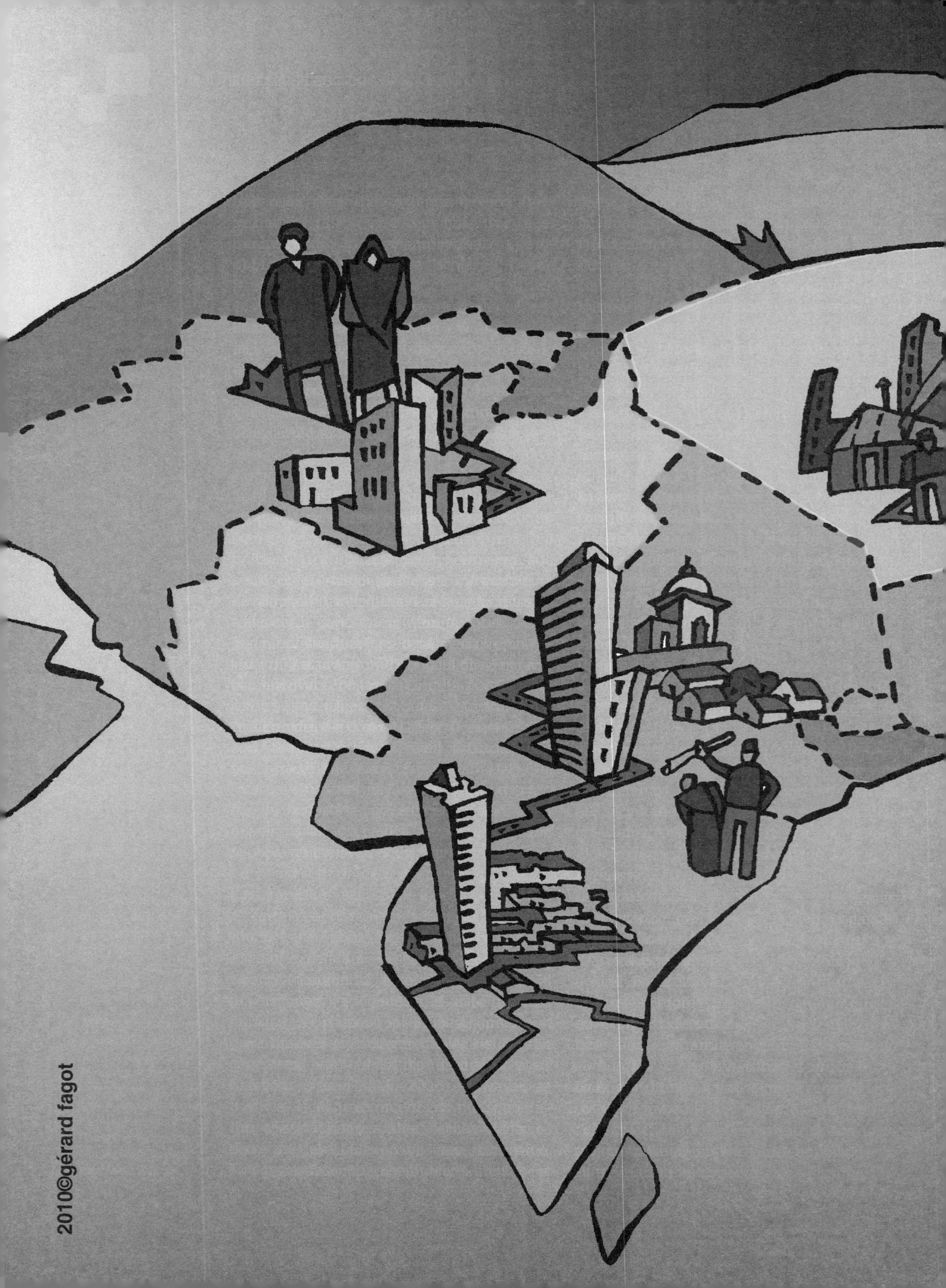

3. Asia-Pacific

Blane D. Lewis*
Lee Kuan
Yew School of Public Policy
National University of Singapore
Singapore

Bob Searle*
Consultant
Australia

* *The authors thank participants in the UCLG GOLD II ASPAC Workshop in Guangzhou, China, on 10 November 2009 and attendees at the UCLG ASPAC Workshop on Local Finances in Batam, Indonesia, on 25-26 June 2010 for useful comments on drafts of this Chapter, especially Sung Il Lim of the Korea Research Institute for Local Administration. Blane Lewis was principally responsible for the work on South Asia, East Asia and South East Asia; and Bob Searle for Australia and New Zealand.*

In most countries in the Asia-Pacific Region, the context in which fiscal decentralization policymaking and implementation takes place does not usually change radically over short periods of time. Nevertheless, a number of countries in this region have recently seen quite significant changes to the structure and use of local government.

In July 2009, the President of Pakistan postponed local elections based on the unanimous decision of governors. In the meantime, governors appointed "non-political" administrators to replace elected mayors and vice mayors; and the magistracy system has been revived. As such, the very existence of local government in Pakistan is under debate.

In China, the intergovernmental system has in the recent past concentrated on promoting economic development, and this emphasis has generated a number of noteworthy successes. Given these achievements, Chinese leaders now appear poised to re-focus their decentralization program on delivering quality local public services. The change will be operationalized as part of the government's renewed attempts to address equity and poverty concerns in the context of its recently initiated program to "build a harmonious society".

In 2003, Japan's government launched a broad set of "Trinity Reforms", which it hoped would ease many of the long-standing constraints on local government operations. The overarching goal of the reforms is to provide sub-national governments with more fiscal autonomy: particular objectives focus on reducing sub-national government reliance on specific purpose transfers from the central government, increasing access to own-source revenue and streamlining the untied equalization grant. It is too early to judge whether these objectives have been achieved.

In Indonesia, recent changes to laws envision the eventual decentralization of property tax to the local level. This change has the potential to significantly increase the amount of own-source revenues available to local governments but also portends some daunting administrative challenges. More broadly, the government has begun to outline revisions to its laws on both administrative and fiscal decentralization with a view to again improve the legal framework introduced in 1999.

Cambodia passed an Organic Law on Decentralization and Democratic Development in early 2009 and is now in the process of formulating the implementation plan to establish district and provincial administrations as intermediate tiers between the central government and the communes. In Nepal, the writing of a new constitution is progressing (with completion due in 2011) and will include, a clarification of the roles and responsibilities for the tiers of local government, provisions for a more secure base for local elected officials, and make funds transfers more transparent and formula-based.

In general, it might be said that local government in the countries with more developed economies is undergoing reform to the structures and procedures within which it operates. On the other hand, local government in the nations with developing economies is at an earlier stage in its development.

This chapter describes and analyzes local government finances in the Asia-Pacific region. It is divided into separate sections for South Asia, East Asia, South East Asia, Australia and New Zealand. Each section concentrates on the experience of the countries for which a reasonable amount of reliable primary and secondary information is available. In South Asia, the local government finances of India, Pakistan, and Bangladesh are highlighted, with some comments also provided on Nepal and Sri Lanka. In East Asia, the fiscal decentralization systems of China, Japan, and Korea are reviewed. The section on South East Asia examines the intergovernmental framework in Indonesia, Philippines, Vietnam, and Thailand, and provides comments on Cambodia and Malaysia. The countries covered in Asia are among the most prominent in their respective regions and account for over 50 percent of the world's population. The section on the Oceania sub-region covers Australia and New Zealand. It has in some cases been difficult to differentiate between local government and other levels of sub-national government. Generally, it can be assumed that the lower tier of sub-national government equates to local government.

In examining the structure and performance of each country's intergovernmental fiscal system, the chapter focuses on expenditures, revenues, intergovernmental transfers, and debt finance. A variety of input and output criteria are taken into account in evaluating performance, including the adequacy of local government resources, local tax and spending discretion, incentives in the intergovernmental transfer system, local government administrative and management capacity, and the quality of local public services. In addition, the chapter highlights a number of pressing constraints on local finances across sub-regions and countries, and provides observations for improving fiscal decentralization policy for selected countries where sufficient data were available. A final section of the paper makes some broad conclusions that may be important for the reform of decentralization policy across countries in the Asia-Pacific region.

South Asian Local Governments Finances

Structure

Expenditure[1]

Sub-national governments in India contribute up to about two-thirds of consolidated government spending, one-third of which comes from states and local governments (i.e. "local bodies"). State governments are empowered to constitute lower level governments, including urban and rural local bodies (ULBs and RLBs)[2]. Of total local expenditure, 85 to 90 percent—is ULB spending concentrated in the largest urban centers; the remainder is from RLBs, with village *Panchayats* responsible for about 85 to 90 percent of rural local government expenditure. There is, however, a great deal of variation across states and local governments. Approximately 60 percent of total local government spending goes to "core functions", including water supply, street lighting, sanitation and roads. Not surprisingly, ULB spending is more concentrated than RLB spending on these core functions.

Legally, Pakistan has a three tier system of sub-national governments although these were all dissolved as elected bodies in July 2009. Prior to that, sub-national government spending amounted to about one-third of consolidated public sector expenditure, with most sub-national spending carried out by provinces as opposed to local governments (Districts, Tehsil Municipal Administrations—TMAs, and Unions[3]). In theory, districts have expenditure responsibility for elementary and secondary education, primary health care, and the environment; in practice

1. *See Table 3.1.*
2. *The 3682 Rural Local Bodies are either Panchayats (of which there are three tiers) or Autonomous Rural Councils; while the 247 033 Urban Local Bodies are known either as Municipal Corporations, Municipalities or Nagar Panchayats.*
3. *There are, in total, over 6600 local government units in Pakistan.*

these functions appear, for the most part, to be carried out exclusively by or in concurrence with provinces. TMAs are responsible for basic municipal services and building control. Unions perform very few minor functions.

The sub-national government share of total spending in Bangladesh is more limited than that of India and Pakistan, amounting to 15 percent or less. Local governments (Union *Parishads*, *Pourashavas* and City Corporations) account for an estimated two-thirds of the sub-national total. Union *Parishads'* spending focuses on agriculture, road construction and maintenance, and health and sanitation; *Pourashavas'* expenditure is mostly devoted to waste management, water supply, sanitation, and drainage; City Corporations concentrate their spending on the usual urban infrastructure services. Many of these functions are carried out concurrently with deconcentrated agencies of the central government.

In Nepal, the local governments' share of total public sector expenditure is also very small, but perhaps surprisingly high considering the state of development of local government and the uncertainty surrounding future levels and spheres of activity under the constitution now being rewritten. The pressure from local government is for the constitution to limit the functions of the central government and, under the subsidiarity principle, give more responsibilities to sub-national government.

Own-Source Revenues

Indian state and local government own-source revenues comprise just over one-third of total consolidated public revenues. State governments assign revenue sources to local governments but only municipalities have any real tax powers. The local governments' share of total sub-national own-source is 10 percent or less, dominated by ULBs, which collect over 90 percent of local government revenue. Property taxes are the most important urban government own-source revenues. The *octroi* (a tax on goods brought into the locality from outside) was important in the past but has now been abolished in all but one state. RLBs derive most of their own-source revenue from various minor licenses, fees, and charges. The small share of rural local government own-source revenue is concentrated at the *gram parachat* level, with the vast majority of all rural revenue being derived from transfers.

Revenue raised by the sub-national government in Pakistan is only about seven percent of total public revenue. Again, the majority of sub-national own-source revenue is from provinces. Local own-source revenues were only 8 percent of local budgets in 2008-09, suggesting that such revenue is less than one percent of total public revenues (Bahl and Cyan, 2008). Most district revenue comes from a variety of charges and fees. In theory, the property tax has been assigned to TMAs but the provinces administer this tax in most areas. Unions have no revenue raising authority.

Sub-national government own-source revenues in Bangladesh are even more limited than in India and Pakistan. Total sub-national government own-sources amount to less than two percent of consolidated public revenues and there is no information on how the sub-national total is distributed across different levels of governments. For Union *Parishads* the most important own-source revenue is the holding tax on the value of land; for *Pourashavas* and city corporations, the major own-source revenues are those

Table 3.1: Sub-national Government Share of Total Public Expenditure and Revenue – South Asia

Country	Share of Total Public Expenditure (%)			Share of Total Public Revenue (%)		
	Sub-national	Upper Tier	Lower Tiers	Sub-national	Upper Tier	Lower Tiers
India	66	33	33	33	30	3
Pakistan	33	28	5	7	6.5	0.5
Bangladesh	15	5	10	2	1	1
Nepal	9	--	9	14	--	14

Source: UCLG data files and other sources. Figures are approximations. Data is from most recent year available: India 2004, Pakistan 2004, Bangladesh 2005, Nepal 2008.

from the property tax, land transfer tax and building permits.

Intergovernmental Transfers[4]

As Table 3.1 shows, local governments in India experiences a very high level of vertical fiscal imbalance (revenue is only 3 percent of total public revenue while expenditure is 33 percent of national total). Intergovernmental transfers to local governments in India make up nearly 90 percent of their total revenues, with transfers being received from both central and state governments but most coming from the latter as central transfers to local governments are mostly distributed through states. State transfers to local governments, including both revenue sharing and grants, comprise around one third of total state expenditures. Both types of transfers appear, in most cases, to be rather ad-hoc and tied to particular kinds of spending mandated by the grantor. On a per capita basis, transfers to rural local governments are significantly larger than those to ULBs but there are significant deviations from these norms (Rao, 2000b; Oommen, 2008). In part these variations relate to the differential roles played by the State Finance Commissions (SFCs), which are charged with determining appropriate revenue sharing and grants-in-aid allocations.

Service delivery by Pakistani local governments is also financed largely through intergovernmental transfers. At the district government level, transfers make up 90 percent or more of total revenues (Kardar, 2006), but Karachi is the exception to this rule with about 20 percent of its revenue coming from own-sources. TMAs are somewhat less reliant on provincial transfers, with transfers comprising 60 to 80 percent of total revenues, depending on the province and district of location. Unions are financed exclusively by a grant from provinces. Most intergovernmental transfers to the local level are general-purpose in nature, although provinces also provide specific project grants.

Intergovernmental transfers also dominate local government revenues in Bangladesh, with transfers constituting 90 percent or more of the total. There is considerable variation, however, with rural local governments (Union *Parishads*) being particularly dependent on grants and urban local governments (*Pourashavas* and City Corporations) somewhat less so. The most important transfer is the block allocation. While it is the largest grant, it is still very small from a national perspective, making up less than two percent of the state

4. *See Table 3.2.*

Table 3.2: Intergovernmental Transfers as Local Government Revenue Source – South Asia

Country	Share of Transfers in Total Local Revenue (%)	Relative Importance of Type of Transfer		
		Revenue Sharing	General Purpose	Special Purpose
India	90	Medium	Low	High
Pakistan	90	Low	High	Medium
Bangladesh	90	Low	High	Medium
Nepal	n.a. (but heavily dependent)	n.a.	n.a.	n.a.
Sri Lanka	n.a. (but heavily dependent)	n.a.	n.a.	n.a.

Source: UCLG data files and other sources. Figures are approximations. Data are for most recent year available: India 2004, Pakistan 2004, Bangladesh 2005.

budget. This general-purpose transfer is intended to fund local development activities. Other development grants are specific-purpose in nature, often focused on particular projects (some of which are funded by international donors). Local governments in Bangladesh also receive small grants to support the salaries and allowances of local civil servants.

Debt Finance[5]

Indian sub-national governments are permitted to borrow and many do so. Resources borrowing include central government, donors (indirectly), public and private financial institutions, and capital markets. Returns to bondholders are tax free. Borrowing to cover budget deficits is common at all levels of government, and consolidated borrowing to cover deficits has recently reached around 15 percent of GDP. About 80 percent of this borrowing is done by state and local governments. Most worryingly, much of the borrowing appears to finance recurrent rather than capital expenditures. The majority of local borrowing is by urban local bodies, with much of it concentrated in the states of Andhra Pradesh, Gujarat, Karnataka, Madhya Pradesh, Maharashtra, and Punjab, and the widely disseminated experience of Tamil Nadu with the Tamil Nadu Urban Development Fund (see box 3.1). States formally guarantee the repayment of local government loans. The totality of outstanding state guarantees extended to local governments may amount to as much as 10 percent of GDP or slightly less (Pradhan, 2004).

Although Pakistani provinces may legally assume debt, local governments may not. Local governments in Bangladesh are permitted by law to borrow in order to finance capital development. There is no data on amounts borrowed by local governments of any type, although it is clear that it has not amounted to much. It seems all local government borrowing is done through the central government's on-lending channels (Boex et al, 2002).

In Nepal, the Town Development Fund lends to municipalities for infrastructure development, but other tiers of local government have no access to borrowing. In Sri Lanka, local government borrowing is from the Local Loans and Development Fund of the central government but there are insufficient funds to meet local government demand.

5. See Table 3.3.

Table 3.3: Legal Authorization and Extent of Local Government Borrowing – South Asia

Country	Borrowing Legally Authorized	Extent of Borrowing
India	Yes	Moderate
Pakistan	No	None
Bangladesh	Yes	Very Limited
Nepal	Yes (but only by Municipalities)	n.a.
Sri Lanka	Yes	limited

Source: UCLG data files, among others sources.

Box 3.1. Municipal Bonds in India

The Tamil Nadu Urban Development Fund (TNUDF) was established in 1996 for development of urban infrastructure at the state level. It was the first public-private partnership providing long-term debt for civic infrastructure and was not state guaranteed. The unit capital is contributed by the government of Tamil Nadu (49 percent) and three Indian Financial Institutions with international finance support (World Bank, Japan Bank for International Cooperation and the German KfW). The TNUDF also raises funds from capital markets.

This fund has been an important first step towards linking domestic capital markets and the financing need of small cities. The eligible borrowers are urban local bodies (Corporations, Municipalities and Town Panchayats) and private institutions creating urban infrastructure.

Since the launch of the Jawaharlal Nehru National Urban Renewal Mission (JNNURM) in 2005, the role of financial markets in financing sub-national governments has increased sharply. The JNNURM has two main missions: a) the development of urban infrastructure and governance, and b) the development of basic services for the urban poor.

More generally, municipal issues are provided as revenue bonds, with fixed interest rate of around 12-14 percent, with or without government guarantee. Their maturity is between 7-15 years and they are structured obligations. Investor income can be either taxable or tax free.

Performance[6]

Current and Capital Resource Adequacy

In India, municipal governments generally operate under severe fiscal constraints. This can be attributed both to their narrow and inelastic tax base and an indifferent attitude to the use of funds. Within this context, local governments are not able to generate sufficient resources to meet even the operating and maintenance costs of the

6. See Table 3.4.

services they provide. Only a few large urban local bodies in India (the million plus cities) appear to have sufficient revenue for service delivery. Large urban centers can have significant own-source revenues, making up well over 50 percent of their total revenues, but some of this flows to parastatals they use to provide services on a cost-recovery basis. Nevertheless, they are less dependent on transfers than other local governments, which are severely resource constrained, especially in rural areas. Rural bodies have few own-source revenues and are almost completely dependent on transfers from the central and state governments. Most state governments also find themselves in precarious fiscal conditions and this in turn limits the extent to which they can transfer resources to local governments, thereby extending fiscal constraints to the lowest levels (Rao, 2000b; Oommen, 2008).

In 2005, the Indian government began a large urban renewal program and extended grant assistance to municipalities for urban infrastructure and governance. Based on city development plans, tied grants will be made available for better basic services for the poor, urban land development, and major infrastructure developments.

Local governments in Pakistan also suffer from harsh resource constraints. Access to tax revenue is very limited at the local level, as noted above, and transfers from provinces to local governments are not usually sufficient to meet residual funding needs. As expected, the more constrained a Pakistani province is due to lack of transfers received from the central government, the more constrained its transfers are to local governments. Local government capital needs must be met out of own-source revenues and transfers as they are not allowed to borrow. This further exacerbates their capacity to produce adequate levels of services (Manning et al, 2003; Bahl and Cyan, 2008).

Bangladeshi local government resources are also extremely constrained. The resources available are exceptionally limited to allow them to satisfy the meager service responsibilities that have been assigned to them at minimally acceptable levels (Boex et al, 2002; Fox and Menon, 2008).

In Nepal, local governments cannot fund all their recurrent expenditure, so that revenue reassignment or grant increases must be achieved if services are to be provided. In Sri Lanka, the provision of services and maintenance of infrastructure are among the most important issues facing local government.

Taxing and Spending Discretion

State governments in India determine the kinds of services that local governments should deliver and the particular taxes that they may levy (based on recommendations from the SFCs). The central government has allowed for reasonably significant expenditure responsibility and tax autonomy to be decentralized to local governments in recent amendments to the constitutions. Decisions regarding implementation of these provisions, however, rest with the states, which generally have not assigned extensive fiscal powers to local governments. Of course there are exceptions to this rule, including Karnataka, Madhya Pradesh and Kerala for example, which have been more proactive in devolving expenditure and revenue assignments (World Bank, 2007).

Indian local governments have limited discretion over the taxes assigned to them. State governments exert much control over defining bases and setting allowable rates of tax. Local governments do, however, have reasonable spending autonomy over their own source revenue where restrictions do not seem particularly onerous. This is not the case with transfers. The vast bulk of revenue sharing and grants-in-aid is tied to particular types of spending or projects that the states deem important. In this regard, local governments are better viewed as implementing agencies of the states than autonomous local entities. Service delivery discretion is further constrained by the concurrent nature of almost all assigned functions and the parallel institutional arrangements (essentially local level para-statal bodies of the states) that have been developed for the delivery of services such as slum improvement and water provision.

Law allows for significant fiscal responsibilities to be devolved to the local level in Pakistan, but provinces determine precise expenditure and revenue assignments of local governments under their purview. Expenditure assignments could vary quite widely across provinces but are in general quite limited. Pakistan's constitution allows for the complete separation of tax bases across levels of government but provincial governments have access to very limited sources of revenue. This in turn constrains revenue assignments at the local level.

As is the case in India, local governments in Pakistan have little discretion over the taxes that are assigned to them by provinces and can only change taxation arrangements with the approval of the provinces which define local tax bases (including exemptions) and set local tax rates. In addition, provinces have authority to assess property values used in determining liabilities related to the property tax, ostensibly a TMA revenue.

Local governments in Pakistan also have limited control over spending on service delivery. Provinces exercise significant controls over both recurrent and development (capital) spending. Provinces prescribe spending priorities in local budgets and sometimes even require ex-ante approval for local governments to incur expenditures. Provinces specify in detail the expenditure objects targeted in transfers that they make to local governments, especially those for capital spending, and make balanced budgeting a condition of grant receipt. In extreme cases, provinces have used assessments of poor performance to take back control of functions originally decentralized.

Most employees of local governments in Pakistan are provided by other tiers of government. Local governments have little or no authority over assigned staff and cannot fire civil servants appointed by other tiers. Federal and provincial pay increases established in law are simply passed through to local governments without regard to the local budget or to local government's ability to pay. This constitutes a significant unfunded mandate.

As is clear from previous discussion, public expenditures and revenues are very centralized in Bangladesh. The central government dominates service delivery even in education and health where related functions in other nations have been devolved to local governments. Similarly the central government keeps a tight reign on almost all sources of revenue.

Bangladeshi local governments have very little decision-making authority, even over taxes and services under their responsibility. The district council (a deconcentrated unit at the regional level) must approve all local budgets and local tax and fee rates are set by the central government. In addition, most block grants are earmarked. Central officials are actively engaged in local government decisions on spending priorities and the central government must also approve development projects prior to implementation. Essentially all local government staff

Table 3.4: Performance of Intergovernmental System – South Asia

	Resource Adequacy	Fiscal Discretion	Performance Incentives	Management Capacity	Service Outcomes
India	Large urban LG resources reasonably adequate; small urban and rural governments severely resource constrained.	LGs have very little fiscal discretion. States control local taxing and spending to large extent.	States have made significant use of incentives but rewards focus on past not future behavior.	Weak tax administration and expenditure management.	Weak service outcomes.
Pakistan	Most local governments suffer harsh resource constraints.	Limited LG discretion over taxes and spending. Provincial control ubiquitous.	No experience with performance incentives.	Reasonably sound tax administration at district level. Decent expenditure management but mostly carried out by central employees.	Weak service outcomes.
Bangladesh	Resources of LGs severely constrained.	LG discretion extremely limited. LGs essentially deconcentrated units of CG.	Some effective use of incentives to encourage "local" revenue effort.	Weak and corrupt deconcentrated tax administration. Management of service delivery mostly a CG concern.	Weak service outcomes. Overt focus on magisterial and police functions.
Nepal	Grossly inadequate.	Limited discretion and confused mandates.	These have only recently been introduced.	Very limited outside large Municipalities.	Weak outcomes.
Sri Lanka	Inadequate.	Limited discretion and confused mandates.	n.a.	Very limited outside large Municipalities.	Weak outcomes.

Source: Author's assessment based on UCLG data files, among other sources (see bibliography)

members are employees of the central government so, while mayors and councils are popularly elected, they have very little authority over their staff. Mayors cannot appoint independent (i.e. non central government) staff without the approval of the center and such approval is very difficult to obtain. In many ways, local governments in Bangladesh are deconcentrated units of other tiers of government.

In Nepal, local governments have very little power to set the taxes and fees for the revenue sources available to them, and lack of clarity of revenue assignments results in government Ministries encroaching on local government revenue mandates. There is similar overlapping of responsibilities for service delivery that creates confusion and non-provision by the poorly-resourced local government sector. In Sri Lanka, there is also confusion in the allocation of revenue bases between the central and local spheres of government.

Incentives in the Intergovernmental Framework

Many Indian states have integrated performance incentives into revenue sharing schemes for local governments. These incentives are operationalized as weights to variables used to allocate revenue shares and are intended to encourage good local government behavior in revenue effort, service management, etc. However, the weights are developed exclusively, based on past behavior and may therefore be seen as rewards for past behavior rather than encouraging future performance. Generally, empirical evidence suggests that transfers are negatively associated with local own-source revenue generation (Mathur and Peterson, 2006).

Pakistani provinces have not, in general, made much use of performance incentives in their dealings with local governments. Most provinces have not incorporated incentives into the allocation of transfers that they make to local governments (Peterson, 2002).

The Bangladeshi experience with incentives has been somewhat more positive. The local revenue raising incentives created by the intergovernmental transfers, for example, appear to be relatively constructive, or at least benign. Transfers are unlikely to discourage local revenue efforts and may even encourage it. It's clear at least that increasing grant levels are positively associated with local own-source revenues. On the other hand, the limited discretion local governments have over spending, including those from their own-sources, may well dampen enthusiasm for increasing collections (see Fox and Menon, 2008).

In Nepal, the grant system is supposed to be formula based but is ad-hoc in practice, with no criteria specified in legislation or policy documents. They are, however, experimenting with minimum conditions and performance measures in village and district development committees and municipalities. In Sri Lanka, local governments are overly dependent on transfers, but their lack of regularity and predictability is a problem for fiscal management.

Tax Administration and Expenditure Management

Indian local government tax administration and expenditure management is quite weak: a prescribed budget process, which includes formulation of a plan, its approval by local elected officials and implementation, is not generally operational (Bahl et al, 2005). A study in Rajasthan found that local governments there made no use of optional taxes under their authority. The local officials' explanation was that councils and/or citizens would be reluctant to pay, even if they resulted in improved service delivery. This attitude could also explain local tax collection inefficiency. On the service side, local governments do not generally seek additional responsibility, a function of their unwillingness to assume either greater management burdens or the financial costs associated with the increased responsibility. There are, however, some reforms and innovative experiences (see Box 3.2) that could be used as examples by other states and local governments (Mathur and Peterson, 2006).

The system of local tax administration in Pakistan is unusual. District governments have two types of tax collection units, one to collect provincial taxes and another that focuses on the administration of district revenues. The capacity of both tax administration agencies is reasonably sound, although districts themselves only benefit to a certain extent from such capabilities. TMA tax administrative systems have a long history but their administrative capacity is weaker than that of district governments. Lack of training among tax collectors is a particular problem (Peterson, 2002; Bahl and Cyan, 2008).

The quality of local expenditure management capacity is also reasonable at the local government level, at least from a technical perspective. Unfortunately, most civil servants working in district and TMA governments are federal or provincial employees (but paid from local budgets) and can be transferred at the discretion of federal or provincial managers. As such, existing local management capacity can be illusory and temporary.

Box 3.2. Reform of Property Taxation in Andhra Pradesh

Prior to the changes, property taxes were only 13 percent of municipal revenue and 0.1 percent of State GDP. The tax suffered from being based on difficult annual rental valuation provisions, a complex set of exemptions and high administrative costs.

The state clarified and simplified the valuation system, to make it more objective, standardized but widened the exemption scope to improve cost: benefit ratios, made payment easier by involving the banking sector and provided grant incentives to councils to improve collection rates relative to demand notices. Increases in collections were generally over 25 percent.

While the revenue authority of local governments in Bangladesh is limited, they could be getting more out of their revenue sources than they do. Many municipal governments have made little effort to expand the property tax database or conduct valuations in a timely manner, and collection efficiency is low. Moreover, there are widespread reports of corruption in tax collection and an apparent culture of tax avoidance and evasion adds to the problem. Some estimates indicate that only about one quarter of the businesses in *Pourashavas* regularly pay their tax liabilities (Fox and Menon, 2008).

The management of spending and service delivery is the responsibility of higher tier rather than local governments in Bangladesh. Local governments seem to be held responsible for the local accountability function but not for the management and delivery of services. This "implicit bifurcation" of regional and local public administration has long been an issue and creates poor incentives for management performance and service quality (Fox and Menon, 2008).

In Nepal, the very limited capacity of local government staff is currently being addressed through donor funding, but much still needs to be done. As might be expected after a prolonged period of civil unrest, Sri Lanka has a particularly large need for capacity development within local government staff.

Service Delivery Outcomes

Local public service outcomes in India are generally inadequate (World Bank, 2004). Basic education, health, water and sanitation have been judged to be some of the weakest in the world. Illiteracy is high, local public health systems are non-functional in many parts of the country, quality of drinking water is less than minimally adequate and general living conditions are often unsanitary. Access to social services by the rural poor is particularly problematic. There are, of course, exceptions.

Pakistani local public service outcomes are similarly sub-standard, but variation is extreme across provinces and local governments. A contributing factor to poor public services is the apparent indifference and corruption of the nation's bureaucrats: a problem for all tiers of government. Citizen surveys in Pakistan rate the honesty and responsiveness of their civil servants much lower than do the citizens of other countries in South Asia (Peterson, 2002).

Bangladeshi service outcomes are very weak across the board. Local governments in

Bangladesh are reputed to be inefficient and unaccountable providers of public services. Local bureaucracies tend to be isolated from citizens and are, in general, seen to be highly politicized and corrupt. Local administrations are more given to political and social control than they are to the delivery of typical public services. To the extent that public services are emphasized at all, they tend to be more related to magisterial and police functions rather than those that might be more useful in raising the welfare of citizens (Boex et al, 2002; Fox and Menon, 2008).

Selected Pressing Issues and Binding Constraints

The most pressing issue in India is the general lack of fiscal decentralization to urban and rural local bodies. Despite having the constitutional power to devolve significant spending and revenue authority to local governments, the states have not done so in any meaningful way. While some local governments have unilaterally started taking on more responsibility for service delivery and tax collection a more proactive policy needs to be adopted. Nevertheless citizens often seem to be reluctant to pay for more and/or better local services (and where they may be more willing they have few mechanisms through which to register their willingness). For decentralization to proceed, improving the cooperation between local governments and their citizens must be a priority (Mathur and Peterson, 2006).

A second area of concern relates to the performance of the State Finance Commissions (SFC). As noted above, SFCs are charged with a wide range of duties, including determining local tax assignments, deriving appropriate local shares of state revenues, and establishing the appropriate amount of grants-in-aid to local bodies. The performance of SFCs on all these counts has often been disappointing. Where SFCs have been proactive and focused, their recommendations have largely been ignored by the states.

Since July 2009 when the President of Pakistan dissolved elected local governments, reportedly based on the unanimous decision of provincial governors, the very existence of local governments in Pakistan has been under debate. Beyond that most basic of issues, two others deserve to be highlighted. One is the role of the provinces in decentralization. Similar to their state counterparts in India, provinces in Pakistan determine the extent to which decentralization proceeds within their jurisdiction. So far, they have decided that decentralized public service provision and financing stops, for the most part, at the provincial level; and the central government has not stepped in to override this stance. The second issue concerns the extremely low level of local government own-source revenues and the lack of any linkage it has to service delivery and cost recovery. Although limited own-source revenue is often a problem in developing countries, it is especially acute in Pakistan. Moreover, it has not been a priority of central policy-makers in the past and it is not clear that they see lack of tax authority and discretion as a problem (Bahl et al, 2008).

The key issue in Bangladesh is the extent to which government wishes to genuinely decentralize its public sector to the local level. Currently, the system for the provision and financing of public services is more akin to deconcentration rather than decentralization. Local governments have very limited responsibility for delivering services and raising revenues and next to no discretion over the services and taxes that have been assigned to them. All civil servants at the local level are essentially central government employees. Significant reorganization would be necessary to implement a more decentralized system.

A second set of important issues relates to the complexity of the Bangladeshi government structure. The five separate levels of operation results in increased costs of administration, and an excessive number of official levels of government. This is further complicated by the existence of other, parallel institutional arrangements for service delivery operating alongside the official structure. In addition, the complex structure seems itself to be constantly in flux, as each new governing administration seeks to use the system to further its own and different political ends. Again, the effective operation of any system of service delivery and governance, regardless of its deconcentrated or decentralized orientation, is made difficult by the consistent and sweeping changes over time (Fox and Menon, 2008).

In both Nepal and Sri Lanka, the pressing issues relate to the current state of development of local government and the need to clarify legislation and improve the capacity of local government to manage and provide service delivery. Nepal particularly needs to give more responsibilities and revenue sources to local government.

Conclusions and Observations on South Asia

India may wish to revisit the strategy of letting states decide on the extent of allowable decentralization to local bodies. The voluntary approach has so far resulted in little success. Policymakers might consider whether a mandatory approach, under the careful direction and guidance of the center, might be a more viable way to proceed.

In this regard, the Indian Federal Government should consider a number of actions:

- Devolve specific functions to local governments to reinforce local democracy: where concurrent responsibilities are deemed necessary, respective responsibilities of the states and local governments should be defined;
- Award more revenue autonomy and discretion over the use of revenue instruments to local governments;
- Give exclusive authority to local governments over the property tax and taxes on motor vehicles; and give access to personal income tax, via a piggyback scheme, at least to some urban local governments;
- Develop a transparent and predictable system of formula based transfers to local governments, so as to provide adequate revenues, equalize fiscal capacities to meet expenditure responsibilities and improve fund distribution;
- Provide local urban and rural bodies with capital grants;
- Promote a more structured budget process, along with improved auditing;
- Facilitate access to loan funds for local governments to finance capital expenditure, and develop their creditworthiness and administrative capacity. Existing regulations concerning municipal access to borrowing should be reduced or streamlined.

In addition, the central government could be more pro-active in supporting and guiding State Finance Commissions (SFCs). SFCs need increased capacity to carry out their assigned roles more effectively and, with increased capacity, the government might consider making SFC recommendations binding like those of the Central Finance Commission.

In Pakistan, the first policy priority for the country should be to revive the system of elected local governments. In particular, Pakistan should:

- Reconsider the practice of allowing provincial governments to decide the extent of decentralization at sub-provincial levels, which has led to limited decentralization.
- Revisit the basic objectives on which intergovernmental fiscal relations are based.
- Devolve more expenditure responsibilities and tax authority to local governments.
- Assure the development of a modern system of fiscal transfers.

Bangladesh first needs to decentralize their system of public service provision and finance. Then a number of policy questions automatically present themselves. Like other nations in south Asia, these relate to expenditure assignments, tax assignments, intergovernmental transfers, local borrowing and methods of vertical and horizontal accountability. A first priority, however, should be to make local officials more accountable to their citizens by having them engaged by the local governments and giving elected officials more control over the hiring and firing of these staff.

East Asian Local Governments Finances

Structure

Expenditure[7]

Expenditures are extremely decentralized in China, where sub-national governments[8] are responsible for about 70 percent of recorded total public spending. Local (i.e. sub-provincial) governments account for most of this, contributing about 50 percent of the recorded total, but there are also substantial amounts that are not recorded. Local government expenditure budgets focus on education and health services: and the bulk of public sector spending in education and health —as much as 85 percent— is carried out by local governments. Chinese local governments are internationally different from most in that they also devote reasonably large shares of their budgets to social insurance schemes of various kinds (including unemployment compensation, health insurance, and pensions), functions usually carried out by the central government (Bahl and Martínez-Vázquez, 2009).

Expenditures are also quite decentralized in Japan. Japanese sub-national governments (47 prefectures and 1820 municipalities) comprise about 60 percent of total public expenditure, about two-thirds of which is done by municipalities. Sub-national governments focus on infrastructure, education and social welfare, which respectively constitute 25 percent, 18 percent and 18 percent of local government expenditure. These shares are reasonably similar for both prefectures and municipalities.

Following the strong move towards decentralization in the 1990's, spending is also quite decentralized in Korea. The relative size of Korean sub-national government has increased over 5 fold since these reforms and sub-national governments (special metropolitan area of Seoul, 6 metropolitan cities and 9 provinces) and lower-level sub-national governments (75 cities, 86 counties and 69 districts) now account for about 45 percent of total public expenditure. Adding expenditure by local education authorities, which are independent of local governments, would increase this to about 60 percent, such that local governments dominate the public sector. The upper level of sub-national

7. See Table 3.5.

8. There are 34 provinces, 333 prefectures, 2862 counties or districts and 41 636 townships in China.

Table 3.5: Sub-national Government Share of Total Public Expenditure and Revenue – East Asia

Country	Share of Total Public Expenditure (%)			Share of Total Public Revenue (%)		
	Sub-national	Upper Tier	Lower Tiers	Sub-national	Upper Tier	Lower Tiers
China	70	20	50	40	15	25
Japan	60	20	40	40	20	20
Korea	45	17	28	35	22	13

Sources: UCLG Data Files among others. Figures are approximations. Data are the most recent available: China 2005, Japan 2007 and Korea 2010.

government spends about 40 percent of the sub-national total. Local government expenditure traditionally focused on public works and economic development but social services, including safety, health, housing and community development, have recently become the priority.

Own-Source Revenues

Taxes are somewhat centralized in China, although not as much as in some other countries with the same degree of expenditure decentralization. The sub-national portion of total public sector tax revenues amounts to about 40 percent. The shares of total public revenues of provinces, prefectures and counties/townships are approximately 15 percent, 15 percent and 10 percent respectively, although there seems to be some annual variations (Shen and Zou, 2006). Many taxes are assigned to provinces, including land use, property, and vehicle taxes and stamp duties. Provinces have discretion in assigning these taxes to lower levels and some do so, but lower level tax assignments vary widely. Four of the major taxes in China, including Value Added Tax and Corporate Income Tax, are shared between the central and local governments – these constitute substantial parts of local finance.

Sub-national governments in Japan collected approximately 40 percent of total tax revenues in 2007, split about equally between prefectures and municipalities. This is expected to increase to 50 percent under the 2003 Trinity Reforms. Noteworthy prefecture taxes include an enterprise, consumption and inhabitants' (income) tax. The most important local taxes are the residential and non-residential property (fixed asset) tax and the inhabitants' tax. Own-source revenues comprise slightly more than one-third of total revenues of both prefectures and municipalities. This relatively low level persists even after the Trinity Reforms, which were a response to excessive centralization in its public revenue collections and over-reliance of local government on grants. The reform increased local government own-source revenue and commensurately reduced the local tax allocation (untied revenue sharing) grants and to national government subsidies (tied grants) to local government.

Revenues are quite centralized in Korea compared with other countries in the sub-region. Korean sub-national governments account for about 35 percent of national public revenues, with upper and lower tiers respectively raising about 22 and 13 percent. Property taxes are the most important source of own revenues for local governments, making up over half of the total. Income and consumption taxes are also important. Own-source revenues make

Table 3.6: Intergovernamental Transfers as Local Government Revenue Source – East Asia

Country	Share of Transfers in Total Local Revenue (%)	Relative Importance of Type of Transfer		
		Revenue Sharing	General Purpose	Special Purpose
China	60	High	Low	Low
Japan	40	High	Low	Medium
Korea	40	High	Low	Medium

Source: UCLG data files and other sources. Figures are approximations. Data are for most recent year: China 2005, Japan 2006, Korea 2010.

up about 60 percent of total local government revenues. As part of the central government's fiscal decentralization policy, a Local Consumption Tax was introduced in 2010. As a result, the revenue share of local government is expected to increase by about 3 percent.

Intergovernmental Transfers[9]

Intergovernmental transfers of various kinds make up around 60 percent of total sub-national level revenues in China where the system is very complex and non-transparent (Bahl and Martínez-Vázquez, 2009). The most important transfers are revenue sharing mechanisms (including VAT, business tax, individual income tax and enterprise income tax), tax rebates and earmarked grants. These make up about 80 percent of local government grant revenue, whereas equalization grants amount to only about 5 percent. A myriad of other intergovernmental transfers comprise the remainder. There is little official information provided about the allocation of transfers among levels of sub-national government.

Japanese sub-national governments also receive almost 40 percent of their revenue in the form of transfers from the central government – both local tax allocations and tied subsidies – or the prefectures. The Local Allocation Tax (LAT) is by far the most important transfer, followed by various special purpose grants. The LAT is a fiscal support and equalization transfer. Special purpose grants are used largely to fund delegated functions, although some address spillovers or provide fiscal performance incentives. Conditional grants target specific sectors and require compliance with tight operational standards. The Trinity Reforms discussed earlier reduced the amount of the tied grants to local government as well as changed (simplified) the basis on which the LAT is distributed. The Ministry of Home Affairs, however, does not manage distribution transparently.

Intergovernmental fiscal transfers account for about 40 percent of Korean local government revenue. The current transfer system, established by structural changes in 2005, consists of Local Shared Tax (LST), National Treasury Subsidies (NTS) and the Special Account for Region-wide and Regional Development (SARRD). It is overly complex and compromises the consistent measurement of the fiscal effects of grants. Under the LST, there are 4 types of grants: Ordinary Local Shared Tax (OLST), Special Local Shared Tax (SLST), Decentralization Shared Tax (DST) and Real Estate Shared Tax (REST). Prior to 2005, the LST consisted only of OLST and SLST and operated as an instrument of fiscal support and equalization, similarly to the LAT of Japan.

9. See Table 3.6.

Table 3.7: Legal Authorization and Extent of Local Government Borrowing – East Asia

Country	Borrowing Legally Authorized	Extent of Borrowing
China	No	Significant
Japan	Yes	Significant
Korea	Yes	Moderate

Source: UCLG data files and other sources.

The 2005 increases in DST and REST were designed to compensate for expenditures incurred for additional NTS projects transferred to local government and for the fiscal loss to local governments caused by national tax policy.

NTS are essentially special purpose grants designed to support costs of delivering mostly delegated services. A majority of NTS projects are subject to matching and other conditions stipulated by the central government. SARRD is a grant to support regional development projects to enhance competitiveness. Transfers between upper and lower-local governments include Metropolitan and Provincial Subsidies (M&PS), Provincial Revenue Sharing (PRS) and Metropolitan Revenue Sharing (MRS). M&PS is a conditional grant distributed to cities, counties, and districts together with NTS funds. PRS is a general grant to lower level local governments based on population, tax collection costs and other factors. MRS is a general grant to support basic fiscal needs of districts and to mitigate fiscal inequality among them.

Debt Finance[10]

Under existing laws, sub-national governments in China are not allowed to borrow. Nevertheless, many do borrow, both to cover operational deficits and to finance capital spending. Sub-national governments borrow directly from commercial banks and other financial institutions, or indirectly through their locally owned Trusts and Investment Companies (TICs). In turn, the latter borrow from banks and through capital markets. It is estimated that in 2004, total outstanding debt of sub-national governments was about $120 billion USD, about one-third of which was due to borrowing (Shen, Jin, and Zou, 2006).

More recently, economic commentators have estimated the outstanding debt of China's local government investment companies to be about 11.4 trillion yuan (about $1.7 trillion), with additional commitments of a further $1.9 trillion, much of it tied to infrastructure projects. Other sources talk about $880 billion, a figure approximately corroborated by China International Capital, an investment bank.[11] These loans are backed by assets (typically land) or supported by implicit government guarantees and have been used to develop local transportation, energy, water, urban infrastructure, and public housing. There are concerns that the proceeds from land sales used to repay these bank loans may fall short, especially if the country's bubble-prone real estate market tumbles.

Japanese sub-national governments are legally allowed to borrow from commercial banks and to issue domestic bonds; the latter are becoming increasingly more common.[12] The traditional permission system has been abolished but a "prior consultation" system still gives the central

10. See Table 3.7.

11. "Shell Game", The Economist, March 11th 2010.

12. In 2003, the Financial Investment Local Fund covered 60 percent of local bonds, private financial institutions covered 30 percent and the market covered the remaining 10 percent.

government some control over sub-national borrowing. This could be because, while local governments secure their borrowing with own-source revenues, local borrowing is also implicitly guaranteed by the center (Mochida, 2008). Government claims to be moving increasingly toward a system that is based more on fiscal rules and market discipline. Sub-national governments in Japan borrow significant amounts. The sub-national share of public capital spending is around 70 percent of the consolidated public sector total and almost all of this is financed by borrowing. Outstanding sub-national debt was about one-third of GDP in 2005, which is very high by international standards (Mochida, 2008).

Korean sub-national governments may borrow to finance capital spending and recovery from natural disasters. They can source funds either via direct loans (public loan funds or bank loans) or the issuance of bonds. The former process (particularly, public loan funds) is more common. In recent years, local governments' access to public loan funds, relative to the central government, has decreased sharply but access to the special account, the "Regional Development Fund" operated by upper-level local governments, is still possible. Traditionally, Korean local governments have tended not to borrow for capital financing, except for some relatively rich upper-level local governments and large cities. Korea maintained a very strict "permission system" on local borrowing. This was softened in 2005, by the introduction of the "total volume control system" under which local governments may borrow, subject to quotas set by the central government. In 2007, total outstanding debt of sub-national governments represented 2.1 percent of GDP, and local borrowing represented about 3 percent of local annual revenue throughout the 2000s (Lim Sung Il, 2010).

13. *See Table 3.8*

Performance[13]

Current and Capital Resource Adequacy

Given the vastness of China and the diversity of local governments, it is difficult to generalize about local resource adequacy. However, it does appear that resource constraints have become generally more problematic since the 1994 reforms under which revenues became more centralized, expenditure responsibilities remained essentially the same and intergovernmental transfers failed to adequately replace the lost own-source revenue of many sub-national governments. On the other hand, this period coincided with a very rapid expansion of the Chinese economy and improvements in the standards of living, and the resultant additional demand for services could be the cause of additional pressure on local budgets. Whatever the cause, resources generally become more constrained as you move down the hierarchy of government tiers. Given the ineffectiveness of equalization grants due to their small volume, current and capital resource constraints are particularly binding for rural areas and for less economically developed regions. Thus, there are substantial disparities between urban and rural areas in service provision levels by local government, especially in education, health and water supply (Bahl and Martínez-Vázquez, 2009).

Local governments in Japan appear to have sufficient current and capital resources to deliver services with which they have been charged. Grants seem to adequately fill the vertical fiscal gap, although one objective of the Trinity Reforms is to make local governments more self sufficient and efficient by limiting access to transfers and forcing them to collect more revenue. In principle, the support and equalization grant (the LAT) assures adequate current

Table 3.8: Performance of Intergovernmental Systems – East Asia

	Resource Adequacy	Fiscal Discretion	Performance Incentives	Management Capacity	Service Outcomes
China	LG resource constraints increasingly problematic, especially at lowest levels of government.	Limited formal fiscal discretion. Off budget activity significant.	Performance incentives have focused on economic development.	Good quality tax administration and expenditure management, although significant variation.	Significant variation across regions but generally low in rural areas.
Japan	LG current and capital resources adequate.	Tax authority over rates and bases limited. Spending controlled to large degree by CG through delegation of responsibilities and mandates.	CG uses incentives in block grant to encourage local revenue effort. Some performance incentives incorporated into specific purpose grants, as well.	High quality tax administration and expenditure management, within narrowly assigned responsibilities.	High quality service outcomes.
Korea	LG current and capital resources seem adequate, although increasing fiscal pressure from additional demand for social welfare services.	Authority over local tax bases and rates is limited. LG have reasonable control over spending their own-source revenue but other spending is controlled to large degree by central government.	There are some incentive mechanisms to encourage better performance, but experience is limited.	Good quality tax administration, although perhaps too little use of tax rate authority. Good expenditure management.	High quality service outcomes.

Source: Author's assessment based on UCLG data files, among other sources (see bibliography)

revenues for all local governments to deliver services at basic or standard levels and the central government's implicit guarantee of local borrowing allows local governments to raise sufficient capital to meet financing needs, but this is not always the case. The "Trinity Reform" resulted in fiscal pressure, particularly on local governments with relatively poor fiscal capacity. This pressure, worsened by the increasing demands of an aging society and the impacts of the global financial crisis, has differentially affected local governments.

In general, local governments in Korea also seem to have adequate resources to deliver their assigned services, although there is some variation. While own-source revenues are insufficient to fund routine service delivery, transfers appear to fill the vertical fiscal gap reasonably well, at least in the aggregate. The equalization transfer (LST) also seems to meet its intended purpose. Although borrowing has not been substantial, intergovernmental transfers have, again, proved to be more than adequate to compensate for any shortfalls in accessing capital finance. Nevertheless, recent developments, including a sharp increase in demand for social welfare services and other unfunded mandates, have increased fiscal pressures on local governments.

Taxing and Spending Discretion

Formally, local governments in China have little tax and spending discretion. Local tax assignments are allowed by higher level governments but all tax bases are defined and rates are officially set by the center. Local expenditure responsibilities are also assigned by higher level governments and the central government has a variety of mechanisms to otherwise influence local spending, including expenditure laws and regulations, spending mandates and overt political control. Nevertheless, in practice, many local governments appear to have significant discretion, as indicated by the "illegal" use of loan funds and the use of off-budget solutions to overcome fiscal constraints and meet service delivery ambitions. In general, local governments in China enjoy (or take) a high degree of freedom in the use of non-tax revenue items: with the application of land development and real estate business fees being particularly important sources of revenue in some areas.

Japanese local governments have reasonable control over most taxes assigned to them. Although the central government defines the tax bases, local governments set rates within ranges formulated by the center. Local governments are also allowed to create their own taxes under certain well-defined conditions codified in law, but very few have utilized this capacity. Local governments have also traditionally used "extra-legal taxes" but these have been in decline since the 1990s and are now insignificant. Examples of those that still exist include prefectures taxes on the nuclear fuel industry and municipal taxes on vacant houses, small living spaces and to support the historical and cultural environment.

Local governments in Japan have limited expenditure discretion. The center determines spending levels and standards and can mandate local governments to assume other (nominally "autonomous") functions, thus creating unfunded mandates. In recent years, such requirements have increased sharply, particularly in the social welfare. Because of the level of control, sub-national expenditure responsibilities in Japan may best be seen as centrally delegated functions and not genuine decentralization (Mochida, 2008).

Local governments in Korea have reasonable control over most of their own revenues (Lee, 2003; An, 2003). Central government sets the types, base, and range of local tax, however local governments determine the tax rate applied with the centrally set range. In practice, most local governments do not use this flexibility. Currently, a tax simplification process is under way. In 2011, tax sources will be reduced from 16 to 11, with a further simplification of local taxes expected to occur at a later date.

Korean local governments have both autonomous and delegated functions. In theory local governments have complete discretion over spending on autonomous tasks; but spending on delegated functions is influenced significantly by central government, as are the projects funded by the National Treasury Subsidies. As such, local governments appear to have a reasonable degree of discretion over their expenditures. The discretion is, however, constrained somewhat by the fact that the center sets sub-national civil servant wages and pension benefits, which comprise a large portion of autonomous spending.

Incentives in the Intergovernmental Framework

The intergovernmental system in China has, in the recent past at least, provided significant incentives for economic development in the regions, taking precedence over equalization. The extent to which these incentives have stimulated economic growth is the subject of great debate. On the fiscal side, the effect of local tax rate competition on economic development has been clearly documented. There has been a "race to the bottom" among local governments in regions with favorable economic conditions and a "race to the top" for local governments in less well developed regions (Yao and Zhang, 2007).

Japan incorporates some incentives into its transfer system. The support and equalization grant (the LAT) ostensibly provides an incentive for local tax effort by increasing the amount of the grant as fiscal capacity declines. The latter is estimated as a function of "standard" rather than actual revenues. Like many such calculations, standard own-source revenues are those that would be derived if the local government used the standard tax rate. If a sub-national government sets a higher rate, it keeps the associated extra revenue. In practice, the effects are unclear since most sub-national governments use the standard rates. In addition, some analysts argue that the equalization grant provides an incentive for local governments to over-borrow, since grant increases with expenditure needs, which are determined in part by the size of standard interest and principal repayments. But the effects of such an incentive are also unclear since the central government still controls the amounts that municipalities can borrow. Some special purpose grants provide performance incentives but there is little information on the objectives, design or implementation of such incentives.

Korea has gone relatively far in attempting to establish incentives in its intergovernmental system. For instance, some of the specific purpose grants in Korea have matching components that are designed to stimulate spending of certain kinds. In 2010, a new block grant is set to be implemented with incentive mechanism for own-source revenues.

Tax Administration and Expenditure Management

The quality of tax administration and expenditure management varies widely across local governments in China. The overall system of tax administration appears to have improved somewhat since the 1994 reforms. Prior to that time China operated a unified central tax administration system that was reasonably efficient in collecting taxes, but created significant rent seeking behavior and divided loyalties among tax administrators vis-à-vis their central and local "clients" (Shen, Jin, and Zou, 2006). Expenditure management policies in recent times have tended to focus on the stimulation of economic growth to a much greater extent than on the delivery of public services, but this does seem to be changing.

Japanese local government tax administration and expenditure management appear to be of reasonably high quality, at least within the limited bounds within which municipalities are allowed to operate. Much local government taxation and spending is "co-managed" by or "integrated" with the central government.

Local government tax administration and expenditure management also appear to be sound in Korea. Administration of taxes and expenditures makes extensive use of computerized systems, and a simplification of the tax system commenced in 2011 will further assist in efficient tax administration. One remaining problem may be that local tax authorities seem to make insufficient use of the control they have over the rates of their assigned taxes, but this may be due to the disincentives imposed by the transfer system and not because they lack capacity of making such adjustments (Lee, 2006).

Service Delivery Outcomes

The quality of local public services in China varies a great deal across the country. In the east and southeast regions, services appear to be of good quality: elsewhere and especially in rural regions, service quality lags. Broadly speaking, those regions that are growing well economically have access to relatively more resources, at least some of which are devoted to service delivery; in poorer regions, particularly in rural and remote areas where own-source resources are much more limited, local public service delivery is very weak.

The quality of local public services in Japan is very high. Public service outcomes for education, health and infrastructure are among the best in the world. Access to services is fairly equitable across sub-national jurisdictions, indicating that the intergovernmental fiscal system designed with this goal in mind has been working well (although very recently it has been under some strain).

The quality of public services in Korea is very good. The country's infrastructure and social service outcomes are consistently ranked among the best in the world for countries with a similar level of income. Like Japan, Korea has a strong tradition of assuring equitable access to public services and the geographic distribution of service outcomes is quite even, notwithstanding some concentration of quality public services in Seoul. In addition, local governments appear to have become increasingly accountable to citizens in the recent years and this helps to assure quality services.

Selected Pressing Issues and Binding Constraints

China's current system of intergovernmental fiscal relations needs to be improved to balance economic development and equalization, and a higher average quality of public services. The system has recently focused more on economic development and less on public service outcomes. This may now have changed with government's renewed focus on addressing equity and poverty concerns, and the "building of a harmonious society".

Several issues stand out as China moves to concentrate more on local public service delivery. First, the high level of debt of sub-national government in China must be corrected as it poses threats to both the national and international economies. Second, while the assignment of expenditures needs clarifying, central and local governments need to find a more adequate equilibrium in the responsibilities assigned to sub-national governments. For example, social insurance schemes (especially pensions) should probably not be a local responsibility (Bahl and Martínez-Vázquez, 2009). Third, the lower levels of government lack sufficient revenues, in general, to cover their expenditure assignments. They have very few taxes at their disposal and very little official control over those available to them: and the transfer system fails to address vertical imbalances and is ad-hoc and overly complex. Fourth, the distribution of grants should be more transparent and predictable as between the levels of sub-national government and between units of local government. A final concern relates to the tight accountability to central officials, which must be reduced if autonomy of local government is a real objective.

The critical fiscal decentralization issue in Japan concerns the degree of control exerted by the central government over local governments. For a mature, developed country, municipalities still have very little discretion over their fiscal affairs (Mochida, 2008). The second and related issue concerns the "one-size fits all" approach to service provision and financing, and there is growing concern that the varied preferences of residents across the country are not being addressed by the overly centralized system (Aoki, 2008). Although local governments would appear to be well placed to respond to local demand, they have not been given sufficient authority to do so. As Japan increases fiscal decentralization under the Trinity Reforms, the fiscal relationships between the central and local government will need to be reassessed. Widening fiscal capacities of local government will mean changes to the distribution of LAT funding if equality of service provision is to be maintained. Japan's high dependency on debt funding will also need critical evaluation.

A key issue in Korea concerns the assignment of service responsibilities across levels of government. As in many countries, there is some lack of clarity regarding service assignment, but the major problem appears to be some mis-assignment of functions: the practice of "revenues are owned by the central government, but executions are done by local governments" needs to be changed to give better fiscal balance. The central government seems to play a relatively large role in the delivery of health, environmental and police services compared to some other countries. A second concern, even after the 2011 tax simplification initiatives, may be the proliferation of taxes at the local level. A final problem concerns the system of inter-governmental transfers where the issue is the existence of multiple transfers with the same objectives, some of which are allocated by the center and others by regional governments (Lee, 2003; Lee, 2004).

Conclusions and Observations on East Asia

China appears ready to re-orient its intergovernmental system to focus more on the delivery of public services. Policymakers could begin by reducing higher level subnational government authority to assign expenditures and revenues to lower level governments (Shen and Zou, 2007). In addition the following objectives should be considered:

- Building a stronger consensus between central and sub-national governments on the assignment of local level service responsibilities and tax authorities to the different levels of local government, particularly concerning the service responsibilities of local governments for the provision of social insurance;
- Assigning more substantial tax and non-tax revenues to local governments and considering allowing at least some discretion for tax rates and fee schedules;
- Restructuring the system of intergovernmental transfers with a view to making it simpler and more fiscally equalizing both between different levels of government and across the country;
- Formalizing local government borrowing authorities (and introducing rules for the size and use of loan funds) and more generally bringing all fiscal and financial operations on budget;
- Developing improved measures of horizontal accountability (such as the Local Congress of People).

In Japan, the results of the Trinity Reforms (Doi, 2004) have so far been mixed. Transfers to local governments were reduced and own-source revenues have risen by a commensurate amount, but the reduction in special purpose grants, relative to the support and equalization grant, has been somewhat disappointing. In addition, while the overall vertical fiscal gap did not increase with the reforms, some sub-national governments did experience a net loss in revenue. As such, inequality in resources and levels of service delivery has, for the first time, become an issue. Finally there is some evidence that the reduction in block transfers has led to increased borrowing by sub-national governments. This may be worrisome given the already high level of local debt, especially at a time when the central government is turning away from administrative supervision to market discipline as the main mechanism of control. This suggests that the future policy agenda in Japan may wish to increase efforts in:

- Providing sub-national governments with more fiscal autonomy by replacing specific purpose grant with own-source revenues,
- Clarifying the twin roles of the LAT distribution and improving its equalization performance to improve equity in the distribution of resources for service delivery as own-source revenues increase and LAT transfers decrease,
- Taking steps to ensure that local governments do not borrow excessively, and
- Eliminating unfunded mandates associated with social welfare services.

Although Korea's system of public service provision and financing appears to function reasonably well, there are several improvements that the government might consider:

- Realigning its assignment of service responsibilities across levels of government, withdrawing itself from the provision of some services while still maintaining its responsibility for policy.
- Balancing functional and fiscal distributions to guarantee full coverage of the costs in the case of transfers of functions from central to local governments.
- Further restructuring of the National Tax and Local Tax System and improving the taxing power of local government by eliminating nuisance taxes (i.e. those that do not generate much revenue net of collection costs) at the local level. Aspects of revenue assignment, tax base structure, tax payer's rights and convenience should be reconsidered and property, income and consumption taxes need to be harmonized. The fiscal accountability to local residents should also be considered.
- Revisiting the system of intergovernmental transfers. Here the focus would be on consolidating the number of transfers that focus on similar goals, streamlining the design of individual transfers to reduce conditions and the number and complexity of tied grants, increasing the equalization attributes of the Local Services Tax distribution and clarifying the relationship between this and other transfers.
- Enhancing the links between the tax system and the grants system with the aim of improving local autonomy, accountability and efficiency.
- Introducing differentiated policy on fiscal decentralization to allow for the application of differentiated fiscal autonomy, considering fiscal capacity, economic conditions, population and other factors across local governments.
- More autonomy in local borrowings and its linkage with the citizen's burden.

South-East Asian Local Governments Finances

Structure

Expenditure[14]

In Indonesia, expenditures have been devolved to sub-national levels to a significant extent. Sub-national government (of which there are 33 provinces, 349 regencies

14. *See Table 3.9*

Table 3.9: Sub-national Government Share of Total Public Expenditure and Revenue – South-East Asia

Country	Share of Total Public Expenditure (%)			Share of Total Public Revenue (%)		
	Sub-national	Upper Tier	Lower Tiers	Sub-national	Upper Tier	Lower Tiers
Indonesia	35	7	28	8	5.5	2.5
Philippines	25	11	14	10	2.5	7.5
Vietnam	45	30	15	35	25	10
Thailand	26	n.a.	n.a.	15	n.a.	n.a.
Cambodia	Less than 5	n.a	Less than 5	Less than 1	n.a.	Less than 1
Malaysia	n.a	n.a	Less than 5	n.a.	n.a.	Less than 1

Source: UCLG data files and other sources. Figures are approximations. Data are for most recent year available: Indonesia 2006, Philippines 2005, Vietnam 2008, Thailand 2010 actual and 2011 budget.

(*kabupaten*) and 91 cities (*kota*)) spending makes up about 35 percent of total public expenditure; and spending by local governments (kabupaten/*kota*) is about 80 percent of the sub-national total. The most important local service in Indonesia is education: local governments spend about 35 percent of their budgets on primary and junior secondary school education. Infrastructure is next most important with a budget share of around 15 percent.

In the Philippines, sub-national spending makes up about 25 percent of total public expenditure (net of debt service). Local government (i.e. 1,496 municipalities, 138 cities, and 42,025 *barangays*) expenditure contributes about 55 percent of Philippine sub-national totals. Health and infrastructure are the most important services among local governments in the Philippines, each making up about 11 percent of total expenditure budgets. In education, they have responsibilities only for the construction and maintenance of schools.

Local budgets in Vietnam increased from about 26 to more than 45 percent of total public expenditure from 1992 to 2008. Data are not available nationally to disaggregate sub-national spending among provinces and central cities (63), provincial cities and towns (93), rural districts (550) and the communes (more than 10,600 communes and wards). Information for two provinces (Ninh Thuan and Thai Binh), however, suggests that in 2008, provincial, district, and commune spending made up about 75, 15, and 10 percent of the sub-national total respectively (Hanai and Hugen, 2008). Since provinces are responsible, in large measure, for assigning particular expenditures to district and commune levels, significant variation across provinces is likely, but it seems that provinces are dominant. Available information suggests that districts and communes focus their spending in the education and health sectors.

Sub-national spending in Thailand[15] makes up about 26 percent of total public sector expenditure (including state owned enterprises) in the 2011 budgets. There are no precise data on the local government (i.e. municipal and sub-district) portion of the sub-national total (Amornvivat, 2004). Most local spending is focused on education and health, which account for about 20

15. In Thailand, the sub-national government sector is made up of 75 provincial administrative organizations, 2006 municipalities and 5,742 tambon administrative organizations or special types of local governments.

percent of local budgets: the composition of local expenditure varies greatly, however, depending on the degree of urbanization of the jurisdiction.

In Cambodia, provincial and district administrations above the 1,630 elected commune and *sangkat* councils (urban commune) have long been deconcentrated entities of the central government. Communes account for a very small share (less than 5 percent) of total public expenditures. They mostly finance councilor allowances and small infrastructure development projects funded through transfers from the central government and, indirectly, from donors. The 2009 Organic Law on Decentralization and Democratic Development created indirectly elected councils at the provincial and district level and foresees specific functions and resources being given to all sub-national levels, including the communes.

In Malaysia, the application of the "One Malaysia" policy has resulted in a more centralized form of government within the Federation and a very small local government sector. Local government is seen as a service delivery arm of the central government (deconcentration). There are, however, some calls from local government for more autonomy and specific expenditure assignments being provided.

Own-Source Revenues

As in many developing countries, Indonesian tax revenues are very centralized, especially given the level of expenditure decentralization. Provincial and local government own-source revenues comprise only about eight percent of government revenues; and local government own-sources contribute just under a third of the sub-national total. The tax on electricity sales is the most important own-source revenue in Indonesia, making up about 20 percent of the total. Local taxes on hotel and restaurant sales and public health center charges are also noteworthy; each comprises about 10 percent of total own-source revenues.

Philippine sub-national government own-source revenues contribute around 10 percent of consolidated public revenue. Unlike Indonesia, however, the bulk of sub-national revenue generation —about 75 percent— derives from local (municipal, city, and *barangay*) government collections. The real property tax is the most significant own-source revenue, respectively accounting for about 30 and 40 percent of own-source revenues of municipalities and cities. The business tax is also important for some local governments. One concern is that elected councilors often lack knowledge on sources of finance for local government.

Sub-national revenue in Vietnam is reasonably important. Own-source revenues at the provincial, district, and commune level have been increasing rapidly, from about 35 to 44 percent of total public revenue from 2008 to closer to the present. At the provincial level, the most important taxes are the VAT (excluding imports), corporate profit tax, personal income tax on high incomes, gasoline and oil fees. Data from the two provinces noted above suggest that most, perhaps just under 85 percent, are collected by provinces with the remainder coming from districts (Hanai and Huyen, 2008). Revenues of communes are negligible. Again, given provincial discretion to assign local taxes, some variation across provinces is likely. Overall, land-based taxes dominate local own-source revenues. The current tension in public revenue collection in Vietnam is that the central government wants large cities to be more self-reliant while they see a need for greater financial assistance.

Sub-national revenues in Thailand comprised about 15 percent of the consolidated total in

Table 3.10: Intergovernmental Transfers as Local Government Revenue Source – South-East Asia

Country	Share of Transfers in Total Local Revenue (%)	Relative Importance of Type of Transfer		
		Revenue Sharing	General Purpose	Special Purpose
Indonesia	90	Medium	High	Low
Philippines	70	Low	High	Low
Vietnam	50	High	Medium	Medium
Thailand	85	Low	Low	High
Cambodia	Very high	n.a.	High	Low
Malaysia	Very close to 100	n.a.	n.a.	High

Source: UCLG data files and other sources. Figures are approximations. Data are for most recent year available: Indonesia 2006, Philippines 2005, Vietnam 2008, Thailand 2011.

2010. The most important local taxes are the building and land tax, the land development tax and the signboard tax (a local advertisement tax). Local governments also levy license fees and fines but these are not important quantitatively. There is considerable variation between local governments, with major cities obtaining a significantly larger proportion of their total funding from own source revenues.

In Cambodia, there is currently very little revenue collected by the commune/*sangkat* councils and the future of revenue collection by them and the newly established district councils is yet to be determined. In Malaysia, in line with the nation's "One Malaysia" policy, there is heavy centralization of revenue management. There are, however, some calls from local government for greater revenue autonomy to be given and local government being able to fix tax rates without state approval.

Intergovernmental Transfers[16]

Intergovernmental transfers dominate local government revenues in Indonesia, making up at least 90 percent of the total. The general-purpose equalization grant (DAU) is legislated to be at least 25 percent of national general revenue and is the largest transfer, comprising about two thirds of local revenues. Central government tax (property and income) and non-tax (natural resource) sharing with local governments is also important and comprises the bulk of the remainder. There is also a small special purpose capital grant (DAK).

In the Philippines, transfers contribute up to 70 percent of local government revenue, although there is significant variation regionally and between the two lower tiers. The formula-based Internal Revenue Allotment (IRA) is by far the most important revenue source[17]. The share of the IRA in total revenues of cities and municipalities is about 50 percent and 75 percent, respectively. National revenue sharing and categorical (tied) grants of various kinds are considerably less important to local budgets.

Intergovernmental transfers in Vietnam comprise half of total local revenues. Shared taxes distributed to provinces include VAT (except on imports) and those on corporate

16. *See Table 3.10.*

17. *At each level of local government, the distribution is based on population (50%), area (25%) and an equal share (25%). Due to the size of the grants pool and the distribution formula, it does not cover the costs of devolved functions, has resulted in greater disparities between rich and poor local governments and has been incapable of encouraging local revenue collections.*

Table 3.11: Legal Authorization and Extent of Local Government Borrowing – South-East Asia

Country	Borrowing Legally Authorized	Extent of Borrowing
Indonesia	Yes	Limited
Philippines	Yes	Limited
Vietnam	Yes	Limited
Thailand	Yes	Very Limited
Cambodia	No	None
Malaysia	Yes	n.a.

Source: UCLG data files and other sources.

and personal income, profits, consumption, and gas and oil. The sharing rate is the same for all taxes but varies across provinces, depending on differential expenditure needs and fiscal capacities. Other transfers to provinces include an equalization grant and various categorical transfers (e.g. for national programs and emergency needs). Provinces, in turn, make transfers to district and commune governments within their jurisdictions. Transfer objectives and mechanisms are often unclear, although provinces claim to allocate grants to lower levels for both general and specific purposes.

Intergovernmental grants make up the bulk of local government revenues in Thailand, comprising nearly 85 percent of total budgets. Three main types of transfers are made to local governments: general-purpose grants, specific purpose grants, and subsidies. Nearly all grants are tied to particular types of expenditures (even so-called general-purpose grants). The total grants allocated to local government in Thailand fell by nearly 30 percent between 2008 and 2010.

In Cambodia, commune revenue assignments defined in the original 2001 decentralization legislation have never been implemented. Most funding for the councils derives from the Commune/*Sangkat* Fund as untied transfers. In turn, that Fund receives resources from both the central government budget and from international donor agencies, though donor funding is declining and is now only about 30 percent of the total. Although the funds are received as untied transfers, about one third is needed for administration costs and the remainder mostly finances small infrastructure projects. The future design and scale of transfers to commune/*sangkat* and district councils is currently under discussion as part of the plan to implement the 2009 law noted above.

In Malaysia, local government receives very close to all its funding in the form of grants and contributions from the federal and state governments. These enable both infrastructure development and recurrent service provision. That the federal grants pass through the state governments causes a problem of funds flow to local governments.

Debt Finance[18]

By law, Indonesian local governments are allowed to borrow for capital development from government sources, private financial institutions or capital markets. In practice, local borrowing to finance capital spending has been limited and has been exclusively from the government or from international donors through the government's on-lending

18. See Table 3.11

Box 3.3: The Local Government Unit Guarantee Corporation (LGUGC) in the Philippines

Established in 1998, the LGU Guarantee Corporation (LGUGC) is a private financial credit guarantee institution owned by the Bankers Association of the Philippines (38 percent), the Development Bank of the Philippines (37 percent) and the Asian Development Bank (25 percent).

Its primary goal is to make private financial resources available to creditworthy local governments (LGs) through its credit guarantee. The LGUGC's credit enhancement facilitates LGs infrastructure development projects in the capital market. Over the past decade, the LGUGC has supported LGs to mobilize capital from a range of banks and bond investors for all types of infrastructures projects.

Three main services provided are:

- A *guarantee mechanism. The* LGUGC guarantees the debt of LGs, water districts, electric cooperatives, renewable energy technology providers and state universities and colleges. The guarantee fees range from 1 percent to 2 percent per annum.
- *Credit rating services*. In the absence of an entity specialized in LG risk evaluation, the LGUGC has established an internal LG credit screening and rating system. The system evaluates the LG's capacity to pay and willingness to honor contractual obligations.
- *Program management*. The LGUGC manages the guarantee fund for the Electric Cooperative System Loss Reduction Project of the World Bank - Global Environment Facility and is the program manager for the Capacity Building to Remove Barriers to Renewable Energy Development - a Loan Guarantee Fund of the UNDP.

Out of the 26 projects that the LGUGC has guaranteed, nine have been related to water (for example: Indag Water District for about $315,000 USD). Of the municipal bonds floated in the Philippines market since 1998, increasingly more have had an LGUGC bond guarantee. As of January 2009, closed deals totaled about $60.4 million USD.

mechanisms. Over the past twenty five years *kabupaten/kota* and their water enterprises have borrowed, in total, less than one percent of GDP, and current outstanding debt is considerably less than this (Lewis and Woodward, 2010).

Philippine local governments have access to a similar set of loan mechanisms but appear to have borrowed from a wider array of sources than their counterparts in Indonesia. Some local governments have issued bonds and many have borrowed from either government or non-government institutions, with the bulk of local borrowing in the Philippines —about 80 percent— coming from government sources. One interesting loan mechanism is outlined in Box 3.3. Outstanding debt of Philippine local governments has recently been estimated at about 0.6 percent of GDP. Elected councilors are said to be wary of taking on debt that extends beyond their period of office and this fear needs to be overcome if more appropriate use of debt financing is to be achieved (Asian Development Bank, 2008).

Provincial governments in Vietnam are allowed to borrow in domestic markets (either bank loans or bonds) to finance capital expenditures, and some have done so. District and commune governments are not allowed to take on debt.

Municipalities and sub-districts in Thailand need higher-level government approval to borrow, with borrowing restricted to financing local capital development. In practice local government borrowing has been very limited and most infrastructure development has been funded through transfers, donors or from local fiscal reserves. There are no data available on the level of borrowing by Thai local governments (Amornvivat, 2004).

In Cambodia, the Organic Law on Decentralization and democratic development prevents local government from accessing debt. In Malaysia, local governments may borrow from either the federal or state governments, as either overdrafts or mortgages, but only with the approval of the state government.

Performance[19]

Current and Capital Resource Adequacy

The distribution of resources across local governments in Indonesia is quite skewed. As such, it appears that at least some local governments in Indonesia have insufficient resources with which to discharge their functions (World Bank, 2006). However, as a whole, local governments do not spend all the operating funds that are available to them and are building up large surpluses. This is partly a capacity problem.

Access to local government capital financing in Indonesia is insufficient relative to infrastructure needs at the local level. Central government allocates only a small capital grant (DAK) to *kabupaten/kota*. Currently the DAK makes up less than five percent of total *kabupaten/kota* revenues and local governments have not borrowed significantly to finance capital development. Operation and maintenance of infrastructure and public investments by local government is a particular concern in Indonesia (Lewis, 2003a; Lewis, 2007a).

In the Philippines studies suggest that current local government funding is insufficient to cover the cost of delivering services under their authority (Manasan, 2004; World Bank and Asian Development Bank, 2005). Inadequacy of funds seems to be a particular problem for municipalities, although perhaps less so for cities (Manasan, 2004).

Resources for local capital development in Philippines are perhaps slightly less constrained than in Indonesia, although some of this apparent adequacy may be being forced on local governments, which are required to use 20 percent of their IRA for capital development (Manasan, 2004). Philippine local governments also receive a variety of capital transfers from the central government, but these are mostly small. Other capital grants are allocated as part of a grant-loan mixed distribution package from the Municipal Development Fund (World Bank, 2009). The larger variety of financing sources notwithstanding, local government debt finance in Philippines has been similar in size to that in Indonesia.

It is difficult to judge current and capital resource adequacy of local governments in Vietnam. On the current side, the maintenance of infrastructure appears to be somewhat of a concern but this may be

19. *See Table 3.12*

either a problem of resource constraints or a difficulty with expenditure assignments. In terms of capital requirements, there are no capital transfers in the Vietnamese intergovernmental system and, as noted, local governments are not permitted to borrow to finance capital development; as such any local capital spending needs have to be met out of general resources (Martínez-Vázquez, 2005). In any case, since district and commune expenditure and revenue assignments vary across provinces, resource adequacy probably also varies across local governments.

As local government's functions in Thailand have not yet been very clearly identified, it is difficult to assert the adequacy of resources to assure local responsibilities are fulfilled, but some sources say local governments have run quite substantial budget surpluses in recent years (Amornvivat, 2004; JICA, 2008). However the National Municipal League of Thailand contest this and claim that local governments have had recurrent revenue problems as central government has not provided the amount of shared taxes defined in the Decentralization Act of 1999. This was originally set at 35 percent, although this level has never been reached, and it was only 25 percent in 2009. If surpluses are being experienced they could be indicative of capacity constraints as much as over-funding. Unfortunately there is insufficient information with which to make a judgment on this.

In Cambodia, the central government's Commune/*Sangkat* Fund makes up nearly all local government revenue. It is received as untied funding and is used nearly entirely for administrative expenses and small infrastructure projects. There is effectively no recurrent service delivery undertaken by local governments, partly a result of the lack of clarity in functional assignments as well as resource and capacity constraints. In Malaysia as in most nations, finance is said to be a major constraint of local government performance.

Taxing and Spending Discretion

Indonesian local governments have little discretion over their tax resources. Central government enumerates allowable taxes and charges and defines tax bases, although local governments have some flexibility in setting tax rates up to limits set by the center. In the early years of decentralization, local governments were allowed to create their own taxes and charges, but this authority was rescinded by legislative change. Sub-national governments need to have their budgets approved by the central government but recent changes to legislation seem to have made this much more of a formality than it has been.

Once budgets are approved, Indonesian local governments have complete expenditure authority over their own-source revenues and their DAU transfer revenue. Even for the small DAK capital grant, which is tied to specific spending sectors, local governments have quite wide latitude in choosing specific spending activities within the designated sectors. They are required by law to spend 20 percent of their total budgets on education, but this is rather easily achieved now that teacher salaries are included in the calculation under a recent change in the interpretation of the law. Unfunded mandates are not a problem for local governments. The central government is, however, developing "minimum service standards" which, if enforced as currently designed, would cost more to achieve than the resources available to many *kabupaten/kota* (World Bank, 2006).

In the Philippines also, central government strictly defines allowable local government taxes and their bases, and local

Table 3.12: Performance of Intergovernmental Systems – South-East Asia

	Resource Adequacy	Fiscal Discretion	Performance Incentives	Management Capacity	Service Outcomes
Indonesia	Some LGs have insufficient funds.	LGs set tax rates under centrally imposed ceilings; LGs have (almost) complete discretion over spending.	Minor and ad-hoc experience with performance incentives. Formal encouragement of local revenue effort through block transfers discontinued.	LGs need to reinforce their capacities to administer taxes and spend resources. As significant accumulation of cash reserves demonstrate.	Service outcomes need to be improved.
Philippines	Inadequate resources for significant number of LGs, particularly municipalities.	LGs set some tax rates but can make changes only every 3 years. CG heavily influences LG spending; Unfunded mandates a particular concern.	Explicit use of incentives limited to employment of transfer intercept in cases of non-repayment of loans.	LGs need to improve taxes and spending management. Significant cash build-ups.	Service delivery needs to be improved.
Vietnam	LG resource adequacy questionable, especially for development and maintenance of infrastructure.	LGs have very limited tax authority. Moderate discretion over management of service delivery.	No experience with performance incentives.	Tax administration completely centralized. Spending reasonably well managed—low wage bills.	Significant improvements needed. Little horizontal accountability in most provinces.
Thailand	LGs resources need to be linked to responsibilities and the legislated amount of the shared tax transfer should reflect these responsibilities.	Taxing discretion limited to minor charges/fees; spending heavily influenced by CG.	No experience with performance incentives.	Local efforts to improve tax administration and expenditure management in evidence—tax system computerization and contracting out services.	Generally weak outcomes but improving responsiveness.
Cambodia	LGs are extremely poorly resourced	LGs have very little revenue or expenditure discretion.	Incentives within the grant system are currently being considered.	Generally very limited.	Generally poor service outcomes.
Malaysia	LGs have very few resources that are not grants from other spheres of government.	Very little.	Some relationship of grants to financial position and revenue collection, but not strong.	Capacity is limited to that necessary to enable them to be arms of the central government.	

Source: Author's assessment based on UCLG data files, among other sources (see bibliography)

governments are also quite constrained in setting tax rates. The tariffs for some local taxes are fixed by the center and local government rate flexibility for other taxes is bound at the upper end to limits which appear to be quite low by international standards. Finally, local governments are only allowed to change rates of taxes over which they have authority once every five years and then by no more than 10 percent. On the other hand, local governments appear to have quite wide purview in establishing and developing fees and charges, but these do not result in much revenue (Manasan, 2004).

The central government in Philippines exerts control over local spending in several ways. In some cases, it limits the amounts that local governments can spend on certain classes of expenditures and in other instances it prescribes minimum levels on particular types of spending. For example, spending on personnel services is limited to

45 percent or 55 percent of budgets, depending on the income class of the local government and, as noted above, 20 percent of a local government's IRA must be set aside for development spending and five percent of total local revenue must be reserved for a "calamity fund" (World Bank, 2009).

Philippine local governments also face a number of significant unfunded mandates. The most binding of these include local civil servant salaries in general, and benefits for health sector employees in particular. Local governments have also recently been required to fund health insurance premiums for their impoverished residents. Finally, local governments are expected to offer financial support for many central government agencies operating in their jurisdictions, such as for police, fire protection, and the courts.

Vietnamese local governments have very limited tax autonomy. The central government determines all allowable sub-national taxes, defines tax bases, sets tax rates and higher level governments in the hierarchical structure approve the budgets of levels of government "below" them. Provinces assign taxes to district and commune levels at their own discretion, with few exceptions, passing on the centrally defined bases and rates. Such local revenue assignments are fixed for "stability periods" of three years but can be changed thereafter. The only revenue authority local governments have relates to their ability to establish relatively minor toll road, school, and health fees (Hanai and Huyen, 2008).

Local governments in Vietnam have significantly more expenditure autonomy than either Indonesia or the Philippines. Although provinces establish the service responsibilities of districts and communes, they do not micro-manage service delivery. Somewhat unusually in the region, all sub-national governments, including districts and communes, have discretion to make decisions regarding staffing and remuneration (above minimum levels set by the center). Local unfunded mandates are illegal under current law (Martínez-Vázquez, 2005).

Thai local governments have limited taxing and spending discretion. The central government assigns allowable taxes, defines their bases and sets rates (or ceilings). As in Vietnam, the only revenue authority that local governments have is in developing user fees and charges. Local governments in Thailand have limited discretion in setting spending priorities and allocating funds across expenditure types. All local government budgets must be approved by higher level governments, which often insist on significant changes. Almost all grants are tied to particular types of spending. On the other hand, local governments do have some discretion in deciding how particular services can be delivered. Many local governments have, for example, contracted out delivery of some services (Weerasak, 2006; JICA, 2008).

In Cambodia, the limited resources of the communes/*sangkats* and their responsibility for councilors' remuneration means that even though their transfers are untied and their expenditure decisions are not interfered with, they have limited resources with which to exercise their expenditure autonomy. At this stage in the development of decentralization, they have no revenue-raising autonomy.

In Malaysia, the discretion of local government is limited by the fact that the executive is an appointed arm of the state (intermediate level) government in the federation rather than an elected sphere of government. The main own-source revenues of local government are property taxes, rents, license fees and fees for services. Local government needs the approval of the state before changing tax rates or introducing new taxes.

Incentives in the Intergovernmental Framework

Indonesian has had only limited experience with structuring performance incentives into the intergovernmental fiscal system. However, the central government does allocate 10 percent of the national property tax to local governments based on their previous year's tax collection performance and the DAU grant was increased in line with the extent to which own-source revenues exceed "potential revenues". However, the mechanism was dropped, at least in part due to local government complaints (Lewis and Smoke, 2009).

Interestingly, research has shown that the size of the DAU is, in any case, positively associated with local own-source revenues, even without the incentive (Lewis, 2005). A likely explanation for this outcome is that increased transfers and under-spending lead to increased reserve funds, which in turn lead to increased interest earnings, a form of own-source revenue. Finally, a more positive experience with incentives is illustrated by a recent (partial) withholding of DAU untied transfers to local governments that did not comply with budget reporting requirements. After delaying transfer payment, the noncompliant local governments almost immediately conformed to the relevant regulations.

In the Philippines, experimentation with performance incentives has been even less common than that in Indonesia. Evidence suggests, however, that larger block grant allocations are associated with less local revenue generation (Manasan, 2004). Thus, larger transfers provide a disincentive to local tax effort. More positively, as mentioned above, the central government's prerogative of withholding a local government's IRA if it fails to repay a loan on time or in full has encouraged good debt repayment performance by local governments.

No specific performance incentives have been integrated into the intergovernmental framework in Vietnam. On the other hand, the lack of clear expenditure and tax assignments may create disincentives to improve spending efficiency and revenue mobilization. The centralization of tax administration may also provide disincentives for local tax collection, and negotiations involved in determining many transfers may provide incentives for lobbying behavior at the expense of local revenue effort. Regarding the equalization transfer, the use of outdated expenditure norms to determine spending needs may create negative incentives in service planning and decision-making; and the fact that equalization transfers are reduced if local own-sources increase sends the wrong signal regarding local revenue effort (Martínez-Vázquez, 2005).

The central government in Thailand has not yet used explicit performance incentives in the intergovernmental transfer system and little information exists on the general incentive effects of the central-local decentralization framework. However, it has been hypothesized that excess slack in the fiscal system has induced reasonably significant innovation among some local governments in developing their fiscal strategies (Weerasak, 2006).

Cambodia does not yet have any experience with performance incentives within its fiscal transfer system but is considering this development. Malaysia measures local government performance through a "Local Government Star Rating" classification introduced in 2008 and some of the grants to local government rely on a council's financial position and revenue collection performance, but incentive structures are not a feature of grant distribution.

Tax Administration and Expenditure Management

Indonesian local government revenue planning and tax administration are insufficiently developed and these processes are not standardized to one set of financial reports and a fixed timetable for their production. A desirable annual level of tax revenues is not estimated by local officials and most local governments simply target a fixed percentage increase in own-source revenues each year, then meet the target with relative ease (Lewis and Oosterman, 2009). Another issue is the excessive cost of tax administration. Currently, the ratio of the cost of administering taxes to revenue yield, across all local governments in Indonesia, is well over 50 percent and more than 10 percent of local governments have cost-to-yield ratios exceeding 100 percent (Lewis, 2006).

Similarly expenditure management suffers from weaknesses. As noted above, many Indonesian local governments do not fully spend the resources to which they have access and have accumulated a surprisingly large stock of fiscal reserves since decentralization began in 2001. Currently, *kabupaten/kota* fiscal reserves are equal to about 25 percent of annual local government expenditure. As is the case for revenues, the distribution of fiscal slack across Indonesian local governments is skewed: the fiscal reserves ranging from about five percent to nearly 80 percent of annual expenditure. Even so, only a few Indonesian local governments have drawn down on these reserves to finance needed capital spending (Lewis and Oosterman, 2009). On the expenditure side of their budgets, Indonesian local governments spend a significant amount on government administration (25 percent of local expenditures) but also spend about 35 percent of total budgets on education, often more than the pre-determined optimum amount (Lewis, and Pattinasarany, 2009b).

While Indonesian local government borrowing has been limited, as noted above, repayment of loans has been weak overall (Lewis and Woodward, 2010). Over forty percent of total principal and interest repayments that have fallen due are in arrears. Most outstanding loans to local governments and their water enterprises (especially) would be considered non-performing by normal definitions (although such loans are referred to as merely "stuck" in Indonesia). The Indonesian central government appears to be addressing the problem, however, with an extensive program of local debt restructuring.

Local tax administration in the Philippines has seen improvements made but there remain important challenges. As little as 60 percent of total own-source assessed revenue is collected by local governments and collection efficiency appears to have declined in recent years. Many local officials do not use the tax authority that is available to them. In addition, local governments collect many nuisance taxes and, although hard data are lacking, tax administration cost efficiency is low (Manasan, 2004).

In terms of expenditure management, Philippine local governments spend, on average, about 25 percent of their budgets on administration (Manasan, 2004) and like those in Indonesia, have accumulated quite large fiscal reserves. The stock of sub-national reserves in the Philippines is between 35 percent and 40 percent of annual expenditure. However, unlike the situation in Indonesia, local government reserves in the Philippines are not fully available for appropriation, owing to requirements regarding the maintenance of liquidity sufficient to cover long-term liabilities. Finally, as already mentioned, the central government can cut the IRA allocations due to non-payment of debt and this has undoubtedly encouraged timely and full loan repayment (World Bank, 2009).

Tax administration is centralized in Vietnam. Thus tax administrative effectiveness and efficiency are not issues for local governments. Local officials do sometimes attempt to improve the performance of central tax administrators by limiting their salaries and benefits but this has little overall impact in improving tax administration. On the other hand, Vietnamese local governments do have some control over spending and seem to do a reasonably good job in terms of managing their expenditures. By international standards, local governments spend less on wages and salaries and significantly more on capital development (Martínez-Vázquez, 2005).

Despite having limited discretion over their revenues, local government tax administration in Thailand appears to be quite competent and many local governments have modernized their tax administrative systems with a view to improving collection efficiency (Weerasak, 2006; JICA, 2008). Others have embarked on successful civic education schemes to encourage residents to pay their tax liabilities (Weerasak, 2006). Thai local governments have also been innovative on the expenditure side, with many now contracting-out the delivery of some services and improving cost efficiencies. Some local governments have also adopted medium-term expenditure frameworks and others have engaged in genuine participatory budgeting, becoming more responsive in the process (Weerasak, 2006).

In Cambodia, tax administration by local government is restricted by the delay in passing local government finance legislation to clarify assignments and give legal capacity to collect. Until this happens, local governments' in Cambodia have little authority and capacity. On the expenditure side, the small projects undertaken by the communes are included in their development plans and budgets, but these Councils generally have only one staff member so administrative capacity is very limited.

In Malaysia, the "One Malaysia" policy has led to local governments having very few duties in revenue collection, so they have very little capacity. On expenditure management, local government's major task is to deliver functions that are controlled by the central government so while they have some service delivery experience, their overall capacity in service delivery management, including policy determination and the setting of standards, is limited.

Service Delivery Outcomes

As in other developing nations, local public services in Indonesia need improvement, although since decentralization a decade ago, citizens have become more satisfied with the level of service provided by local government, (for example a recent study estimated that over 85 percent of citizens are at least somewhat satisfied with local public school education), social service outcomes rank disappointingly low from both regional and international perspectives (Lewis and Pattinasarany, 2009a). Infrastructure quality is, on average, sub-standard and deteriorating, but citizen satisfaction with low quality services, which may in part be related to improvements they perceive in the role of local governments and governance, creates few incentives for local governments to improve service delivery performance.

Philippine residents, like their counterparts in Indonesia, appear quite content with the quality of public services. A recent survey of health services indicates that just less than 90 percent of Filipinos are at least somewhat satisfied with quality (Azfar and Meagher, 2001), but a recent World Bank Report qualified the situation of public service delivery in Philippines as quite poor (World Bank, 2009). As with Indonesia, it is likely that low expectations explain high levels of satisfaction, but these low expectations engender little support for service improvements.

Information on the quality of local public services is lacking for Vietnam but sources suggest that significant improvements are needed (Martínez-Vázquez, 2005). Improving service delivery at the local level, however, is constrained by the almost total lack of horizontal accountability. Vietnam has started to experiment with local service score-cards and this is a useful beginning in establishing local government accountability to citizens, but much remains to be done.

There is a similar lack of information about local public service outcomes in Thailand. Performance of local governments is not monitored and outcome data are not regularly collected. It does seem, however, that local governments are becoming more accountable to their citizens. Local governments, for example, are increasingly using public hearings to seek opinions on and experience with particular development projects. While public participation in budget decisions is still somewhat limited, the positive experience of some local governments gives cause for some optimism (Weerasak, 2006).

In Cambodia, the level of resourcing of the communes, the lack of clarity in their expenditure assignments, and limited capacity have led to ad hoc provision of a rather limited range of small-scale services. Some of what is delivered is of poor quality and has limited impact.

Selected Pressing Issues and Binding Constraints

The most critical local government issues in Indonesia are related to the distribution of revenues across local governments and to the quantity and quality of spending by local governments. The max-min ratio of per capita own-source to shared revenues among local governments is nearly 400:1, quite large by international standards (Lewis, 2002). This overstates the inequity problem since such revenues make up a relatively small portion of total revenues, but even after accounting for the equalizing DAU grants, there is a great disparity in local government access to revenues (Lewis, 2003).

At the same time, Indonesian local government's management capacity is weak, and while some municipalities have made significant improvements in this domain, across the board this translates into low spending efficiency. There is the potential for reaching higher levels of service delivery with existing resources if spending is refocused (especially away from administrative tasks) and efficiency is improved. Weak intergovernmental performance incentives and inadequate efforts to build capacity have contributed to this shortcoming.

Another related set of constraints in Indonesia relates to local own-source revenues. Like most developing countries, the level of Indonesian local government own-source revenues is very low and this constrains accountability. Just as important is the fact that Indonesian local governments lack access to any good source of own revenue that can be used to respond to citizen demand (Lewis, 2009). A new Indonesian law on sub-national taxation asserts that authority over the urban and rural property tax will be decentralized to local government within five years, but implementation during the indicated time frame is far from certain. If it does eventuate, it will be necessary to reinforce the capacity of Indonesian local governments to use the property tax revenue effectively (Lewis, 2009).

In the Philippines, the most pressing issue is arguably the under-funding of local governments relative to their service responsibilities, especially in municipalities. Local tax administration also appears to be the binding constraint. A particular problem in this regard concerns the property tax, which is not used as a local revenue source. Unfunded mandates by the center further constrain resources.

A second major concern in the Philippines is local governments' lack of fiscal autonomy. As mentioned above, the central government maintains significant control over both local revenues and expenditures. Over-control of local fiscal operations constrains the achievement of efficiency and accountability objectives.

Perhaps the most important issue in Vietnam relates to the structure of the intergovernmental system, particularly the role of provinces. Currently, Vietnam is allowing provinces almost complete discretion in setting the fiscal agenda for district and commune governments. A related issue is the hierarchical relations among levels of government, particularly with regard to the budget preparation and approval process. This model, under which the budget at each level must be approved by the next higher level government (in addition to the People's Council), limits planning and budgeting autonomy, which in turn constrains the attainment of efficiency and accountability objectives. Finally, the relatively large number of sub-national tiers increases administrative costs and distorts implementation of central, regional and local policies and programs (Martínez-Vázquez, 2005).

A particular constraint to effective decentralization in Thailand is the number and size of local governments. Thailand has over 7,800 local governments at the bottom tier, making the average size of a local unit little more than 8,000 residents, with many being much smaller. This constrains the proper decentralization of many services and possibly increases the costs of service delivery. Another problem relates to the parallel structure of deconcentrated offices of the central government operating alongside decentralized governments. Such a structure creates confusion in service delivery and fiscal operations and constrains the development of horizontal accountability. Besides these institutional problems, some technical concerns also exist. There is a particular problem with the assignment of functions, which have not been clarified since the basic legislation was passed in 1999. Lack of revenue decentralization and discretion is also problematic. Finally, the system of transfers is complicated and fragmented and constrains local decision-making; transfers also lack transparency, predictability, and timeliness in their allocation (Martínez-Vázquez, 2005).

In Cambodia, the most pressing issue is to get the 2009 Organic Law on

Decentralization and Democratic Development implemented. A plan to achieve this was adopted in June 2010 and the period to 2013 should see significant change. The newly created district councils will, however, remain indirectly elected by the elected councilors of the communes and *sangkats*, a situation that raises questions about their accountability to the people.

In Malaysia, clearly the most pressing matter is to reintroduce elected local governments. Once the councils are back in place, they need to be given sufficient autonomy to function effectively as representatives of the people and providers of services.

Conclusions and Observations on South-East Asia

The foregoing discussion suggests a number of different priority areas for policy reform across the countries of South-East Asia.

In Indonesia, government might consider:

- Revising allocation procedures of the main DAU untied grants to improve equalization (including removal of the counter equalizing wage payment component);
- Revising and eliminating the many inefficient local taxes and levies (estimated to number 9,715 and account for 36 percent of local taxes and levies);
- Prioritizing expenditure management through increasing awareness of operation and maintenance needs, better identification of investment opportunities, and improving service delivery outcomes;
- Requiring relevant central ministries to work with local government to build local administrative capacity (for general purposes and on the assumption the property tax will be decentralized and need to be well managed);
- Opening a dialogue with local governments to design and integrate a consistent set of performance incentives into the intergovernmental fiscal transfer framework and working with local governments to further develop horizontal accountability.

In the Philippines, the central government could consider ways to improve the funding situation of local governments, especially cities. This might include:

- Increasing the IRA allocations;
- Decentralizing additional tax bases, including a piggy back scheme on the national income tax;
- Building capacity of local governments in tax administration and other own revenue generation;
- Discontinuing its practice of making unfunded mandates;
- Removing some controls over local government revenue generation and spending and replacing them with performance incentives.

In Vietnam, the government may want to rethink the controlling role provinces play in district and commune fiscal affairs. Possible reform to consider might be:

- Explicitly assigning expenditure and revenue responsibilities to sub-provincial levels;
- Providing more autonomy in expenditure planning and decision-making, and in

revenue generation to districts and communes;

- Implementing a modern property tax over which some rate authority would be granted to sub-national government.

Vietnam may also like to revisit the multi-level and nested national budget preparation and approval process as well as the need for four levels of government.

In Thailand, the government might consider following the Indonesian example and eliminate its deconcentrated offices. A priority policy concern is clarifying the service responsibilities of local governments, which are poorly defined. Currently, services are assigned in individual local government acts and sectoral laws rather than in consolidated national legislation. If that were done, a more appropriate assignment of revenues could be made and a system of intergovernmental transfers developed. Local governance and accountability should be developed, strengthening horizontal structures and avoiding excessive bureaucracy. In addition, it will be necessary to improve the efficiency of local government operations, possibly through the amalgamation of some smaller municipalities.

In Cambodia, the most important action required is the implementation of the 2009 Organic Law, which is underway. That process should involve clarification of the status of provincial, district and commune councils and definition of revenue and expenditure assignments for each. The fiscal transfer system should then be developed so as to ensure each sphere of government in Cambodia is equitably (though probably not fully) funded.

In Malaysia, the priority would be to provide for elected local governments with genuine autonomy. Following this, the government could increase the clarity in the division of responsibilities between local, provincial and central government and work towards eliminating overlaps to improve efficiency.

Australia and New Zealand Local Government Finances

Australia and New Zealand differ from other nations in the Asia-Pacific Region in that only a small percentage of their population is descended from the indigenous people. In both nations, the general government sector is about 35 percent of GDP but local government is small, making up only about 6 percent of total government expenditure in Australia and about 9 percent in New Zealand (2 percent and 3 percent of GDP respectively).

Australia is a federation in which local government is not mentioned in the national Constitution. In each of the six states and the northern territory, local government exists under State[20] legislation and each council is subject to the same legislation, irrespective of its population size, area, degree of urbanization and range of services. In the Australian Capital Territory, municipal functions are performed by the territory government. The number of councils in Australia remained fairly stable between 2000 and 2008 at about 700, but changes in Queensland and the Northern Territory in that year resulted in a reduction of over 100 in the number of councils.

In New Zealand, there are two tiers of local government, both of which operate under the same national legislation. Most of the nation is covered by both regional councils, of which there are 12, and territorial authorities, of which there are 73. Five of the territorial authorities also have the powers of a regional council and are known as "unitary authorities". The structure

20. Unless the context indicates otherwise, the term 'State' is used in the Australian context to include either or both of the Northern Territory and the Australian Capital Territory.

Table 3.13: Sub-national Government Share of Total Public Expenditure and Revenue – Oceania

Country	Share of Total Public Expenditure (%)			Share of Total Public Revenue (%)		
	Sub-national	Upper Tier	Lower Tiers	Sub-national	Upper Tier	Lower Tiers
Australia	36	30	6	20	17	3
New Zealand	9	n.a.	9	8	n.a.	8

Source: UCLG data files and other sources. Figures are approximations. Data are for most recent year available: Australia 2006-7; New Zealand 2007-8.

of local government has been stable since the late 1980s but there is now some pressure to reduce the number of regions and form more unitary authorities, with major changes already agreed for the Auckland area. The unitary nature of government makes this process of overall reform much easier than in the Australian federation where each state is responsible for local government.

The separation of powers between the two spheres of local authorities in New Zealand is, in theory, that the regions are the regulatory authorities and the territorial authorities provide the services. Below the territorial authorities is a tier of local organization that exists at the discretion of those authorities – community boards. About half the territorial authorities have chosen to establish these and in 2006 there were about 150 community boards. Some councils also have formal relationships with local indigenous Maori Liaison committees. At both the regional and territorial authority tiers of local government, there is considerable variation in area and population size.

All councils in Australia and New Zealand are made up of elected officials, and with the exception of setting rate levels in New South Wales, councils in both nations have a very high level of autonomy within the activities legislated for local government. In terms of supervision, New Zealand councils are largely left to the scrutiny of citizens and the electoral process, the state of South Australia operates a self-regulatory system through the local government association while other Australian states use a more legislative supervisory model.

Expenditure[21]

Traditionally, the major responsibilities of local governments in Australia have been local roads, recreational facilities, and community amenities (including waste removal). Recent times have seen an expansion into a wider range of activities in the social security and welfare areas but these are still a minor task overall. The atypical structure of the population in the northern territory –high proportion of poor indigenous people in the territory's small and scattered population– results in councils in that jurisdiction having more roles than elsewhere. The increasing proportion of local government expenditure spent on general administration in Australia is of some note and seems to be related at least in part to greater regulatory requirements being imposed on councils by state legislation. Possibly resulting from these extra administrative costs, the share of councils' expenditure spent on roads –a basic municipal service– has been reducing over the last decade.

As in Australia, the main functions of local government in New Zealand are roads and

21. See Table 3.13

transportation; activities associated with culture, recreation and sport; water and waste water, and solid waste management. General governance is about 17 percent of total local expenditure and further amalgamation of regional and territorial councils may result in this being reduced. In both countries, there has been some cost shifting to local government by other spheres of government in recent years, but these have been incremental and regulatory in nature rather than a major unfunded mandate being deliberately transferred to the local sector.

Under the principle of subsidiarity, it seems unlikely that either nation has gone as far as it could to get service delivery down to the lowest level of government that could reasonably provide it. However, both nations have taken the view that services such as education and health should be provided on a more uniform basis than can be achieved if they were transferred to local government. In Australia, the greater uniformity the community expects is achieved through agreements between the commonwealth and state governments and through conditions the commonwealth attaches to tied grants it provides the states. There is no move towards giving these types of services to local government and, if any change were to be made, it would probably involve a greater concentration of power at the central government level. In New Zealand, the national uniformity of education and health services is achieved though their assignment to the national government and there is no pressure to change these arrangements.

Own-Source Revenues

The revenue sources of local government in Australia and New Zealand are shown in Table 3.14 and 3.15. In both cases, the tax base is the value of real property but, in Australia, the state governments also use this revenue base and their absolute revenue flow from property is greater than that of the local government sector. Councils generally decide on the size of the rate levies and user fees, and collect their own revenue. The only exceptions being that councils in the Australian state of New South Wales have a limit imposed by the state government on the size of annual rate increases[22] and some regional councils in New Zealand arrange to have their revenue collected by the territorial authorities. The flexibility given to councils in New Zealand to use different valuation bases and create different property-based taxes is wider than that available in Australia, and greater flexibility given to some Australian states coincides with higher levels of rate revenue in those states.

Current reviews of taxation in both nations may impact local government. In New Zealand, there is some talk of the national government levying a valuation-based tax on rural properties, and in Australia there is a quite radical proposal that all public sector taxation might be collected by one agency, whether the revenue flow is for the central, state or local government sector.

Although the New South Wales State Government imposes a limit on the annual increase in rates, councils can apply for special exemption and the great majority of such applications are successful. Nevertheless, it does appear that the restriction has some impact as the growth in rate revenue in New South Wales over the last decade has been significantly lower than in all other states. The use of the property value as a revenue source by the state governments may be a much larger and more widespread incursion.

In Western Australia, the legislative requirement to use unimproved value as the basis of valuation in all rural areas, results in

22. *This is also the case in the Northern Territory until 2013.*

Table 3.14: Australian Local Government Revenue Sources, by State, 2006-07 (%)

State	Source of Revenue					
	Property Rates	Sale of Goods and Services	Interest and Dividends	Other Revenue	Self Funding Ratio	Grants and Subsidies
New South Wales	35.7	32.0	4.3	12.0	84.0	16.0
Victoria	47.7	17.9	1.3	12.9	79.8	20.2
Queensland	27.4	39.0	2.4	19.3	88.1	11.9
Western Australia	40.2	20.7	3.2	15.7	79.8	20.2
South Australia	59.2	16.3	1.2	5.7	82.4	17.6
Tasmania	31.4	39.0	3.8	8.3	82.4	17.6
Northern Territory	17.2	16.5	1.9	12.9	48.4	51.6
Total	37.4	28.9	2.8	14.1	83.1	16.9

Source: UCLG data files and other sources.

Table 3.15: New Zealand Local Government Revenue Sources, 2007-08 (%)

Source of Revenue	Regional Councils	District/City Councils
Municipal Rates	43.9	61.0
Regulatory Income	4.3	6.4
Investment Income	7.9	5.1
Sale of goods and services, and other income	14.4	17.6
Self-funding ratio	70.5	90.1
Grants and subsidies	29.5	9.9
Total	100.0	100.0

Source: UCLG data files and other sources.

very productive mining properties on poor quality rural land being grossly under-valued and under-taxed. Notwithstanding this restriction, Western Australia has had one of the highest rates of property tax growth since the mid 1990s.

The pattern of revenue sources for councils in the northern territory differs from other Australian states because of the high proportion of poor indigenous people in the territory's small and scattered population, and the way other levels of government use councils to provide non-municipal services on an agency basis, financed through subsidies. Associated with the revised structure of local government, a three-year period of limiting rate increases is currently in operation in the northern territory but there are, as yet, no data available to measure the impact of this state policy decision.

Revenue from the sale of goods and services is an important supplement to rate revenue in both nations, but is more important in Australia where it is close to 30 percent of total revenue. Part of the difference between the two nations in the importance of this revenue (and between States in Australia) is due to some utility services, such as water and sewerage, being funded through rate revenues in some jurisdictions and by consumption-based charges in others. It had been anticipated that, in New Zealand, revenue from sales of goods and services might have been higher for regional councils because of the enterprises such as ports and public transport they provide, but these seem to be managed outside the general government accounts of the councils unless they need supplementation or provide support funding for other council activities.

Income from interest and dividends is relatively high in both nations, but higher in New Zealand where councils have accumulated relatively large surpluses over time and have considerable investments. Interest and dividend revenue is over 10 percent of the own-source revenue of the New Zealand regional councils, indicating that they have been able to accumulate substantial investments – possible resulting from their trading enterprise activities. For this reason, the size and importance of the grants provided to the regional councils in New Zealand is somewhat surprising.

The impacts of the recent global financial crisis on councils' capacity to raise revenue in both Australia and New Zealand have been relatively small. Some councils suffered a temporary reduction in residents' capacity to pay rates and charges, but the greater impact has been the lower interest rate received on investments and, in a few Australian cases, their investment portfolios were grossly reduced in value through the collapse of international banks. The longer-term impact, at least in Australia, may be a reduction in the spread of values between the lower and higher ends of the property market that will result in a redistribution of a council's total rate impost away from those with greater capacity to pay, towards those with less.

Intergovernmental Transfers

Councils in Australia receive grants from both the central and state governments, with the largest program being the untied funding from the central government. This program provides about a third of all grants to councils and is distributed by state grant commissions based on principles of fiscal and service delivery capacity equalization specified by the central government. This structure does not work particularly well as the different state commissions interpret the principles differently and similar councils in different states sometimes receive very different levels of per capita funding. The annual increases in the size of the grants pool is determined by formula but the original amount was based on a self-assessment of the Australian government's fiscal capacity many years ago, so the pool has no direct relationship to levels of current fiscal stress (if any) within the three spheres of government. Another 15 percent of Australian grants are provided by the central government as tied grants for recurrent service delivery –particularly road maintenance. These grants are managed by line agencies within the central bureaucracy which at least partly follow the distributional patterns decided by the state grants commissions, i.e. limited equalization.

At the state level, the largest program is the untied subsidy to councils for reducing or exempting those in need from council rates, although these have been declining in real value in some states and no longer cover the full cost of the states' policies. Two states also provide untied funding for more needy councils with large indigenous populations. Tied grants from the state governments are most frequently provided for capital infrastructure development and for services provided on a cost recovery basis. The distribution is most frequently based on relative needs as expressed in submissions to state government agencies responsible for program management.

There are very few incentive mechanisms included in the grant arrangements in Australia. The federal government uses agreements rather than strict conditions to ensure that its objectives are achieved by grant recipients and the state funding is rarely tied to local government achieving greater efficiencies.

For councils in New Zealand, almost all grants to local government are provided as tied grants for local road maintenance and construction. The grants are funded from national fuel excise, road user charges, and vehicle registration fees, and there is some equalization of service capacity within the distribution so that poorer councils receive a higher percentage of their total road expenditure budgets from grant funding. The overall size of the pool of grant funding provided to councils in New Zealand varies over time as expenditure priorities of the national government change.

In fact, changes in central government policy in the eight years after 1999-2000 saw grants to regional councils increased from 15 to nearly 30 percent of their total revenue while grants to territorial councils remained stable at about 10 percent of revenue. As a result, rates have reduced in importance from over 50 percent to less than 44 percent in the regional councils, while remaining much more stable at about 57 to 60 percent in the territorial councils. While these movements are associated with the different functions performed by the regional and territorial councils, it is an issue requiring further analysis and negotiation with the government of New Zealand.

The extent to which councils in Australia and New Zealand are self-funded acts against the likelihood that municipal services are of roughly the same standard within each of these nations. Self-funding must result in richer councils being able to provide better services and the equalization mechanisms operating through the grants systems are insufficient to overcome the differences in fiscal capacity. Clarity is needed in both nations as to where the policy objective of equalization fits in relation to the provision of municipal services, and changes may be necessary to expenditure assignments between spheres of government, revenue assignments, or both. In both nations, the local government structure and management capacity do seem to be underutilized and diseconomies of small scale are obvious in many councils.

Debt Finance

All local authorities in both Australia and New Zealand have capacity to borrow, but the level of debt is exceptionally low in Australia where gross debt is about 25 percent of the annual operating revenue, and also low in New Zealand where it is about 70 percent of the annual operating revenue. In both cases, borrowing is much more likely to be used to fund infrastructure for cost-recovery rather than social activities.

Overall, with self-funding ratios being very high, with large investment portfolios and very low debt levels, it must be assumed that the local government sectors in Australia and New Zealand are under little stress in funding their service delivery responsibilities. At a minimum, a different approach to intergenerational funding of infrastructures would see greater use of debt and higher rate imposts (or lower investments) to fund more social developments.

Conclusions and Observations on Australia and New Zealand

Australia claims that the most important negative feature of the framework within which local government operates is its lack of national constitutional status. If this is the case, it does not seem to be associated with fiscal management, as councils have a high level of autonomy and the grants system has been designed to by-pass any constitutional difficulties. More work is needed by local governments to identify the implications of the lack of constitutional status. Such status may, for example, make changes to expenditure assignments easier to achieve and this would result in a more active and influential local government sector.

Local government representatives highlight the fiscal difficulties that councils are facing, being squeezed on the one side by rising community expectation, increasing responsibilities and compliance requirements and on the other by only modest revenue growth. Local governments in larger urban and regional councils have far fewer economic constraints than small rural and remote councils; especially indigenous councils in the more remote regions.

Work is needed to improve the long-term planning in local government in Australia. The system of fiscal transfers for local government is too cumbersome and creates difficulties for local government's acceptance of grant distribution results, especially for the untied grants. More work is also needed by the central government to see that the principles for distribution that it has agreed to with the states are interpreted uniformly and applied similarly by the seven state grants commissions.

Along with the development of policy on the constitutional status of local government, work is necessary in Australia on examination and clarification of the vertical imbalance within the federation to see that the revenue and expenditure assignments to each of the three spheres of government are those that best serve the nation. The rate pegging actions of the New South Wales government also need to be abolished so that true autonomy is provided to local government in that State. Clarification is needed on where equalization of service provision by local councils fits into national objectives as this will impact on grant systems, revenue assignments and the spread of revenue between rates and fees from the sale of goods and services.

In New Zealand, the major policy development must relate to the future role of regional councils and their amalgamation into unitary authorities. These councils currently appear to have too limiting a range of functions and suffer substantial diseconomies of scale. The extent to which equalization of the capacity of local governments is an objective of the central government also needs policy clarification as the current system of grants cannot achieve equalization and greater inequities are developing over time: to the detriment of the more needy sectors of society. Policy may also be necessary on the accumulation of investment assets by councils to see that intergenerational equity of citizens is better achieved, but this should result from agreement of councils through their association rather than being imposed by the national government.

Conclusions

The above review demonstrates the significant variation in fiscal decentralization frameworks and outcomes across and within sub-regions of the Asia Pacific region. The differences extend across standard variables such as local governments' shares of consolidated public expenditure and revenue, local dependence on intergovernmental transfers, and local government access to and use of capital finance. Differences also span across an assortment of performance indicators related to resource adequacy, fiscal discretion, incentives, capacity and service delivery. This diversity is at least in part dependent on the level of development of the nations' economies and their historical backgrounds, making it nearly impossible to generalize about fiscal decentralization in the Asia Pacific.

Difficulties in making generalizations notwithstanding, findings are summarized in three broad conclusions that may be important for policymakers in the region to consider as they develop their decentralization reform agendas going forward. The first relates to the appropriate economic objectives of decentralization. One of the principal arguments in support of decentralization is that it can improve public service delivery to citizens. As such, it makes sense for countries to design and implement their decentralization programs with an explicit view to making improvements in basic public services. China, for example, has tied its recent decentralization agenda more towards economic development goals (and this policy is also being emulated in Cambodia), though public services are now becoming a more significant concern. Bangladeshi policymakers have ignored service delivery in the design and implementation of their decentralization program, using decentralization more as an instrument of control than as a mechanism for the improvement of local services. Orienting a decentralization program toward the objectives of improving services would appear to be a necessary starting point in the achievement of the objective.

A second conclusion also relates to decentralization strategy. Here the issue is the extent to which it is the central government or middle tier governments that lead the design and/or implementation of decentralization programs. In unitary nations, it appears that strong central government guidance of decentralization is needed for its more successful implementation. In federal nations and elsewhere where decentralization decision-making is a mix of central and middle-tier government policy implementation, decentralization often seems to get stuck at the middle tier. However Australia has proved an exception to this rule and Vietnam seems to be making efforts to move beyond this dynamic. In any case, the general point is that when decentralization stops at the middle tiers, the achievement of service delivery outcomes is constrained. As such, central governments need to develop mechanisms to ensure that provision and financing of public services is devolved to the lowest levels feasible.

A final conclusion concerns accountability. This review has shown that where countries in the region have paid attention to accountability in the design and execution of their fiscal decentralization, they have most frequently stressed vertical accountability to other governments. Horizontal accountability is somewhat weak throughout the Asia subregions, although it is stronger in the older developed democracies of Australia and New Zealand. It is difficult for decentralization programs to deliver quality local public services in the absence of strong accountability to the people. Part of the problem in Asia may be technical in that the link between service delivery and tax payment is not strong; and this certainly constrains accountability. The larger issue lies outside the realm of the strictly fiscal, however, and relates more to the political environment in which local governments operate. It is often argued that democratic elections at the local level are necessary for the establishment of horizontal accountability and to create a robust citizen demand for quality services. To deepen local democracy, more active citizen engagement and government responsiveness is also needed.

UCLG ASPAC Policy Recommendations for Fiscal Decentralization

After discussion at the Workshop on Local Government Finances held at Batam, Indonesia, on 25-26 June, the members of the UCLG-ASPAC Region agree that the basis of its policy on Fiscal Decentralization is as follows.

1. That local government be given greater autonomy by having its powers widened to decide all tax bases and tax rates, and the level of fees for service, within its mandate.
2. That there be a review of the current allocation of revenue sources and service delivery responsibilities to each sphere of government and that they be reassigned so as to:
    a. Reduce vertical fiscal imbalance;
    b. Better match expenditure responsibilities with own-source revenues;
    c. Ensure all spheres of government share in natural resource revenues; and
    d. Reduce the impact of economic cycles on any one sphere of government.
3. That local government be provided with an increased and fixed share of national public sector revenue through grants and transfers, but with a reduced number of grants and a larger proportion being provided as untied funding.
4. The grants distribution to local government be managed by an institution that is independent of government, has membership acceptable to grant recipients and operates in a transparent manner to provide funds directly to the bank accounts of the recipients.
5. That there be more widespread application of horizontal fiscal equalization principles within the distribution of grant funding for local government.
6. That all local governments have access to loan funds, under conditions and limits that are acceptable to both the national and local governments.
7. That where one does not already exist, there be a local government finance corporation or equivalent established to ensure local government has access to loans at lower than commercial rates of interest.

UCLG ASPAC Policy Recommendations for Fiscal Decentralization (continued)

8. That all unfunded mandates of local government be removed by increased funding or reallocation of responsibilities, and that future unfunded mandates be made illegal.

9. That "finance follows function" in any future reallocation of responsibilities between spheres of government.

10. That consultative mechanisms be established to ensure that all spheres of government work together to coordinate development and infrastructure planning and renewal, and budgeting, and that local government has an increased role in determining national service delivery objectives.

11. That other spheres of government review and amend their policies and procedures to remove unnecessary restrictions on local government fiscal autonomy.

12. That where not already done, standard accounting and financial management practices be introduced for local government; that there be clear procedural instructions for practitioners implementing these standards and that both elected officials and local government staff be trained in their application.

13. That national constitutions be amended where necessary to give local government appropriate status, that all sectoral legislation be examined to ensure its consistency with local government legal requirements and that local government revenue management be firmly based in the law.

14. That local government associations be recognized by other spheres of government as the appropriate bodies to represent local government in intergovernmental discussions on policy and fiscal arrangements.

For its part, local government will work with other spheres of government to achieve these objectives, will re-examine its own policies, by-laws, regulations, procedures and practices to see that they best meet the overall objectives of government in providing services to the people in an efficient manner.

Local government will also take steps to improve the transparency of its operations, involve the people more in its planning, budgeting and other activities, and will introduce programs to encourage the payment of local taxes and charges.

4. Eurasia

Natalia Golovanova

and

Galina Kurlyandskaya

Center for Fiscal Policy (Moscow), Russia

The countries reviewed in this chapter include those belonging to the Caucasus region (Armenia and Georgia), Central Asia (Kazakhstan and Kyrgyzstan), Eastern Europe (Moldova, Belarus and Ukraine), and Russia, which covers Eastern Europe and Northern Asia.

Local governments in the Eurasia region have faced major challenges over the last 20 years due to the rapid adjustment of a diminished size and role of government. This problem has been encumbered by the concurrent attempt on the part of most national governments to retain responsibility for the large amounts of social services that usually were provided by local governments during the Soviet period.

Concurrently local governments across the region have been coping with a dramatic increase in migration, both domestic and international. This has resulted in a redistribution of service needs in relation to these positive and negative net-migrations, which no longer match the existing infrastructure. At the same time, the social infrastructure (schools, hospitals etc.) in localities that have lost population has been preserved in order to reduce social tensions, as budget-supported institutions have become almost the only area of employment.

In the early 1990s, despite the fact that Eurasian countries developed local self-governments from a common framework, each of the eight countries examined in this chapter has responded to those challenges in its own way and has selected its own model of local self-governance and intergovernmental fiscal relations. For instance, Kazakhstan has adopted a system of deconcentrated state bodies for local administration; a rather centralized hierarchical system of public authorities was selected in Belarus; and a two-tier system of local self-government was implemented in Russia and Moldova. In between, there are states where local self-governments exist autonomously (Armenia, Georgia) or alongside state bodies of local administration (in Ukraine at the *oblast* and *raion* level, in Kyrgyzstan - at the *raion* level).

Positive trends towards greater decentralization can be traced in some of the Eurasian countries: Local taxes were adopted in 2010 in Armenia and in Belarus a law On Local Government and Self-government was adopted.

However, in other countries an inclination towards centralization is being observed; local tax reduction in Russia, Kyrgyzstan, and Georgia; nomination by the center of local self-government heads in Kyrgyzstan; reorganization of local governments in Georgia; and limitations to local government autonomy in Russia.

The recent financial crisis revealed weaknesses within the local finance system of some Eurasian countries, while in other countries local budgets faired much better than central/regional ones due to the more stable revenues assigned to local level. For example while in Moldova, transfers to local governments were proportionally cut by 20 percent, in Kazakhstan, where grants were set up for a three-year period, they remained stable. In Russia, the revenue of settlement budgets (*poselenie*) grew, in nominal terms, in 2009 by 22 percent, however some large industrial cities (e.g., Yaroslavl, Orel, Kursk) faced shortcomings due to the reduction of Personal Income Tax revenue resulting from growing unemployment.

It should be noted that despite local finance problems in Eurasian countries, significant progress has been made since the early 1990s in a number of areas:

- Explicit assignment of expenditures have been put into law in all these countries;
- Meaningful revenue decentralization has taken place;
- Transparent equalization transfer mechanisms have been developed in most of these countries.

In this chapter we review how particular countries in Eurasia have addressed their local finances in different ways. We also take into account the common difficulties that local governments in the region continue to face and are hopeful that effective solutions can be found for improving the local finance systems in Eurasia.

Territorial Organization and the Size of Local Governments

Across the region there is a wide variety in the size of the public sector as well as in the division of spending across the levels of government. The territorial and economic features of the countries under review in this chapter are presented in Table 4.1.

As shown in Table 4.2, the size of the public sector ranges from 23 percent of GDP in Kyrgyzstan to 45 percent of GDP in Ukraine. Across the Eurasian government sector, local government spending make up a relatively small percentage of total government spending, with Armenia having the lowest share at 6 percent.[1] This trend reflects the low level responsibilities assigned to the local level across all Eurasian countries. Countries with budgets allocated to local levels, cities, and *raions* can be united into one group for comparison. The category of local budgets in Ukraine, Belarus and Kazakhstan include *oblast* budgets thus making the expenditure share of these combined local budgets the highest: 31 percent, 36 percent and 53 percent respectively. *Oblast* executive authorities in this group of countries are subordinates to the central government which retain control

1. *The share of local government in the general government budget according to the IMF data differs from, figures found in selected publications (e.g. Tumanyan, 2009 [2]). The difference could appear due to the country's accounting features. Besides, researchers often use the share of local budgets in the consolidated budgetary government but not in the general government.*

Table 4.1: General Country Statistics, 2008

Countries	Population (thousands)	Urban population (% of total)	Capital City Population (thousands)	Total Area (km²)	Population Density (persons per km²)	GDP per capita (2008 US$)	GDP per capita, PPP (current international $)
Armenia	3,234.2	63.9	1,113.3	29.8	109.1	3,872.7	6,074.7
Belarus	9,671.9	73.5	1,829.1	207.6	47.7	6,230.1	12,278.2
Georgia	4,382.1	52.7	1,106.7	69.7	62.0	2,969.9	4,965.5
Kazakhstan	15,766.5	57.9	633.7	2,724.9	5.8	8,513.1	11,323.2
Kyrgyzstan	5,276.0	36.3	785.1	198.5	27.5	958.4	2,192.6
Moldova	3,572.7	41.8	592.9	33.8	110.5	1,693.8	2,979.4
Russia	142,008.8	72.8	10,470.3	17,098.2	8.7	11,831.5	15,922.5
Ukraine	46,143.7	68.0	2,765.5	603.7	79.8	3,898.9	7,276.8

Data source: WDI, capital city population and territory - countries' statistical offices

Table 4.2: The Size of Government Expenditures

Countries	Armenia (2008)	Belarus (2008)	Georgia (2007)	Kazakhstan (2007)	Kyrgyzstan (2006)	Moldova (2008)	Russia (2008)	Ukraine (2008)
Total Expenditure of General Government (% of GDP)	23.9	48.7	29.0	20.6	23.3	41.4	42.9	45.4
Expenditure of Local Government (% of GDP)	1.3	17.3	6.1	11.0	5.5	10.2	7.8	14.2
Local Expenditures as a Share of General Government (%)	5.5	35.5	21.2	53.4	23.8	24.6	18.3	31.2

NOTE: Data for Belarus, Kazakhstan and Ukraine include oblast level figures. For Kazakhstan general government figures are not available, figures refer to the budget of the government.
Data source: for Kyrgyzstan – Ministry of Finance data, for other countries – Government Finance Statistics Yearbook 2009 (IMF)

Figure 4.1: Local Government Outlays as a Share of General Government Outlays (%)

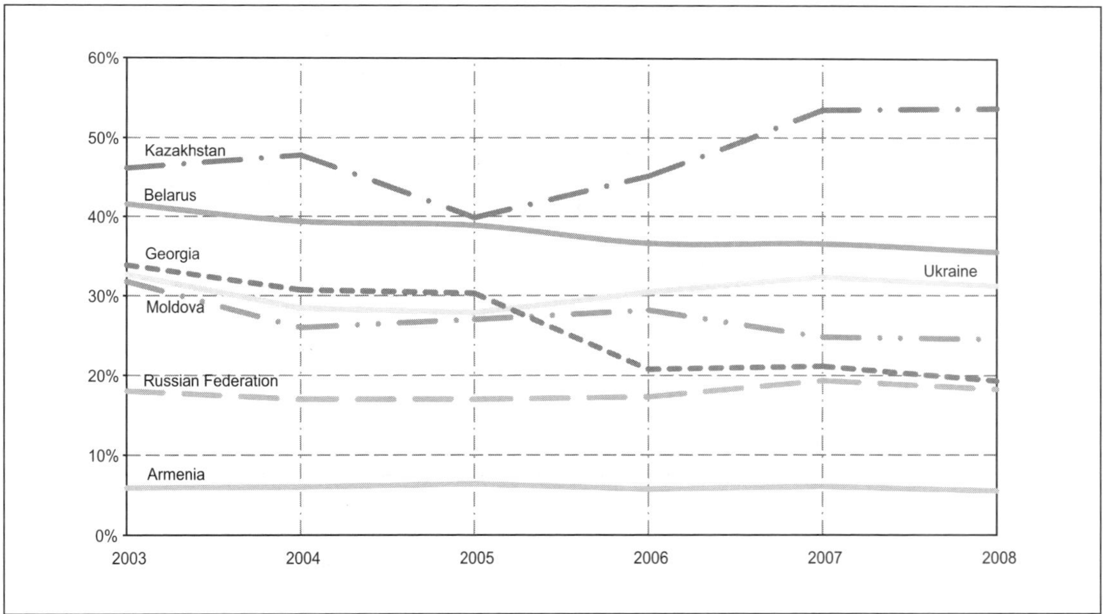

Data source: for Russia for 2003-2004 author's calculations based on the RF Ministry of Finance data, for other countries – IFS database (IMF).

over the execution of functions even if it transfers many of them to the lower level.

All countries under review became independent after the disintegration of the Soviet Union. With the exception of the Russian Federation, all of them are unitary states[2], and adopted their constitutions between 1993 and 1997. These constitutions laid the foundation of local self-governance to be further developed in laws on local self-governments or state local governments. Belarus was the last country to introduce the law On Local

2. *Although Ukraine, Georgia and Moldova are unitary states, the asymmetric assignment of powers with the special rights for the autonomous territorial units (republics) allows regarding them as an intermediate step between the unitary and federal state. For discussion on asymmetric decentralization in Georgia see Kirn and Khokrishvili (2008). The idea of federalization of Ukraine is discussed widely between the experts and politicians.*

Table 4.3: Territorial Organization of Local Governments [4](2009)

Countries	Regional level	Intermediate level	Local level
Armenia	10 *marzers* (administrative regions without budget rights)		City of Yerevan (capital) 48 urban and 866 rural communities
Belarus	6 *oblasts* City of Minsk (capital)	118 *raions* 23 cities	1,524 rural municipal units (cities/towns of *raion* subordination, villages, settlements)
Georgia	9 administrative regions (administrative regions without budget rights) Autonomous republics of Abkhazia and Adjara[5]	5 cities: Tbilisi (capital), Batumi, Rustavi, Poti, Kutaisi 4 communities (Eredvi, Kurta, Tighvi and Azhara) 60 *raions*	
Kazakhstan	14 *oblasts* 2 special status territories: Astana (capital) and Amaty	160 *raions* 39 cities	45 cities and towns about 2,500 rural settlements without budget rights
Kyrgyzstan	7 *oblasts* (administrative regions without budget rights) 2 special status territories: Bishkek (capital) and Osh	40 *raions* 12 cities of *oblast* subordination	11 cities of *raion* subordination 472 settlements (*ayls*)
Moldova	1 autonomous territorial unit Gagauzia (Gagauz Eri)[6]	32 *raions* 2 municipium (Chisinau and Balti)	3 municipium (Comrat, Bender and Tiraspol) 51 towns 847 villages (communes)
Russia	83 subjects of RF: 21 republics, 46 *oblasts*, 9 *krais*, 4 autonomous *okrugs*, 1 autonomous *oblast*, 2 federal cities: Moscow (capital) and St. Petersburg	1,799 *raions* 521 cities (*"gorodskoi okrug"*)	21,595 (1,734 urban and 19,861 rural) settlements
Ukraine	25 regions: 24 *oblasts* and Autonomous Republic of Crimeria 2 special status territories: Kiev (capital) and Sevastopol	488 *raions* 176 cities	243 towns 657 settlements 10,222 villages

Source: compiled by authors (see bibliography).

Government and Self-Governance in 2010.[3]

As former republics of the USSR, these countries had, at one point, a common system of administrative and territorial division. The USSR's republics were divided into regions (*oblasts*, *krais*, and autonomous republics). Regions were further divided into *raions* (the equivalent of counties or districts) and cities of regional subordination. *Raions*, in their turn, included cities of *raion* subordination, towns, and villages, rural and urban settlements. This administrative

3. *Belarus regulated its local governments by a normative act (1991) that was enacted before its constitution was adopted.*

structure became the starting point for establishing local governments throughout the region and remained relevant during the first years of independence.

Although the countries originally had a uniform administrative and territorial division, later, in the course of decentralization, they preferred different options for territorial organization of local authorities (see Table 4.3).

Local authorities in Eurasia do not always take the form of countries with a long tradition of local self-government. In many countries (Belarus, Kazakhstan, Kyrgyzstan and Ukraine) the executive bodies of local governments are subject to the executive bodies of the higher level (embedded in the "vertical power structure"). At the same level of administrative-territorial division, there are elected councils, who adopt the budget prepared by the executive authorities, and take other decisions according to the powers assigned to them. The degree of accountability of the executive local body to the higher level of government and the degree of influence of elected councils at the executive local body varies in different countries of Eurasia. Such an organization of local self-government is a compromise between deconcentration and the devolution of powers. Under such arrangement local authorities have the greatest attributes of local self-government: an elected local council, local ownership and local budgets while under a deconcentrated system the local budget is usually a part of the central budget (as the budgets of *marzers* in Armenia or the budgets of *oblasts* in Kyrgyzstan).

In Kazakhstan, local governments do not have the official status of local self-governments. According to the law they are called local bodies of state government, though they do have elected local councils and expenditure responsibilities and revenue sources assigned to them. Local authorities include *oblasts* and cities of republic subordination (Astana and Almaty) as well as *raions* and cities of *oblast* subordination. At the same time, the central government directly interacts only with the *oblast* level, while *oblasts* build intergovernmental fiscal relations with *raions* and cities of *oblast* subordination. There are local councils at the sub-*raion* level but as they have no budgets of their own they cannot be considered a full-fledged level of public administration.

In Armenia, the *raion* level was abolished. The territory of the country is divided into administrative provinces (*marzers*), and each province includes several former *raions*. *Marzers* are deconcentrated subdivisions of the central government. Local self-government units have been established in the City of Yerevan (law adopted in 2009, before which the territory of Yerevan was divided into 12 neighborhood communities), and in local communities at the level of rural and urban settlements (first law adopted in 1996, new law in 2002).

Georgia has administrative subdivisions of central government at the regional level (*krais*, autonomous republics and the city of Tbilisi). Initially, Georgia had two subnational administrative levels, the *raion* and the local self-governments at the settlement level. Only the settlement level had some degree of autonomy.[7] Since 2006 the new Organic Law on Local Self-Government introduced a one-tier system of local self-government. Today the municipalities at the *raion* level (including large cities) constitute the only territorial level of local self-governance. However the dissatisfaction with the reform results, calls for the necessity of further local self-governance reform since the number of residents in newly

4. *In some countries (e.g. Russia and Ukraine) the large cities (Moscow and St. Petersburg, Kiev) could be divided further into municipalities according to the special laws but these municipal units have very limited powers so we do not consider them in the Chapter.*

5. *There is also one breakaway Republic of South Ossetia on the territory of Georgia. According to the Organic Law "On Local Self-Government" "On the territory of Georgia which is not under Georgia's jurisdiction, the authority and rules of establishing the local self-government bodies will be determined after restoration of Georgia's jurisdiction in compliance with conditions set by this law"*

6. *Territorial unit Stinga Nistrului (Transnistria) is not included into the intergovernmental relations system of Republic of Moldova.*

7. *See Shergelashvili and Narmania (2006).*

formed municipalities is too large to allow populations to feel represented (Losaberidze, 2009).

In the Republic of Kyrgyzstan the system of local government was introduced in 1995 for Bishkek city. By 2001, all cities, towns and villages received the right to local self-governance. Initially Kyrgyzstan had a system in which *oblasts* and *raions* had local bodies of state executive power while cities, towns and settlements (*ayls*) set up local self-governments with their own responsibilities and revenue sources. Later *oblasts* became administrative subdivisions of the central governments without budget rights and without their own representative bodies. According to the legislation *raion* councils (*kenesh*) consist of representatives of sub-*raion* municipalities and, therefore, express the interests of local self-governments. Heads of the executive authorities of the cities (mayors) are "elected" by the deputies of the local *keneshes* after nomination by the President of the Republic. Since 2009 the heads of the cities of *raion* subordination, villages and settlements are approved by the deputies of the local *keneshes* on the proposal of the head of *raion* administrations.[8] However with the recent government overthrow (2009), new processes or restrictions may be on the horizon.

In 1998 the territory of the Republic of Moldova was organized into 11 units, of which 9 were regions (*judets*), one was the autonomous territorial unit Gagauzia, and the other was Chisinau municipality. In 2001 the regional level (*judets*) was abolished and the *raion* system was adopted. The *raions* were endowed with effectual power after the local elections of 2003 (Veverita, 2006).[9] As a result, the central government directly interacts with local self-governments in the *raions*, the two municipalities outside *raions* (Chisinau and Balti) and in the one autonomous territorial unit of Gagauzia. *Raions*, in turn, interact with local governments in settlements and sub-*raion* cities. Transnistria, a breakaway territory on the border of Ukraine, though formally a territory of the Republic, is not currently included into the budgetary system of the Republic of Moldova.

Initially, the subjects of the Russian Federation, in compliance with the principles of federalism and on the basis of the old Law on General Principles of the Organization of Local Self-Government (1995), set up various models of local self-government. In most regions, local governments were established mainly at the level of large cities and *raions* (the so-called "*raion* model" of local self-government). In other regions, local self-governments were, for the most part, set up at the level of large cities and settlements (the "sub*raion* model"), while yet other regions had a combination of *raion* and sub*raion* types of local self-government (the "two-tier model").[10] Starting from 2006, a two-tier model of local self-governance has been introduced in the country in accordance with the new Law on General Principles of the Organization of Local Self-Government (2003): local self-governments at the level of large cities ("*gorodskoj okrugs*"),[11] *raions* and settlements.

In Ukraine local self-government is exercised by territorial communities of villages, settlements, and cities, both directly through village, settlement, and city councils, and their executive bodies, and through *raion* and *oblast* councils that represent the common interests of the territorial communities of villages, settlements, and cities. Bodies of executive power in *oblasts* and *raions*, similarly to those in Kazakhstan and Belarus, are embedded in the state "vertical power structure". The central government directly interacts with *oblasts*, *raions* and cities while basic levels of local self-governments (towns, settlements and villages) interact only with the *raion* bodies of state power. In Ukraine a draft Concept on Local Self-Government

8. *Initially head of the cities of raion subordination, villages and settlements were elected by direct elections.*
9. *This story has evolved since: under the Law on Regional Development (2006), 6 development regions were established. These regions are not administrative territorial units and have no legal authority, however in the context of actual initiative to reform the Moldovan constitution there have been proposals to reorganize raions into large regions more viable from an economic point of view.*
10. *See for additional details: Kurlyandskaya at al. (2001), Martínez-Vázquez at al. (2006) or De Silva at al. (2009).*
11. *Some regions with the low population density have tried to avoid negative consequences of the fragmentation of local governments. They have organized "gorodskoj okrugs" across the whole territory of the former raions preserving one-tier local government structure on the territory. An example of this can be seen in the Far-East regions with low population density (e.g. Sakhalin and Kamchatka).*

Reform in 2009 envisaged the creation of elected councils in the oblast and raions, giving them new responsibilities and resources. However this project was abandoned in 2010, and a program of mergers between small municipalities was begun. The new budget code (adopted July 8, 2010), which entered into force on 1 January 2011, introduced no major changes to the system of state funding. As long as cities receive direct resources from the State budget, the local government framework is unlikely to change. Concurrently there is increased encouragement for joint funding initiatives between local governments for investments.

The Republic of Belarus has preserved the old administrative division with regard to local authorities. Although *de jure* local councils called "bodies of local self-governance"[12] exist, *de facto* they are included in the overall public administration system. Decisions on territorial development, such as the construction of schools, care centers, or the infrastructure of facilities (roads, transport) etc., flow down from the upper tiers of government. The same administrative practice applies to the financial resources that support these decisions. Local councils have neither real authority to make decisions nor the resources to execute them, though the language used in local administration leads one to assume the existence of local self-governance is plausible based on such terms as "local councils", "executive committee" or "the head of the city". The new law *On Local Government and Self-Governance* (introduced in January 4, 2010, and coming into force six months after its official publication) has not made any changes to this situation. The new law regulates the responsibilities of local councils and the responsibilities of the executive committees of *oblast*, basic (*raions*) and primary (settlements) levels. According to the new law "The *oblast* councils are superior to the councils of the basic and primary levels" and "basic level councils are superior to the councils of the primary level". Executive

Table 4.4: Legal Status of Local Governments

Countries	Regional level	Intermediate (raion) level	Settlement level
Armenia	D		LSG
Belarus	LG/LSG	LG/LSG	LG/LSG
Georgia	D	LSG + Autonomous Republics (LSG)	
Kazakhstan	LG	LG	LG (without budget rights)
Kyrgyzstan	D	LG/LSG	LSG
Moldova		LSG (include Autonomous Republics)	LSG
Russia	Subjects of Federation	LSG	LSG
Ukraine	LG/LSG	LG/LSG	LSG

D – deconcentrated units of central government
LG – local state government bodies
LSG – local self-government bodies
LG/LSG – local executive bodies included into hierarchical "vertical power structure" and local representative bodies (councils) with a status of local self-government

Source: compiled by authors.

12. *See the Constitution of the Republic of Belarus and the law On Local Government and Self-government in the Republic of Belarus.*

committees could cancel the decisions of lower executive and administrative bodies, and the decrees of their heads, if they do not comply with other acts of legislation or the decisions of the council or the executive committee of the regional level.

Most Eurasian countries consider settlements and cities the main level of local self-governance closest to citizens. However, the question of the territorial level suitable for setting up local self-governance remains open for discussion. On the one hand, settlement authorities are closer to the population and therefore have a better understanding of popular concerns; on the other hand, *raion* self-governments can ensure more effective services due to economies of scale, higher levels of staff competency, and the remains of the traditional *raion*-level orientated budgetary system in former USSR countries. At the same time, *raions* are often called on to fulfill many mandates delegated by the regions or central government (e.g., the social security function). Compromises have been found: such as two-tier systems of local self-governance or in combining executive bodies to include both representatives of higher levels of government (from the hierarchical "vertical power structure") and local council members (from local self-government) at the *raion* level (see Table 4.4).

Local Finance

Expenditure Assignment

Initially, the assignment of expenditure responsibilities between the levels of government in the countries of the former USSR corresponded to the ownership of infrastructure and other properties: the central budget funded institutions belonging to central government, and local budgets were responsible for local institutions irrespective of the services rendered by them. Often laws were amended to include provisions that assigned the same responsibilities to different levels of government. It was therefore difficult, when the new states were dividing central and local responsibilities, to decide what to allocate to each level of government and, accordingly, to estimate expenditure needs in building a system of equalization transfers.

Gradually, however, the Eurasian countries have come to recognize the need for a clearer assignment of expenditure responsibilities in the creation of an effective system of intergovernmental fiscal relations. Most of the countries under review regulate expenditure assignments by means of the Budget code or the Law on Local Self-Governance. The only exception to this is Moldova where issues of local responsibilities are determined in the Law of Local Public Administration and the Law on Administrative Decentralization (both enacted in December, 2006), while the Law on Local Public Finance sets the public expenditure assignments.

In Russia, the laws establishing a new system of expenditure assignment were adopted in 2003. The law On Local Self-Government that formally outlined the responsibilities of cities, *raions* and settlements came into force in 2006.

In Armenia and Georgia local self-government responsibilities are listed in the laws On Local Self-Government. For Armenia this law was adopted in 2002 and replaced an earlier 1996 law, in Georgia the Organic Law was signed in December, 2005.

In Ukraine, the Budget Act of 2010, like that of 2001, is based on the distinction between on the one hand, income and expenses for services considered guaranteed by the State, which are based on a national equalization system (first "fund"), and on the other expenditure and revenue for local needs, which is

Table 4.5: Expenditure Assignment Among Levels of Government

Expenditure/Countries	Armenia	Belarus	Georgia	Kazakhstan	Kyrgyzstan	Moldova	Russia	Ukraine
Public Order								
Security, police	C	C, R	C	C,R	C	C, L2	C, (L2)	C, R, L2
Fire protection	C	C, R, L2	(L2)	C	C, L2, L1	L1	R	R, L1
Civil protection	L1		C	C	C	C, L1		
Education								
Kindergartens or pre-school education	L1	*	L2	L2, L1	L1	L2–>, L1	L2	L1
Primary and secondary education	C	*	C	L2	L1	L2–>, L1	R–>, L2	L2, L1
Vocational and technical education	C	*	C	R	C	L2	R	C, R
Higher education	C	*	C	C	C	C	C ,(R), (L2)	C
Specialized or additional/off-school education	L1	*	C	L2	C	L1	L2	L1
Public Health								
Emergency assistance	C	*	C	L1	C	C	R(aviation), L2	L2, L1
Primary care	C, (L1)	*	C, (L2)	R	C	C	L2, L1	L1
Hospitals	C	*	C	C, R	C, L2, L1	C	R, L2	R, L2
Social Welfare								
Family welfare services	C	L2	C	L2, L1	C	L2, L1	C, R	R, L2
Welfare homes	C	R	C	R			R	R, L2
Social security	C, L1		C	C	C, L2, L1	C, L2, L1	C	R, L2
Housing and town planning								
Housing	L1	L2		L2	L1	L1	L1	L1
Town planning	L1	L2	L2	L2	L1	L1	L1	L2, L1
Cemeteries & crematoria	L1		L2	L2, L1	L1	L1	L1	L1
Utilities								
Gas	L1	L1		R, L2	L1	C, L2, L1	L1	R, L2, L1
District heating	L1			L2	L1	L1	L1	L1
Electricity	L1	L1		L2	L1	C, P	L1	L1
Water & sewage	L1	L2, L1	L2	R, L2, L1	C, L2, L1	C, L1	L1	L1
Refuse collection	L1	L2, L1	L2	L2	L2, L1	L1	L1	L2, L1
Refuse disposal	(L1)	L2, L1	L2	L2	L2, L1	L1	L2	L2
Culture, leisure & sports								
Theatres & concert halls	C, L1	C, R, L2	C, L2	R, L2	C, L2, L1	C, L1	R, L2, L1	R, L2
Museums	C, L1	C, L2	C, L2	R, L2	C, L2, L1	C, L1	R, L2, L1	R, L2
Libraries	C, L1	C, L2	C, L2	R, L2	C, L2, L1	C, L2–>, L1	R, L2, L1	R, L2, L1
Parks & open spaces	C, L1	C, L2	C, L2		C, L2, L1	L1	L1	L1
Sports & leisure	L1	L2	C, L2	R, L2	C, L2, L1	L2, L1	R, L2, L1	R, L2
Other cultural facilities (clubs)	L1	L2	L2	R, L2	C, L2, L1	L2–>, L1	L1	R, L2, L1
Roads, transport								
Local roads	L1	L2, L1	L2	L2, L1	L1	L2, L1	R, L2, L1	L1
Transport	L1	C, R, L2	L2	L2	L1	L1	L2, L1	R, L2, L1

L1 – settlements; L2 – raions; R – regions; C – central government.
(...) – voluntary/discretionary authority;
** – expenditures are assigned according to the allocation of institutions (property);*
–> – responsibility for financing salary and some other expenses through earmarked grants to other level of government.

In countries with a multi-tier system of local government, the list of responsibilities of cities of oblast subordinations usually combines the lists of responsibilities for raions and settlements, cities of oblast level subordination fulfill the lists of responsibilities for raions, settlements and oblasts unless otherwise stated.

Source: analysis of country legislation, UCLG country data files, publications listed in bibliography and comments from the UCLG workshop participants.

not part of the matching system (this includes housing and municipal services, infrastructure and transport).

In Belarus, prior to the new 2010 law On Local Government and Self-Government, expenditure responsibilities were not delineated (see Bakanova and Martínez-Vázquez, 2007), and the assignment of functions were made in accordance with assignment of institutions. The new law places more attention on the division of powers between executive authorities and local councils than on the vertical assignment of responsibilities.

In Kyrgyzstan, the responsibilities of local self-governments were outlined in 2008 in the law "On Local Self-government and Local State Administrations". Meanwhile in Kazakhstan, the expenditure assignments of all levels of government were assigned in the Budget Code (2007). Sub-*raion* municipalities in Kazakhstan have no budgets of their own; however according to the Budget Code, *raions* and cities of *oblast* subordination provide in their budgets for the expenses of city districts, cities of *raion* subordination, settlements and *auls* (villages).

Across the Eurasian countries the wording of expenditure responsibilities in legislation can be quite vague, and it is sometimes very difficult to determine which level of government is responsible for the provision of a certain service. In addition, in many countries, there are exceptions to the general rules of expenditure responsibility allocation, where an authority can take on additional (discretionary) obligations, usually financed from the budget of another level. Nevertheless, according to the legislation, the general scheme of allocation of expenditures is as follows (see Table. 4.5).

The Ukraine budget code delineates "own" and "delegated" responsibilities. The latter includes education, health care and social protection. "Delegated" responsibilities are financed through the general budget funds and are taken into account in the process of the allocation of equalization grants.

In some countries responsibilities are unclear: it is difficult to find out which level of government is responsible for what service. For example, in Georgia local government "Performs social-cultural activities and supports the activities of the relevant objects (educational and educative institutions, *etc.*) having local importance" and "establish pre-school and other education institutions"; following this arrangement general education could be provided by local or central government (*de facto* it is provided by central government). In Moldova the legislation on local self-government assigns the same powers to local authorities of the first and second levels (see Popa, 2007).

In Eurasian countries there are also some cases of local governments financing issues that do not belong to their exclusive authority. In Georgia local budgets finance local police departments but according to the Organic Law on Local Self-Government maintenance of the public order does not belong to the exclusive authorities of local government.[13] According to the same law, local governments could also have *voluntary authority*, within which authority "the local self-governing unit shall be entitled as its own initiative to make decision on funding in social, cultural and educational spheres". It is questionable though, if financing the police could be considered the social spheres. Before 2009 the definition was even stricter: voluntary authority could include issues "*not belonging to its exclusive authorities or to the authorities of the state body and those not prohibited for the self-governing unit*".[14] According to this former definition financing the police by the local self-governing units could not be considered as an execution of voluntary authority, be-

13. *In Georgia according to the legislation local governments could have "own", "voluntary" and "delegated" responsibilities.*

14. *The similar restrictions are pointed out in the law "On general principles of the organization of local self-governance in the Russian Federation". But in the Russian law some exceptions are made.*

cause according to the Georgian Constitution (Article 3), criminal police and investigation is an exclusive responsibility of Georgia's higher state bodies (see CIESR, 2009 for detailed discussion on the topic).

The issue of local police funding is a complicated one for more countries than simply Georgia. According to the Russian Constitution (Article 132) "the local self-government bodies ... ensure the protection of public order", and according to the law On Local Self-Government in the Russian Federation (RF) local government issues include "providing municipal police", however, implementation of this issue required amending the existing law enforcement system as public order and safety was, prior to these legislative changes, provided by the Federal Ministry of the Interior. Some localities (usually large cities) historically finance their "own" municipal police but the police force follows the instructions of and reports to the Ministry of the Interior. Now instead of separating police into the federal and local (as it was the intention at the time of the reform of responsibility assignment) federal government is planning to simply recentralize the police force.[15]

Another problem of expenditure assignment in Eurasia arises from unfunded mandates.[16] Unfunded mandates exist in Armenia, Kyrgyzstan and Moldova. In Armenia, for example, of the 19 delegated responsibilities given to local governments, only 2 are financed from the central budget. In Kyrgyzstan, central government instead of transferring funds for delegated responsibilities simply converted the unfunded mandates into official local government responsibilities without making any modification to the revenue assignment of local government. The central government's decision on the growth of salaries in Moldova could be taken as an example of unfunded mandate.

In Kazakhstan, Russia, Ukraine, Belarus[17] and Georgia unfunded mandates are forbidden but *de facto* some legislative decisions of higher levels of government do result in additional financial burdens to the local level.

In Russia, for example, if federal government increases the salary of federal police, regional and local government must also increase their expenditures on public order and safety. In the year that this change is implemented the federal government provides a special grant for increasing salaries but in the following years subnational budgets must find their own revenue sources to cover this additional expense. This practice hits local budgets especially hard during times of economic crisis (a recent example is Yaroslavl city).[18] In Kazakhstan, hot breakfasts at school were introduced by the central government without additional funding assigned to the local governments providing the services.

Despite the formal delineation of authority, central governments often seek to retain control over local spending. One way to do so is to allow the central treasury to manage (meaning control the allocation of) public expenditures (Armenia, Russia) even though, on paper, the treasury is simply supposed to manage the internal control of funds and never decide on the priorities for the allocation of resources, it can, and often does, exert quite significant influence over these. For example, Armenian observers have noted that the treasury often intervenes in the financial operations of the local communities.[19] In Russia, the Federal Treasury asks for detailed assignments of budgeted expenses and requires exact execution of those expenses which reduces flexibility within the budget execution process.

Another method used by Federal or Central governments to exercise control over local expenditure is to regulate by law the number of

15. *Regional governments co-finance the federal police. In the initial version of the legislation on assignment of expenditure responsibilities the cross-subsidizing of functions of other levels of government was forbidden. However an exception was later made for police financing.*
16. *The obligation for local governments to provide a service or perform a task without full or adequate funding from the upper-level government that introduces the requirement or obligation.*
17. *It is not easy to determine if the responsibility could be considered as a mandate in Belarus due to unclear expenditure assignments and vertical subordination of the executive authorities.*
18. *Another example of unfunded mandates in Russia can be found in the laws devoted to the quality of services and safety standards. While rendering public services, local governments fall within these federal normative acts. However, they often do not have the funds to comply with all the requirements of the federal legislation. If the federal prosecutor's office (the main authority that oversees the compliance with the federal legislation) finds violations of federal norms and standards by a municipality, the local government must eliminate the provision of those services. But other agencies could continue to render the same services, with the same violated standards of federal laws unless or until they are themselves evaluated by representatives of the prosecutor's office.*
19. *UCLG Country data file on Armenia.*

Box 4.1. Restrictions to Local Government's Autonomy in Russia

Share of grants (including tax transfers) in total revenues of a local government	Restrictions
0 ≤10%	None
> 10% for two consecutive reporting years	Salary of local officials shall not exceed the ceilings established by the regional council.
> 30% for two consecutive reporting years	Local spending is limited to matters explicitly listed as local expenditure responsibilities in federal and regional legislation.
> 70% for two consecutive reporting years	• The local government shall sign an agreement with the regional government to increase the efficiency of local spending and enhance collections. • The local government's budget is submitted to the regional government for approval. • The regional government audits end of year local budget execution reports at least every other year.

Source: De Silva at al. 2009, based on the Budget Code of RF.

local government and public sector employees. This can be found in all the countries with executive bodies with vertical power structures such as Belarus, Kazakhstan and Ukraine, and this is also true for Kyrgyzstan. The expenditure autonomy in terms of personnel at the settlement government level in Moldova is limited due to the high share of expenditure financed through earmarked grants coming from the *raion* level (specifically for wage payments in the social sphere).

In Georgia, according to the law on State Supervision over Activities of Local Self-government Bodies, central government bodies that execute control over the local governments have the right to cancel local normative acts (see Losaberidze, 2009).

In Russia, the Budget Code imposes constraints on municipalities depending on their share of intergovernmental transfers in total revenues, discounting any grants for financing delegated responsibilities (see Box 4.1). As local government budgets strictly depend on intergovernmental transfers it is little wonder that local governments are under strict control.[20]

The expenditure structure of local governments depends on the assignment of responsibilities between the different tiers of government and between the public and private sectors.[21] Expenditure outlays include both the amounts related to own and delegated responsibilities and budgetary reports do not distinguish between spending on these (see Figure 4.2).

20. *The same norms exists for the regional governments (see De Silva at al. 2009).*
21. *The share of health care expenditures also depends on the existence of the Medical Insurance Funds, while social protection expenditures depend on the existence of the Pension Fund and other funds of accumulated resources for social protection.*
22. *In transitional countries the low qualifications of the public sector employees at the settlement level could also contribute or be a principal reason for the small number of functions assigned to the local level.*

Figure 4.2: **The Structure of Local Government Outlays (2008)**

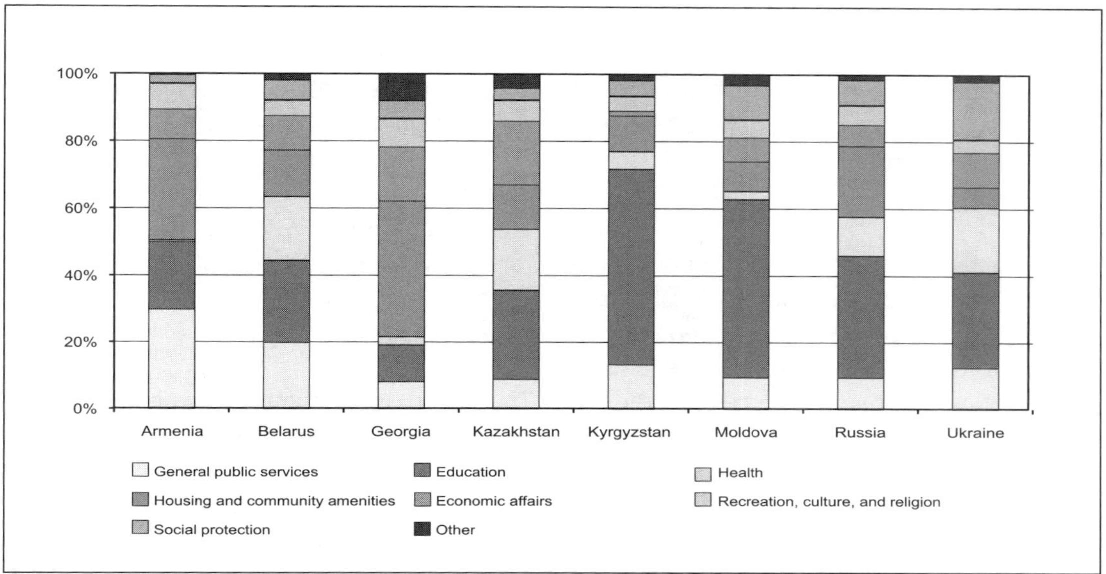

Source: Authors' calculations based on IFS database, for Armenia – on "Local Self-Government Reforms in Armenia (2007 and 2008) Book 3", for Russia – on RF Ministry of Finance reports. Data for Kyrgyzstan is for 2006 (cf. Annex 4.1).

The list of local expenditure responsibilities is significantly impacted by the administrative-territorial division. Thus, the number of functions assigned to settlements is usually not large due to the diseconomies of scale and spillover effects.[22] Typically settlements are assigned responsibility for housing and community amenities, pre-school education and recreation. If *raion* budgets are included in the local government category, the list of responsibilities can include, in accordance with expenditure assignment criteria, general education and primary health care. If *oblast* budgets are regarded as local, expenditures on health care and education will constitute a large portion of total outlays, and will support many related responsibilities. Due to economies of scale, services provided at this level will be less expensive and will reach a greater portion of the population.

In the presence of a large number of thinly populated municipalities, per capita management costs will grow, together with the share of expenditures on general public services in local budgets. This is illustrated by the case of Armenia where the main expenditure line items are general public services (26 percent)[23] and housing and community amenities (26 percent). The share of education is also important at 18 percent (see Figure 4.2).

In Georgia, where there are no settlement governments, local budgets spend much less on general public services – 8 percent of expenditures.[24] The main share of expenditures falls on Housing and community amenities (40 percent). 16 percent of expenditures in Georgia go to economic affairs. In comparison, expenditures on culture (8 percent) and education (11 percent) look relatively small.

In spite of the fact that both Russia and Moldova have a two-tier system of local self-government, the difference between these two countries in responsibilities assigned to the local level results in different expenditure structures. In Russia, education (general and

23. This share becomes even greater if the additional 11.9 percent from "Expenditures not classified elsewhere" is taken into consideration, as most of these expenditures can be attributed to General Public Services.

24. It is difficult to compare revenue and expenditure structures in different countries especially when dealing with transitional countries. As a result of differences in budget classifications, expenditures on the same function can be assigned to different functional groups in budgets of various countries. The IMF database could be a good source as countries provide data according to common standards in comparable budget classifications. However, excessive consolidation of the data in the GFS causes other problem. The data gives one figure for all local governments. This is is not a significant problem when we look at a country with one-tier subnational government (such as Armenia or Georgia) or a country with a two-tier local self-government structure (Russia, Moldova). However, for countries where the state local government system is supplemented with local self-government bodies (Belarus, Ukraine) it is better to distinguish between the different levels of the budgetary system.

preschool) accounts for 37 percent of all expenditures, in Moldova more than 50 percent, while Russia spends 12 percent of local budgets on health care and Moldova only about 2 percent. In Russia housing and community amenities accounts for 21 percent of total outlays while in Moldova this is only 9 percent.

In Kyrgyzstan, where *raion* budgets belong to the local level, local spending on health care was not high (only 5 percent of expenditures). At the same time, the share of expenditures on education reached 59 percent. Later the Medical Insurance Fund was created in Kyrgyzstan and health care expenditure were centralized.

Expenditures on general public services amount to between 11-13 percent in Kazakhstan, Kyrgyzstan and Ukraine, while in Belarus they are as high as 20 percent, this can be attributed both to a high number of administrative staff and also to different approaches to the classification of expenditures.

In Belarus, Kazakhstan and Ukraine, where the expenditure of local government includes those of *oblasts*, the local level supports not only pre-school and general education but in some countries even vocational training; this adds to spending on education and the share of this line item in expenditures is larger (25 percent - 29 percent). Healthcare is another important expenditure item in this group of countries (19 percent - 20 percent). Economic affairs remain at 11 percent of expenditures in Belarus and Ukraine and reaches up to 20 percent in Kazakhstan.

One should also note the tendency towards low spending on social protection: in countries with one-tier local governments (Armenia, Georgia) and countries with *oblast* budgets (with the exception of Ukraine), relevant expenditures constitute 2-5 percent.[25] The low share of this line item can be explained by the fact that social support is financed through special funds. In Russia and Moldova, the share of social protection is about 8-10 percent; while social protection is not assigned to local governments, in Russia, however, regional governments often delegate social protection functions to the local level along with earmarked grants for its funding. On the other hand, local governments in Ukraine spend 17 percent on social protection.

The ideal assignment of expenditure responsibilities does not exist. The scope of responsibilities in each of the countries under observation depends, among other things, on the territorial organization of authorities, and on the readiness of the central government to transfer them to the subnational level. In countries with local bodies of state power (Belarus, Kazakhstan), more responsibilities are assigned to the local level through the decisions of executive bodies of power. Also, *raion* governments have more responsibilities assigned to them than settlement governments. This approach can probably be explained by economies of scale or low staff qualifications at the settlement level.

Revenue Assignment

In discussing effective intergovernmental fiscal relations the next issue to examine is revenue assignment. Some countries (for example in Kyrgyztan) even began the assignment of revenues before that of expenditure responsibilities of local governments had been determined. In the Russia of the 1990s, regions and local governments first competed for revenue sources before addressing the question of what should be funded by these moneys. The RF Budget Code provided for the federation and regions to share tax revenues in a 50:50 division,[26] while the Law on Financial Foundations of Local Self-Government

25. *At the same time, one should remember that per capita spending in absolute terms is higher in countries with multi-tier budgetary systems.*

26. *In practice, however, the normative had never been observed.*

assigned shares of federal taxes to local governments (e.g., 50 percent of regional enterprise property taxes were to be transferred to all local budgets).[27]

To assess the actual level of revenue autonomy, one has to distinguish between own taxes (taxes for which local governments have authority/discretion to change tax rates and/or tax bases) and shared taxes (taxes shared between different levels of government whose rates and bases cannot be changed by local government). From the point of view of local governments' fiscal autonomy, the difference between taxes that are allocated to local governments on a permanent basis and those where the percentage received is set annually by a law on budget of a higher level of government is important. However, not all countries have legislation that clearly distinguishes between own and shared taxes. Many view all taxes that go to local governments as own taxes, and distinct from transfers and grants allocated as a sum of money. For example, under the RF Budget Code own revenues include not only tax and non-tax revenues but also budget revenues in the form of

Box 4.2. Tax Reform in Russia: Reduction of the tax burden at the expense of sub-national governments

The history of the tax system reform in Russia has amounted to a gradual reduction of the tax burden for taxpayers at the expense of regional and local government incomes.

Before 2004, the list of local taxes, according to the law On the Foundation Principles of the Tax System in the Russian Federation, included 22 taxes and fees. Fifteen taxes and fees from this list were cancelled for a Subject of the Federation in the case of it introducing the sales tax of which 60 percent was due to local governments. However, in 2004, the regional sales tax and the fifteen local taxes and fees that it substituted were abolished by federal law.

In 2001, local governments were due 5 percent of the federal profits tax (which could be reduced to 0 percent if the local government so choses), in 2002-2004 this was reduced to 2 percent.

Starting in 2004, only four taxes were remitted to the local budgets: the land tax, the personal property tax, the registration fee paid by individuals engaged in entrepreneurship and the tax on advertising. From 2005 on, the Tax Code only assigned local government the land tax and the personal property tax.

As a result of the almost total lack of own revenue sources and administrative rights over their collection, local governments are deprived of the flexibility to manage the revenue side of their budgets; moreover, the *raion* level of local government is left without any own revenue sources.

The desire of the central government to cut the list of local taxes was partly a result of the centralized collection of local taxes: tax authorities were not interested in improving local tax compliance and local taxes were abolished due to expensive tax administration.

27. *Some regions, such as Rostov Oblast broke this mandate, leaving Rostov on the Don City, for example, with 36 percent to 40 percent of collections in 1997–2000.*

grants, i.e. all revenues except for subventions (transfers to support delegated expenditure responsibilities).

The search for stable revenue sources with an evenly distributed tax base represents a great challenge for transitional countries. However, due to spatial disparities across the countries examined, and their resulting differences in ability to raise taxes, regional inequalities are growing. Also, the smaller the size of a municipality (settlement, village), the more difficult it is to find suitable revenue sources.

There is no doubt that property taxes are the best alternative for local taxes. In the USSR, the group of property taxes included the personal property tax, the legal entity property tax and the land tax. Currently, some Eurasian countries are still in the process of separating property taxes from land tax[28] (Russia[29], Armenia, Kyrgyzstan), others have combined these revenue sources into a single tax. Also, in Moldova, Russia, Kyrgyzstan local authorities can vary the tax rate within the limits established by law, while in Armenia and Ukraine they have no control over property tax revenues. In all of these countries the tax base for property taxes is set by Central government.

In Moldova and Ukraine local authorities, apart from property taxes, may impose local taxes and fees from a list, established by law by the central government. Usually, they can change the rates of such taxes and fees within the limits established by the Central government. In Armenia and some other countries local governments can introduce and regulate local duties.

There has been a recent trend towards the abolishing of local taxes in some countries of Eurasia as some local taxes were considered nuisance taxes due to their high compliance costs. For example, in Russia, the list of local taxes was reduced from 22 to 4 in 2004 and, finally, to 2 taxes in 2005 (see Box 4.2); in Kyrgyzstan the number of taxes was reduced from 16[30] to 8, and then in 2009, to 2, the local tax list was also cut in Georgia in 2004.[31]

Armenia provides an opposite example to this trend: both land and property taxes are local as of 2011 and two additional local taxes (hotel tax and parking tax) are to be introduced for 2011 (see Tumanyan, 2010).

Despite the obvious advantages of real estate (property) taxes as sources of local budget revenues, these taxes are not sufficient to compensate the vertical imbalance in the budget system of Eurasian countries. There are two reasons which contribute to this: (1) the significant amount of expenditure responsibilities legally assigned to local governments and (2) the impossibility of gathering high tax revenues from property, owing to the poverty of many jurisdictions or as a result of ineffective assessments of the tax base (for instance, in Russia the tax base for the personal property tax is assessed according to the booked[32] rather than market value). Additional local taxes and fees collected in Ukraine, Moldova and some other countries cannot solve this problem of vertical imbalance. For this reason the countries under review also assign percentages of shared taxes to local governments.

The personal income tax (PIT) is often used as the second-best choice to provide revenue autonomy to local governments. If paid at the place of residence the PIT can be viewed as a benefit tax, or as a payment for public services funded by local governments. Unfortunately, in some countries (e.g., Belarus, Russia, Ukraine) the tax, calculated on wages, is still paid at the place of employer's registration rather than at the place of employee's residence. This practice results in an unevenly distributed tax base and a disrupted relation between the amount of taxes paid and the amount of services received.

28. *This distinction has its roots in the former USSR's system of taxation, where before the transition land was publicly owned while property could be private. This was the reason for creation of two separate taxes.*

29. *In Russia real estate tax was introduced as an experiment in 2 cities: Novgorod and Tver. According to the RF Government, property tax in Russia may be introduced after the presidential elections in 2013.*

30. *Local taxes included dog licenses; fees for the organization of local commercial auctions, lotteries, competitions and exhibitions; tax on the use of local symbols; fee on transactions made on commodity and raw materials exchanges; tax collected on growing flowers in greenhouses and the sale of them to the public; hunting and fishing licenses; tax on tourists travelling abroad; tax on video salons and concert performances.*

31. *The list of taxes included taxes on economic activity, gambling business, resorts, hotels and advertisements. To replace these incomes local government was assigned shares from the central tax.*

32. *Booked value is the value estimated at the moment of the creation of an asset, then corrected through amortization and the use of some coefficients to update it. So the market value of the property often is far from the booked value estimated for the purpose of taxation.*

Small business taxes (special tax regimes) are another good candidate for the source of local revenue. But successful applying of this tax depends on the establishment of a proper tax base. In situations where the local government can administer the tax base for small business this tax could be a good source of local income.

Many countries also assign the enterprise profits tax to local governments. However, this leads to a growth of revenue disparity due to uneven distribution of the tax bases. The assignment of the profit tax at the local level also exposes local governments to greater revenue volatility; this has resulted in a shortfall of local revenues during the recent economic crisis.

In addition to the central government, regional or *raion* authorities also can assign shared tax rates to local governments. In Russia, subjects of the Federation can assign local governments shares of any taxes in the regional budgets. This means that local government across the country have different taxes assigned to them. The RF Budget Code only requires that municipalities of the same type must be assigned the same sharing rates of shared taxes and that taxes must be imposed by a long-term normative act rather than a law on budget. In Kazakhstan, *oblasts* can set sharing rates of the PIT and the social tax for *raions* and cities of *oblast* subordination. In Moldova, authorities of the second level (*raions*) can assign taxes to authorities of the first level. But the most complicated system of shared taxes is in Belarus: some shared rates are established by the budget code, others by the Republic's and *oblasts*' annual budget laws.

Of the countries under consideration, in Armenia, Moldova and Kyrgyzstan collection of local taxes (duties) has been transferred or delegated to the local level. In Armenia local government monitors the tax base and controls the collection of land and property taxes. 75 inter-municipal inspections were created to fulfill this function. The delegation of property tax collection to the local level in 2003-2005 resulted in a 38 percent increase in collected tax revenue. The delegation of land tax collection in 2006 resulted in a 36 percent increase in collected tax revenue.[33]

In Kyrgyzstan, after the introduction of the Tax Code in 2009, local taxes and fees have been collected by the National Tax Service. However, according to the Law on Local Self-Government and Local State Administration the collection of taxes and duties is considered a responsibility delegated from the state level and before 2009 the local government collected its own tax revenues. The centralization of sales tax (which was converted from a local to a state tax) in 2009 resulted in a decrease in the amount of collected tax.

Financing local services through shared taxes and grants often results in a blurring of the relationship between taxes paid to and services rendered by local governments. Local authorities blame higher governments for failure to allocate funds and residents do not demand qualitative services in return for the taxes they have paid.[34]

From the point of view of fiscal autonomy, we are interested in the estimation of local government own revenues. However, the available reports do not allow revenues to be identified separately. At first sight, it appears that local authorities can have more influence on revenues than on grants. In the case of shared taxes, however, local governments have little to no control or impact, and if their fiscal autonomy is analyzed on the basis of their share of tax and non-tax revenues in the budget structure it can be easily overestimated.

Unfortunately in Eurasia local taxes are not really "local"; central government can grant

33. *For both taxes estimation was made for 2008 in real terms (Tumanyan, 2009).*

34. *It is also important to remember the mentality of those who grew up under the Soviet system, which cannot be changed easily. There is a tendency to think that budgetary services mean services provided free of charge and the fact that they have paid for municipal services by paying their taxes is not well recognized (this is especially true in the case of indirect taxes that are passed on to consumers of goods and services).*

Figure 4.3: The Structure of Local Tax Revenues (2008)

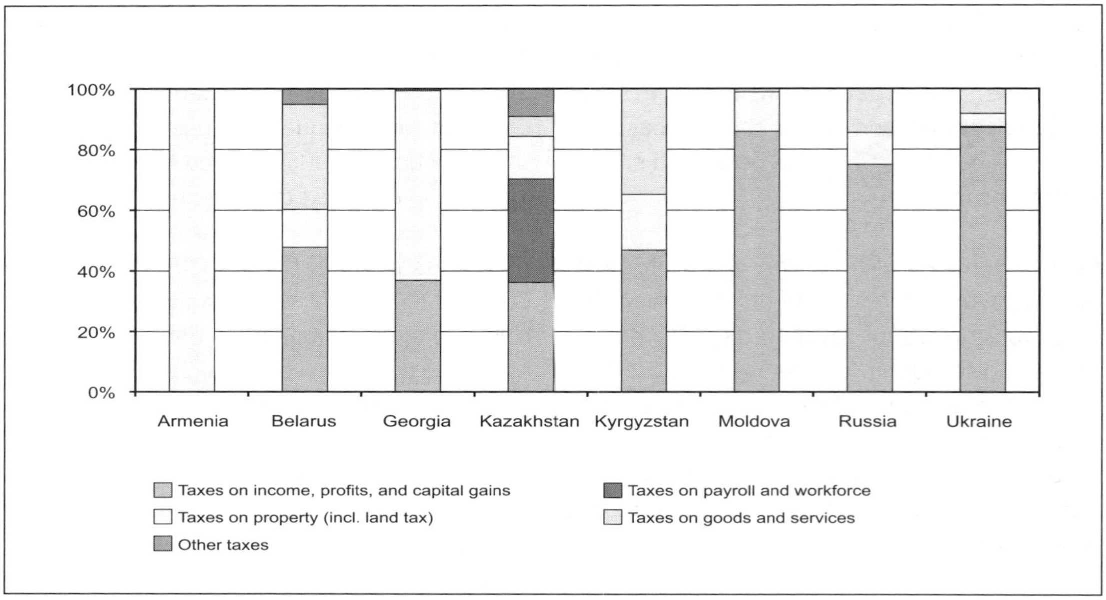

Source: Authors' calculations based on IFS database. (cf. Annex 4.2)

tax benefits at the cost of local taxes, thus reducing the local tax base and fiscal autonomy. For example, in Georgia and Russia, the central (federal) government legislation establishes tax exemptions on local property taxes.

In Russia, for instance, before 2005 subjects of the Federation were able to set differentiated sharing rates for taxes due to local government (different rates were adopted for various municipalities in the jurisdiction of the same region). As a result, if a region assigned sharing rates, the portion of taxes in the structure of its local budgets was higher than in a region where grants-in-aid were allocated. But it would be an exaggeration to assume that municipalities in the first region enjoyed greater fiscal autonomy than in the second.

It is also difficult to distinguish between tax revenues and grants, especially if we deal with tax revenue in the place of grants. In Russia, starting from 2005, subjects of the Federation could substitute the equalization grant by a share in the personal income tax (and prior to 2009, by shares of any federal and regional taxes due to a subject of the Federation). In this case, the grant amounts due to a municipality is substituted by the tax calculated on the basis of estimated tax receipts according to the sharing rate established in the regional budget law. If actual tax receipts in the jurisdiction of a municipality are higher than estimated receipts, the income of the municipality will not be withdrawn into the regional budget. However, if a collected amount of a tax is below estimations, the municipality's losses will not be compensated. Also, and more relevant to our discussion here, such incomes will be shown as tax revenues, not grants.

Income taxes provide the greatest share of local government revenues in most Eurasian countries (with the exception of Armenia where only taxes on land property were assigned to local budgets). In Moldova, Russia, and Ukraine income taxes account

Figure 4.4: Structure of Local Transfers

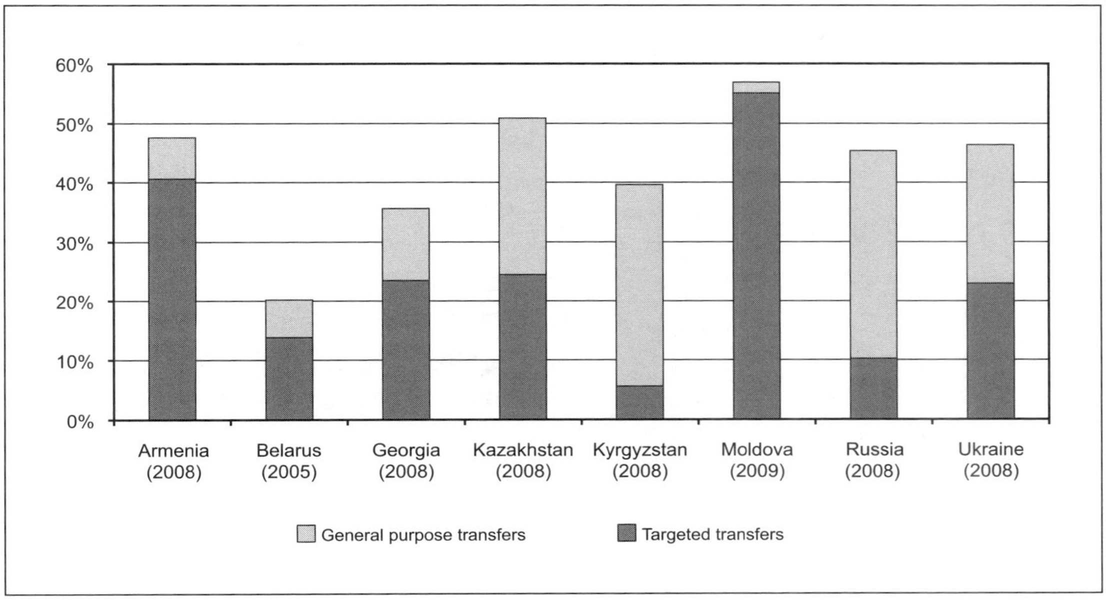

Source: Authors' calculations based for Armenia – on "Local Self-Government Reforms in Armenia (2007 and 2008) Book 3", for Georgia – on "Local Self-Government in Georgia" for other countries – on the countries' Ministry's of Finance reports. (cf. Annex 4.3)

for 75-87 percent of all local tax revenues, of which the largest part is paid by individuals (see figure 4.3). Income taxes paid by legal entities include the small business tax and taxes under the simplified taxation scheme and the profits tax. The latter does not occur very frequently owing to its unevenly distributed tax base. In Kyrgyzstan and Belarus income taxes amount to 47-48 percent, but taxes on goods and services also constitute a significant proportion of tax revenues in these countries (about 35 percent). In Kazakhstan, where income taxes account for 36 percent of tax revenues, there is also a social tax in addition to the income taxes; actually, this is a wage tax, i.e. an income tax paid by the employer.

Property taxes account for only 4 percent of tax revenues in Ukraine (where real-estate tax has not yet been introduced), 11 percent in Moldova, 14 percent in Kazakhstan, 13 percent in both Russia and Belarus, 63 percent in Georgia, and 18 percent in Kyrgyzstan. In Armenia, the proportion of these taxes in local budgets is 100 percent as they are the only taxes assigned to the local level in the country.

Intergovernmental transfers

Intergovernmental transfers are used in order to reduce vertical and horizontal imbalances, to stimulate local governments to follow the central (or regional) government's policies, or to ensure equal access to public services for all citizens. Local governments in all the countries under review receive general purpose equalization grants. In Russia, half of the regions' local governments, in addition to equalization grants, receive compensatory transfers for balancing the budgetary system. Local governments in all the countries under review also receive earmarked grants (capital grants, transfers for financing delegated responsibilities, etc.).

Box 4.3. Main Characteristics of the Equalization Grants to Local Governments in Russia

In Russia, different formulas are used in different regions to determine equalization grants, however according to the Budget Code they should be based on either:

- A tax capacity index (where objective factors affecting the per capita cost of municipal services are considered);

  or

- A per capita equalization.

Revenue

The Tax Capacity Index (TCI) is used to estimate local government revenue. General formulas are used where the tax capacity for a given municipality, divided by its population, is compared to the same equation for the region.

For specific taxes, tax capacity is calculated by multiplying the specific tax rate by the municipalities' tax base.

Expenditure

Estimations of expenditure are usually based on the Expenditure Needs Index (ENI). Different formulas are used in different regions to calculate expenditure needs. Usually the formula is based on one (or more of the following):

- the number of consumers of the state services in a given municipality;
- the weighted sum of the expenditure factors (most common);
- the expenditure norms, established by the regional legislation.

Different factors can be taken into account for different expenditure items, the most common are: size; proximity; level of urbanization; utility cost; population age structure; and remote area wage differences.

Transfer allocation formula

The most common transfer formulas are:

- Proportional equalization
- Full equalization
- Per-capita allocations

Usually the formulas applied to *raions* and cities ("*gorodskoy okrugs*") are different from those applied to settlements (where per-capita allocations are most frequent). In addition, the responsibility for settlement budgets equalization is often delegated to *raions*.

Source: Author's analysis of the RF regions' legislation.

Table 4.6: Characteristics of Negative Transfers

Countries	Formula to Determine Excess	% of Excess Reassigned	Funds Assigned to
Belarus	$Rev_j / Exp_j > 1$	100%	Central Budget
Kazakhstan	$Rev_j / Exp_j > 1$	100%	Central Budget
Moldova	$Rev_j / Exp_j > 1.2$	100%	Equalization Fund
Russia	$Rev_j / Exp_{j\ average} > 2$ (established by the law of the RF subject, but not less than 2)	≤50% (established by the law of the RF subject but not more than 50%)	Equalization Fund
Ukraine	$Rev_j / Exp_j > 1$	93% for Kiev 95% for other donors 60% for the capitals of the oblasts with population more than 950 thousand	Central Budget

Rev_j – revenue estimation used for grant allocation, Exp_j – expenditure estimation used for grant allocation

Sources: Authors' analysis of the countries' legislation

The low proportion of transfers in local budgets of Belarus (20.9 percent, see Figure 4.4) is not surprising as, given the political regime in this highly centralized structure, the center is likely to be much less afraid that the decentralization of revenues will lead to a loss of control over vertically aligned bodies of executive power. In addition, the central government has a legislative opportunity to withdraw revenue surpluses in the form of negative transfers.

At the same time in Kazakhstan the proportion of grants is much higher than in Belarus (56 percent of revenues) although Kazakhstan also uses sharing rates of taxes and negative transfers. In Moldova, the proportion of grants in the structure of budgets is also high (57 percent).

In Russia, grants account for 46 percent of consolidated local government budgets; but the share would be higher if the amounts of shared taxes that replaced grants were included.[35]

Equalization grants

The equalization grant methodology used by most countries is based on the estimation of revenue (or tax) capacity and the estimation of expenditure needs. In some countries (Belarus, Moldova, Kazakhstan, Georgia), grants are allocated to cover the difference between estimated revenues and expenditure assessments. Another possible approach is to compare the indicator of revenues (adjusted on the cost of expenditures) with the target value (this approach was used in Georgia and is still used in 2010 in Armenia). A more sophisticated approach is based on using a dimensionless fiscal capacity index based on per capita tax capacity of local government and expenditure needs index. This latter approach is used in Russia (see Box 4.3); a similar formula is used in Kyrgyzstan and suggested in the draft Law on Financial Equalization in Armenia.[36]

Since the countries of Eurasia shared the same budgetary system in the past and face

35. *Figures are not available due to reporting standards.*

36. *According to the draft Law on Financial Equalization (Armenia) part of the fund is allocated according to the scale coefficient, another part – according to the fiscal capacity index, for details see Movsisyan (2007). For more details on equalization in Russia see Slavgorodskaya et al. (2008).*

similar challenges in the sphere of intergovernmental fiscal relations, it is no wonder that best practice and experience in the field of equalization grants is shared among the former USSR neighbors. Most of these countries have also had methodological support from international organizations.

In some countries, municipal governments pay negative grants in cases where their revenues exceed predetermined level (see Table 4.6). The Russian Budget Code permits the withdrawing of negative grants into the local government equalization fund if per capita tax revenues of a municipality are in excess of the per capita double average tax revenues in the latest reporting year. The amount of grants should not exceed 50 percent of the difference between the per capita local tax revenues and the double average tax revenues. Though many regions have included such provision in their laws, no more than 6 subjects of the RF currently employ it.

Belarus, Kazakhstan, Ukraine and Moldova all also use different variants of negative grants with regard to relatively better off local governments, within a stricter framework of rules. For example, in Belarus and Kazakhstan, with their centralized budgetary system, local governments remit to the central budget any sums of estimated revenues in excess of estimated expenditures. In Moldova local government revenue estimations can exceed expenditure estimations by 20 percent; any local revenues in excess of that figure are to be transferred to the central budget. In Russia and Ukraine there are limits established for the amount of excess revenue that can be taken, while in other countries this is not the case and all surpluses are collected. In Russia and Moldova revenues are taken into equalization fund and redistributed between other local governments, while in other countries these revenues go directly to the central budget.

Local experts have observed that negative transfers reduce the incentive for own tax base development in Eurasian countries, while advocates of the negative transfer system note that in the countries with the uneven distribution of tax base negative transfers with moderate withdrawals can allow for a greater over all assignment of tax revenue to the local budgets.

In countries with a multi-tier system of local government, the hierarchical model[37] of transfer allocation is predominant (Belarus, Kazakhstan, Moldova). However, starting from 2008, transfers to settlements in Kyrgyzstan have been allocated directly from the budget of the Republic, not from the budget of the *raion*. In Ukraine, the central government allocates equalization grants to *oblasts* and *raions* and *raions*, in turn, allocate grants to municipalities at the sub-*raion* level. In Russia, the subjects of the Federation use various models: both regions and *raions* have the right to equalize budgets of settlements and a subject of the federation may delegate responsibility for the equalization of local settlement budgets to *raions*. As a result, Russian settlements can receive equalization grants only from regional governments, or only from *raion* governments, or from both of them (in which case the grants from the *raion* budget will be allocated taking into account equalization grants from the regional government).

Countries also differ in their treatment of different types of local governments. Kyrgyzstan has three separate funds: for the equalization of cities, *raions* and settlements, respectively, while in Russia cities can receive grants from the equalization fund for *raions* and *gorodskoy okrugs* and from the equalization fund for settlements.

Other transfers

As distinct from general-purpose equalization grants, special-purpose grants often have no

37. When local government of lowest level receive transfers from the local governments of the intermediate level.

transparent allocation methodologies. In all Eurasian countries under observation, special-purpose grants are provided for capital investments, for salary payments and for specific policy stimulation.

At best, capital grants are allocated on a competitive basis, but clear provisions concerning capital grant allocation procedures are absent in budget legislation. At worst, their distribution is a result of lobbying on the part of individual municipalities.

In Moldova, special-purpose grants are provided to local governments of first tier (settlements) from administrative-territorial units of second tiers (*raions*) to cover wages, state obligatory social insurance contributions to the budget of the state social insurance institution, and medical insurance contributions of staff in pre-schools, primary schools, general education schools, lyceums, clubs and libraries.

Regional governments in Russia and the central government in Kyrgyzstan[38] allocate categorical grants to local budgets to fund general education services.[39] Grant money is used to pay wages and some other operating costs in educational institutions. Grants are calculated upon a minimum standard of educational expenditures per student. Some regions in Russia use similar grants to co-finance expenditures on pre-school education (kindergartens).

Russia also uses the co-financing mechanism to support current expenses in the social sphere. The Federal center and subjects of the federation can provide financial support to local self-governments for the execution of their expenditure responsibilities. While doing this, they do not necessarily stipulate a co-financing input from local governments; the federal or regional government often simply assumes the funding of a certain responsibility. Examples of such grants include additional payments to teachers for classroom management under the National Education Project, additional payments to general practitioners under the Health Care National Project, subsidies from a number of regional budgets to pay for school meals, and so on. It should be noted that in Russia the financial crisis has reduced the number of earmarked grants (above all for capital purposes) coming from federal and regional budgets. Other examples of specific grants in Russia are transfers from regional and municipal finance reform funds (see Box 4.4).

Grants for financing delegated responsibilities (mandates) should be viewed separately. As a rule, such transfers are calculated based on estimated responsibility costs. The responsibility for social protection regarding certain groups of citizens or the responsibility to fund the privileges of various populations, are often delegated as mandates. For instance, in Russia and Ukraine regions often delegate such responsibilities to *raions* and cities.

All countries in question exercise strict control over public expenditures funded by earmarked transfers.

Local Borrowing

Along with analyzing revenue and expenditures structures it is significant to discuss the general rules of sub-national borrowing. Two main types of external funding are available for local governments: borrowing from financial organizations and budget loans from upper level budgets. Short term borrowing to cover cash gaps should usually be repaid in the current fiscal year.

In Kazakhstan local authorities can borrow in the form of budget loans or issue securities. The debt limits of local executive bodies for the respective financial year is set by the Central Government taking into consideration the

38. *There used to be a grant for salary payment in health care but since 2008 health care is financed through the Medical Insurance Fund.*

39. *Uzbekistan uses the same approach to funding school education from budgets of different levels through special-purpose grants.*

Box 4.4. Russian Regional and Municipal Finance Reform Funds: Success or Failure?

The Regional Finance Reform Fund was established in 2000 with the support of a loan issued by the World Bank to the RF Government. The Fund's grants were awarded to competing regions for the chance to co-finance and implement reform programs. Subsequently, having recognized the success of the regional finance reform program, the Ministry of Finance started to finance the regional Fund from its own resources and founded a Municipal Finance Reform Fund in addition to it.

There was a special selection procedure for regions and municipalities. To participate in the programs, they had to comply with certain criteria of financial management and develop a program for reforming a regional or a municipal finance management system including measures to increase expenditure effectiveness. Any RF subject and/or municipality with a population of over 100,000 as well as capitals of RF subjects were eligible for taking part in the federal Program of Finance Reform. During the time of the Fund existence, 54 RF subjects were selected for funding, though later 5 were disqualified for failure to comply with criteria.

Not all the activities that were to be carried out under the grant program contributed to the effective performance of the authority (participation required a huge number of reports and following the completion of the reform program some regions annulled normative acts adopted for the program, demonstrating the ineffectiveness of part of the activities). Still, the Fund stimulated implementation of good management practices including creating transparent systems of intergovernmental fiscal relations and implementation of performance-based budgeting. Non-participating regions were able to copy successful behavior models of the program participants and use their normative acts as examples for developing own legislation. Thus, one of the most important advantages of federalism, the possibility to copy innovations, was realized.

Some efficient mechanisms developed under the Program of Regional Finance Reform (such as transparent methods of intergovernmental transfer allocation, local responsibilities inventory list, standards for local services quality, etc) were included into the Budget Code and became obligatory for all subjects of the Federation.

In response to the success of the Federal Program of Municipal Finance Reform, RF subjects started their own municipal finance reforms. For instance, Stavropol Krai has demonstrated good results in the regional municipal finance reform program.

Unfortunately, during the recent financial crisis the federal government decided to cut funds allocated under the program, and in 2009 competitors received less funding in comparison to previous years. The federal government did not provide grant financing in 2010 but in 2011 the Fund will probably be restored.

Box 4.5. Municipal Development Fund of Georgia

The Municipal Development Fund of Georgia (MDF) was established in 1997 in the course of the implementation of the World Bank project aimed at reconstructing municipal infrastructure.

The MDF is governed by the Supervisory Board approved by presidential decree and includes representatives of the Government of Georgia, relevant delegates of the President of Georgia and local self-governments. The Supervisory Board makes final decisions on funding municipal investment projects.

As a result of successful MDF project implementations, the government decided to place other capital projects under the MDF management. Thus, the activity of the MDF was further diversified.

The MDF had now been institutionalized; which has resulted in its own expert opinion taken into account due to the sound relationship created with central and regional authorities of Georgia and donors, as well as being able to implement projects of different categories.

The main objective of the MDF is to mobilize funds from international financial institutions, donor agencies, central and local governments, and to make them available to local governments and self-governments for investments in municipal infrastructure and services. The MDF also assists local self-governments in management optimization and introduces international practices in the field of local self-government. The MDF established an additional source of funding for projects to be implemented under the supervision of municipalities. Its structure perfectly meets the requirements of local self-governments that lack access to management expertise and financial markets.

The activity of the MDF is a considerable step towards improving municipal infrastructure investment in Georgia, particularly in view of the actual output being seen in the development of city road infrastructure, improved operation in water supply systems, enhanced quality of services provided by the educational and health institutions and generation of employment opportunities.

purposes and tasks defined by the mid-term fiscal policy (three-year period). The amount spent on debt repayment and services should not exceed 10 percent of the local budget revenue in the corresponding financial year.

In Belarus borrowing is allowed only in the form of budget loans from higher-level budgets and loans, implemented through the issuance of securities. The provision of loans by banks to local executive and administrative bodies is not allowed. The maximum local government debt size for the next fiscal year should not exceed 30 percent of forecasted local budget revenues without intergovernmental transfers.

Armenian legislation allows municipalities to borrow from the budget of higher level governments, as well as from commercial banks. But in practice, municipalities do not have access to the credit market.[40] Instead, in Armenia, there is a practice of inter-municipal lending, where one municipality can receive an interest free loan from another. To date, there has been no case of default on these debts. While this type of loan is generally not a large amount, this could be an interesting case of best practice and a model for other countries; though unfortunately it may be hard to replicate.

In Georgia local governments can borrow from the Georgian Municipal Development Fund (see Box 4.5). These loans are limited to infrastructure development: repair of existing service infrastructure and roads, replacement of equipment necessary for water supply, etc. Borrowing levels are limited by the amount of discretionary budgetary resources available. Local government funds 20 percent of the cost of a project, 40 percent is provided as a grant, and 40 percent is financed by a loan at the interest rate of 15 percent annually with 10 years maturity.

In Kyrgyzstan local government can receive loans under agreement of the Ministry of Economics and Finance, and under government guarantee. Short-term loans should be repaid during the fiscal year. Middle-term and long-term borrowing can only be used for development projects. Local self-government bodies are prohibited from borrowing in cases where the total debt service obligations exceed 20 percent of the local government annual revenue.

In Moldova local governments (both tiers) can borrow funds for current expenditures from financial organizations and from upper-levels budgets, under the condition that these should be repaid during the current financial year. The total amount of loans should not exceed 5 percent of the total revenues of the administrative unit receiving the loan. For capital expenditures loans can be taken for short-term and long-term period. In this case the amount of outstanding loans already received (together with interest) as well as the amount owed on the loans to be obtained (together with interest) can not be in excess of 20 percent of total annual revenues of the respective budgets.

In Russia only domestic borrowing is allowed for local governments. The total amount of the municipal debt should not exceed the total amount of local revenue not considering intergovernmental transfers. For the municipalities that have a share of grants (including tax transfers) as part of their total revenue less than 70 percent for two consecutive reporting years the total amount of the debt should not exceed 50 percent of the total amount of local revenue less intergovernmental transfers (see Box 4.1). Municipalities can also receive budget loans from higher level budgets. Normally, budget loans should be repaid during the same financial period they are taken, but as a result of the financial crisis this term has been extended to up to three years.

In Ukraine local governments can borrow from financial and banking organizations to cover cash gaps for a period of no more than 3 months and within the current fiscal year. Local governments (cities and Crimea) can also take loans for capital purposes (or development budgets) in the domestic market. The total amount of these loans should not exceed 10 percent of the administrative unit's total expenditures. All borrowing must be approved by the Ministry of Finance. Only

40. Tumanyan (2009) wrote on this issue "The Article 59 of law on Local Self-government and Article 30 of the law on Budgetary System of Armenia state that municipal securities are issued in accordance with relevant law. Clause 6, Article 57 of the law on Local Self-government states also that the procedures of issue and allocation of municipal securities are established by the government, but there is no law or procedure adopted... and the communities did not issue municipal securities..."

cities with a population over 800,000 are allowed to borrow abroad. In the case that a regional or local government body defaults on a loan, they are prohibited from borrowing for the next five years. The maximum amount of debt is fixed annually in the Law on Budget. The total debt of central, regional and local governments must not exceed 60 percent of the GDP of Ukraine.

In addition to the shortage of own revenue sources, limited borrowing rights hamper the ability of local authorities to fund capital expenditures. While the theory behind these limitations is intended to protect local governments from harmful debt practices, when debt limits are set up as a share of annual budgets it is difficult if not impossible to finance long-term investment project. As a result, local governments find it easier to access funds for capital expenditure from higher level government budget than from the financial sector. Public Private Partnerships (PPPs), an alternative that has been used with some success in other regions as a way of financing investment, is not widely used in Eurasia.

Main Positive and Negative Features of Local Finance in Eurasian Countries

Decentralization in the countries of Eurasia was a spontaneous process based on the trial-and-error that led to changes in the status of administrative-territorial entities, municipality borderlines, and assignment of expenditure responsibilities and revenue sources. Although formal local self-governance in some countries is nearly 20 years old, the decentralization process has not been completed. There are however common elements that can be found throughout the region with regard to local finance.

In some countries positive trends can be traced in the field of decentralization. In Armenia the list of local taxes and duties will be enlarged as of 2011. In 2010 Belarus adopted the law On Local Government and Local Self-government.

However, in other countries recentralization tendencies have been observed, specifically in recent years in Kyrgyzstan (establishing of appointed heads of local self-governments) and in Georgia (annulment of settlement level of government). In Russia the nomination process for regional heads has affected the regional level, but has yet not reached the local self-government level.[41] In all three countries local tax lists were cut over the last years.

A huge impact on the pace of local government establishment has been made by international assistance projects. External support for decentralization and local government reform provided by the World Bank, USAID, UNDP, EBRD, the Council of Europe EU and other international organizations included both consultative and financial assistance. Although the formation of local self-government is not possible without an informed population and the support of central government (one may refer to Kazakhstan, a centralized state without local self-governments but with clear expenditure assignment between levels of governments), the assistance in the development of transparent legislation, creation of democratic institutions and support to local initiatives have provided an invaluable contribution to the decentralization processes in Eurasia.

In all the countries under review expenditure responsibilities are assigned to different levels of government by legislation but the assignment is not

41. *Unification of the local self-government model in Russia resulted in centralization of powers in some regions because former own responsibilities of local governments became delegated ones and local tax lists were cut while in other regions local self-government were first established only.*

always clear. Sometimes the same definitions occur among the responsibilities of authorities of different levels (e.g., Moldova), also some responsibilities are still assigned according to the old method of institutional delineation (property ownership) (e.g., in Belarus). Sometimes *de facto* assignment differs from that outlined in the legislation: local governments finance responsibilities that do not belong to the local government authority (e.g., Georgia). Co-financing of expenditure from different levels of government is rare but still exists (e.g. in Russia, Moldova).

Unfunded mandates have been significantly cut. In many Eurasian countries unfunded mandates are forbidden by the legislation. However there remain responsibilities that, while not legally considered unfunded mandates, place significant additional burdens on local government budgets and reduce their expenditure autonomy.

The central government has tried to exercise control over local spending. In some countries (e.g., Kazakhstan, Belarus, Kyrgyzstan, Moldova) the number of local staff is established by the central government through law or by imposing limits on local budgets for certain expenditure line items (e.g., Russia). In Russia, according to the President's decree, regional governments must evaluate the performance of municipal *raions* and city governments.

Fiscal autonomy of local governments is restricted in most countries of the region. All countries under review have a closed list of local taxes, some countries (Belarus, Kazakhstan, Kyrgyzstan) set the sharing rates of shared taxes in the budget law. In Russia, *raion* governments have a significant amount of expenditure responsibilities assigned to them but no taxes of their own. Besides, central (federal) governments can establish tax benefits (exemptions, etc.) for local taxes (e.g. Georgia, Russia).

Delegation of tax collection powers is not a common. Only in Armenia, Kyrgyzstan and Moldova can local governments collect local taxes. The experience of these countries has shown that tax collections at local level increase tax compliance.

There has been significant improvement in the design of equalization grants. All the countries under review have legally adopted formula-driven methodologies for allocating equalization grants from the central budget. The ability of coefficients to adequately reflect capacities or needs of local governments can be discussed but the rules of the game are the same for all grant recipients. However local experts note that negative transfers in Belarus, Kazakhstan, Moldova and Ukraine create disincentives for the development of the local tax base.

The design of conditional grants has not moved along equally well. At best, capital grants are allocated on a competitive basis, but clear provisions with regard to capital grant allocation procedures are absent in budget legislation. At worst, their distribution is a result of lobbying on the part of individual municipalities. All countries in question exercise strict control over public expenditures funded by earmarked transfers.

Borrowing powers are limited in all Eurasia countries. For some countries limitations are set as a percentage of annual local revenue, for others – as a share of local expenditure. In most countries (Russia, Kazakhstan etc), the capital expenditures of local governments are often co-financed by higher level governments.

Despite a number of unresolved problems in local finance in Eurasian countries, significant progress has been made over the last twenty years.

Conclusions

Expenditure responsibilities have been assigned to different levels of government in Eurasia, however, decentralization of revenue sources is still a great challenge. Not only have the transitional economies faced a difficult problem of "ideal" local taxes, but the uneven distribution of tax bases and administrative costs associated with tax collections result everywhere in greater levels of decentralization of expenditure responsibilities than that of revenue powers. In addition to this, transitional economies are confronted with effectively influencing their national tax systems, tax base estimation, tax evasion by large taxpayers, and uncoordinated reform policies.

For local self-governments to become more autonomous it is necessary to enlarge the list of local taxes (specifically, in Russia, Kyrgyzstan, Georgia) or to assign for long periods those shared taxes whose sharing rates are currently established in annual budget laws (Kazakhstan, Belarus, Moldova). Local real estate tax should be introduced instead of separate taxes on land and property. Personal income tax is a good source for local revenue if combined with a flat rate and payments according to the residence principle. Small business taxes are another good instrument if local government could establish the tax base and the tax rates. Central government should not set tax exemptions on local taxes.

The administration and collection of local taxes and fees should be carried out at the local level, delegation of the tax collection to the local level increases tax compliance and resulting revenues.

The recent financial crisis has revealed weaknesses in the local finance systems of some Eurasian countries, while in other countries local governments faired much better then central ones. During an economic downturn, the situation of public sector revenue assignment is highlighted, and the necessity of stable sources of income for public sector revenue becomes crucial for local governments. Widely used property and land taxes are the most stable sources of budget revenues, especially if the tax base is not estimated on the basis of the market value (as is the case for Russia and some other Eurasian countries). One of the main sources of local government revenues in Eurasia (except for Armenia), personal income tax also remained stable in Russia (except for large industrial cities) and Kazakhstan, however Ukraine reports significant downturns in revenue collection. Small shares of stable local taxes in the total amount of local revenue and strong dependence on the decisions of the higher level authorities endanger the stability of local finance.

Another important issue is the stability of the rules for allocations of intergovernmental transfers that prevent local budgets from unexpected changes in the amount of transfers. In Moldova, for example, transfers to local governments were cut by approximately 20 percent due to the crisis (Expert-Grup, 2009), so local governments have had to significantly cut expenditures. At the same time in Kazakhstan the amount of transfers, having been set for a 3-year period, was not reduced, and additional grants were transferred to the *oblast* level. In Ukraine in 2009 "local budgets missed about 3.7 percent of their expected grant revenues" (Slukhai and Tsekhanovskiy, 2009), however local budgets in the Ukraine were also confronted by an additional problem: "permanent delays in payments to local governments by the State Treasury ... which almost paralyzed local government functioning".

In Russia the crisis mainly influenced federal and regional budgets, while local self-government budgets (especially those of settlements) were not much affected by the crisis; only a number of large industrial cities faced budget problems due to falls in revenue. In most of the region's countries equalization transfers were not cut in 2009, capital transfers were reduced in the first half of the year but were restored by the end of 2009.

Commercial credit shortages should not cause significant problems for local governments in most Eurasian countries because local borrowing powers were already restricted by the national legislation. In Russia federal governments provided budget loans to regional governments, and regions, in turn, can provide loans to local governments. Budget loans were also enlarged in Ukraine.

It should be noted that prior to the crisis Eurasian countries have created effective mechanisms to address pressing issues of local self-governance. For example, the Municipal Development Fund of Georgia brings together funds from various sources to be used for municipal infrastructure development. A similar mechanism can be recommended to other transitional economies provided it is supported by the central governments and international financial organizations.

The Russian Fund for Regional and Municipal Finance Reform is also a good example of best practices that allows new mechanisms of public financial management to be tested in pilot jurisdictions and then includes successful instruments into common practice. Another useful example is the experience of inter-municipal loans in Armenia. Different municipal best practice programs in Eurasian countries (e.g. in Moldova) add to the improvement of local government performance.

Inter-municipal cooperation is an effective instrument to reduce costs associated with the provision of municipal services taking advantage of the available economies of scale, while at the same time allowing individual local self-governments to retain control over functions. This approach can be used effectively in other countries, especially those where local self-governments exist only at the settlement level and are therefore not able to realize economies of scale. Inter-municipal tax inspections in Armenia could be mentioned as an example of these types of economies of scale. In Russia, in some regions, *raions* and cities finance ambulance services together but the Russian Budget Code does not provide a mechanism for allocation transfers between budgets of the same level of government, so some municipalities are afraid that the joint provision of services will cause difficulties due to its co-financing.

Of all countries under consideration, Belarus has the least effective system of intergovernmental fiscal relations in the region. First, the republic should decide on further developing its local authorities. Belarus has recently started a set of reforms, including the development of a new law on local self-government, the adoption of the second part of the tax code, and starting the process of developing a new equalization grants mechanism. Given political realities, one can assume that Belarus would benefit from the experience of other Eurasian countries where bodies of local power, albeit subordinate to the central government, nevertheless, have legally assigned responsibilities and own revenue sources.

Kazakhstan does not plan to set up local self-governments in the near future. In spite of their absence, however, the centralized system of the country promotes other reforms to enhance performance of the public sector (performance-based budgeting, PPP mechanisms development). It is possible that in the future, upon completion of the budgetary reform, at the next stage of development, the central government will reconsider the issue of local self-government.

Moldova needs to make intergovernmental fiscal relations between *raions* and settlements in their territory more transparent and formula-driven. Settlements should receive more expenditure and revenue autonomy for the provision of effective services.

In Russia, it is necessary to assign own taxes to *raion* governments (the transport tax was the most suitable candidate for decentralization but federal government is planning to cancel it) and introduces the real estate tax. As in other Eurasian countries, the Russian central government should entrust tax administration to the local level.

Armenia needs clear legislation on financing delegated responsibilities. Municipalities need additional support in accessing financial markets; as while they are allowed access by law, in practice this has yet to be effectively implemented.

Ukraine seems to have renounced radical reforms. Instead of an overall reform of territorial organization, the national government is currently supporting voluntary association to improve the efficiency of local management. The focus is on certain key sectors such as the management of housing and the improvement of municipal services rather than a full institutional reform. The new Organic Budget Law, adopted in 2010, does not introduce any changes in the principles that govern local government, but it does reopen the debate on the formula for calculating equalization transfers.

It is difficult to predict the local self-government development in Kyrgyzstan, but with the current political instability central government can hardly be interested in strengthening the local government level. The internal problems of Georgia are also not a good environment for building strong local governments.

The countries of Eurasia cannot avoid problems while developing local self-governments, however, the success of neighboring countries facing similar challenges and the analysis of best practices in countries with a long history of local self-government should help in finding effective solutions. The main recommendations for the Eurasian countries have been summarized in the box which follows.

UCLG Euro-Asia Regional Policy Recommendation

- *Administrative-territorial division and the status of local government should be clarified*: local executive bodies should be accountable to the local representative bodies and thus to the citizens;
- *Clear assignment of expenditure responsibilities should be established;*
- *Unfunded mandates should be eliminated* not only on paper but in the everyday practice, delegated functions must be supported with adequate financial resources;
- *Local governments should have autonomy over local budgets*: expenditure autonomy should be supported by revenue autonomy with sufficient revenue sources;
- *Local government responsibilities at the lowest level (that closest to citizens) should be increased* and matched with adequate funds;
- *Transfer allocations should be transparent* and should not contain negative incentives;
- *The administration and collection of local taxes should be transferred to the local level;*
- *Inter-municipal cooperation should be developed*: local governments should work together for better services provision;
- *Inter-municipal short-term loans can be recommended* as a good system of mutual assistance;
- *Evaluation of the quality of local services and sufficiency of funding* should be provided by external non-partisan entity;
- *Access to capital markets should be provided for local governments.*

Recommendations developed by the participants of the UCLG GOLDII Eurasia Workshop in Moscow (February 2010).

5. Europe

Luiz de Mello*
Economics Department, OECD

* *The opinions and analyses presented in this chapter are the author's own and do not necessarily reflect that of the OECD or the organisation's Member countries. The author is indebted to DEXIA for compiling the data set used in this chapter, providing background information on recent decentralization initiatives in Europe and updating the country-specific information reported in DEXIA (2008) on revenue-sharing coefficients and fiscal rules.*

This chapter deals with local government finances in Europe. The set of countries under examination includes the European Union Member States, and to further extent Iceland, Norway, and Switzerland. These countries offer a rich array of experiences with fiscal decentralization but face common policy challenges, which the chapter aims to highlight. The institutional underpinnings of fiscal decentralization are strong in Europe. For several decades, the continent has seen a continuing, though sometimes uneven, trend towards greater democratic decentralization to the local and regional levels, as evidenced by the European Charter for Local Self-Government of 1985, which came into effect in 1989 and has been ratified by all European Union (EU), and almost all Council of Europe, member States.

The GOLD I report provides a comprehensive review of the history of fiscal decentralization in Europe, reported recent country experiences and described the political empowerment of local governments in the region. The Report recognises that, to a large extent, the institutional arrangements currently in place in different countries – such as the tax bases assigned to the local authorities, the expenditure functions under their remit and the financial relations among the local jurisdictions and between them and higher levels of government – are rooted in history, culture and local traditions. But intergovernmental fiscal institutions are far from immutable, because the role of local governments is also shaped by evolving social, economic and demographic forces that affect citizens' demands for goods and services provided locally.

A number of broad trends are shaping the outlook for local government finances in Europe. First, European local governments have been hit hard by the global crisis that erupted in 2009 and the subsequent recession.[1] Several EU countries have been developing fiscal consolidation plans to restore longer-term fiscal sustainability, which affect local and regional governments through increased pressure for tax hikes and expenditure restraint. For example, the fiscal consolidation programs announced during 2009-2010 have included tax hikes, especially the value added tax (as in Croatia, Czech Republic, Estonia, Hungary, Ireland, Latvia, Lithuania, Poland, Portugal, Romania, Spain and United Kingdom), pay freezes in the public sector (as in Italy, Latvia, Romania, the United Kingdom) and more general expenditure cuts (as in the United Kingdom). Intergovernmental fiscal relations have also been affected through a reduction in central government grants and transfers to the local authorities.[2] Fiscal consolidation has also implied a curtailment by the central government of local government financial autonomy in some countries, such as Spain.[3]

Second, several territorial and tax reforms have been announced or implemented in Europe over the last years with a direct bearing on local governments. They include Greece's administrative and territorial reform (the Kallikratis Project) aiming to reduce the number of municipalities through mergers and to replace the prefectures by regional authorities with extended powers; Latvia's abolition of regional governments; and France's plans to merge the *départements* and *régions* to reduce the number of territorial counsellors and to set up "community of municipalities" for the major cities with a broader set of competencies transferred to them from the regional and departmental authorities. Municipal merger programs are also in place in Finland, Luxembourg, Sweden and Norway. In the same vein, the new government in the United Kingdom has

1. *According to the Council of European Municipalities and Regions (CEMR) and Council of Europe's surveys, Europe's local governments have, for the most part, been pessimistic about the outlook for their financial position since the eruption of the global crisis.*
2. *This is the case of Bulgaria, for example, where central government transfers to the municipalities will be cut by 2015 and the VAT rate may be raised if the planed expenditure cuts are not enough to reduce the public deficit.*
3. *To limit the public deficit, the central government of Spain has restricted access to credit for local authorities and their dependent public agencies to finance investments as of 2011.*

abolished the Regional Development Agencies and the Government Offices and all the regional strategies for economic development and housing, with the central and council governments, as well as business-led partnerships, picking up many of the functions. In Norway, competencies and corresponding revenue have been transferred from the national government towards the county councils to reinforce decentralization and local democracy, as well as to streamline the share of competencies between the different levels of authorities.

Finally, European local governments will need to deal with emerging challenges. They include in some countries a reduction in local revenue sources imposed by the central government (for example, in Greece, as part of the fiscal consolidation program in France, as a result of phasing-out of the *taxe professionelle*; and in Germany as a reduction in intergovernmental transfers). At the same time, there is an increased pressure for value for money from local governments – a centralising trend of the last UK government in particular, but also in different forms seen in Scandinavia and the Netherlands – which may also lead to more pressure towards outsourcing or privatization. Local governments will also have to deal with the emergence of new claims on local budgets, including in the areas of social protection in times of crisis and in a context of rapidly ageing populations. Demands associated with the need to integrate immigrants into the social fabric of the recipient countries also take a toll on local governments.

The focus of the chapter will be on the local level of government (municipalities and cities), rather than the middle-tier jurisdictions (such as, states, provinces, autonomous regions, etc.), although the analysis of intergovernmental fiscal relations will sometimes take into account other levels of government. Different country experiences in the areas of expenditure commitments, revenue assignment, including intergovernmental revenue sharing, and financing arrangements, especially local government borrowing, will be analysed with a view to highlighting common policy challenges, while recognising that generalizations are often difficult. This is because common trends may sometimes mask very different underlying forces shaping the public finances at the local level of government.

The paper is organised as follows. The following section builds on the GOLD I Report and provides an overview of the structure of local government finances in Europe. The third section is related to the expenditure side of local budgets, and attention is focused on the composition of local government outlays by functional and economic classification, as well as the main policy issues related to local government expenditure policy. The fourth section delves into the revenue sources of local governments, including taxes, non-tax instruments and intergovernmental revenue sharing, highlighting the main policy issues related to the assignment of revenue sources to local governments. The fifth section deals with the design of intergovernmental grants and transfer systems needed to bridge the gap between locally raised (or shared) revenue and the expenditure mandates assigned to local governments. The sixth section focuses on local government budget outcomes and indebtedness, with special emphasis on the fiscal rules governing local government financial management. The seventh section emphasises the short-term policy challenges facing European local governments, including those related to the recovery from the global financial and economic crisis, as well as longer-term challenges related to population ageing and immigration. The

Table 5.1: Socio-economic and Political Indicators

	Population (millions, 1st January 2009)	Population growth rate (%, 1999-2009 average)	Urban population (% of total pop., 2005)	Pop. in the largest city (% of urban pop., 2005)	Old dependency ratio (pop. 65+ to pop. 15 to 64, 2008)	Net migration stock (net migration as % of pop., 2008)	GDP (billions of current euros in PPP terms, 2008)	GDP per capita (thousands of current euros in PPP terms, 2008)	Structure of government (number of sub-national layers, 2009)	Average population of municipalities (2008-2009)
Austria	8.4	0.5	66.0	41.6	25.4	0.4	258.2	31.0	Federal (2)	3,540
Belgium	10.8	0.5	97.2	9.9	25.8	0.5	309.1	28.9	Federal (3)	18,180
Bulgaria	7.6	-0.8	70.0	20.2	25	0.0	78.8	10.4	Unitary (1)	29,015
Cyprus	0.8	1.6	69.3	34.7	17.8	0.1	19.1	24.0	Unitary (1)	1,510
Czech Rep.	10.5	0.2	73.5	15.6	20.5	0.7	210.2	20.2	Unitary (2)	1,670
Denmark	5.5	0.4	85.6	23.5	23.6	0.5	165.4	30.1	Unitary (2)	56,040
Estonia	1.3	-0.3	69.1	43.6	25.3	..	22.6	16.9	Unitary (1)	5,910
Finland	5.3	0.3	61.1	34.0	24.8	0.3	155.7	29.3	Unitary (1)	15,265
France	64.4	0.7	76.7	21.0	25.1	0.1	1,735.8	27.1	Unitary (3)	1,750
Germany	82.0	0.0	75.2	5.5	30	-0.1	2,380.4	29.0	Federal (3)	6,655
Greece	11.3	0.4	59.0	49.3	27.8	0.3	265.6	23.6	Unitary (2)	10,870
Hungary	10.0	-0.2	66.3	25.3	23.5	0.2	162.0	16.1	Unitary (2)	3,160
Ireland	4.5	1.8	60.5	41.2	15.9	0.4	150.8	33.9	Unitary (2)	38,975
Italy	60.0	0.5	67.6	8.5	30.4	0.8	1,526.9	25.5	Unitary (3)	7,395
Latvia	2.3	-0.6	67.8	46.1	24.9	-0.1	32.6	14.4	Unitary (1)	19,205
Lithuania	3.3	-0.5	66.6	19.1	23	-0.2	52.1	15.5	Unitary (1)	55,965
Luxembourg	0.5	1.4	82.8	21.3	20.6	1.6	33.9	69.3	Unitary (1)	4,215
Malta	0.4	0.9	95.3	5.8	19.3	0.6	7.9	19.1	Unitary (1)	6,060
Netherlands	16.5	0.5	80.2	8.8	21.8	0.2	552.3	33.6	Unitary (2)	37,280
Poland	38.1	-0.1	62.1	7.1	18.9	0.0	539.3	14.1	Unitary (3)	15,380
Portugal	10.6	0.5	57.6	45.4	23.4	0.1	202.4	19.1	Unitary (2)	34,485
Romania	21.5	-0.4	53.7	16.6	21.3	0.0	259.0	..	Unitary (2)	6,760
Slovak Rep.	5.4	0.0	56.2	14.4	16.6	0.1	97.9	18.1	Unitary (2)	1,870
Slovenia	2.0	0.3	51.0	32.4	23.3	1.4	46.1	22.8	Unitary (1)	9,630
Spain	45.8	1.4	76.7	16.8	24.1	0.6	1,173.3	25.7	Quasi-federal (3)	5,620
Sweden	9.3	0.4	84.2	22.5	26.7	0.6	278.6	30.1	Unitary (2)	31,790
United Kingdom	61.6	0.5	89.7	15.7	24.3	0.4	1,788.7	29.1	Unitary (3)	151,110
EU 27	**499.7**	**0.4**		..	**25.2**	..	**12,501.7**	**25.1**		
Iceland	0.3	1.5	92.8	39.0	17.1	0.4	9.7	30.3	Unitary (1)	4,150
Norway	4.8	0.8	77.4	22.4	22.1	0.9	228.6	47.9	Unitary (2)	11,020
Switzerland	7.7	0.8	75.2	20.5	24.1	1.2	269.9	35.3	Federal (2)	2,950

Sources: Eurostat, World Bank (World Development Indicators, 2009), Dexia and CEMR (2009a).

eighth section summarises the main policy considerations raised in the paper and highlights key policy recommendations. The final section concludes.

Structure of Local Governments in Europe: an overview

Institutional Arrangements

The GOLD I report noted that institutional environments differ among the European countries. First and foremost, variations in the definition of local authority depend essentially on the territorial organisation of different countries and their institutional settings, which are shaped by history.[4] Institutional arrangements depend on whether the country is a federation (Austria, Belgium, Germany and Switzerland), a quasi-federation (Italy and Spain) in the sense of having regional authorities enjoying comprehensive legislative, financial, and executive autonomy while not being defined *de jure* as a federal country, or a unitary State (Table 5.1). Even among the unitary States, there are countries with a long tradition of decentralised fiscal and financial management and empowerment of local authorities, such as the Nordic countries. The United Kingdom has a particularly interesting arrangement that could be described as a case of asymmetric decentralization by combining a quasi-federal setting for Scotland, Wales and Northern Ireland (since 1998) with a unitary structure in England.

There is in addition considerable heterogeneity in Europe in the number of layers of administration within each country. This makes it difficult to put forward an all-encompassing definition of local government that could be applied to the entire continent.[5] In some cases, there are

Box 5.1. Middle-tier Jurisdiction in Countries with Three Levels of Subnational Government

In 2009, there were approximately 980 middle-tier jurisdictions in Europe. They are situated between the local and regional (or federated) levels of administration in the 7 European countries that have three sub-national layers of government (Belgium, France, Germany, Italy, Poland, Spain and United Kingdom).

The institutional underpinning of middle-tier jurisdictions are also changing. In Belgium, a debate was launched in 2009 on the transformation of provinces into "territorial communities" in Wallonia and in "urban regions" in Flanders, both with redefined mandates. In Italy, the reform of local governments approved by the Council of Ministers in July 2009 foresees a rationalisation of the provincial map. In England, the policy of mainstreaming "unitary authorities" should have led to the abolition of county councils; however the Cameron government decided not to proceed with this process (law of December 16, 2010). In France, the law of December 16, 2010 provides for the creation of new regional directors, elected at the cantonal level, but who will participate in both departmental and regional level councils, which implies a redefinition of the role of these two levels of government. It also allows for mergers between departments and between regions and between a region and the departments that are part of its territory.

Source: Dexia

4. *See also DEXIA (2008) and CEMR (2009a) for more information on institutional arrangements in the European Union countries.*
5. *To deal with this difficulty, this chapter uses to the extent possible the classification used by Eurostat.*

Box 5.2. Municipal Restructuring in Europe: Ongoing and planned reforms

Recent initiatives

In Latvia, a local authority merger programme, which had been in place for more than 10 years, came to an end in July 2009, resulting in the replacement of 524 local authorities by 118 new entities. In Finland, the PARAS project for restructuring municipalities and services was launched in 2007. At the end of 2012, when the project is due to come to completion, Finland is expected to have 337 local authorities instead of 416 in 2007. In Northern Ireland, a local government restructuring programme adopted in 2008 will come into effect in May 2011 with the replacement of the 26 current districts by 11 new districts with a broader array of responsibilities. In England, restructuring of the remaining two-tier system in some rural regions (county and district councils) resulted in the replacement of 44 local councils by 9 new authorities in April 2009. In February 2010, new mergers were agreed for Norfolk, Suffolk and Devon.

Ambitious municipal merger programmes were launched in Greece and Luxemburg. In Greece, the Kallikratis institutional reform voted in 2010 plans to reduce the number of local authorities from 1,034 to 370, as well as to strengthen their responsibilties. In Luxemburg, a project launched in 2008 aims to reduce the number of municipalities from 116 to 71.

In Iceland, the number of local authorities is planned to be reduced from 78 in 2009 to less than 40 in the next 5 years. Finally, in France the law of December 16, 2010 renewed the mechanisms for municipal fusion, allowing for the creation of "new municipalities", based on the current metropolitan areas. However this process can be blocked if the majority of the elected officials of the municipalities concerned vote against it. The "new" local authority will have the ability to create "devolved administrations" whose bodies issue from the new municipalities.

Inter-municipal cooperation

In Hungary, the government is reinforcing the system of "micro-regions with multiple purposes" in its public services reform. In other countries, inter-municipal cooperation can be fostered as a preliminary step towards municipal mergers. This is the case in Luxemburg and Finland, where the municipalities that are not ready for merging are required to create "partnership areas" to implement basic services, such as health care and social services.

In countries where inter-municipal cooperation is already well developed, there is a tendency to rationalise these ventures whilst reinforcing their democratic legitimacy. In Italy, the reform of local government approved by the Council of Ministers in July 2009 plans the suppression of Mountain Communities. In France, the law of December 16, 2010 plans to consolidate the inter-municipal cooperation (90% of the local governments and 95% of the population are already parts of metropolitan areas), to ensure that by 2013 no local government is working alone (with the exception of Paris). The members of the deliberative assemblies of the municipal associations with own revenue will be elected by direct universal suffrage from the same list of candidates presented for municipal elections.

Source: Dexia

two easily identifiable sub-national levels of government, such as middle-tier jurisdictions (Box 5.1), including the *comunidades autonomas* in Spain and the *régions* in Belgium, and local authorities, which in turn encompasses municipalities, communes, local councils or districts, and provinces in some countries (such as Spain). In other cases, there are countries with local governments which have similar legal status, such as France (municipalities, departments and regions), but which in other countries may have special characteristics, particularly in the different laws applicable to urban and rural municipalities, as in Cyprus and Poland, or in the duality of the county-district and unitary councils in England (but also in other regions of the United Kingdom). In some countries, cities can gain additional municipal powers and those of other intermediate levels of government (eg the cities of Germany, Poland, which are also districts, and in Hungary where cities can assume the rank of department).

There are other complexities too, related to the special status of local authorities in a number of countries. Capital cities may enjoy a different status among local governments, as in France, Hungary, Italy, Poland and the Slovak Republic. Capital cities can also take on the role of a middle-tier jurisdiction, as in Austria, Belgium, Czech Republic and Germany (regional status). In addition, other non-capital cities or urban areas may be defined as middle-tier jurisdictions. Cases in point are Bremen and Hamburg in Germany, which have a double status of local and middle-tier jurisdictions. This is not to be confused with particular administrative arrangements, including those of a supra-municipal nature, such as metropolitan areas, which are not considered to be a separate stratum of administration. Geographically isolated areas, such as islands and mountainous regions, are often treated differently in some countries (Greece or Italy, for example), on account of their special needs and economic structure.

The boundaries of local governments have evolved over time in line with changes in the territorial organisation of a number of countries, as well as evolving demands for local goods and services. In some countries, where local authorities are deemed too small, there have been efforts towards the amalgamation of local jurisdictions, as in Austria in the 1950s, Sweden in the 1950s and 1970s, Denmark and Belgium in the 1970s, and Finland and the Netherlands more recently (Box 5.2). The number of local jurisdictions was reduced sharply in Greece and Lithuania in the 1990s, Denmark in 2007 and Latvia in 2009. Amalgamations have also taken place at the regional level, as in Denmark.[6] Initiatives in this area have been motivated by the need to enhance efficiency in service delivery through the territorial enlargement and consolidation of local jurisdictions (discussed below in the context of local government expenditure policy). By contrast, in some Central and Eastern European countries, a number of mergers of local jurisdictions carried out during central planning have been reversed since the return to democracy in the 1990s. The average population of local jurisdictions is well below 10,000 in many European countries, often making it difficult for these local authorities to reap the benefits of economies of scale in the delivery of local services.

A final consideration when illustrating the diversity in institutional settings among local governments in Europe is related to the legislative and executive structure of local governments. As noted in the GOLD I report, all European governments are administered by elected councilors, however the methods of appointment of

6. *See CEMR (2009a) for more information.*

their executives can vary: they may be elected by the council or directly by the people or appointed by the government; the executive can be individual or collegiate. As a general trend, the decentralization of revenue and expenditure functions to the local governments cannot be dissociated from stronger demands for self-government and the devolution of political powers to the local jurisdictions.

Support for Local Governments

There seems to be strong support for local authorities in Europe. A number of initiatives have been put in place in support of local governments, including first and foremost at the supra-national level the European Charter of Local Self-Government, which came into effect in 1988 under the auspices of the Congress of the Council of Europe. By guaranteeing local governments' political, administrative and financial autonomy, the Charter contributes to strengthening local authorities politically and institutionally. Within the treaties of the European Union, and as is clear from the Treaty of Lisbon, local and regional autonomy is part of the "fundamental political and constitutional structures" of the Member States which the EU must respect (Article 4).

"Europeanization", as the process of accession to the European Union and the consequent adherence to the EU's *acquis* is sometimes known, is affecting self-government at the sub-national level in many countries. This is especially the case of the new member States in the Baltic region and in Central and Eastern Europe, where EU integration has been an important catalyst for political and economic reforms. In these countries, it can be argued that fiscal decentralization has contributed to fostering democratic governance through greater political representation at the sub-national level – albeit often only half-heartedly at the beginning in some countries.

Notwithstanding an overall fairly strong political commitment to self-government, local governments are confronted with the emergence of middle-tier jurisdictions in many countries (Box 5.3). Important expenditure mandates were devolved to the German *Länder* in 2006 and to the Italian regions since the 1990s. The Danish reform of 2007 replaced the counties by fewer regional jurisdictions, while maintaining the local authorities and allocating to them most of the tax bases of the former counties. Regional jurisdictions have been created in the transition economies that have recently joined the European Union, such as the Czech and Slovak Republics, in part as a means of facilitating access by these countries to financial support from the European Union's structural and cohesion funds, which are disbursed at the regional, rather than local authority, level. Political decentralization in the United Kingdom also illustrates the empowerment of regional jurisdictions, with the devolution of important prerogatives to Scotland, Wales and Northern Ireland since 1998.

Local Government Expenditure

The Assignment of Expenditure Mandates to Local Governments

The allocation of spending responsibilities to local authorities often follows two principles. On the one hand, they may intervene on any subject of local public interest which does not interfere with the jurisdiction of other administrative authorities and respects the legal framework. This principle, known as the "general competence clause" is enshrined in Article 4 of the European

Box 5.3. The Regionalisation Process

Regionalisation has been in place in a number European countries for over twenty years to strengthen the competencies of the existing regions, to create or to reshape the regional level of government and to launch new initiatives.

Recent initiatives are noteworthy. For example, Lithuania will have two levels of local government instead of one from 1 July 2010. Five self-governing regions were created and the 10 State regional administrations were suppressed. In Greece, as noted in Box 5.2, the Kallikratis reform replaces the existing 54 counties by 13 regional governments elected by direct universal suffrage. In Norway, the regional reform in place since 1 January 2010 maintains the current 19 counties (instead of replacing them by 5 or 6 new regions, as originally envisaged), while reinforcing their responsibilities in the fields of road maintenance, land settlement, environment protection and innovation.

Several countries are considering regional reforms. In Poland, the government has recently announced its intention to strengthen regional competencies and to reshape their organisation. In Romania, the government announced in January 2009 that it intended to replace the counties by regions before 2013 (the most recent version of the draft law refers to 16 to 20 regions). In Slovenia, despite failure of the 2008 regionalisation project, the government is preparing a new plan based on the creation of 6 regions from 2011 (instead of 14, as announced in 2008). A debate is under way on the creation of regions in continental Portugal, and a new project refers to 3 to 5 regions, instead of 8, as planned in 1998, the year when the original regional reform law was rejected by referendum.

Regionalisation is ongoing in Sweden, where the government announced its intention to merge from 2011 the 24 counties into 6 to 9 regions with special competencies in the fields of health care and regional planning. In Finland, an independent assessment of the pilot project implemented in the region of Kainuu was to be released in the spring of 2010. On the basis of this evaluation, the government will present additional measures.

Regionalisation is neither linear nor general in Europe. In Latvia, for example, the 2009 territorial reform originally aimed to create self-governing regions to replace the 26 districts. In the end, the responsibilities of the districts were reassigned to the municipalities and to the five State regions created in 2002 for regional development. In France, the 2003-2004 reforms were favorable to the regions, however the succesive local finance reforms and in particular the elimination in 2010 of the tax on economic activities –*taxe professionelle*–, has progressively limited their fiscal power.

Source: Dexia

Charter of Local Autonomy. On the other hand, they exercise powers assigned them by law, which generally represent the bulk of local government spending. They may also assume other duties delegated to them by the State which they execute in its name. In most countries, local governments are responsible for primary education, including the construction, operations and maintenance of schools. In some new European Union Member States, including Estonia, Latvia, Lithuania, Slovak Republic and Slovenia, education alone accounts for at least one-third of local government budgets (Figure 5.1). Other responsibilities that are in general under the purview of local governments include the supply of urban amenities and planning, waste collection and treatment, and distribution of drinking water and treatment of waste water. In some cases, payment of social benefits adds to local government spending, including in selected Western European countries, such as Denmark, Germany, Iceland, and the remaining Scandinavian countries. The provision of social services, including child care and income support for the elderly and the disabled, is another area where local authorities are engaged heavily in service delivery.

In the case of health care, which accounts for a large share of expenditure, the role of local government is less uniform across countries. In some cases, local authorities are responsible for primary and preventive care, in particular in the Nordic and some Eastern and Central European countries. The case of Finland is interesting; health care accounts for a large share of local government budgets because the municipalities (through municipal boards) are responsible for managing health care centres. By contrast, in Norway, health care was recentralised in 2002 as a means of boosting cost-efficiency in service delivery through greater reliance in activity-based funding for the allocation of health care resources.[7]

The part local government spending makes up of total public spending reflects the

Figure 5.1: Local Government Expenditure: Functional classification, 2007

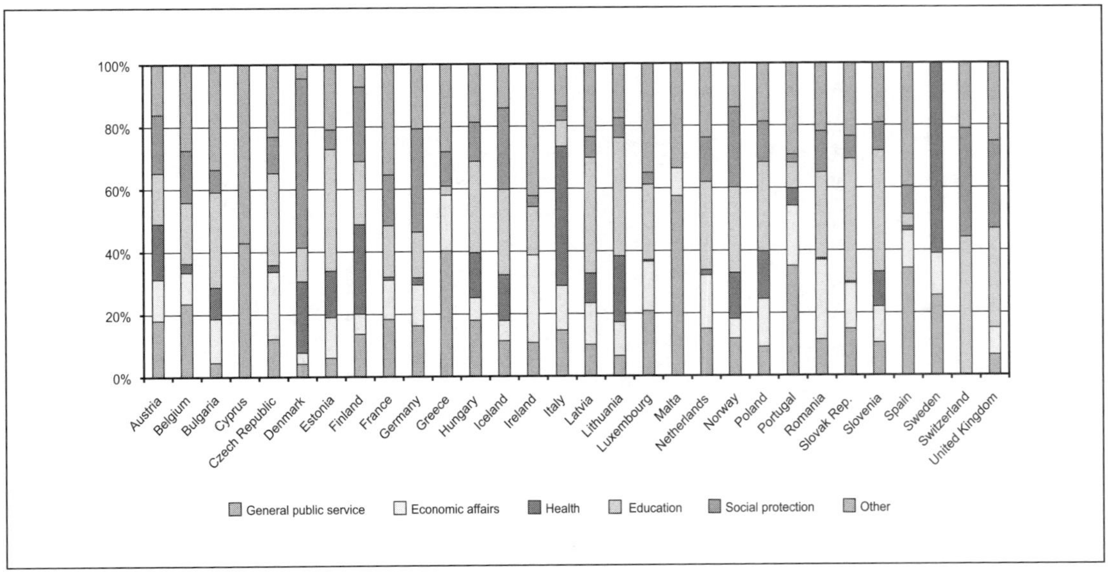

Sources: Eurostat (February 2010), national sources and DEXIA calculations. (cf. Annex 5.3)

7. *An evaluation of the reform carried out by the Norwegian Research Council for the Ministry of Health and Care Services notes an improvement in access, an increase in productivity and a reduction in waiting times after the reform. The evaluation nevertheless did not cover important areas, such as equity of access and quality of health care services. See also Magnussen et al. (2007) for more information on the Norwegian experience, and WHO (2008) for a discussion of country experiences and common policy challenges in the decentralization of health care systems in Europe.*

difference in assignment of expenditure functions to local governments (Figure 5.2 and Table 5.2). Local government expenditure is comparatively high in proportion to GDP and general government outlays in the Nordic countries. In other countries, where middle-tier jurisdictions are important providers of public goods and services, the relative size of local governments is typically lower, as in Austria, Germany and Spain. Most importantly, cross-country variations in the relative size of local governments reflect differences in the assignment of expenditure functions across the various levels of government.

Rather than being immutable, local expenditure patterns evolve over time. Local government spending has risen in many countries in part because expenditure mandates have changed over the years. In some cases, increase in local spending reflects changes in the composition of overall expenditure and are matched by lower spending at higher levels of administration. This is the case of community services, including social protection, for example, which were fully decentralised to the local governments in Denmark in 2007. Non-tertiary education was decentralised to the local governments in Italy during the 1990s, a trend that almost doubled the relative size of local governments.[8] In the case of Spain, several functions were decentralised to the middle-tier jurisdictions following the country's comprehensive decentralization program implemented in the 1990s, although there is much less clarity in the assignment of

Figure 5.2: Local Government Expenditure, 2008

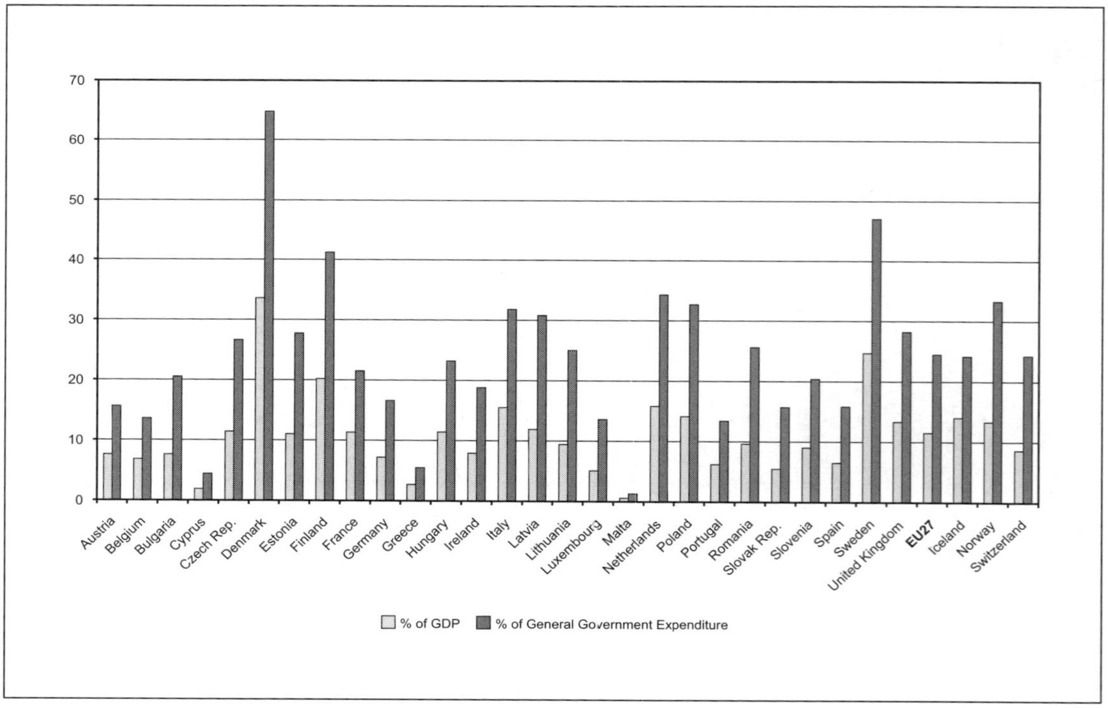

Source: Eurostat (February 2010), national sources and DEXIA calculations (cf. table 5.2).

Table 5.2: Local Government Expenditure: Economic classification, 2008

	Expenditure		Composition of expenditure (% of local government expenditure)				
	% of GDP	% of general government expenditure	Compensation of employees	Use of goods and services	Gross fixed capital formation	Social benefits	Other
Austria	7.6	15.6	23.8	18.0	6.6	18.0	33.6
Belgium	6.8	13.6	53.5	14.1	11.6	11.6	9.2
Bulgaria	7.6	20.5	35.3	36.8	26.8	0.2	0.8
Cyprus	1.9	4.4	38.1	23.0	30.6	0.0	8.2
Czech Rep.	11.4	26.6	31.8	28.2	20.4	5.6	14.1
Denmark	33.6	64.8	36.6	17.6	3.7	36.1	6.0
Estonia	11.0	27.7	41.5	26.9	19.3	3.2	9.1
Finland	20.2	41.2	48.9	30.0	8.7	8.0	4.4
France	11.3	21.5	29.0	19.7	20.6	8.3	22.4
Germany	7.2	16.6	22.9	21.9	11.9	26.6	16.7
Greece	2.7	5.5	42.4	27.5	22.7	0.1	7.4
Hungary	11.4	23.2	49.1	24.8	10.7	5.0	10.4
Ireland	7.9	18.8	21.2	17.6	45.2	10.1	5.9
Italy	15.5	31.8	30.3	25.2	11.0	18.4	15.1
Latvia	11.9	30.8	46.0	23.8	25.5	2.9	1.8
Lithuania	9.4	25.0	51.5	19.0	21.3	4.8	3.4
Luxembourg	5.1	13.6	32.4	22.6	31.2	1.2	12.7
Malta	0.6	1.3	12.8	63.9	22.9	0.0	0.3
Netherlands	15.8	34.3	38.5	28.3	15.1	10.0	8.0
Poland	14.1	32.7	40.3	23.5	18.6	8.2	9.4
Portugal	6.2	13.4	30.3	25.6	24.0	5.8	14.2
Romania	9.6	25.6	35.7	22.8	25.5	10.0	6.0
Slovak Rep.	5.5	15.7	42.3	27.9	20.4	1.1	8.3
Slovenia	9.0	20.4	41.3	20.7	23.9	4.3	9.8
Spain	6.5	15.8	28.4	28.1	16.4	1.6	25.5
Sweden	24.7	47.0	46.3	24.5	7.3	14.4	7.4
United Kingdom	13.3	28.2	37.9	35.7	8.9	11.2	6.2
EU27	**11.5**	**24.5**	**33.6**	**25.3**	**13.2**	**14.5**	**13.4**
Iceland	14.0	24.2	40.3	28.3	17.0	3.4	11.0
Norway	13.3	33.3	50.9	19.3	11.8	7.4	10.6
Switzerland	8.6	24.3					

Source: Eurostat (February 2010), national sources and DEXIA calculations.

expenditure functions to the local governments. Policing was devolved to the municipalities in Belgium in 2002.

Rising expenditure can be attributed to some extent to an increase in delivery costs. It is difficult to compare unit costs across countries, given the enormous diversity in norms and standards applicable to local government provision, and information is not readily available for most countries. The extent to which the local authorities can exploit economies of scale in service delivery contributes to reducing the cost of locally provided goods and services (discussed below). But, in general, there is likely to have been considerable cost changes over time, reflecting the increased importance of old age-related outlays, especially in countries where local governments are important providers of health care and social protection services.

Because the services delivered by local governments tend to be intensive in labour, payroll accounts for the lion's share of local government outlays in most countries, followed by purchases of goods and services needed for government operations. Related to the cost of payroll at the local level of government is the labour market status of local employees. In most countries, local officials are civil servants and therefore enjoy a different employment status to those working in the private sector. This is nevertheless not the case in Cyprus, Czech Republic, Ireland, Italy, Latvia, Malta, the Netherlands, Poland, Slovakia, Sweden, and the United Kingdom (CEMR, 2009c). The share of local government employees with a separate employment status also varies among the different layers of sub-national government. In Germany, for example, 61 percent of those employed by middle-tier jurisdictions, such as teachers and police officers, have a specific status, against only 14 percent of those employed at the municipal level. There is, nevertheless, a clear downward trend in the number of employees with this specific status in many countries.

Local governments also play an important role in public investment, which accounts for 13 percent of local government spending on average in the EU countries. Gross fixed capital formation carried out at the local level accounts for the lion's share of total public investment, or about two-thirds on average among the EU countries and as high as 70 percent in countries, such as Italy and France. The European local governments are key players in non-residential construction, including development, improvement, operations, and maintenance of infrastructures in areas as diverse as public transport, roads, urban amenities, and in network industries, most notably water and sanitation. Local governments also contribute to residential investment in the area of social housing.

Main Issues in Local Government expenditure

Dealing with benefit spillovers across local government borders

Certain services that are provided and financed by a given local authority may benefit residents from adjacent jurisdictions. There are numerous practical examples of such benefit spillovers. Access to urban facilities, such as parks and leisure areas, is open to non-residents, even though they do not share the associated provision costs by paying taxes to the supplying authority. By the same token, individuals are often allowed to seek health care in jurisdictions other than the one where they live, even when inter-jurisdictional refunding mechanisms are absent. The problem associated with these benefit spillovers is that they discourage the local authorities from supplying the service in

8. *See Bibbee (2008) for more information.*

Box 5.4. The Metropolisation Process in Europe

Several countries have aimed to strengthen the institutional framework for inter-municipal cooperation. Recent initiatives include:

- Following the mid-term evaluation of Finland's PARAS project (report released in November 2009), the government announced legislation to promote cooperation in the 7 largest urban regions, including the Helsinki metropolitan area, in the fields of land use, transportation and housing.

- France's territorial reform law, passed 16 December 2010, creates two new types of inter-municipal cooperation for metropolitan areas: the "Metropolis" a supra-metropolitan area for agglomerations of more than 450,000 inhabitants, which is the case of 8 French cities, which will benefit from the transfer of powers from the departments and the region, and for those agglomerations of more than 300,000 inhabitants, including a member city of more than 150,000 inhabitants. With the Law of Greater Paris, passed on June 3 2010, the State takes back the management of development planning for the Paris region with the creation of two public entities, the strengthening of the role of the regional prefecture and through development contracts with the municipalities affected by the new regional express metro.

- In Italy, Article 23 of Law 42 (May 5, 2009) relaunched the creation of "metropolitan cities" (Città metropolitana) provided for by law since 1990 and included in the 2001 Constitution, which gives an additional impulse, and facilitates the creation of these in nine major cities. These metropolitan cities will immediately assume the functions of territorial planning and infrastructure development, the organization of system coordination, the management of public services, and support to economic and social development. Article 24 creates a more detailed interim status for immediate application in Rome. The implementation of this reform would lead to the disappearance of the corresponding provinces.

- Legislation was adopted in Luxembourg in November 2008 to create urban communities. It defines the basic rules for the creation and functioning of these communities, which are public entities for inter-municipal cooperation among cities of more than 20,000 inhabitants.

- Among the reform proposals made by Poland's Joint Commission of the Central and Local Governments established in May 2008, there is a proposal for adoption of a special status for the 12 metropolitan cities.

Source: Dexia

question when they have to bear the corresponding delivery costs in full.

Likewise, the costs of local services, in addition to their benefit, can be exported to neighbouring jurisdictions. Social protection is a case in point. What happens in practice is that local governments may be allowed to set benefit rates while relying on funding from other levels of government. In this case, they face the incentive to set a rate above those of neighbouring jurisdictions while exporting the cost of provision elsewhere. There are numerous examples in Europe of countries where local governments have prerogatives over welfare programs, such as Denmark, Netherlands, Sweden, and Switzerland.

Several European countries have devised ingenious ways to mitigate the perverse incentives associated with such benefit and cost spillovers. For example, the local governments concerned may agree to share at least part of the provision costs in recognition of mutual benefits. In the case of

Box 5.5. Inter-municipal Initiatives: A few examples

Europe has well developed structures in support of inter-jurisdictional ventures at the local level.*

In most cases, inter-municipal initiatives are voluntary. In other cases, arrangements are institutionalised, and selected responsibilities are legally binding, as in the case of health care in Finland. Inter-municipal structures are sometimes imposed upon smaller municipalities, as in Italy and Germany, whereas in France they may be set up by a majority vote among the participating jurisdictions and have significant tax powers. They are the only metropolitan administrations with fiscal powers in Europe. Inter-municipal arrangements are well developed in Austria, Belgium, France, Gemany, and Southern Europe, but they are at their infancy in the new member countries of European Union in Central and Eastern Europe. The case of inter-municipal arrangements for water supply in Czech Republic and hospital management in Estonia are nevertheless instructive.

Inter-municipal ventures can be institutionalised as a legal entity that has managerial and financial responsibility for the shared provision of a service. They can be of a public nature, as in the case of syndicates of different local governments, or semi-private. Semi-public arrangements are common in nearly all European countries and more prevalent in the areas of water/sewerage, waste collection, energy and public transport. Such arrangements are often multi-purpose and cover areas related to network services that cut across municipal borders, such as the management of water and transport networks, which are subject to inter-jurisdictional externality effects.

Public-private partnerships, which are not equivalent to the inter-municipal cooperation arrangements referred to above, are gaining ground, following the pioneering experience of the United Kingdom, especially in Germany, France and Southern Europe.

** See Hulst and Montfort (2007) for more information on the experiences of Belgium, Finland, France, Italy, Germany, Netherlands, United Kingdom and Spain.*

9. Large urban areas can also straddle international borders. This is the case of the Eurometropole Lille-Kortrijk-Tournai, which includes cities on both sides of the France-Belgium border. International initiatives to improve accessibility, quality and efficiency of cross-border health care include the EUREGIO Rhein-Waal created by German and Dutch local authorities.

health care and urban facilities in general, arrangements have been put in place in large metropolitan areas, where there is plenty of room for inter-jurisdictional spillovers, as in France, Spain, and Portugal (Box 5.4).[9] Cross-border compensation for the costs of health care is available in Denmark and Sweden when patients chose to seek care in a different jurisdiction, a practice that can be considered exemplary in this area. In the case of welfare programs, benefit rates are set and service delivery is carried at different levels of administration.

Lowering delivery costs through economies of scale

Another important policy challenge for local governments in Europe is to make the most of economies of scale in service delivery. Local governments are often too small to reap the benefits of economies of scale in the provision of local services, which drives up unit delivery costs. Operating costs are likely to rise among smaller jurisdictions in the case of education, because teacher/student ratios are higher than in communities with larger schools. Excess capacity, on the other hand, may also push up operating costs, as in the case of health care facilities in some of the countries of Central and Eastern Europe, whose ratios of hospital beds to population tend to be higher than in Western and Southern Europe.

There are options for lowering delivery costs through gains in economies of scale. Local jurisdictions that are considered too small can be amalgamated (forcibly or not), as in the case of Belgium, Finland, Netherlands, and Norway, for instance.[10] Political resistance to such amalgamations by local civil servants and residents alike should nevertheless not be underestimated. Central government grants can be introduced to encourage amalgamations, although the experience of Estonia suggests that these financial incentives may not be sufficiently strong.

Another option is to encourage local authorities to deliver services jointly, as in the experience of inter-municipal cooperative ventures in many European countries (Box 5.5), where local governments join forces to provide common services.[11] The cases of transport, urban waste management, water supply, fire fighting and hospital administration are illustrative of efforts in this area. Joint ownership of power plants in Norway also allows neighbouring jurisdictions to cut costs in providing energy services. In some cases, however, regulations on government procurement pose obstacles to cost-effective inter-municipal cooperation, as argued by local governments in Sweden and other Nordic countries. An alternative strategy to tackle excess supply is through the closure of underutilized facilities. This is the case of schools in small communities in Portugal, for example. Of course, measures should be put in place to ensure access to services in the case of residents that may be affected adversely by the closure of local facilities.

Solving coordination problems across different levels of government

The assignment of expenditure functions across levels of government is not always well delineated. Arrangements are particularly complex in federations, given the institutional autonomy enjoyed by the different layers of government. In Germany, for example, the federal government sets norms and regulations for the provision of health care and finances the operating costs of hospitals. The regional governments (*länder*) finance hospital investment and manage capacity, and services are delivered by the local governments.[12] Yet even in

10. *For example, in Ireland, according to the Local Government Efficiency Group, a number of local authorities should be merged in order to trim the number of civil servants and streamline expenditure.*

11. *Empirical evidence, at least for school cleaning services in Denmark, shows that the ability to exploit economies of scale is the main factor explaining cost differentials between public (centralized and decentralized) and private provision. See Christoffersen et al. (2007). The evidence for other sectors and other Scandinavian countries reported by Blom-Hansen (2003) is nevertheless less conclusive, although the author finds a cost advantage for private providers in the case of municipal road maintenance.*

12. *See Wurzel (1999) for more information.*

unitary countries, assignments often overlap in the areas of regulation, management and service delivery, because it is often increasingly difficult to unbundle the different functional areas of expenditure. In France, for example, where current arrangements work rather well, the central government sets school curricula and administers personnel, the regional governments are responsible for the construction and maintenance of upper-secondary schools and for vocational training, the *départements* are in charge of construction and maintenance of lower-secondary schools, and the municipalities deal with the construction and maintenance of primary education schools. A lack of clarity in the assignment of expenditure in increasingly complex functional areas may also undermine the accountability of local governments to their citizenry.

Institutional arrangements are often complex and create room for cost shifting among the different layers of government. A case in point is when services are delivered and norms and standards are set by different levels of government. For example, education is provided essentially at the local level in most countries, at least up to the secondary level, subject to curricula set by middle-tier jurisdictions and the central government. Of course, some degree of uniformity is required in service delivery both within local jurisdictions and across the national territory, but adherence to norms and standards set by higher levels of government and the European Union may place an undue financial burden on local budgets. In that respect, by exercising the regulatory powers attributed to them and understating the attendant financial burden, higher levels of government may end up off-loading expenditure entitlements or shifting provision costs to the local authorities, which need to be financed locally.

Coordination failures between different levels of government often result in unfunded expenditure mandates at the local level. In Austria, child care entitlements introduced by higher levels of government have been deemed unfunded by the local authorities. In some countries, however, the local authorities are fully compensated for initiatives taken at higher levels of government that would create claims on local budgets. This is the case of Denmark, where a commitment to full compensation has mitigated perverse incentives for cost-shifting and the offloading of expenditure commitments by higher levels of administration on local governments. A best practice in this area is therefore to ban the creation of unfunded mandates across the different levels of administration.

Local Revenue Assignments

The Mix of Revenue Sources Across Countries

Because the assignment of expenditure functions varies across countries, so does the mix of instruments available to local governments for financing provision. In general, this mix of financing instruments reflects decisions on the breadth and depth of the taxes to be assigned to the local authorities. It also depends on the corresponding transfers needed to bridge the gap between revenue from own and shared sources, on the one hand, and local expenditure commitments, on the other, which are based on the allocation of functions across levels of government.

Local government revenue – including local taxes, non-tax instruments (such as user charges and fees for services), and intergovernmental grants and transfers – accounts for close to 10 percent of GDP on average in the countries under examination. Nevertheless, there are differences across countries (Figure 5.3). Local government revenue, is much higher on average as a share of general government receipts – a conventional gauge of the relative size of local governments – in some unitary States, such as the Nordic countries (except for Norway), than in the federal countries (Germany, for example). The relative shares of local government revenue are particularly low in some Southern European countries, such as Cyprus, Greece, and Malta, reflecting, as discussed below, differences in the assignment of revenue sources across the different layers of government among the European countries. Of course, these quantitative indicators need to be interpreted with caution, because they do not reflect the degree of autonomy enjoyed by local governments in tax policy. While taxes and grants account for the bulk of local government revenue, other sources, such as user charges and fees, are additional important sources of local government revenue (Figure 5.4).

Local Taxes and Shared Revenue

The assignment of tax bases to local governments

A case can be made for relying on local taxes, rather than on revenue mobilised elsewhere, to finance the provision of local services. It can be argued that such reliance tightens the link between the benefits and costs of local services, which is likely to make local officials more accountable to their taxpayers. Local governments are best equipped to tax immobile bases, because their revenue yield tends to be fairly insensitive to cyclical fluctuations in economic activity. This facilitates fiscal

Figure 5.3: Local Government Revenue, 2008

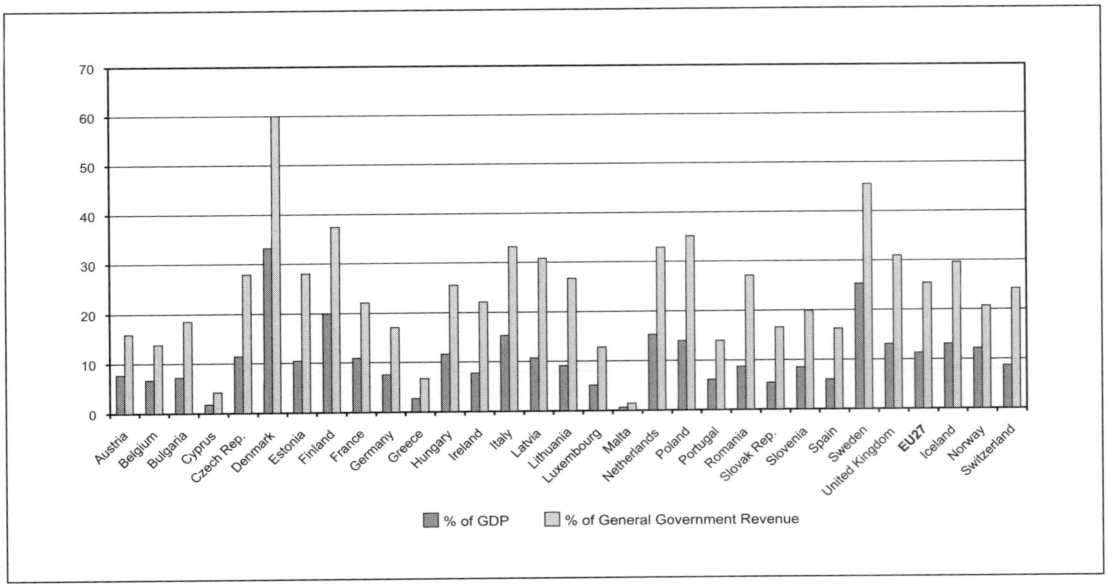

Sources: Eurostat (February 2010), national sources and DEXIA calculations. (cf. Annex 5.4)

Figure 5.4: Local Government Revenue Composition, 2008

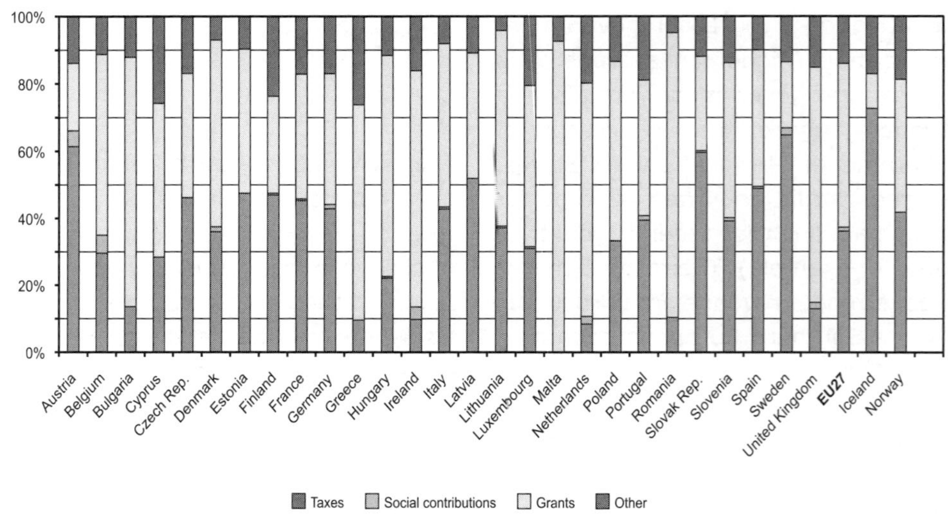

Sources: Eurostat (February 2010), national sources and DEXIA calculations. (cf. Annex 5.4)

Figure 5.5: Local Government Tax Revenue as a Percentage of Local Government Revenue, 2008

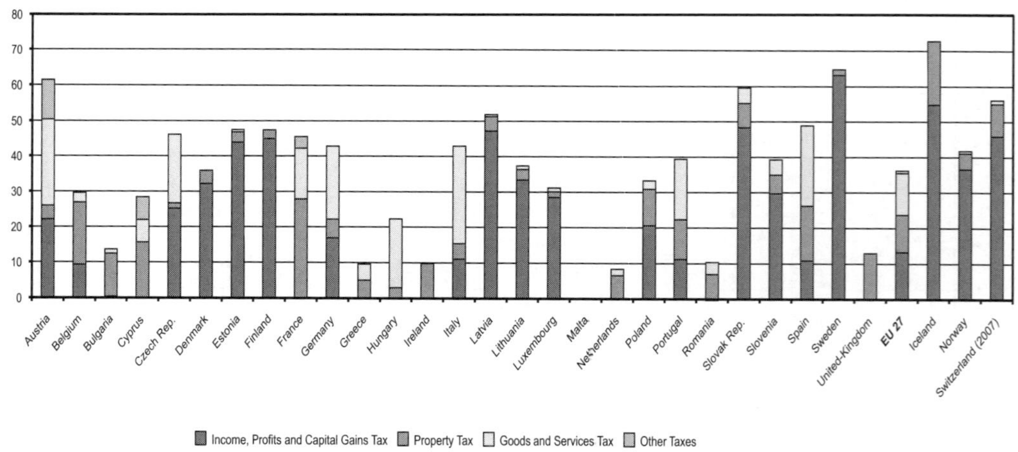

Sources: Eurostat and DEXIA calculations. (cf. Annex 5.5)

management over the business cycle, given that local governments are often constrained from borrowing to finance budget deficits of a recurrent nature. As a result, property tax revenue accounts for a large share of local government revenue in several European countries, including Belgium, France and Iceland (Figure 5.5).

Other tax bases are also important for local government taxation in some countries. This is the case of mobile taxes, such as the personal and corporate income taxes (PIT and CIT, respectively), in the Nordic countries,[13] Iceland, and most new European Union Member States, such as Estonia, Latvia, Lithuania, and Slovak Republic. Whereas PIT is a local tax in the Nordic countries and Belgium, local governments can levy a surcharge on the central government PIT in Italy. In most other countries, PIT and CIT revenue is shared among different layers of administration, rather than being assigned exclusively to local governments. The federal and quasi-federal countries (Austria, Belgium, Germany, Italy and Spain) tend to rely on formula-based, fixed-coefficient arrangements for sharing PIT revenue among the different levels of government (Table 5.3). A large proportion of PIT revenue is also shared with the local authorities in the Central and Eastern European countries.

PIT and CIT revenue-sharing parameters are cast in law in most countries, but they are not immutable. The criteria conventionally used for sharing these revenues include derivation (when revenue is allocated to the jurisdiction where the tax is collected), the size of the recipient jurisdiction (based on population, for example) and estimates of expenditure needs, when equalisation efforts are pursued (discussed below). The overall percentage of revenue to be shared across layers of administration may also change over time. For example, the Portuguese reform of 2007 allows the municipalities to receive a small share (2-5 percent) of PIT receipts collected by the central government. Revenue from other taxes, such as the corporate income tax (CIT), is shared with the local authorities in Denmark and Finland.

In some cases, taxes on goods and services are additional important sources of local government revenue. This is the case in Austria, Italy and Spain. As with PIT and CIT receipts, revenue from the value-added tax (VAT) is shared among different levels of government in several countries, including Germany and Spain. With regards to levies on business transactions, several countries have phased them out, or are in the process of doing so, including Belgium, Germany, Spain and, more recently, France, and Hungary.[14]

Main issues in local taxation and revenue sharing

An important consideration in a decentralised policy setting is the extent of autonomy that local governments should have in tax matters. It can be argued that autonomy is beneficial, because it may enhance tax competition among the local governments, which may help to constrain increases in public spending and taxation. When sub-national expenditure is financed predominantly with resources mobilised locally, policymakers face an incentive to evaluate the benefits of an increase in spending against the costs of incremental taxation. It should nevertheless be noted that autonomy in income and property taxation, where applicable, does not often lead to significant variation in tax rates among local governments in most European countries.[15] In some cases this may be due to the fact that local tax autonomy is curtailed by higher

13. In Finland, a proposal has been made recently to reduce the tax burden on labour income, a measure to be compensated by greater reliance on value added taxation. Likewise, in Romania, the law on local public finances was amended in June 2010 to, among other things, reduce the local tax burden on personal income.

14. An example is the phasing-out of the taxe professionelle in France from 2010. To compensate at least in part for the associated revenue loss, the real estate tax will be transferred from the départements to the "communities of cities" and other municipalities. The real estate tax may well have to be raised, even if the central government is committed to maintaining municipal revenue through additional transfers. In Germany, the local business tax is the main source of revenue for local governments and the only tax rate the local authorities have the autonomy to set. A reduction of local revenue autonomy is therefore posing challenges for German local governments due to increasing pressure for spending on social benefits, especially within the context of the economic crisis, which are partly financed at the local level.

15. Empirical evidence on tax competition among European local governments includes Heyndels and Vuchelen (1998) and Richard, Tolkens and Verdonck (2002) for the property tax in Belgium, Buettner (2001) for the business tax in Germany, and Solé-Ollé (2003) for a few municipal taxes in Spain, among others.

Table 5.3: Revenue Sharing Coefficients, 2009 (% of tax receipts)[1]

	PIT/wage taxes				CIT				VAT			
	Central state	Federated states/regions	Intermediary governments	Municipalities	Central government	Federated states/regions	Intermediary governments	Municipalities	Central government	Federated states/regions	Intermediary governments	Municipalities
Austria	73.2	15.2	-	11.6	73.2	15.2	-	11.6	73.2	15.2	-	11.6
Belgium	Variable	Complex formula[2]	0	0	100	0	0	0	Variable	Complex formula[3]	0	0
Czech Rep.	70.0	9.0	-	21.0	70.0	9.0	-	21.0	70.0	9.0	-	21.0
Denmark		[4]			86.6	0	-	13.4	100	0	-	0
Estonia	88.6	-	-	11.4	100	-	-	-	100	-	-	0
Finland		[4]			78.0	-	-	22.0	100	-	-	0
Germany	42.5	42.5	0	15.0	50.0	50.0	0	0	53.1	44.8	0	2.1
Hungary	60.0	1.0	-	39.0	100	0	-	0	100	0	-	0
Italy	92.5	0[5]	1.0	6.5	100	0[5]	0	0	100	0	0	0
Latvia	17	0	-	83	100	0	-	0	100	0	-	0
Lithuania	42.5	-	-	57.5[6]	100	-	-	0	100	-	-	0
Poland	48.8	1.6	10.3	39.3	76.0	15.9	1.4	6.7	100	0	0	0
Romania	18[7]	13.0	-	47.0	100	0	-	0	72.5	1.5	-	26.0
Slovak Rep.	6.2	23.5	-	70.3	100	0	-	0	100	0	-	0
Slovenia	65.0	-	-	35.0	100	-	-	0	100	-	-	0
Spain[8]	64.3	33.0	1.0	1.7	100	0	0	0	62.1	35.0	1.1	1.2

PIT= Personal Income Tax; CIT = Corporate Income Tax, VAT = Value Added Tax

1. *Surtaxes are not considered as shared taxes but as own-source taxes if local governments have some fiscal discretion, as the municipal PIT surtax in Belgium and Italy and the municipal CIT surtax in Portugal.*
2. *For the Belgium regions, the fraction of PIT receipts is based on the consumer price index and real GDP growth. The regions can also apply a surtax. For the communities, the fraction of PIT receipts is based on several economic and demographic criteria.*
3. *VAT is shared only with the Belgium communities. The sharing coefficient depends on fluctuations in the consumer price index and the under-18 population headcount.*
4. *In Denmark, Finland and Sweden, there is a local PIT in addition to the national PIT.*
5. *In Italy, PIT and CIT receipts are shared between the central government and the five regions with special status (according to variable percentages).*
6. *In Lithuania, this percentage is applied to a lump-sum representing 70% of total PIT receipts. The precise percentage of PIT transferred to the municipal budgets varies from 40% for Vilnius to 100% for small municipalities after deducting payments to the Compulsory Health Insurance Fund and the State budget.*
7. *In Romania, the central government percentage is 18%, because 22% of PIT receipts are redistributed for equalisation.*
8. *In Spain, for the regions, the PIT and VAT shares differ according to the autonomous communities. The percentages reported apply to most regions. For some other regions, the percentages are higher (Catalonia for example). The two foral regions (Basque Country and Navarre) have a special tax regime and raise their own PIT and CIT locally for which they set rates and bases. In return, they reimburse the central government for services provided. For the municipalities, only provincial capitals and cities with over 75 000 residents are affected by the PIT and VAT sharing mechanisms.*

Source: DEXIA.

levels of government through a reduction in grants and transfers when sub-national governments cut their own tax rates. Another consideration is that tax competition can be predatory, as when local governments are free to set tax bases, rather than rates. In this case, they may try to attract businesses and households by granting tax breaks for enterprise relocation, which results in an erosion of some tax bases.

Tensions often arise between the local authorities and higher levels of government in local tax policy. The central government may wish to prevent an increase in the local tax take or to alleviate the tax burden on businesses as a means of fostering entrepreneurship. This is the case of the scrapping of business taxes in many countries, as discussed above. In the United Kingdom, there is a cap on annual increases in the council tax levied by the local governments.[16] While initiatives in this area are in line with central government objectives, they impinge on local budgets by restricting the scope for the local authorities to mobilise revenue from their own sources.

The local property tax base is sometimes underexploited. This is because rates may be set too low and/or the local authorities may be unable or unwilling to keep up-todate registers of property values. Of course, as with other taxes, it is difficult to estimate empirically the extent of underutilisation of the local property tax base. To do so, actual collections would need to be compared to estimates of the potential tax base, a task that is methodologically complex.

Formula-based revenue-sharing arrangements have the disadvantage of linking local government receipts to central government revenue. This is the case of VAT revenue sharing in Germany and Spain, for example, which makes local budgets sensitive to cyclical fluctuations in central or middle-tier government revenue. If local governments have limited financial room for smoothing transitory budgetary slippages associated with the business cycle, due to a ban on borrowing, for example, revenue sharing may also make local finances pro-cyclical: spending rises with economic upswings and contracts in downturns. Another consideration is that revenue sharing often creates incentives for higher levels of government to focus their revenue raising efforts on non-sharable receipts so as not to export part of the benefits of their own tax effort to other jurisdictions.

Bridging the Gap Between Local Revenue and Expenditure Mandates

The Use of Intergovernmental Grants and Transfers

The allocation of revenue sources to local governments and the financial arrangements needed to bridge the gap between locally raised revenue and expenditure commitments varies considerably across countries. It is often difficult to draw a precise line between the various types of revenue accruing to local governments, especially in so far as own, shared or transferred revenue are concerned (Annex 5.1). For example, VAT revenue is accounted for as own revenue in Germany, because it refers to an intergovernmental revenue-sharing arrangement, whereas it is treated as an intergovernmental transfer in Italy. The distinction between grants and transfers is also blurred in many cases, and revenue sharing is treated as grants in countries such as Greece, Portugal, and Spain. Typologies of revenue structures are therefore often fraught with problems, because quantitative indicators invariably fail to capture important qualitative distinctions in the assignment of revenue sources across the different layers of

16. *At the same time, efforts to prevent excessive tax rises at the local level have included the need to call a referendum in those local authorities that raise their Council tax above a ceiling approved by Parliament each year.*

Figure 5.6: Local Government Grants as a Percentage of Local Government Revenue, 2008

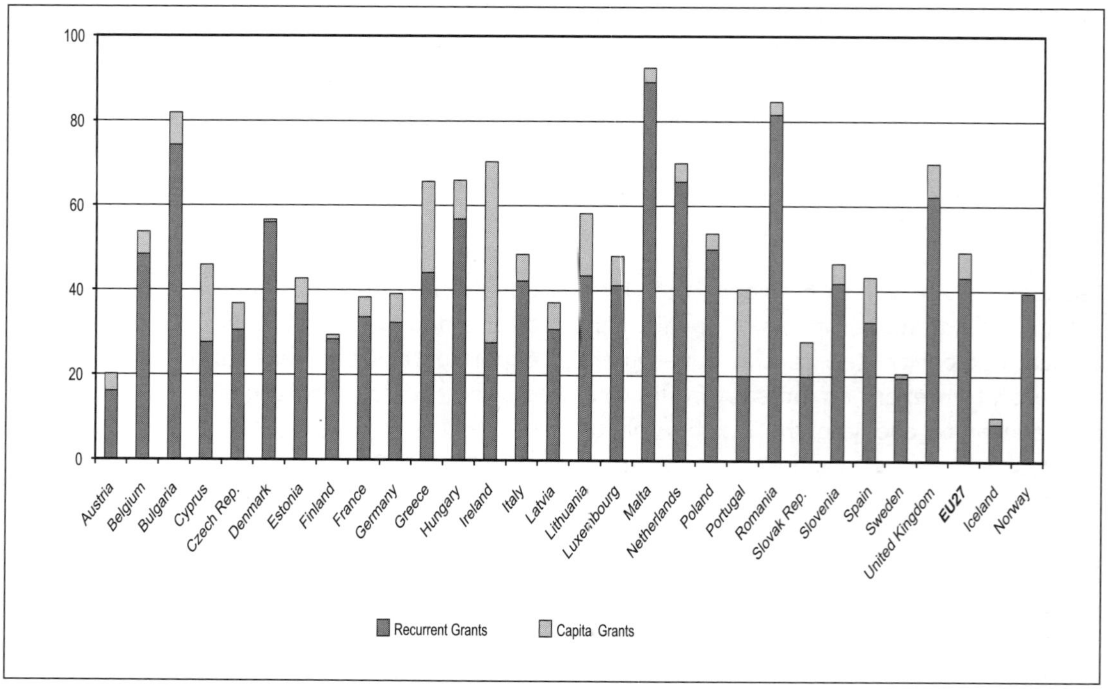

Sources: Eurostat (February 2010) and DEXIA calculations. (cf. Annex 5.6)

government.

Notwithstanding these methodological difficulties, grants and transfers account for the bulk of local government receipts in many countries. This is the case in most Western European countries, as well as a few Eastern European countries, such as Romania and Bulgaria. These countries are characterised by large vertical imbalances in intergovernmental fiscal relations, as local provision is financed by revenue collected at least in part in jurisdictions other than that where the services are provided. The United Kingdom stands out among the more populous European countries on the basis of its local governments' reliance on grants and transfers from the centre. By contrast, local governments tend to rely more heavily on locally raised revenue in the Nordic countries (except Denmark), Iceland and a few transition economies of Central and Eastern Europe, such as Estonia and Slovak Republic.

Local governments in member states also benefit from transfers from the European Union. Structural and cohesion grants focus predominantly on financing for investment projects. They are disbursed in general to middle-tier jurisdictions and regions, and are often shared with the local authorities responsible for project implementation.

Equalisation Grants and Transfers

Schemes are in place in many countries to equalise revenue capacity among the local governments. This is to ensure that expenditure needs are met across the country in spite of differences in revenue capacity among the local jurisdictions arising from the fact that economic activity, and therefore tax bases, is distributed unevenly. In addition to using the tax system, equalisation is carried out predominantly through intergovernmental grants and transfers, which may be vertical, when based on receipts from higher levels of government, or horizontal, when resources are shared among same-level jurisdictions. For example, Germany has a complex vertical transfer system combining arrangements between the central government and the states, and between the states and the municipalities located in their jurisdictions, as well as horizontal transfers among the states. Horizontal transfer arrangements are also in place in Austria, Denmark, Germany, Latvia, Lithuania, Poland, Sweden and Switzerland. Cost equalisation was introduced in Sweden in addition to revenue equalisation in 2004.

A problem that arises in the design of equalisation grants and transfers is that they are often calculated on the basis of actual revenue and spending, rather than estimated revenue capacity and expenditure needs. As such, they rely on historical budgeting, rather than on an assessment of potential collections and normative costs per unit of service delivered. If service delivery is inefficient, a grant system based on actual expenditure, rather than on estimated expenditure needs, would perpetuate deficiencies, rather than equalising spending capacity on the basis of common standards and norms. If local tax bases are underexploited, the use of actual, instead of potential, collections would overestimate the need for equalisation of revenue capacity without creating incentives for local effort in raising revenue. To overcome this problem, equalisation is based on potential average, rather than actual, revenue in the Nordic countries. Another option for dealing with perverse incentives for local tax effort is to centralise collections. This is the case is some countries, even where local governments are allowed to piggyback on central government taxes.

An interesting policy question is how much equalisation of revenue capacity should be pursued. It can be argued that full equalisation would discourage recipients from raising local revenue, if donors adjusted the level of transfers in tandem with the increase in local revenue from own sources (the effective withdrawal rate). Partial equalisation could therefore be pursued to mitigate the tax effort disincentive arising from full equalisation. In fact, the survey conducted by Bergvall *et al.* (2006) shows that full equalisation is rare in Europe.

Earmarking of Grants and Transfers

Grants to local governments are earmarked in many countries. Based on a recent survey of intergovernmental transfer arrangements in the OECD area, it appears that all or nearly all grants are earmarked in Czech Republic, Greece, Ireland and the Netherlands, whereas local governments in Finland, France and Portugal tend to rely predominantly on general-purpose (non-earmarked) grants.[17] Earmarked grants are also often of the matching type, when they are designed to complement local financing by requiring the recipient jurisdiction to match at least a share of the grant using local sources, as in the case of the Netherlands and Switzerland. The use of grants also varies across countries. Although most earmarked transfers to local governments are used to finance the provision of general public services, these resources are also often allocated to more specific functional areas, such as environment protection (Italy), recreation

17. See Bergvall et al. (2006) for more information.

and culture (France and Italy), economic affairs (Spain), housing (France), social protection (Poland), education (Belgium, Czech Republic, Finland and Sweden), and health care (Sweden), for example.

Earmarking is particularly common in the case of investment programs. This is despite the fact that most transfers to local governments tend to be of a recurrent nature (Figure 5.6). Only in a few Western and Southern European countries, such as Cyprus, Greece, Ireland and Portugal, and new European Union Member States, including Hungary and Lithuania, do capital grants account for a larger share of receipts. The cases of Ireland and Portugal are noteworthy, given the role played by local governments in infrastructure development, an area where they act on behalf of higher levels of government.

Main Issues in the Design of Grant Systems

Dealing with benefit and cost spillovers

The design of intergovernmental grant and transfer systems is not without practical implications for local government finances. The main consideration is that these transfers drive a wedge between the costs and benefits of local provision. While the benefits can be internalised by local residents, the corresponding provision costs can be "exported" to taxpayers residing elsewhere. Because of these externalities, local governments may face a number of perverse incentives, including to spend beyond their means and to under-utilise their own tax bases. Alternatively, as noted above, the benefits, rather than costs, of service delivery can be exported to other jurisdictions, an externality that would in general discourage local provision. Of course, the experience of different countries shows that there are options for mitigating these perverse incentives through practical solutions tailored to different country circumstances and institutional settings.

Conditionality can be introduced in intergovernmental transfer systems to deal with externalities in local government provision. Earmarked or matching grants can be used to ensure that at least part of the costs and benefits of provision can be fully internalised by local residents. As a result, the service provider is compensated by having the share of delivery costs that exceeds the benefits of provision that can be internalised by local residents covered by the donor. Of course, in practice, the design of such grants is complicated by the fact that externalities are not directly observable. Matching grants may therefore exceed the level required for mitigating the disincentives for provision arising from cross-border spillovers. These grants may also be complex to administer.

There are a number of successful country experiences in the use of grants and transfer schemes to internalise inter-jurisdictional benefit and cost spillovers. The Dutch reform of 2004 is instructive in this regard. The pre-reform grant system had encouraged the municipalities to overspend in social protection, because they could set the level of benefits and the central government would reimburse them for the attendant expenditure needs in the form of grants. The current system attenuates this perverse incentive by introducing a block grant for social protection based on risk factors related to income and unemployment levels in different jurisdictions. Another example is the introduction of a block grant in Denmark in 2002-04 to finance municipal spending on old-age care, which aimed at encouraging cost-effectiveness in local government provision.

Ensuring transparency and administrative simplicity

Transfer systems tend to be formula-based, especially in so far as general-purpose grants are concerned. This makes arrangements transparent and predictable, which facilitates budget planning at the local level. However, formula-based systems are not without pitfalls. In some cases, formulas are based on parameters such as the size of the resident population. An example of this practice is the calculation of grants to finance local government administrative costs in the Czech Republic, in place since 2005. This mechanism assumes that service delivery costs rise monotonically with population; as such, it may discourage the local authorities from cutting costs on the basis of gains of economies of scale, unless they are free to allocate the associated cost savings to alternative uses.

There is a trend towards simplification of grant and transfer systems. This is especially so in countries where current arrangements are administratively cumbersome and where local government autonomy is curtailed by restrictive conditionality in the design of intergovernmental grants and transfers. Simpler systems based on block, as opposed to conditional, grants and transfers go in the direction of enhancing local self-government by allowing recipients greater autonomy in setting local policy and the level of provision.[18] Nevertheless, the use of a single transfer instrument to meet different objectives (equalisation and subsidisation of service delivery to correct for spillover effects, for example) may pose problems.[19] The Swiss reform of 2004 addressed this issue by replacing earmarked grants by general-purpose transfers for equalisation and using earmarking for the attainment of policy objectives other than equalisation.

Another consideration is a possible loss of accountability to donors, which would run counter to efforts to use grant/transfer systems to align policy objectives across the different layers of administration.

Local Government Indebtedness and Financial Management

The level of local government indebtedness in relation to GDP does not elicit concern about the longer-term sustainability of local public finances in Europe. The implications of local government indebtedness for macroeconomic fiscal management are therefore limited. Only in a few countries, such as Denmark, Iceland, Italy and Netherlands, does the stock of local government liabilities amount to close to or above 10 percent of GDP (Figure 5.7 and Table 5.4). Local governments in these countries, with the exception of Latvia, also hold sizeable assets, such that their net debt position is low in relation to GDP. In other countries, net local asset-to-GDP ratios are large, as in France and Italy.

Low debt positions are due to a large extent to restrictions on local government borrowing. In some countries, fiscal rules may ban local governments from borrowing altogether or issuing bonds, whereas in others there are constraints on the size of local government budget deficits (Annex 5.2).[20] In most cases, local governments are only allowed to borrow to finance investment (golden rule). In some countries, golden rule provisions apply to long-term borrowing, whereas short-term loans (often in the form of bridge financing across budget years) may be used to finance operating expenditures. This is the case of Estonia and Lithuania, for example.

Local government borrowing is also subject to prudential regulations. These regulations are often based on debt service and loan repayment capacity, as well as the level of

18. *For example, Norway's system of revenue sharing has changed, resulting in an ongoing reduction in the municipal spending share and less reliance on earmarking of transfers from the central government. Furthermore, following the changes in the cost calculation system for the municipalities, additional funds have been set aside by the central government to compensate individual municipalities penalised by the new system.*
19. *See Carlsen (1995) for a discussion of the Norwegian reform of 1986.*
20. *See Sutherland et al. (2005) for a typology of sub-national fiscal rules in OECD countries.*

Figure 5.7: Central, Regional and Local Debt as a Percentage of GDP

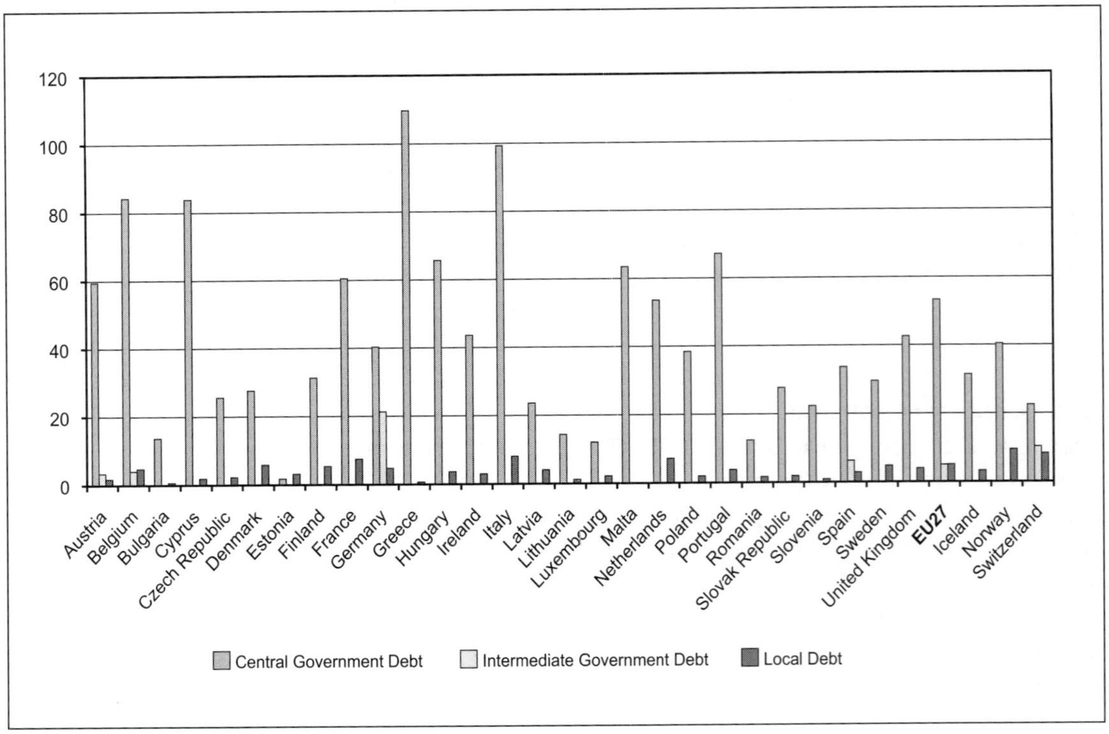

Sources: Eurostat (February 2010), national sources and DEXIA calculations

indebtedness in relation to local revenue. Guarantee of local government liabilities by higher-level jurisdictions is often banned as a means of safeguarding overall fiscal sustainability and imposing hard budget constraints at the sub-national levels of government. Restrictions are also in place in most countries on the type of collateral allowed in local government debt issuance. Guidelines and recommendations on local government indebtedness are also available from the Council of Europe.

Administrative controls on local government financial management are being replaced by prudential regulations. A case in point is that of the United Kingdom's 2004 Local Government Act, which replaced pre-approval requirements for local government borrowing in England, Scotland and Wales by prudential regulations on debt service capacity. The legal framework for local government borrowing has also been strengthened in many countries, as illustrated by Bulgaria's Municipal Debt Act of 2005 and a government resolution issued in the Czech Republic in 2004. Administrative restrictions have also been loosened in the Greece with the issuance of the 2006 Municipal Code.

Restrictions on local government borrowing and access to financial markets have implications for financial management, including over the business cycle. Such restrictions often make local budgets overly pro-cyclical, because local governments may find it difficult to smooth cyclical fluctuations in revenue associated with the business cycle.

Table 5.4: Local Government Indebtedness, 2008 (% of GDP)

	Budget balance (Net borrowing/lending)				Consolidated gross debt (Maastricht definition)				Local government net debt[1]		
	General	Central	State	Local	General	Central	State	Local	Assets	Liabilities	Net debt
Austria	-0.4	-0.6	0.1	0.1	62.6	59.5	3.4	1.8	6.0	1.8	-4.1
Belgium	-1.2	-1.6	-0.1	-0.1	89.8	84.3	4.1	4.8	2.1	4.9	2.8
Bulgaria	1.8	2.0	-	-0.4	14.1	13.7	-	0.7	2.0	1.3	-0.7
Cyprus	0.9	-2.6	-	0.0	48.4	83.9	-	1.9	0.3	2.1	1.7
Czech Republic	-2.1	-2.4	-	0.0	27.8	25.6	-	2.3	11.0	4.1	-6.8
Denmark	3.4	3.8	-	-0.4	33.4	27.6	-	5.9	10.1	10.3	0.1
Estonia	-2.7	-2.4	-	-0.6	4.6	1.8	-	3.2	2.9	4.0	1.1
Finland	4.5	0.9	-	-0.2	34.2	31.3	-	5.4	9.9	8.5	-1.4
France	-3.4	-2.9	-	-0.4	67.4	60.5	-	7.5	3.5	8.3	4.7
Germany	0.0	-0.6	0.0	0.2	65.9	40.3	21.3	4.8	5.1	4.7	-0.4
Greece	-7.7	-8.3	-	0.0	99.2	109.7	-	0.7	0.8	0.7	0.0
Hungary	-3.8	-3.6	-	0.2	68.7	65.7	-	3.7	5.7	4.7	-1.0
Ireland	-7.2	-6.8	-	-0.2	44.1	43.6	-	3.0	3.6	3.8	0.2
Italy	-2.7	-2.7	-	-0.2	105.8	99.3	-	8.1	3.3	9.9	6.6
Latvia	-4.1	-4.4	-	-1.3	19.4	23.6	-	4.1	7.2	5.7	-1.5
Lithuania	-3.2	-2.0	-	-0.2	15.6	14.4	-	1.2	3.0	1.2	-1.8
Luxembourg	2.5	-0.2	-	0.0	13.5	12.1	-	2.2	3.4	2.6	-0.9
Malta	-4.7	-4.6	-	0.0	63.6	63.5	-	0.0	0.3	0.2	-0.1
Netherlands	0.7	0.5	-	-0.4	58.2	53.6	-	7.2	7.4	8.9	1.5
Poland	-3.6	-3.9	-	-0.2	39.9	38.4	-	2.0	8.9	3.7	-5.2
Portugal	-2.7	-3.3	-	-0.1	66.3	67.2	-	3.8	1.6	4.5	2.8
Romania	-5.4	-4.4	-	-0.9	12.2	12.4	-	1.7	1.5	2.5	1.0
Slovak Republic	-2.3	-2.7	-	-0.1	28.7	27.7	-	1.9	4.1	2.5	-1.6
Slovenia	-1.8	-1.2	-	-0.6	22.5	22.3	-	0.9	2.9	2.0	-0.9
Spain	-4.1	-2.8	-1.6	-0.5	39.7	33.7	6.3	2.9	2.3	4.7	2.4
Sweden	2.5	1.4	-	0.1	33.6	29.6	-	4.8	11.0	9.4	-1.6
United Kingdom	-5.0	-4.8	-	-0.2	43.5	42.6	-	4.0	2.7	5.5	2.8
EU27	**-2.3**	**-2.3**	**-0.1**	**-0.2**	**61.5**	**53.3**	**5.0**	**5.1**	-	-	-
Iceland	-13.6	-13.0	-	-0.9	34.7	31.4	-	3.3	9.2	10.6	1.4
Norway	18.8	20.0	-	-1.2	49.9	40.4	-	9.5	8.5	12.8	4.2
Switzerland	2.2	1.1	0.8	1.1	41.1	22.5	10.3	8.3	-	-	-

1. Refers to 2005 for Luxembourg and 2007 for Cyprus, Iceland and United Kingdom.

Sources: Eurostat, national sources and DEXIA calculations

Local governments are often called upon in support of nation-wide fiscal stabilisation programs. In Portugal, for example, constraints began to be imposed on local government indebtedness in the context of the adjustment efforts that were put in place in 2001, when the budget deficit ceiling under the Stability and Growth Pact was first breached. The Austrian National Stability Pact of 2005 is another initiative towards sharing the burden of adjustment across the different levels of government, with the introduction of budget balance targets for the three layers of administration. Italy's Internal Stability Pact introduced constraints on sub-national debt and expenditure growth, including for the municipalities with at least 5,000 inhabitants. Germany's reform of 2006 also introduced provisions for sharing the burden of adjustment under the Stability and Growth Pact between all levels of government (Table 5.4).

Policy Challenges for European Local Governments

The Effects of the Global Crisis on Local Government Finances

Short-term effects of the global crisis

The global financial and economic crisis that erupted with the collapse of Lehman Brothers in September 2008, and the ensuing sharp slowdown in economic activity in 2009-10, put pressure on local government finances.[21] The main channels through which local governments have been affected by the global crisis are *i*) lower revenue (from own taxes, shared taxes and transfers from higher levels of government, which are only in part mitigated by stimulus packages in some countries); *ii*) higher spending associated with rising unemployment and heightened demand for social protection; and *iii*) tighter financial conditions, including through a shortage of credit and costlier borrowing, where allowed, in the aftermath of the crisis. Needless to say, the relative importance of these channels has varied from country to country and among local governments.

The slowdown in economic activity, which was very pronounced towards end-2008 and in the first half of 2009, took its toll on local tax revenue. This is especially the case in countries, such as the Nordic countries and some transition economies in Central and Eastern Europe, where local governments rely on taxes on income, profits and capital gains, which are very elastic to fluctuations in the business and financial cycles. A weakening of construction activity and falling housing prices are also affecting local revenue performance in countries that have experienced housing booms in recent years, including Iceland, Ireland and Spain, where local governments are particularly reliant on property or property transfer taxes.

At the same time, local budgets have suffered from poor collection performance at higher levels of government, even in countries where own local tax bases are not particularly sensitive to fluctuations in business activity and in the price of financial assets. This is because in most countries local governments rely on revenue-sharing schemes, grants, and transfers from higher levels of administration, often in the form of a fixed share of revenue. Uncertainty over the level of transfers from the central government is also expected to have a bearing on local budget-making and planning in countries where such transfers are negotiated, rather than based on a fixed proportion of central government revenue, and account for a large share of local budgets, as in Lithuania and Greece, for example. This is especially so as post-crisis fiscal consolidation is pursued in earnest in

21. *See CEMR (2009b) for an analysis of the effects of the global crisis on Europe's local authorities and for the Council's views of how the local governments could be involved in the nation-wide policy responses to the crisis. See also CDLR (2009) for more information based on a survey of European local administrations.*

those countries where the effects of the crisis on public finances have been most adverse.

Turning to expenditure, local government finances have been affected adversely by heightened demand for selected social assistance and labour market-related services, whose provision is under their purview. A number of labour market programs, including unemployment insurance, in some countries, reintegration programs and training facilities for the unemployed, have traditionally been delivered by local governments, the role of higher levels of administration being restricted typically to setting benefit rates and (partially) funding provision.[22] Demand for these services has risen in tandem with the unemployed rate, which the OECD projects to peak among the organisation's member states in 2010 (OECD, 2010). Expenditure on these services is likely to be particularly onerous to local governments in countries where these authorities play a leading role in the provisions of social programs, such as Belgium, France, Germany, Netherlands, and the Nordic countries.

Local governments have participated in the implementation of stimulus packages that have been put in place in many countries in response to the global crisis. To the extent that these packages have included public investments that are delivered through the local authorities, they have required financial assistance from higher levels of government – often in the form of conditional grants and liquidity support, by bringing forward the payment of transfers and allocation from higher levels of administration – to ensure a smooth implementation of the support packages, as in most European countries.[23] According to OECD estimates (OECD, 2009b), public investment hikes accounted for most of the spending programs announced during 2008-10 in Czech Republic, Finland, Germany, Netherlands, Poland, and United Kingdom. Support for local public investment was particularly strong in Austria, Germany, Portugal, and Spain. This is important, because local governments account for about two-thirds of public investment in Europe (over 70 percent in France and Italy).

Post-crisis budget sustainability considerations

Local governments in most European countries were hit by the global crisis in a fairly benign fiscal environment. As a result of steady growth and comfortable financial conditions, public finances in most Western and Southern European countries had strengthened considerably prior to the crisis. Budget outcomes had improved in general, and public indebtedness had fallen in relation to GDP. By contrast, many countries in Central and Eastern Europe were undergoing comprehensive fiscal consolidation to ensure the sustainability of their public finances. Fragile fiscal positions had made these economies particularly ill-suited to weather the effects of the global financial turmoil that culminated with the crisis in September 2008 and the ensuing rapid deterioration in investor sentiment.

Public finances deteriorated sharply following the crisis. The OECD projected the headline budget deficit of the Euro-area countries to rise from close to 2 percent to about 7 percent of GDP during 2008-10 (OECD, 2010). Budget deficits rose sharply in Europe as a whole in 2008-09 as a result of the economic slack brought about by the crisis and to accommodate a wide range of anti-crisis measures. Given that there are lags in tax collection and in the implementation of stimulus packages, the effects of the crisis on the budget (at all levels of administration) are likely to persist over the near term.

22. See OECD (1999) for more information.

23. See Blochliger et al. (2010) for more information on the policy responses at the local level of administration on the basis of a survey conducted with local authorities. Despite considerable differences among the local governments across – and often within – countries in the mix of instruments used, the policy responses to the crisis appear to be counter-cyclical in most countries.

The sharp deterioration in budget positions across the continent will call for remedial measures in the form of fiscal retrenchment over the medium-to-longer term. The magnitude and timeframe of fiscal consolidation will vary from country to country, depending primarily on the initial level of debt, the size of the stimulus packages put in place in response to the global crisis and the speed of recovery in economic activity. In any case, fiscal consolidation efforts are likely to affect local governments. This is particularly the case of local authorities that are heavily reliant on discretionary grants and transfers from higher levels of government, which may also be unable, or unwilling, to support local authorities financially and may have strong incentives to offload unfunded expenditures on local budgets in the course of adjustment. More recently, several European countries have announced fiscal consolidation programs to restore the longer-term sustainability of their public finances, which was compromised by the effects of the global crisis and the ensuing recession, including cuts or freezes in transfers to sub-national levels of administration.

But local budgets may also stand to gain from fiscal consolidation at higher levels of government. Those local authorities that rely on a fixed share of revenue collected elsewhere may actually benefit from revenue raising measures implemented at higher levels of government in support of fiscal adjustment. Local governments that rely on market-based sources of finance would also benefit from nationwide fiscal retrenchment to the extent that it improves financial conditions and contributes to a recovery in credit growth and an improvement in market sentiment towards riskier assets, such as local government debt.

Long-term Challenges Facing Local Governments

Most European countries are confronted with the challenge of coping with the effects on public finances of a rapidly ageing population and the need to integrate immigrants into the labour market and society at large. These are long-term challenges that cut across the different layers of government and are particularly important at the local level. This is because, in many countries, the provision of social services, including active labour market policies, are under the remit of the local authorities.

In many countries a rapidly ageing population is continually shifting the demand for goods and services provided by local governments. The share in population of individuals aged at least 65 years is close to 16 percent on average in the European countries under examination in this chapter, which is among the highest in the world. The United Nations projects the old-age dependency ratio to nearly double to 46 percent of the European population during 2010-50. Demographic trends are particularly trying in Southern Europe, where birth rates are well below replacement ratios and population growth rates (excluding immigration) are already negative. This is also the case of the transition economies of Central and Eastern Europe, where demographic decline can be attributed only in part to net emigration.

Demand for health and old-age care is rising and delivery costs are putting increasing pressure on the public finances, often at the local level of administration. The OECD estimates that, even with cost containment measures, public (all levels of government) spending on health and long-term care could rise from 6-7 percent of GDP in 2005 in the OECD area as a whole to around 10 percent by 2050.[24] In some countries, the increase could be dramatic. At the same time, the provision of other services, such as child care and education, which has traditionally been in the remit of sub-national governments, continues to weigh on local governments. To a certain extent, demographic decline will alleviate some spending pressures, especially if selected services, such as primary schooling, are scaled back in tandem with falling demand.

Immigration and the integration of long-term residents are creating claims on local budgets. In Southern Europe, where net emigration was the norm until relatively recently, immigrants already account for a high share of the labour force. The proportion of foreign-born individuals in the population of Greece and Spain, for example, is over 10 percent. Immigration is particularly challenging for local government finances in countries where the local authorities play a leading role in the provision (and financing) of housing, employment and related social assistance services, which are in high demand among immigrants. This is despite the fact that immigration is mitigating some of the effects of adverse demographics in many countries, including labour shortages in selected sectors, rising age dependency ratios and a contraction in the pool of workers contributing to social security.

Overall Assessment

Local Government Expenditure Mandates

There is a great deal of variation in the assignment of expenditure functions to local governments among European countries. In general, local governments focus on expenditures that are local in nature, so that the benefits of provision can be internalised by residents. But it is rather difficult in practice to unbundle expenditure functions according to the geographical reach of the benefits they generate. In some cases, not only the benefits, but also the costs of local government expenditures spill over across jurisdictional borders. This possibility calls for intergovernmental financial arrangements to remedy the incentives that local authorities would otherwise face to refrain from supplying these goods and services or to shift the burden of provision to other constituencies. The examples discussed above illustrate the numerous arrangements put in place in several European countries to deal with these important policy issues.

Improved inter-governmental coordination is needed to deal with rising expenditure pressures at the local level of government. Demand for local services, including the provision of selected health care, is rising due to population ageing and technological change. This trend is particularly challenging in Europe, where many countries are already facing the difficulties arising from a rapidly ageing population. This is also the case of social services associated with the absorption and integration of immigrants in some countries, who already account for a comparatively large share of the labour force in many European countries. Dealing with these challenges goes beyond the realm of policies that can effectively be put in place by local governments. But *there is a need to boost coordination among the different levels of government to devise workable, cost-effective solutions to these problems that would take into account local government expertise in service delivery and their ability to extract information on residents' preferences and needs.*

Regulation of service delivery by higher levels of government needs to recognise the benefits of local self-government. It is important to rely on regulations and norms set by higher levels of government to

24. The OECD argues that most of the upward pressure on long-term health care will come from non-demographic factors, including effects from technology and relative prices. See OECD (2006) for more information.

ensure that minimum standards are met throughout the national territory. But overly restrictive, top-down regulations often thwart the potential for decentralised provision to enhance cost-effectiveness by exploiting differences in regional preferences, in addition to undermining the scope for decentralization to strengthen accountability of local officials to taxpayers. This drawback is particularly important in the case of intergovernmental financial arrangements that focus on the equalisation of expenditure and/or the use of conditional grants for the financing of local government expenditure. *Policymakers should therefore make sure that top-down regulations do not curtail their ability to tailor service delivery to local preferences and needs, which may vary across regions, especially in territorially diverse countries.* A related issue is that of cost shifting across levels of government, which often arise when top-down regulations impose a financial burden on local budgets. *When unfunded, such intergovernmental cost shifting should be banned.*

At the EU level, efforts to expand the internal market need to take local choice into account. The provision of public services has come under increasing scrutiny from the European authorities as they seek to expand the European internal market.[25] Tensions have therefore often arisen with sub-national governments in matters that they perceive as within the remit of their self-government prerogatives. A European Charter on Local and Regional Services of General Interest was proposed in 2009 to deal with this matter. Against this background, *effort should be stepped up to reconcile initiatives towards building an internal market with the need to preserve local preferences and choice.*

Options will need to be considered for dealing with inter-jurisdictional spillovers and economies of scale in service delivery. For example, there may be cases where local provision creates considerable inter-jurisdictional externalities that cannot be solved effectively through the use of earmarked, conditional or matching grants, and/or where options to allow local governments to make the most of economies of scale to reduce service delivery costs may be limited. In these cases, there can be a rising temptation to recentralise service delivery. Nevertheless, an option that is more in tune with local government preferences in most countries includes an array of cooperative ventures among local governments, such as inter-municipal consortia. *While taking country specificities into account, greater cooperation is needed among local governments, and between local governments and higher levels of administration, to search for mutually beneficial solutions.*

Local Government Revenue

As in the case of local government expenditure functions, there are important differences in the assignment of revenue to local governments in Europe. In some cases, local budgets are financed by local sources, as in the case where broad tax bases are delegated to the local authorities or shared among the different layers of government. An alternative arrangement is to assign a limited number of sources of revenue to the local authorities, which would then rely predominantly on transfers and grants from higher levels of administration. But, as far as the experience in Europe is concerned, there does not appear to be a strong relationship between the composition of local government revenue and budget outcomes, including the size of budget imbalances, the level of

25. *Public services, including those that affect individual citizens' quality of life, sustainable economic development or social/regional cohesion, are known in EU jargon as Services of General Interest (SGIs) or Services of General Economic Interest (SGEIs).*

26. *See de Mello (2000) for a review of the literature and some cross-country empirical evidence.*

indebtedness, and the level of local government spending. This is not the case for other parts of the world, where the design of intergovernmental fiscal relations has often not been conducive to fiscal discipline at the different levels of administration.[26]

With regard to own revenue sources, the assignment of tax bases across the different layers of government is in general broadly in line with public finance principles. Local governments tend to collect immobile taxes, such as those on property, and fees for services provided locally, which are the ideal sources of revenue for local governments. In some cases, nevertheless, as in the Nordic countries and transition economies of Central and Eastern Europe, mobile bases, such as personal and corporate income, are assigned to the local governments. *The experience of several countries suggests that, while the PIT works quite well as a local tax or when its revenue is shared between different levels of government, the CIT is best managed by the central government*.

There may be scope for raising local revenue through user charges and fees for services. The experience of several countries is that the provision of local services free of charge (without making the corresponding costs perceptible to users) encourages excessive demand. Co-payments may therefore be used to extract information on users' willingness to pay, which is useful for local government to gauge the marginal cost of services that would otherwise be difficult to price, and to raise revenue that could be used to alleviate supply constraints. But concern that co-payments may hinder access by selected social groups to local services has often discouraged local governments from levying charges and fees for services. *While recognising the constraints imposed by specific country environments, local authorities should continue to evaluate the costs and benefits of user charges in their efforts to raise revenue.*

Fiscal Rules and Intergovernmental Financial Arrangements

Fiscal rules are effective in instilling fiscal rectitude at lower levels of government to the extent that they are complemented by effectively designed intergovernmental financial arrangements. Constraints on local government borrowing and indebtedness should therefore be accompanied by effort on the part of policymakers at all levels of government to enhance the incentive structure underpinning the assignment of revenue and expenditure functions to local governments and the complementary arrangements for intergovernmental transfers and grants. As a general principle, intergovernmental grants and transfers should not be perceived as gap filling or vehicles for higher level of government to bail out jurisdictions in financial distress. European countries fare well in this regard, as evidenced by the comparatively sound financial position of local governments before the crisis.

There is nevertheless scope for improving the design of fiscal rules for local governments. On the one hand, rules that restrict local government access to credit markets may encourage local governments to rely on bank lending as a source of finance or to bypass restrictions on debt issuance. In this case, *the option of replacing such restrictions by more comprehensive prudential regulations based on debt repayment capacity that do not distort policymakers' choice over financial instruments should be considered*. On the other hand, borrowing constraints or balanced budget provisions make it difficult for local governments to smooth the budgetary impact of fluctuations in the business cycle. This is especially the case of local authorities that rely on cyclical revenue, through own collections or sharing arrangements with higher levels of government. Thus *balanced budget provisions could be redefined on a cyclically adjusted basis, so long as local governments have access to budget financing from non-government sources in bad times and instruments to save cyclical revenue windfalls in good times*.

Conclusions

Europe has a long tradition of decentralised fiscal management. There now appears to be a broad commitment to self-government, reinforced by the issuance of the European Charter of Local Self-Government and the recognition by the European Union of the principle of subsidiarity in the treaties of Maastricht, Amsterdam, and Lisbon. Nevertheless, tensions sometimes understandably occur between the local authorities and higher levels of administration, including middle-tier governments, on policy areas where the assignment of functions across the different levels of administration is not easy to delineate or rapidly evolve. To a large extent, existing intergovernmental fiscal relations are rooted in history, but they are not immutable. The return to democracy in many countries (such as in Central and Eastern Europe), the need to deal with regional diversity, and the ensuing pressures for policy autonomy (as in Belgium, Italy, Spain, and the United Kingdom), or economic imperatives, such as the recognition that public provision may be more cost-effective when it best reflects local preferences and needs, have sustained the momentum of decentralization in Europe.

Notwithstanding considerable achievements in this area, this paper argues that important policy challenges remain for local governments in Europe. In particular, emerging expenditure pressures, such as those related to population ageing and immigration, are already bearing down – and will continue to do so – on local budgets. At the same time, local governments are being affected by fiscal consolidation in most countries following the sharp increase in public indebtedness as a result of the global crisis and the ensuing recession. Moreover, continued effort will be needed to align policy objectives across the different layers of administration in the design of intergovernmental financial arrangements so as to ensure that decentralised fiscal management and service delivery are cost-effective, cooperative and consistent with principles of local self-government.

European Regional Policy Recommendations

Europe's local and regional governments will wish to respond to the major fiscal challenges and pressures which now confront them. In particular, they will need to consider how to engage effectively with central governments, with a view to maintaining the maximum scope for local and regional self-government for the coming decades. Some key points are likely to be:

- Local and sub-national governments should not take a disproportionate share of the fiscal reductions over the coming years, whether via reduced local revenue or through cuts in inter-governmental transfers;
- There should be recognition that local governments have generally less fiscal flexibility than national governments, and for the most part have not incurred high levels of indebtedness;
- Central governments should also recognize that local authorities generally have major social welfare obligations, which cannot be escaped while unemployment and other poverty indicators are high, are pro-cyclical in impact, and over which they have little direct control;
- Central and sub-national governments should together recognize the need for good quality future-oriented capital investment, mainly financed by new debt, e.g. on greening the future economy and urban infrastructure;
- In most countries, the local government tax base should be broadened to give more fiscal room for maneuver and protection from excessive income losses from any one source;
- Local governments should have more freedom to raise fees and charges;
- Grants from central governments should be fewer (i.e. of a more general character), only ear-marked in exceptional cases, and provided without imposing undue administrative and regulatory burdens;
- The EU needs to make its internal market and public procurement rules less centralised and intrusive, with more scope for local choice on local services, and with less detailed prescription. The cohesion policies must be preserved.

At the same time, local and regional governments will need to think very carefully about how to do the best for their citizens within the reduced resources available. This means that they may have a common interest in looking at new ways of delivering public services cost-effectively, and at new ways of reducing administrative costs. The range of options must depend on local choices, whether by increased inter-communal cooperation, by some outsourcing or PPPs, by sharing some services between different levels of government, and so on. There will need to be an even greater emphasis on being responsive to the citizens and users of services.

European Regional Policy Recommendations (cont.)

The important point will be for local and regional governments to be proactive in all of these issues, and not cede the initiative to central governments. The role of national associations of local and regional governments is of particular importance, since they can give advice and training to their members, directly or through daughter companies, as well as negotiate with central governments.

Amongst the points for discussion with central governments, local authorities will often wish to emphasize that:

- Where territorial reforms are being considered in order to enhance efficiency and cost-effectiveness, priority should be given to supporting inter-municipal forms of co-operation, rather then centrally imposed amalgamations which often do not respect local needs and identities.

- It is essential that there are effective and fair arrangements, involving all levels of government, for co-ordination and negotiation on financial and fiscal issues, in particular on the rules for and amounts of financial transfers, grants and redistributed resources (in particular equalisation processes), but also covering the policy frameworks for all major services / competences.

- It will probably be wise or even necessary to try to reach some form of "settlement" or compromise with central governments, based on protecting key principles of self-government (see Article 9 of the European Charter of Local Self-government, 1985).

We should also not ignore the European Union, which is playing an increasingly important role in relation to economic policy, cohesion funds as well as the rules for public services. Here too, there is a need for effective and fair co-ordination arrangements, involving the European Commission and the representative associations of local and regional government. The purpose would be to evaluate the financial, administrative and regulatory impact of EU laws and policies on sub-national governments and seek improvements in the framework.

Recommendations developed by the representatives of European Local Governments Associations in the workshop on GOLD II in the city of Sceaux (Paris, March 2010)

2010©gérard fagot

6. Latin America

Jorge Martínez-Vázquez*
Georgia State University, U.S.A.

* *I am thankful to Gustavo Canavire-Bacarreza and Gabriel Leonardo for very able assistance and Harold Vasquez-Ruiz and Mark Curtis for conducting additional background research. I am also thankful to Andrew Nickson, Paul Smoke, Edgardo Bilsky, Claire Frost, Eduardo Stranz, the FLACMA technical team, and many others attending the UCLG regional workshop in San Salvador in February 2010 for helpful comments on previous drafts.*

Local governance and the municipality have a long history and tradition in Latin America going back to colonial times.[1] It was only after the 1980s, and for many countries only in the last decade, that genuine decentralization reform efforts have come to invigorate and enhance the role of local governments. However, despite some significant progress to date, many challenges still remain for municipalities to play a vibrant and meaningful role in the delivery of public services and to contribute to improve the daily lives of Latin American citizens.[2]

In the last two decades the Latin American region has seen a general trend toward an increased level of fiscal decentralization. Using the measure of sub-national expenditures as percent of national expenditures, fiscal decentralization increased from an average of 13 percent in 1985 to 19 percent in 2005; using the measure of sub-national expenditures as percent of GDP decentralization increased from 5.5 percent in 2000 to 6.6 percent in 2007. However, there are significant variations in these trends across countries in the region.[3] Overall, increased decentralization can be detected in the devolution of new responsibilities which includes the environment, the fight against poverty, and an increase in decentralized expenditures for education, health, etc. Less progress can be detected in the devolution of autonomous revenue sources.

Recent times have seen a variety of innovations in the region that have attracted interest from all corners of the world, such as ranking systems' local performance in Brazil and Colombia, per client based transfers for health and education in Chile, or fighting poverty with direct transfers to families administered by municipalities in Brazil. A good number of countries have embarked or are considering significant reforms that that will further strengthen municipal autonomy. For instance, Bolivia has recently approved a new Constitution to allow for better representation of different ethnic groups at the sub-national level; Uruguay lately introduced a third tier of government made up of 89 new municipalities; and Costa Rica only just approved the "*Ley General de Transferencia de Competencias y Recursos a los Municipios*" which provides the ability to transfer 10 percent of the national budget resources to the municipalities, clearing the way for local governments to assume new competencies and improve the quality of services and infrastructure. In El Salvador the association of municipalities (COMURES) is maintaining an active dialog with central authorities to increase the funding and general stability of the general transfer system (FODES) which represents between 70-80 percent of local budgets, and was expected to reach 9 percent of the national budget in 2009 but because of the crisis it attained only 7.5 percent of the national budget.

On the other hand, there are countries in the region where some trends have moved toward some forms of recentralization. For example, in Argentina the Law of Economic Emergency of 2002 and the Budget Law of 2006 have given central authorities increased discretion to assign federal funds or unilaterally interrupt their disbursement. In the Dominican Republic there have been elements of recentralization with the Municipal Law of 2007 establishing fixed budget shares for different types of expenditures on personnel, services, public infrastructure, and so on; it is also feared that the new constitution will lead to the general transfer fund of 10 percent of the state budget established in 2003 (but never implemented). Similarly, in Peru recent

1. *See United Cities and Local Governments 2008 GOLD I report.*
2. *The effectiveness of decentralization efforts has varied considerably across countries of the Latin America region. In the last decade, decentralization has moved at a fast pace in countries such as Colombia and Peru but it continues to be stagnant after several decades of planning and legal measures in countries such as the Dominican Republic and Haiti. Besides Brazil and all the Spanish-speaking countries of Latin America, this paper covers also Haiti, Jamaica, and Trinidad and Tobago. As shorthand, all the countries will be addressed in this paper as Latin America.*
3. *See, for example, Daughters and Harper (2007).*

legislation has revoked the municipalities' prerogative to issue building licenses and rezoning of land use. The regular transfer funds allocated to municipalities have been significantly reduced from 2009 to 2011 (a decline of 22 percent in the last five years). In Colombia, the central government has recently decided to directly allocate resources for water and sanitation that until then had been assigned to municipal governments (through a fiduciary fund administrated by Central Government). Finally, in Venezuela the municipal authorities have been denouncing the continuous curtailment of competencies and resources and the increasing encroachment of the central authorities in local matters.

This report takes an in-depth look at the current state of the local public finances in the Latin America region, identifies and analyzes some of the main challenges for improving efficiency, equity and effectiveness in the delivery of public services and for promoting development and it closes by offering a set of observations concerning policy reform.[4]

Structure and Performance of Local Government Finances in the Region

Countries in the region are highly diverse along a number of dimensions: federal versus unitary, size, colonial tradition, etc. This diversity is found first among the four federal countries in the region: Argentina, Brazil, Mexico and Venezuela. Among the countries with a unitary system we can identify clusters of countries with more similar institutions and current challenges, including the Andean countries (Colombia, Ecuador, Peru and Bolivia), the generally smaller countries of Central America, the Island States with non-Iberian traditions,[5] and what we could call the southern cone exceptions (Paraguay, Uruguay and especially Chile) because of their approach to fiscal decentralization. The diversity is also found in population size (from the 196 million of Brazil to the one million of Trinidad and Tobago), in real GDP per capita (from $9,357 in Argentina in 2007 in constant 2000 US dollars to $884 in Nicaragua and only $411 in Haiti), and in other dimensions.

However, there are also many common features in the way municipalities are structured, which enables us to observe all municipal governments in the region from a common perspective. An important feature is that for those countries with more than one tier of sub-national government, the relationship between the central government and the municipalities is for the most part directly between these two levels as opposed to the central government dealing exclusively with the regional and local governments and then the latter dealing exclusively with the municipalities.[6] In most cases, the legal status of the municipalities is clearly stated in the constitution or specialized laws, such as municipal codes. The most important exception to this rule is Argentina where the constitution gives the intermediate level government, the provinces, discretion to structure the fiscal arrangements with the municipalities.[7] To a lesser extent the same story is repeated in Mexico.[8] Thus, the key difference in explaining the different approaches to central-local relations is between "federal" and "unitary" nations. But even in the federal cases, the issues currently facing municipal governments are not essentially different from those being faced by the rest of the municipalities in the region. For this reason, the report will not make a point of identifying the different groups of country experiences but instead we will use a common framework for all countries,

4. *The focus of this report is on fiscal decentralization. Issues of political and administrative decentralization for the most part are not covered.*
5. *Naturally, these countries are not usually classified as "Latin" America.*
6. *In the technical parlance the vertical relationships between different levels of government are bifurcated (central to local and central to regional, separately) as opposed to hierarchical (central to regional to local, all linked).*
7. *In contrast, for example, the Brazilian Constitution defines its political system as the union of the central government, the states, and the municipalities, thus giving local governments an autonomous standing vis-à-vis the intermediate level governments.*
8. *Brazilian states also have some limited role in managing the municipalities.*

Table 6.1: Decentralization in Latin America: Political and Territorial Organization (2007)

Country	Levels of gov. (#)	Govt. level names	Intermediate Level (level 2)	Local Level (level 3)	Average Population Level 2	Average Population Level 3	Population in the largest city (% of urban population)	Population in urban agglomerations > 1 million (% of total population)	GDP per capita (current US$)
Argentina	3	federal, provincial, municipality/department	24	2218	1,654,436	18,804	35	39	6645
Bolivia*	4	national, department, municipality/canton	9	327	1,058,277	29,126	26	32	1378
Brazil	3	federal, state, municipal	27	5564	7,041,481	34,169	12	39	7013
Chile	3	national, region, municipality	(15)	345	1,109,075	48,220	39	34	9851
Colombia	3	national, department, municipality	32	1102	1,386,232	40,253	23	35	4684
Costa Rica	3	national, canton	(7)	81	636,968	55,046	46	29	5891
Dominican Republic**	3	national, province, municipality	(32)	155	306,677	63,314	32	22	4210
Ecuador	3	national, province, canton	22	221	606,446	60,370	29	32	3432
El Salvador	3	national, department, municipality	(14)	262	436,197	23,308	39	23	3336
Guatemala	3	national, department, municipality	(22)	333	606,989	40,101	16	8	2548
Haiti	3	national, department, commune	10	140	97,008	6,929	45	21	640
Honduras	3	national, department, municipality	(18)	298	398,563	24,074	..	..	1671
Jamaica	2	national, parish		14		191,128	..	..	4802
Mexico	3	national, state, municipality	32	2454	3,290,016	42,902	23	34	9715
Nicaragua	3	national, department, municipality (+ 2 special regions)	(17)	153	35,003	3,889	..	..	1023
Panama	3	national, province/comarca, district	14	75	238,810	44,577	53	38	5828
Paraguay	3	national, department, canton	17	231	360,390	26,989	51	30	1995
Peru***	3	national, region/special province, province/district	26	1834	1,096,480	15,544	39	28	3771
Trinidad and Tobago	2	national, region/borough/city		16		83,013	..	..	16351
Uruguay****	2	national, department (municipality)	19	89	174,942	37,347	49	45	7297
Venezuela	3	national, state, municipality	24	335	1,145,125	82,038	12	32	8299

Note: # computed using the number of jurisdictions in level. Between brackets when the authorities are not elected.

* *In Bolivia, there are departments, provinces (not elected authorities: 112), municipalities and territories of traditional peoples "territorios indígenas originarios campesinos" (incorporated in the new constitution)*

** *In the Dominican Republic, recent constitution reforms recognize 229 municipal districts as local governments*

*** *In Peru, are two kinds of municipalities: provincials and districts.*

**** *In Uruguay, municipalities were created in 2009 by constitutional reform.*

Sources: UCLG data collection, World Bank

identifying particular country experiences as lessons of what needs to be avoided or what may be replicated.

The Structure of Local Governments

As a rule the vertical structure of government in Latin America is organized in three tiers of government (Table 6.1), with the exceptions of Bolivia that has four levels, and Jamaica and Trinidad and Tobago that have two levels[9]. The focus of this paper will be almost exclusively on the lowest tier of government: the municipalities. The intermediate levels (States, provinces, regions and departments) will be referred to only in issues relevant to the municipalities.

As of 2010, there were over 16,000 municipal governments in Latin America. Their number by country obviously varies with population size and territory, with Brazil counting 5,564 municipalities and at the other extreme 16 municipalities for Trinidad and Tobago. Local governments vary considerably in size in each country (Table 6.1).

Even though a significant share of the Latin American countries' population live in the largest cities (for example, 53 percent in Panama, 49 percent in Uruguay, 40 percent in Peru, and 35 percent in Argentina), the majority of municipalities in the region remain, for the most part, small in size and of a rural nature. For example, in Peru over 200 municipalities have populations under 1,000 inhabitants, and over 50 percent of all municipalities have fewer than 5,000 inhabitants. Thus the region faces challenges at the two extremes: massive metropolises with high levels of population density, congestion and rings of urban poverty; and very small municipalities in rural areas with low density, little administrative capacity and lacking an appropriate scale for the provision of many basic public services.

In many Latin American countries the structure of local governments continues to be work in progress. In the case of Bolivia, the new 2009 Constitution declares autonomous governments at the regional, municipal, and indigenous community level, with the added facet that indigenous communities may fit in one or more municipalities or regions. The legal norms regulating this structure have not yet been enacted. The proliferation of new local governments, almost always through the fragmentation of existing ones, continues to be quite common in the region. For example in the Dominican Republic, between 1995 and 2006 the number of municipalities rose from 108 to 155.[10]

Local Expenditures and the Assignment of Competencies

The scope of local government expenditures: The local government share in total public expenditures and in GDP differs significantly by country but they are generally lower than those observed in other regions of the world. However, as shown in Figure 6.1, the share of the public sector in GDP as measured by total expenditures of the general government is rather high, and at levels above those of other countries in the world at similar levels of per capita income. This contrast of proportionately smaller local government sectors in otherwise larger overall public sectors may be explained first, by fewer functional expenditure responsibilities being assigned to local governments in comparison with other regions of the world, and second, by relatively lower levels of expenditure and service provisions in those expenditure

9. In the case of Bolivia, the provincial level may not be interpreted as an additional autonomous level.

10. A recent law in that country has imposed stricter requirements for new potential municipalities requiring that they have 15,000 residents and be able to generate at least 10 percent of the revenue that their previous municipality was raising.

Figure 6.1: Local Expenditure as a Percentage of GDP and General Government

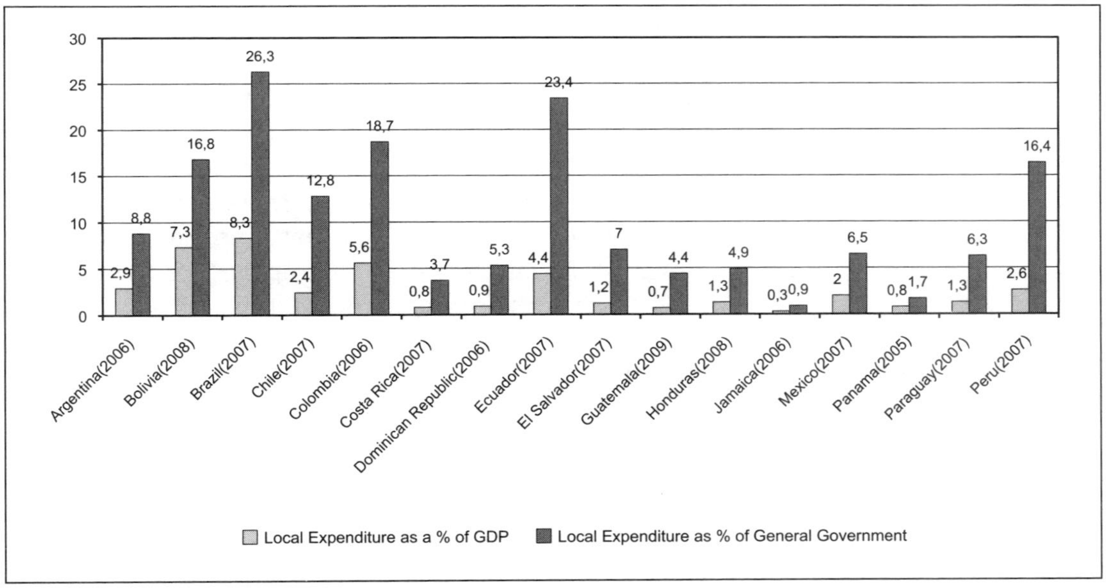

Sources: IMF, Ministries of Finance of Argentina, Bolivia, Guatemala and Peru, UCLG data collection (cf. Annex 6.2)

responsibilities actually assigned to local governments, as discussed below.

As shown in Figure 6.1, there are large differences between the share of local governments in total public expenditures and the relative importance of local government expenditures in GDP. Among the most decentralized countries, as measured by the municipal share in total public expenditures are: Brazil, Ecuador, and Colombia[11] at around 20 percent, followed by Peru and Bolivia at about 16 percent and Chile with 12.8 percent. Two large federal countries, Argentina and Mexico stand at 8.8 percent and 6.5 percent, respectively. At the low end we find unitary countries that are still highly centralized such as many Centro-American and Caribbean countries (from 7 percent in Salvador, to 1.7 percent in Panama and 0.9 percent in Jamaica and between them Dominican Republic, Honduras, Guatemala, Costa Rica).

Perhaps a more meaningful measure of local governments' role as providers of public services is the share of local expenditures in overall GDP (Figure 6.1). This variable measures the percentage of national resources channelled through local governments. From this perspective, Brazil at 8.3 percent and Bolivia at 7.3 percent, Colombia at 5.6 percent (see note 14) and Ecuador at 4.4 percent are currently the most municipally decentralized countries in the region, while Argentina, Peru, Chile and Mexico account for between 2 and 3 percent of the GDP. At the bottom stand more centralized countries: Paraguay, Honduras, El Salvador, Dominican Republic, Costa Rica, Panama, Guatemala, and Jamaica, around 1 percent of GDP.

The assignment of expenditure competencies: Several features characterize expenditure assignments in Latin American countries. First, with the exception of Argentina,[12] all countries have explicit

11. *For Colombia, if departments as intermediate local governments are added to the municipalities, then in 2008 local expenditures represent as much as 29 percent of general government expenditure and 9.5 of GDP.*

12. *In Argentina, each province regulates the expenditure responsibilities of municipalities differently. The provinces, in general, tend to enumerate a set of general functions accompanied by a clause that may be used to expand local competencies. Much less frequently the provinces explicitly enumerate the functions that municipalities must fulfill or functions exclusively assigned to them.*

assignments for municipalities in their national laws. In most countries, as shown in Annex 6.1, the expenditure assignments are defined in the country's constitution; otherwise, the assignments are specified in special laws, most commonly some form of municipal code.[13] Often, in these formal assignments, municipalities are allowed to provide any services not specifically assigned to any other level of government.[14]

Second, there are enormous variations in the assignment of responsibilities to municipalities; the assignments represent a mosaic of approaches, which as shown in Annex 6.1 defy generalization. Most countries provide for a set of obligatory functions, often exclusively assigned to municipalities. These range from basic urban services such as garbage collection, road maintenance, parks, market stalls and slaughter houses, and so on, as well as some administrative functions such as, civil registry, land planning, and housing permits. In addition, most countries provide voluntary functions, which often are co-shared with other levels of government. These may include some social services, such as basic education, primary health services, and public utilities, such as water and sewerage services. But as can be seen in Annex 6.1, in some countries (Colombia, Guatemala, Jamaica) basic education and primary health can also be designated as obligatory and exclusive responsibilities of local governments.[15]

Third, in some countries (for example, Bolivia and Chile) the central governments, while retaining the obligation of financing social welfare services (such as social security, unemployment compensation, and welfare payments), have delegated the implementation and management of several social programs (e.g., family welfare services) to local governments in order to exploit the advantage of proximity and better information local governments have.[16] Municipal governments in many Latin American countries play a large role in the public investment of infrastructure at the sub-national level often as equal partners with upper level governments in patterns similar to those observed in European countries. For example, in Brazil local governments in recent years have undertaken close to 45 percent of all public sector investments.

Finally, many countries in Latin America have concurrent or shared expenditure responsibilities, which generally results in less clarity and potentially more conflict than exclusive assignments.

Revenue Assignments

Practically all countries of Latin America assign certain taxes to local governments; some exceptions are Jamaica, and Trinidad and Tobago. As shown in Table 6.2, the most commonly assigned type is the property tax, although it varies in name and scope across countries.[17] Other local taxes include betterment levies, car registration and car permits, real estate and land transfers, different forms of business licenses,[18] taxes on gambling, and in some form of sales tax or business tax.[19] Practically all local governments are allowed to charge fees for particular public services such as building licenses, refuse collection, public utilities, slaughter houses, and public markets.

Revenue assignments are formalized in different ways, usually in the general tax laws or in special municipal laws. The exceptions are Brazil, where it is established in its national constitution, and Argentina and Mexico, where the constitution delegates to the provinces or states the authority to determine local revenue assignments. This arrangement results in

13. *There are some qualified exceptions to the rule. For example, in the case of Colombia there is no special law assigning expenditure responsibilities at different levels of government, but there are several laws (60 of 1993 and 715 of 2001) that specify certain norms regarding the assignment of competencies.*
14. *A clear exception to this rule is Chile, where municipalities are circumscribed to a closed list of functions.*
15. *In El Salvador basic education and primary health are assigned to the local level, but actual service delivery works through special local mechanisms administrated jointly by the State, the communities and the private sector.*
16. *On the whole these experiences appear to have been positive (Bolivia, Brazil, Mexico and Peru). In the case of Mexico some programs have been critiqued because of partisan interference by central authorities in the deployment of funds.*
17. *Of significant importance is that just a handful of countries allow for the taxation of both urban and rural property. Those countries allowing only the taxation of urban property leave rural municipalities in a disadvantage. Note that the property tax is still assigned to the El Salvador's central government and that there appears to be no property tax in the Dominican Republic, only a property transfer tax.*
18. *A good example is the "patente municipal" in Chile which is paid annually at rate based on the declared own capital assets. This tax is further discussed in the next section.*
19. *In the cases of Brazil's ISS (tax on services) and Colombia's ICA (tax on trade and industry), municipal collections exceed those from the property tax (IBI, impuesto sobre bienes inmuebles). The two countries' experiences with these taxes are also further discussed in the next section.*

Table 6.2: Assignment of Taxes and Fees to Local Governments in Latin America

	Type of Tax		Type of Fees
Country	Property	Others	
Argentina	urban/rural property (and its increased value because of public investment)[1]	car registration, turnover tax	public utilities, fines
Bolivia	urban/rural property	car registration, car/property transfers, slaughterhouse, construction	
Brazil	urban property (including increased value due to infrastructure improvement)	tax on service sector (ISS), registered goods tax, real estate transaction tax [2]	fines, public utilities
Chile	urban property	car registration, alcohol	public utilities, fines, permits
Colombia	urban property (and its increased value because of public investment)	surtax on gasoline, tax on industry/commerce, mineral extraction, slaughterhouse, gambling	public utilities, fines
Costa Rica	urban property		public utilities
Ecuador	urban/rural (and its increased value because public infrastructure investment)	car tags, permits (business, construction),	fines, utilities
El Salvador		Specific taxes for each municipality based on congress approval such as business taxes on industrial, trade, and financial activities	fines, public utilities, fees for services rendered
Guatemala	urban property[3]	tax on wages, advertising (banners), extraction of products/economic activity, alcohol	
Honduras	urban/rural property (and its increased value because of public investment)	tax on turnover of industry and trade, extraction of natural resources (fishing, minerals, oil), slaughterhouses	public utilities, firefighters, fines
Jamaica		Parochial revenue fund	
Mexico	Urban property	Car registration (all other taxes are centralized)	Varies by state
Nicaragua	Urban/Rural property	Sales tax (recently eliminated); patents and business licenses	fines, public utilities
Panama	tax on unused land (urban/rural)	tax on alcohol, economic activity and vehicles	fines, fees (cattle slaughter)
Paraguay	urban property (and its increased value because of public investment)	car registration, games/gambling, wealth tax (corporate), land transfers/subdivision	public utilities

Table 6.2: Assignment of Taxes and Fees to Local Governments in Latin America (cont.)

Country	Type of Tax		Type of Fees
	Property	Others	
Peru	urban/rural property	car registration, car transfer, construction	public utilities, fines
Uruguay	urban property (and its increased value because of public investment)	car registration, gambling, shows	fines, fees for services
Venezuela	urban/rural property	car tags, gambling, economic activity	fines, fees for services

Notes:

1. *Argentina: Not all provinces have delegated property taxes to their municipalities*
2. *Brazil: The ISS is assessed and collected by the municipality at rates set by the municipality but subject to a maximum fixed by federal law*
3. *Tax collection authority is only given to local governments that prove to have the capacity to collect the tax*

a variety of *de facto* assignments in those two countries.[20]

The level of autonomy granted to local governments also varies. As summarized in Table 6.3, most countries use a "closed list" approach and do not allow the introduction of new taxes to local governments; some exceptions include Ecuador and Uruguay.[21] On the other hand, about two-thirds of the countries in the region allow local governments the ability to set the rates of some taxes; this practice is widely accepted as the most desirable form of tax autonomy that can be granted to local governments. It is interesting that countries such as Bolivia and Peru, where decentralization reforms have advanced rapidly in recent years, still grant no discretion to set tax rates. A reduced number of countries in the region grant local discretion to modify tax base. Most countries in the region allow local government discretion in fixing the levels of fees and user charges for local government services. Nevertheless, an important restriction on the revenue autonomy of local governments is the practice by several countries to require local government revenue budgets ("plan de arbitrios") to be previously approved by a higher tier of government prior to the start of the fiscal year. Table 6.3 shows this is still practiced in Costa Rica, Nicaragua, Panama, and Paraguay; in Mexico approval comes at the intermediate level from state governments. In terms of fiscal administration (Table 6.3), the general rule is local government is responsible for the administration of local taxes, fees and charges, although in some cases, tax administration responsibility is shared with the central authorities.[22]

In most countries in the region, the yield from property tax remains far below its potential (Figure 6.2). While on average property taxes raise revenues representing 2.12 percent of GDP in OECD countries, 0.68 percent in transition countries, and 0.60 percent in developing countries, the average yield in Latin America is only 0.37 percent of GDP. The reasons for low performance are multiple, including low political will from national governments, local governments,

20. *In the case of Mexico, the constitution assigns only the real estate tax to the municipalities.*

21. *In Argentina, some provinces may also allow their local governments to introduce new taxes but under quite restrictive guidelines.*

22. *As an exception, it appears that in Bolivia all local taxes are collected and administered by the central authorities.*

Table 6.3: Autonomy Granted in Revenue Assignments to Local Governments and Responsibility for the Collection and Administration of Local Taxes and Fees

Country	Ability to introduce new taxes	Ability to set tax rates within legal limits	Ability to change tax base	Control or veto over local govt. budgets by Central/Regional govt.	Responsibility for the collection of	
					Fees	Taxes
Argentina	Yes	Yes	Yes	No	L	L
Bolivia	No	No	No	Central	C/R	C
Brazil	Yes	Yes	Yes	No	L	L
Chile	No	Yes	Yes	No	L	L
Colombia	No	Yes	No	No	L	C
Costa Rica	No	No	No	Central	PS*	PS*
Dominican Republic	No	No	No	No	C	C
Ecuador	Yes	Yes	No	No	L	L
El Salvador	Yes	Yes	No	No	L	L
Guatemala	No	Yes	No	No	L	C/L
Haiti	na	na	na	na	na	C
Honduras	No	Yes	No	No	L	L
Jamaica	No	Yes	Yes	Central	L	C/L
Mexico	No	No	No	Regional	L	L
Nicaragua	No	Yes	Yes	Central	L	L
Panama	No	Yes	No	Central	L	C/L
Paraguay	No	No	No	Central	L	C/L
Peru	No	No	No	No	L	L
Trinidad and Tobago	No	No	No	No	L	C/L
Uruguay	Yes	Yes	No	Central	L	L
Venezuela	Yes	Yes	Yes	No	L	L

*Note *: Costa Rica collects, in some municipalities, through the private sector.*

L= local, C= central, R=regional, PS= private sector

Figure 6.2: Average Property Tax Revenue Raised as a Percentage of GDP

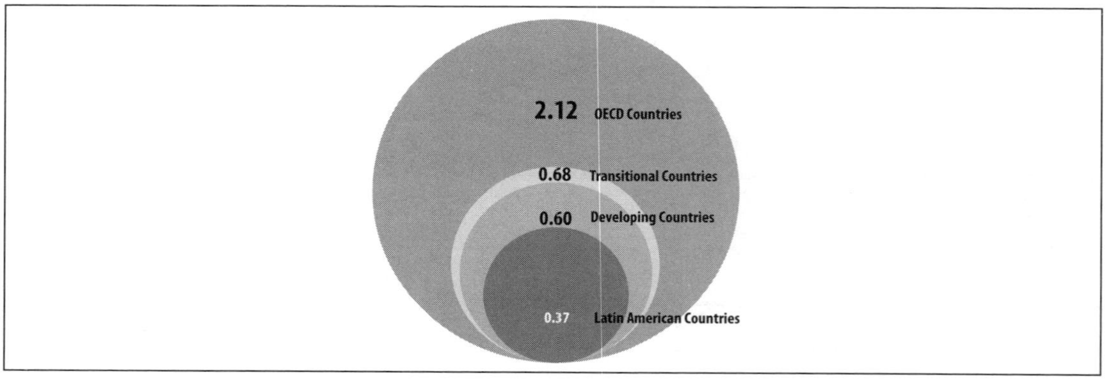

Figure 6.3: Local Revenue as a percentage of GDP and General Government

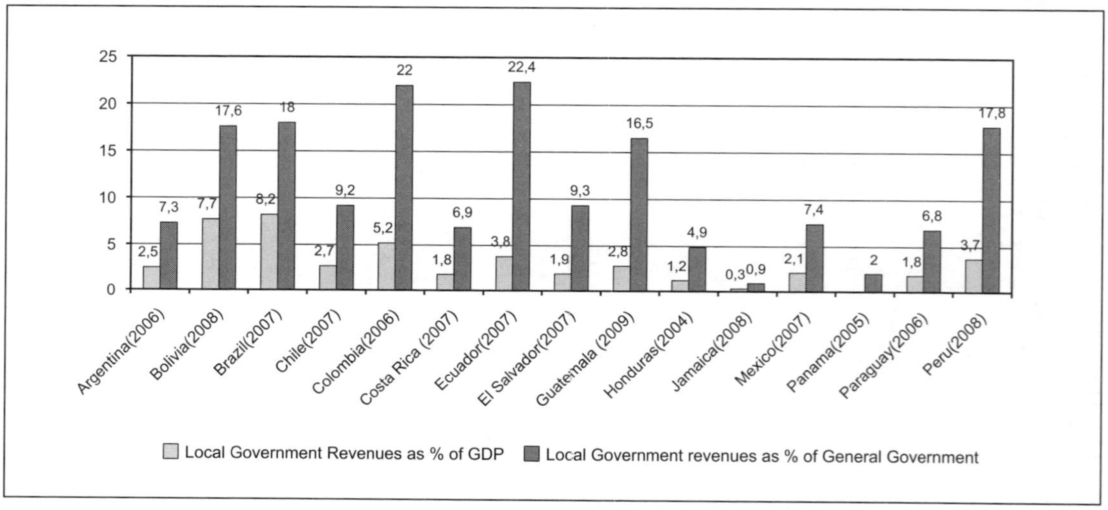

Sources: IMF, Ministries of Finances of Argentina, Bolivia, Guatemala and Peru, UCLG data collection, (cf. Annex 6.2)

Parliament and the disincentive effects of revenue sharing and inter-governmental fiscal transfers (IGFTs), not to mention outdated and poorly equipped tax administrations. These factors translate into generous exemptions and low tax rates, obsolete and infrequent property value assessments, incomplete registries and cadastres and a lack of willingness and means to enforce collections. This lacklustre performance varies little with the different arrangements in the region for discretion on rate setting or administering property tax.[23]

Generally, the range of locally raised revenues from own taxes and fees represent a relatively small share of total consolidated revenues in the public sector, although in terms of local budget shares, these revenues are relatively large.[24] Of course there is a large variation in execution from country to country. Figure 6.3 shows that as percent of national GDP, local governments in Brazil raise 8.2 percent, Bolivia 7.7 percent, Colombia 5.2 percent. Ecuador and Peru stay at 3.8 - 3.7 percent followed by Guatemala and Chile 2.8 - 2.7 percent and then Argentina and Mexico 2.5

23. *For a discussion of the issues, see Sepulveda and Martinez-Vazquez (2009) and De Cesare and Lazo Marín (2008).*

24. *These two effects are compatible if we recall our discussion in the previous section that local government budgets represent a relatively small share of the general government budget.*

Table 6.4: Shares of Local Own Revenues (in percentages)

Country (Most recent year)	Own taxes and fees as % of local revenues	Local own taxes and fees as % of GDP
Argentina (2006)	49.8	1.2
Bolivia (2008)	11.4	2.7
Brazil (2007)	20.1	1.8
Chile (2007)	63.0	0.7
Colombia (2006)	41.2	2.1
Dominican Republic (2006)	58.4	0.7
Ecuador (2007)	34.6	1.6
El Salvador (2007)	13.2	0.3
Haiti (2004)	25.0	0.5
Honduras (2004)	11.1	0.2
Jamaica (2008)	100.0	0.2
Mexico (2007)	15.6	2.4
Nicaragua (2002)	44.0	0.6
Panama (2005)	49.0	0.3
Paraguay (2006)	34.1	1.2
Peru (2008)	43.2	2.6
Trinidad and Tobago (1995)	52.9	0.1

Sources: UCLG data collection.

- 2.1 respectively. At the lower end stand El Salvador, Paraguay, Costa Rica, Honduras, and Jamaica (less than 2 percent).[25]

However, on average, municipalities raise a higher percentage of their budgets from their own revenues similar to Africa, Asia and a good portion of European countries. As shown in Table 6.4, the percentage of local budgets financed out of their own taxes and fees is quite high, at or above 25 percent for many countries.[26] However, in Bolivia, Brazil, El Salvador, Honduras, and Mexico the share is much lower in relation to the other countries in the region.

Intergovernmental Transfers

As a result of limited fiscal autonomy, practically all local governments suffer from vertical imbalances, i.e. the expenditure needs arising from their functional competences exceed their ability to self finance. Although the existence of vertical imbalance is not in dispute, their actual measure is generally a polemical issue because practically no country in the region has introduced explicit methodologies to measure the expenditure needs of local governments in a transparent and objective manner. In order to address the exis-

25. *See Annex 6.2 for the breakdown of revenues collected by each tier of government.*

26. *See Annex 6.3 in the Appendix for the breakdown of sources for revenues of local governments.*

ting vertical imbalances, practically all countries in the region should implement a range of fiscal transfers, often consisting of different forms of revenue sharing, an array of specific or conditional grants, and in some cases, equalization grants.

In addition to vertical imbalances, in practically all countries in the region there are also significant horizontal imbalances between local governments. These imbalances are the result of the different tax capacities and economic development of local governments, and the different expenditure needs arising from disparities in the service delivery costs and the differing resident populations' needs arising from their diverse characteristics. Horizontal imbalances are most pronounced between urban and rural municipalities and between smaller and larger urban centers. As we see later, different approaches are used in the region to address these horizontal imbalances.

The emphasis throughout the region has been to address the problem of vertical imbalances through different forms of revenue sharing via central government tax collections. There has been less emphasis on the design of explicit equalization grants, although, quite often, revenue sharing formulas contain equalization features. Conditional grants are less common in Latin America than in other regions of the world, but here again there are important exceptions.

Most countries in the region use some form of *general revenue sharing.* The pool of funds to be shared is most frequently defined by total central government revenues, although in some cases particular taxes are excluded from the pool. This is the case for Bolivia, Colombia, Dominican Republic, El Salvador, Guatemala, Honduras, and Nicaragua. In other cases, the pool is based on specific central government taxes; for example, 20 percent of oil production fees derived by the Mexican states must be passed on to their municipalities; Nicaragua's additional tax sharing with municipalities is based on revenues from natural resources; and in Peru, some of the tax sharing is from portions of the sales tax, and proceeds from gas and oil extractions (*canon*, *sobrecanon*, and *canon petrolero*). In the latter, actual shared revenues are subject to considerable market fluctuations, for example, international price levels for natural resources.

In some cases, shared revenues are distributed on a derivation (i.e. origin) basis, for example, the *canon*, *sobrecanon*, and *canon petrolero* in Peru. This approach (sharing revenues from natural resources on a derivation basis) has become a significant factor for regional horizontal fiscal imbalances. Most often some sort of formula is used for the distribution of resources that includes several variables, some of which, as noted above, may have equalizing features.[27] For example, in Bolivia revenue sharing is based solely on population; in Ecuador it is according to population and relative poverty levels; in El Salvador it is according to population, "equity" (a fixed amount for each municipality), poverty, and land surface area; in Guatemala it is distributed according to a formula that includes equal shares (fixed amounts), population, number of settlements, and per capita income; in Honduras it is according to population and equal amounts for all municipalities; in Nicaragua it is according to population and several other criteria; and in Peru it is according to population and infant mortality rates. Frequently, the formulas are also employed by central governments

27. In some cases, like in Paraguay, the allocation of funds is still ad-hoc at the discretion of the central authorities.

Figure 6.4: Composition of Local Government Revenue

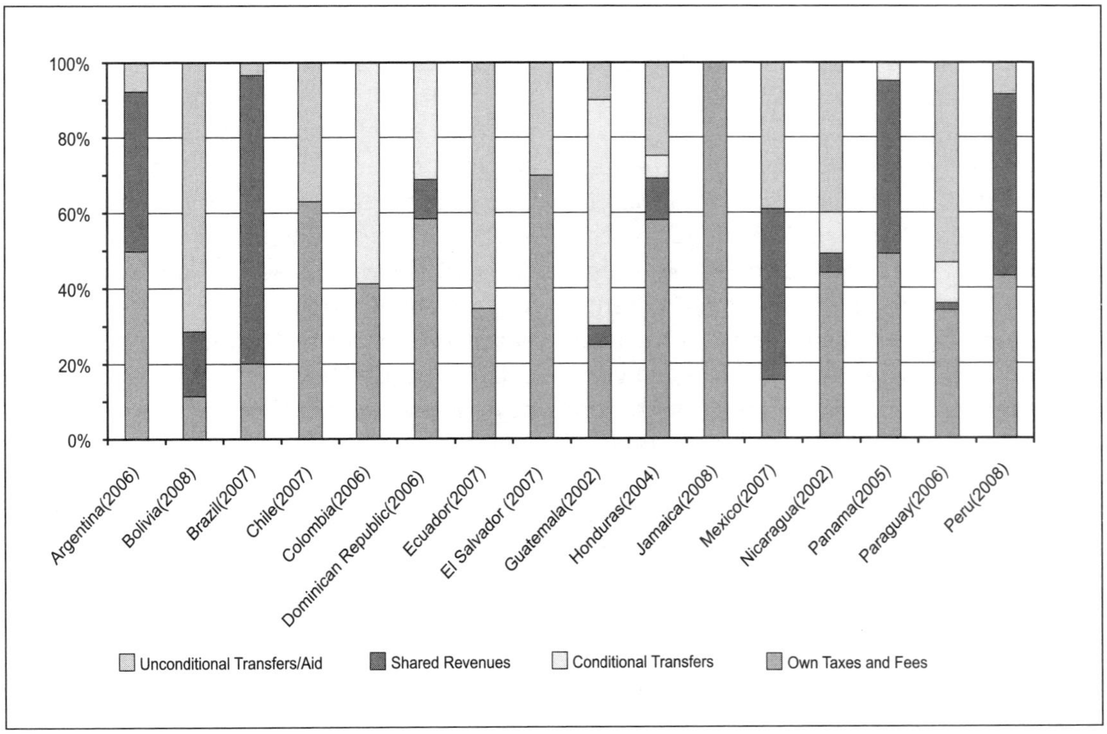

Source: UCLG data collection, (cf. Annex 6.6)

to pursue several objectives other than equalization. For example, in Ecuador the sharing formula includes elements for rewarding administrative effort and achieving goals in the national development plan, while in Nicaragua the formula provides incentives for increasing revenues from property tax and for achieving more effective budget execution.

Some countries allow unconditional use of shared revenue, including Bolivia, Ecuador, El Salvador, and Honduras. In other cases the use of funds is conditional; Colombia uses revenue sharing funds earmarked for basic education, health, and water and sewerage; Guatemala, for education, health and infrastructure; while in Nicaragua and Paraguay, a share of the funds –80 percent in the latter case– must be spent on infrastructure investment.

Revenue sharing practices in the federal countries also have different features. In Argentina, tax sharing with local governments is carried out exclusively by the provincial governments, which can decide how to distribute their share of federal VAT and income taxes. The Brazilian states also have a tax sharing system funded with 25 percent of their regional VAT revenues, which distributed 75 percent on a derivation basis according to value added in the municipalities, and 25 percent by a formula based on population, land area, and other variables. This same formula is used to distribute federal tax sharing with the states (cooperation funds) to the municipalities. In Mexico, the states are required to distribute to their municipalities at least 20 percent of the income that they receive from revenue sharing in the federal funds (*Fondo de Fiscalización and Fondo General de participaciones*). Mexico also has a federal grant, amounting to 1 percent of federal collections (*Fondo de Fomento Municipal*) that is distributed on the basis of municipal revenue collections.

Conditional or specific transfers are less extensively used in Latin American than in other regions of the world,[28] nevertheless their use is increasing, especially in those countries where central governments count on being associated with local governments as partners for the delivery of certain services and the implementation of national programs. For example, Bolivia has introduced a conditional health transfer for a national program in support of infants and mothers (*seguro materno infantil*). In Brazil, several conditional grants have been introduced for public transport (funded by the sharing of federal fuel levies), basic education, and health services, including hospitals from the national health system. In Chile several highly conditional grants have for many years funded local governments' activities in education, health, and other social programs. Some conditional grants are earmarked for certain geographical areas that are deemed to be lagging behind. For example, in Ecuador there is a conditional capital investment grant for the Amazon region.[29]

A particular subgroup of conditional grants is earmarked for investment in local infrastructure. For example, El Salvador offers grants for municipal capital infrastructure based on the presentation of project proposals. In Guatemala one-eighth of VAT revenues go to infrastructure in social and basic services, while a share of vehicle taxes is earmarked for maintenance of roads and drainage. In Mexico, at least 20 percent of the investment grants (*Fondo de Compensación*) from the federal government must be assigned to the poorest ten states in the country and used by the municipalities of those states.

The practice of explicitly addressing horizontal disparities among local governments through equalization transfers is still not common but it is taking hold in the region. One reason for the slow introduction of explicit equalization grants is that often revenue sharing schemes do incorporate some equalization elements in their allocation formulas. Several examples of existing equalization grants (above and beyond revenue sharing schemes with some equalizing elements in their formulas) are worth mentioning. One is Bolivia's HIPC (Heavily Indebted Poor Countries Initiative) transfers started in 1997 with funds from international organizations (the World Bank and the IMF) that is distributed by the central government to local governments using a formula based on the poverty level and population of municipalities. In Brazil, there is a federal equalization transfer to the municipalities funded with a share of federal VAT and income tax revenues; the fund is split into two parts, with 10 percent going to state capital municipalities (distributed according to population and the inverse of per capita income) and the other 90 percent to the rest of the municipalities (distributed according to an index that favours municipalities with smaller populations). An interesting approach is that of Chile, where the formula driven equalization grant (the Common Municipal Fund) is funded by the municipalities' own revenues from different sources in what is known in the technical parlance as a "fraternal" (or Robin Hood) system, in which the relatively richer municipalities finance the transferred amounts to the poorer municipalities. The allocation formula includes population size, poverty levels, exempted real estate property, and past revenue collections. One key positive feature in all these examples is the recognition of the need to introduce a

28. *Here we are referring in a conventional way to specific funds assigned to particular objectives and administered separately by central government agencies. This is interpreted as being different from the conditioning or earmarking of revenue sharing funds. As we have seen above, a number of countries in the region condition the use of revenue sharing funds to investment in infrastructure and so on. If the restrictions in the use of revenue sharing funds were included in the general category of conditional transfers then the practices in the regions would not be that different from those in other regions of the world.*

29. *This is a specific instance of larger developmental goals that can be addressed by conditional transfers, such as arid areas, poor areas, unexploited high potential areas, etc.*

Table 6.5: Authority to Borrow by Local Governments in Latin America

Country	Access to Financial Markets	Municipal Bank	Limitations
Argentina	Y	Y	Y
Bolivia	Y	N	Y
Brazil	Y	N	Y
Chile	N	N	n.a
Colombia	Y	n.a	Y
Costa Rica	Y	n.a	n.a
Dominican Republic	N	Y	Y
Ecuador	N	Y	Y
El Salvador	N	Y	Y
Guatemala	Y	n.a	Y
Haiti	n.a	n.a	n.a
Honduras	Y	Y	Y
Jamaica	N	N	Y
Mexico	Y	N	Y
Nicaragua	Y	n.a	Y
Panama	n.a	n.a	n.a
Paraguay	Y	N	n.a
Peru	Y	N	Y
Trinidad and Tobago	N	N	n.a
Uruguay	Y	N	Y
Venezuela	Y	Y	na

Source: UCLG data collection.

separate instrument (equalization grants) to address the separate objective of horizontal inequalities arising from different expenditure needs and fiscal capacity.[30] A key common challenge ahead is the need to improve the methodologies used to quantify the expenditure needs and fiscal capacity of the different local governments. [31]

Borrowing

Given their expenditure responsibilities, most municipalities have a long-term need to finance capital infrastructure. Local borrowing can be considered a legitimate, efficient, and equitable source for financing this local infrastructure. However, it is also widely accepted that the local borrowing process must be subject to explicit rules and limitations in order to ensure fiscally responsible behavior by local officials and to guarantee macroeconomic stability in the country.[32] Commonly applied rules include those about expected behavior, such as the "golden rule" that long-term borrowed funds must be used for capital infra-structure only, and not for recurrent

30. *The use of a fraternal system to fund the equalization transfers in Chile is a promising innovation. This is a common system to a number of European countries but it is uncertain how easily it will be adopted by other countries in the region.*

31. *For the available methodologies used in other regions of the world see, for example, Martinez-Vazquez and Searle (2007).*

32. *Historically this wasn't always widely accepted in some countries in the region, which in past decades saw an accumulation of macroeconomic difficulties associated with unfettered sub-national borrowing in some of the federations and politicized government-run municipal development banks.*

expenditures, and different quantitative budgetary limits on borrowing. Among the latter, there are rules on non-negative current budget balances, limits on the level of total debt and debt-service payments as a percent of budget revenues, as well as restrictions on borrowing abroad.

For a variety of reasons, ranging from fiscal conservatism to negative past experience, not all countries in the world allow their local governments to borrow. Yet in the case of Latin America, as shown in Table 6.5, most countries do allow local governments to borrow.[33] Practically all countries allow such borrowing even though they impose rules and limitations on local borrowing similar to the above-mentioned international "good practice" guidelines. In most cases, foreign borrowing is not allowed, in some cases it is allowed with permission of the higher authorities, and in other cases even domestic borrowing requires administrative approval by higher level authorities.[34] Over time, national systems have adapted to idiosyncrasies. For example, in Nicaragua, municipalities are able to contract short or medium term loans from public and private banks for public works, with long-term loans for large-scale public works approved by the National Assembly. Loans must be repaid within the term of the elected officials; mayors and municipal councils may not leave debts to their successors, except for long-term loans approved by the National Assembly. In Colombia, law 358 from 1997 introduced a system of "semáforos" (traffic light) restricting the level of local debt according to the ability to pay by the local units; if interest payments are below 40 percent of the operational surplus and if the debt level is under 80 percent of current revenues, local governments are free to borrow according to the law; however, they require permission from the Ministry of Finance if any of those limits is exceeded. With law 819, which came into effect in 2003, the need to have a primary surplus sufficient to cover on going debt service was added to the existing indicators. The three indicators must be positive in every year of the loan, and this must be reflected in the medium term fiscal framework of the municipality or department. In El Salvador, municipalities can borrow from commercial banks once they receive the proper quality ranking from the Ministry of Finance and the semi-official organization charged with the physical distribution of the general transfer funds. The municipalities then establish an intercept agreement for those transfers to work as collateral for the loans from the commercial banks. As in other countries around the world, it is common to impose limits on annual debt service as percent of revenues (for example 20 percent in Argentina and Bolivia or 40 percent in Ecuador) and/or the total stock of debt as percent of total revenues (120 percent in Brazil or under 100 percent in Ecuador and Peru).

The actual amount of sub-national debt, which includes local and provincial/state debt, is quite low in most countries, with the exception of Brazil and Argentina, where sub-national debt represents in recent times between 10 and 15 percent of GDP; Mexico, Colombia and Bolivia come behind with sub-national government debt representing less than 2 percent of GDP as of 2007. However, for municipal governments alone in recent years, Bolivia is first in debt service (interest and repayment of principal) at around 9 percent of total municipal expenditures, followed by Ecuador at around 8 percent, and Argentinean and Brazilian municipalities, where debt service stands at around 4 percent.[35]

33. *The exceptions include Chile, Dominican Republic, El Salvador, Ecuador, Jamaica and Trinidad and Tobago.*
34. *For example, foreign borrowing by the municipalities in Argentina requires administrative approval at the provincial level and by the Ministry of Economy at the national level, which it has been argued has been subject to political criteria beyond technical aspects.*
35. *See Porto (2009).*

Budgeting

The budgeting process at the local level in most Latin American countries is still carried out along traditional lines with heavy emphasis on incremental budgeting and ex-ante financial audit controls for the disbursement of funds. Much less attention is given to the planning of expenditure programs and ex-post evaluation of the effectiveness of funds disbursed on programmatic goals.[36] One positive aspect without exception is, local budgets need to be approved by democratically elected local councils. However, as we have seen above, in a significant number of countries (Bolivia, Costa Rica, Jamaica, Mexico, Nicaragua, Panama, Paraguay) at least some components of the local budgets need to be approved ex-ante by higher level authorities at the central or regional levels. It is questionable whether or not these approvals are really needed; the best practice internationally is to rely on horizontal accountability mechanisms ex-ante, and on the ex-post audit and to grant full budgetary autonomy to local governments.[37]

"Participatory budgeting" is an area of innovation in the region that has attracted much international attention. The specific meaning of this term varies among countries introducing this type of reform, but generally means additional mechanisms for citizens to influence local budgetary decisions beyond the conventional vehicle of democratic elections for municipal councilors.[38] For example, in Bolivia a 1994 law established citizen committees (*comités de vigilancia*) and community-based organizations (OTBs—*organizaciones de base*), that are social organizations of peasant communities, the indigenous population, and neighborhood groups. Citizen participation at the local level is also important in Brazil, but varies considerably across states and municipalities. One experiment involves groups of citizens empowered to address social and political inequalities by influencing the allocation of budget resources through neighbourhood meetings.[39] Even some provinces in Argentina, have formally adopted participatory budgeting.[40] On the other hand, participatory budgeting is generally appropriate for only certain elements of the budget; thus, even in Porto Alegre (Brazil) the share of the budget subject to this process is limited (see Box 6.6). Nevertheless, the implementation of participative budgeting often depends on the will of the Mayor and the City Council since it is not a compulsory or permanent tool.

As for the composition of municipal budgets, our discussion is based on a small number of countries where data availability varies. In terms of the economic classification of local expenditures, the high share of capital infrastructure expenditures in the municipal budgets of a significant number of countries is notable (Figure 6.5). For example, in both Chile and Ecuador, local governments spend 55 percent of their budgets on capital expenditures; in Guatemala this figure is 64 percent and in Peru, 58 percent. Of course, there are large variations for these figures across countries, including the assignment of expenditure responsibilities—what tier of government is responsible for capital infrastructure in the different areas of responsibility: schools, roads, etc –and the legal restrictions imposed on local governments for how to spend revenue sharing and other types of funds— as in Peru, where local governments only can spend funds from the *canon* and *sobrecanon* from natural resources on capital investments. There is also the possibility that capital expenditures are over reported.[41] Whatever the explanation, it is clear that many local

36. The strong emphasis on ex-ante treasury controls has not, on the other hand, reduced corruption, which, with some exceptions, still appears to be extensive among local governments (and the rest of the public sector) in the region. The difficulties lie more in poor execution of the ex-ante controls than in a deficient design.

37. In some cases controls for checking the legality of actions, as opposed to changing budget allocation decisions, can be justified when horizontal accountability and audit mechanisms are deficient or not present at all.

38. Somewhat related, citizen participation mechanisms such as referendums, "popular initiatives," and elected representative recalls have been operating in other regions of the world.

39. See Afonso (2006).

40. For a positive assessment in the case of Bolivia, see Faguet (2004). See also Goldfrank (2006) and Shah (2007) for general assessments.

41. There are incentives in many countries in the region to report some current expenditure as capital expenditure. For example, in some cases central legislation restricts the share of budgets that can go to recurrent purposes. In other cases, practically all kinds of current expenditures have been demonized as being inefficient so local authorities actually report some current expenditure as actually being some form of capital expenditure. But, fortunately there does not appear to be a problem in Latin America with the off-budget programs and expenditures that are common in other regions of the world, for example Africa and Asia.

Figure 6.5: Budget Expenditure by Economic Classification of Local Governments

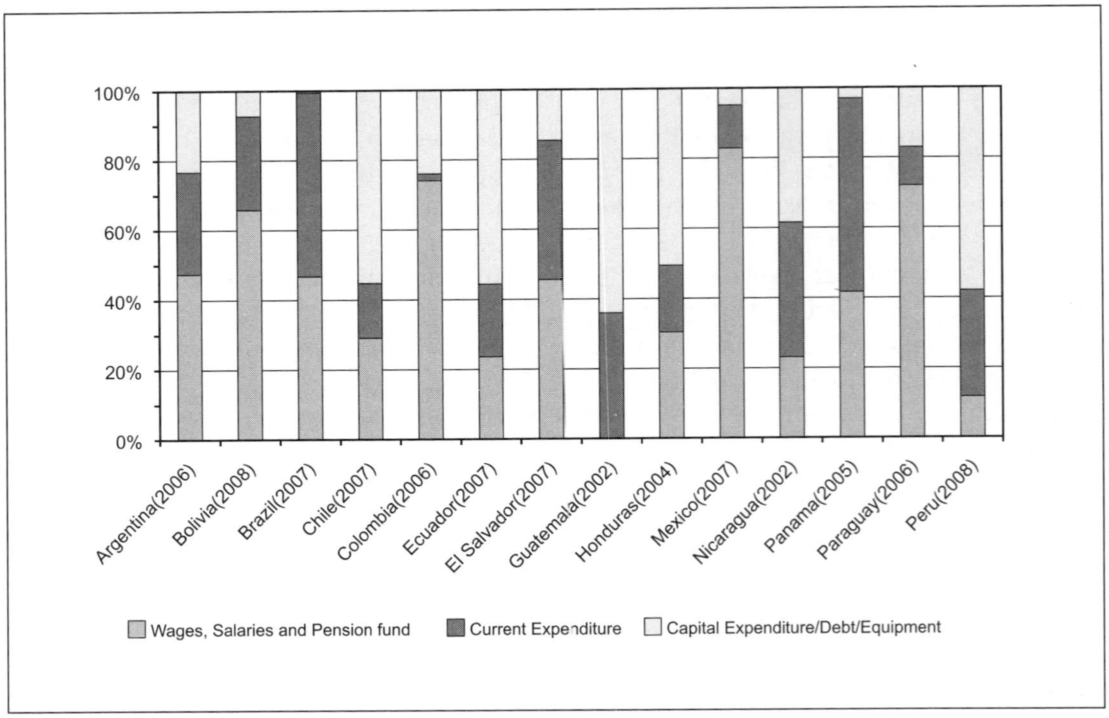

Source: UCLG data collection (cf. Annex 6.4)

governments in Latin America have been given an important role to play in the task of providing much needed infrastructure. This highlights the importance of finding more stable and potent instruments for infrastructure finance.

As we have seen, the movement toward open and participatory budgeting is spreading, increasing budget efficiency and accountability in general. Although participatory budgeting is not directly about decentralization itself, the movement toward participatory budgeting has tended to reinforce decentralized institutions. There are, however, exceptions; for example, in the Dominican Republic, Law 176 of 2007 goes a long way to introduce participatory budgeting but the actual level of decentralization to local governments in that country remains quite weak.

Even less data are available to obtain a panoramic view of the functional classification of local budgets in the region; for countries where individual municipalities' data are available, comparisons are hard because of the different classification methods used in each country. As shown in Figure 6.6, education expenditures, deriving from the assignment of expenditure competencies, are important items in the local budgets of Bolivia, Brazil, Chile and Colombia. For the same reason, expenditures on health services are relatively important in the local budgets of Brazil, Colombia, and Peru, with budget shares here ranging between 16 and 22 percent. It is noteworthy that in most of these countries for which disaggregated data are available, not surprisingly "general administration" is the most important expenditure item in terms of budget shares.

Figure 6.6: Shares of Local Government Expenditure by Functional Classification

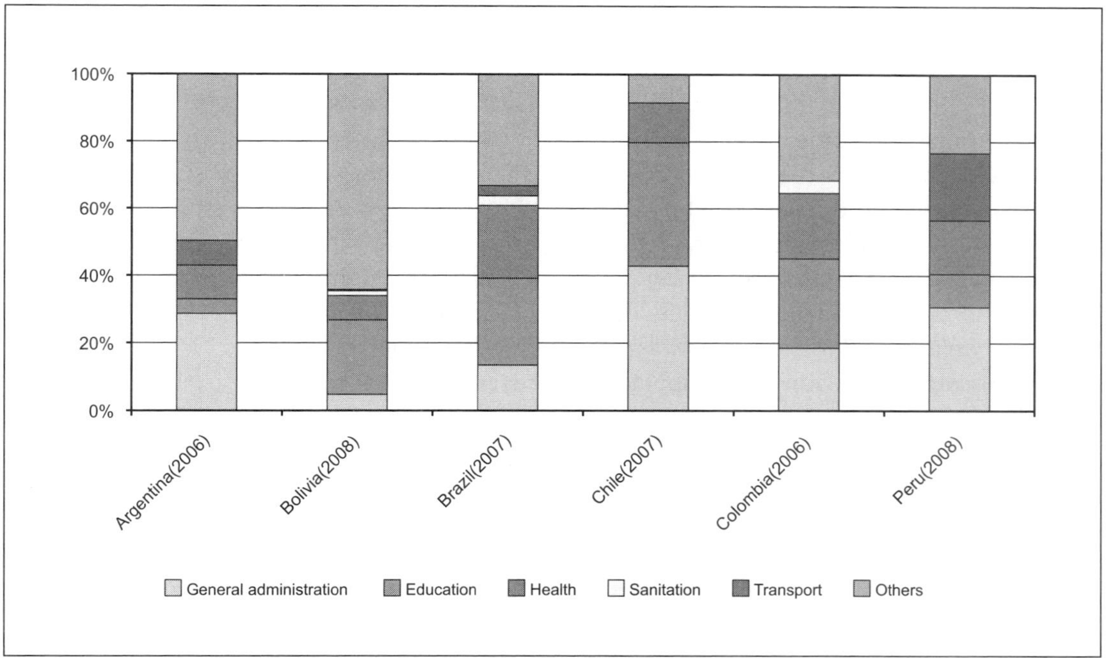

Source: UCLG data collection (cf. Annex 6.5)

Special Issues, Constraints and Opportunities for Local and Intergovernmental Finance in the Region

As shown in the introductory section, the Latin American region offers a vast array of different experiences and approaches to local finance. The kinds of issues facing local governments in large federal countries such as Argentina, Brazil, and Mexico are often very different from those affecting local governments in small countries such as El Salvador, Nicaragua, or Paraguay. Furthermore, there is also significant diversity among the large federal countries as well as among the unitary countries. Hence, the attempt to generalize analysis of local problems and their solutions is neither always possible nor desirable. Nevertheless, some themes common to a significant number of countries in the region clearly emerge from the description of the local finance system presented in Section 1. In this section we identify some of the special issues, constraints and opportunities for the development of local finance in Latin America. It is organized around four major themes: (a) Organizational Structure; (b) Intergovernmental Fiscal System Design; (c) Budget Process and Transparency; and (d) Short Term and Long Term Structural Challenges.

Issues on Organizational Structure

Fragmentation and sub-optimal scale[42]

In many countries there is an ongoing debate on the number and size of local governments related to the issues of economies of scales to deliver public services, which typically improve with size, and citizen representation, which generally deteriorates with size. Citizens that feel marginalized frequently call for the

42. The issues of local fragmentation and administrative capacity have a significant political component and from that perspective they were reviewed in GOLD I. Our main perspective here is on how fragmentation and administrative capacity may affect the fiscal sustainability of local governments.

creation of new municipalities. As the current legal frameworks guarantee a minimum amount of funds to each municipality regardless of size, this has promoted the creation of new municipalities.[43] In response to this problem some countries have introduced legislation requiring minimum population size in order to ensure the future fiscal viability of any new local government. This action can be effective in slowing down the process of further fragmentation but it does not help to address the inadequate scale of the already existing municipalities.

Perhaps a more attractive and potentially equally effective approach is the promotion and creation of associations of municipalities into *mancomunidades* for the delivery of certain public services requiring certain minimum scale.[44] This is an approach still largely unexploited but it is currently being developed in some countries, especially in some provinces of Argentina, southern Brazil, Ecuador, and Peru.[45]

The trade-off between economies of scale and representation[46]

The issue of an optimal scale of local governments presents an inherent tradeoff between the (potential) better political connection in terms of representation and accountability of smaller jurisdictions with the (potential) greater fiscal viability of larger jurisdictions (in particular with regard to population size).

The essence of this trade-off between the greater efficiency of smaller governments that can better match the preferences and needs of local residents in their expenditure allocation and economies of scale in production with lower costs associated with larger governments implies a compromise solution between the two objectives. In particular, it implies that lower cost effectiveness in the delivery of public services may be offset by greater efficiency in responding to the needs and preferences of local residents.

Local administrative capacity

The problem with local governments' administrative capacity is closely associated with their small size (in number of inhabitants). Central governments (or state or provincial governments in the case of federal countries) spend little time and resources in developing the capacity of local governments.[47] Some of the slack has been taken up by local government associations, which, for example in some of the Andean countries and in Central America, provide their members with assistance and training. However, these associations often lack the resources necessary to address this issue. Central (or provincial–state) governments can do much more.

To summarize, there are no exact answers or methodologies to address the issue of optimal size for municipalities. Several goals need to be pursued including cost efficiency and representation and accountability and several constraints need to be met regarding fiscal viability and administrative capacity. See Box 6.1.

Issues on Intergovernmental Fiscal System Design

Lack of clarity in the assignment of expenditure responsibilities to local governments

One of the weakest points of many decentralization programs in Latin America has been the scant attention given to clear assignment of expenditure responsibilities of sub-national governments, which is a crucial first step in the design of any system of intergovernmental fiscal relations. Instead, the focus has been

43. *For example, in El Salvador, the Fund for Economic and Social Development (FODES), which is the main source of local revenues, is distributed according to a formula that distributes 25 percent of the funds evenly to all municipalities.*
44. *However, these programs can be difficult to implement. For example, in El Salvador, the National Plan for Territorial Development and Organization (PNODT) was supposed to promote mancomunidades and general cooperation among local governments which would allow them to lower administrative costs by working together to print jointly needed forms and gathering regularly to share ideas. However, the results are very limited.*
45. *Other approaches to dealing with the problem of inadequate scale include the contracting out to private companies of some services, so that private companies can benefit from sufficient scale by supplying different municipalities, or the creation of 'sector specific' service governments or districts. The privatization of services is being used in several Latin American countries. See Martinez-Vazquez and Gomez (2008) for a discussion of the issues and solutions.*
46. *See Martinez-Vazquez and Gomez (2008) and Imansyah and Martinez-Vazquez (2009) for a more extensive discussion of this issue.*
47. *The Latin America region shows a lower prevalence for Ministries of Local Government/Interior/Home Affairs that are more prevalent in other regions of the world and have a higher presence of special agencies designed to exclusively address the needs of local governments, such as ISEDM y FISDL in El Salvador or INIFOM in Nicaragua. In general, it is easier for these types of specialized agencies to play a supporting and capacity development role than it is for sectoral ministries; the downside is that the specialized agencies tend to pull a lower rank within the government administrations in the bargain for additional resources.*

Box 6.1. Four Possible Criteria to Consider for the Minimum Size of Municipalities

Although the desirable minimum size of municipalities is a complex issue that must be addressed in the historical and political contexts of each country, there are four basic criteria that can be followed as guideline for policy decisions:

(1) *The production/cost efficiency/population criterion.* The international experience shows that unit costs for some public services (such as water or public transportation) can be much affected by scale. Depending on the assignment of expenditure responsibilities, in order to arrive at the lowest cost of production it is required to reach a minimum size in terms of population. Yet we must note that there are other ways to provide services in a cost efficient manner, including buying the services from a larger local government, creating an association between several smaller local governments to produce the service, or even buying the services from a large privatized producer. What this means is that this criterion of a minimum population size should be administered intelligently with flexibility to allow for these other service delivery possibilities.

(2) *The representation/political responsiveness/accountability criterion.* The general presumption is that smaller local governments will generally tend to be more representative and accountable to the residing population. But consideration must also be given to the fractionalization of the population and adequate representation of the minority groups' interest. Population density should also be considered. From an accountability and representative focus it would seem that a simple but useful rule of thumb will be the time required to travel to the location of the municipality building.

(3) *The financial/fiscal capacity criterion.* It seems reasonable to require that any new local government have a minimum level of economic capacity to self finance some of its service needs. Measuring this capacity is not always an easy matter, but it should involve some approximation to the "expenditure needs" and the "fiscal capacity" of each potential municipality and the setting of some threshold for the difference between needs and capacity.

(4) *The administrative capacity criterion.* This can be measured in a number of different ways, but fundamentally qualified personnel available to run the business of the local government efficiently is required.

almost exclusively on putting in place some form of financing scheme.[48] At present, there continues to be too much emphasis in many countries of the region on the decentralization processes simply understood "as the provision of some of revenue sharing and transfers" to local governments, ignoring the fundamental rule that "finance should follow function."

On closer analysis, the assignment of functional responsibilities remains in many cases too general and vague. For example in El Salvador, the municipal code gives authority to municipalities to perform a list of responsibilities that clearly overlap with those also assigned to central government; the same is true in Uruguay. In other cases, the vagueness lies in the

48. *See Bahl and Martínez-Vázquez (2006) for a discussion of the proper sequencing of decentralization reforms.*

way that legislation is implemented (or not implemented). For example, Law 66 of 1997 in the Dominican Republic added primary and secondary education to the responsibilities of local governments; yet real power and decision-making remain with the regional Education and Culture committees, which may be considered a deconcentrated tier of the central government.[49]

Beyond the operational inefficiencies associated with the unclear assignments of functions, an important consequence is the ambiguity in political accountability this situation introduces. The governance implications for attaining the purported benefits of decentralization are quite considerable.

Another problem is that the assignment of expenditure responsibilities in practically all Latin American countries is uniform for all local governments, regardless of their size and administrative capacity. As aforementioned, a good way to address these shortcomings is the creation of associations of local governments into *mancomunidades*. Alternatively, there may be room for asymmetric assignments for municipalities of different size and administrative capacity.

Nevertheless, the highly asymmetric assignment of expenditure responsibilities can lead to confusion. For example, in Ecuador, the Constitution (Article 226) establishes the obligation of central government to transfer functional competencies at the discretion (by voluntary request) of sub-national governments. This means that any sub-national government can request a full or partial competence in a particular area at their discretion, leading to great heterogeneity in central-local relations, thereby compromising the overall effectiveness of intergovernmental coordination. A better practice could be to design two or at most three different packages of expenditure responsibilities that can be devolved to local governments depending on their administrative capacity. However, an important issue with asymmetric approaches is the need for using verifiable criteria, that is, differential assignments must be grounded in something other than political connections.

Another factor contributing to confusion in the assignment of expenditure responsibilities is the common practice of unfunded mandates. Frequently, line ministries may partially decentralize certain competencies to local governments without providing the required resources to implement them properly. There may also be increased reporting requirements on local governments without adequate coordination among central government agencies or the provision of the technical and financial means to make that reporting possible.

A workable system of expenditure assignments, no matter how specific, is developed in the laws and regulations, which always requires coordination and effective dialog between the different levels of governments. Because of the larger number of municipalities, it is important that the voice of these local governments be represented by associations of municipalities. On this front there has been considerable progress since practically all countries in the region have developed effective municipal associations.[50] However, central authorities have not always recognized these associations as strategic partners in improving policy design in expenditure assignments and the strengthening of other components of the fiscal decentralization systems.

49. Although the trend in the region has been toward more devolution of responsibilities to local governments, there are exceptions. For example, Jamaica has been recentralizing functions previously assigned to the local governments (Parish Councils) through the creation of national entities under the tutelage of the Ministry of Local Government, which is in charge of fire protection services, parks and markets.

50. See, for example, the discussion in Porto (2009).

One final issue in the practice of expenditure assignments is the practically universal lack of effective and transparent methodologies to translate the assignment of functional responsibilities into expenditure needs. Sometimes, historical costs (or levels of expenditures prior to decentralization) are used as a guide. Different methodologies are used in other countries around the world, such as the use per-client spending norms or bottom-up cost estimates that could be successfully implemented in the region. The advantage of having some effective method to calculate expenditure needs is that the discussions on and ultimate design of revenue assignments, whether through own revenue or fiscal transfers, becomes more informed and rational.

Insufficient revenue autonomy

The level of tax revenue autonomy of local governments differs quite significantly across Latin American countries. Countries such as Brazil and Chile have relatively high autonomy and countries such as El Salvador, Mexico and Peru have significantly less. But, in general, as it occurs in some other regions of the world (Africa, Asia and many European countries), local revenue autonomy in Latin America remains below what is desirable.

The lion's share of financing for local governments in the region continues to come from different forms of central government transfers including revenue sharing. Transfers have experienced an increase as the most often used form of newly devolved financing responsibility for local governments. With this in mind, some important and correct policies have been adopted for various countries in the region. For example, many countries in Latin America have taken steps to increase their share of own taxes in local budgets. Most have now assigned the property tax to the local level, which is excellent because there are many features that make it an ideal tax.[51] Unfortunately, the property tax remains highly underutilized for a variety of reasons.[52] Several other taxes have been assigned to local governments, including vehicle tax, betterment levies, and different forms of business taxes and licenses. These positive measures should be imitated by countries that still allow little local tax autonomy. Another practice to emulate is the allowance of a certain degree of discretion for municipalities to set the rates of their local taxes, between some maximum and minimum approved levels.

Nevertheless, it is difficult to make a strong case for policy design that allows for a greater degree of tax autonomy when there is a perception that many local governments in the region do not make effective use of the tax autonomy law granted to them. This is most clear in the case of the property tax for which actual revenues collected are a small fraction of the revenue potential.[53] So the realization of more revenue autonomy for local governments may need to be accompanied by a significant improvement in local tax effort. However, it is important to note that low tax effort (known in the region as "pereza fiscal") is a complex problem. First, there is often confusion between low tax effort ("pereza fiscal") and low tax capacity or economic/fiscal poverty of jurisdictions. Establishing the presence of "pereza fiscal" requires a comparison between actual tax collections and potential tax collections of every particular jurisdiction; this is a complex task in many cases. Second, once the presence of "pereza fiscal" can be established, it is important to understand its multiple roots, from simple political economy issues (local officials may simply be happy spending funds but never raising

51. The property tax is highly visible and because of the low geographical mobility of its base and because property values tend to reflect well in general the quality of local services, the property tax can approximate well the concept of a benefit tax, where residents pay for the services they receive (see Sepulveda and Martinez-Vazquez, 2009). All of this is likely to increase political accountability of local officials. The property tax may also have relatively low efficiency losses compared to other local taxes. In terms of administration, there can be flexibility in taking advantage of a mixed local and central administration and enforcement approaches See Bahl, Martinez-Vazquez and Youngman (2008 and 2010).

52. See Sepulveda and Martinez-Vazquez (2009) for an evaluation of the performance of property taxes in the region.

53. See Sepulveda and Martinez-Vazquez (2009).

Box 6.2. A Tale of Two Cities: Bogotá's Success Story in Raising Local Tax Effort and Lima's Success with a New Approach to Tax Administration

Bogotá provides an example of a local government that has had success in raising local tax effort (the city was awarded a prize by the United Nations in 2002 for being the most improved local government in the world.) Starting in the late 1980s, The Municipality of Bogotá began a program of civic education during which it emphasized the importance of paying taxes and the accompanying benefit for citizens that derives from a stronger local government. It significantly increased property tax collections through a series of administrative improvements, including enforced business taxes, privatizing certain government run organizations, and successfully issuing own bonds, some times in foreign markets receiving a AAA rating,[54] Particularly noteworthy is that the Municipality of Bogotá in 2006 raised 42 percent of its tax revenues from the local business tax (Impuesto de Industria y Comercio, ICA). Updating the fiscal cadastre in 2009 has also produced significant increases in revenues from the property tax. It is expected that the assessed tax base for this levy will increase by more than 50 percent by 2010, bringing an additional $51 million in revenues or a 13.3 percent increase over collections before the updating of the cadastre.

In 1996 Lima, along with other provincial Peruvian municipalities, introduced a semi-autonomous Tax Administration Service (SAT in Spanish), with the goal of increasing collections for own local taxes. This followed the model of a national-level SAT. The SAT of Lima is autonomous in its financial and human resource management and it is financed through a share of the taxes and fees commission it collects. The shared collections by Peruvian municipalities range from 3 percent to 10 percent. But note that the local authorities are still responsible for regulating and controlling the SATs' work. There have been some clear benefits for those Peruvian municipalities that, like Lima, adopted a SAT approach. For example, between 1998 and 2007 those municipalities that adopted a SAT increased their own revenue by 80.9 percent, or 9 percent of the annual average, by comparison over the same period the municipalities that did not adopt a SAT saw their revenues increase by 61.2 percent, or 6.8 percent of the annual average. The empirical studies show that the trust in tax administration in Lima and other municipalities where a SAT was adopted has increased. This could be attributed to lower political intervention in administrative processes, higher client focus management, improved public relations, and a reduction of corrupt practices. But not all have been highly regarded for their new local tax administration. The same empirical survey studies identify some issues associated with the SATs: such as a limited link between the revenue collection and public services, and the public perception of tax administration as "insensible." But some of this is to be expected since the SATs have gone against the conventions and took advantage of not always well defined rules, especially in the SAT of Lima. One of the key characteristics of the SAT agencies has been their innovative drive, including internal processes, the use of modern technologies, human resource development, improved financial management, and the collaboration across tax administrations.

54. *See Acosta and Bird (2005).*

them), to lack of economic resources (building an updated fiscal cadastre is expensive), to inadequate methodologies for evaluation, to the lack of skilled human resources, or even to the negative incentives for local tax effort provided by the central government's existing fiscal transfer system. However, the region offers success stories in raising local tax effort, as provided by the recent experiences of Bogotá and Lima (see Box 6.2).

A third issue is the need to explore taxes with significant revenue potential that could possibly be assigned to local governments in order to increase their revenue self-sufficiency, akin to a flat-rate piggy back personal income tax or local surtaxes on some excise duties, such as those on vehicle fuel. Another possibility is a more intense use of betterment levies, which can complement annual real property taxes. Betterment levies are being used quite successfully in Colombia (See Box 6.3). A different option is the adoption of some form of final retail tax such as in the case of Brazil's ISS (Tax on Services, as discussed in Box 6.4.) Except that this type of tax, although fine within the Brazilian tax system where the federal and state VAT levies exclude many important services from their bases, may be problematic because it would overlap with other countries' existing VATs.[55]

An alternative to the ISS that would not present potential conflicts with the existing national VATs, is the broader base local business tax (*Impuesto de Industria y Comercio,* ICA) in Colombia. This is a

Box 6.3. Betterment Levies ("Contribución de Valorización") in Colombia

In general terms, a betterment tax recoups some of the benefits accrued by property owners due to adjacent public investment that increases the value of that property (Bird & Slack 2006). Since most real estate property is significantly affected by public facilities surrounding it, this tax has significant revenue potential. In Colombia, this tax receives the name *Contribución de Valorización* and it has been in operation for a long time. The constitution gives municipalities and other public entities the right to a share on the added value produced by investments made in urban settings (e.g. infrastructure works). The tax is being looked at with interest by other countries and in the first Latin American conference of Valorization, held in Bogotá (Colombia) in 2009.[56] The levying of the tax implies a series of steps including, the determination of the costs and benefits of the project, the geographical area that is expected to benefit, and a method to distribute the costs and benefits of the project among the different properties. This distribution can use an array of "benefit factors" (use of property, closeness, access, etc.) or simply a land area, linear size of lot front, etc.

Bogotá also levies a tax called *Participación en Plusvalia*[57] defined as the contribution owed to owners of real estate property as a result of modifications that increase the value of property. This is similar to the betterment tax except that it captures only changes in urban codes that affect the ways the property can be used or the intensity of its use (how much can be constructed) that may increase its value.

55. *For example, in the recent past Nicaragua eliminated a productive local sales tax as part of a policy conditionality given by the International Monetary Fund precisely because of the conflict presented by the existing national VAT.*

56. *I Congreso Latinoamericano de Valorizacion; http://www.lonjadebogota.org.co/Portals/0/Docs/*

57. *Information about this tax may be found at: http://www.shd.gov.co/portal/page/portal/portal_internet/impuestos/impuestos_imp/Plus valia/INFO%20PLUSVALIA*

Box 6.4. The ISS in Brazil[58]

The ISS (*Imposto sobre Servicos*/Tax on Services) is a municipal level tax levied on those services that are left out of Brazil's state value added tax (ICMS). The services that may be taxed under ISS are defined by federal law, but the states may decide whether to tax or exempt some of those services. The base covers a wide range of services including, IT services, rental of premises, medical services, veterinary services, personal services (barber shops, etc), professional services (engineering, architecture, law, accounting, etc.), education and training, hotels and tourism, parking, leisure entertainment (movies, shows), repair services, financial services (by banks, etc.), municipal transportation, port, terminal, and airport services. The tax base is the revenue generated from the provision of services. The rate that municipalities may charge for ISS is locally set but cannot exceed 5 percent (in the past, it could go as high as 10 percent). Although the tax rate to be applied is the one charged by the municipality in which the business resides, there are exceptions in which the tax rate is the one belonging to the municipality where the service is rendered (e.g. construction). Producers of services are charged with paying and recordkeeping of the ISS. Buyers of services do not directly see the tax they pay as it is included in the price charged to them by vendors.

Although the ISS collects at the municipal level, its importance varies greatly across local governments; according to the Receita Federal (national tax administration) 1 percent of municipalities (out of more than 5,500) account for 73 percent of the tax collection. The ISS collected approximately 0.5 percent of the GDP in the mid-to-late 1990s and more recently, the tax collections are nearer to 0.8 percent of the GDP. As the maximum tax rates were lowered sometime in the early 2000s, the observed increase in collections as a share of GDP might come either from an expanded tax base and/or better efforts in collecting the tax. There is some evidence of the expansion of the tax base; when the rates were lowered in 2003. The ISS was also extended to services provided by financial institutions, banking services in particular.

The ISS is not without its problems. One issue is the increased tax on the production of products/services for future use, since users of these services cannot identify the ISS balance to be paid against the ISS they would receive; remembering that the price for the services are ISS inclusive. Another issue has been the management of exports. The import of services is subject to this tax, and although it should not apply to exported services, it may become subjected to this tax.[59]

With regard to the future of the ISS, there have recently been calls in Brazil for the simplification of the tax system where–one way or another- the elimination of the ISS was contemplated. This viewpoint supports the integration of the federal-based IPI and state-based ICMS (both value-added type taxes) and the locally-based ISS within a general VAT whose revenues could be shared by all three levels of government. However, the increasing importance of ISS in municipal budgets, with regard to the potential loss in local autonomy and the difficulties of coordination at different levels of government, weigh-in on the other side of the argument.

58. *See, among others, Deloitte (2010), Government of Brazil (2009), KPMG (2006), Banco Central do Brasil (2000) and Purohit (1997).*

59. *See KPMG (2006).*

local "direct" tax on all business activities (industry, trade and services) that uses as its presumptive tax base the monetary value of annual transactions. It is also levied at different rates depending on the sector. The production of food pays a rate of 0.41 percent, the sales of alcoholic beverages, tobacco products, and fuels pay a rate of 1.38 percent, and financial transactions pay a rate of 1.1 percent. The ICA is one of the most important sources of municipal tax revenues in Colombia, on average representing approximately 42 percent of municipalities' annual tax revenues, but as much as 72 percent in the Municipality of Cali.

Another form of local business tax with revenue potential is Chile's "patente municipal." This annual levy, administered by the municipalities, is paid for any commercial activity (trade, professional, industrial, and sale of alcoholic beverages) that requires a permanent office location; municipalities select rates between 0.25 and 0.5 percent that fall on the declared (to the national tax administration) own capital of the business. The "patente municipal" raises approximately the same amount of municipal revenues in Chile as the property tax ("impuesto territorial.")

In terms of revenue collection hierarchy in Latin America, the two sets of taxes that are generally of equal importance are the property taxes (*impuesto sobre los bienes inmuebles*, IBI) and the different taxes on business activities and services. In a distant third place we find those taxes falling on the use of motor vehicles. Generally, there would appear to be room to increase local revenues for taxes on motor vehicles. This is also the case for local fees and charges in many countries in the region; often the levels of fees and charges are completely out of date.[60]

Unbundling revenue sharing

Revenue sharing is the most common mechanism for arranging fiscal transfers to sub-national governments in Latin America and in many countries provisions for revenue sharing are enshrined in the constitution. As mentioned in Section 1, fiscal decentralization has often been understood simply as the sharing of central government revenues without relating the additional revenue to any particular local and regional expenditure assignments.

One of the most negative aspects of revenue sharing in other parts of the world is that it can exacerbate the substantial horizontal disparities across local governments when carried out on a derivation (i.e. origin basis). Fortunately, this has generally been avoided in Latin American countries.[61] An important exception has been the revenue sharing in natural resources, which in countries such as Peru and Ecuador is fundamentally implemented on a derivation basis. This has led to significant horizontal disparities among municipalities.[62] In most Latin American countries fiscal transfers from revenue sharing are distributed according to a set of parameters or formulas that try to achieve several objectives, one of which is some degree of equalization. One of the positive aspects of revenue sharing is that it manages to combine the unconditional use of funds with rather plentiful sources of revenue.

The main problem with general revenue sharing is that there is some confusion over the exact achievement of distribution formulas; pursuing many objectives with essentially one instrument tends to be the source of that confusion. It isn't always best to give local governments the unconditional

60. For example, reportedly in the case of El Salvador municipal fees and charges date from 1954.

61. Note that this does not mean that there are no significant regional disparities in the region; it simply means that the more frequent use of the derivation would have made things worse. As discussed above, regional fiscal disparities arise from the differences in economic bases and the more tax autonomy provided, the higher the potential for enlarged fiscal disparities which require a higher need equalization grants.

62. In the case of Peru, the evolution of international prices for natural resources had a significant impact on the transfers system. The Ministry of Economy and Finance (MEF) currently shares 50 percent of mining and hydrocarbon revenues with local governments. Transfers from central government to regional/ local governments increased exponentially after 2000 but plummeted in 2009. This experience has given rise to very significant horizontal imbalances between municipalities because shares of mining revenues are highly concentrated on seven departments, accounting for close to 80 percent of the total. This has created problems with increased unspent balances during the boom years and it has continued to expose local governments to high volatility in revenue streams.

use of all of these funds.[63] The reforms being introduced or contemplated in some Latin American countries consist fundamentally of the unbundling of the revenue sharing system into two additional separate transfer mechanisms, namely: (i) an equalization transfer with unconditional use of funds and financed from a pool extracted from the shared revenues, which would exclusively pursue the goal of equalization of horizontal fiscal disparities, or (ii) a system of specific or conditional grants for current expenditure and investment purposes, financed with some of the revenue sharing funds. The use of these funds would be earmarked in pursuit of a variety of sectored objectives. Advances in this general direction have been made in countries like Brazil and Chile, while countries like Ecuador, El Salvador and Honduras are still using an unbundled revenue sharing scheme as the main funding source of local governments.

The need to rationalize the transfer system

The system of transfers plays a pivotal role in drawing together the other elements of the intergovernmental fiscal system. It makes up for the vertical and horizontal gaps that own source revenues and revenue sharing cannot meet, and when it is designed properly it does not undermine local tax effort or the incentives for creditworthy municipalities to borrow.

With the exception of a few countries, the current system of transfers to local governments in Latin America lacks a clear orientation. Most countries have yet to introduce unconditional equalization grants that incorporate some formula-based measures for expenditure needs and fiscal capacity.[64] When some equalization elements are introduced into the revenue sharing formulas, actual revenue collections are often used instead of measures of tax capacity, thereby creating a negative incentive for tax effort. The current methods used to incorporate different expenditure needs in the revenue sharing formulas are also problematic. For example, population, which is commonly used as a good approximation for some services needs, is not the right factor to be considered for other services. For example, the number of school age children provides a better approximation for basic education needs than population as a whole. The relative share of infants and the elderly in the population provides a better approximation for health care needs than the whole population per se. In some cases, especially in Central American countries like El Salvador and Nicaragua, the existing formulas favor small municipalities, which in turn create problems of fairness and economic viability and regional development.

Even though many countries have some form of conditional grants, they lack structure and consistency, especially in the area of capital grants. When conditional grants are used, the complex system is often a problem.[65] Compliance-administrative costs by local governments which is intricate, in many cases penalizes smaller jurisdictions with low administrative capacity and dilutes the achievement of central government goals. A remedy to these problems, following best international practice, has been to consolidate many of these specific or conditional programs into block grants. While specific conditional grants narrow the use of funds (e.g. funds to buy furniture for primary schools), block grants, while still conditional, have a much broader scope for the use of funds (e.g., the funds must be spent on primary education). The advantages to

63. *The point is to quickly achieve a more appropriate mix of unconditional and conditional grants, without losing sight of the fact that, in the long term, it is desirable to increase unconditional local governments funding.*

64. *Some exceptions include Chile's revenue equalization grant.*

using just a few block grants are the simplification and expansion of local government choices, thus aligning the final allocation of public resources more closely to the priorities of individual local governments (e.g., repairing the school building instead of buying new furniture), without unduly compromising the general goals of central government's policies (e.g., promoting the quality and standards of primary education in the country).

Increasing fiscally responsible local borrowing

Historically, the Latin American region has suffered some of the worst incidences of fiscally irresponsible sub-national borrowing in the world. The negative experiences of Brazil and Argentina, with uncontrolled sub-national borrowing and hyperinflation during the 1980s and 1990s, are still examples of what can go wrong in this area of sub-national finance. One consequence of those experiences is that the borrowing policy towards local governments in the region has become excessively conservative and restrictive.

For example, in Chile, local governments are —in principle— not allowed to borrow or take out loans of any kind, but either way outright prohibition is unnecessary or effective. In the same country, indirect borrowing through leasing contracts or by delaying the payment of current expenditure makes that norm difficult to enforce. In Uruguay, any domestic or foreign debt issued by a local government needs to be approved by the national congress. Peru also provides an example of legislative conservatism in the matter of local borrowing: The central government has established indebtedness rules to maintain fiscal prudence by two laws (the Law on Fiscal Prudence and Transparency -LPTF- and the Law on Fiscal Responsibility and Transparency -LRTF-). Besides limits on debt service ratios and total debt, the laws also limited the rate of growth for municipal expenditures to a maximum of 3 percent per year. However, this framework has not been fully enforced because of insufficient monitoring, and the lack of effective sanctions. Many local governments in Peru carry large budgetary arrears. At the other extreme, and more like an exception, Paraguay, has practically no restriction on local borrowing.

Thus a pending challenge for several countries in the region is how to set up institutions that effectively regulate borrowing without becoming overly restrictive of local governments. Many countries are still struggling to introduce a credible system of penalties for lack of compliance. The development of information and monitoring systems covering all aspects of borrowing,[65] including budgetary arrears with official institutions and private providers, is urgently needed. But the key ingredient for fiscally responsible behavior of sub-national units remains at the political will of the central government authorities to implement the existing regulatory frameworks.

A second challenge for practically all countries is how to make more credit available to local governments for responsible borrowing.[66] In practice, the level of borrowing by local governments in Latin America is far too low to meet the present large needs for public infrastructure across the sub-continent.[67] The exceptions are large cities, which tend to have ample access to domestic credit markets and in many cases to international markets with accompanying international credit ratings. Thus, the capital cities of La Paz (Bolivia) and Lima (Peru) display a very different picture from that of most other municipalities.

65. *Monitoring systems for local indebtedness have often proved a doubtful utility. In Ecuador and Peru information on debt is taken directly from the financial statements of sub-national governments and is not crosschecked with other sources. In Argentina, the Federal Council for Fiscal Responsibility created by the Fiscal Responsibility Law of 2004 and in charge of monitoring compliance with norms and rules of fiscal and financial behavior does not receive timely information from the majority municipalities as of 2009.*

66. *Part of the solution can be direct on-lending to municipalities by regional-multinational institutions such as the* [Confederation Andina de Fomento] *(CAF) or* [the Banco Centroamericano de Inversiones]*, or international organizations such as the Inter-American Development Bank (IDB) or the World Bank. However, a large part of the solution needs to be the mobilization of domestic credit sources.*

67. *Brazil is an exception.*

The absence of real access to borrowing by the average municipality in the region is a complex issue. It is explained by a multitude of causes, ranging from the lack of tax autonomy for local governments to the lack of national financial market development. One potential remedy for the scarcity of local credit is the creation of semi-official financial intermediaries or municipal banks.[68] As shown in Box 6.5, several Latin American countries have created this type of institution to facilitate long-term credit to local governments. However, the experience of these institutions has been mixed because of the difficulty of maintaining them at arms' length from central government officials and of operating them with strict banking criteria.

Issues on the Budget Process and Transparency

Streamlining the Budget Process at the Local Level

Budgets and the budget process at the local level in Latin America have improved

Box 6.5. Practice with Municipal Development Banks and Funds in Latin America[69]

Experience with municipal development banks in Latin America has been mixed, as has been the case in many other countries around the world. Although quite a few countries have introduced some sort of specialized financial intermediaries or municipal development funds to raise capital financing for local governments, few of those institutions have been transformed into financial institutions with market-oriented practices and controls channelling private savings to finance public infrastructure. The following is a summary of experiences with municipal development banks and funds in the Latin America region.

Brazil

The Integrated Program of State Improvements (PIMES) was established as a municipal development fund administered by BADESUL, the development bank of the Rio Grande do Sul, which owns and controls it. The program has two components: institutional and human resource development and infrastructure investments. The first component comprises of about 10 percent of the total project costs and includes technical assistance, training and equipment for municipalities, the State Water Company (CORSAN), and other state sector agencies, etc. The second component represents about 90 percent of the total program budget and includes the financing of projects in water supply and sanitation, street paving and lighting, drainage and erosion control, and so on. The Municipal Action Program (PRAM) was established in 1991 by the Parana state bank BANESTADO, which originally served as the bank's financial agent. PRAM was eventually converted into a revolving State Urban Development Fund (FDU), administered by BANESTADO with technical assistance provided by a legally autonomous organization that in practice functions as a department of the State of Parana Secretariat of Planning.

PARANACIDADE was created in 1996 as a non-profit corporate entity to provide institutional and technical services to municipalities in Parana; this institution also collects and invests financial resources from the state's urban and regional development

68. *Central governments also guarantee on-lending to local governments from multilateral international organizations, including the World Bank, the IDB, and CAF.*

69. *See Peterson (1996). There are other relevant initiatives in the region that for space reasons are not developed in this box, including the* Banco del Estado *(BEDE) in Ecuador and* La Caixa *in Brazil. At the regional level the CAF and the IDB have been active supporters of on-lending programs for the development of local public infrastructure.*

significantly in recent times. A noteworthy innovation has been the introduction of participatory budgeting (See Box 6.6). Nevertheless, a variety of issues at different stages of the budget process still need to be addressed in several countries in the region. In terms of budget planning and formulation, there are still countries where local governments must have their budgets, or certain aspects of them, approved on an annual basis by higher levels of government.[70] Ex-ante monitoring and approval of local budgets by higher level authorities is not needed where there are local elected councils and an effective ex-post audit system, and courts to address irregularities. Local budget autonomy is often limited in the case of investment projects.[71] Another issue in the preparation stage is the lack of a link between planning and budgeting. Frequently, it is seen that many development plans at the local, regional, and national levels lack coordination and do not relate to actual budgets in terms of the cost of activities for the fulfillment of strategic objectives.

Practice with Municipal Development Banks and Funds in Latin America (cont.)

programs, managing the State Urban Development Fund (FDU), which creates loans for municipalities at maturity ranging from 8 years for urban infrastructure to 10 years for social infrastructure. One of the main explanations for PARANACIDADE's success is its support of capacity building for municipalities.

Colombia

Colombia has been successful in using its Municipal Development Funds to accelerate the development of private credit markets for local government. The Territorial Financing Institution (FINDETER), which began in 1994 as an infrastructure financing window within the National Mortgage Bank, eventually evolved into a development bank for municipalities, working through the commercial banking system. In essence, FINDETER operates as a second-level financing institution which re-discounts commercial bank loans to municipalities. The banks' good credit experience through FINDETER has led them to commit their own resources to municipal lending. Intermediate-sized cities and departments in Colombia now borrow primarily through commercial bank loans, while small cities and towns continue to rely on FINDETER. The largest cities now finance their credit requirements primarily through bonds.

Mexico

The federal public works bank, BANOBRAS, was founded in 1933 as the Banco Nacional Hipotecario Urbano y de Obras Públicas, S.A (National Urban Mortgage and Public Works Bank), and has long had a loan program for municipal development. Its operations, however, became complex and bureaucratic and the allocation of financial resources soon responded more to political than financial criteria. The bank's heavily subsidized loan program used to focus on social housing, water supply systems and the construction of markets and abattoirs. Since 1988, its interest rates have come close to market rates and BANOBRAS has switched its focus to improvements of municipal land registers.

70. *These countries include: Bolivia, Costa Rica, Jamaica, Mexico, Nicaragua, Panama, Paraguay.*

71. *In Peru all public investment projects must be approved by the National Public Investment System (SNIP) which is managed by the Ministry of Economy and Finance (MEF). Through the General Directorate of Multi-Sector Programming (DGPM), MEF has the power to cancel any approval made by regional and local governments if DGPM consider that SNIP criteria have not been properly applied.*

In terms of budget execution, the misappropriation of funds by central government is still a problem in several countries. For example, in Haiti, 90 percent of local government income evidently comes from transfers associated to the Funds for the Operation and Development for the Territorial Collectives (FGDCT), administered by the Department of the Interior. However, recent studies show that these funds are not being distributed as the Department of the Interior claims, and that a significant share is retained by the Department to finance its own projects. The budgets of communes (i.e. the local governments in Haiti) are the most directly hurt, receiving 33 percent less than what they are budgeted to receive. Honduras provides another example, where the law is not respected by the central authorities. In particular, while the Municipal Code establishes that the central government should allocate 5 percent of its tax

Box 6.6. Participatory Budgeting in Porto Alegre (Brazil)[72]

Participatory budgeting has been functioning successfully in the municipality of Porto Alegre, in the state of Rio Grande do Sul (Brazil) for the last two decades. The participatory budget of Porto Alegre, called OPPA, is a process through which ordinary citizens and a team of elected local government officials work together to define a list of projects to be included within the local government budget. Through this mechanism for the shared management of budgetary resources, local residents perform the role of identifying and controlling the implementation of projects. Thus, through the OPPA, local residents are closely associated with the formulation of public policy at the initial stages, including diagnosis and needs assessment, the intermediate phase of monitoring and implementation, and the final phase of control and accountability.

Since its inception the OPPA has contributed to the improvements in the lives of local residents. The number of participants in Porto Alegre has increased year by year, from approximately 1,000 in 1990 to nearly 15,000 in 2004. The process has also brought opportunities to better integrate traditionally marginalized groups of the population in the community's development. In 2002, there was a predominance of women among the leaders of neighbourhood associations, delegates and counselors. In addition, most of the OPPA participants belong to lower income groups. Other groups, such as the black population or, manual and unskilled workers have also seen higher participation rates in the OPPA process (City, 2003). According to Abers (2000), who studied the profile of OPPA's participants, contrary to some expectations, the process has not given rise to the influence of an elite field of people with more education or income. In addition, Santos (2003) has shown that OPPA resulted in an increase in the provision of basic public services. In 1999 the volume of garbage collected and the number of additional lights installed nearly doubled from the annual average for the period prior to the existence of OPPA (1985-1988). In 1996, the sewer lines in the municipality were expanded to cover 98 percent of households up from a coverage of about 50 percent in 1989. The World Bank (1999) also attributed to OPPA the paving of half of the municipality streets and the doubling in the number of students enrolled in primary and secondary schools.

72. See http://www.internationalbudget.org/ for other experiences in participatory budgeting and other innovations for more open and transparent budgeting practices.

revenue to the municipalities, in fact, only 3 percent appears to have been allocated in the most recent years.[73] Other countries, like the Dominican Republic, are experimenting with similar situations; 10 percent of their national budget must be allocated to local governments (according to Law 166-03), but actual transfers have never reached this level and recently they have decreased from 8 percent to 6 percent of the national budget.

Deficiencies related to ex-post audit of local budgets still exist.[74] For example, in Paraguay, many municipalities do not comply with the requirement to send their annual financial reports to the Comptroller General of the Republic.

Addressing the Scarcity of Data on Local Finance

The lack of adequate data on local finance is a widespread problem in the region which has major consequences. Only a handful of countries currently make municipal data openly available to the public. Countries, such as Brazil, Peru and Ecuador provide examples for best practice in this area; for further examples in the region see Box 6.7.

Conclusions

The analysis in the above sections has shown that the Latin America region contains a rich variety of experiences and lessons, good and bad, about decentralization and municipal finance. This assortment of experiences and challenges, sometimes quite unique,[75] has made it difficult to draw up a cross-country analysis. Nevertheless, there are many common themes and challenges facing municipal governments in Latin America and each country has been able to address them with varying degrees of success. For example, in Chile, the central government has made use of municipal governments' ability to increase the effectiveness of social policies and encourage innovation and competition among them. In Colombia,

Box 6.7. Annual Publication of Executed Budgets in Colombia

Law 617, enacted in 2000, charges the National Planning Department (DNP) in Colombia with the annual publication of budget results (revenues, expenditures and financial indicators) for all departments and municipalities, together with an explanation of where there have been problems and where there has been progress. Included in these records is a detailed recording of the municipalities' fiscal performance and information on all income and expenditures during the past fiscal year. This annual publication is of high quality. The DNP collects annual data on revenues and expenditures, as well as the debt levels of all local governments. Each local government reports and certifies the accuracy of its executed budgets to the DNP through an automated system, the *Sistema de Información para la Captura de la Ejecución Presupuestal de Departamentos y Municipios* (SICEP). The DNP also receives information on debt levels from the *Controloría General de la República* (CGR). These data are regularly used by government institutions and nongovernmental organizations to monitor the performance of sub-national governments. The comparisons in performance also allow some form of benchmarking competition among local governments; which governments are doing relatively better and which are doing worse.

73. *See Cardona (2006).*

74. *In El Salvador and other countries in the region, municipalities are required to undergo a full independent audit once a year to search for signs of corruption and misuse of public funds. This practice does not eliminate corruption but it goes a long way to keep it under control.*

75. *For example, the challenges faced by some municipalities in Colombia go beyond fiscal issues. Here, municipalities in the war-torn areas must face the challenge of being on the frontlines against armed actors such as drug traffickers, paramilitaries and the Revolutionary Armed Forces of Colombia (FARC).*

central legislation can provide administrative flexibility, with local governments exercising control over staff hiring and salary decisions, and at the same time provide effective accountability mechanisms to maintain fiscally responsible decisions by local officials. In Honduras, a municipal association can successfully provide technical assistance and training for its members. Changes in the attitudes of municipal officials toward broader community participation in budget decisions have taken place in countries such as Bolivia, Brazil, and Peru.

In this concluding section we offer some observations grouped according to the set of issues examined. Yet, there are challenges remaining which need addressing and it will be necessary to continue looking for new orientations in future research about public local finances in the region.

Observations on Organizational Structure

Countries with problems of fragmentation and small municipalities, should introduce legislation and practical support for the creation of associations of municipalities into *mancomunidades* for the delivery of certain public services requiring a certain minimum scale. Other solutions to the problem of insufficient scale that could be pursued include cooperative services agreements between larger and smaller municipalities, and the contracting of services with private enterprises for the delivery of services. In addition, careful critical study and consideration should be given to the creation of new tiers of vertical government (for example, regional governments) as a solution to some of the weaknesses observed at the existing local governments. A cheaper more efficient solution can be the strengthening of technical assistance and additional funding of existing governments.

In any case, existing potential incentives to further fragmentation should be removed. In particular, those countries with transfer formulas that ensure the same amount of funds to all municipalities independently of their size should discontinue this practice. Where they do not exist now, new legislation with minimum population and fiscal viability requirements should be introduced to prevent any further undesirable fragmentation of local governments.

Most central governments in the region, and provincial or state governments in the case of federal systems, should devote more time and resources to developing administrative capacity, especially in the case of small and rural local governments. Some of this assistance can be provided by working together with and offering support to municipal associations in order to give quantitative and qualitative technical assistance and training to local officials in the most cost-effective manner or by having regional universities and colleges contracted to tutor local governments.

Observations on Intergovernmental Fiscal System Design

Without a clear assignment of expenditure responsibilities to local governments it is not possible to have an informed judgment on whether or not the level of financing of these governments is adequate. Most systems of intergovernmental fiscal relations in the region would benefit from an explicit clarification of the competencies assigned to local governments. First, this will require the clear identification of the exclusive responsibilities of local governments. Second, in the case of concurrent or shared responsibilities between the local and central (or intermediate level) governments, it will be necessary to identify which attributes of the particular competence (regulation, financing, and implementation) are the responsibility of the local governments and which belong to higher levels of government. There will be no clear assignment of responsibilities, especially in the case of concurrent functions, until it is apparent which level of government is exclusively responsible for the different sub-functions involved. Of course, the implementation of services may be done directly by the local jurisdiction or this unit can make arrangements for its provision, for example by a private company or some other jurisdiction.

If there are significant differences in administrative capacity among local governments it may be desirable to temporarily introduce two or at most three different packages of expenditure responsibilities that can be devolved to local governments depending on their administrative capacities and over time, as capacity is acquired, graduate municipalities to the more complete levels of responsibility.

It would also be desirable to adopt transparent approaches to translate the assignment of local functional responsibilities into expenditure needs in order to have a clear idea of the financing requirements for local governments.

Greater local revenue autonomy is a challenge not yet adequately addressed by most countries in the region. However, there is a need to find a better balance between the decentralization of expenditure responsibilities and the authority to collect local taxes from the residents directly benefiting from local services. This will lead to more fiscally responsible and politically accountable forms of decentralization. Several options are open going forward with this agenda.

- First, countries that have not assigned property tax to local governments should do so. Property tax has several characteristics that make it ideal as a local tax.

- Second, other taxes that should be assigned to local governments are vehicle taxes, business licenses, and betterment levies on real estate for financing basic infrastructure improvements.

- Third, for countries that have not done so, some degree of discretion in setting tax rates should be granted to all local governments so that they can adjust their tax bases, within legislated maximum and minimum rates. Other forms of autonomy beyond rate setting (e.g., adjustments to the tax base or the freedom to introduce new taxes) are not generally desirable.

- Fourth, coordinated efforts of local and central governments should be made to increase the revenue yield of property tax and other taxes assigned to local governments. In the case of property taxes, these should include: regularly updated and improved property cadastres and property value assessment methodologies, increased effectiveness in the collection of tax bills, and removal of disincentives for increases in tax effort by local governments i.e. reductions in transfers when more local revenues are collected.

- Fifth, the introduction of new taxes at the local level should be considered, including wider use of betterment levies and local business taxation, such as the ICA (*impuesto de industria y comercio*) in Colombia or Chile's *patente municipal*.

Going forward, to improve the direction of increased local tax autonomy, would be the introduction of a local piggy-back personal income tax with a flat rate collection at the same time national income tax is collected. This latter form of local tax is common, in northern and central Europe, but it is yet to be tried in the Latin American region. Finally, there is a possibility of considering the introduction of environmental or "green" taxes enabled by national legislation on the regulation of the environment. This form of taxation has not taken root in many Latin American countries though it provides several important advantages. The first is the so-called "double dividend" since these taxes not only collect needed revenues but also contribute a cleaner environment. These taxes can also fit well in regional and local contexts. Potential levies in this area would include taxes on the emission of solid waste and water contamination.

In those countries where revenue sharing is a major source of local finance, it would be desirable to un-bundle part of the revenue sharing system into separate transfers, including: (i) an equalization transfer with unconditional use of funds and (ii) a system of block conditional grants for current and capital purposes. An explicit unconditional equalization grant is needed to address the important and increasing problem of regional fiscal disparities in many countries in the region—based on differences in tax capacity or economic base, and differences in expenditure needs due to geography or the population structure. Explicit conditional grants are necessary to ensure national standards and objectives in the provision of important services have been decentralized, such as in education and health.

In those countries where local borrowing is not allowed, new legislation should introduce the possibility of responsible local borrowing. In those countries that already allow municipal borrowing, it would be desirable in many cases to review the current status of regulations, streamlining them when necessary so that they are not overly restrictive. This review should also focus on the monitoring capabilities of the central government (including "floating debt" or budgetary arrears with official institutions and private suppliers, and guarantees through municipal enterprises) and the introduction of a credible system of penalties for lack of compliance.

Beyond the regulation and monitoring of local borrowing, an even more important challenge for most countries in the region is to facilitate a significant increase in credit availability to local governments for responsible borrowing, especially for smaller municipalities. The solution may sometimes be the creation of official financial intermediaries or municipal banks. A large amount of information is available within Latin America and other regions of the world regarding the positive features institutions should replicate (e.g., operating with strict banking criteria) and those features that should be avoided (e.g., operating with less than arms' length distance from political authorities). Policies to encourage the development of private markets for local credit are equally, or even more, desirable. But it must be recognized that local credit from private sources is unlikely to develop without more revenue autonomy and greater transparency of local budgets.

Observations on Budget Process and Transparency

Those countries still requiring ex-ante approval of municipal budgets by higher-level authorities should phase out this practice and increasingly rely on local accountability and effectiveness of ex-post audits and the rule of law in order to keep an eye on the probity of local budget execution. The misappropriation of funds in a selected number of countries is a practice that needs to be stopped and full compliance with ex-post audit rules should be ensured. The ultimate effectiveness of local public expenditures will depend on the adoption of modern budget evaluation practices, which remains a pending assignment for most countries in the region.

The low reliability on municipal finances remains an important problem in the Latin American region, affecting the quality of policy design and of analytical work. Best practice in budget transparency and data dissemination in countries such as Colombia and Peru, for example, should be replicated by all countries in the region where publicly available data on annual budgets and other aspects of the local finances are still missing. An effective way to encourage and sustain good practices in budget reporting and data generation is to make good use of the data, by providing information to experts and ordinary citizens on performance and by publicizing the results in order to create benchmark competition across jurisdictions.

There has been continued progress over the past decade with the institutions that manage finances and with the practice itself of municipal finance in the Latin American region. Nevertheless, there is a long road ahead for further improving the overall efficiency, equity, and accountability of municipal finances in the region.

Latin America Regional Policy Recommendations

Prepared by the technical team of the Federación Latinoamericana de Ciudades, Municipios y Asociaciones (FLACMA), March 2010.

Signs of recentralization in Latin America

In various countries a backward trend has been observed with regard to decisions taken on the handover of responsibilities to local governments, affecting both local autonomy and financing.

National transfers to local governments must be stable and regular

Financial transfers to local government are a mechanism to effectively integrate municipal participation into the national budget and constitute a right for citizens of territories. Universal services such as education and health are nationally designed and financed to ensure equality between territories and, when managed by local governments, merit regular and stable national transfers.

Strengthen collection and take into account the fiscal effort of local governments with regard to local poverty levels

It is often argued that local governments are "fiscally lazy" and invest little in tax collection. These observations do not consider the low yield of economic activity and level of poverty in the majority of Latin American municipalities. As a result, levels of collection in poor areas are often confused with the efforts made to achieve them. To complement these fiscal efforts, systems of income compensation should be favored, such as unconditional transfers from central to local governments that permit a redistribution of resources in favor of more vulnerable, lower income territories.

Increase the participation of local governments in public spending and their autonomy in the management of resources

It is a recurrent theme in Latin America to measure the level of decentralization of diverse countries with indicators such as local expenditure as a percentage of general government spending or local expenditure as a percentage of GDP. Such fiscal observations must be balanced against real levels of local government autonomy in deciding how financial resources will be used, be they collected directly by the local government or transferred from the central level. In addition, access to information on municipal finance must be improved as well as the methodologies for collecting and recording this information.

Promote association and cooperation between municipalities to strengthen municipal capacities

In Latin America and the Caribbean there are more than 16 million local governments. Analyzing, by country, the total number of Latin American municipalities this is not necessarily excessive to respond to the needs of citizens. However, there are significant differences in both the sizes and characteristics of these entities, depending on the country and type of territory as well as the municipal human and financial resources. The most effective manner to balance municipal capacity – without reorganizing the territorial and institutional structure in each country – is through municipal associative movements, that is to say, to encourage inter-municipal cooperation. "Mancomunidades" allow local governments to mutually support each other, manage services jointly, and undertake local development programs and projects.

Increase the sources of own revenues for local government

In Latin America the main sources of municipal income –apart from fees and tariffs for municipal services– are property taxes, business and commercial licenses, vehicle taxes, development charges and transfer systems for equalization purposes to strengthen incomes for less developed municipalities. Property tax is the most common, and is in use across all of Latin America, with some exceptions such as the Dominican Republic, and El Salvador. It is necessary to improve and increase the sources of own revenue for local governments.

Prioritize strengthening and improved functioning of local governments

It is very important for the success of the decentralization process that local governments are effectively strengthened, helping them to better exercise their powers and responsibilities and provide good levels of services.

Improve coordination between ministries and national institutions responsible for sectoral policy and local government; the transfer of responsibilities must be accompanied by corresponding resources

One of the most common conflicts in public policy is that of aligning the generally sectoral visions of national ministries, with the territorial optic of local governments. Municipalities are often assigned partial responsibilities, from national ministries, without the necessary resources to successfully implement them.

Recognize and strengthen the role of local government associations

Local government associations are an important supporting structure for municipal management. The national associations allow for the design and discussion of national policies and regulations on decentralization and local responsibilities, with central government and parliament; the departmental, regional or intermediary municipal associations play a similar role with intermediary governments, and also provide technical support to member governments.

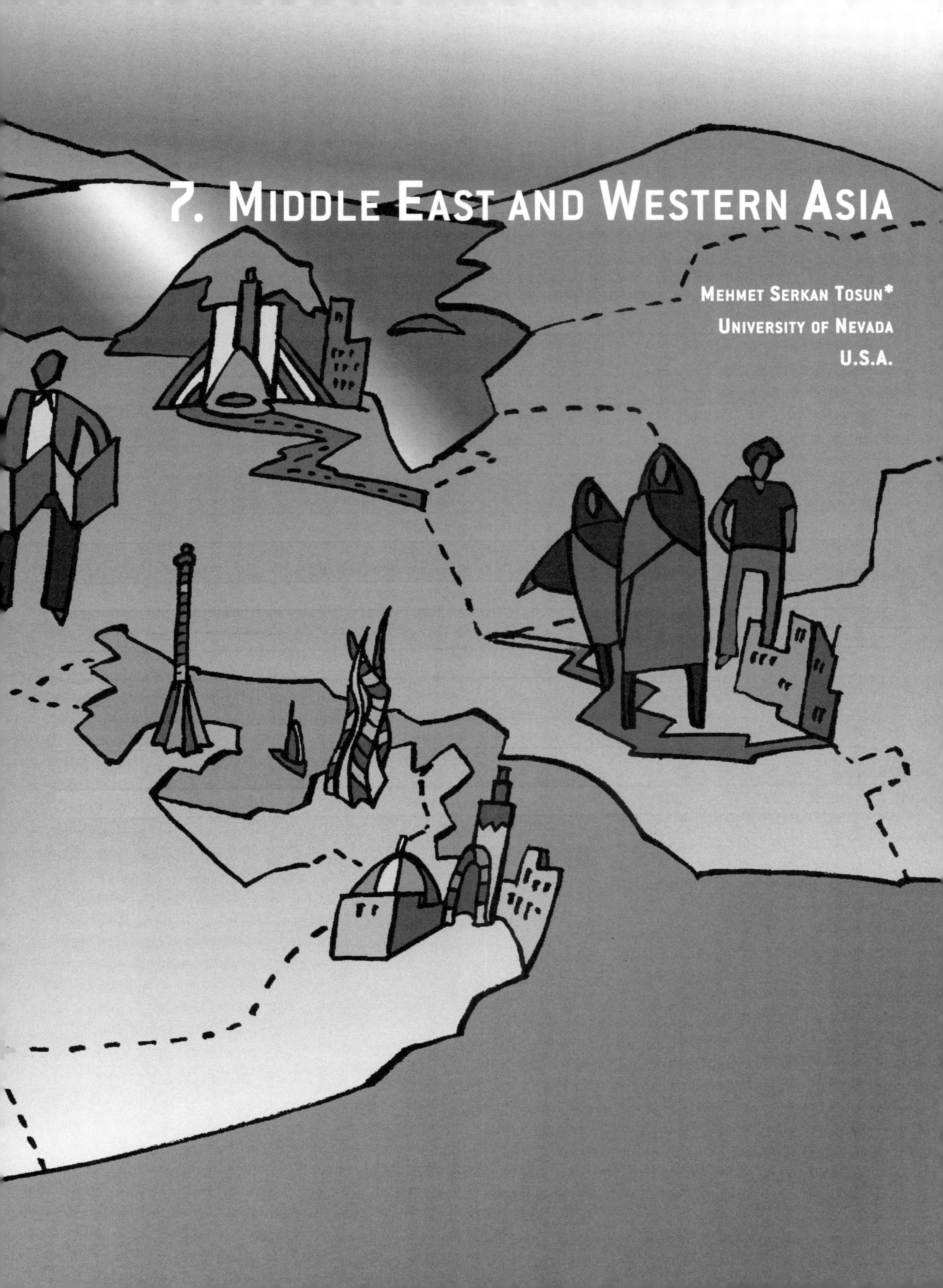

7. MIDDLE EAST AND WESTERN ASIA

MEHMET SERKAN TOSUN*
UNIVERSITY OF NEVADA
U.S.A.

* *The author would like to thank Serdar Yilmaz (the World Bank), Isam Akel (Association of Palestinian Local Authorities), Muaffak Al-Hajaj (Jordan Ministry of Public Sector Development) and other participants of the UCLG Gold II Workshop in Istanbul for their help with this chapter.*

The Middle East and Western Asia (MEWA) region has unique characteristics in terms of its economy, demography, politics, and government structure.[1] Some of the characteristics that distinguish MEWA generally from other regions are economic dependency on sizeable oil reserves, internal and external conflicts, poor governance, and significant growth in the working-age population mainly due to high population growth in the region. The MEWA region is composed of a complex geographical configuration. Turkey and Iran are the largest countries with a combined population of close to 150 million, which makes more than half of the total region population. On the other hand, Bahrain and Qatar are the smallest countries with a combined population of about 2 million (see table 7.1 for basic statistics).

While Turkey, Saudi Arabia, and Iran are the largest economies in terms of total Gross Domestic Product (GDP), other oil exporting economies have higher GDP per capita. Among those, Qatar, Kuwait and the United Arab Emirates are not only the richest in the MEWA region in terms of GDP per capita but they are also among the richest in the world. On the other hand, the region also includes some of the poorest countries in the world such as Iraq, Yemen, and Palestine.

1. *This chapter builds on the MEWA region chapter of UCLG's* Decentralization and Local Democracy in the World, First Global Report (GOLD I) *by Mustapha Adib (2008). That chapter gives a good overview of the administrative and political aspects of decentralization in the MEWA region. The goal of this chapter is to complement previous work by giving a comparison of local government financing and highlighting special issues, constraints and opportunities.*

Table 7.1: General Characteristics of MEWA Countries

Country	Land Area (km²)	Political Regime	Population, 2008	Urban population (% of total population), 2008	Population Growth Rate (%), 2008	GDP per capita (current US$)
Bahrain	710	Constitutional Monarchy	766,926	88.5	2	21,421
Iran	1,745,150	Islamic Republic	71,956,322	68.5	1	5,352
Iraq	438,320	Parliamentary Republic	20,941,720	66.6		
Jordan	88,780	Constitutional Monarchy	5,906,043	78.4	3	3,389
Kuwait (2007)	17,820	Absolute Monarchy (Emirate)	2,728,041	98.4	2	42,102
Lebanon	10,400	Parliamentary Republic	4,139,281	87.0	1	6,924
Oman (2006)	309,500	Absolute Monarchy (Emirate)	2,785,361	71.6	2	13,381
Qatar	11,000	Absolute Monarchy (Emirate)	1,280,862	95.6	12	52,690
Saudi Arabia	2,000,000	Absolute Monarchy (Emirate)	24,645,686	82.4	2	18,973
Syrian Arab Republic	185,180	Presidential Republic	21,226,920	54.2	3	2,601
Turkey	783,560	Parliamentary Republic	73,914,260	68.7	1	10,745
United Arab Emirates	83,600	Federation of Absolute Monarchies (Emirate)	4,484,199	77.9	3	38,436
Palestinian National Authority* (2005)	6,020	Palestinian Authority	3,837,957	71.9	3	1,160
Yemen	527,970	Presidential Republic	23,053,462	30.6	3	1,153

* *Figures for Palestinian National Authority correspond to the West Bank and Gaza.*

Source: World Development Indicators, 2009.

Many studies have noted that countries in the Middle East and North African (MENA) region have very centralized government structures (Tosun and Yilmaz, 2008; Arzhagi and Henderson, 2005). It has been argued that most MEWA countries have based their government organization on the administration structure of the Ottoman Empire.[2] Aside from a few isolated attempts at decentralization, the region inherited a highly centralized system of taxation and public administration which has left very little room for local government autonomy.

To give an overview, we can say that Turkey and Palestine have the greatest degree of decentralization from the perspective of expenditure and revenue allocation. Of the two, it is Palestine that gives the greatest fiscal autonomy to local governments. While this singles out Palestine from the other countries of region, the situation must be given careful consideration as the level of decentralization is the result of very particular political and security situation: strong internal and external conflicts, a weak central authority and discontinuity in its geographic border.

The system of financing local governments in the Middle East and Western Asia must be improved in its entirety. While Jordan, Lebanon, Turkey and Palestine use some form of rule or formula to calculate transfers, in other countries, the intergovernmental transfer process is largely ad hoc. Local access to credit is very limited. In countries where there is a significant level of local government borrowing, this is due to the weak regulatory frameworks set by central governments.

There have been important efforts recently to reform local government finance in the MEWA region. Examples of this include new laws that were adopted in Turkey since 2002 as part of its European Union membership process; a reform project in Jordan to transfer the responsibility of property tax collection and management from the Ministry of Finance to municipalities; the advances accomplished in the modernization of municipal administration in Syria in the framework of the current Five Year Plan (2006-2011); and the 1997 law on local authorities in Palestine. In Lebanon, in October 2009 the National Government, at its highest level, committed to further support decentralization and local government reinforcement during an international Seminar organized by UCLG in Tripoli.

Local democracy is also in progress. Local elections took place in 2010 in Lebanon, allowing democratic renewal of local leaders. In Jordan, a new municipalities' law was issued in the year 2007 that allows for full election of municipal councils and Mayors, and dedicates a 20 percent quota for women. In Iraq and Yemen, provincial councils and governors have been elected for the first time in January 2009 and May 2008 respectively. On the other hand, local elections have not, for the moment, been renewed in Saudi Arabia. While local elections in Iran were scheduled for 2011, they may be delayed until the presidential elections in 2013.

Given this brief background on the region, the following presents a formal overview of the government structure and a cross-country comparison of local government finance through expenditure and revenue assignment, intergovernmental transfers, and borrowing.

Centralized Government Structure and Local Government Finance

This section shows a comparison of subnational government finance in the MEWA region.[3] Measuring fiscal decentralization is especially difficult in this

2. *See Inalcik (1977) and Barkey (2008) for excellent accounts of transformation in the Ottoman administration towards centralization in the eighteenth and nineteenth centuries. Centralization gained momentum particularly during the Tanzimat (Reorganization) period in the nineteenth century when the empire was declining rapidly and consolidation of power at the center was seen as a solution to prevent collapse. Centralization that started in the sixteenth century is, by no means, unique to the Ottoman Empire.*
3. *Ebel and Yilmaz (2003) provide an excellent review of measurement issues in decentralization. See also Hammond and Tosun (2011) for a sensitivity analysis on a variety of decentralization measures at the local government level.*

Table 7.2: Comparison of Decentralization and Centralization Measures for MEWA Countries

Country	Percentage of local government expenditures in GDP	Percentage of local government spending in total public sector spending	Percentage of central government expenditures in GDP
Bahrain			13.92 (2002)
Iran	6 (2004/05)		24.64 (2004)
Jordan	3.5 (2008)	9.6 (2008)	38.00 (2008)
Kuwait			37.20 (2007)
Lebanon			35.72 (1999)
Oman			3.44 (2001)
Qatar			26.23 (2005)
Syrian Arab Republic	5.6 (2007)	15.5 (2007)	36.00 (2007)
Turkey	4.8 (2008)	11.1 (2008)	23.88 (2008)
United Arab Emirates			11.95 (1999)
Palestinian National Authority*	2.3 (1999)	11.1 (1999)	10.68 (2005)
Yemen	6.4 (2004)	11.2 (2004)	27.43 (1999)

** Figures for Palestinian National Authority correspond to the West Bank and Gaza.*
Source: Author's compilation from IMF-GFS datasets and national statistics of countries (for Syria, Ministry of Local Administration). Local government spending figures for Turkey from the IMF-GFS differ from the Turkish Ministry of Finance figure of 4.8 percent for 2008.

Figure 7.1: Local Expenditure as a Percentage of GDP and General Government Expenditure

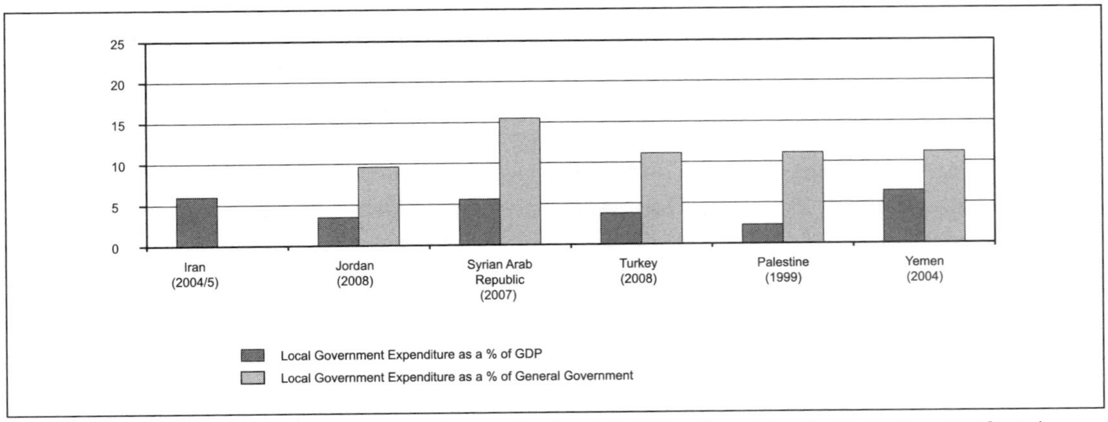

Source: Author's compilation from IMF-GFS datasets and national statistics of countries (for Syria, Ministry of Local Administration). Local government spending figures for Turkey from the IMF-GFS differ from the Turkish Ministry of Finance figure of 4.8 percent for 2008.

region, firstly due to the difficulty in gathering basic data.[4]

Table 7.2 and Figure 7.1 show a comparison of the size of central and local governments.

4. *Jordan and Turkey are somewhat exceptions to this general trend. This is mainly due to Jordan's efforts to meet the International Monetary Fund's Special Data Dissemination Standard and Turkey's reform efforts in the EU membership process.*

Box 7.1. Complex Deconcentrated System in Iran

The Iranian public administration system is composed of the central government and two types of local administrative units—deconcentrated line agencies and the municipal authorities. The Constitution of Islamic Republic of Iran defines the deconcentrated administrative units as governmental and municipalities as non-governmental units. The "public governmental" sector includes the line ministries and central government agencies with offices at sub-national levels. It consists of officials appointed by the central government. At the provincial level, deconcentrated service delivery is coordinated through planning bodies under the supervision of the Management and Planning Organization (MPO), the Ministry of Interior (MOI) and the Ministry of Housing and Urban Development (MHUD). The "public non-governmental" sector includes urban and rural municipalities, as well as the hierarchy of representative, directly and indirectly, elected councils. It consists of the representative bodies which include the directly elected urban and rural local councils (established in 1999) and the indirectly elected hierarchy of Islamic councils (established in 2002 and comprising of County Islamic Councils, District Islamic Councils, Provincial Islamic Councils, and the High Islamic Council of Provinces) as well as the administrative bodies of urban and rural municipalities at the city and village levels.

The subnational administration in Iran is primarily organized at the provincial level. For administrative purposes the country is divided into 30 provinces (*ostan*). The ostans have subdivisions called districts (*shahrestan*). Shahrestans also have further subdivisions called rural counties (*bakhsh*). Ostans, shahrestans and bakhsh are deconcentrated governmental units and cover the whole territory of Iran.

The head of the Ostan administration is Ostandar, who is an official appointed by the central government. Expenditures at the ostan level are organized through line agencies and spending units. These units are responsible for provincial expenditures while national public services such as defense and those public goods with significant externalities are assigned to the central units.

One notices immediately the lack of data on local government expenditures for most of the MEWA countries.[5] This table shows a large variation in the size of central government across countries in the region. In the few countries where local government expenditure data is available, the size of local governments is significantly smaller when compared to what we see in other developed or developing countries.

The Structure of Subnational Administration in MEWA Countries

MEWA countries have a variety of subnational governments. Iran contains four subnational tiers made up of provinces, districts, and rural counties in addition to both urban and rural municipalities (See box 7.1). Both Jordan and Syria have a structure of governorates, districts, and sub-districts. In Palestine, both the West Bank and Gaza are subdivided into governorates and regions. In Turkey both provincial and sub-provincial district governors are appointed by the central government however municipal mayor and council members are elected.[6] Finally, in Yemen while both governors and district governors are appointed by the president the councils at both the governorate and district levels are directly elected by the people (see table 7.3). Heads of provincial governments are not generally elected by the people but are appointed by

5. *Database of Political Institutions (DPI) from the World Bank has a number of federalism indicators that include variables that show availability of elections in municipal governments and authority over taxing, spending or legislating at the local level. MEWA countries have significantly lower federalism scores compared to most of the other countries in the neighboring regions. See Beck et al. (2001) and Keefer (2007) for detailed descriptions of these variables. Tosun and Yilmaz (2010a) use these variables in their study of decentralization in the broader Middle East and North Africa (MENA) region.*
6. *See Tosun and Yilmaz (2010b) for stylized facts on local governments in Turkey.*

Table 7.3: Deconcentration and Decentralization Systems in Selected MEWA Countries

	Iran	Jordan	Lebanon	Syria	Turkey	Palestine	Yemen
Central Government Ministry	Ministry of Interior (MoI)	Ministry of Interior (MoI) / Ministry of Municipal Affairs	Ministry of Interior & Municipalities (MoIM)	Ministry of Local Administration (MLA)	Ministry of Interior	Ministry of Local Government (MoLG)	Ministry of Local Administration (MoLA)
Province District County	30 provinces (Ostan) 318 districts (Shahrestan) 854 rural counties (Bakhsh)	12 governorates 51 districts and 56 sub-districts	8 Provinces (Muhafaza) 25 Districts (caza)	14 Governorates 55 Districts 210 Sub-districts	81 provinces (il) 892 sub-province districts (ilce)	16 governorates (11 in West Bank and 5 in Gaza)	22 governorates
Accountability Arrangements	Provincial governor (Ostandar) is appointed by the President District Governor (Farmandar) is appointed by MoI. Rural county administrator (Bakhshdar) is appointed by the Ostandar	Governors are appointed by the Cabinet based on recommendation from the Minister of Interior.	Provincial Governors (Muhafezs) are appointed by the MoIM with the approval of the government council. District Governors (Kaymakams) are appointed by the Governors with the approval of the MoIM	Governor is appointed by presidential decree	Provincial and sub-provincial governors (vali/kaymakam) are proposed by the Minister of Interior and appointed by the Council of Ministers and the President	Governor is appointed by the President.	Governor is appointed by the President District governor is appointed by the Prime Minister
Council	Provincial Planning and Development Council (Chair: Ostandar; Line Ministry reps) District Planning Committee (Chair: Farmandar; Line Ministry reps)	Each governorate has two councils chaired by the Governor: - *Executive Council* including the heads of the Line ministries directorates.. - *Advisory Council* made up of 25 appointed members, selected from the following bodies: the Parliament members from the concerned governorate, the mayors of municipalities, the private sector organizations, and the civil society.	Reconstruction and Development Council (CDR - at the national level) – appointed by the government council.	Governorate council directly elected by people	Special Provincial Administration (SPA). Provincial general assembly is the legislative body of the SPA and its members are elected by popular vote.		Governorate council directly elected by people District council directly elected by people

Table 7.3: Deconcentration and Decentralization Systems in Selected MEWA Countries (cont.)

	Iran	Jordan	Lebanon	Syria	Turkey	Palestine	Yemen
Urban Municipalities Rural Municipalities	More than 1000 municipalities (Shahr) More than 68,000 rural municipalities (Deh/Roosta)	93 municipalities and Greater Amman Municipality	42 municipal federations 944 municipalities	11 Governorate cities 96 cities 248 towns 207 villages	2951 municipalities 35402 villages	133 municipalities 251 village councils 49 joint service councils	332 districts municipality
Accountability Arrangements	Mayor of an urban municipality (Shahrdar) is jointly appointed by the MoI and City Council, which is directly elected by people. Mayor of a rural municipality (Dehyar) is jointly appointed by the MoI and Village Council, which is directly elected by people.	Municipal mayor and council members are directly elected by people.	Municipal mayor and council members are directly elected by people.	Municipal council is directly elected by people. Mayor is elected by the municipal council, election endorsed by the President for cities and the Ministry of Local Administration for towns and villages	Municipal mayor and council members are directly elected by people.	Municipal mayor and council members are directly elected by people. Village councils and joint service committees are appointed by the MoLG.	N/A

Source: Compiled by Mehmet S. Tosun and Serdar Yilmaz based on World Bank and UCLG consultancy missions and UCLG country datasheets.

the central government ministries and/or the President. Among the countries that have formal provincial councils, council members are directly elected only in Syria, Turkey, and Yemen.

Municipalities are run by elected mayors and council members in most countries, however, there are a few exceptions. In Syria, municipal council members are directly elected by citizens. The mayor is then elected by the municipal council and then endorsed by the President, for cities, and the Ministry of Local Administrations for towns and villages.

In Palestine, mayors and councilors are democratically elected, while village councils and joint service committees are appointed by the Ministry of Local Government. In Iran, there is a complex deconcentrated (and decentralized) system, however representation of people is partial and indirect. First, there is the involvement of the Ministry of Interior (MOI) in both urban and rural municipalities. Second, people elect city or village councils that in turn appoint mayors jointly with the MOI.

Expenditure Assignments

In the region, subnational deconcentrated or decentralized governments have very limited number of "own" responsibilities. Most of the local expenditure responsibilities can be classified as "delegated" expenditures as opposed to "own" expenditure responsibilities.[7] Central government ministries make decisions on most services that are traditionally provided by local governments in other countries (see Table 7.4).[8] Among MEWA countries, Turkey, Palestine, and Syria are

7. *Delegated responsibilities are those transferred to the deconcentrated units of the central government for delivery of services while actual budgeting and financing decisions are carried out at the central level.*
8. *Tosun and Yilmaz (2008) assigned points to central, provincial and municipal government involvement in expenditures and thereby created a basic indicator for expenditure decentralization. According to that indicator, Turkey is the most decentralized in the MEWA group followed closely by Palestine.*

Table 7.4: Responsibility for Financing and Provision of Public Services in Selected MEWA Countries

	Financing								Provision							
Function	Iran	Jordan	Lebanonon	Syria	Turkey	Palestine	Yemen	Worldwide	Iran	Jordan	Lebanonon	Syria	Turkey	Palestine	Yemen	Worldwide
Social Welfare	C	C	C	C,P	C	C	C	C	C	C	C	C,P	C	C	C	C,P,M
Hospitals	C	C	C	C,P	C	C	C	C,P	C	C	C	C,P	C	C	C,P	C,P
Public Health	C	C	C	C,P	C	C	C	C,P,M	C	C	C	C,P	C	C	C,P	C,P,M
Universities	C	C	C	C,P	C,P	C	C	C,P	C	C	C	C,P	C,P	C	C	C,P
Secondary Education	C	C	C	C,P	C	C	C	C,P,M	C	C	C	C,P	C	C	C	C,P,M
Primary Education	C	C	C	C,P	C	C	C	C,P,M	C	C	C	C,P	C	C	C	C,P,M
Housing	C	C	C	C	C,M	C	C	C,P	C	C	C	C	C,M	C	C	C,P,M
Urban Transport	C,P,M	C	C	M	M	C,P,M	C,P	C,P,M	C,P,M	C,P	C	M	M	C,P,M	C,P,M	C,P,M
Railroads	C	C	C	C	C	N/A	C	C,P	C	C	C	C	C	N/A	C	C,P
Airports	C	C	C	C	C	C	C	C,P	C	C	C	C	C	C	C	C,P
Ports and Navigable Waterways	C	C	C	C	C	C	C	C	C	C	C	C	C	C	C	C
Urban Highways	C,P,M	M	C	C,P, M	C,M	C,P,M	C,P	C,P,M	C,P,M	M	C	C,P, M	C,M	C,P,M	C,P,M	C,P,M
Interurban Highways	C	C	C	C,P,M	C,M	C,P,M	C,P	C,P	C	C	C	C,P,M	C,M	C,P,M	C,P,M	C,P
Electricity	C	C	C	C	M	M	C	C,P,M	C	C	C	C	M	C	C	C,P,M
Waste Collection	M	M	C	M	M	M	P	M	M	M	C	M	M	M	P	M
Water and Sewerage	P,M	C	C	C,P,M	M	M	C,P	M	P,M	C	C	C,P,M	M	M	C,P	M
Fire Protection	C	C	C	C	C,M	C,P,M	C,P	M	C	C	C	C	C,M	C,P,M	C,P	M
Heating	C	C	C	C	M	M	N/A	M	C	C	C	C	M	M	N/A	M
Irrigation	C	C	C	C		C,P	C,P	M	C	C	C	C		C,P	C,P	M
Police	C	C	C,M	P,M	C,P,M	C	C	C,P,M	C	C	C,M	P,M	C,P,M	C	C	C,P,M

Source: Compiled by Tosun and Yilmaz based on World Bank and UCLG consultancy missions and UCLG country datasheets.
C= central, P= provincial, M= municipal

more decentralized on the expenditure side than Iran, Jordan, Lebanon, and Yemen.[9]

In the majority of the countries examined, local governments assure infrastructures maintenance (roads, streetlights, and green areas), solid waste and sanitation, public markets, sport and cultural activities, and often urban planning and building control. Expenditure assignments in utility service functions are particularly similar to worldwide practice in Turkey and, in theory, in Palestine. In the latter country, the local government law (1997) lists twenty seven areas of activity relating to municipal powers and responsibilities, including: producing driving licenses, regulating businesses and industries. However in many cases (water and electricity networks, building permits, municipal waste deposits, road planning, etc.), the State of Israel retains control over land within or on the edges of municipal borders. In order to intervene, municipal authorities must obtain their authorization.

In Iran, Jordan, and Lebanon many local services have been significantly centralized. In Iran, the distinction between affairs regulated by the State and local authorities' tasks and responsibilities has resulted in unclear legislative requirements. In Jordan, after 2001, the central government took back 13 of the 39 local government responsibilities listed in law, and many local services were given to the private sector. In Lebanon, the role of municipalities is also very limited. The central authority exercises the majority of powers and responsibilities that are theoretically assigned to the municipal level, particularly in relation to planning, transport, education, social services, public hygiene services, water resource management and distribution, energy and economic development. Even town planning decisions are taken by the High Urban Planning Council, which operates under the authority of the Ministry.

Syrian cities and towns have full or partial responsibilities in local services such as roads, solid waste, water and sewerage, planning, and transportation.

Revenue Assignments

Countries in the region have largely ad-hoc local revenue systems that are under strict central government control (see Table 7.5).

Palestine is the only country where local governments have some control over both the tax rate and the tax base. Furthermore, the municipalities impose new taxes or fees without the explicit approval of the central government and they collect and administer them locally.[10] For certain revenue items, there are differences in practice between West Bank and Gaza. For example, while property taxes are collected and administered by the central government in the West Bank, Gaza municipalities collect and administer property taxes themselves. In Gaza, 90 percent of revenues are kept by municipalities, while the remaining 10 percent are transferred to the national government. Other taxes, such as the fuel tax, are centrally collected and should be partially transferred to the municipalities according to current laws. The enforcement of these provisions remains under discussion. Municipalities implement most infrastructure projects with financing from donor countries which oversee the projects and whose priorities often take precedence.[11]

However, municipal revenue autonomy in Palestine is not something granted by

9. *The 2005 Jordan Country Profile published by the Economic Research Forum (ERF) and the Institut de la Méditerranée (FEMISE) notes that Jordanian municipalities, with the exception of Greater Amman Municipality, have limited financial independence. Local government expenditure is only 6% of total government expenditures (ERF, 2005: 17).*
10. *This is despite the 1997 Law on Local Authorities which established, at least on paper, central authority's strong control of local administrations (see Box 7.3 for more information on this law).*
11. *http://www.pogar.org/countries/theme.aspx?t=6&cid=14*

Table 7.5: Revenue Assignment in Selected MEWA Countries

Country	Revenue Assignment
Iran	All local levies are required to be consistent with the government's annual budget and the National Five Year Development Plans and to be in line with the capacity to pay as determined by the Ministry of Interior (ceiling for local tax/local income ratio). With adoption of the Law on Tax Amalgamation (2003) revenue collection has been effectively re-centralized and almost all taxes are collected by the central government. One of the main locally collected fees is the land use change and density increase tax.
Jordan	Municipalities have some control over the following revenue instruments: solid waste collection fees, business license fees, building permits, property tax (on land and structures), municipal traffic fines, municipal parking fees.
Lebanon	Local governments are not free to introduce new taxes. They are free to set tax rates for some taxes but they are not free to change the tax base of some taxes. Central governments have control over revenue and other budget decisions of local governments. Some local taxes are collected and administered by local governments and local fees are exclusively collected and administered by local governments.
Syria	Local governments are not free to introduce new taxes. They are free to set tax rates for some taxes but they are not free to change the tax base of some taxes (inspection and slaughtering fees, motorcycle fees, fees for the sale/rental/auction of property, fees for public property use, building license fees, fees for services). Central governments have control over revenue and other budget decisions of local governments. Local fees are collected and administered exclusively by local governments.
Turkey	Local governments are not free to introduce new taxes and they are not free to set tax rates or change tax bases. Limitations on these come from separate laws on local governments and municipal budgets. Central governments have control over revenue and other budget decisions of local governments. Some local taxes are collected and administered by local governments and local duties and fees are exclusively collected and administered by local governments.
Palestinian National Authority	According to a World Bank consultancy report, Palestinian regulatory framework provides the greatest autonomy to the local governments. While local governments have a right to set taxes or create new ones, they can only do so through initiating amendments to the tax law. Many taxes and fees are collected and administered locally by local governments.
Yemen	Central government sets both tax rates and base, local governments can make proposals for taxes and fees. Apart from the religion tax ('zakat') most taxes are not collected in many districts, particularly in rural areas.

Source: Compiled by Mehmet S. Tosun and Serdar Yilmaz based on World Bank and UCLG consultancy missions and UCLG country datasheets

laws. Due to special security circumstance and discontinuity in the geographic area of Palestine, municipalities have invented their own ways of raising revenues and they often find ways of rationalizing such practices (World Bank, 2006). In general Palestinian municipalities are very poor financially.

Iran, Jordan, Turkey, and Palestine, have some form of property taxation at the local level. While local property tax is generally known as a key revenue instrument that grants fiscal autonomy to local governments in many developed and developing countries, use of property taxation in the MEWA region is very limited. This is again due to central government's control over both the rate and base of the tax. In Turkey, municipalities have some representation in the property valuation process of the property tax but they have no control over the tax rates. In Jordan, there is a UNDP funded project to move property tax management to municipalities over time. Both Jordan and Turkey have property tax systems that are based on the value of land and structures, whereas Iran has a land-use change and density increase tax.

Municipalities in Jordan rely on the national government for most revenues. Internally generated revenues represent less than 40 percent of municipal finances and come from more than 70 different sources. All municipal budgets must be approved by the Ministry of Municipal Affairs which raises questions about catering to local needs using local budgets. (Al-Hajaj, 2010; UNDP-POGAR, 2010a.)

Municipalities in Lebanon and Syria have some limited control over local tax rates but the central government has control over the tax base and other local budget decisions. In Lebanon municipalities have been assigned 16 direct local taxes (tax on rent value; tax on meeting spaces and clubs; advertising tax; etc), however local governments can not create additional taxes nor can they make changes to the tax base. In Syria local governments have been assigned a series of duties over which they can set the rate level.[12] However these rate changes must be approved by the governorate. In addition to this, local authorities have also been assigned the right to 20 percent of the sale value of electricity. In 2003 local duties collected at the local level represented 9.6 percent of total local budgets.

Approximately two thirds of Lebanese municipalities have revenues less than 65,000 USD per year. It is estimated that only 30 out of 700 local authorities have an adequate tax base to provide local services. Another difficulty in the local fiscal system is that municipal funds come from over 35 different sources (Bassil and Karam, 2009; UNDP-POGAR, 2010b).

Central government has strong control over tax rates and tax bases in Yemen, where local governments can only make proposals for taxes and fees. Throughout the MEWA countries local fees are largely collected and administered by local governments.

A recent UNDP report on governance in Saudi Arabia notes that "there is no fiscal separation between the central and municipal governments" (UNDP-POGAR, 2010c). It was also noted in the same report that "government spending on municipal services, infrastructure development and local subsidies in Saudi Arabia amounted to 7 percent of the government budget for 2003," and that "the Ministry of Municipal and Rural Affairs and the Ministry of Finance are

12. *The main duties are on building and repair licenses, fines, rent registration, spirits, auction sales, street paving, sewerage, street cleaning, vehicles, slaughtering, advertising, street sales, fuel consumption, fuel storing, ports, on documents, improvement duties etc. (Financial law 1/1994)*

currently crafting legislation to privatize municipal tax collection" (UNDP-POGAR, 2010c).

Intergovernmental Transfers

Allocation rules for transfers to local governments are also mainly ad-hoc, except in Jordan, Lebanon, and Turkey and to some extent Palestine (see Annex 7.1). In these countries, the transfer system is based on a formula that uses different revenue sources. They get transfers based on 40 percent of the proceeds from vehicle licensing fees and a special legislation fee of 6 percent on petroleum products produced or imported (except fuel oil) by the Jordan Petroleum Refinery Company. These proceeds are first deposited in a special account in the Ministry of Finance and then transferred to the Cities and Villages Development Bank "on a regular monthly basis to be distributed to the municipalities according to a ratio established by the Prime Ministry based on recommendation from the Minister of Municipal Affairs." (Jordan Ministry of Municipal Affairs, 2009: 8) The ratio (or transfer formula) is determined by taking into consideration such general factors as population, proportion of its contribution in overall revenue generation, particular importance of location and non-local responsibilities.

In Turkey, the transfer and allocation system is based on grants and shared revenues (specific percentages from the general budget tax revenues such as income and consumption taxes) that are set by the central government. Annex 7.1 shows the percentages allocated to specific local government units. Certain criteria such as population, acreage, number of villages in the city, rural population and city development index are used for distribution of transfers among local governments.[13] Palestine uses transport fees for general transfers and a separate account for discretionary/emergency transfers.

In Lebanon, 10 percent of the rates collected by the national telephone, electricity and water public services, as well as 3 percent of taxes on property transfers are supposed to be transferred directly to local governments. However, this payment requires a decision from the Minister, and often undergoes important delays. In addition, the revenue of 13 indirect taxes, collected by the State on behalf of local governments, goes into the Autonomous Municipal Fund (AMF). After deductions for the cost of collection and staff salaries, the remaining funds are transferred to local government (75 percent among municipalities and 25 percent among municipal federations). The Ministry of Finance distributes to municipalities according to a transfer formula which is based on factors such as population, proportion of its contribution in overall revenue generation, particular importance of municipality's location and non-local responsibilities. Allocation rules are decided annually by the Ministry of Interior and Municipalities and the Ministry of Finance with the approval of the central government. Funds coming from the AMF make up approximately 80 percent of local government budgets.[14] But transfers are carried out irregularly and with a lack of transparency (see below, "*Significant Spatial Disparities in Public Expenditures*").

In Syria 90 percent of local government revenue is assigned revenue from the central government[15], which is transferred from the General Budget of the Government, through the Ministry of Finance, to the Ministry of Local Administrations. These funds are redistributed

13. See Tosun and Yilmaz (2010b) for more on recent law changes regarding intergovernmental transfer formula.

independent of the collection share of each municipality, resulting in a disincentive to tax collection and to increased investment that would result in greater local tax revenue.

In Palestine, municipalities have been historically less dependent on central government transfers compared to other countries in the region due mainly to historical, as well as current political and security reasons. In fact, this situation has not been affected significantly by the Intifada period, as there is no difference today in the amount of central government transfers as a share of total local revenues, which remains constant at about 5 percent[16] (World Bank, 2006). While there is a formula for the pooling and distribution of transport fees according to the 1997 Local Government Law, the formula is partially applied, and discretionary/emergency transfers are ad hoc.

In other MEWA countries, there is either no formula or only a non-binding arrangement for transfers. For example, Iran makes development transfers from its oil revenues but allocation rules are not based on a formula, and are decided annually by the parliament. Yemen uses shared revenue from 28 different taxes, the religious tax Zakat being the main source, but the council of ministers uses only non-binding guidelines based on population density, financing gap, degree of deprivation and performance in revenue collection.

Borrowing

Local borrowing is either nonexistent or very limited in most MEWA region countries with few exceptions. In Turkey, local administrations can engage in domestic and foreign borrowing in accordance with the municipalities law (Law no. 5393) and the special provincial administrations law (Law no. 5302). Municipal borrowing is, in principle, capped in proportion to annual revenues (OECD, 2004). Foreign borrowing is subject to approval by the Treasury and it is heavily concentrated on metropolitan municipalities. Besides the Treasury, the Bank of Provinces, under the Ministry of Public Works and Settlement, also play an important role as a lender of short and long term loans to local administrations. The outstanding debt of local administrations to the Bank of Provinces was about Turkish Lira (TL) 5.51 billion or about 0.6 percent of GDP in 2009 (Turkish Ministry of Interior, General Directorate for Local Authorities, 2009). There was a significant increase in municipal borrowing and indebtedness in the post-1980 economic liberalization period, which subsided in the years following the financial crisis in 2001 but has continued since 2005 with a substantial jump in 2008. Recent trends in domestic and foreign debt of local administrations in Turkey are shown in Annex 7.2. Foreign financing of large projects such as subway construction seems to have played a role in the rise in foreign debt stock. Also, short term debt has shown the largest increase compared to long term debt. Overall, total debt has reached about 2.8 percent of GDP in 2008. More than half of this debt has accrued to metropolitan municipalities. The rising indebtedness of municipalities is a serious problem for the local administrations as well as the central government.

Jordan's municipalities can also engage in borrowing. Cities and Villages Development Bank (CVDB) is a state development bank specialized in municipal lending, established in 1979 as an independent public institution. It

14. *This is based on a 2001 questionnaire on 350 municipalities conducted by the Lebanese Centre for Policy Studies as cited in Bassil and Karam (2009).*
15. *As of 2003 transferred taxes in Syria consist of export taxes and customs duties; 10 percent of the corporate profit tax; 10 percent of income tax; 7.5 percent of real estate tax; 5 percent of duties and taxes on cars and their registration and 1 percent of fuel consumption tax (Doherty 2005).*
16. *This is the average figure for Palestine municipalities in the Intifada period.*

provides low interest loans for infrastructure and related projects. The standing loans by the CVDB were JD 61.5 million (0.4 percent of GDP) in 2010. Municipal borrowing from CVDB is subject to approval by the Ministry of Municipal Affairs whereas the board of CVDB approves borrowing from commercial banks or any other financial institutions. Any foreign borrowing is subject to approval by the cabinet. In other MEWA countries, local borrowing is largely non-existent.

In Lebanon, aid obtained by municipalities from the central government through the AMF can also take the form of either credit granted by the Lebanese government or aid given to carry out specific infra-structure projects (public waste, monu-ment restoration, etc.) in one or several municipalities.

Issues, Constraints and Opportunities for Local Government Finance in the MEWA Region

Prevalence of Deconcentrated Government Structure

Local government systems in most of the MEWA region, with the exception of Turkey and Palestine, can be characterized as a form of deconcentration rather than one of devolved local self-government. In general, the public administration system is highly centralized, equipped with an elaborate system of deconcentrated field offices of line agencies. Decisions for the most part, especially service delivery decisions, are made by the central government and the role of subnational authorities is largely confined to carrying these out. In all countries, the de-concentrated units of the central government provide a big chunk of public services, including health and education, under strict guidance of the central government. Whereas, decentralized units (generally municipalities) perform a limited number of functions such as street paving and maintenance, construction of local roads, street lighting, garbage collection, library and park services, and issuing permits for constructions.

A good example of the importance (and prevalence) of deconcentrated systems is the case of Iran which was featured in Box 7.1. In Iran, line ministries providing services, such as gas, electricity, transportation, education and health, are organized by sector at the provincial level. The municipal sector provides urban municipal services including public health, recreational services including parks, public safety including fire stations and local transportation including buses and taxis as well as rural municipal services. While Iran has an elaborate local council structure which is an important component of the subnational administration system, the areas in which the local council can legislate and pass bills is restricted. In fact, in relation to the entire range of issues that impact local economic development, the council and municipality has a secondary or almost no role. The restricted interactions and limited role of elected councils constitute a major obstacle to increased inclusiveness and accountability (Tajbakhsh, 2000). This weak institu-tionalization, in conjunction with the enhanced role of the Ministry of Interior's Municipalities Organization is among the factors that exacerbate Mayor-Council tense relations, primarily because mayors feel increasingly dependent upon the central government and consequently less accountable to the municipal council (Tajbakhsh, 2000).

Significant Spatial Disparities in Public Expenditures

Another important issue is disparity in public expenditures found across regions within MEWA countries. While some expenditure functions are delegated to local governments, provinces, and municipalities, particularly poorer regions have difficulty meeting their expenditure responsibilities due to lack of proper revenue assignment and/or inadequate intergovernmental transfers and borrowing. This is an important issue as such disparities may lead to deterioration in welfare in those regions.

For example, in Jordan the municipal expenditures per capita in 2007 varied between 207 Jordan Dinars (JD) in the province of Karak, followed by Mafraq (146 JD), and 7.30 JD in Aqaba or 14.4 JD in Jarash, with the median falling at 52.7 JD per capita. There are significant variations in the public expenditures per capita both across and within the three main regions.[17] Household expenditures also show significant spatial disparities in such important expenditure items as education and medical care. Hence, despite government transfers, significant spatial disparities remain. Similar spatial disparity is also observed in Syria, where in 2003, local spending per resident went from 55,523 Syrian Pound (SYP) in Al Sweida to 1,575 SYP in Aleppo and Damascus), the average being 2,527 SYP per resident.

Many of the existing revenue systems simply perpetuate these disparities. Syria's transfer system for example, which allocates funding based on tax registered residents, does not take into consideration regional development or the presence of disadvantaged areas with high population growth.

Ad Hoc Intergovernmental Transfers and Borrowing Practices

As shown in Annex 7.1, MEWA countries have largely ad hoc intergovernmental transfer systems where most countries in the region do not use transfer formulas. There is also often significant difference between de-jure and de-facto practices. Lebanon is an example where 75 percent of the Autonomous Municipal Fund (AMF) is invested in large scale development projects by the central government through the Council of Development and Reconstruction (CDR), and other development institutions, and hence not transferred to municipalities. The majority of local governments in Lebanon do not have sufficient resources to meet their needs. This has led in some cases to unsustainable borrowing as depicted in the case of the urban community of d'Al Fayhaa in Box 7.2.

Local borrowing practices are also largely ad hoc. An important problem is lack of transparency in local borrowing which could lead to serious indebtedness and financial crisis. Faced in many cases by an imbalance between responsibilities and revenues along with unpredictable or reduced transfers the environment is ripe for unsustainable debt. Local administrations in Jordan and Turkey have engaged in significant borrowing to meet their rising investment needs. In Jordan, there has been a substantial growth in capital expenditures as the share of capital expenditures rose from 41 percent of total expenditures in 2003 to about 58 percent in 2008, reaching a share as high as 65 percent in 2007. Along with this increase, Jordan municipalities have run substantial fiscal deficits recently with an average deficit of 0.33 percent of GDP. Fiscal deficit in 2007, when capital expenditures showed the largest increase, was 0.62

17. *Note that the expenditure numbers for the Amman region do not include the Greater Amman Municipality which explains the low per capita figures for that region. Amman municipality has a special status and is not counted among the 93 municipalities. Separate data on Amman municipality was not available.*

Box 7.2: The Case of the Urban Community of d'Al Fayhaa

The Urban Community of d'Al Fayhaa is made up of the municipalities of Tripoli, El Mina and Beddaoui and has a total population of 340,000 inhabitants.

The revenue of municipal federations in Lebanon is, by law, made up of: 10 percent of the revenues of member local governments, an additional percentage assigned from the budgets of local governments benefiting from common projects undertaken by the Urban Community and 25 percent of the taxes deposited in the AMF.

In practice, due to the financial constraints of most municipalities, they are neither able to transfer 10 percent of their revenues to the municipal federations nor make additional contributions for service delivery in their area. Transfers from the AMF (which as mentioned above are closer to 2 percent than the legislated 25 percent) are also limited in that only 40 percent of funding can be used to pay for service provision (while 60 percent must be reserved for staff salaries).

Even if it is one of the most important municipal federations in Lebanon, the Urban Community of d'Al Fayhaa is not able to finance the common services it provides (garbage collection, management of slaughter houses, landfills, etc) which have been contracted out to private companies, nor to cover their entire staff salaries. The debt of the Urban Community increases yearly and all new projects of common nature have been cancelled in the last 6 years.

percent of GDP. Following different sources, this debt is due in part to the fact that most municipalities in Jordan, particularly the smaller ones, do not have the resources to pay their employees and must turn to borrowing to pay their current expenditures (UCLG, 2007). A recent report by the Jordan Ministry of Municipal Affairs shows that municipal indebtedness is an important problem in Jordan for which a municipal debt reduction account has been established by the central government (MoMA, 2009).

In Turkey, local administrations had a fiscal deficit of TL 7.1 billion (0.75 percent of GDP) in 2008 while the total outstanding debt, excluding deferred payments, of Turkish local administrations was 2.8 percent of GDP in that same year (Turkish Ministry of Interior, General Directorate for Local Authorities, 2009). An important issue here is that municipalities are not required to have balanced budgets and thereby rely on central government to finance their debt in the case of insufficient resources.

The cases of Turkey and Jordan show that these countries are suffering from fiscal deficits and indebtedness at the local level which is at least partially driven by ad hoc local borrowing practices and soft budget constraints.

Internal and External Conflicts and Decentralization

Conflicts have particular relevance to the Middle East and Western Asia region as

Box 7.3: Conflict, Government Structure and the 1997 Law on Local Authorities in Palestine

The local government system in Palestine reflects the realities of the Israeli occupation. The overriding concerns in the design of local government system have always been providing emergency services and security through central control. As a result, laws, the political system, administrative arrangements and development practices of local governments are geared towards these objectives rather than toward providing services to local communities.

Prior to the 1994 Oslo Peace Accord, in the absence of a sovereign state, Palestinian local governments have had to fend for themselves in providing services to local communities. The Ministry of Local Governments (MOLG) was established in 1994 to help build an effective local government system. However, this current legal framework in Palestine has assigned the central government strong formal controls over local governments (World Bank, 2006).

The Law on Local Authorities of 1997 (LLA) provides the legal basis for the current local government system. LLA draws heavily on other regional country legislative frameworks, particularly that of Jordan. LLA grants significant powers to the central government, primarily Ministry of Local Government in its role as the sector regulatory agency, including provisions for approvals of a wide range of activities of local governments and claw-back clauses where autonomy appears to be granted (World Bank, 2006).

The LLA provides the legal basis for municipal expenditure responsibilities and revenue-raising authorities. However, there is a significant mismatch between the legal assignments to municipalities and the reality on the ground (World Bank, 2006). The absence of an effective public administration system compels the larger municipalities to assume responsibilities that are not necessarily assigned to them by law, such as fire fighting service and maintenance of school buildings (World Bank, 2006).

The LLA grants the central government extensive powers over municipal governments in terms of control over revenue sources. They have to obtain the approval of the central government in setting the tax rates and defining the revenue bases. Mostly within the confines of the centrally defined tax and fee bases, assessment strategies, and rates, the local governments are provided with revenue sources such as property taxes, building permits and utility revenues. They are also allowed to perform certain public functions and market services to raise additional revenues. Yet, in practice, the municipalities invent their own ways of raising revenues and they often find ways of rationalizing such practices in old laws (World Bank, 2006).

it's one of the most conflict-ridden regions in the world.[18] Palestine leads all other countries in the total number of conflicts and, particularly, in number of minor and internal conflicts. Iran and Iraq lead in the number of major conflict (or war) years and follow with Turkey and Palestine in internal conflict years. Studies show evidence of strong negative spillovers from conflicts and point to external conflicts as a significant obstacle to a decentralized government structure in the region (Tosun and Sen, 2008 and Tosun and Yilmaz, 2010a). The special circumstance of Palestine is described in Box 7.3 to show the unique form of government structure in Palestine in the face of a persistent conflict environment.

Capacity Building and Community Participation

Local government officials across the region generally express their need for more data and information. However, they tend to employ insufficiently trained staff, and therefore do not have the capacity to work at a policy level and use local financial data. They simply do not have enough resources (time, money, or people). The need for local data depends not only on the size of local governments, but also on the service responsibilities assigned to them. Better informed and trained decision makers at the local government level would be an important element in implementing a decentralization strategy. In Lebanon for example, local tax collection is hampered by a slow tax evaluation process, non-computerized accounting practice, and a lack of tax collectors (Atallah, 1999). Similar problems are found, at least to some extent, across the countries surveyed.

There are also good practices in the region, particularly regarding capacity building and community participation as depicted in the cases from Jordan, Syria, and Turkey. For example, Eskisehir Metropolitan Municipality in Turkey is a good example of a local administration that gives much importance to capacity building and training of municipal employees.[19] Fuheis municipality in Jordan provides a successful case of local community involvement.[20] Some of the initiatives by the municipality are local community involvement in the planning process (through community proposals), formation of volunteer action committees, capacity building through strengthening of the skills of staff and department heads by holding workshops and training sessions, partnerships with the private sector, access to information (such as financial statistics) and use of computer technology –particularly Geographic Information Systems (GIS)–, and finally integration of gender and youth considerations in the local decision-making process. Box 7.4 describes two other examples of good practices regarding capacity building.

Conclusions

For a variety of reasons (such as tradition, history and culture), the responsibilities assigned to local governments in the MEWA regim have not been as extensive as those in many other parts of the world. In their efforts to reform the local government sector, governments should recognize that decentralization requires sharing of fiscal roles and responsibilities between central and local governments accompanied by a robust capacity to deliver services both centrally and locally. The challenge is to determine how to sort-out the responsibilities and financing among different types of local governments.

One possible suggestion to allow the decentralization process to move forward

18. *See Milton-Edwards and Hinchcliffe (2004) for a chronology and detailed discussion of conflicts in the Middle East since 1945.*

19. *Eskisehir is a city synonymous with higher education and is virtually a city of students. It is home to Anadolu University, which is the largest university in Turkey in terms of student enrollment. The mayor of Eskisehir Metropolitan Municipality, formerly president of the Anadolu University, maintained a good working relationship between the municipality and the university. It is noted that, all contract employees in Eskisehir Metropolitan Municipality have at least Bachelor degrees. http://www.eskisehir-bld.gov.tr/cityiseskisehir/index.html*

20. *Fuheis is a small municipality about 15km northwest of Amman.*

Box 7.4. Good Practice in Capacity Building: Jordan and Syria

Devolution of Property Tax Management to Municipalities in Jordan

In 2004 the Jordanian Ministry of Finance (MOF) and the Ministry of Municipal Affairs (MoMA) began a project to transfer the responsibility for property tax collection from the MOF to the municipalities.

The project, funded by the UNDP, was divided into two phases (phase 1: 2004-2010, phase 2: 2010- 2012) to allow new strategies to be tested in larger municipalities before being implemented in smaller ones with lower capacity.

The project involves:

- Conducting legal and procedural review
- Establishing integrated data base and network for property tax management centers, across the country
- Capacity building for local government staff (600 employees)
- Awareness campaigns for citizens and tax payers
- Development of administrative set up, and restructuring of property tax management units.

To date 47 (out of 93) municipalities have been transferred the responsibility of property tax collection (the remaining 46 are targeted in phase 2 of the project). Large municipalities collect both for themselves and on behalf of the smaller neighboring municipalities.

An increase has been noted in property tax collection since the beginning of this project (Al-Hajaj, 2010).

Municipal Administration Modernization Program in Syria

This joint initiative funded, by the Syrian Arab Republic and the European Union, has as its long range purpose to improve the quality of life of people in urban centers across the country. With an initial focus in 6 cities there are currently projects underway in Damascus, Aleppo, Lattakia, Tartous, Homs, Der Zour and Palmyra.

The goal is to seek out new frameworks and best practices in the long term management of urban growth. The program will deliver a series of interconnected action plans focusing on legislative, financial and management reform. Specific areas targeted by this program include: Decentralized governance; supporting local decision making; institutional development; financial resource management; property management; local development; twinning agreements and partnerships; urban planning and informal settlements; geographic information systems (GIS); public private partnerships; traffic and transportation; solid waste management; Local Agenda 21 and gender.

Source: http://www.mam-sy.org/index.php?p_id=11&lang=en

across the region is the application of asymmetric decentralization. Specific criteria can be set to classify local governments into different categories that have asymmetric taxing and spending responsibilities and borrowing privileges. This would give impetus to decentralization reform processes by which regional governments (governorates) and local governments might be empowered with increased autonomy in expenditure and revenue decisions that remain in line with their capacity to meet these new responsibilities and build toward greater ones. However, there is also a need for systematically reviewing legal and regulatory standards for "sorting out" rules and responsibilities among different types and levels of governments. In addition, existing and future revenue commitments on the part of central governments must be honored both in quantity and timeframe to allow local governments to plan for and deliver their mandated services.

In the long run, the governments in the region need to devolve expenditure responsibilities further to local governments while making them fully accountable before their respective constituencies for policy results, in terms of their effectiveness and efficiency in delivering quality public services. To this end, they should consider strengthening local government accountability mechanisms by systemic collection, analysis, and dissemination of information about local fiscal performance and compliance with financial and policy goals. Such information is essential both to informed community participation through political process and to the monitoring of municipal performance by the central government.

In reforming local government systems the most challenging task for the governments in the region would be restructuring the overall revenue system in a manner that provides local governments "fiscal space" to strengthen own revenue and expenditure arrangements. The governments should first make sure that adequate steps are taken to establish accountability mechanisms, then boost revenue autonomy by giving local governments adequate decision-making powers on tax rates and the determination of some tax bases in order to improve budgetary predictability. They should gradually lift central government controls on local fees and taxes after making sure that local revenue generation is maintained.

The governments in the region should consider establishing a multilevel government coordinating body that would operate across the different tiers of government to launch fiscal decentralization reforms. This coordinating body would be a mechanism for the central government to improve the design and gauge the direction, pace, and extent of decentralization, and disseminate information, provide training and directly engage municipal governments in the decentralization process. This body would be instrumental in developing institutions for intergovernmental cooperation and dialogue. It will be especially central to increasing local public expenditure efficiency in areas of concurrent expenditure responsibilities and creating strong incentives (financial and legal) to promote cooperative arrangements among local governments for service delivery.

In public service delivery, the governments could explore the participation of the private sector in both financing and delivery of public services to improve the overall efficiency of local government expenditures. Inter-municipal cooperation and collaboration with the private sector might be a means of overcoming inefficiencies associated with small size of municipalities. However the choice of management model must remain a local one to ensure the public appropriation and approval of the chosen methods.

The governments should study rationalizing the transfer system so as to make it a more effective instrument for the implementation of policies of national interest at the local level and reduce spatial fiscal disparities. This would include an examination of both conditional and unconditional transfer systems. They should establish transparent rule-based transfer systems with explicit formulas for equalization. They should explore ideas for a combination of unconditional and matching grants that would promote municipal governments to exploit their revenue bases and improve the efficiency of tax collection.

Another important element in the implementation of a decentralization strategy is capacity building through investment in both staff capacity and information technology. The region needs more capacity building initiatives that are supported by domestic and international funds and agencies.

Central governments in the region should also credibly commit to the strengthening of local government management capacity both in terms of long term budget planning and the sustainability of debt. This will involve enforcing hard budget constraints for local governments and ensuring that local governments receive the funds they are assigned under law and that these income sources are sufficient to allow them to provide their mandated services. This process will be important, particularly for local government borrowing as for many local governments in MEWA, unsustainable debt has become one of the only options for continuing to provide service. In some cases, lack of long-term capacity planning has led some local governments to accumulate significant and sometimes unsustainable debt. While the central government should set responsibilities for local government, and ensure matching long-term predictable funding, it should also refrain from bailing out over-indebted local governments. This may mean letting some local governments fail first and then be subject to centrally led financial restructuring rules.

Finally, a critical issue in the MEWA region is the role of conflicts in centralization. It seems external conflicts set a major obstacle to the decentralization process and often is a key impetus for recentralization movements. Regional conflict prevention should be seen as a regional or international public good of which the collective provision would ease the burden on the central and local governments of individual countries.

This chapter presented an overview and comparison of local government finance in the Middle East and Western Asia (MEWA) countries followed by a discussion on some of the issues that are important in local government performance. The chapter also included region-wide proposals for reform. As has been shown throughout the chapter, MEWA countries have very centralized government structures. Some of the challenges facing local government finance and decentralization as discussed in the chapter are the preferences on the part of central governments for deconcentrated government units to provide local services than the devolution of powers to the local level; spatial disparity in public expenditures that require a better (formula based) intergovernmental transfer system; ad-hoc intergovernmental transfer and borrowing practices;

internal and external conflicts that could limit further fiscal decentralization and draw resources away from local government finances; and capacity building and community participation. Despite these challenges and the overall bleak picture on decentralization in the MEWA region, there seems to be a trend towards reforming government structures to allow more flexibility in and less control of local governments by the central authority. It is hard to tell, however, if that trend will continue in the future given the turbulent political and macroeconomic environment in the region.

2007
FOR SALE
2010©gérard fagot

8. North America

William F. Fox
University of Tennessee, U.S.A.

Enid Slack
University of Toronto, Canada

Both Canada and the United States are constitutional democracies with a federal structure of government. Both countries are geographically large but the U.S. has a much larger population than Canada (see Table 8.1).

Canada is a federation with three levels of government: the federal government, ten provincial and three territorial governments,[1] and almost 4,000 local governments (see Table 8.2). Canada's Constitution lists the jurisdictions over which federal and provincial governments have lawmaking authority. Local institutions are listed as one of the responsibilities of the provinces. Each province has separate legislation governing municipalities in the province and, as a result, there are differences across the country.

Table 8.1: Country Characteristics

	Canada	United States
Population (2008)	33,311,400	304,059,724
Area (km^2)	9,984,670	9,161,930
Population density (population per km^2)	3.34	33.19
Urban population (%) (2005)	80.1	79.2
GDP per capita (USD) (2008)	45,127	46,914

Sources: Statistics Canada, CANSIM, Table 051-0001 Estimates of Population, Canada; CANSIM Table 3800030, Gross Domestic Product and Gross National Product at Market Prices and Net National Income at Basic Prices, annually; United Nations, World Urbanization Prospects: The 2007 Revision Population Database.

Table 8.2: Government Characteristics

	Canada	United States
National	Federal government	Federal government
Intermediate	10 provinces and 3 territories	50 states and 1 autonomous city
Local		
· Upper tier	124 regions, 106 counties and municipal districts	3,033 counties
· Lower tier	3,524 cities, towns, villages, townships, rural municipalities, district municipalities, hamlets, parishes, etc.	36,011 cities, towns, and townships
· School boards	375	14,561

Sources: Information provided by the Federation of Canadian Municipalities and Canadian Education Association, Public Education in Canada: Facts, Trends, and Attitudes, Toronto: 2007.

1. *The three territories govern the sparsely populated northern part of the country. Unlike the provinces, they have no constitutional standing, are under the jurisdiction of the federal government and rely more heavily on federal funding.*

The U.S. government structure is composed of one federal government, fifty states, and 89,476 local governments (in 2007). State constitutions and statutes are the primary determinants of local government structure, which means wide differences exist across the country.[2] Local governments were generally created to assist state governments in the delivery of services. The specific role of local governments is given through the state constitutions in some cases and by statute in others.

In contrast to the U.S., direct relations between the federal government and local governments in Canada are limited. Cities remain creatures of the provinces. The federal government can give money to cities but it cannot change their expenditure responsibilities or their revenue-raising tools.

Local Government Finances in the Region

What is true of many countries is also true of the United States and Canada: summarizing the relative service delivery roles played by the federal, state/province, and local governments is not simple because many services have been unbundled, with each arena of government taking responsibility for different components. Data on expenditures and revenues tell part of the story but fail to explain fully the nuances of the intergovernmental relationships (see Figure 8.1).

Assignment of Service Responsibilities

The powers and responsibilities of governments in Canada were set out in the *British North America Act, 1867* and have been revised since then through judicial

2. See Benton, J. Edwin. 2009 "Trends in Local Government Revenues: The Old, The New, and The Future," presented at the 2009 Lincoln Institute of Land Policy Conference, "The Changing Landscape of Local Public Revenues," Cambridge Massachusetts, June 2009.
3. Simeon, Richard and Martin Papillon, "Canada," in Majeed, Akhtar, Ronald L. Watts and Douglas M. Brown (eds.) Distribution of Powers and Responsibilities in Federal Countries. (Montreal and Kingston: McGill-Queen's University Press for the Forum of Federations and International Association of Centres of Federal Studies, 2006)

Figure 8.1: Income and Expenditure Breakdown

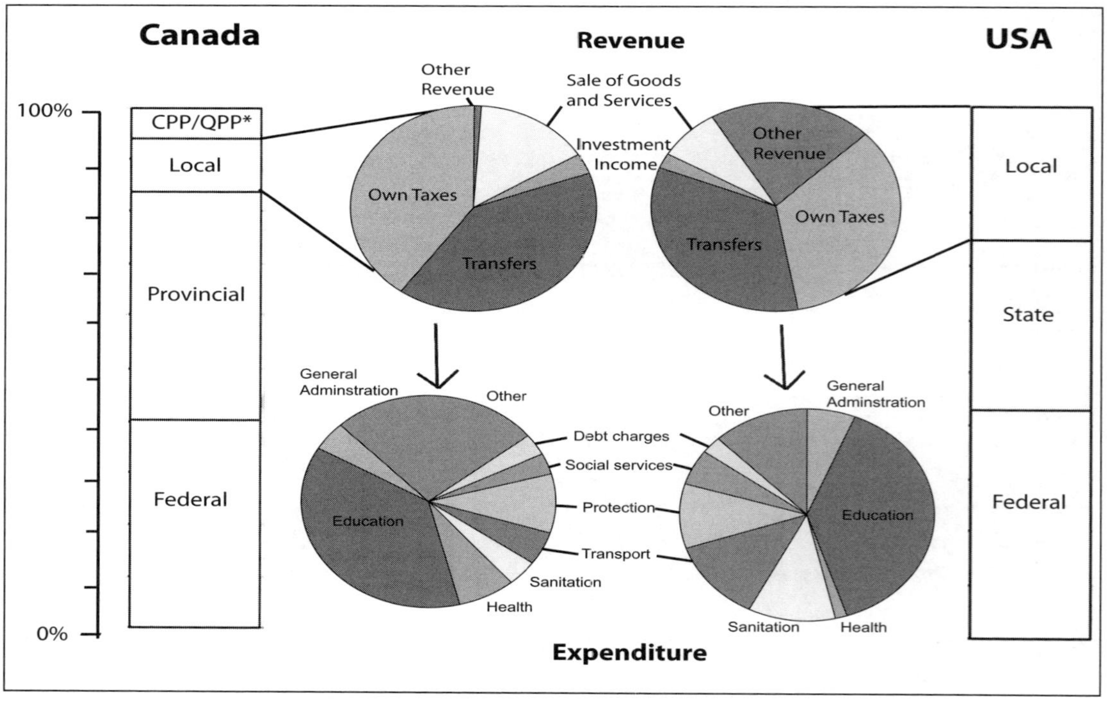

Note: illustration of data presented in Tables 8.3, 8.4, 8.5.
* *CPP and QPP are the Canada Pension Plan and the Quebec Pension Plan respectively*

Table 8.3: Distribution of Local Government Expenditures (%)

	Canada	United States
General administration expenditures	6.1	4.6
Education	38.6	38.5
Health	1.5	7.5
Sanitation (environment)	11.1	4.1
Transport	12.3	5.2
Protection (fire and police)	9.8	9.3
Social services	5.4	3.3
Resource conservation and development	1.3	0.5
Recreation and culture	7.6	2.1
Housing	2.1	2.6
Regional planning and development	1.2	n.a.
Debt charges	2.6	3.4
Other expenditures	0.1	18.7
Total	100.0	100.0

Note: Local government revenues include municipalities and school boards in Canada.

Sources: Statistics Canada 2007. Table 385-0003 - Local government revenue and expenditures for fiscal year ending closest to December 31, CANSIM (database).

U.S. Census Bureau. Table 1. State and Local Government Finances by Level of Government and by State: 2005-06.

interpretation, constitutional amendment, fiscal arrangements, and intergovernmental negotiations.[3] Provincial governments are empowered to control regional and local affairs and have exclusive responsibility for services such as education, health, social services, property rights, administration of justice, local public works (including roads, waterways, natural resources and environmental matters), and municipal government.

Although Canada is a highly decentralized country in terms of federal and provincial powers, it is much more centralized with respect to provincial and local powers. Local governments are often referred to as "creatures of the provinces" because they have no original powers in the constitution and enjoy only those powers that are delegated to them by the provinces. Nevertheless, municipalities are largely responsible for delivering such important services as police and fire protection, roads and transit, water and sewers, solid waste, recreation and culture, and planning. Table 8.3 shows the distribution of expenditures at the local level.

The federal versus state/local role in the United States is generally based on history and practice, and most service delivery is not specifically articulated in the U.S. Constitution.[4] The assignment of service responsibilities at the state versus the local level can vary widely across states based on constitutional and statutory provisions, making generalizations difficult. Some state constitutions provide specific assignments. For example, many state constitutions assign responsibility for education to state governments, but every state except Hawaii either assigns or delegates most provision of primary and secondary schools to local governments. The national, state, and local governments frequently share responsibility, at least to some extent, for delivering most services. The federal government generally plays a much smaller overall role in direct service delivery than do state and local governments, but the federal government often has important influence over service delivery. Federal grants, loans, and cost sharing that come with various restrictions, as well as federal laws and regulations, are frequently used to leverage federal priorities far beyond the narrow area in which the funding is provided.

State and local governments have nearly exclusive responsibility for a number of services, including fire, education, libraries, solid-waste management, sewerage,

4. *The power of the U.S. Congress to deliver national services beyond a narrowly set of enumerated authorities was articulated in an early court decision (McCulloch v. Maryland [1819]). This opinion also limited the states' ability to tax the national government.*

Table 8.4: Summary of Federal, Provincial, and Local Government Finances, Canada 2007-08

	Total government amount ($ USD millions)	Federal (%)	Provincial (%)	Local (%)	CPP/QPP* (%)
Total revenue	596,794	40.2	43.5	10.3	6.0
Tax revenue	424,847	48.1	42.2	9.7	0.0
Property	49,711	0.0	18.7	81.3	0.0
General sales	67,693	49.0	50.9	0.1	0.0
Selective sales/excise taxes	36,864	35.1	64.9	0.1	0.0
Individual income	181,509	61.3	38.7	0.0	0.0
Corporate income	61,909	63.3	36.7	0.0	0.0
Motor vehicle license	3,279	0.0	100.0	0.0	0.0
Other taxes**	23,892	32.5	64.5	3.1	0.0
Charges and miscellaneous revenue	104,652	14.6	62.4	19.1	3.9
Health and drug insurance premiums	3,212	0.0	100.0	0.0	0.0
Contributions to social security plans	64,072	32.1	18.3	0.0	49.6

**CPP and QPP are the Canada Pension Plan and Quebec Pension Plan respectively.*

***Other taxes include mining and logging taxes, taxes on payments to non-residents, payroll taxes, natural resource taxes and licenses, and other miscellaneous taxes.*

Source: Statistics Canada, CANSIM database, Table 385-0001, Consolidated Federal, Provincial and Local Government Revenues and Expenditures.

water supply, and transit. Much of health care is provided through the private sector, but public-sector hospitals and clinics are also common, and regulatory responsibility is vested in all three orders of government. Water, electricity, gas supply, and sewerage are exclusive state and local responsibilities, although the federal government plays some regulatory and fiscal roles in all of these fields. The public sector produces the services in some cases, and the private sector does so in others.

Tax Assignment

Under the Canadian Constitution, the federal government has unrestricted powers

Table 8.5: Summary of U.S. Federal, State, and Local Government Finances, U.S. 2005-06

	Total government amount (USD billions)	State government (%)	Local government (%)	Federal government (%)
Total revenue	5,586,902	31.7	25.2	43.1
Tax revenue	3,303,218	29.3	23.2	47.5
Property	359,109	3.3	96.7	0.0
General sales	282,179	80.3	19.7	0.0
Selective sales/excise taxes	203,897	52.1	11.6	36.3
Individual income	1,312,507	18.7	1.7	79.5
Corporate income	406,846	11.7	1.3	87.0
Motor vehicle license	20,520	92.7	7.3	0.0
Other taxes*	134,668	39.9	21.0	39.1
Charges and miscellaneous general revenue	583,493	43.8	48.5	7.7
Utility revenue	125,265	12.6	87.4	0.0
Insurance trust revenue	1,256,702	29.2	4.2	66.7
Unemployment compensation	36,989	99.7	0.3	0.0
Workers' compensation	21,514	100.0	0.0	0.0
Old-age and survivors insurance	520,069	0.0	0.0	100.0
Hospital insurance	177,429	0.0	0.0	100.0
Disability insurance	88,313	0.0	0.0	100.0

** Estate and Gift Taxes and Customs Duties and Fees*

Sources: http://www.whitehouse.gov/omb/budget/fy2008/pdf/hist.pdf and http://www.census.gov/govs/estimate/0600ussl_1.html

to levy taxes with the exception of taxes on provincial lands and property. Provincial governments are limited to direct taxation (income, sales, property, and commodity taxes) within provincial boundaries. The provinces were not given the power to inhibit interprovincial trade through the use of indirect taxes. Taxes levied by provincial and local governments include the property tax. Provinces have their own taxes such as natural resources and capital taxes.

Municipal governments are largely restricted to property taxes although some municipalities are permitted to levy selective sales taxes. In addition to a property tax, Toronto levies a land transfer tax, a vehicle registration fees, and a billboard tax and has the authority to tax alcohol, tobacco and amusements. Table 8.4 shows the revenues of the federal, provincial, and local governments in Canada.

The U.S. Constitution imposes relatively few limitations on taxation at the U.S. federal (Article 1 Section 8) and subnational government levels. A prohibition against taxing exports from a state is the only notable explicit restriction. The prohibition against state and local taxes distorting interstate commerce arises from the dormant commerce clause and is a very significant limitation on the ability of states to tax. In turn, states generally determine, either statutorily or constitutionally, the authority of local governments to levy taxes. For example, many states have limited the annual growth rate in assessments for property tax purposes.

The federal government raises the greatest share of revenue (see Table 8.5). A limited form of specialization has developed by tax source, though each level of government uses multiple tax sources. Local governments raise almost all of property tax revenue and most utility revenues. Otherwise, local revenues are modest shares of total receipts for the various revenue sources.

Local Government Revenues

Table 8.6 shows the distribution of local government revenues for Canada and the U.S. broken down by municipal revenues and school board revenues. For municipal governments in Canada, by far the largest source of revenue is property and related taxes which includes the general property tax as well as land transfer taxes (which are levied by municipal governments in only two provinces), payments in lieu of property taxes on federal and provincial/territorial government properties, lot levies (or development charges), and special assessments. Property and related taxes account for more than half of municipal revenues. Municipal governments levy few other taxes and those taxes (such as taxes on hotels, restaurant meals, and liquor) result in limited revenues. The heavy reliance on property taxes has meant that Canadian municipalities have not experienced significant revenue losses as a result of the recent economic crisis.

Municipal governments receive less than 20 percent of their revenues from provincial and federal transfers with the bulk of the transfers coming from the provincial/territorial governments. The majority of grants are conditional (specific purpose). User fees are also an important source of revenue for municipal governments. For school boards, the main source of revenue is provincial transfers which account for almost three-quarters of total revenue. The property tax is the next largest revenue at 20 percent although these estimates do not reflect provincial property taxes for education in some provinces.

Table 8.6: Distribution of Local Government Revenues (%)

	Canada			United States
	Municipal	School	Total Local Government	Local Government
Own taxes				
- Property and related taxes	50.7	20.6	39.3	24.7
- Consumption taxes	0.1	0.0	0.1	5.6
- Income	0.0	0.0	0.0	2.0
- Other taxes	1.4	0.0	0.7	2.1
Conditional transfers	16.0	74.0	38.7	
- Federal	1.6	0.2		
- Provincial	14.4	73.4		
- Municipal	n.a.	0.4		
Unconditional transfers	2.9	n.a.	1.7	
Total transfers	18.9	74.0	40.4	33.9
Investment income	5.3	0.3	3.3	2.4
Sales of goods and services	22.2	5.0	15.2	8.1
Other revenue	1.5	0.1	0.9	21.3
Total revenue	100.0	100.0	100.0	100.0

Sources: Statistics Canada 2007. Table 385-0009 - School board revenue and expenditures, year ending December 31, CANSIM (database); Table 385-0024 - Local general government revenue and expenditures, current and capital accounts, year ending December 31.

U.S. Census Bureau. Table 1. State and Local Government Finances by Level of Government and by State: 2005-06.

U.S. local governments generally raise revenue using four sources: property taxes, sales taxes, income taxes, and user fees and charges (Table 8.6). Different types of local governments may be empowered to use different tax sources. For example, no state allows cities unfettered use of all three taxes, but at least five states allow some cities a form of access to all three taxes[5]. Property taxes are used almost exclusively by local governments and generate nearly three-fourths of local revenues. Some states also raise modest revenue with property taxes. Most local governments with taxing authority can levy property taxes. For example, municipalities in all states except Oklahoma are empowered to raise property taxes. Thirty-six states allow local sales taxes, and fourteen permit local income taxes, which are often wage taxes rather than broad-based income taxes.[6] About one-half of local sales tax revenue is collected by municipalities and somewhat more than one-third by county

5. *Hoene, Christopher and Michael A. Pagano, Cities and State Fiscal Structure, Research Report on America's Cities, (Washington, DC: National League of Cities, 2008).*
6. *State and local income and sales tax data are taken from Mikesell, John,"State Sales Taxes in the Great Recession," State Tax Notes, July 19, 2010.*

governments. Special districts and school districts collect modest amounts. Local income taxes are even more concentrated, with about 80 percent collected by municipalities. Still, municipalities obtain only 26.6 percent of their tax revenues from sales and income taxes, and counties receive only about 20.6 percent of their revenues from these sources, but this differs dramatically across the country. Local governments in some states, such as Arkansas and Louisiana, and some large cities, such as New York City and Philadelphia, use sales or income taxes heavily. But, many other cities raise very little revenue from these sources.

The recent economic crisis had a very uneven effect on local governments. Property tax revenues rose 6.0 percent on average during fiscal year 2009 and continued to rise during the last half of calendar year 2009. On the other hand, combined state and local personal income tax revenues fell 13.8 percent and sales taxes 4.5 percent during fiscal 2009. Thus, most local governments that are very dependent on property taxes have not experienced substantial revenue losses, but those dependent on sales and income taxes have been more severely impacted.

U.S. cities also have additional powers to provide tax incentives to attract investment: for example, tax increment financing, which is used in most U.S. states but is only beginning to be used in a few cities in Canada.[7] Development charges ("impact fees", "lot levies") are levied by municipalities in most Canadian provinces.

State and local user fees and charges generate 19.3 percent of total revenues. Local governments collect 25.7 percent of revenues from user fees versus 14.2 percent for states. Local government charges are diverse, with hospital services representing 26.3 percent and sewerage another 17.1 percent. Local governments, and to a much lesser extent states, deliver a number of utility services including electricity, water, natural gas and transit. These generated $125.3 billion in revenue of which 87.4 percent is collected by local governments.

Municipal Borrowing

Municipalities use debt financing to pay for at least part of the costs of major public capital works. Repayment of borrowed funds comes from operating revenues such as property taxes and user fees. U.S. cities borrow more heavily than Canadian cities, on average.[8]

The amount that municipalities can borrow for capital projects is almost always controlled by the province.[9] These controls are in place because cities are "creatures of the province" and provinces do not wish to be responsible for unlimited borrowing and possible repayment of debt. Moreover, unrestricted access to capital markets might, in some circumstances, crowd out private sector borrowing. The methods that provinces use to control municipal long term borrowing vary and may be categorized as: permitting borrowing only for provincially-approved capital projects; requiring prior approval of provincial authorities for borrowing; requiring prior approval (through a referendum) by local taxpayers for borrowing above a specified limit; restricting annual debt servicing costs to some percentage of municipal own-source revenues; restricting the amount of debt to some percentage of assessed property values; and permitting (or requiring) borrowing from a provincially controlled "municipal fund."

U.S. municipalities are permitted to issue revenue bonds but Canadian municipalities

7. *Although legislation in one province (Manitoba) permits the use of TIFs, none exist in that province. Recent legislation in Alberta permits municipalities to use a form of TIF known as the "community revitalization levy." The Province of Ontario has introduced legislation to allow Toronto to use TIFs in two neighborhoods.*

8. *U.S. cities have USD1.3 trillion in long term debt outstanding and USD22 billion in short term debt compared to only C$30 billion in Canada. See TD Economics, Mind the Gap: Finding the Money to Upgrade Canada's Aging Infrastructure, Toronto, May 2004: 16 and http://www.census.gov/govs/estimate/0600ussl_1.html. Even accounting for the difference in population size, U.S. cities borrow more than Canadian cities, on average.*

9. *Bird, Richard, M. and Almos Tassonyi. "Constraints on Provincial and Municipal Borrowing in Canada: Markets, Rules, and Norms ." Canadian Public Administration 44, 2001: 84-109.*

are not. Revenue bonds, unlike general obligation bonds, are legally secured by a specific revenue source. For example, a revenue bond issued by a water utility could be backed only by the specific revenues of that utility. The advantage is that these bonds promote full-cost pricing of services and shift the risk to the investors. The disadvantage is that the market interest rates are often higher because the loans are not backed by the "full faith and credit" of the governments.

Municipalities in the U.S. are also permitted to issue tax-exempt bonds but these are not permitted in Canada. Tax-exempt bonds enable municipalities to issue bonds at a lower interest rate because the interest earnings are tax-free. Tax-exempt bonds tend to work best in larger municipalities that have access to capital markets and their application to smaller municipalities has been limited.

Intergovernmental Grants

For Canadian municipal governments, federal and provincial transfers account for less than 20 percent of their revenues. Transfers to school boards, on the other hand, account for three-quarters of their revenues. The bulk of transfers to municipalities and school boards come from the provincial/territorial governments with federal transfers only accounting for 1.6 percent of municipal revenues and 0.2 percent of school board revenues, respectively. Federal funding is usually channeled through the provinces but there are some exceptions. The relatively good fiscal situation of the federal government in recent years, combined with the fiscal pressures on provincial governments (particularly to fund health), has resulted in a "... growing range of federal government initiatives that bypass the provinces and deal directly with citizens and cities."[10]

The federal government responded to local demands by introducing a number of initiatives directed to cities (and other municipalities), including such measures as a proposal to share the equivalent of up to 5 cents per liter of gasoline on a (roughly) per capita basis to municipalities,[11] a rebate on the Goods and Services Tax (GST) for municipalities,[12] more funding for public transit and housing, and a commitment to renew existing infrastructure funding programs.

Provincial transfers are a combination of specific-purpose and general-purpose. For all of Canada, provincial/territorial unconditional grants accounted for less than 3 percent of all revenues in 2007, whereas provincial conditional grants accounted for more than 15 percent. In terms of provincial conditional transfers, as in the U.S., the largest transfers by far are for primary and secondary education. The predominant transfers for municipal purposes are for transportation and water and sewers. The dependence on conditional transfers by municipalities is not the same across all provinces and territories. In New Brunswick and Manitoba, for example, unconditional grants are proportionately more important than conditional grants.

At the moment, there are a variety of provincial/territorial-municipal unconditional grant programs. Some provinces provide per capita grants. Some provinces/territories allocate grants to municipalities with inadequate or insufficient fiscal capacity. Still others consider expenditure needs and the municipality's ability to raise its own revenues. Some provinces pool municipalities into different groups – arranged by population, functions or services provided, rural versus urban and so on. Two provinces use a weighting factor to differentiate the treatment of municipalities. Some provinces have more than one unconditional grant program. Finally, the territories take cost

10. Courchene, Thomas, J., "Hourglass Federalism – How the Feds Got the Provinces to Run Out of Money in a Decade of Liberal Budgets." Policy Options, April, 2004: 12.

11. In response to the federal gas tax initiative, some of the provinces have offered to share their fuel tax revenues with municipalities.

12. Although commonly viewed in Canada as a federal transfer, this rebate is actually a logical feature in the federal value-added tax (the GST), as noted in Gendron, Pierre-Pascal, "Value Added Treatment of Public Sector Bodies and Non-Profit Organizations: A Developing Country Perspective," Bulletin of International Fiscal Documentation, 59 (12): 2005: 514-26.

differences into account in their unconditional grant formulas.

As in nearly every country, the U.S. federal government finances much more expenditures and services than it delivers. Total federal grants in 2006 represented about 20.7 percent of total state and local revenue. Local governments only received 12.1 percent of these transfers, but some of the grants to state governments are subsequently forwarded to local governments.

Over 600 federal grant programs exist for state and local governments. The grants are provided in many different forms, including project, categorical, and block grants. Some have matching components and others are structured through formulas. Still, except for a few specific areas, the overall federal-to-subnational intergovernmental grant system is relatively small compared with many other countries.[13] Grants are increasingly focused on a small number of functional areas, and particularly health care. There is no form of general revenue sharing. The federal intergovernmental grant system is primarily intended to provide a degree of equalization across people, not to equalize subnational government service delivery, with most of the money intended to support low-income people.

The composition of federal grants has changed radically in recent years. Grants to state and local governments for redistribution to individuals have risen, and other types of grants have fallen. The rapid rise in health care costs, and therefore in the Medicaid program, has been the driving force behind the growth in transfers for people. Transfers for health care have risen from about 21.9 percent of total grants in 1983 to 48.2 percent in 2008.

The amount of transfers is decided annually by congressional decisions. However, some programs, such as Medicaid and TANF, have been established as entitlements (with carefully established eligibility requirements), and the basic structure is changed infrequently. The other large grant categories, transportation and education, are more likely to support state and local service delivery, and these programs generally do not have strong equalization components. Rather than being entitlement payments, the specific amounts are often determined through the annual budget process or by agency decisions.

State and local governments have sought to leverage federal grants in a number of ways. First, some states appear to claim a wide range of expenditures as being appropriate for the Medicaid program and, thus, eligible for the federal matching grant. Second, states have sought to provide their matching component through various creative means. For example, Tennessee created a "services tax" on hospital health care during the early 1990s and used this revenue to finance the state's share of the Medicaid program. Hospitals made the payments but received the money back in Medicaid revenues, allowing the state to draw down the federal funds with no state share. The federal government disallowed this scheme based on the argument that the state was not in fact matching the federal grant.

Unlike in Canada, state and local income, sales, and property taxes are deductible expenses in determining federal individual income tax liabilities. Various interpretations are given to the linkage that this establishes between the federal and state and local governments, one of which is that deductibility is a form of grant to the state and local governments, although it may be better seen as a tax expenditure. All U.S. states provide grants and shared taxes to local governments. State grants to local governments are nearly of the

13. For some comparisons across countries, see Bird, Richard M., and Francois Vaillancourt, "Fiscal Decentralization in Developing Countries: An Overview," in Fiscal Decentralization in Developing Countries, ed. Richard M. Bird and Francois Vaillancourt, (Cambridge: Cambridge University Press, 1998).

Box 8.1: The American Recovery and Reinvestment Act (ARRA) and beyond

The **American Recovery and Reinvestment Act (ARRA)** was passed in February of 2009 and was worth a total of $787 billion U.S.

While the bulk of the ARRA was not specifically intended to prop up local budgets, $144 billion was specifically targeted to state fiscal stabilization to prevent cuts to health and education programs and state and local tax increases. The state fiscal stabilization funding indirectly assisted local governments by mitigating potential cuts in state aid and funding for local programs that might otherwise have occurred in response to the recession. In some cases, ARRA funding for specific programs, such as infrastructure, broadband deployment, and green energy initiatives also was allocated through grants and formulas to local governments. In total, to date, the White House Recovery.Gov website, created for the purpose of tracking ARRA funding and usage, reports that 682,000 jobs have been saved or created nationwide.

While ARRA funding had some positive impacts on local government, other large portions of the ARRA went toward entitlements, tax cuts and assistance to individuals. In addition, the obligation for rapid spending of the ARRA funds means that funding plummets in 2011, after peaking in mid-2010. With U.S. cities facing the worst economic downturn in 50 years, the end of ARRA funding is expected to coincide with increasing financial difficulties and budget short falls extending into 2011. Incomes from tax collections, lagging behind the overall economy due both to payment periods and reassessment schedules, are expected to continue decreasing even if employment rates begin to rise. Local taxes will be especially hit by property reassessment as more houses are foreclosed upon and homes are reassessed to lower values.

The National League of Cities (NLC) annual State of the American City Survey on Jobs and the Economy found that 3 out of 4 local government officers reported that the economic and fiscal conditions of their city had degenerated over the last year. And 7 out of 10 city officials indicated that they are responding to the ongoing crisis through personnel cuts, layoffs, hiring freezes and furloughs. Many will also be cutting public safety spending and healthcare benefits. In total, the NLC estimates that city governments will face shortfalls between $56 billion and $83 billion over 2010-2012, with the range of shortfalls depending on cuts in state aid over this period.

The NLC is currently supporting legislation that would provide additional stimulus funding to state and local governments, including additional fiscal stabilization for states through health care and education investments and the **Local Jobs for America Act (LJAA)**. LJAA would provide funds to states, local government units, and community-based organizations to save and create local jobs through the retention, restoration, or expansion of services needed by local communities. Without additional stimulus for state and local governments, NLC predicts that city leaders will have to lay off more employees, cut essential services and cancel projects.

Information facilitated by the National League of Cities

same magnitude as federal grants to states, totaling USD 421.6 billion in 2006.[14] However, some of these grants may be the pass-through of federal grant funds. Federal and state grants together provide 38.3 percent of local government revenue, with 33.9 percent coming from the states and 4.4 percent from the federal government. Shared tax revenues are often provided to local governments as one form of grant. The dominant state transfer program in nearly every state is for financing primary and secondary education. The specific grant structure differs across states, but similarities exist in the basic design. A number of states build the grant around ensuring that local governments have sufficient resources to deliver an adequate level of education. Some degree of equalization is usually built into the grants, along with incentives to achieve certain objectives (such as to meet class-size expectations). Equalization is frequently based on both the capacity to raise revenues locally and the expenditure needs in the community.

Major Issues and Constraints for Local Finance in the Region

Nine issues in local government finance are discussed in this section including:

- The contribution of property taxes to local finance
- Sales tax base erosion in the United States
- The limited set of revenue sources available for Canadian local governments
- Vertical and horizontal tax relationships between governments
- Federal limitations on sub-national taxation
- The role of intergovernmental transfers
- Federal mandates
- The importance of infrastructure finance
- Pricing of local government services

These nine issues generally apply to governments across North America, but some are more generally applicable to Canada, such as the limited set of available revenue sources, and others are more applicable to the U.S., such as erosion of sales tax bases. These differences are highlighted throughout the section.

Property Taxes

The property tax is the largest local revenue source in both countries, accounting for 25 percent of local government revenues in the U.S. and 39 percent of local government revenues (municipal and school) in Canada (see Table 8.6). At the municipal level in Canada, property taxes account for more than 50 percent of revenues. The heavy reliance on property taxes has generated considerable controversy in both countries, particularly when property values have risen rapidly. A number of issues are addressed here including shifts in the tax's contribution to local finance, limitations on imposition of property taxes, and the erosion of the base.

Although the property tax has been around for a long time in North America and funds important local services, it is a very unpopular tax, at least in part, because of its visibility. Unlike the income tax, the property tax is not withheld at source. Unlike the sales tax, it is not paid in small amounts with each daily purchase. Instead, the property tax generally is paid directly by taxpayers in periodic lump sum payments. This means that taxpayers tend

14. See the U.S. Bureau of the Census at http://www.census.gov/govs/estimate/03s l00us.html.

often to be more aware of the property tax than they are of other taxes, though it is also possible in most places to have a monthly property tax charge folded into mortgage payments making each payment smaller and less visible. To a considerable extent, the property tax finances services which are also very visible, such as roads, garbage collection, and neighborhood parks. Visibility is clearly desirable from a decision-making perspective because it makes taxpayers aware of the costs of local public services. This awareness increases taxpayer scrutiny and enhances accountability, which is obviously a good thing from both an economic and political perspective. It does not, however, make the property tax very popular. On the contrary, it often appears to be harder to raise (or reform) property taxes than other taxes.[15] Property tax rate changes can be easier than sales or income tax changes, however, because the former tend to be small often annual changes and less subject to media scrutiny while the latter are infrequent, discrete, and normally subject to considerable attention.

Erosion of the Property Tax Base

Changes in the economy, combined with conscious efforts to reduce property taxes through tax incentives and tax and expenditure limits, have resulted in a reduction in property taxes in the U.S. from 87.2 percent of local government revenues fifty years ago to 72.4 percent in 2005.[16] In Canada, however, the use of limits on property taxes has been much less widespread and property taxes have actually increased as a percentage of municipal revenues over the last 20 years. In 1988, property taxes accounted for 48.4 percent of municipal revenues whereas they accounted for 50.7 percent in 2007. School board property taxes, however, decreased from 31 percent of total revenues in 1988 to almost 21 percent in 2007, in large part, because provincial governments took over the funding of education in many provinces during that period. There has, nevertheless, been some erosion in the property tax base even in Canada.

The erosion of the property tax base derives from a number of sources, some of which governments have control over and some of which they do not. For example, state/province and local governments have no control over the shift from a goods-based economy to a service-based economy to a knowledge-based economy. These changes in the economy have resulted in lower property tax collections in both countries because, in the new information-based economy, there are fewer plants and less machinery and equipment to tax.[17]

The property tax base is also declining in the U.S., though much less so in Canada, because of policy decisions to limit the use of property taxes by local governments. These policies include, for example, property tax incentives and tax and expenditure limits. Governments have control over these sources of tax base erosion which are discussed below, though it is often in the hands of state rather than local governments.

Narrowing the property tax base means that tax rates have to be higher to collect the same amount of revenue. Higher tax rates increase the excess burden of the property tax, make the tax even more unpopular, and can result in greater tax arrears if there is reduced compliance. Narrowing the tax base by targeting relief to particular taxpayers can result in an inequitable tax system, for example, by shifting the burden from existing to new businesses or by shifting the burden from those with rapidly growing market values to those with stagnant market values.

15. *See Bird, Richard, M. and Enid Slack, International Handbook on Land and Property Taxation, Cheltenham, UK: Edward Elgar, 2003.*

16. *Augustine, Nancy, Y., Michael E. Bell, David Brunori, and Joan M. Youngman (eds.) Erosion of the Property Tax Base, Trends, Causes, and Consequences. Cambridge, Mass.: Lincoln Institute of Land Policy, 2009: vii.*

17. *See, for example, Augustine, Nancy, Y., Michael E. Bell, David Brunori, and Joan M. Youngman (eds.) Erosion of the Property Tax Base, Trends, Causes, and Consequences. Cambridge, Mass.: Lincoln Institute of Land Policy, 2009 and The Conference Board of Canada, "How Can Canada Prosper in Tomorrow's World?" Performance and Potential 2004-05, Ottawa, 2004.*

Property Tax Incentives

Property tax incentives to stimulate economic growth are used widely in the U.S. but, until recently, Canadian municipalities were not permitted to offer fiscal inducements (such as property tax reductions and exemptions) to new firms or businesses. A study of stand-alone property tax abatements in the U.S. indicates that over 40 states allowed for these abatements in 2007.[18] The goal set out for most of these incentives is to increase employment and/or income generated in the jurisdiction and, in many cases, to increase the property tax base of the jurisdiction and property tax revenues.

Some authors believe that tax incentives are justified because the firms that receive them provide benefits to the community that exceed the costs to the municipality both for business services and environmental degradation caused by the businesses.[19] Moreover, new investment results in benefits from agglomeration economies.[20] When a large number of firms are clustered together, the cost of production will be lower because firms will have many different competing suppliers, they can take advantage of greater specialization, and they will have a larger market for their goods and services. Although there is some validity to this argument, it is not clear the extent to which an individual city will be able to determine which firms should receive the tax incentive and how much that incentive should be. From a political perspective, tax incentives are an indication that the municipality is pro-business and politicians can take credit for job creation and investment.[21]

Notwithstanding the arguments in favor of tax incentives, there are several disadvantages. Property tax incentives can result in a zero-sum game whereby development at one location is at the expense of development to another location. The underlying assumptions are that the overall supply of capital is fixed and that it is unresponsive to price (tax) changes. Under these assumptions, tax competition would not increase the national capital stock but, rather, only move it around. Tax competition would simply result in a redistribution of resources from local taxpayers to industry.

Tax incentives are often wasted on firms that would have located there anyway. If the economic activity would not have occurred "but for" the tax incentive, proponents argue that the tax incentive is a good thing. If, however, the economic activity would have occurred even without the tax incentive, the tax incentive is probably wasteful.[22] Moreover, tax incentives can lead to unfair competition among businesses and can lead to a situation where no major investments occur without them.

Tax competition can result in inefficiently low taxes and public services. Tax cuts need to be financed in some way and, if they are financed by cutting public services that businesses want, the net effect on economic development could be negative.[23] The provision of services that, at the same time, provide direct benefits to existing residents and firms is preferable to tax incentives. Moreover, a number of studies argue that lowering non-residential property taxes for all businesses in the municipality is preferable to tax concessions to any specific business.[24]

Tax and Expenditure Limits

Tax and expenditure limits (TELs) are state-imposed limitations on the ability of local governments to raise property taxes.

18. *Wassmer, Robert W., "Increasing Use of Property Tax Abatement as a Means of Promoting Sub-National Economic Activity in the United States." Sacramento, CA: California State University, 2007.*
19. *Glaeser, Edwin, Comment on "Tax Incentives and the City," Brookings-Wharton Papers on Urban Affairs , 2002, 115-24.*
20. *Garcia-Mila, Teresa, and Therese J. Mc Guire "Tax Incentives and the City," Brookings-Wharton Papers on Urban Affairs , 2002, 95-132.*
21. *Brunori, David, Local Tax Policy: A Federalist Perspective. Washington, DC: The Urban Institute Press, 2003.*
22. *Wassmer, Robert W., "The Increasing Use of Property Tax Abatement as a Means of Promoting Sub-National Economic Activity in the United States," Sacramento, CA: California State University, 2007.*
23. *Bartik, Timothy J., Who Benefits from State and Local Economic Development Policies? Kalamazoo, MI: W.E. Upjohn Institute, 1991.*
24. *Wasylenko, Michael, J. "Taxation and Economic Development: The State of the Economic Literature," New England Economic Review , March/April, 1997: 37-52.*

TELs include caps on assessment increases, tax rates, property taxes revenues, and expenditures. Although limitations have been used for many years, the proliferation of TELs in the U.S. really began when voters passed Proposition 13 in California in 1978 limiting property taxes to no more than 1 percent of property values. Since that time, most states have introduced some form of TEL. The political costs and benefits of imposing TELs can be imbalanced because the state political leaders receive most of the benefits of cutting taxes, but may not bear any of the revenue consequences of their actions. Some states have made an explicit effort to fund TELs with additional state transfers. But, many other states have reduced the local revenue stream with no explicit plan for financing any problem created for the local governments.

Tax and expenditures limits are not common in Canada but, in some provinces, reassessments are only performed every few years with the result that there is an assessment freeze for the period between assessments. Similar reassessment cycles exist in most U.S. states. The impact of not having annual reassessments is similar to capping assessments at a zero increase for the years between reassessments. Legislation in some provinces requires municipalities to reduce the property tax rate following a reassessment so that the reassessment is revenue neutral (known as "truth in taxation" in some U.S. states) but municipalities are not restricted from increasing property tax rates for budgetary reasons.

Tax and expenditure limits have severely constrained the growth in property tax revenue in U.S. local jurisdictions and particularly where assessment limits and tax rate limits are used in combination.[25] There is some evidence in the U.S., for example, that TELs have severely limited spending on local public schools and lowered educational outcomes.[26] The greater the increase in property values and the lower the assessment increase permitted, the greater will be the erosion of the property tax base.

Notwithstanding the pervasive use of assessment limits, they are probably the least effective, equitable, and efficient strategies for providing property tax relief.[27] Assessment limits are inequitable because properties with similar market values may not be paying the same taxes. Assessment limits shift the property tax burden from those properties whose values are increasing rapidly to those properties whose values are stagnant.[28] And, the most relief goes to those properties who appreciate the most quickly. Assessment limits also shift the property tax burden from those who have owned property for a long time to recent buyers.[29] In California, for example, it was found that by 1991 taxes on newly purchased property in Los Angeles County were more than five times the taxes on property of equal market value owned since 1975.[30]

There are at least three other concerns with assessment limits. First, if imposed until time of sale, assessment limitations reduce the incentive to move and result in a misallocation of resources. Second, assessment limits complicate the administration of the property tax and create confusion among taxpayers because the taxes paid are no longer calculated simply as a tax rate multiplied by the tax base. Moreover, there is no incentive to review one's assessment. Third, it is very difficult to remove a freeze: "once a freeze is imposed, the

25. *The limits may not be binding if, for example, assessment growth is limited but rates are not. Where a reduction in assessment is matched by an increase in the tax rate, there would be no overall decline in revenue, although there would be distributional implications. Thirty-three states place potentially binding constraints on the ability of cities to levy property taxes. See Hoene, Christopher and Michael A. Pagano, Cities and State Fiscal Structure, Research Report on Ailing Cities.Washington, DC: National League of Cities, 2008.*

26. *Yuan, Bing, Joseph Cordes and David Brunori, "Tax and Expenditure Limitations and Local Public Finances," in Augustine, Nancy, Y., Michael E. Bell, David Brunori, and Joan M. Youngman (eds.) Erosion of the Property Tax Base, Trends, Causes, and Consequences. Cambridge, Mass.: Lincoln Institute of Land Policy, 2009.*

27. *Sexton, Terri A, "Assessment Limits as a Means of Limiting Homeowner Property Taxes," In Augustine, Nancy, Y., Michael E. Bell, David Brunori, and Joan M. Youngman (eds.) Erosion of the Property Tax Base, Trends, Causes, and Consequences. Cambridge, Mass.: Lincoln Institute of Land Policy, 2009.*

28. *Ibid*

29. *Winters, John. "An Overview of Property Tax Limitations." State Tax Notes, 2008.*

30. *O'Sullivan, Arthur, Terri A. Sexton, and Steven M. Sheffrin. Property Taxes and Tax Revolts: The Legacy of Proposition 13. New York: Cambridge University Press, 1995.*

process of thawing may be too painful to bear."[31]

Sales Tax Base Erosion

Thirty-six U.S. states (including 35 of 45 states that impose sales taxes) permit at least some local governments to impose sales taxes. States normally include limitations on the operation of these taxes, such as on the maximum rate that can be imposed. Erosion in the underlying tax base has been an important implicit limitation on these taxes. Data are not available for local sales tax bases but the sales tax bases defined for a state and its local governments are normally, though not always, defined by the state and are generally very similar. The average state sales tax base has fallen from 53.2 percent of personal income in 1979 to 39.2 percent of personal income in 2007. At least in part as a result, state sales tax rates have risen from a median rate of 3.25 percent to 6.0 percent today and average local sales tax rates can exceed 4.0 percent.[32]

Three factors explain the base erosion. First, state governments have chosen to narrow the base by granting a seemingly ongoing set of exemptions. In some cases these were good policy choices, such as the exemption of certain business input purchases. Exemption of manufacturing equipment is a key example.[33] Also, many consumer goods have been exempted. Food for consumption at home has been exempted by many states and clothing by a small set of states. The solution to this problem is for local governments, and particularly states, to exert the political will to maintain the tax bases.

Second, although differences exist across states, sales taxes are broadly imposed on goods, but relatively narrowly on services. For example, a review by the Federation of Tax Administrators finds that the median state taxes 55 of 162 itemized services.[34] Service consumption growth has outstripped goods consumption growth in recent decades, causing the relative taxable base to fall. In general, states have found it politically very difficult to broaden the base to additional services because it requires identifying specific industries to draw under the tax base.

Third, the tax is generally collected by vendors but a Constitutional provision against states taxing interstate commerce has been interpreted by the U.S. Supreme Court to mean that states can only require vendors to collect the tax when they have physical presence in the state. Buyers are expected to pay a parallel use tax if the vendor has not complied, but use tax compliance is nearly nonexistent for individuals and relatively weak for businesses.[35] Combined state and local sales tax rates can be as high as 11 percent, so this can be an important advantage for remote vendors. As a result, rapid growth of Internet-based transactions has cost states a significant share of sales tax receipts (effectively the base is narrowed), estimated at approximately USD12.0 billion in 2012.[36] In addition, states lose tax base because of physical cross border shopping and mail order sales. State and local governments have appealed to the federal government to require remote vendors to collect the tax on their behalf, but so far to no avail.

Higher rates combined with narrowing bases likely have increased the tax's excess burden, reduced equity, and raised compliance and administrative costs. Excess burdens rise more than proportionately to the tax rate, and occur as the increasing wedge between taxable and non-taxable purchases encourages consumers to

31. *Youngman, Joan. "The Hardest Challenge for Value-Based Property Taxes: Part I." State Tax Notes, March 1999.*
32. *See http://www.taxch.com/STRates.stm*
33. *Nonetheless, the average tax base is still thought to be composed about 40 percent of input purchases. See Ring (1999).*
34. *See http://www.taxadmin.org/fta/pub/services/services.html*
35. *See http://dor.wa.gov/Docs/Reports/Compliance_Study/compliance_study_2008.pdf*
36. *See Bruce, Donald, William F. Fox, and LeAnn Luna, "State and Local Government Sales Tax Revenue Losses from E-Commerce," State Tax Notes, May 18, 2009: 537-53.*

purchase more non-taxable goods. For example, one study found that one-eighth of the relative growth in the service sector can be attributed to the lack of taxation.[37] Administrative and compliance costs rise with the narrowness of the base since the number of decisions on whether a transaction is taxable or not increases dramatically as more exemptions are allowed.

Inadequate Revenue Tools to Meet Expenditure Requirements

Municipalities in Canada complain that they do not have adequate revenue tools to meet their expenditure requirements. Several commentators have also questioned whether municipalities will be able to provide the services that people want at reasonable tax rates in the future.[38] This problem is more significant in Canada than the U.S. because Canadian municipalities have access to a narrower range of revenue tools.

These concerns originate from a series of events that have had an important impact on the municipal fiscal environment. First, the "offloading" of services by the federal and provincial governments has meant increased responsibilities for municipalities throughout the country. Second, the future of most countries is increasingly linked to the fortunes of its large cities where employment, wealth, and productivity growth are generated. In the new global environment, cities have to compete in the international marketplace to attract business and skilled labor. To do this, they not only have to provide sophisticated transportation and communications infrastructure but they also have to deliver services that enhance the quality of life in their communities. Third, municipalities that are facing rapid growth are also, in many cases, experiencing the higher costs associated with urban sprawl. The literature on the costs of sprawl in both Canada and the U.S. suggests that infrastructure and service costs are higher in sprawl developments than compact developments.[39] Fourth, at the same time that municipalities are facing and will continue to face increased pressures on the expenditure side of their budget, there has been no parallel diversification of their revenue sources in Canada.

Some authors have argued that municipalities in most provinces simply need to raise property taxes (on residential properties but not on commercial and industrial properties for the reasons noted earlier) and user fees to solve the problem.[40] There is some truth to this argument at the municipal level – residential property taxes have not increased dramatically over the last 20 years and user fees could probably be expanded to include a few more services. Correct pricing, in many cases, would also result in reduced demand for services and infrastructure and remove some of the pressure on expenditures. Nevertheless, all of these measures are still likely to fall short of meeting existing expenditure requirements.[41] Although municipalities have not run deficits on operating accounts because they are not permitted to by law, there is evidence that the infrastructure deficit is rising as a result of insufficient revenues at the local level. This issue is discussed further below.

Vertical and Horizontal Tax Relationships

U.S. federal and state governments have independent control over their tax bases and rates, given the limitations described above. Governments are not required to coordinate their tax bases or rates, and differences exist in the tax bases used by

37. *Merriman, David and Mark Skidmore, "Did Distortionary Sales Taxation Contribute to the Growth of the Service Sector," National Tax Journal, March (2000) 53(1): 125-142.*
38. *See, for example, TD Economics, Mind the Gap: Finding the Money to Upgrade Canada's Aging Infrastructure, Toronto, 2004; Kitchen, Harry M. and Enid Slack, "Special Report: New Finance Options for Municipal Governments." Canadian Tax Journal, Volume 51, Number 6, 2003; and Van der Ploeg, Casey. 2004. "No Time to be Timid: Addressing Infrastructure Deficits in the Western Big Six," Western Cities Project Report #30, Calgary: Canada West Foundation, 2004.*
39. *Slack, Enid, Municipal Finance and the Pattern of Urban Growth. Toronto: C.D. Howe Institute, 2003.*
40. *Mintz and Roberts note two important exceptions to this recommendation, however: Alberta where municipal user fees are relatively high and Ontario where the cost of social services is shared with municipalities. In those two provinces, the authors recommend consideration of a new tax on earned income. See Mintz, Jack M. and Tom Roberts, Running on Empty: A Proposal to Improve City Finances. Toronto: C.D. Howe Institute, 2006.*
41. *Courchene, Thomas J., "Citistates and the State of Cities: Political-Economy and Fiscal-Federalism Dimensions." Montreal: Institute for Research on Public Policy, 2005.*

every state and by the national government. Similar or identical bases are more common for local governments within states, but wide differences exist across states and in some cases within states.

Federal, state, and local tax structures are often intertwined, despite their legal and constitutional independence. Most states require individuals and corporations to begin calculation of their income taxes with some variant of the federal definition of taxable activity. The relationships between federal, state and local personal income taxes extend to administration as well. Each state has its own tax administration but relies heavily on federal audits and databases to assist in collection. In many cases local governments administer their income tax but also can benefit from administrative data collected by other governments.

In the Canadian context, all municipal governments levy property taxes, provincial governments levy property taxes in eight provinces, and school boards levy property taxes in five provinces. To minimize the possibility of unintended variation in provincial assessment practices within each province and to attempt to achieve intended variation where it is desired, a central assessment authority has been established in each province. Every province maintains an assessment manual for the guidance of its assessors and it is the practice that assessors follow the manual.[42] In addition, all provinces exercise a certain measure of control through the establishment of compulsory educational standards and training courses for provincial assessors. Similar standards have been laid down where the cities rather than the provinces assume responsibility.

In terms of property tax rates, each taxing authority is free to set its own rates to meet budgetary requirements. In many provinces, however, the provincial government imposes restrictions on the relationship between tax rates for different classes of property. In particular, there are often limitations placed on the extent to which non-residential property tax rates exceed residential tax rates.

The institutional linkages between tax bases mean that tax policy decisions made by one level of government frequently have implications for other levels. There is scant evidence that these vertical and horizontal externalities are given serious consideration when policy decisions are made. The federal government has made numerous tax policy changes in recent years by changing tax bases (frequently narrowing them) and lowering tax rates with little discussion of how other governments are impacted.

Vertical competition between governments may also exist, and it is an empirical question as to how one level of government responds to policy decisions at another level. The notion is that imposition of a tax by a higher level of government reduces the tax base available for lower governments, and vice versa.[43] The affected local governments could either raise their rate to offset the revenue loss or lower their rate because the tax is less productive. Research has yet to reach a solid conclusion regarding the direction of these relationships. Most of the research suggests that lower level governments raise their rates after increases by higher levels, but most of the published research has been outside of North America and the limited North American research has tended to be at the state/federal levels. Some evidence suggests that states tend to raise their gasoline and tobacco tax

42. Some U.S. states also have central assessment authorities that oversee local assessment and assess some properties, such as statewide utilities.

43. Other relationships could also exist, such as leader/follower responses or demonstration effects.

44. See Besley, Timothy and Harvey Rosen, "States' Responses to Federal Tax Setting: Evidence from Gasoline and Cigarettes," Journal of Public Economics 73 (1998): 383-98.

rates in response to federal increases,[44] suggesting that states raised their rates to offset the base decline. Also, research on the U.S. and Canadian corporate income, personal income and sales taxes have found that states tend to increase their tax rates in response to federal income tax rate increases.[45] Nonetheless, there has been too little research to reach a firm conclusion on how federal and state tax changes affect local governments.

Horizontal relationships between local governments can also be important, both in terms of how revenues are distributed across governments and how the governments compete for the tax base. Sales taxes are due in the state where the goods and services are to be enjoyed or used – that is, on a destination basis. This is normally presumed to be the place where possession of the goods takes place.[46] But, the local tax is often collected at the origin, creating an inconsistency. Origin taxes are well known to create the potential for tax competition.

More than forty states, in an extraordinary act of cooperation, worked together over the past nine years to create the Streamlined Sales and Use Tax Agreement (SSUTA).[47] On October 1, 2005, nineteen states signed on as initial members by enacting the legislation that was developed through the process and three more states have joined subsequently. The SSUTA is intended to simplify the sales tax and structure it on a destination basis so that state and local governments are better able to collect their sales taxes on remote transactions. The SSUTA is a wonderful example of government cooperation, but cartels of this type are difficult to develop and hold together, even when the related structures represent good tax policy (which is generally true of the SSUTA).

Federal Limitations on State and Local Fiscal Activities

The U.S. Constitution imposes two basic constraints on state and local government fiscal actions. First, state and local governments are prohibited from discriminating against interstate commerce. Canadian provinces are precluded from imposing indirect taxes, which is a stronger tool preventing them from distorting interprovincial trade. Second, state and local governments are prohibited from taxing international trade. In addition, the U.S. Constitution supersedes the state constitutions when conflicts arise between them.

Limitations arising from state and local governments' inability to distort interstate commerce are imposed both by federal court constraints and by congressional legislation. The U.S. Constitution gives Congress control over interstate commerce, which means that congressional legislation can define when state or local governments violate interstate commerce. Many examples of congressional and judicial constraints exist, but only a few are mentioned here. The constraints on state/local governments almost always prevent them from being advantaged at the expense of others. The courts have generally ignored cases where national or state policies may cause the home state to be disadvantaged relative to others.

The U.S. Supreme Court ruled that state and local governments can only require vendors with physical presence in the state to collect the state's sales tax.[48] Congress has not acted to require remote vendors to collect the state sales tax despite the admonition by the Supreme Court to address the issue. This limitation allows easy tax planning because vendors can purposely sell into a state/city from remote

45. *See Esteller-More, Alex and Albert Sole-Olle, "Vertical Income Tax Externalities and Fiscal Interdependence: Evidence from the U.S.," Regional Science and Urban Economics 31 (2001): 247-72 and Karkalakos, Sotiris and Christos Kotsogiannis, "A Spatial Analysis of Provincial Corporate Income Tax Responses: Evidence from Canada," Canadian Journal of Economics 40 (2007): 782-811.*

46. *Some states have traditionally taxed services based on the place of production.*

47. *The SSUTA was formed primarily as a state response to the Supreme Court ruling in the Quill case and in light of the rapidly growing extent of cross-border shopping.*

48. *Quill v. North Dakota, 112 U.S. 298 (1992).*

locations and avoid the compliance responsibility as well as the tax burden (which is either a legal burden of the vendor or the consumer, depending on the state in question).

The U.S. courts have in some cases also required state and local governments to provide non-residents with equal access to services. Thus, residents can move from one state to another and can gain access to services such as education, welfare, and health care for the poor within thirty days. This appears to have limited the extent to which some state and local governments are willing to expand delivery of certain services.

Congressional legislation can preempt state or local governments from imposing taxes in cases where Congress believes that state or local taxation would distort interstate commerce. The Federation of Tax Administrators (an association of state revenue departments) has identified twenty-eight examples of preemption.[49] Congress passed the "4-R Act" to prevent state and local governments from taxing railroads differently than other commercial and industrial firms of the same class. An example of the effect is that local governments are prevented from imposing heavier property taxes on railroads than on other industrial property.

Intergovernmental Transfers

Both Canadian and U.S. municipalities depend on transfers from provincial/state governments and, to a lesser extent, from the federal government. In Canada in 2007, for example, transfers accounted for over 40 percent of local government revenues; in the U.S., transfers accounted for almost 34 percent of local government revenues. In most cases, these transfers are for specific purposes (for example, to pave roads or subsidize recreation programs) but, in some cases, they are general purpose grants (for example, they can be used for any expenditures or to reduce taxes).

A more detailed breakdown of transfers for Canada in Table 8.6 shows that school boards depend much more heavily on provincial transfers than do municipalities. Moreover, for municipalities, the bulk of transfers comes from provincial governments (14.4 percent of revenues compared to 1.6 percent of revenues from the federal government). The bulk of transfers is also conditional (16 percent of revenues are conditional grants compared to 2.9 percent that are unconditional grants).[50] All federal transfers to municipalities in Canada are conditional transfers and are mainly for targeted to infrastructure.

Over the last 20 years, overall transfers to municipalities in Canada in constant dollars per capita have fallen at the annual average rate of 0.1 percent. This decline represents a 2.7 percent annual average decrease in unconditional transfers and 0.6 percent annual average increase in conditional transfers. Unconditional transfers as a proportion of municipal revenues have remained both low and constant over the last 20 years and, indeed, over the entire post-war period. Money from the provinces has come with restrictions and controls designed to "meet provincial wishes at the local level."[51] Transfers to local governments in the U.S., on the other hand, rose 2.3 percent annually in constant dollar per capita terms between 1992 and 2006. Federal transfers have risen most rapidly (3.9 percent versus 2.1 percent), but state transfers still represent 88.5 percent of total transfer to local governments. As with Canada, most of these transfers are conditional.

49. *Federation of Tax Administrators, June 2003.*

50. *Conditional transfers to municipalities exceed 50 percent of total transfers in all provinces except for two – Manitoba and New Brunswick.*

51. *Bird, Richard M. and Almos Tassonyi, "Constraining Subnational Fiscal Behavior in Canada: Different Approaches, Similar Results?" in Rodden, Jonathan A., Gunnar S. Eskeland, and Jennie Litvack (eds.) Fiscal Decentralization and the Challenge of Hard Budget Constraints. Cambridge, Mass.: MIT Press, 2003.*

Although there are valid economic and political justifications for intergovernmental transfers, grant funding is not always the best way to address municipal fiscal problems. First, conditional, matching grants lower the price of the aided service and encourage municipalities to spend more on that service. Where there are no externalities, or where the amount of the grant exceeds the amount of the externality, the resulting distortion in municipal behavior is inappropriate. Many of the matching grants in Canada have matching rates that exceed 50 percent but it is unlikely that the externalities are that high. Matching grants in the U.S., at least in cases where states are willing to match local contributions at the margin, are often at lower rates.

Second, transfers can get in the way of proper pricing of municipal services. There is no incentive to use proper pricing, however, when grants cover a large proportion of operating and capital costs.[52] In parts of Canada, for example, large grants for water treatment plants in the past reduced the incentives of municipalities to use volumetric pricing to reduce the demand for water or to engage in asset management.[53]

Third, transfers can reduce accountability. When two or more levels of government are funding the same service, accountability problems can arise. Fourth, transfers are rarely a stable and predictable source of revenue for local governments. Lack of predictability makes it difficult for municipalities to plan expenditures.

Federal and State Mandates

Higher level governments can alter local behavior through either a carrot or a stick approach. The carrot approach often involves providing grants that include conditionalities that require local governments to spend the money in a particular way or alter the local price of delivering services that the higher government would like provided. The stick approach often means requiring local governments to deliver specific services, to use specific approaches to deliver the services, or to meet certain input or output standards as the services are produced.

Whether or not delivery of a service is mandatory, once the municipality delivers the service, provincial/state or other standards often have to be met. For example, there are standards for fire protection, water and sewerage services, solid waste disposal, building inspection, local education, day care, and housing for the elderly. Municipalities in both Canada and the U.S. may be more concerned with finding sufficient funds to meet the service standards associated with all of these functions than they are with the distinction between mandated or non-mandated services. For example, water quality has been a particular concern in recent years. The result is higher provincial standards for water treatment and operations, sewerage treatment and facilities, and solid waste handling and disposal. Higher standards have led to higher costs but not necessarily to higher provincial funding. Municipalities often find such requirements and changes in those standards difficult to meet both in terms of qualified staff and capital demands.

The mandates are a troubling practice when federal/state governments impose responsibilities without providing funding to meet the related expenditure requirements. Unfunded mandates can be an important source of expenditure growth for local governments. The U.S. Congress

52. Bird, Richard M. and Michael Smart, "Intergovernmental fiscal transfers: International lessons for developing countries." World Development, 30 (2002): 899-912

53. Federation of Canadian Municipalities, Innovative Mechanisms for Fiscal Transfers to Municipalities – The Canadian Experience in Municipal Financing, Ottawa: FCM, 2008.

enacted legislation in 1995 requiring the federal government to determine the costs of such mandates, whether by congressional or administrative action. This legislation provides some information on the costs of federal decisions.[54] Gallo examines the act and applauds the increased supply of information, but she questions the long-term effect on federal decisions as the legislation is narrowly constructed.[55]

Mandates come in two general forms. In some cases, Congress, using its control over interstate commerce, directly requires state or local governments to provide certain services in certain ways. Restrictions on drivers' licenses and voter registration are examples. Alternatively, Congress may link conditions to grants, which state/local governments often view as mandates, though these are variants on the carrot approach. The No Child Left Behind education links receipt of federal education grants to states establishing measurable standards of achievement and making progress to achieve these goals.

Infrastructure Funding

Most public infrastructure is the responsibility of municipal governments. In Canada, for example, the local government capital stock represented 48 percent of the total capital stock of all three levels of government in 2002 compared to 34 percent for the provincial government and 18 percent for the federal government.[56] Local public infrastructure largely comprises roads and highways followed by sanitary sewers and sewage treatment. Most of the infrastructure was built between the 1950s and 1970s and much of it is now in need of replacement.

A number of Canadian studies have attempted to measure the magnitude of the "infrastructure gap" or "infrastructure deficit" and they have come up with estimates ranging from $60 billion to $125 billion. [57] Moreover, the trend in the deficit has also been increasing from $12 billion in 1985 to $60 billion in 2003 to $123 billion in 2007. Notwithstanding the differences in estimates of the infrastructure deficit, there is a consensus that there is a significant deficit and that it is growing.

In the U.S., the American Society of Civil Engineers estimated that $2.2 trillion needs to be invested over five years to bring the nation's infrastructure up to a good condition.[58] Since current spending amounts to about half of the needed investment, they estimate that an additional $1.1 trillion needs to be invested over the next five years. At the federal level, the investment gap is also significant – long-term annual average Highway Trust Fund revenues are estimated to be $32 billion compared to required investments of nearly $100 billion per year.

Some authors have argued that infrastructure is in a state of disrepair because the municipal financing of infrastructure is in a state of disrepair.[59] Some of the reasons include: politicians prefer to support short-term projects because of re-election rather than long-term capital projects; accounting practices fail to include replacement costs for depreciating assets resulting in a fiscal shock when it is time to replace the asset; and inadequate user fees and local taxes promote over-consumption of local services and an increased demand for infrastructure.[60]

A number of different tools are used by North American cities to finance municipal capital infrastructure: property taxes (in-

54. *However, the legislation does not regard conditions on grants to be mandates and an argument can be made that the lower level government could choose not to accept the funds.*

55. *See Gallo, Theresa. "History and Evaluation of the Unfunded Mandates Reform Act," National Tax Journal 57, 2004: 559-70.*

56. *Harchaoui, Tarek, M., Faouzi Tarkhani, and Paul Warren, "Public Infrastructure in Canada, 1961-2002," Canadian Public Policy, 30 (3), 2004: 303-18.*

57. *See, for example, Mirza, Saeed, "Danger Ahead: The Coming Collapse of Canada's Municipal Infrastructure," A report prepared for the Federation of Canadian Municipalities, November 2007.*

58. *American Society of Civil Engineers, 2009 Report Card for America's Infrastructure, March 25, 2009 (www.asce.org/reportcard).*

59. *Kitchen, Harry, M., A State of Disrepair: How to Fix the Financing of Municipal Infrastructure in Canada (Toronto: C.D. Howe Institute, 2006).*

60. *Ibid.*

cluding special assessments), user fees, development charges (lot levies) and other exactions, federal and provincial/state grants, borrowing, tax increment financing,[61] and public-private partnerships.[62]

Governments in both countries are looking at ways to improve infrastructure financing. The National Surface Transportation Infrastructure Financing Commission in the U.S., for example, is calling for the federal government to move away from the current funding approach based on declining federal motor fuel taxes towards a new system that is built around more direct user charges in the form of fees for miles driven (known as a vehicle miles travelled fee system).[63] The Commission proposes that state and local governments piggyback their own mileage based systems on the federal system to raise their own revenues.

Canadian municipalities use mainly property taxes, user fees, and federal and provincial transfers to pay for infrastructure costs. Since 2005, for example, the federal government has directed the equivalent of a portion of federal gas tax revenues (now $2 billion CAD per year) on a per capita basis to municipalities for environmentally sustainable municipal infrastructure (including roads). Canadian jurisdictions are beginning to think about tax increment financing which is used in most U.S. states. Perhaps the most important source of financing infrastructure, which has been largely overlooked in Canada, is proper pricing of local services – tolling roads, charging for water according to use, etc. Proper pricing would result in more efficient use of infrastructure and enable more efficient investment thus reducing the need to build additional capacity.

Pricing Policies

Collecting user fees is generally the preferred mechanism for financing local government services wherever possible. But, services can only be priced when non-payers can be excluded from consuming the service and should only be used in cases where a marginal cost is associated with each additional user. These factors suggest that user fees apply best in cases where the local government services have some characteristics of goods and services provided through the private sector. U.S. local governments generate 25.7 percent of their own source revenues with user fees and charges and 35.0 percent when local public utilities are included.[64] Canadian local governments raise a similar 25.6 percent from user fees.

Water, sewerage, electricity, solid waste disposal, higher education and urban mass transit are services that can be substantially or totally financed with user fees. Health care is often financed with a combination of user fees and insurance in the U.S. User fees are also important financing sources for parks and certain aspects of K-12 schools (books and meals). U.S. local governments raise the most user fees from electricity, hospitals, water, sewerage, and education.

Financing service delivery with user fees offers a number of financial and economic benefits for local governments. First, properly set fees allow service delivery to be (at least partially) self financing, and preclude the need to impose additional taxes. Second, economic efficiency is enhanced by setting user fees at the marginal cost of producing and distributing the services. These fees allow the local government to establish the appropriate amount of services to deliver (the amount that people want to buy at

61. Forty-seven states and the District of Columbia have TIF enabling legislation. In Canada, a form of TIFs is used in the Province of Alberta and TIFs are being considered for two major projects in the City of Toronto. There is extensive literature on TIFs in the U.S. See, for example, Wassmer, Robert, "Can Local Incentives Alter a Metro City's Economic Development?" Urban Studies, 1994: 1251-1278 and Anderson, John, "Tax Increment Financing: Municipal Adoption and Growth," National Tax Journal, 1990: 155-164.

62 Slack, Enid, "Municipal Financing of Capital Infrastructure in North America," Journal of Property Tax Assessment and Administration, Volume 2, No.1, 2005.

63. National Surface Transportation Infrastructure Financing Commission, 2009.

64. See http://www.census.gov/govs/estimate/0600ussl_1.html

the cost of provision) and ensure that those who most value the services obtain them. Third, user fees follow the benefits-received principle: only recipients pay for the services and non-consumers are not charged. Properly set fees for utility services (such as for water and electricity) are an excellent example of all three advantages.

Conclusions

This section contains five recommendations for enhanced operation of the local public sector including:

- Providing a richer mix of taxes for Canadian cities
- Reducing the over-taxation of business
- Slowing or eliminating erosion of the tax bases
- Enhancing the pricing of services
- Designing an appropriate role for federal and provincial/state governments

A Mix of Taxes for Canadian Cities

Revenues from a mix of taxes would give Canadian cities more flexibility to respond to local conditions such as changes in the economy, evolving demographics, and expenditure needs. Other taxes are more effective than property taxes at linking the costs and benefits of services when people commute to work from one jurisdiction to another. Taxes that grow with the economy could provide cities with an incentive to make the kinds of investments (in infrastructure, for example) that stimulate economic growth. Currently, the contribution that municipal infrastructure makes to economic growth is felt more by the federal and provincial governments that have access to income and sales taxes than by municipal governments. Finally, any single tax like the property tax is almost certain to create local distortions (such as discouraging investment in housing), some of which could be offset by other taxes.

In principle, an income tax 'piggybacked' on the federal or provincial tax with locally set rates has clear advantages in terms of local autonomy, accountability, and revenue elasticity, but there are obviously some problems in imposing such taxes at the local level. Business income is especially difficult to tax both because of its mobility across jurisdictions and because business properties are already generally over-taxed by the property tax. Solutions such as taxing only employment income (as is done in a number of U.S. cities) are possible, but have their own problems. Local surtaxes on the provincial tax in those provinces with a retail sales tax would be technically feasible but would again clearly be economically a bad idea, not least because these taxes would again tax business inputs heavily. In provinces with value-added taxes (which do not tax inputs), local surtaxes may also be technically feasible.

Selective sales taxes, used by some municipalities in Canada, could be extended to all municipalities. For example, hotel and motel occupancy taxes (which are widely used by U.S. local governments) could be an additional levy on the provincial retail sales tax rate on hotels and motels. The usual justification for imposing this tax at the local level is to compensate cities for the services they provide to tourists or visitors (additional police and fire protection, transit capacity, etc.). A municipal fuel tax piggybacked onto the provincial tax, if the funds are earmarked for local roads and transit, can be viewed as a benefits tax. Moreover, it should help curb urban sprawl by discouraging road use (although with the effect of lowering available tax revenues for continued investments).

Reduce the Over-taxation of Business

There is no economic justification for the high taxation of businesses either through the property tax or the sales tax. Local governments should reduce the property tax burden on non-residential properties to be more closely related to the benefits received from local services. Of course, a reduction in property taxes on non-residential properties will necessarily mean an increase in taxes on residential taxpayers. To minimize the impact on residential taxpayers, a phased implementation is suggested along the lines of what is currently being done in cities such as Vancouver and Toronto.

Although some states in the U.S. have exempted certain business input purchases from the sales tax and some provinces have harmonized their sales tax with the federal GST in Canada, many states (and some provinces) still need to eliminate the sales tax on intermediate transactions. However, a case can be made for taxing the intermediate transactions in situations where the final goods consumption is not part of the taxable base. Many services are exempt from U.S. sales taxes, and taxation of the intermediate transactions is likely to be efficiency enhancing in these cases.

Eliminate or Reduce Erosion of Tax Bases

Property and sales tax base erosion have resulted from a number of factors including political decisions (either at the state or local level) and underlying economic trends that lower the taxable bases relative to economic growth. The result is either declining revenues relative to the economy or higher tax rates to maintain revenues. Higher rates and narrow bases increase the distortions arising from the taxes and declining revenues could result in under production of local public services.

The best approach is to keep the bases broad to the maximum extent possible. State and national governments play imperative roles in maintaining the bases. The political courage to maintain the bases is the most important step to maintain the revenue bases. In many cases (though not all) higher level governments make decisions that narrow local tax bases because they bear little or no revenue consequences of their decisions and gain the political benefits. There is also need for political decisions to broaden the bases to cover evolving parts of the economy. For example, federal legislation in the U.S. is necessary to allow local governments to collect sales taxes on remote transactions effectively. The federal government has failed to act thus far, despite requests from many states and their advocacy groups.

Price Services Properly

Services should be priced to the maximum extent feasible since the prices provide an effective means of financing service production, providing service delivery to those who most value the services, and helping determine how much service to produce. North American local governments rely on pricing for many services, but should continue to seek cases where tax financing can be replaced with user fee financing. Further, prices should be set at marginal cost to achieve the benefits of pricing.

Cities should also expand pricing in new and innovative ways. Congestion pricing of access to cities during peak times is an example that has been used in some places around the world. Technologies exist to charge vehicles that enter the cities during certain hours. These charges can provide financing for substitute services, such as urban transit, and ration automobile usage to those who most value access to cities during peak windows.

An Appropriate Role for Federal and Provincial/State Governments

Cities need to be empowered to meet their expenditure responsibilities with adequate and appropriate revenue sources. Only in this way can they be responsible for their own actions. To get to this point, cities (at least in Canada) likely need more fiscal power than they now have. The federal government is very much a third wheel when it comes to municipal fiscal issues – only the provinces/states can change the expenditure responsibilities and revenue raising tools of local governments.

Federal and provincial/state governments also have an important role to play in cities because they are involved in policy areas that have a direct impact on cities. In Canada, for example, the federal government is responsible for immigration settlement, urban Aboriginals, and payments in lieu of taxes on government properties. If the federal and provincial/state governments provide adequate funding in the areas under their own jurisdiction, local governments would be relieved of responsibilities that are not rightly theirs and local revenues would be released for truly local functions.

Regardless of the tax sources made available to local governments, federal and provincial/state transfers will continue to provide an important source of revenue to local governments in Canada and the U.S. In 2009, the U.S. implemented a countercyclical program (American Recovery and Reinvestment Act of 2009) that is intended to distribute $787 billion USD across 10 years, with 71 percent to be expended in the first two years. Local governments are generally not direct beneficiaries of the ARRA but indirectly benefit in many ways. For example, 14.7 percent of ARRA funds finance infrastructure, much of which may be directed through local governments. Also, 26.7 percent of ARRA funds are transfers to state governments, and these are allowing states to limit reductions in transfers to local governments. Similarly, as part of Canada's $28 billion Economic Action Plan, the 2009 federal Budget established a $4 billion Infrastructure Stimulus Fund to provide funding for the rehabilitation or construction of provincial, territorial, municipal, and community infrastructure projects over a two-year period.[65]

Transfers are needed for those municipalities that do not have the fiscal capacity to provide adequate local services with their own-source revenues. Transfers are also needed in cases of externalities because municipalities generally do not consider the benefits of their services to people outside their jurisdiction. But, transfers can also distort local decision-making in ways that create inefficiencies in service delivery. Transfers should be designed so that they do not get in the way of municipalities charging appropriate user fees for services, where appropriate.

65. *The Federation of Canadian Municipalities has expressed the concern, however, that federal and provincial governments could cut funding to municipalities and impose unfunded mandates as part of a deficit-cutting program coming out of the economic crisis.*

9. FINANCING METROPOLITAN AREAS

ROY BAHL*

GEORGIA STATE UNIVERSITY, U.S.A.

* *Regents Professor of Economics, Andrew Young School of Policy Studies, Georgia State University.*
Tetyana Zelenska provided valuable research assistance for this paper.

The world population will approximately double by 2050 and virtually all of this growth will be absorbed by urban areas in less developed countries, (United Nations, 2008). The number of megacities (population greater than 10 million) is projected to increase from the current 19 to 27 in 2025. By 2025, about 10 percent of the world's urban population will reside in these cities.

Metropolitan area governments in many countries will need to find a way to manage populations of 5 to 20 million, and provide affordable services (Figure 9.1). To arrive at the right formula for governance and finance they will be required to settle on the right degree of fiscal decentralization within the metropolitan area, coordinate the work of many different government agencies and public companies, and find a viable plan for resource mobilization.

The financing of government services in large urban areas is more complicated than resolving the problem of financing the expenditures of a single city government because the common pattern is for many different governments and public enterprises to provide services within a single metropolitan area. It involves a balancing act in determining who governs, who manages and who pays. Furthermore, at almost every turn, there is a political dispute about the "right" balance of power among these governments.

Figure 9.1 Population size of the 11 Largest Metropolitan Areas

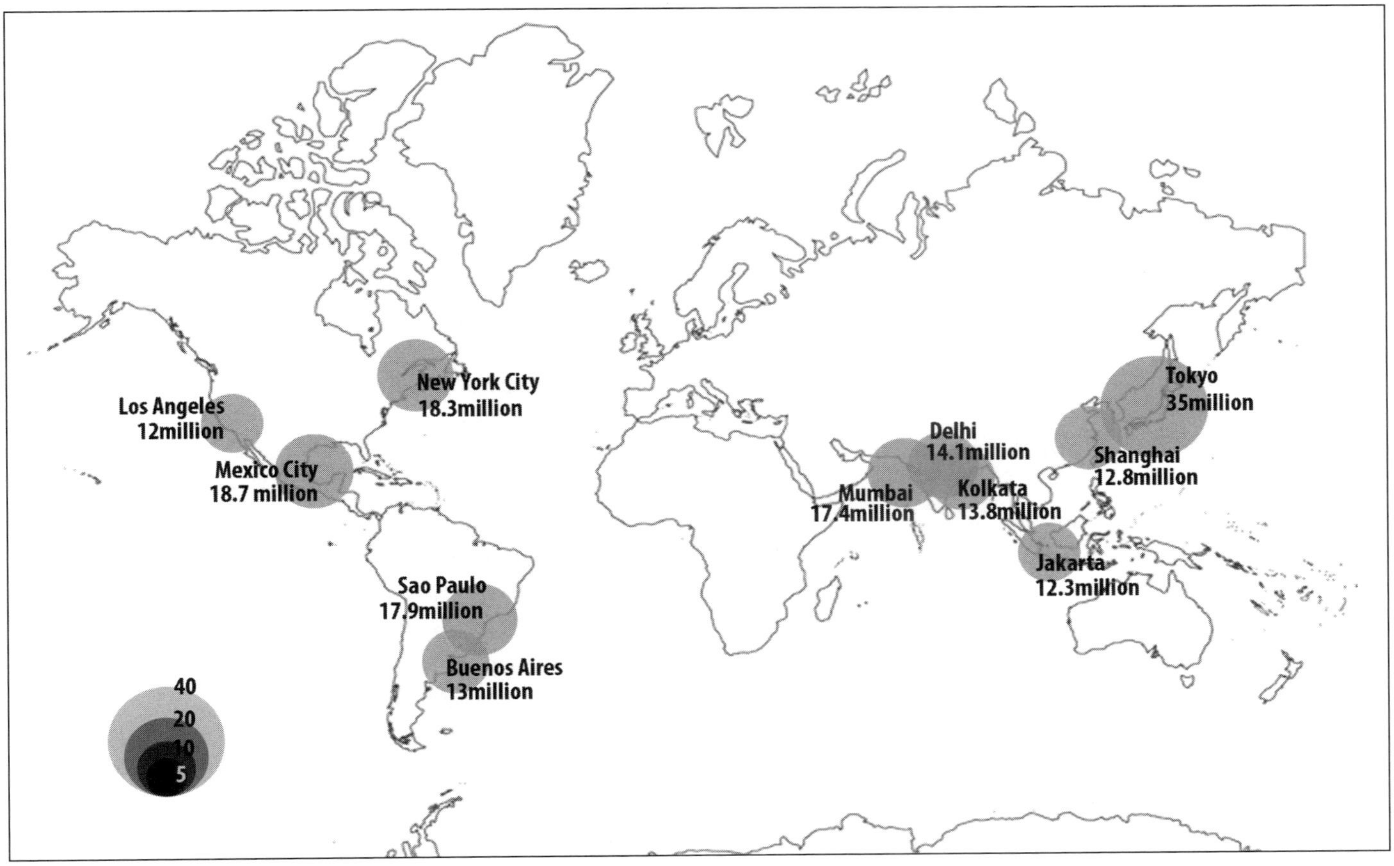

Source: *http://www.metropolis.org/publications/metropolitan_regions*

This chapter is about the financing of government services in metropolitan areas. The scope of this review is both governance and finance. These two topics cannot be separated because the arrangements for financing public services in metropolitan areas are largely driven by the service delivery responsibilities assigned to the various governments and enterprises. But, countries make different choices for structuring and financing their service deliveries, and so the problems that arise can differ greatly from country to country. In this review we consider a sample of metropolitan areas in both developed and emerging and developing economies. The choice of the sample is based on the availability of information rather than on any formal attempt to have a "representative" coverage.[1]

In the next section of this chapter, we consider the theoretical underpinnings for choosing among the various possible metropolitan governance structures. In sections following, the governance and finance models that are used around the world are reviewed, and their advantages and disadvantages are discussed. The chapter concludes with a discussion of the range of policy reform options that appear to be open.

Theory and Metropolitan Governance

Can economic theory point the way to best practice metropolitan governance and finance? Certainly not in any precise way, because the political economy dimension is so important. Still the economic model can provide a useful framework for evaluating the practice.[2] The problem is often defined as choosing the population size of a local government that will maximize the welfare of its residents. The core argument is the now-familiar "decentralization theorem", the basic rule of efficient expenditure assignment is to assign each function to the lowest level of government consistent with its efficient performance. The apt phase is that "people get what they want" so the overall public welfare is enhanced (Bahl and Bird, 2008). If the story ended here, metropolitan governance would be in the hands of small, independent municipal governments.

For some functions, however, assignment to the lowest level of government does not lead to an efficient performance. One reason why, is the presence of external effects in the delivery of the service, and the other is the presence of economies of scale. This pretty much defines the questions to be answered in structuring metropolitan public finances: should individual local governments carry the public financing load, is a metropolitan government necessary for managing and financing area-wide services, what physical area should the regional government encompass, and how important should state/federal vertical programs be?[3] Once these questions are answered, expenditure responsibilities can be assigned and finance will follow function.

Government Structure in Metropolitan Areas

Countries and metropolitan areas have reacted differently in deciding on a governance arrangement for service delivery. Some have created very fragmented structures with strong decentralization of responsibility and power, while others have created a more regional approach. Almost all have tried to strike some balance between capturing the efficiencies of area-wide government and maintaining local control.[4] If there is a general conclusion that can be drawn about the

1. *Ideally, we would include a comparative analysis of fiscal indicators for governments providing services in metropolitan areas. Unfortunately there are no such data available other than in individual case studies, and even these are not readily comparable. The IMF (various years) provides a compendium of government finances for all countries in the world, reported in a specified format, but no data are reported for individual local governments.*
2. *Oates (1972) has offered an approach that serves as a starting point for most students of this subject. For application to metropolitan areas, see Bahl and Linn, 1992; Bird and Slack, 2004; and Slack, 2007.*
3. *A vertical program is one where the service is delivered in the metropolitan area by a higher level government, and where the funds do not pass through the budget of any local government budget.*
4. *For discussions of metropolitan area governance, see OECD (2006), and Jouve and Lefèvre (2002).*

choices actually made, it would seem to be that the sentiments for local control have largely held off the formation of metropolitan governments. One way to think about the various approaches to metropolitan governance is in terms of the *emphasis* of the structure adopted: jurisdictional fragmentation, functional fragmentation, or metropolitan government.

Jurisdictional Fragmentation

Under this approach, many general purpose local governments operate in the same metropolitan area with some degree of independence in choosing their package of public services and their tax, user charge, and debt financing arrangements. In some cases there also is an overlying metropolitan government, and in most cases there are region-wide special districts.

The advantage of the jurisdictional fragmentation model is that it keeps government close to the people, but, the welfare gains from this "home rule" model will come at some cost, usually failure to capture economies of scale and operating within a set of boundaries that are often too small to internalize important external effects or to allow coordinated service delivery. Jurisdictional fragmentation can lead to large fiscal disparities among local governments in the metropolitan area, since they almost surely will have different financing and service delivery capacity.

Developed Countries

The jurisdictional fragmentation model best characterizes governance in most U.S. metropolitan areas. The traditions of home rule in the U.S. are strong; there is an acceptance of competition among local governments and a higher tolerance for fiscal disparities than is the case in many European countries. There have been numerous attempts to establish metropolitan governments in the U.S. but almost no successes.[5] The typical arrangement is well illustrated by the New York City region which includes over 2,000 governments (Benjamin and Nathan, 2001).

Strong traditions of home rule are also found in Europe. "Local Governments in the Nordic countries fiercely defend their rights to collect own-source taxes. They argue that their own-source taxation results in accountability and makes the behavior of the local population and local councils more responsible" (Lotz, 2006, p236).

The Copenhagen metropolitan region is an example of a jurisdictionally fragmented structure. Its population of 2.4 million is governed by 45 municipalities, which are the dominant tier in terms of service delivery and taxation, and by a National Capital Region. The Capital Region is an elected area-wide government that has health care as its primary responsibility, but it has no taxing powers.

The population of the city of Paris is about 2 million, but another 6 million people live in the inner suburbs. Local governance in this agglomeration is kept by 80 municipalities, 3 departments, and numerous companies that provide public services. The Stockholm metropolitan region includes 65 municipalities and five counties (OECD, 2006a), and 50 municipalities are contained in the Randstad (Holland) metropolitan region (OECD, 2007a). Metropolitan Vancouver includes 21 municipalities and about 2 million people.

Emerging and Developing Economies

The core provision of many local services in Manila is the responsibility of 11 cities

5. *For a discussion of the history of reform of local governance in the U.S., see Campbell and Birkhead (1976). For a discussion of recent efforts, see Phares (2009).*

and 6 municipalities whose boundaries are contained within the metropolitan area. Each has a local council that is popularly elected, and a defined set of expenditure responsibilities and revenue entitlements. These 17 local governments are overlapped by a supra Metropolitan Manila Development Authority which is responsible for planning and coordinating area-wide functions.

Governance in the Mexico City metropolitan zone is another example of jurisdictional fragmentation (OECD, 2004a). The metropolitan area is overlapped by a Federal District and its 16 municipal-like sub units, the States of Mexico and Hidalgo with their 59 municipalities, and the federal government. All of the lower-tier local units in the two states have elected governments but the boroughs within the Federal District have no taxing powers.

The metropolitan municipality of Istanbul overlaps with 73 municipalities. The municipalities, however, have no legislative powers. The Sao Paulo metropolitan region, with a population of about 18 million, is made up of 39 municipal governments with no overlapping metropolitan government. Coordination is attempted by agreement or compact among these municipalities, through a number of agencies and councils (World Bank, 2007).

Functional Fragmentation

A second approach to metropolitan governance is to emphasize *functional fragmentation*. Under this model, the delivery of a single function or a particular set of functions is placed under the control of either a public company, or a special district government. In fact, some degree of functional fragmentation exists in almost all metropolitan areas, but the way in which this is done varies widely.

A main advantage of functional fragmentation is that the autonomous agency is likely to be more technically efficient because it is specialized. The salary schedule may be outside the normal civil service so that the agency can attract and retain higher quality workers. It also may be more efficient in its operations because it has a large enough area of coverage to capture economies of scale. Because it is usually the only entity in the urban area responsible for the function, the problems of coordination for that function are considerably less than under a jurisdictionally fragmented model. Finally, a public company may have access to a dedicated revenue stream (e.g., an earmarked tax, a compulsory transfer from the city government, or user charges), and if well-run, has arguably a greater potential for debt finance than would a general purpose local government.

There are drawbacks to the functional fragmentation model, depending on the approach taken. First, it will almost certainly be less under the direct control of local voters as would be an elected municipal council, for example. In this respect, some degree of local autonomy is lost. A second concern is that the autonomous agencies may be single purpose and therefore unable to contribute to coordination of service delivery across functions. Although there are some exceptions, most special districts are single purpose.

Developed Countries

Functional fragmentation can take a number of forms, including the assignment of several area-wide functions to a single government or agency. The Greater Vancouver regional district consolidated all functions provided previously by special districts, most notably hospitals, water and sewer, capital expenditures, and solid waste management. The governing board includes elected local government representatives, but it is a voluntary organization and has no authority to implement policies.

The financing of special districts and public companies can take many forms. Since the services delivered are often amenable to pricing (e.g., public transportation, garbage collection), user charges provide a base level of revenues. In other cases, they are partially financed by compulsory transfers from the city budget, or they might be profitable enough to subsidize the city budget.

In Stockholm, a holding company was organized by the city to manage several city owned companies that provide services such as public housing, real estate management, port operations and water utilities. These public companies are in a surplus position and have been paying dividends to the city budget. The same is true in the case of two energy companies in which the City of Oslo holds equity.

The City of Paris participates (or is part owner) in several enterprises that provide services ranging from transportation to social services. These are financed by user charges and by compulsory transfers from the city budget. The City of Paris pays about one-third of its subsidies to the public transport companies and covers almost half the budget for the *Prefecture de Police*. Transfers to the municipal company in charge of social programs accounts for a significant percent of budget expenditures by the city government.

The City of Madrid makes compulsory transfers to the two public companies that provide transportation services. In the Italian metropolitan cities, the transfers to the companies providing transportation, waste collection and disposal, and water treatment services account for about 25 percent of total metropolitan city government expenditures. Milan, however, earns significant dividends from its companies. The City of Lausanne has fully incorporated the electric company into its budget, and the company maintained a surplus position during the late 2000s.

The water boards in the Randstad region in the Netherlands – with responsibility for flood control, water quality, and wastewater treatment – are another example (OECD, 2007a). These are local, independent public authorities that are democratically elected. The eleven boards in the Randstad region do not have administrative boundaries that are coterminous with municipalities. The water boards have taxing powers: a water board charge and a pollution levy.

Emerging and Developing Economies

Public companies play an important role in delivering services in the metropolitan areas in transition countries. Sometimes the relationship between the city government and the public companies is quite complex. For example, the City of Riga provides services through 42 companies in which it holds ownership and through the heating company where its equity stake is 49 percent. Most of these companies are self-supporting, but the transport enterprise claims about 10 percent of the operating budget of the city.

In Zagreb, most capital spending (and some current spending) is the responsibility of a holding company that was created following the merger of 22 municipal companies. The City of Zagreb uses more than 15 percent of its budget for subsidy payments to the holding company. In other eastern European metropolitan cities, it is more a matter of the city supporting the loss-making activity of a single company, notably transportation. The metropolitan cities of Sofia, Budapest, and Odessa are examples.

Special purpose agencies can be important in managing and financing public service delivery in developing countries. Sometimes this is because the special district status gets the service delivery function separated from the politics at the local level, sometimes it makes management easier and arguably more professional, and sometimes it is an easier route to a dedicated revenue stream and debt finance.

Public companies are set up by the local governments, as is the case of public transportation in Bogota, Colombia. They also can be multi-function, as for the water, energy and telecommunications company in Medellin, Colombia. In some cases, the special purpose agencies can become the dominant player in local government finance. Webster (2000, p7) points out that over 65 percent of urban infrastructure expenditure in metropolitan Bangkok is made by state enterprises, as compared with approximately 25 percent by the national government and less than 10 percent by the city government.

Metropolitan Government

The third general approach is *metropolitan government*. Under this model, general services are provided by an area-wide metropolitan government. Typically the metropolitan government is elected and has significant powers to regulate the service delivery and financing in the metropolitan area. While there are a number of area-wide governments in large urban areas, few of them have this range of powers. More often, they have a limited range of functional responsibilities, and govern alongside lower tiers of government. The emphasis under this approach is regional governance but usually with some degree of local autonomy protected.

There are significant advantages to this approach, most notably a built-in coordination in the delivery of all functions assigned to the metropolitan government. This gives a potential for better resource allocation by comparison with the case where responsibility for local services is divided among multiple municipalities and special purpose governments. The metropolitan government form also offers a greater *potential* for equalization because the quality of local services is not tied to the wealth of each local jurisdiction as it is in the case of jurisdictional fragmentation.

Metropolitan governments often have a large enough area of coverage to capture economies of scale and to internalize externalities. This could result in both lower costs of service delivery and efficiency gains.[6] Finally, because factors are less mobile across than within metropolitan areas, there are more choices for efficient taxation. There also may be significant tax administration economies in an area-wide approach to revenue raising.

The metropolitan form of governance also has significant drawbacks. The most important is that it diminishes the power of local voters to influence the local budget. In effect, the election of the local council is replaced by election of local representatives to the more distant metropolitan council. A second drawback is that metropolitan governance often brings intergovernmental conflict. If lower tier local governments exist under a metropolitan arrangement, they may resist the leadership (and especially the dominance) of the metropolitan government.

Finally, the boundaries of the metropolitan government may not be drawn large enough to fully capture the benefits of area-wide governance. In this situation, one of the most significant advantages of metropolitan government may be substantially diminished.[7] For example, New York City

6. *If it does not result in lower cost of providing services, it may result in the provision of a higher level of services due to a "leveling up" effect.*
7. *A comparison of metropolitan area boundaries with governance boundaries in many cities is given in OECD (2006).*

has a population of 8 million but accounts for less than 40 percent of the population of the New York metropolitan region. In this case, services provided outside the metropolitan government boundaries are not coordinated with those provided inside and some of the advantages of area-wide governance are lost. A similar situation exists in Toronto, which holds only about one-third of the population of the metropolitan region. In Copenhagen, where 45 municipalities make up the greater Copenhagen metropolitan area, the region-wide government – the National Capital Region – includes only 33 of these.

Developed Countries

About the closest the U.S. has come to area-wide governance is the Metropolitan Service District in Portland, Oregon. This metropolitan government includes 25 cities and provides area-wide services for transportation, solid waste and a number of environmental concerns. But Portland ("metro") is a far cry from a comprehensive regional government. As Lefèvre (2008) notes: "By U.S. standards, metro is an innovative metropolitan arrangement; yet by European standards, it is critiqued as a weak metropolitan governance arrangement with limited responsibilities and resources."

Canada presents some interesting contrasts in the structuring of metropolitan government. Toronto approximates a true metropolitan government. It replaced the former two-tier metropolitan government with a single tier metropolitan city in 1998 (Slack, 2000; OECD, 2009a). All local government functions, including those previously invested in special districts and underlying municipalities, rest with the new metropolitan government. Two other structural reforms in Canada, however, took a less centralizing approach. Vancouver created a regional government with some service delivery responsibility but the lower tier municipalities were left as the dominant local government units. Montreal used an amalgamation of municipalities to create two stronger core cities, but left in place a fragmented local government structure.

There are other examples of area-wide governments in OECD countries. In Madrid, the Autonomous Community of Madrid is responsible for the metropolitan area, which is about the same size as the functional urban region of Madrid (OECD, 2007). Underneath the Community is 179 municipalities, including the City of Madrid, which accounts for about half of the population of the metropolitan area. The functions of the Community are broader than those of the municipalities.

The Tokyo metropolitan government has substantial responsibility for service provision to a population of about 12 million persons (Togo, 1995; Tokyo Metropolitan Government, 2010). It has a prefecture (state) status in Japan's intergovernmental fiscal system. Below the metropolitan government are 23 special wards in the core area, in addition to 26 cities, 5 towns and 1 village. All have elected assemblies. The special wards carry out service delivery for designated functions on behalf of the metropolitan government, while the municipalities are general purpose local governments.

The Greater London Authority (GLA) was created in 1999, as a senior level of government in metropolitan London, with a provision to elect a mayor and, separately, an assembly. The GLA is responsible for a number of functions, including transport, economic development, environmental protection, and police. About 80 percent of expenditures are made for transport and police. It is financed by central government grants (63 percent), user charges (20 percent) and property taxes (10 percent) (Bird and Slack, 2004). In part because resources are so limited, it would be difficult to classify London as a strong metropolitan government. The underlying 33 boroughs are independent of the GLA and provide basic urban services such as education, housing, social services, street cleaning, and roads. There is a clear separation of expenditure responsibilities between the upper and lower tiers of government in the metropolitan area.

Emerging and Developing Economies

Metropolitan government has had an easier road in many emerging and developing economies. Oftentimes, area-wide governments were in place and their boundaries simply grew with their populations, while in other cases they were created to meet specific needs. In many cases, democratically elected local governments are relatively new, and home rule traditions are much less entrenched. Moreover, the weak level of infrastructure in place and the strains placed on city finances by migration, make area-wide government an easier sell.

Before 1994, Cape Town, South Africa was composed of 61 local government entities. This number was reduced to 6 general purpose governments and a metropolitan authority in 1996, and finally to a single local authority, the "Unicity" of Cape Town in 2000 (OECD, 2008). The gross inequity in services provided and the need for local input and coordination of area-wide services, were driving forces behind the consolidation.

A somewhat different model was adopted in Manila, where the Metropolitan Manila Development Authority (MMDA) exists to manage area-wide functions while the local government units are responsible for local functions. The local government units (cities and municipalities) are governed by elected councils while the Chair of the MMDA is appointed by the President and its membership is prescribed by law. The formation of the MMDA (and its predecessor bodies) was a result of the concern for delivery of area-wide services and the perception of government that the well-being of Metropolitan Manila is a national priority. The history of metropolitan governance in Manila has been one of a struggle for power between the metropolitan government and the lower level local governments.

Taxes, Charges, and Transfers[8]

Culture, economic structure, and politics all play a role in determining the particulars of a public financing regime in metropolitan areas. But there also is a theory of tax assignment that points the way to "best practice" in financing metropolitan services.[9] The guidelines from this theory are generally followed in many (most) developed countries, but are less often followed in the emerging and developing countries.

The Theory of Tax Assignment

Is there a best way to finance public service provision in metropolitan areas? Are there guidelines for identifying those tax revenue sources most appropriate for financing local and area-wide governments in metropolitan areas? The answer to both questions is a qualified "yes".

Four considerations might guide tax assignment decisions in metropolitan areas. The first is accountability. In order to make elected local government officials more accountable to their voting constituents, it is

8. *For other papers on this topic, see Bahl and Linn (1992), Bird and Slack (2004) and Chernik and Reschovsky (2006).*
9. *One of the best statements of the theory is McLure (1998). For reviews and applications, see Musgrave, 1983; and Martinez-Vazquez, 2008.*

necessary to give these officials some independent taxing powers. The accountability rule for tax assignment fits lower tier local governments in those metropolitan areas where the city council is elected. Those who hold fast to the representation rule of taxation would tend to limit non-elected governments to cost-recovery user charges. If there is to be general taxation by a non-elected body, it should be enabled by a referendum.

The issue is more complicated when it comes to metropolitan government or area-wide special purpose governments. If the area-wide government is elected, taxing powers will enhance accountability to voters. This would apply, for example, to the cases of the Portland, Toronto, or London metro areas, where the leadership of the metro government is elected. Some area-wide governments (special districts such as New York's Port Authority or Toronto's Services Board) are led by appointed officials. In this case, accountability to voters will not be enhanced by taxing powers. These agencies should charge for services rendered, but their monopoly powers should be regulated. In yet another arrangement, the council of the metropolitan government may be made up of all elected mayors in the metropolitan area. Because of the large membership of the council, this arrangement may allow a single elected mayor to hide from being accountable to his home constituency. There are many examples here, including the Greater Vancouver Regional District.

A third principle, and the one that seems to be followed most religiously in developed countries, is "correspondence", i.e., local governments should not levy taxes whose burden can be exported to those who do not benefit from services delivered by the local government (McLure, 1998). This principle imposes a tight restriction on local governments in jurisdictionally fragmented metropolitan areas. It suggests that lower tier local governments should rely only on benefit taxes[10] and on taxes on immobile factors. Metropolitan governments and area-wide special districts, on the other hand, can be given access to some broader-based taxes because labor is less likely to cross jurisdictional boundaries.

Finally, the theory of tax assignment also calls for consideration of the relative costs of tax administration in deciding on the level to which a tax will be assigned. Local governments, particularly in developing countries, might be denied access to certain taxes for this reason, while area-wide governments in metropolitan areas could have some inherent advantages in tax administration.

Tax Assignment: The Practice

Do countries follow the general "rules" laid down by the theory discussed above? Most developed countries do make tax assignments that are in step with good practice (though there are exceptions). Metropolitan area governments in developing countries have many fewer taxing options, and appear to be less in step with what many policy analysts see as best practice.

Developed Countries

Higher income countries appear to have given more attention to the issue of structuring governance in large metropolitan areas and to finding ways to finance these structures. Examples of the "special" financial arrangements that have been put in place include (a) granting metropolitan governments both city and state level status (Tokyo, Shanghai, Berlin), (b) providing for special taxing powers (New York City) and (c) instituting special intergovernmental transfer arrangements (London, Rome). A

Table 9.1: Selected Special Revenue Treatments for Metropolitan Local Governments

Government	Special Treatment
Copenhagen National Capital Region (OECD, 2007)	Financed 75 percent by Central Transfers and 25 percent by Municipal Transfers
Tokyo Metropolitan Government (Tokyo, 2010)	Metropolitan government has both prefecture (state) and municipal taxing powers and expenditure responsibilities
Toronto (Slack, 2000)	Metropolitan City with no underlying tier of government, created by a Provincial Act.
Community of Madrid (OECD, 2007)	Has both State and Metropolitan Government Features, and State Taxing Powers
London (GLA)	Special central Transfers cover about two-thirds of Expenditures
Netherlands: Independent, elected Water Boards	May impose a water board charge and a pollution levy.

Source: http://www.metropolis.org/publications/metropolitan_regions

sample of such special arrangements is described in Table 9.1.

One underlying objective in many developed countries is to increase the fiscal self-sufficiency of metropolitan local governments. In some countries in the sample reported in Figure 9.2, this strategy has succeeded. The Tokyo metropolitan area government has both city and prefecture (state) status, hence it has access to a broader tax base than do other local governments in Japan. About 70 percent of all metropolitan government revenue is from local taxes.[11] Toronto has a more traditional financing structure for a local government. It relies primarily on the property tax and user charges. The Toronto metropolitan city funds about 60 percent of its budget from property taxes and user charges. The property tax alone accounts for about 41 percent of revenues (OECD, 2009a).

Metropolitan local governments in some the Nordic countries and Spain rely primarily on individual income taxes, and New York City makes heavy use of a combination of retail sales tax, personal and corporate income taxes, and business taxes. Stockholm's local governments cover about 80 percent of their expenditures from local sources, primarily from an earned income tax. In Paris, the principal local tax was applied on economic activities –a tax on inmobile capital but limited to added value. This was replaced in 2010 by combination of a tax on property, a share of locally collected VAT and a variety of low return charges on network activities, which

10. A "benefit tax" in this case could refer to any tax where the revenues raised are borne by those who benefit from the services financed. A residence-based income or payroll tax would qualify, but an origin based business tax would not.

11. The largest revenue source is the corporate income and registration tax. Tokyo and New York are the largest metropolitan governments studied here that rely to any significant degree on taxes on corporations.

globally have meant a loss of autonomy and a drop in revenue.

Metropolitan local governments in other developed countries do not have significant taxing powers (Slack, 2007). The Greater London Authority receives most of its revenues from central government grants. The Stuttgart Regional Authority has no taxing authority. The Greater Vancouver Regional District is financed primarily by user fees and intergovernmental transfers.

Emerging and Developing Economies

In practice, large urban governments in most emerging and developing economies do not rely heavily on local taxation. Despite the arguments that local governments in metropolitan areas could feasibly handle a greater range of taxes, most are limited to property taxes and user charges as the main sources of revenue. There are some exceptions to this general pattern, notably Brazil, and these are taken up below.

Property Tax

Almost everyone's choice for a major instrument of local government taxation is the property tax. It passes many of the theoretical tests of a good subnational government tax, but it is costly to administer and it is politically unpopular.

Developed Countries

Among the developed countries, property tax is a favorite among the English speaking federal countries, but it is much less important among non-English speaking countries and unitary countries in general

Figure 9.2: Percent of Revenues Raised from Own Sources by Selected Metropolitan Local Governments

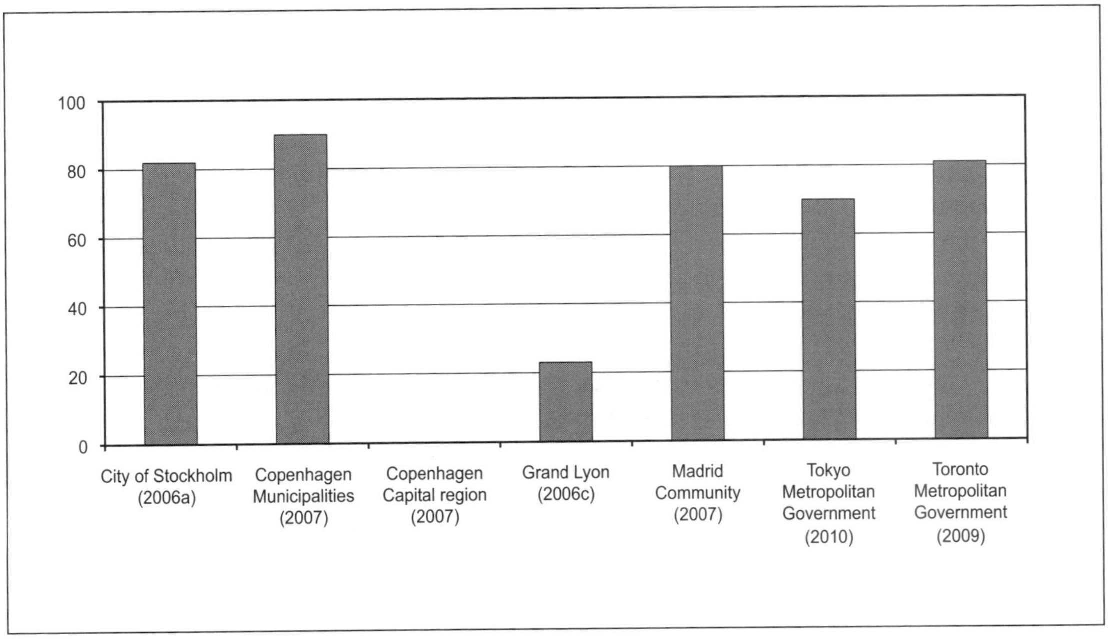

Source: *All information taken from OECD Territorial Reviews with the exception of the Tokyo Metropolitan Government taken from (http://www.metro.tokyo.jp/ENGLISH/PROFILE/index.htm)*

(Lotz, 2006). Property tax revenues account for one-half or more of local government financing in the Toronto, Montreal, and Melbourne metropolitan areas, and it accounts for 34 percent of the budget in New York City.

Different patterns emerge for some metropolitan area local governments in other OECD and transition countries. Municipalities in the Netherlands, including those in the Randstad region, receive less than 5 percent of revenues from the property tax. There is no local government property tax in Sweden or Norway (OECD, 2006a, p176). In Copenhagen, the primary revenue source of municipalities is the income tax, and property taxes play only a minor role. The same is true in Stockholm, Tokyo, and in the Swiss cities. The property tax is somewhat more important in Madrid at the city level, but financing is dominated by income taxes levied at the regional government level. In Busan and Daegu, Korea, the property tax is an important source of local financing, but most of the revenue is derived from property transfers.

Emerging and Developing Economies

Governments in most emerging and developing countries do not seem to have bought into the idea that the property tax is a good fit for financing services provided in metropolitan areas. While it is true that property values are growing in most metropolitan areas, valuation in most countries fails to capture this growth. This seems to be the case even in countries with large metropolitan areas (Mathur, et. al., 2009; de Cesare, 2004). Moreover, delays in general revaluation are commonplace, significantly lowering the revenue-income elasticity of the property tax. The property tax as practiced in developing countries generally fails the tests for a good subnational government tax in terms of its high administrative cost and its unpopularity with voters.

There is a great deal of variation in the extent to which the property tax generates meaningful revenues for metropolitan cities. In Cape Town, about 20 percent of metropolitan government revenues are derived from a tax levied against the capital value of land and improvements. This is about the same share of revenues that is received from intergovernmental transfers.

The primary source of revenue for municipalities in the Mexico City metropolitan area and in the Istanbul metropolitan area, is the property tax. However, in neither case are the local governments empowered to set the tax rate or determine the tax base. The result is that there is relatively little autonomy for the metropolitan local government to determine its revenue level, and in both cases the property tax falls well short of its potential. There is some local government discretion in metropolitan cities in India but the results are much the same. The low yield is largely attributed to the poor administration of the tax. For example, in Mumbai only about 70 percent of properties pay taxes, and in Kolkata properties are assessed at about 20 percent of their value (Mathur, et. al., 2009).

Income and Payroll Taxes

The individual income tax can meet many of the tests for a good metropolitan government tax. It can generate significant revenue from an elastic tax base. It is roughly consistent with the correspondence principle in that the burden falls mostly on those who benefit from the services provided, though correspondence problems do arise with respect to those who cross provincial borders to reach their place of work.[12] Its administration can be simplified by a direct piggyback on the income tax of a

12. *The correspondence principle would call for a residence-based income tax, and for non-residents to file returns and pay an amount that would serve as a benefit charge for local services received. For a discussion, see McLure (1998).*

higher level government, or by information sharing with a higher level government.

Perhaps the major drawback of the personal income tax, as a metropolitan local government revenue, is that it is cyclically sensitive and can leave a local government in a difficult financial position during an economic contraction. This sensitivity is of greatest concern where there is little diversification in the city revenue structure and where the central government does not have the financial strength to compensate for the revenue losses. During the recent economic down turn, personal income taxes in the cities of Riga, Bucharest, and Budapest all declined significantly and had a major budget impact. By contrast, Stockholm and Lausanne also rely on income taxation, but neither suffered as much budgetary stress during the economic contraction because their revenue structures were more diversified.

Developed Countries

New York City has long levied an earnings tax, and until 1999, the liability was with commuters as well as residents. The earnings tax now finances about 16 percent of the city budget. The major source of local government revenue in Cleveland is an earnings tax.

Urban government income taxes are more prevalent in Europe than in the U.S. and Canada, and in many cities are the dominant sources of local government revenue. The piggy back approach to income taxation offers considerable advantages to some metropolitan local governments. It allows local rate determination while avoiding the issue of defining the tax base or administration of the tax. The primary revenue source for Swiss cities is a piggyback personal income tax. Rome levies a residence-based income tax, on a base defined by the central government. The principal municipal government revenue source in metropolitan Copenhagen is the individual income tax (OECD, 2009). The tax base is defined by the central government, and collections are made by the central government. In theory, the 45 municipalities in the metropolitan area are free to set the tax rate, but since 2002 a centrally imposed freeze on the tax rate has been in place. About 80 percent of municipal revenue is raised from the income tax. The Capital Region, the metropolitan area-wide government in Copenhagen, has no taxing power.

Local governments in the metropolitan region of Stockholm rely almost exclusively on a local tax on the earned income of residents. The base is defined by the national government, but local governments are free to set the tax rate. The major concerns with the earnings tax in Stockholm are (a) that such complete reliance on it leaves the municipalities vulnerable to cyclical movements in the economy, and (b) the equalization formula that limits the revenues a local government can receive, provides a significant disincentive to revenue mobilization.

The area-wide government in Madrid (The Community of Madrid) relies on the individual income tax for most of its revenues. The tax base is defined by the central government,[13] but the regional government (community) may choose the tax rate (subject to some restrictions) and is entitled to one-third of revenue collections (OECD, 2007).

There is less use of corporate income taxes at the local government level in metropolitan areas, arguably because of cyclical sensitivity of the revenues and of a fear of driving away investment. However, there is some practice. Both Geneva and Lisbon

13. The Community may provide certain preferential treatments, thereby lowering the tax base.

derive significant revenue from a surcharge on the corporate income tax. New York City derives a significant amount of its budget revenue from the corporate income tax.

Emerging and Developing Economies

The Eastern European Cities use a different model of local income taxation. In these cases, it is a sharing of central income taxes based on collections in the city (Zagreb and Bucharest) or collections from residents (Riga). The central government sets the "local" tax rate, e.g., 26 percent in Riga in 2008. The City of Zagreb may levy a surtax of up to 30 percent on personal income tax collections, and presently it levies a rate of 18 percent.

In general however, subnational government income taxes are rarely found in emerging and developing economies. There are four reasons for this. The first is the administrative problems that would be posed. The second is tax competition. Central governments in some developing countries rely heavily on this source of revenue, and even have trouble collecting much from the personal income tax (Bird and Zolt, 2005). The third reason is that income taxes often carry income distribution goals and these are perceived to be the exclusive responsibility of the central government. Finally, income generation in the formal sector is concentrated in most developing countries, and it is not likely that much revenue would be generated outside the metropolitan areas.

States and the Federal District within metropolitan Mexico City, finance a part of their budgets from a payroll (wage) tax. They are free to choose the tax rate, define the tax base and administer the tax. The tax is collected from employers. There are three problems with the Mexican payroll tax that need to be reckoned with. First, it is a tax on wages, and if levied at a high enough rate, could drive some employment to the informal sector. Second, since it is levied at the place of work, it will result in some tax exporting to non residents.[14] Third, it is cyclically sensitive and can create significant budget problems during an economic contraction.

14. *For a discussion of the payroll tax in Mexico, see Diaz-Cayeros and McLure (2000)*

Sales Taxes

Sales taxes are an attractive option for financing the provision of local public services in metropolitan areas, because with a significant share of consumption taking place within the large urban areas, the revenue potential is considerable. Also, as the point of tax collection for most transactions is identifiable, administration is feasible in developed countries and in some developing countries. However, metropolitan government sales taxes raise the possibility of introducing unwanted distortions in resource allocation, if they are not properly structured.

Developed Countries

The retail sales tax is an important source of revenue for many local governments in U.S. metropolitan areas (e.g., about 11 percent of the total revenue budget in New York). In Canada, local governments in metropolitan areas are mostly limited to the property tax, and cannot levy a general sales tax, though many local governments do impose various selective sales taxes. In Italy, regional governments levy a value added tax on an origin basis (Bordignon, Giannini and Panteghini, 2001). Bird and Slack (2004) have argued that this form of business taxation deserves wider attention. Local government sales taxes are not widely used in the metropolitan areas of Eastern Europe.

Emerging and Developing Economies

In theory, a destination-based sales tax could satisfy the conditions for a good local government tax in emerging and developing economies. In theory, it could be levied at either the metropolitan government level or at the lower tier of metropolitan government. Theory and practice, however, do not always come together because of administrative constraints in most emerging and developing economies.

A value added tax (VAT) is usually levied by central governments as a destination-based sales tax. Unfortunately, in most developing countries, there is no realistic prospect that the tax administration will be able to support a subnational government VAT.[15] A value-added tax levied at the metropolitan city level is almost certainly not feasible, except perhaps in the special case where a metropolitan city covers a large area and has the legal status of a state/province, e.g., Shanghai or Berlin. A better route would be a surcharge on the state government levy or a revenue sharing arrangement with the state government. Here there is some experience. One fourth of the state value added tax in Brazil is distributed to municipalities on a basis of point of collection. A similar arrangement exists for province-level cities in China (Fu, 2007).

Retail sales taxes are not administratively feasible in developing countries, even in large metropolitan areas. A large percent of sales takes place in the informal sector, and a destination-based retail sales tax would likely swell this number even more. Informal sector retailers usually do not keep accurate books of account, and small merchants often keep a "special" set of accounts for tax purposes.

A gross receipts tax levied on all sellers in the formal sector, on an origin basis, can be revenue productive. But, this will create distortions by shifting tax burdens from producing to consuming regions, by introducing a cascading effect on prices, and by discriminating against formal sector sellers. An origin-based sales tax is also subject to the "headquarters problem" or the problem that arises when firms pay their tax bill at the central office location. While all of these reasons suggest that a gross receipts tax is not a good choice for financing governments in metropolitan areas, reason is sometimes outweighed by the appeal of a significant revenue take.

The major own source revenue of Brazilian municipalities is a tax on services (ISS), almost all of which is collected by the largest municipalities (Rezende and Garson 2006). The ISS and the urban property tax together account for about 60 percent of total local tax revenue. Buenos Aires, both city and province, levy a gross receipts tax. The tax is complicated because the tax rate varies widely by type of product. Bogota derives much of its revenue from a gross receipts tax. The business tax in the Philippines is levied on gross receipts and accounts for about 30 percent of local revenues (Taliercio, 2005).

Charges and Fees

Most analysts argue that benefit charges of one form or another are the most appropriate revenue source for local governments (Oates, 1972; Musgrave, 1983; Bahl and Bird, 2008). It constitutes a charge for benefits received, and may lead to recovery of the cost of providing the service in question. Central governments in many countries cede this revenue source to urban local governments because it does not crowd out central revenues as might a local income tax or a consumption tax.

15. *There are efforts and even some experience with implementation. Brazil has long relied on a state level value added tax. India also has implemented a state level value added tax, but is still working out the details of how it will operate, particularly with respect to interstate trade.*

Figure 9.3: User Charges as Share of Total Revenue for Selected Metropolitan Local Governments

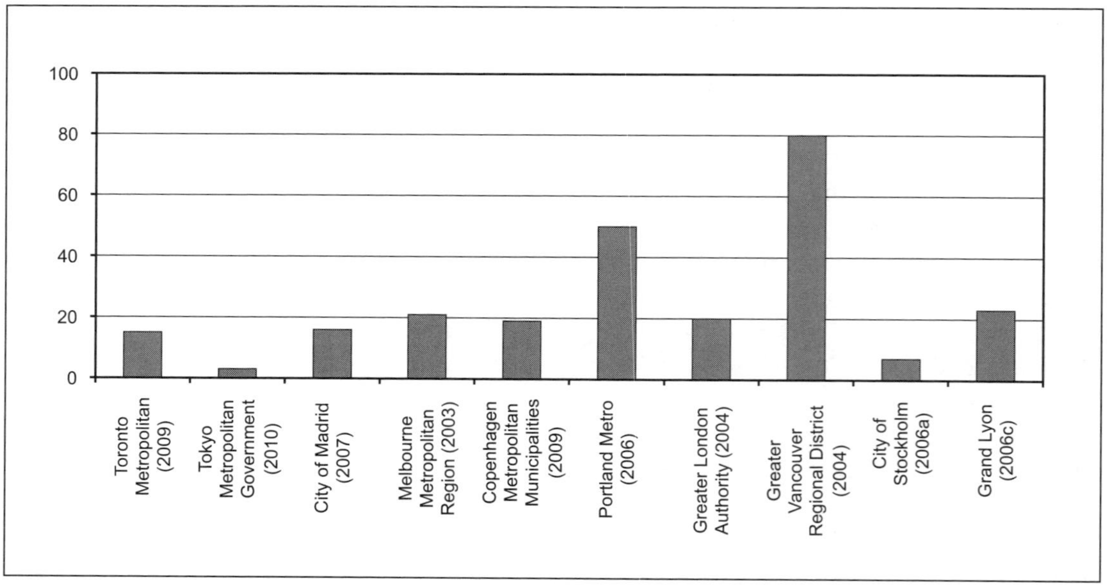

Source: *All information taken from OECD Territorial Reviews with the exception of Tokyo (http://www.metro.tokyo.jp/ENGLISH/PROFILE/index.htm) and Greater London Authority and Greater Vancouver Regional District (Bird and Slack 2004)*

Developed Countries

User charges are particularly important for financing the operating expenditures of special purpose districts and public companies in metropolitan areas. The comparison for selected metropolitan areas presented in Figure 9.3 gives some idea of the relative importance of user charges in financing metropolitan services. Even these amounts are an understatement, however, because they do not include the user charges levied by public companies. European cities often are full or partial owners in various types of public service companies (e.g., public transit, water, energy, housing) that finance their operations with user charges. Sometimes the charges are supplemented by a subsidy paid from the city budget, and other times the user charge revenues generate a surplus that is distributed back to the city.

Emerging and Developing Economies

User charges are a particularly attractive revenue option for metropolitan local governments in emerging and developing economies. The levy can be linked to service benefits, hence there is more willingness to pay, and both assessment and collection can be easier than in the case of general taxes. On the other hand, charges often are made for essential services, and sentiments can run high when increases are necessary to cover rising costs. Public housing rents, water rates and bus fares are examples.

The City of Cape Town collects about 35 percent of revenues from user charges, mostly electricity, water, sanitation, and refuse collection. While the revenue take is quite large by comparison with other metropolitan cities, there is poor compliance and low collection rates (OECD, 2008). This is a not uncommon outcome in emerging and developing economies. For example, the Bangkok Metropolitan Administration collects only about 20 percent of charges due for garbage pickup (Webster, 2000, p17). Mohanty, et al. (2007) reported a low rate of cost recovery for the Indian metropolitan cities of Mumbai and Kolkata. By contrast, user fees in Bogota are sufficient to cover operating costs for the city's urban bus transport company (RTI, 2005).

Intergovernmental Transfers

A special treatment as regards the flow of intergovernmental transfers may be reserved for metropolitan cities, sometimes to exclude them from certain flows to encourage self-sufficiency, and sometimes to recognize their special needs. In Rome, for example, a special central transfer equivalent to about 15 percent of the current revenues of the city is given as a recurrent grant to recognize Rome's capital city status. Some metropolitan areas have the same status as states or provinces, in which case they have both a state and a city entitlement to intergovernmental transfers. Also different from other local governments, a special program of intra-metropolitan government revenue sharing may be in place.

Developed countries

Metropolitan area governments in some developed countries do not depend as heavily on intergovernmental transfers as do other local governments. For example, the cities of Stockholm, Paris, Madrid, and Lausanne all raise more than two-thirds of their own financing from local taxes and charges.

A few illustrations may help describe the general practice. Grants play a minor role in financing municipalities in metropolitan Copenhagen. Specific grants account for about 10 percent of revenues, and these are primarily for reimbursement of agency functions performed on behalf of the central government. On the other hand, the area-wide capital region government, which is primarily responsible for health care, has no independent taxing powers. About 75 percent of its financing comes from central government transfers and 25 percent from municipalities' transfers.

The Madrid regional government receives about 20 percent of its revenues in shared taxes and grants. The municipal governments, however, depend on transfers for about 40 percent of revenues. Large municipalities receive most of their transfers in the form of shared taxes, while smaller municipalities receive formula grants based on indicators of expenditure need and tax effort. Melbourne and Toronto finance only about 15 percent of their respective budgets with intergovernmental transfers.

There are some exceptions to this general pattern. One is Germany, where local governments have few independent revenue sources, and rely almost exclusively on transfers. In the Netherlands, local governments have only limited taxing powers. Equalization is done through transfers.

Emerging and Developing Economies

Metropolitan local governments in emerging and developing economies are heavily reliant on intergovernmental transfers from federal and state/provincial governments though usually less so than are other local governments. There are several reasons for this. Metropolitan cities have a stronger tax base and are sometimes given more legal taxing powers than other local governments. Often times large urban governments have a better ability to collect taxes. They also may have more incentive to levy taxes than do other local governments. If the higher level governments use equalization grants, metropolitan cities will receive less relative to their population size and therefore will be pushed toward raising more own source revenues.

In Cape Town, only 20 percent of metropolitan city revenues are derived from grants. The major transfer in the system – "the equitable shares grant" – is allocated on an equalizing basis. The result is that Cape Town and the other metropolitan cities in South Africa receive about half the per capita amount that goes to smaller cities.

The Metropolitan Manila Development Authority has no taxing powers and limited authority to levy user charges. It relies almost exclusively on grants from the central and provincial governments and on mandated contributions from the underlying local government units. In effect, the lower tier local governments pay the metropolitan governments for services delivered.

Mexico has a highly centralized financing structure. Sub-national government taxes account for less than 1 percent of GDP. Most metropolitan services are financed from conditional (22 percent of spending) and unconditional transfers. However, the dependence on transfers is significantly less in the Federal District of Mexico than in the other states in Mexico.

About 50 percent of revenues of the metropolitan municipality of Istanbul come from intergovernmental transfers. The most important of these (50 percent of revenue) is the revenue sharing grant which is distributed on a derivation (origin of collection) basis. This basis for distribution favors Istanbul greatly because of its large tax base, and because it receives a share of the tax paid by all companies that are headquartered in Istanbul.[16]

Brazil uses both discretionary grants and equalization grants to support local governments. The former, for education and health, probably favor metropolitan cities, but the latter do not. Rezende and Garson (2006, p20) report that the ten largest metropolitan areas, which house 30 percent of the Brazilian population and generate about half of the national GDP, receive only about 13 percent of the divisible pool from shared income and industrial products tax.

The core municipalities in metropolitan areas in Eastern Europe are heavily financed by intergovernmental transfers, often in the form of a shared personal income tax (e.g., Bucharest, Budapest, and Zagreb). Revenues from these transfers were buoyant during the economic expansion of the early 2000s, but contracted significantly in the later part of the decade. In other cases, the transfers take the form of conditional grants that are restricted to particular uses. The City of Zagreb provides decentralized services, but under a strict set of central government earmarks. The revenue structure of Budapest is dominated by intergovernmental transfers of various forms, including both revenue sharing and conditional grants. The central government provides about 70 percent of Sofia city revenues through intergovernmental transfers.

Conclusions: Is There an Easy Way Forward?

Removing the constraints to providing an adequate level of public services in metropolitan areas is a subject that is high on the policy reform list in many countries. But the "right" way to deliver public services in large urban agglomerations, and to finance these services, is still an open question. This review shows that the international practice is quite diverse.

16. For a discussion of this "headquarters problem" see Bahl and Solomon (2003).

What is the Real problem?

The underlying problem to deal with in metropolitan governance and finance is finding a way to marry two very different spatial units. The functional economic region has boundaries that are informal and always changing, as one would expect of a labor market area. The "champion" of the region as a government entity is the planner or social reformer who sees the great efficiency and equity gains that would come with regional service delivery. The other spatial unit, the local government, has fixed boundaries. The champions of the local government are voters and their elected officials, who want to maintain control over services provided in the local area. It seems unlikely that these two units, with their differing priorities, will come together easily in support of a general purpose region wide government. The issue is even more complicated by overlapping special districts or public companies whose service boundaries may not be coterminous with either the metropolitan area (labor market area) or the general purpose local governments.

The public policy solution lies in finding a way to deliver some services with a degree of local control and financing, while delivering others on a region wide basis and with a broader finance base. All governments will likely identify with a model that produces better prospects for long run economic growth, and better transportation services and public amenities. Local governments can be moved by strategies that give them some voice and a promise to hold a lid on taxes. But none of these arguments seem to be convincing when it comes to moving basic services away from the local level, or more drastic yet, abolishing local units of government. The practice shows that governance and finance in some metropolitan areas have moved toward this solution, but almost no one would declare that the delivery of regional services is properly coordinated.

Is there a next step in improving and rationalizing the financing of large cities in metropolitan areas? Three policy directions would seem worth considering.

Governance

It may be time to move away from the good but academic advice that area-wide, general purpose local government are the answer to the public financing problems in metropolitan areas. Home rule is too firmly entrenched to be dismissed, at least in the foreseeable future. Where this shift in emphasis would take public policy is toward emphasizing a two-tier metropolitan structure, probably overlaid by a capital infrastructure district(s) for services that lend themselves to pricing, and a regional coordination and planning district. Attention could then shift to designing a system of taxing and charging that would best fit a two-tier governance.

The above model might also work in emerging and developing economies where there is a tradition of local government, e.g., Manila, Calcutta or São Paulo. In all three metropolitan areas, a kind of two-tiered governance is in place but the revenue mobilization system is not well designed. Where something akin to a metropolitan government is in place, it could be overlapped with an infrastructure district(s) and a coordinating body. A major struggle in such cases would be to insure that the government boundaries grow with the boundaries of the economic region. Again, the question would be how to design a financing system that would match up with the governance system.

How would this differ from the present system? One difference is that the regional districts would need to be elected and to be viewed as financing districts as well as service delivery areas. Enabling legislation by higher level governments would be required to make this happen. Second, the taxation instruments used by the lower tier governments should be designed to fit the basic efficiency rules of taxation, e.g., no tax exporting. Some sort of monitoring might be put in place to regulate intra-metropolitan practices that distort trade between the member communities. Third, higher level governments should ensure a better match between expenditure assignment and revenue assignment. This would require important changes on the expenditure side – more clarity and fewer mandates – and would require passing more economic growth-responsive tax bases to the metropolitan local governments. Finally, the provincial and national intergovernmental system should be redesigned to give more autonomy to metropolitan area local governments, and at the same time to limit the flow of grants to them in order to encourage local revenue mobilization.

Metropolitan Finance

As always, part of the problem in metropolitan areas is that resources are scarce and do not match up well with the demand for public services. But the level of taxation in some OECD countries is very high and additional taxing space may be limited. In the United States, there may be room for tax increases, but a combination of the federal deficit and political backlash may crowd out most opportunities for increased local government taxation.

Ideally, one could compare the level and structure of taxation across metropolitan areas. Unfortunately, there is scant evidence on the finances of overlapping governments in metropolitan areas, as indicated by the relatively few (and somewhat dated) special studies reviewed above. More timely evidence is available for core city governments and from the credit rating agencies that regularly evaluate these municipalities.[17]

The major stumbling block in developing a model system of metropolitan finance is the lower tier local governments. Those wedded to fiscal decentralization within metropolitan areas will argue for heavy assignment of expenditure responsibility to these local governments. If these local governments are to be moved toward budgetary independence, significant tax assignment is implied. The property tax and user charges alone will not likely carry the expenditure load, so long as the property tax remains so politically contentious. But broad-based taxes in jurisdictionally fragmented metropolitan areas are likely to be characterized by a significant amount of exporting of burdens to residents in other jurisdictions. The recourse is to use a residence-based earnings tax with some sort of compensating mechanism as is the case in Denmark, or to rely heavily on intergovernmental transfers to finance local services.

There is room for metropolitan (area-wide) governments to contribute more to the financing of services in the metropolitan area. A residence-based income tax, with an appropriate commuter charge, would be an attractive alternative. This might be justified first, on grounds that area-wide services provide benefits to non-users, hence less than full financing from user charges would be efficient. Second, this tax could support an intra-metropolitan equalization fund. This would remove the disincentive to lower tier tax effort, as has been observed in some Nordic countries. Intra-metropolitan revenue sharing has much to recommend it relative to a national or provincial program of grants.

17. *The credit rating data, however, is focused on individual local governments. It does not take account of the impact of overlapping governments on core municipalities. For example of a credit rating report, see Standard & Poors.*

Some other taxes that might be appropriate for a metropolitan taxing district are the property tax, or at least the commercial-industrial portion of it, and taxes on motor vehicle licenses. User charges would continue to play a major role in financing the regional district, but grants from higher level governments would not.

For single purpose special districts, revenue mobilization could continue to be centered on user charges, as is the case now. Special benefit taxes, raised within the metropolitan area, could be dedicated to the special district. There is much more room here for public financing. Finally, general taxation to support a service is a possibility (and one that has been tried in several places), but should only be done if authorized by a voter referendum.

In emerging and developing economies, metropolitan cities need to ratchet up the level of own source revenues but have less administrative capacity or legal authority to do so. Unfortunately, the will to increase local taxes is often not in place. If some of these constraints are removed, significant revenues might be raised in the largest metropolitan cities. The most viable options for increasing the rate of revenue mobilization might include:

- Increase the rate and the collection efficiency on user charges. Give metropolitan local governments discretion to set the level of user charges.

- Improve the administration of the property tax so as to raise the overall effective rate. There are many ways to do this, and there is a literature that has explored this at length in developing countries. Among the options that might be considered, in most countries they are removing preferential treatments, increasing valuation rates, bringing untapped properties into the base, installing a "payment in lieu" for government properties, simplifying payment options and increasing penalties for non-payment.

- Levy taxes on wage income, either directly or as a piggyback on the national government income tax.

Intergovernmental Transfers

Central and state (provincial) governments might adopt an explicit strategy of using equalization grants to discriminate against large cities in order to induce them to make a greater level of tax effort. This is already done in some developed countries. In fact, integrated transfers might be limited to conditional grants that would stimulate spending for a national priority. This financing strategy will of course be limited by the extent to which expenditure responsibilities have been assigned to local governments in metropolitan areas.

In the emerging and developing economies, the metropolitan local governments tend to be more dependent on transfers from higher level governments. This often dampens the enthusiasm of local governments to mobilize more revenues from their own sources. A strategy of replacing most transfer revenue with increased local taxing power would not be met with great enthusiasm by local politicians, because of the political pain associated with imposing taxes. It has been argued in many countries that a significant amount of untapped taxable capacity resides in the metropolitan cities. Authorization of a model of local government taxation, such as that discussed above, could provide an incentive for metropolitan area governments to find a way to tap this capacity.

10. Conclusion

Jorge Martínez-Vázquez
Georgia State University, U.S.A.

Paul Smoke
New York University, U.S.A.

Overview

Local governments around the world have become key public sector actors during the past two decades, and decentralization now ranks among the most common and consequential global reforms (See First GOLD Report on Decentralization and Local Democracy). This trend could ultimately be as influential as other major institutional transformations of the past century, such as decolonization in Africa and Asia or the transition from planned to market economies in the former Soviet Union, China, and elsewhere. Indeed, local governments have in many respects truly come of age. Their role is reinforced in global policy circles, including through major multilateral proclamations, such as the *European Charter of Local Self-Government* (1985) and the UN Habitat Guidelines on Decentralization and Reinforcement of Local Governments (2007).

In many regions of the world decentralization has enhanced the functions and autonomy of local entities. Local governments play increasingly more critical roles in delivering basic infrastructure services, such as roads, transportation and water, and social services, such as education and health. These developments have contributed in minor and major ways to the progressive deepening of local democracy, the alleviation of internal regional tensions in conflict prone areas, the promotion of broader and deeper citizen participation in public affairs, and the overall strengthening and efficiency of the public sector.

Decentralization has also generated a dramatic upsurge in expectations. Citizens look more to local governments for those public services that improve daily living conditions. Central governments depend on local governments to support priority development and poverty reduction goals. Private firms increasingly rely on local governments to deliver infrastructure and other services that support production and stimulate job creation.

One of the most critical factors underlying the ability of local governments to meet the growing expectations placed on them is the quality of the architecture and operation of the intergovernmental fiscal system. This Second GOLD Report focuses on local government finance worldwide. Local government finance is important not only because the role and impact of local governments have dramatically increased, but also because this progress has recently been confronted by daunting challenges.

The global economic and financial crisis that emerged in 2008 —the most significant crisis since the Great Depression— has imposed major financial constraints on local governments in many countries. Equally important, central authorities in some countries have responded to the crisis by taking recentralization measures to deal with their own fiscal problems and increasing control over local governments. It is too early to say whether these actions represent a durable change in the decentralization trend, but they clearly pose immediate challenges to the viability and effectiveness of local governments. Resource constraints during a period of greater responsibility and need pose obvious threats, but so does the damaging curtailment of local government autonomy, which is a necessary condition for the full realization of the promise of decentralization.

Beyond the impact of the global financial crisis, local governments are confronted with other significant structural challenges. As substantial urbanization continues unabated in some parts of the world, public service demands are growing faster than many local governments can keep up with. New needs are also arising as a result of an emerging understanding of the onerous implications of global environmental challenges, as well as from major demographic changes, such as the increasing number of the elderly in some countries and the explosion of youth as a share of the population in others. These challenges, however, also present opportunities to strengthen and boldly reinvent the role of local governments. They are often in a unique position of strength to deal with pressing local problems, the solutions to which have important national consequences.

The preceding regional chapters document strengths and weaknesses of local government fiscal frameworks in different parts of the world and examine the capacity of local governments to mobilize resources and manage expenditures. The chapters also assess intergovernmental relations and developments in governance, such as broader and deeper citizen participation in local planning and budgeting. This chapter summarizes key challenges and issues discussed in the preceding regional chapters, and points to possible broad-based policy solutions that could both alleviate problems and weaknesses experienced to date and help to improve overall local government performance.

The next section outlines basic contextual factors that affect fiscal decentralization worldwide. This is followed by a summary of recent influential trends, experiences, and policy issues. Building on the review of fiscal decentralization parameters outlined in the introduction and discussed in the regional chapters, common and noteworthy local government finance issues and challenges are considered. Finally, the chapter closes with recommendations and concluding thoughts on the way forward in local finance reform and the next steps for UCLG.

The Context of Reform: Diversity, Politics and Change

The potential for local governments to serve as full partners in managing public functions and to contribute to local governance and improved service delivery remains a promising, but only partially fulfilled process in many countries. To some extent this should be expected, as decentralization occurs under different circumstances, is subject to powerful political forces, and requires some minimum capacity to be effective. Even in the most conducive environments, decentralization is a highly dynamic process that demands ongoing adaptation to evolving economic, social and political conditions.

Understanding Diversity

As highlighted in the introductory chapter, countries have been subject to different historical influences, so they are building from diverse institutional and governance traditions. This includes their experiences with and inclinations towards decentralization, as well as their ability to absorb decentralization reforms. The role of local governments in public finance varies considerably across regions (Figure 10.1 & Table 10.1), and there are also large differences within regions. An important implication of these various differences is that desired local finance reforms vary considerably across regions and countries. Clearly, the reforms needed to strengthen local finances differ between countries that have a long tradition with decentralization and those with a shorter history of relevant experience.

Local government finance is prospering in much of Europe, North America, and parts of East Asia and the Pacific (Korea, Japan, Australia, New Zealand). It remains at an early stage in some regions, such as the Middle East & Western Asia, where most local governments are deconcentrated units of the central government with limited autonomy. South Asia has a recent tradition of democracy, but local governments face controls by higher level governments. In Latin

Figure 10.1 The Comparative Fiscal Role of Local Government: Expenditure and Revenue as a Percentage of General Government Expenditure and Revenue

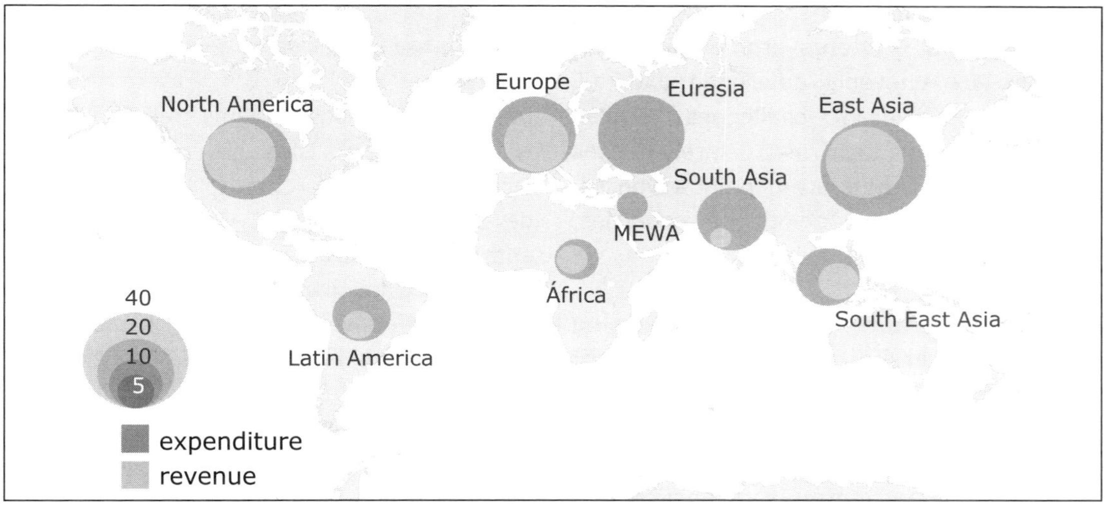

Note: while local expenditures as a proportion of public expenditure may be relatively high in East Asia, Eurasia, and South Asia this does not necessarily mean that local goverments have autonomous control over spending, which is an important aspect of decentralization (devolution).

Source: Data from Table 10.1

Table 10.1: The Comparative Role of Local Government

	Local expenditures as percentage of total revenues	Local expenditure as percentage of total expenditures
Africa	3.2 (3.6)	7.9 (6.8)
Asia		
South Asia	1.5 (0.9)	16.0 (0.9)
East Asia	20.0 (0.3)	40.0 (0.3)
South –East Asia	5.3 (0.8)	15.5 (0.6)
Eurasia	N.A.	26.5 (15.1)
Europe (2008)	13.0 (0.7)	23.9 (0.5)
Latin America	4.0 (4.5)	11.1 (7.3)
Middle East & Western Asia	N.A.	4.6 (1.7)
North America	17.8 (0.6)	26.8

Notes: Coefficient of variation in parentheses. The means include : Africa: Benin, Burkina Faso, Egypt, Ethiopia, Gabon, Ghana, Kenya, Malawi, Mali, Morocco, Mozambique, Niger, Nigeria, Senegal, South Africa, Tanzania, Togo, Tunisia, Uganda, Zambia, Zimbabwe. South Asia: Bangladesh, India, Pakistan; East Asia: China, Japan, Korea; South -East Asia: Indonesia, Philippines, Vietnam, Thailand. Eurasia: Armenia, Belarus, Georgia, Kazakhstan, Kyrgyzstan, Moldova, Russia, Ukraine. Europe: Austria, Belgium, Bulgaria, Cyprus, Czech Rep., Denmark, Estonia, Finland, France, Germany, Greece, Hungary, Iceland, Ireland, Italy, Latvia, Lithuania, Luxembourg, Malta, Netherlands, Norway, Poland, Portugal, Romania, Slovak Rep., Slovenia, Spain, Sweden, Switzerland, United Kingdom, Iceland, Norway, Switzerland ; Latin America: Argentina, Bolivia, Brazil, Chile, Colombia, Ecuador, El Salvador, Honduras, Jamaica, Mexico, Panama, Paraguay, Peru. Middle East and Western Asia: Bahrain, Iran, Jordan, Lebanon, Palestine, Syrian Arab Republic, Turkey, United Arab Emirates, Palestine, Yemen. North America: Canada, U.S.A.

America and Eurasia, local finances are generally improving, but still face challenges associated with past centralized traditions. China and most of Southeast Asia have made progress, but intergovernmental fiscal relations are unevenly developed and still experience significant challenges. African local governments are rarely well empowered, but there are hopeful advances, especially in some Anglophone countries, such as South Africa or Tanzania.

One of the critical inferences emerging from the diversity of local government systems is that there is a need for diverse approaches to deal with fiscal challenges, even those that are relatively common. There is no magic formula to ensure that local government systems will function effectively. The road to success requires consistent and appropriately sequenced application of basic local public finance principles outlined in the introductory chapter. These are relatively few, and they leave adequate flexibility for each country to structure its intergovernmental finance system to fit its history and national goals.

Responding to Political Reality

Decentralization is an intensely political process since it involves the central government assigning powers and granting autonomy to local governments. While political forces can often open the door to decentralization, as discussed throughout this report, they can also pose challenges. These include reluctance of central politicians to devolve powers to local governments for fear of losing control, the opposition of central bureaucrats whose institutional and personal goals conflict with decentralization, or resistance to legally mandated decentralization reforms during implementation from elites and pre-existing deconcentrated agencies. At the local level, local politicians can undermine decentralization if they are not sufficiently accountable to their constituents. These political realities must be understood and responded to if decentralization is to be effective and prosper.

Developing Capacity

Effective local governments require administrative capacity. Local government capacity can be an important constraint, particularly in developing countries. At times, perhaps somewhat paradoxically, decentralization underperforms because of weak central institutions, either due to political instability or a lack of control of basic functions of government, such as unified tax administration or treasury and budget implementation controls. If decentralization is to meet its promise, capacity constraints and their consequences must be recognized and efforts to develop appropriate capacities need to be adopted.

Adapting to Change

Conditions and motivations for decentralization change, sometimes rapidly and dramatically. These changes can be relatively routine, such as the adoption of new legislation or the turnover of a government power after an election. They can also be momentous, such as a major political shift or a sudden economic and financial crisis. Local government policies and systems need to respond effectively to these changes, and adapt as necessary to shifting circumstances. At the same time, the 2008 global financial crisis showed that adapting to shifting circumstances can also damage local governments. Local governments and their advocates must be vigilant and be prepared to defend their legitimate interests when they come under threat.

Broad Policy Trends and Issues

Before reviewing major findings on local government finance, it is important to contextualize those findings by noting some broader trends and common decentralization issues the report shows can affect local fiscal performance. Some of these are experienced globally, while others are particularly relevant in certain regions or some subset of countries across regions.

Global Crisis

The financial and economic crisis noted above is affecting local governments globally. Emerging countries of Asia and some in Latin America have been less impacted, but others have suffered drastic effects. In March 2010, for example, the Greek government reduced by decree the number of local governments from 1,034 to 355 in order to save an estimated 1.2 billion euros annually.

The pains of fiscal adjustment due to the crisis are being strongly felt by local governments in all the continents. In a number of countries in Africa, Eurasia, and Latin America, central governments have cut transfers or introduced recentralization measures. In some regions, the effects of the crisis simply compound the effects of existing challenges. In Africa, for example, trade liberalization and fiscal transition, and in less developed countries more generally, poverty and informality have long presented challenges for public finance in general and local governments in particular.

Even in the most advanced countries, stabilization policies to reduce public indebtedness, such as those being adopted in Europe and North America, are deeply impacting local finances. Local governments in many of those countries fear that a disproportionate share of the costs of further fiscal consolidation will fall on them in the form of cuts in intergovernmental transfers, restrictions on local credit, and other austerity measures.

The financial and economic crisis is not the only global crisis with relevance for local governments. Financing climate change mitigation policies and the investments required for the associated risk management would considerably increase the resource needs of local governments worldwide. The financial implications for local governments of the response to environmental challenges are only beginning to be understood.

Partial or Interrupted Decentralization Reform

The global crisis provides one example of how decentralization can be stalled or reversed, but this is a more general problem taking different forms as evidenced in the regional chapters. Fiscal decentralization frameworks involve complex systems with many interrelated components, and some are easier to implement or politically more feasible than others. Thus, some local finance systems are only partially designed (relative to best practice principles) and some are only partially implemented even if they are mandated in the legal framework design.

If only certain elements of the system are implemented or partially implemented, problems can arise because of the interdependencies involved. Deficiencies with one component often undermine the ability of the overall system to function effectively. For example, lack of clarity with functional assignment can lead to uncertainty regarding the financial needs of local governments. Similarly, problems with the design and implementation of intergovernmental transfer systems can compromise incentives and capacities for local service delivery, local revenue generation, and local borrowing.

Among the most pervasive and damaging instances of incomplete decentralization is the assignment of too few revenues to finance assigned functions. At a global scale, very few countries escape dealing with major gaps between local expenditure and local revenues. This can result from a flaw in system design, but revenue inadequacy tends to occur for political or capacity reasons even in countries where constitutional or legal provisions prohibit unfunded local government mandates. The problem tends to be more significant in some regions. African countries, for example, generally have much less decentralization of revenues than of expenditures, leading to particularly severe revenue-expenditure gaps.

Demographic Shifts

Many European countries are confronted with the challenge of coping with the effects on public finances of a rapidly ageing population and the need to integrate immigrants into the labor market and society at large. The ageing population challenge is also relevant in several countries in Asia, such as China and Japan, and in Eurasia, such as Russia and Ukraine. In some developing countries, the growth of youth as a share of population poses different types of service challenges that also have serious financial implications.

Rapidly increasing urbanization, particularly in many of the developing countries of Africa, Asia, and Latin America, continues to create demand for public services and infrastructure that requires a huge volume of resources. The needs are even larger if investments for climate change adaptation are included. Given available information on maintenance and development costs of urban investments, it would seem reasonable to expect a need for about 200 billion USD per year over the next 25 years for the developing countries alone[1] ; this represents only one-third of the total spending need for total public infrastructure spending estimated by the World Bank.[2]

Jurisdictional Fragmentation

Fragmentation is a major issue for many countries in most regions of the world. In many countries the appropriate structure and size of local governments is an ongoing debate. Small local governments cannot independently take advantage of economies of scale in the delivery of some services, resulting in higher costs. Smaller local governments, however, generally provide a stronger political connection to citizens and may be better able to respond to local demands. Getting the right balance, e.g. by maintaining smaller local governments but providing mechanisms for cooperative arrangements among them and links to higher levels for large scale services, is a critical challenge in many counties.

Thailand has more than 7,500 bottom tier local governments with an average population of less than 10 000, and there are concerns that these are too small for service delivery. In some cases, such as Uganda or Dominican Republic, new local governments are being constantly created, diluting the capacity of local governments that were only recently empowered. In a number of countries perverse incentives, such as offering equal lump sum transfers to all local governments regardless of size, create incentives for further jurisdictional fragmentation.

On the other hand, in countries such as France (with 36,600 local governments), citizens strongly identify with smaller local governments (communes). These are said to bring greater representation and accountability, thus potentially balancing the additional costs represented by the inability to realize economies of scale, particularly if the latter can be realized by creating cooperative arrangements among the smaller units. When local governments in South Africa were substantially consolidated in 2002, some analysts expressed concern that the new larger, more fiscally viable local governments had damaged political connectivity to citizens in some areas.

Deconcentration and Devolution

Devolution of spending and taxing powers to autonomous local governments is generally

1. *UCLG. 2007.* UCLG Policy Paper on Local Finance. *UCLG.*
2. *World Bank (2005) estimated the investment needs in public infrastructure in developing countries, amounting to 600 billion USD per year over the next 25 years. However, these figures include all public infrastructures, whether national (energy, communications and information technology, transport, water and sanitation, etc.) or urban (local roads, local water supply, and sanitation, waste disposals, schools, street lighting...). (World Bank. 2005.* Infrastructure and the World Bank: A progress report. *The World Bank). The UCLG Committee on Local Finance estimated one third of this amount, i.e. 0.4 percent of World GDP, needs to be channeled to urban infrastructure (UCLG. 2007.* UCLG Policy Paper on Local Finance. *UCLG).*

held up as the standard for decentralization, but even some countries with elected local councils maintain deconcentrated administration. In Kenya, for example, district administrations exist in the same territory as elected county councils. There is little clarity with respect to their distinct functions, sometimes resulting in service redundancy or gaps (although this situation should be corrected by forthcoming reforms based on the 2010 constitution).

In other cases, empowered local governments have not been created. In the MEWA region, for example, deconcentrated local administration prevails except in Turkey and Palestine. Similar situations can be found in countries in other regions, such as Egypt, Pakistan, Bangladesh, Thailand, and Kazakhstan. The use of local governments as deconcentrated units of the central administration leaves unexploited efficiency gains in the delivery of public services that are achievable with devolved systems by better matching the needs and preferences of local residents and making local officials more accountable to citizens.

Intermediate Governments in Federal and Hierarchical Systems

While a federal country is often associated with high fiscal decentralization, many federal constitutions do not recognize directly the right of local entities to self government. Instead, they empower states or other intermediate governments to establish fiscal relationships with local governments. This approach has led to considerable fiscal powers for local governments in Brazil, Canada, South Africa, and the United States.

In other cases, such as Argentina, Australia, India, Mexico, Nigeria, Pakistan, and Russia, local governments enjoy (often considerably) less fiscal autonomy even than those in some unitary countries with more centralized traditions. Depriving large populous countries like India or Pakistan (in the latter local authorities were suspended in 2009 by agreement between federal and provincial authorities) of accountable local governments diminishes their chances for attaining the potential benefits of decentralization. Limited authority for local governments is also present in unitary systems with strong hierarchical links between intermediate and local tiers of governments, such as China or Vietnam.

The Role of International Development Agencies

International development agencies often create challenges for the very developing countries in Africa, Asia, and Latin America that they are supposed to be assisting through support for decentralization and local government reforms. There are various issues in this regard, but two are particularly important. First, these agencies have often pushed particular types of reforms, sometimes based on particular objectives of the agencies or simply what has worked in other countries. As a result, in some cases, the reforms being promoted have been inappropriate for recipient countries or have proven unsustainable because there is no strong national ownership.

Second, the donors have commonly created parallel mechanisms to implement programs that support the financing and delivery of local services because of concerns about low local administrative capacity, corruption, and other institutional weaknesses in the host country. These mechanisms can be based at higher levels or at local levels, but in either case they bypass the regular decision-making and resource management procedures of local governments. They can improve service delivery and may be appropriate in some form at early stages of decentralization when local governments are weak, but they ultimately undermine the legitimacy and effectiveness of local governments unless the systems and procedures they use are adapted and institutionalized into regular government operations.

Local Government Finance: Main Issues and Challenges

As outlined in the introduction of the report, several key aspects of fiscal systems need to be in place and meet certain basic principles for local governments to perform effectively. These include expenditure assignments and management; local own source (autonomous) revenues; properly structured intergovernmental transfers; and, where appropriate, access to borrowing and other alternatives to mobilize resources for development expenditures. This section outlines key issues and challenges identified in the regional chapters with respect to each of these issues.

The emphasis in this section is on identifying problems and challenges that require attention, but it is important to acknowledge, as noted in the Introduction and some regional chapters, that there have been very significant improvements in local finance over the past decades in many developed and also developing countries. These improvements range from increased efficiency in public expenditures to greater revenue mobilization, and to innovations in public management, such as the more general adoption of the type of participatory budgeting that began in Latin America.

Expenditure Assignment and Management

A clear assignment of responsibilities and explicit methodologies to translate expenditure responsibilities into financial needs are fundamental for local finance. Deficiencies on this front weaken local governments and undermine the rest of the local fiscal framework. The challenges commonly fall under a number of categories outlined below.

Clarity in expenditure assignment: Insufficient clarity occurs in many regions, particularly in developing countries in Africa, Asia, Eurasia, and Latin America. This results from poorly drafted laws and conflicts between decentralization laws and sectoral laws regarding specific services. Sectoral responsibilities may continue to be implemented by line ministries without coordination or in competition with local governments, duplicating efforts by keeping deconcentrated offices and staff at pre-decentralization levels; this is a common occurrence, for example, in African and Latin American countries. The ambiguity of expenditure assignments can be more severe where there are more levels of government, as in China, and in federations where intermediate levels have significant but inadequately defined control over local governments under their jurisdiction, such as in the case of India. A related institutional issue in some countries, such as Australia and Argentina, is whether local governments should obtain separate legal status from their intermediate level governments, provinces, or states.

Suitability of and compliance with expenditure assignment: In some cases central authorities still play an unwarranted role in the delivery of basic local services, sometimes contrary to decentralization law. This can result in levels and types of services that differ from those desired by local people. In other cases, services with benefit spillovers (affecting people of jurisdictions beyond direct beneficiaries) or a heavy focus on redistribution lack coordination of tasks with higher levels of government; this can result in insufficient or uneven provision of services. This happens, for example, in China, which assigns responsibility for social security and public pensions to local governments.

Funding expenditure mandates: Lack of clarity in functional assignment creates room for cost shifting among levels of government, often through unfunded local expenditure mandates that can be can be extremely burdensome. These can involve requiring local governments to deliver specific services, use particular delivery approaches, or meet certain input or output standards in service delivery. This is a common occurrence among developing and developed countries. Sometimes such mandates may involve services that local governments are not required to provide under local government legislation.

Budget approval and control by higher level authorities: The central or regional authorities assist with and closely oversee —and ultimately may even approve— the budgets voted on by local elected councils in many countries, particularly in Africa, Asia, Eurasia, Latin America, and MEWA regions. This practice of ex-ante control weakens the budgetary autonomy of local authorities.

Incentives for local expenditure efficiency: Particularly in developing countries, local government spending quality is often low in terms of the outcomes produced relative to the costs incurred. This is partly attributable to resource constraints and the often-excessive administrative shares of the local government budget. But other factors noted above (lack of clarity in functional assignments, unfunded mandates, etc.) and below (conditional transfers and low revenue autonomy) also undermine local accountability and incentives to use resources efficiently.

Local Revenue Generation/Autonomy

Local revenue generation and autonomy are critical for local governments to be able to meet their expenditure responsibilities in an accountable and efficient way. Yet there are very few countries in the world that so far have provided local governments with the means and autonomy needed to raise adequate revenues. This problem is manifested in various ways related to the design and use of local revenue systems.

Vertical fiscal imbalances: The transfer of expenditure responsibilities to local governments has often not been accompanied by devolution of corresponding revenue sources (including intergovernmental transfers, which are discussed below). As noted above, local government revenues in many regions play a minor role in national public budgets. This has resulted in increasing financial pressures on the local government expenditure, and even where resources are more adequate, greater local government dependence on central transfers.

Revenue autonomy: Autonomy is highly constrained in most of Africa, Asia, and the Middle East and West Asia. The situation is better in Eurasia and Latin America, but not uniformly. Local governments have limited or no authority to introduce new taxes, and to decide on some or all tax rates, fees, and user charges. Even some decentralized countries, such as Australia, limit local revenue autonomy. A number of prominent attempts to enhance tax autonomy and reduce transfer dependence, such as recent "Trinity Reforms" in Japan, have only partially succeeded. Revenue autonomy is stronger, but not without challenges, in advanced economies of Western Europe and North America.

Property taxation challenges: The property tax is the most commonly recommended and globally used local government tax, but its significant revenue potential often remains unrealized. On average developing countries raise 0.5 percent of GDP from property tax compared to two percent in developed countries. This is partly because the tax is unpopular— even in some developed countries where it plays a significant role (U.S., Canada, U.K.), citizen opposition has been strong. In addition, it is difficult and expensive to administer, all the more so in many developing countries without well defined property registers, with sizable informal areas, and with weaker local capacity for value assessments, enforcement, and collection.

Diversification of the local tax base: Local tax bases are often narrow, especially given the problems with heavy reliance on the property tax. A number of countries in Europe and North America use local personal income taxes. A local piggyback, flat-rate personal income tax is collected with the national income tax in Nordic countries and some transition economies of Central and Eastern Europe. In Latin America, several countries, such as Brazil, Chile, and Colombia use various types of local business taxation. Local sales taxes are used in a few countries, notably in Canada, with the presence of a national VAT, and in the United States, where there is no VAT. Poor diversification of the local tax base is often aggravated by the lack of flexibility to adapt to evolving circumstances (for example, growth in the service sector). Inelasticity (lack of revenue response to changes in the economic base) of many local taxes over time is problematic as progressively increasing demand for services and costs outstrip revenue growth. In a number of African countries (Tanzania, Uganda, and Zambia) some viable local taxes have been recently eliminated and partially replaced with transfers, and many countries, prominently Korea, suffer from a proliferation of "nuisance taxes" that yield low revenues relative to collection costs.

Fees and user charges: Local governments need to establish fees for services, ideally on a cost-recovery basis where this is feasible. In Canada and the U.S., local governments generate one-quarter of their own revenues with fees and charges, which is all the more significant given their broad high levels of local own tax revenue. The situation is very different in many developing countries. In some African countries, such as Algeria, Benin, Egypt and Tunisia, local governments have no authority to set local fees and charges.

Politics of local revenues: Political barriers to local revenue generation can be seen in both the reluctance of local government to raise taxes (for instance, in some EU countries) as well as in the limitations imposed on local revenue generation legislated by higher levels of government or citizen referendums (in many states in the U.S.). To some extent these phenomena result from poor taxpayer education and general expectations by citizens for more and better quality services with the same or lower taxes.

Local and central roles in revenue collection: International practice varies as countries seek to maximize revenues while minimizing administration and compliance costs (which favor a role for higher levels in administration and enforcement) and maximizing local accountability and local information advantages (which favor local governments' direct involvement in administration and enforcement). Although centralized mechanisms are in principle desirable for certain taxes, central agencies do not in some regions, including MEWA and West Africa, transfer the resources they collect to local governments in a timely manner. The lack of incentives for central tax authorities to collect local revenues can also be a problem. The experience of a variety of countries (Costa Rica, Jordan, and some countries in Eurasia) shows significant increases in revenue collections when tax administration responsibilities are transferred from central to local authorities.

Intergovernmental Transfers

A properly structured system of intergovernmental transfers is a critical component of a local finance system. The use of transfers, however, faces a number of challenges that are dealt with in different ways and to varying degrees across regions and countries.

Appropriate and stable revenue sharing: Most countries share some central taxes with local governments, an arrangement that is simple and has high revenue potential. This can be a partial solution to vertical imbalances, but shared revenues suffer from various constraints. Revenue sharing on a derivation basis can be seen as a stimulus for local economic activity, but it can also reinforce horizontal disparities and leads to higher volatility of local revenues. Particularly in developing countries, the amounts shared may be uncertain or lack transparency, making long term planning difficult for local governments. This is the case in a number of West African countries, where central governments withhold for their own purposes or delay resources to which local governments are entitled. Perhaps most importantly, substantial revenue sharing can create perverse incentives for local revenue generation, undermining both local autonomy and the accountability of local governments to their constituents.

Horizontal fiscal imbalances: Despite the often significant differences across local governments in expenditure needs and the ability to finance them, many countries lack effective equalization grants. In Africa, just a few countries (Morocco and South Africa) have introduced them, and in MEWA there are none. The situation is a little better in Latin America, where a few countries (e.g. Brazil and Chile) use explicit equalization schemes, although more countries in the region employ only limited redistribution elements in revenue sharing schemes. Some Asian countries use equalization transfers (e.g. Australia, Indonesia, Japan), while others virtually ignore fiscal disparities (e.g. China, India, Philippines, New Zealand). Equalization grants are common in Eurasia, Europe, and North America (except at the federal level in the United States), but with varying effectiveness. Some Eurasian countries have not used transparent methodologies for equalization transfers, although the situation is improving.

Equalization transfer design: Where equalization schemes exist, they often present problems; for example, (1) only differences in fiscal capacity or expenditure needs, instead of both, are considered; (2) actual revenues, instead of fiscal capacity, are measured, creating disincentives for local revenue mobilization; (3) the pool of funds are not stable or well defined, or (4) the use of funds is subject to rigid conditions that in effect make the equalization grants, which are normally general purpose grants without use restrictions, into conditional transfers. In federal countries, such as Australia, there are issues regarding how second tier governments (the states) interpret federal policies regarding equalization.

Conditional transfer design: Conditional grants from upper level governments are a key element of local fiscal frameworks. Such grants can (1) promote national standards and goals in the provision of important services that have been decentralized, for example, some aspects of education and health; (2) address inter-jurisdictional externalities with respect to, for example, environmental concerns; or (3) support local government infrastructure investments. Conditional or earmarked grants exist in many countries, especially for capital infrastructure purposes. However, in certain regions, such as Eurasia, conditional grants are not well developed. In other countries, such as Egypt, Nigeria, Tanzania, and Uganda, conditional transfers excessively dominate total transfers. Several problems are often associated with this type of grant, including their number and complexity, which impose high compliance costs on local governments; lack of transparency, stability or timeliness; and sometimes political manipulation. In addition, excessive reliance on conditional grants can overly constrain local government autonomy and move their focus from local to national priorities, potentially reducing their own comparative advantage in focusing on local needs.

Performance based grants. A relatively recent innovation in the field of transfers has been the introduction of performance based transfers in some African and Asian countries with support from international organizations. Performance based grants condition the transfer of funds to meeting certain standards and objectives, generally leaving local governments to decide how best to use the funds. This type of transfer combines the flexibility of unconditional grants with an unconventional form of conditionality. On the downside, these transfers may privilege jurisdictions with greater administrative capacity, and they may suffer from the problems associated with voucher programs. Thus far they have been used more to promote compliance with financial and administrative management procedures than to improve service delivery outcomes. It is too early to definitively judge the effectiveness of performance based transfers but they are a promising mechanism and further trials are certainly desirable.

Local Government Borrowing and Access to Financial Markets

Perhaps the most neglected aspect of local government finance in many regions of the world is borrowing. In the context of the rapid urbanization discussed earlier, especially developing countries in Africa and Asia, the need for infrastructure investment is paramount. In this context, borrowing, with the intergenerational equity that it entails, is potentially an important means to finance longer term investments. At the same time, there are multiple factors that need to be considered.

Local government borrowing and fiscal responsibility frameworks. These frameworks are often weakly developed and poorly implemented. Some frameworks are highly restrictive, effectively precluding local government borrowing (e.g. Denmark, Chile, Kenya and Tunisia). Other frameworks are too lax, potentially allowing for the type of risky behavior that occurred in the 1990s in Brazil and Argentina. In a few case such as South Africa, robust frameworks that promote responsible borrowing have been developed.

Access to credit. In many cases, especially in poor developing countries, local governments often have poor and unreliable access to credit. Financial markets are not well developed, and many local governments do not have credit histories or do not meet technical standards required by lenders. The situation is brighter in the short and medium term in emerging economies where financial markets tend to be more developed with the introduction of systems for disclosure, credit ratings, pricing benchmarks, and so forth.

Special institutions. Special credit institutions that have been set up to lend to local governments (as is the case in more than 60 countries, often with support from international organizations in developing countries) have rarely performed well. Their often disappointing results have been associated with the politicization of lending decisions and problematic design issues. Many of the intermediary institutions are not sufficiently independent from the government, and they are not allowed or have not attempted to link with domestic credit markets. In this regard, local governments are not supported in learning how to become familiar with and develop capacity to comply with market expectations regarding financial capacities, disclosures, provisioning, and so on.

Central government practices. A number of central government practices, such as weak appraisal mechanisms for loans from government affiliated credit institutions, local government bailouts and automatic intercepts, have disrupted the normal development of local credit markets. There has been a pervasive problem with approval by government associated lending mechanisms of inadequately vetted loans for non-viable projects. The practice of bailouts when local governments cannot or will not repay their loans undermines their fiscal discipline and distorts the credit market. Although reliance on automatic intercepts from transfers are generally associated with better repayment to special credit institutions and can help to develop access to credit, maintaining them for long periods without encouraging local government graduation to more market oriented sources can create poor incentives for local governments to properly consider and lenders to properly appraise local government projects.

Links to the broader intergovernmental fiscal system. Other aspects of local government finance covered above are sometimes not conducive to borrowing. Borrowing can be curtailed if local governments have insufficient access to discretionary sources of revenue to make loan payments or if intergovernmental transfers undermine incentives for even relatively wealthy local governments to borrow, for self-financing development projects. Lack of appropriate financial management practices also undermines the ability of local governments to properly prepare development projects, qualify for credit, and manage their debt portfolios.

Recommendations

The findings of GOLD II clearly indicate that local governments around the world -from the most industrialized to the least developed countries- suffer from problems and challenges in their local government finance systems, and in some respects the situation has stagnated or worsened in recent years. In Africa local governments represent well under 10 percent of public expenditures and less of pubic revenue. MEWA countries also have limited resources and even more limited autonomy. In many countries in Latin America, Asia, Eurasia, and even in Europe, local governments lack legitimacy because they cannot meet important responsibilities with available resources. Although some needed actions will be difficult to quickly implement, there is much that can be done.

Expenditure Assignment and Management

A clear assignment of expenditure responsibilities should be at the top of national reform agendas for local government finance. There are some important political economy issues noted throughout the report that often make this step difficult. Several basic measures need to be followed for this foundational reform that will in some cases require a revision of the legal framework and harmonization of decentralization and sector laws.

Identify the exclusive responsibilities of local governments is needed to increase the clarity required for accountability. In cases where there is legal clarity and the assignments have not been implemented, action is needed to enforce the provisions of the legal framework. In cases where it is deemed necessary to have concurrent responsibilities for particular services, it is important to identify which level has specific responsibilities for various aspects — i. e. regulation, financing, and implementation.

Limit higher controls on local expenditures. In the EU, for example, the Commission should not excessively control or interfere with local service delivery. In multi-tier systems the role played by intermediate tiers (states and provinces) in controlling local expenditures should be appropriate and restrained. There should be limited infringement on local autonomy, and with specifically local services, intermediate levels should not be interfering. In developing environments where there are significant differences in administrative capacity across local governments, asymmetric assignment of responsibilities may be justified, at least temporarily. Over time local governments can graduate —with appropriate incentives and support— to more complete levels of responsibility as their capacity is developed.

Determine financial requirements. For a clear assignment of expenditure responsibilities to become useful for other aspects of the local fiscal framework, they must be *translated into expenditure needs/financing requirements* through application of an appropriate standardized methodology. A systematic evaluation of the cost of transferred responsibilities should precede the transfers of task and resources.

Fund all mandates. It is important to be explicit that the level of government with the power to regulate a function also has the obligation to pay for it. Increasing coordination and dialogue among levels of government regarding functional assignment is also needed, and there should be ex-ante review of all government legislation regarding local governments to detect any unfunded mandates.

Ensure that human resources follow functions. Funding/staffing of deconcentrated offices of line ministries should be downscaled or eliminated. This will reflect the functions transferred to local governments and ensure that they have the staff to execute them, while at the same time reducing the existence of staff at other levels who might interfere with local government functions.

Reduce and progressively eliminate ex ante control of local government budgets. In some developing environments this may not be possible to do quickly, but as the local finance system matures it is important to shift from an emphasis on ex ante control to an emphasis on ex post control, such as audits, and to a greater focus on developing accountability to the citizens.

Implement expenditure decentralization strategically. It may be appropriate to use the type of asymmetry noted above, and both performance incentives and capacity building may be needed. Capacity building and technical assistance should support local governments to establish a foundation in the first stages of decentralization and then help them adapt to performance incentives in later stages.

Local Revenue Generation and Autonomy

Autonomous local revenue generation is the most serious fiscal challenge faced in a majority of countries globally. Althought the exact set of revenue reforms will vary across countries, this type of reform is to some extent needed in most countries.

Increase reliance on own revenues with meaningful discretion. This strengthens the link between benefits and costs of local services, making local officials more accountable to taxpayers and more fiscally responsible. This can be done through reforms to existing sources of revenue and/or the addition of new sources, and appropiate systems and capacity must be developed in conjunction with expanded revenue authority.

Reform and modernize property tax administration. Clearly the poor revenue performance of the property tax has a heavy administrative component. But there are political limits to using this source, so the nature and extent of reforms must be decided on a case-by-case basis.

Diversify the local tax base. This is needed in many countries but reforms should target viable and productive local revenues (i.e. not nuisance taxes) as well as ensure that local economic activity will not be impeded.

Only a limited number of local taxes meet these criteria, including vehicle taxes, business license taxes, piggyback income taxes and betterment levies on real estate. Vehicle taxes can be based on registration, licensing, parking and similar bases. Business taxes can take different forms, but typically use sales turnover as a proxy for the tax base; care must be taken not to convert them into sales taxes that conflict with other consumption taxes, particularly national VAT. Going further in the direction of increasing local tax autonomy would be the introduction of a local piggy-back personal income tax with a flat rate collected at the same time as the national income tax is collected. Betterment levies are an important means for financing infrastructure investments in countries where they are used. All of these sources can be extremely productive, but they are most relevant for urban and intermediate-level (states, provinces) governments.

In addition to these more traditional resources, a potentially valuable but relatively unexploited source in most regions is environmental or "green" taxation related to waste management, water and air polluting activities, and the production of energy. Green taxes would provide a so-called "double dividend" since they promote both revenue generation and a cleaner environment. There are also opportunities to develop sources of revenue based on the increasingly important knowledge economy.

There is often an opportunity to adapt the fiscal system to include some taxation on activities from the informal sector, particularly in developing countries.

Increase freedom to raise fees and user charges. There are economic, technical, and political challenges and limitations associated with such revenues, but they could be more extensively used in most countries. Better and more explicit pricing for public services may help to improve efficiency if political obstacles to charges can be overcome. The principle of cost recovery on public services should be promoted where feasible, but in a way that does not undermine access to basic services by the poor.

Carefully organize local tax collection responsibilities. The challenges of getting the right arrangements between central and local governments, as noted above, are considerable. With local collection, robust systems and incentives are needed for the potential benefits to be realized. When centralized administration of local taxes is appropriate, it is important to establish the right incentives for central tax administrations. Extensive dialogue and cooperation between different levels of tax administration is always desirable and should be institutionalized. This includes information sharing on collections with local governments and allowing their participation in some aspects of management.

Engage local government officials more fully in mobilizing local resources, linking them to service delivery, and using them more transparently. Local officials must assume their responsibility to mobilize the local resources required to improve local service provision. The tax morale of local residents and their willingness to contribute to the local funds can be improved through campaigns of fiscal awareness that inform citizens about how resources are used and how decisions are made. Local officials should also ensure the transparent management of funds and encourage citizen participation in order to increase their confidence on the budget process.

Intergovernmental Transfers

Considerable challenges and weaknesses in intergovernmental transfer systems were outlined above. Multiple steps could commonly be taken to improve the structure and operation of intergovernmental transfer systems.

Assure predicable, regular, and transparent transfer mechanisms. A legal framework should establish a minimum level of public resources that the central government must transfer every year to local authorities and offer sufficient assurance that they will be allocated in a clear and fair manner.

Secure an appropriate balance among the various types of transfers. There is no hard and fast rule about derivation based versus formula allocated tax sharing, although the former may worsen fiscal disparities, reinforcing the need for equalization (see below). Similarly, there is no normatively ideal balance between unconditional and conditional transfers. A significant share of unconditional funds hovever reinforces local government autonomy and accountability and it is the better option to support local autonomy and locally driven development when local governments have acquired minimum capacities.

Expand and improve the use of equalization transfers. Countries that do not use them should consider doing so to offset the differential abilities of local governments to meet basic service needs. Countries that do use them should take stock of their approach and move towards a system that uses an explicit and stable rule to determine the pool of funds; takes expenditure needs and revenue capacity (as opposed to actual expenditures or revenues) into account when allocating funds; and allows unconditional use of transferred funds. In countries where elements of equalization are imbedded in revenue sharing, as is common in Latin America, it would be desirable, following the rule of using a single instrument for each objective, to unbundle those schemes and separately introduce an explicit equalization transfer with the properties listed above.

Review and improve mechanisms used for allocating resources under conditional grants. Beyond the basic guidelines on equalization grants noted above, best practice for conditional grant systems calls for simplification, moving toward using fewer separate block grants with clear sectoral objectives and providing governments with sufficient flexibility for deciding on the best use of the funds while meeting the broader sectoral objectives defined by the upper level authorities.

Consolidating grants where large numbers of poorly coordinated programs exist. In some countries in Europe and Asia, for example, there are too many grants that are not clearly distinguished and the resources could be more productively used in a more consolidated system.

Local Government Borrowing and Investment Finance

In many countries, there are considerable opportunities for increasing the use of borrowing and other investment finance mechanisms as well as expanding and improving sources of funding for this purpose. A number of specific policies and reforms can often support this goal.

Promote local government borrowing. Borrowing is one of the necessary pillars of local finance. Responsible local borrowing, guided by prudent rules and regulations (a fiscal responsibility framework) should be allowed where feasible, in parallel to the strengthening of local capacities.

Develop and strengthen legal and regulatory frameworks for local government borrowing. Rules regarding debt level and debt service ratios need not be overly restrictive, but central authorities need to enforce hard budget constraints and avoid bailouts. Central monitoring of local borrowing is critical, especially where private market discipline is not operational. Such monitoring should cover not only regular debt but also "floating debt" or budgetary arrears with official institutions and private suppliers, and local government guarantees for municipal enterprises. Monitoring should be complemented with a credible system of penalties for lack of compliance.

Expand and improve options and support mechanisms for local government borrowing, including support where appropriate to intermediate financial institutions or municipal development funds. Beyond the regulation and monitoring, an even more important challenge for most developing countries is to facilitate a significant increase in credit availability to local governments for responsible borrowing, especially for smaller municipalities. The solution may be the creation of official financial intermediaries or municipal lending institutions, such as Municipal Development Banks or Funds. International experience, however, suggests that they must focus on lending operations rather than get involved in other matters (such as technical assistance to local governments), should be operated following strict banking criteria (including project appraisal), and should increase the share of private capital in their pool of resources over time. Policies to encourage the development of private markets for local credit are equally important. The exact mix of these activities will depend on the context of a particular country following the general rule to use the market to the extent feasible and to use public or mixed lending mechanisms in a way that prepares local governments for eventual commercial borrowing.

Reform other aspects of the local finance system as necessary to enhance the prospects for local government borrowing. Local governments must have access to and effectively use existing (and as needed additional) local taxes, user charges, and central government grants earmarked to local infrastructure. In addition, it is necessary to have good financial management practices in place.

Consider other investment financing mechanisms where feasible. Tax increment financing, betterment levies (valorization), and public private partnerships can also provide necessary investment finance for local governments. These mechanisms, however, also require certain capacities and conditions and should not be seen as an easy alternative to borrowing.

Determine an appropriate role in infrastructure finance for International Financial Institutions and other development agencies. These institutions have long played an important role in developing and some transition countries, and in many cases they will continue to do so for the foreseeable future. Such resources have traditionally flowed to central governments with onlending to local governments. Such onlending should comply with the basic principles outlined above, and there should be an increasing role for direct sub-sovereign lending, especially to larger cities in countries where this is feasible.

Framing Institutional Reform

The finance system reforms outlined above will need to be reinforced by other measures of a more institutional nature, most of which were discussed earlier in this chapter to set the stage for the discussion of fiscal decentralization. A number of key institutional issues often impact local finances and merit consideration.

Assess and respond as necessary to local government jurisdictional fragmentation. Fragmentation is neither inherently desirable nor undesirable, but as discussed above it can create problems. There are two types of issues.

The first is ensuring that any creation of new jurisdictions is done according to clear criteria to prevent the proliferation of non-viable entities. In some cases there are perverse incentives (e.g. in the transfer system) to create new jurisdictions. These should be avoided.

The second is coping with existing fragmentation that is deemed to be problematic. Where politically feasible, consolidation of small, non-viable units may be considered, but this can undermine political connection and local accountability. An alternative policy is to enable the creation of voluntary municipal partnerships to deliver public services requiring a minimum scale. Such associations and agreements can also help to address benefit spillovers across local government or the exporting of the costs of local services to neighboring jurisdictions by, for example, through agreements that provide for sharing service provision costs in accordance with benefits. Other solutions include voluntary jurisdictional consolidation, the creation of special districts to take advantage of economies of scale in selected services, or jointly contracting with private firms.

Identify the right roles for and interactions between deconcentrated and devolved government entities. In cases where both deconcentrated and devolved entities coexist side by side, it should be made clear what functions each is responsible for, and they should respectively be provided with appropriate staff, funding, and capacity to meet their obligations. In countries where there has been heavy reliance on deconcentration alone, consideration could be given to introducing democratically elected local governments with devolved autonomy to prioritize their budgets in accordance with the expressed needs of local residents. It is important to note that there can be room for both deconcentrated and devolved levels in some cases, but the system must be set up to tap the advantages of each and prevent one type —usually deconcentrated administration— from undermining the other.

Assess the appropriate role for and operations of external development assistance agencies and financial institutions in developing countries. As discussed earlier, there are two broad types of problems —the heavy handedness of external agents in promoting certain types of decentralization reforms, and their tendency to create parallel institutions and mechanisms for implementing their programs that at least partially bypass normal decision making and resource allocation procedures of local governments. The latter measure is generally intended to compensate for real and perceived problems, such as weak local government capacity, corruption, and ineffective and bureaucratic central government agencies. Parallel mechanisms can help to deliver services and may be appropriate in some form at early stages of decentralization when local governments are very weak, but ultimately they undermine the legitimacy and effectiveness of local governments. Neither of these donor approaches is consistent with current thinking on aid effectiveness, as reflected in the Paris Declaration on Aid Effectiveness (2005), Accra Agenda for Action (2008) and the upcoming Seoul High Level Forum on Aid Effectiveness (2011). The underlying philosophy highlights the harmonization of development assistance with national policy and stresses the importance of using national systems to deliver services, thereby reinforcing both national and subnational governments' capacity development and their accountability to citizens.

Ensuring that external development partners follow national policies is ideally the role of the national government. In countries with weak capacity and significant need for assistance, however, this may be difficult. Under such circumstances, the development partners themselves need to take steps to ensure that they align with national priorities.

Ideally parallel institutions should not be used. If it is necessary to use them for reasons noted above, they must be framed as temporary arrangements with a clear plan for phasing them out in favor of greater reliance on local mechanisms as they become institutionalized. When local mechanisms are sufficiently credible, external agencies should foresee budget support that empowers local decision making.

International agencies need to ensure that budget support programs contribute to the strengthening of local governments and the development of their autonomy. Likewise, sector-wide approaches are often a centralizing force in practice, but they can be instrumental in strengthening and implementing the specific local powers and responsibilities as defined in the legal frameworks for decentralization.

Create a regular and systematic dialogue between local governments and the central government on intergovernmental and local financial policy. Although this has not been previously discussed in an extensive way, this report clearly leads to the conclusion that local governments in many countries are not sufficiently consulted on national policies of great consequence for them. Local governments could be consulted annually during the national budget process on all questions that directly or indirectly affect their financing. This would require a mechanism created to bring together the national actors (legislature and executive) and local governments. For such an approach to be effective, it would be important to ensure access to appropriate information on public finances, both in general and specifically regarding local government matters.

The Way Forward

Local governments have become more important and more autonomous in many countries around the world and higher expectations have been placed on them. Because this has happened in a challenging global environment of substantial urbanization, demographic shifts, climate change, and increasing risk, more attention needs to be given to developing the basic fiscal architecture that serves as a foundation for good local government performance. As highlighted throughout the report, there has been good progress on many fronts in many countries, but there are still major deficiencies and challenges in most cases, both in terms of the elements of the fiscal system that need to be in place and the capacity of local governments to function effectively. Unless these are confronted head on, there are great dangers of social and economic decline in the more advanced economies and a failure to meet key increasingly urgent needs in developing countries, including poverty reduction targets and the Millennium Development Goals.

Although diversity is great across countries, there are some shared challenges common to many places. Clarity of functional assignment in law and practice is a challenge in many developing countries, and unfunded mandates are a more general problem. In many countries there is a pressing need to reassess the structure of local taxes, and the degree of autonomy that local governments have in defining and using them. In many cases it will be desirable to move beyond traditional local revenue bases, and to search for a more appropriate distribution of transferred and own-source resources between national and local governments, as well as among subnational governments in the context of the emergence of new tiers and new units at particular levels. Growing investment requirements necessitate an expansion of local government access to capital, increasingly through market-oriented an non-traditional mechanisms. There is also a need for developing more innovative approaches to raising resources and delivering services, including through new and expanded forms of partnership with different actors (private sector and civil society).

As countries around the world strive to improve their local government systems, they will have to keep in mind some daunting short-term and longer term challenges. The most immediate challenge is the global financial and economic crisis that started near the end of 2008, which has resulted in revenue shortfalls for many local governments and even attempts to recentralize in some cases. Countries also face longer term challenges that cut across all levels of government, some of which can have particularly important implications for local governments because of the increasing role this government level plays in the provision of social services, environmental control, and so on. Some of these challenges are common (global warming, energy crisis, etc.) but others differ by region of the world. Rapidly increasing urbanization, for example, particularly in many of the developing countries of Africa, Asia, and Latin America, is creating complex demands on public services and infrastructure, yet local governments in many countries in these regions do not have the necessary authority and autonomy to meet these demands. In addition they too frequently cannot even cover the operating costs of existing services much less the costs of the substantial additional investments needed.

Although many suggestions to improve local government finance systems have been made in the regional chapters and in this concluding chapter, in closing this volume it is important to reiterate again a few fundamental points regarding the approach to reform.

First, each country is unique and the basic principles for reform need to be tailored to the economic, political, fiscal, and social realities of individual countries. In Europe, for example, substantial capacity exists, but there is a need for system reforms and increased access to investment finance. At the other end of the spectrum, less developed countries in several regions need to build basic institutions gradually if reforms are to take root and be sustained, although more capacity may exist in larger cities for more immediate assumption of functions and resources.

Second, consultation and collaboration among levels of government and other actors will be critical as efforts to strengthen local finance systems advance —each actor has an important role, but no actor alone can do what needs to be done. In particular, central governments need to treat local governments as partners, with full consultation in all issues of shared responsibilities. Local governments also need to continue the efforts they are already pursuing in many countries to reach out to citizens, to develop partnerships with non-governmental organizations and private firms, and to seek innovative means to deal with the challenges they face.

Third, while political factors are critical and there is no point in pursuing reforms that are politically infeasible, it is also important to make decisions about reform based on good information and evidence, the lack of which created considerable challenges for the preparation of this report. Better information and analysis and broader and more transparent dissemination of such inputs can create and nurture a better environment for pursuing the right reforms over time. In addition, the success of initial modest reforms can create political momentum for the adoption of more advanced reforms with greater impact over time.

Finally, there is considerable value added from regional and global cooperation, sharing experiences, and learning by doing in pursuing local finance reform. The role of UCLG, its regional member organizations, and their individual country members, provides a strong foundation for collaborative learning at various levels, and these actors need to continue to strengthen those links going forward. Global and regional events, online access to information, country specific, regional and global networking activities, diagnostics to help countries and local governments to plan concrete productive action, and forums and mechanisms for sharing experiences and expertise would all be productive ways to support better local government finance. Some opportunities in these areas already exist, but much remains to be done to consolidate and improve knowledge about them, enhance access to them, and deepen an understanding among all stakeholders of how to effectively use them.

ANNEX

2. AFRICA

Annex 2.1: Three indicators of expenditure jurisdiction for 21 African countries, 2009

	Legality/reality indicators		Budgetary autonomy indicator	Personnel autonomy indicators	
	Written into the Constitution	Difference between Constitution and Reality (1)	Restrictions imposed by higher-level authorities (2)	Responsibility in hiring local managers	Responsibility in fixing salaries
Algeria	Yes	No	Lines	State/Region/LG	State/Region/LG
Benin	Yes	Yes	Structure	Local authorities	Condition
Burkina Faso	Yes	Yes	Structure	State/ LG	State/ LG
Côte d'Ivoire	Yes	No	Line/structure	State/ LG	State/ LG
Egypt	Yes	No	Line/structure	State	State
Ethiopia	Yes	No	No	Local authorities	Regions
Kenya	Yes	No	Structure	State	Local authorities
Ghana	Yes	Yes	Line/structure	State/ LG	State/ LG
Malawi	Yes	Yes	Lines	State/LG	State
Mali	Yes	Yes	Line/structure	State/ LG	State/ LG
Mauritania	Yes	Yes	Line/structure	State/ LG	State/ LG
Morocco	Yes	Yes	Line/structure	Local authorities	State
Mozambique	Yes	Yes	No	State	State
Niger	No	Yes	Line/structure	State/ LG	State/ LG
Rwanda	Yes	No	Line/structure	LG	State
Senegal	Yes	Yes	Line/structure	State/ LG	State/ LG
South Africa	Yes	No	Lines	LG	LG
Tanzania	Yes	Yes	Lines	LG	LG
Togo	Yes	Yes	Line/structure	State/ LG	State/ LG
Tunisia	No	Yes	Line/structure	State	State
Uganda		Yes	Structure	Local authorities	State

Source: Compilation by authors, from data collected at national level by UCLG and from other sources (see bibliography).

(1) "yes" means that the reality differs from that of the Constitution

(2) The supervisory authority exercises control on the budget "Lines" or on the overall budget "structure" or both

Annex 2.2: Some characteristics of transfers to municipalities for 20 African countries, 2008

Country	Number of transfer systems	Number of conditional grants/ Number of unconditional grants	Number of transfers with ad hoc financing/ number of transfers financed by % of taxes	Brief observations about transfer systems
Algeria	2	2/0	2/0	One of the funds does not have a formula, the other is linked to fiscal balance (revenues)
Benin	5	4/1	5/0	The Fund of support to the development of local governments (FADeC) was created in 2009. Two funds use the population criteria. One is a fiscal balance fund and the other replacement a former tax
Burkina Faso	8	7/1	2/0	General endowment fund and general capital expenditure grant (GDF/DGE) allocated according to population size; payments for salaries and payments for capital expenditure and operating expenses. Only one (investment) fund takes poverty into account.
Côte d'Ivoire	4	4/0	3/1	A system for sharing local taxes based on the origin of the tax and three other funds. One of these, the DGF uses a formula based, in practice, on the population.
Egypt	1	1/0	1	A system for sharing some surtaxes based on population size, surface area, needs and fiscal balance transfers. The surtax associated with the Suez canal is shared between the governorates that lie along the canal
Kenya	2	2/1	2/2	A system that takes into account the share of the population and the proportion of the urban population and a system based on road construction projects
Malawi	3	2/1	2/1	An unconditional transfer based on population and poverty, a transfer that finances devolved agriculture expenditure and a transfer for education based on the number of children of school-going age
Mali	3	3/0	3/0	No formula would be used
Mauritania	1	1/0	1/0	The FRD is divided into an operating grant and a capital expenditure grant. It is distributed according to population size, poverty and infrastructure
Morocco	3	0/3	0/3	30% of VAT goes to municipalities and provinces/prefectures. Municipalities receive a lump sum, a tax equalisation and a tax effort, while P/P receive funding to cover payroll expenses. 1% of income tax (CIT and PIT) goes to regions
Mozambique	3	2/1	2/1	The FCA (Municipal Compensation Fund) transfer distributes 1.5% of state revenues based on population (75%) and surface area (25%). The other two do not use formulas.
Niger	2	1/1	2/0	No formula would be used
Senegal	2	2/0	0/2	There is a Decentralisation grant (FDD) distributed according to population size and the FECL that finances the domestic counterparty of internationally funded projects
South Africa	15	14/1	13/0/Other single formulas	Most funds have precise formulas that factor in population and needs; some are ad hoc (FIFA 2010)

Annex 2.2: Some characteristics of transfers to municipalities for 20 African countries, 2008

Country	Number of transfer systems	Number of conditional grants/ Number of unconditional grants	Number of transfers with ad hoc financing / number of transfers financed by % of taxes	Brief observations about transfer systems
Tanzania	3	2/1	3/0	The three transfers are each distributed using a formula, which include such elements as population, poverty, rurality
Togo	1	1/0	1/0	The FACT is not operational.
Tunisia	3	3/0	3/0	A general transfer (FCCL) is used, based on population size and revenues, a transfer via grants and reduced interest rates for investments (CPSCL) and transferred ministerial credits
Uganda	3	2/1	3/0	88% of grants are conditioned for sectoral spending in reduction of poverty, 11% of transfers are unconditioned, and 0.5% of the amounts are used for equalisation
Zambia	3	3/0	3/0	Since 2007 there are two grants for restructuring and functioning. This was subdivided in 2010 into three components: institutional support, service provision and abolished tax replacement. The portion on services considers 6 variables including population and poverty index. The 3rd grant is for investment but to date it has had a weak impact.
Zimbabwe	2	2/0	2/0	Payment of salaries of health staff and granting of financing depending on rural council budgets

Source: National information collected by UCLG; Hugouneng, Rocaboy and Vaillancourt 2010 (Kenya); Dafflon and Madies 2009 (Burkina Faso); Gilbert, Hugouneng Taugourdeau 2009 (Senegal); Vaillancourt 2008 (Côte d'Ivoire); Martinez-Vazquez and Timofeev 2008 (Egypt)

Annex 2.3: Public Finance Indicators for 18 countries

	Expenditure					Revenue				
	General Government		Local Government			General Government		Local Government		
Africa	Million USD	% of GDP	Million USD	% of GDP	% of GG (1)	Million USD	% of GDP	Million USD	% of GDP	% of GG
Benin (2007)	1301	23.5	53	1	4.1	1149	20.7	49	0.9	4.3
Burkina Faso (2007)	1820	26.9	45	0.7	2.5	1407	20.8	31	0.5	2.2
Cote D'Ivoire (2007)	3826	19.3	237	1.2	6.2	3775	19.1	252	1.3	6.7
Egypt (2007)	55600	42.1	6067	4.6	10.9	36496	27.6	na	na	na
Kenya (2007)	5541	20.4	252	0.9	4.6	na	na	na	na	na
Malawi (2007)	1312	36.6	111	3.1	8.5	na	na	99	2.8	na
Mali (2007)	1858	27.1	64	0.9	3.4	1599	23.3	57	0.8	3.6
Mauritania (2008)	957	33.4	5	0.2	0.6	691	24.1	5	0.2	0.8
Morocco (2007)	21929	29.2	1680	2.2	7.6	27691	36.8	2912	3.9	10.5
Mozambique (2009)	3568	34.1	86	0.8	2.4	na	na	28	0.3	na
Niger (2007)	877	20.7	21	0.5	2.4	640	15.1	23	0.5	3.6
Rwanda (2008)	1188	26.7	274	6.1	23.1	1246	28	264	5.9	21.2
Senegal (2007)	3017	26.6	95	0.8	3.2	2369	20.9	97	0.9	4.1
South Africa (2007)	94625	33.3	16513	5.8	17.4	104826	36.9	18633	6.6	17.7
Tanzania (2007)	4008	23.8	647	3.8	16.2	na	na	707	4.2	na
Togo (2006)	522	20.9	9	0.4	1.8	482	19.3	8	0.3	1.6
Tunisia (2008)	7906	19.6	762	1.9	9.6	12394	30.7	1020	2.5	8.2
Uganda (2007)	2011	16.4	684	5.6	34	na	na	901	7.3	na

(1) General Government

4. EURASIA

Annex 4.1: The Structure of Local Government Outlays (2008)

Expenditure/Countries	Armenia	Belarus	Georgia	Kazakhstan	Kyrgyzstan	Moldova	Russia	Ukraine
General public services	26.3%	19.9%	8.1%	9.1%	13.4%	9.5%	9.5%	12.5%
Defense	0.1%	0.1%	0.3%	0.7%	0.5%	0.1%	0.1%	0.0%
Public order and safety	0.0%	1.6%	2.3%	3.0%	1.4%	3.2%	1.3%	1.6%
Economic affairs	8.0%	10.5%	16.4%	19.8%	1.7%	7.4%	6.6%	10.6%
Environmental protection	incl. in "Economic affairs"	0.3%	5.5%	0.7%	0.0%	0.0%	0.2%	0.5%
Housing and community amenities	26.4%	13.8%	40.5%	13.5%	10.6%	8.8%	21.0%	6.0%
Health	0.1%	18.9%	2.4%	18.6%	5.2%	2.3%	11.5%	19.2%
Recreation, culture, and religion	6.7%	4.5%	8.3%	6.3%	4.3%	5.2%	5.7%	3.8%
Education	18.0%	24.6%	11.1%	27.6%	58.8%	53.4%	36.6%	28.7%
Social protection	2.5%	5.9%	5.3%	3.6%	4.7%	10.2%	7.5%	17.1%

Source: Authors' calculations based on IFS database, for Armenia – on "Local Self-Government Reforms in Armenia (2007 and 2008) Book 3", for Russia – on RF Ministry of Finance reports. Data for Kyrgyzstan is for 2006.

Annex 4.2: The Structure of Local Tax Revenues (2008)

Expenditure/Countries	Armenia	Belarus	Georgia	Kazakhstan	Kyrgyzstan	Moldova	Russia	Ukraine
Taxes on income, profits, and capital gains:	0.0%	47.8%	36.9%	36.2%	46.9%	85.9%	75.0%	87.2%
payable by individuals	0.0%	26.2%	36.9%	36.2%	28.0%	69.6%	60.3%	84.8%
payable by enterprises	0.0%	18.0%	0.0%	0.0%	15.7%	5.7%	14.7%	2.2%
Taxes on payroll and workforce	0.0%	0.0%	0.0%	34.0%	0.0%	0.0%	0.0%	0.3%
Taxes on property (incl. land tax)	100.0%	12.5%	62.5%	14.0%	18.3%	13.0%	10.5%	4.3%
Taxes on goods and services	0.0%	34.6%	0.0%	6.6%	34.8%	1.1%	14.5%	8.2%
General taxes on goods and services	0.0%	30.0%	0.0%	0.0%	31.0%	0.0%	1.6%	0.0%
Excises	0.0%	1.1%	0.0%	4.8%	1.8%	0.1%	0.2%	0.2%
Other taxes	0.0%	5.1%	0.6%	9.1%	0.0%	0.0%	0.0%	0.0%

Source: Authors' calculations based on IFS database.

Annex 4.3: Structure of Local Transfers

Country Revenue item	Armenia (2008)	Belarus (2005)	Georgia (2008)	Kazakhstan (2008)	Kyrgyzstan (2008)	Moldova (2009)	Russia (2008)	Ukraine (2008)
Transfers	47.6%	20.9%	35.6%	55.8%	39.6%	56.9%	45.5%	46.4%
General purpose transfers	40.6%	13.8%	23.5%	24.5%	5.6%	55.1%	10.2%	23.0%
incl. equalization grants	40.6%	13.8%	23.5%	24.5%	5.6%	55.1%	10.1%	22.4%
Targeted transfers	7.0%	6.4%	12.1%	26.4%	34.0%	1.8%	35.2%	23.4%
Incl. financing of delegated responsibilities	1.8%	n.a.	11.3%	n.a.	n.a.	n.a.	18.8%	n.a.

Source: Authors' calculations based for Armenia – on "Local Self-Government Reforms in Armenia (2007 and 2008) Book 3", for Georgia – on "Local Self-Government in Georgia" for other countries – on the countries' Ministry's of Finance report.

5. EUROPE

Annex 5.1: Local Government Revenue, 2009

	Main own-source taxes (by order of importance in revenue)	Main shared taxes (by order of importance in revenue)	Main grants/transfers
Austria	Municipal business tax, real estate tax.	VAT, wage tax, property acquisition tax, CIT, petrol tax, PIT	General purpose, support based on financial need, earmarked grants and equalisation grants (from the middle-tier jurisdictions and other municipalities).
Belgium	Surtaxes on PIT, vehicle traffic circulation tax, regional withholding tax on real estate, wide range of local taxes.		General purpose (municipal and provincial funds) and earmarked grants (operating and capital expenditure subsidies).
Bulgaria	Tax on the acquisition of property by way of donation, real estate property tax, transport vehicle tax, inheritance tax, patent tax (since 2008)	PIT (until 2008).	Since 2008, general supplemental subsidy, general equalisation grant, capital investment grant.
Cyprus	Waste collection tax, municipal corporate tax, property tax.		General purpose, compensation for the abolition of taxes and earmarked grants (for capital spending).
Czech Rep.	CIT paid by municipal companies, property tax.	VAT, PIT and CIT.	Most are earmarked, designed for current spending (State delegated functions) and capital expenditure.
Denmark	Municipal PIT, land tax, business property tax.	CIT	General purpose, equalisation and earmarked grants (including VAT compensation, reimbursement of social welfare expenditure and municipalities with specific needs).
Estonia	Land tax.	PIT	Block grant , specific purpose (education and social services), equalisation fund, earmarked grants (for capital spending) and amalgamation grant.
Finland	Municipal PIT, real estate tax.	CIT	General purpose, specific purpose (education, health care, social welfare) and equalisation.
France	Local business tax (until 2009), property tax on buildings, residence tax, property tax on land, transfer taxes on property transactions, transport contribution.	Domestic tax on petroleum products, special tax on insurance contracts.	General purpose, equalisation, general decentralisation grant, vocational training grant, and capital expenditure grants (VAT compensation and specific purpose such as rural development, school equipment).
Germany	Local business tax, property tax on real estate.	PIT, VAT and tax on interest.	General purpose, compensation for functions delegated by the middle-tier jurisdictions, investment transfers (from middle-tier jurisdictions).

Annex 5.1: Local Government Revenue, 2009 (cont.)

	Main own-source taxes (by order of importance in revenue)	Main shared taxes (by order of importance in revenue)	Main grants/transfers
Greece	Waste management and street cleaning fee, street-lighting fee, property tax, charge on hotel and restaurant.		General purpose (Central Autonomous Funds composed of the shares of national taxes such as PIT, vehicle tax, property sales tax, VAT, etc.) and earmarked grants (for capital spending).
Hungary	Municipalities : local business tax, property tax on buildings (from 2010, a new property tax will replace other taxes related to property), tourism tax.	PIT and motor vehicle tax.	Normative grants (both general and earmarked), other earmarked grants ("targeted" and "addressed" for capital spending) and grants for municipalities in financial trouble.
Iceland	Local PIT, real estate tax.		Municipal equalisation fund, housing fund, general purpose fund.
Ireland	Commercial rates tax (business property tax).		General purpose (Local Government Fund – General Purpose Grant financed partly by the full proceed from the motor tax) and earmarked grants (roads, housing, water supply and sewerage).
Italy	Municipal property tax, municipal tax on building licenses, household waste tax, surtax on PIT. Provincial vehicle insurance tax and registration tax, surtax on electricity consumption. Regional tax on productive output, surtax on PIT, regional automobile tax, fuel duty	PIT (municipalities and provinces). PIT and CIT (regions with special status).	Municipalities and provinces : operating grants (ordinary fund, consolidated fund and equalisation fund). Regions : operating grant coming partly from the VAT transfers, national health fund, administrative federalism fund. Capital expenditure grants.
Latvia		PIT and real estate tax.	General purpose, earmarked grants (teachers' compensation, road maintenance, public investment programme), Local government Finance Equalisation Fund.
Lithuania	Tax on the immovable property of enterprises and organisations, land tax.	PIT and tax on pollution.	General purpose (based on equalisation), specific purpose (for most delegated responsibilities, including schools and social benefits) and health care.
Luxembourg	Municipal business tax, property tax.		Municipal grant fund (composed of the share of the PIT, VAT, vehicle tax and a flat-rate amount), operating and capital earmarked grants.
Malta	–	–	General grant, funds for special needs.
Netherlands	Municipal property taxes, refuse collection rate, sewer tax. Provincial surtax on the national motor vehicle tax.		General purpose (Municipal and Provincial Funds based on a equalisation system), specific purpose (numerous grants but mainly targeted at education and social services).

Annex 5.1: Local Government Revenue, 2009 (cont.)

	Main own-source taxes (by order of importance in revenue)	Main shared taxes (by order of importance in revenue)	Main grants/transfers
Norway	Local PIT, property tax (municipalities), natural resource tax.	CIT, wealth tax.	General purpose grant, earmarked grants to kindergartens (to be included in the general purpose grant system form 2011)
Poland	Municipalities : property tax, farming tax, tax on vehicles.	PIT and CIT.	General purpose comprising 4 shares (balancing, regional, education, equalisation); Earmarked grants, notably to carry out State delegated responsibilities and own specific responsibilities.
Portugal	Municipal property tax, property transfer tax, vehicle registration tax, surtax on CIT.	Since 2007, possibility to retain 2% of the PIT of local residents.	General block grant made of shares of state taxes (PIT, VAT, CIT) and divided into the General Municipal Fund, the Municipal Cohesion Fund and the Social Municipal Fund.
Romania	Building and land taxes held by legal persons and by individuals, patent tax	VAT and PIT.	Earmarked grants and special funds (e.g. support for the disabled).
Slovak Republic	Real estate tax, vehicle tax.	PIT	Earmarked grants to cover delegated responsibilities (mainly education and social services).
Slovenia	Property tax, gift and inheritance tax, tax on profits from gambling, sales tax on immovable property	PIT	Equalisation grant, investment grant and specific grant (support for ethnic minorities).
Spain	Municipalities : tax on property, tax on constructions, installations and works, tax on motor vehicles, tax on economic activities, tax on capital gains in urban areas. Provinces: surtax on the municipal tax on economic activities.	Municipalities with more than 75 000 inhabitants and provinces : PIT, VAT and excises.	Municipalities and provinces : general grant (composed of shares of central State taxes) based on a equalisation system and specific purpose grants (transport infrastructure).
Sweden	Local PIT, property tax (since 2008).		Equalisation grants for both municipalities and county councils, a grant for pharmaceutical benefits for county councils , several targeted grants to municipalities and a VAT refund.
United Kingdom	England, Scotland and Wales : Council tax (tax on property paid by residents). Northern Ireland: district rates (property tax)	England, Scotland and Wales : business rates (business property tax).	England, Scotland and Wales: "Aggregate External finance" comprising a general purpose grant (Revenue Support Grant), redistributed business rates (Formula Grant) and specific purpose grants (unfenced and ring-fenced). Northern Ireland: general grants and various specific grants.

Sources: National sources and DEXIA (see bibliography).

Annex 5.2: Local Government Long-term Borrowing Rules, 2009

	Golden rule[1]	Approval required from higher-level jurisdiction[2]	Debt ceiling in place
Austria	Yes	Depending on the Länder regulation	Depending on the Länder regulation
Belgium	Yes	No	No
Bulgaria	Yes	No	Cap on debt service
Cyprus	Yes	Yes	No
Czech Rep.	Yes	No	No
Denmark	Yes	No	No
Estonia	Yes	No (Yes, on an interim basis since 2009 and until 2012)	Caps on debt service and on outstanding debt
Finland	No	No	No
France	Yes	No	No
Germany	Yes	Depending on the Länder regulation	Depending on the Länder regulation
Greece	No	No	No
Hungary	No	No	Cap on new annual borrowing
Iceland	No	No	No
Ireland	No	Yes	Cap on new annual borrowing
Italy	Yes	No	Cap on debt service
Latvia	Yes	Yes	Cap on new annual borrowing
Lithuania	Yes	Yes	Cap on outstanding debt and on new annual borrowing
Malta	Yes	Yes	No
Netherlands	Yes	No	No
Norway	Yes	No	No
Poland	No	No	Caps on debt service and on outstanding debt
Portugal	Yes	Yes	Cap on outstanding debt
Romania	Yes	Yes	Cap on debt service
Slovak Republic	Yes	No	Caps on debt service and on outstanding debt
Slovenia	Yes	Yes	Caps on debt service and on outstanding debt
Spain	Yes	Depending on the Autonomous Communities regulation	Cap on outstanding debt and on new annual borrowing
Sweden	Yes	No	No
Switzerland	Depending on the cantons regulation	Depending on the cantons regulation	Depending on the cantons regulation
United Kingdom	Yes	No	No

1. According to the golden rule, borrowing is allowed only to finance capital expenditure.

2. In general and for ordinary loans. For other types of loans (e.g., in foreign currency, in foreign markets, bonds, for a non-eligible spending, exceeding debt ceilings, etc.) or for local governments in financial difficulty prior approval of the supervisory authority may be necessary.

Sources: National sources and DEXIA.

Annex 5.3: Local Government Expenditure: Functional classification, 2007

Composition of expenditure (% of local government expenditure)	General public services	Economic affairs	Health	Education	Social protection	Other
Austria	18.1	13.2	17.7	16.2	18.7	16.1
Belgium	23.5	10.0	2.9	19.5	16.6	27.5
Bulgaria	4.6	14.1	10.0	30.4	7.2	33.6
Cyprus	42.9	0.0	0.0	0.0	0.0	57.1
Czech Republic	12.2	21.5	2.2	29.3	11.7	23.1
Denmark	4.2	3.6	22.8	10.8	54.1	4.5
Estonia	6.1	13.0	14.9	38.9	6.3	20.9
Finland	13.7	6.5	28.5	20.2	23.8	7.3
France	18.4	12.5	1.0	16.4	16.2	35.4
Germany	16.3	13.1	2.3	14.6	33.0	20.7
Greece	40.2	17.8	0.0	2.9	11.0	28.1
Hungary	18.0	7.2	14.4	29.2	12.5	18.7
Iceland	11.4	6.5	14.6	27.3	26.0	14.2
Ireland	10.8	28.0	0.0	15.4	3.5	42.3
Italy	14.7	14.3	44.5	8.3	4.5	13.7
Latvia	10.1	13.3	9.5	37.0	6.6	23.5
Lithuania	6.5	10.8	21.1	37.8	6.3	17.5
Luxembourg	20.8	15.8	0.5	24.1	3.8	35.0
Malta	57.5	8.9	0.0	0.0	0.0	33.6
Netherlands	15.0	17.1	1.7	28.1	14.2	23.8
Norway	11.9	6.3	14.7	27.3	25.7	14.2
Poland	9.2	15.3	15.2	28.5	12.9	18.8
Portugal	35.0	19.2	5.5	8.3	2.6	29.3
Romania	11.5	25.5	0.5	27.5	13.2	21.9
Slovak Rep.	14.9	14.6	0.5	39.3	7.2	23.5
Slovenia	10.5	11.5	11.1	38.8	8.9	19.2
Spain	34.3	11.9	1.3	3.9	9.1	39.6
Sweden	11.3	5.9	27.0	21.4	26.8	7.7
Switzerland	23.5	8.7	20.2	21.0	16.5	10.1
United Kingdom	6.5	8.6	0.0	31.8	27.9	25.2

Sources: Eurostat, World Bank (2009), Dexia and CEMR (2009).

Annex 5.4: Local Government Revenue, 2008

	Revenue		Composition of revenue (% of local government revenue)			
	% of GDP	% of general government revenue	Taxes[1]	Social contributions	Grants	Other[2]
Austria	7.7	15.9	61.4	4.7	20.0	13.9
Belgium	6.7	13.8	29.6	5.4	53.7	11.3
Bulgaria	7.2	18.5	13.6	0.0	74.3	12.1
Cyprus	1.8	4.2	28.4	0.0	45.8	25.8
Czech Rep.	11.4	27.9	46.2	0.0	36.9	16.9
Denmark	33.2	60.0	36.0	1.5	55.5	7.0
Estonia	10.4	28.0	47.5	0.0	42.8	9.7
Finland	20.0	37.4	47.4	0.1	28.8	23.7
France	10.9	22.1	45.5	0.3	37.0	17.1
Germany	7.5	17.1	42.9	1.3	38.9	17.0
Greece	2.7	6.7	9.6	0.0	64.2	26.2
Hungary	11.6	25.5	22.4	0.2	65.8	11.6
Ireland	7.7	22.1	9.8	3.7	70.4	16.1
Italy	15.3	33.2	42.8	0.6	48.5	8.1
Latvia	10.7	30.8	51.9	0.0	37.2	10.9
Lithuania	9.1	26.7	37.5	0.2	58.1	4.2
Luxembourg	5.1	12.8	31.3	0.2	48.0	20.5
Malta	0.6	1.4	0.0	0.0	92.6	7.4
Netherlands	15.3	32.9	8.4	2.3	69.6	19.8
Poland	14.0	35.2	33.2	0.0	53.3	13.4
Portugal	6.1	14.0	39.4	1.4	40.3	18.9
Romania	8.7	27.1	10.4	0.0	84.7	4.9
Slovak Rep.	5.4	16.6	59.6	0.5	27.9	11.9
Slovenia	8.5	19.9	39.2	1.0	46.1	13.8
Spain	6.0	16.3	48.9	0.6	40.5	10.0
Sweden	25.3	45.5	64.8	2.1	19.6	13.5
United Kingdom	13.1	31.0	13.0	1.9	70.0	15.1
EU27	11.3	25.4	36.1	1.2	48.7	14.0
Iceland	13.1	29.6	72.7	0.0	10.3	17.0
Norway	12.2	20.7	41.8	0.0	39.5	18.7
Switzerland	8.7	24.2				

1. Includes own-source and shared revenue, even where a sub-national government has virtually no power to set rates or bases.
2. Includes primarily fees and user charges, but also revenue associated with physical and financial assets (such as sales, dividends and interest).

Sources: Eurostat (February 2010), national sources and DEXIA calculations.

Annex 5.5: Local Government Tax Revenue, 2008 (% of local government revenue)

	Total	Taxes on:[1]			
		Income, profits and capital gains[2]	Property[3]	Goods and services[4]	Other[5]
Austria	61.4	22.1	3.9	24.4	11.0
Belgium	29.6	9.3	17.6	2.7	0.0
Bulgaria	13.6	0.4	12.0	1.2	0.0
Cyprus	28.4	0.0	15.6	6.4	6.4
Czech Rep.	46.2	25.2	1.5	19.4	0.0
Denmark	36.0	32.2	3.7	0.0	0.0
Estonia	47.5	43.9	2.9	0.7	0.0
Finland	47.4	44.9	2.5	0.0	0.0
France	45.5	0.0	27.9	14.3	3.3
Germany	42.9	16.9	5.3	20.6	0.0
Greece	9.6	0.0	5.1	4.5	0.0
Hungary	22.4	0.0	3.0	19.3	0.0
Ireland	9.8	0.0	9.8	0.0	0.0
Italy	42.8	11.1	4.3	27.5	0.0
Latvia	51.9	47.2	4.1	0.6	0.0
Lithuania	37.5	33.4	3.0	1.0	0.0
Luxembourg	31.3	28.5	1.6	1.1	0.0
Malta	0.0	0.0	0.0	0.0	0.0
Netherlands	8.4	0.0	6.6	1.8	0.0
Poland	33.2	20.6	10.3	2.4	0.0
Portugal	39.4	11.2	11.1	17.1	0.0
Romania	10.4	0.1	6.9	3.4	0.0
Slovak Rep.	59.6	48.3	6.9	4.4	0.0
Slovenia	39.2	29.7	5.3	4.3	0.0
Spain	48.9	10.9	15.3	22.7	0.0
Sweden	64.8	63.2	1.6	0.0	0.0
United Kingdom	13.0	0.0	13.0	0.0	0.0
EU 27	36.1	13.3	10.4	11.8	0.7
Iceland	72.7	54.8	17.9	0.0	0.0
Norway	41.8	36.6	4.5	0.7	0.0
Switzerland (2007)	56.1	45.9	9.1	1.1	0.0

1. *Includes own-source and shared revenue, even where a sub-national government has virtually no power to set rates or bases.*
2. *Includes all taxes on income (d51 in ESA95 classification)*
3. *Includes taxes on land, buildings and other structures (d29a), current taxes on capital (d59a), other current taxes n.e.c. (d59f) and capital taxes (d91).*
4. *Includes taxes on products such as VAT, import taxes and other consumption taxes (d21), taxes on the use of fixed assets (d29b), business and professional licences (d29e), taxes on pollution (d29f) and other taxes on production (d29h).*
5. *Includes taxes on payroll and workforce (d29c).*

Sources: Eurostat (Feb. 2010) and DEXIA calculations.

Annex 5.6: Local Government Grants, 2008 (% of local government revenue)

	Total	Current	Capital
Austria	20.1	16.1	4.0
Belgium	53.7	48.4	5.3
Bulgaria	81.8	74.3	7.6
Cyprus	45.8	27.6	18.3
Czech Rep.	36.9	30.5	6.3
Denmark	56.5	56.0	0.6
Estonia	42.8	36.6	6.1
Finland	28.8	28.5	0.3
France	38.3	33.6	4.7
Germany	39.1	32.3	6.8
Greece	65.8	44.1	21.6
Hungary	66.0	56.8	9.2
Ireland	70.4	27.6	42.8
Italy	48.5	42.2	6.3
Latvia	37.2	30.8	6.3
Lithuania	58.2	43.5	14.7
Luxembourg	48.0	41.2	6.9
Malta	92.6	89.2	3.4
Netherlands	70.0	65.7	4.4
Poland	53.5	49.7	3.8
Portugal	40.3	20.0	20.3
Romania	84.7	81.6	3.1
Slovak Rep.	27.9	19.9	8.1
Slovenia	46.4	41.7	4.7
Spain	43.3	32.6	10.6
Sweden	20.0	19.7	0.3
United Kingdom	70.0	62.2	7.8
EU27	49.2	43.1	6.0
Iceland	10.3	8.7	1.6
Norway	39.5	39.5	0.0

Sources: Eurostat and DEXIA calculations.

6. LATIN AMERICA

Annex 6.1: Assignments of expenditures functions

Functions	Argentina	Bolivia	Brazil	Chile	Colombia	Costa Rica	Dominican Republic	Ecuador	El Salvador	Guatemala	Honduras	Jamaica	Mexico	Nicaragua	Peru	Uruguay	Venezuela
Constitution defines assignments	No	Yes	Yes	Yes	Yes	Yes	Yes	Yes	Yes	Yes	Yes	No	No	Yes	Yes	Yes	Yes
General administration																	
Security, police	C/R	C	R	C	C	C	C	C/L	NA	L	L	C	C/R/L	C	C/L	C	C/R/L
Fire protection	C/R	C	R	C	L	C	L	NA	L	C/L	L	L	L	C	L	C	C/R/L
Civil protection	C/R	C	R	C	L	C	C/L	C/L	L	C	L	C	C/R/L		C/R/L	C	C/L
Justice																	
Civil status register	C	C	C	C	C	C	C	C	L	L	L	C	R/L	L	C/L	C	L
Statistical office	C/R	C	C/L	C	C	C	C	C	L	C	L	C	C/R/L		C	C	C
Electoral register	C/R	C	C	C	C	C	C	C	L	C	L	C	C		C	C	C
Education																	
Pre-school education	R	C/L	L	C	L	C	C	C	L	L	C/L	L	C/R/L		C/R	C/L	C/R/L
Primary education	R	C/L	L	C	L	C	C	C	L	L	C/L	L	C/R/L		C/R	C/L	C/R/L
Secondary education	R	C/L	R	C	L	C	C	C	L	NA	C	L	C/R/L		C/R	C	C/R/L
Vocational and technical	R	C/L	R	C	L	C	C	C	L	NA	C	C	C/R		C/R		C/R/L
Higher education	C	C/L	C	NA	C	C	C	C	C	NA	C	C	C/R		C/R	C	C
Adult education	R	C/L	R/L	NA	C	C	C	C	C	L	C	C	R		C/R		C
Public Health																	
Health protection	R	C/L	C/R/L	NA	L	C	C	C	L	NA	C/L	L	C/R		C/R	C/L	C/R/L
Primary care	R	C/L	C/R/L	C/L	L	C	C	C	L	NA	C/L	L	C/R/L	C/L	C/R	C	L
Hospitals	R	C/L	C/R/L	C/L	R	C	C	C	NA	NA	C/L	C/L	C/R		C/R	C	C/R
Social Welfare																	
Kindergarten and nursery	R	C/L	L	L	C	C	NA	C	L	NA	NA	C	C/R			C	C/R/L

C=central, R=regional, L=local

Source: IMF; Ministries of Finance of Argentina, Bolivia, Guatemala and Peru, UCLG data collection.

Annex 6.1: Assignments of expenditures functions (cont.)

Functions	Argentina	Bolivia	Brazil	Chile	Colombia	Costa Rica	Dominican Republic	Ecuador	El Salvador	Guatemala	Honduras	Jamaica	Mexico	Nicaragua	Peru	Uruguay	Venezuela
Family welfare services	C/R	C/L	C/R/L	L	C	C	NA	C	L	NA	NA	C/L	C		C/L	C	C/R/L
Welfare homes	C/R	C/R	C/R/L	NA	NA	C	NA	C	L	NA	NA	C	C/R		L	C	C/R/L
Social security	C/R	C	C	C/L	C	NA	C	C	NA	NA	NA	C	C			C	C
Housing and town planning																	
Housing	L	C/L	C/L	L	C/L	C	C	L	L	L	L	C	L	L	C	L	C
Town planning	L	L	C/L	L	L	C	L	L	L	L	L	C/L	L	L	L	L	L
Regional/spatial planning	R	C/L	C/L	R	C/R	NA	NA	L	L	NA	L	C/L	R		R	L	R/L
Environment, sanitation																	
Water & sewage	R	C/R/L	L	L	R/L	C/R	C	L	L	L	L	C/L	R/L	L	C/R/L	L	L
Refuse collection & disposal	R	C/R/L	L	L	L	L	L	L	L	L	L	C/L	L	L	L	L	C/L
Cemeteries & crematoria	R	C/R/L	L	L	L	L	L	L	L	L	L	NA	L	L	L	L	L
Slaughterhouses	R	C/R/L	L	L	L	L	L	L	L	L	L	NA	L	L	L	L	L
Environmental protection	R	C/L	C/L	L	R/L	C/R	C/L	L	L	L	L	C	C/R/L	L	C/R/L	L	C/L
Consumer protection	C	C	L	NA	C	C	NA	NA	L	NA	L	C	C/R/L		C		C
Culture, leisure & sports																	
Theatres & concerts	NA	C/R/L	R/L	NA	L	L	C	NA	L	L	L	NA	R/L		C/L	L	C/R/L
Museums & libraries	NA	C/R/L	C/R/L	NA	L	C	C	NA	L	L	L	NA	R/L	L	C/L	L	C/R/L
Parks & open spaces	NA	C/R/L	C/R/L	L	L	C\L	L	NA	L	L	L	C/L	L	L	L	L	R/L
Sports & leisure	NA	C/R/L	C/R/L	L	L	NA	C/L	NA	L	L	L	C/L	C/R/L	L	L	C/L	C/R/L
Religious facilities	NA	C/R/L	C/R/L	NA	NA	NA	NA	NA	L	NA	L	NA	C	L	L		
Other cultural facilities	NA	C/R/L	C/R/L	L	NA	NA	NA	NA	L	NA	L	C/L	C/R/L	L	L	L	

C=central, R=regional, L=local

Source: IMF; Ministries of Finance of Argentina, Bolivia, Guatemala and Peru, UCLG data collection.

Annex 6.1: Assignments of expenditures functions (cont.)

Functions	Argentina	Bolivia	Brazil	Chile	Colombia	Costa Rica	Dominican Republic	Ecuador	El Salvador	Guatemala	Honduras	Jamaica	Mexico	Nicaragua	Peru	Uruguay	Venezuela
Traffic, transport																	
Roads	C/R/L	C	C	L	C/R/L	C/L	C	R/L	NA	C/L	L	C/L	L	C/L	C/R/L	L	C/R/L
Transport	C/R	C	C/L	L	C/L	NA	C/L	R/L	NA	L	L	C/L	C/R	C/L	C/R/L	L	C/R/L
Urban road transport	C/R/L	C	L	L	L	C/L	C/L	R/L	NA	L	L	C/L	R/L	C/L	L	L	L
Urban rail transport	C	C	C	NA	L	NA	NA	NA	NA	NA	C	C/L	L				L
Ports	C	C	C	NA	C/L	C	C	NA	NA	NA	C	C	C	L	R		C/R
Airports	C	C	C	NA	C/L	C	C	NA	NA	NA	C	C	C		C		C/R
Utilities																	
Gas	R	C	C	NA	C/L	NA	NA	NA	L	NA	L	C			C	L	C/L
District heating	R	C	C	NA	NA	NA	NA	NA	L	NA	L	C				L	
Electricity	R	R	C/R/L	NA	C/L	C	C	NA	L	NA	L	C	L	L	C/R/L	C/L	C/L
Water supply		R	R/L	NA	R/L	C	C	L	L	L	L	C	L	L	C/R/L	L	C/L
Economic																	
Agriculture, forests, fishing	C/R	C/R/L	C/L	NA	C/L	C	C	L	L	NA	L	C	C		C/R	L	C
Economic promotion	C/R	C/R/L	C/L	NA	C/R/L	C	C/L	L	L	NA	L	C	C/R/L		C/R	L	C/R/L
Trade & industry	C/R	C/R/L	C/L	NA	C/L	C	C	L	L	NA	L	C	C/R		C/R	L	C/R/L
Tourism	C/R	C/R/L	C/L	NA	C/R/L	C	C	NA	L	NA	L	C	C/R	L	C/R	L	L
Other economic services	NA	C/R/L	C/L	NA	L	C	NA	NA	NA	NA	L	C	C/R/L				C/R/L
Employment	NA	C/R/L	C/L	L	C/L	C	C	NA	NA	NA	L	C	C/R/L				C

C=central, R=regional, L=local

Source: IMF; Ministries of Finance of Argentina, Bolivia, Guatemala and Peru, UCLG data collection.

Annex 6.2: Public Finance Indicators

Country	Total Expenditure in General Government (Mill USD)	Total Expenditure in General Government (% of GDP)	Local Expenditure (Mill USD)	Local Expenditure (% of GDP)	Local Expenditure % of General Government	Local Revenues (Mill USD)	Local government revenues as % of GDP	Local government revenues as % of General Government
Argentina (2006)	70,468	32.9	6,204	2.9	8.8	5,277	2.5	7.3
Bolivia (2008)	7,262	43.6	1,223	7.3	16.8	1,278	7.7	17.6
Brazil (2007)	420,253	31.5	110,693	8.3	26.3	108,748	8.2	18
Chile (2007)	31,094	19.0	3,982	2.4	12.8	4,417	2.7	9.2
Colombia (2006)	48,405	29.8	9,046	5.6	18.7	8,451	5.2	22
Costa Rica (2007)	5664	21.5	208	0.8	3.7	468	1.8	6.9
Dominican Republic (2006)	7,612	17.9	403	0.9	5.3	na		
Ecuador (2007)	10,357	18.9	2,423	4.4	23.4	2,087	3.8	22.4
El Salvador (2007)	3,533	17.3	249	1.2	7.0	385	1.9	9.3
Guatemala (2009)	5,620	15.5	245	0.7	4.4	1,016	2.8	16.5
Haití (2004)	802	15.0	na	na	na	na		
Honduras (2008)	3,770	26.6	184	1.3	4.9	177	1.2	4.9
Jamaica (2006)	3,912	32.6	34	0.3	0.9	34	0.3	0.9
Mexico (2007)	339,502	31.2	21,969	2.0	6.5	23,007	2.1	7.4
Nicaragua (2006)	1,461	28.0	na	na	na	na	na	na
Panama (2005)	6,855	44.9	137	0.8	1.7	na	na	2.0
Paraguay (2007)	2,109	20.3	133	1.3	6.3	182	1.8	6.8
Peru (2007)	17,137	15.9	2,812	2.6	16.4	3,977	3.7	17.8
Uruguay (2007)	8,611	30.8	na	na	na	na	na	na
Venezuela (2007)	58,888	25.8	na	na	na	na	na	na

Source: IMF; Ministries of Finance of Argentina, Bolivia, Guatemala and Peru, UCLG data collection.

Annex 6.3: Revenues and Expenditures by Government Level (%)

<table>
<tr><th>Country (Most recent year)</th><th colspan="3">Revenues (% total)</th><th colspan="3">Expenditures (% total)</th></tr>
<tr><th></th><th>Federal / Central</th><th>Regional</th><th>Local</th><th>Federal / Central</th><th>Regional</th><th>Local</th></tr>
<tr><td>Argentina (2006)</td><td>55</td><td>38</td><td>7</td><td>58</td><td>33</td><td>9</td></tr>
<tr><td>Bolivia (2008)</td><td>71</td><td>12</td><td>17</td><td>72</td><td>11</td><td>17</td></tr>
<tr><td>Brazil (2007)</td><td>54</td><td>28</td><td>18</td><td>45</td><td>29</td><td>26</td></tr>
<tr><td>Chile (2007)</td><td>91</td><td></td><td>9</td><td colspan="2">87</td><td>13</td></tr>
<tr><td>Colombia (2006)</td><td>64</td><td>14</td><td>22</td><td>67</td><td>14</td><td>19</td></tr>
<tr><td>Costa Rica</td><td>93</td><td></td><td>7</td><td>96</td><td></td><td>4</td></tr>
<tr><td>Dominican Republic (2006)</td><td></td><td></td><td></td><td>95</td><td></td><td>5</td></tr>
<tr><td>Ecuador (2007)</td><td colspan="2">78</td><td>22</td><td colspan="2">77</td><td>23</td></tr>
<tr><td>El Salvador (2007)</td><td>91</td><td></td><td>9</td><td>93</td><td></td><td>7</td></tr>
<tr><td>Guatemala (2002)</td><td colspan="2">84</td><td>16</td><td colspan="2">96</td><td>4</td></tr>
<tr><td>Haiti (2004)</td><td>100</td><td></td><td></td><td>100</td><td></td><td></td></tr>
<tr><td>Honduras (2004)</td><td>95</td><td></td><td>5</td><td>95</td><td></td><td>5</td></tr>
<tr><td>Jamaica (2008)</td><td>99</td><td></td><td>1</td><td>99</td><td></td><td>1</td></tr>
<tr><td>Mexico (2007)</td><td>68</td><td>25</td><td>7</td><td>69</td><td>25</td><td>6</td></tr>
<tr><td>Panama (2005)</td><td>98</td><td></td><td>2</td><td>98</td><td></td><td>2</td></tr>
<tr><td>Paraguay (2006)</td><td>93</td><td></td><td>7</td><td>94</td><td></td><td>6</td></tr>
<tr><td>Peru (2008)</td><td>66</td><td>16</td><td>18</td><td>66</td><td>18</td><td>16</td></tr>
</table>

Annex 6.4: Budget Expenditure by Economic Classification of Local Governments

Country (Most recent year)	Wages and Salaries/ Pension funds (% of total)	Current expenditure other than wages and salaries (% of total)	Capital Expenditure/debt/ equipment (% of total)
Argentina(2006)	47.40	29.27	23.33
Bolivia(2008)	65.80	26.90	7.30
Brazil(2007)	46.74	53.05	0.21
Chile(2007)	29.11	15.66	55.23
Colombia(2006)	74.05	1.96	23.98
Ecuador(2007)	23.60	20.80	55.60
El Salvador(2007)	45.61	39.78	14.60
Guatemala(2002)	0.00	36.00	64.00
Honduras(2004)	30.42	19.03	50.55
Mexico(2007)	82.83	12.29	4.88
Nicaragua(2002)	23.08	38.46	38.46
Panama(2005)	41.68	55.24	3.08
Paraguay(2006)	71.99	10.94	17.07
Peru(2008)	11.73	30.31	57.95

Source: UCLG data collection.

Annex 6.5: Share of Local Government Expenditure by Functional Classification

Country (Most recent year)	General administration (% of total)	Education (% of total)	Health (% of total)	Sanitation (% of total)	Transport (% of total)	Others (% of total)
Argentina(2006)	28.69	4.31	9.93	na	7.35	49.72
Bolivia(2008)	4.77	22.15	7.20	1.41	0.4	64.47
Brazil(2007)	13.6	25.99	21.94	2.97	3.05	33.6
Chile(2007)	42.84	36.86	11.89	na	na	8.42
Colombia(2006)	18.56	26.51	19.58	3.76	na	31.58
Peru(2008)	30.72	9.79	16.06	na	20.08	23.35

Source: UCLG data collection.

Annex 6.6: Origin of Revenues of Local Governments (millions US$)

Country (Most recent year)	Own taxes and fees (% of the total)	Shared revenues (% of the total)	Conditional Transfers (% of the total)	Unconditional transfers/Aid (% of the total)	Own taxes and fees (% of GDP)	Shared revenues (% of GDP)	Conditional Transfers (% of GDP)	Unconditional transfers/Aid (% of GDP)
Argentina(2006)	49.80	42.40	0.00	7.80	1.22	1.04	0.00	0.19
Bolivia(2008)	11.40	17.20	0.00	71.40	2.65	4.01	0.00	16.63
Brazil(2007)	20.10	76.50	0.00	3.40	1.75	6.67	0.00	0.29
Chile(2007)	63.00	0.00	0.00	37.00	0.66	0.00	0.00	0.39
Colombia(2006)	41.20	0.00	58.80	0.00	2.11	0.00	3.02	0.00
Dominican Republic(2006)	58.40	10.40	31.20	0.00	0.69	0.12	0.37	0.00
Ecuador(2007)	34.60	0.00	0.00	65.40	1.62	0.00	0.00	3.07
El Salvador (2007)	69.90	0.00	0.00	30.10	0.00	2.07	0.00	3.51
Guatemala(2002)	25.00	5.00	60.00	10.00	0.53	0.11	1.28	0.21
Honduras(2004)	58.10	11.00	6.00	24.90	0.95	0.18	0.10	0.41
Jamaica(2008)	100.00	0.00	0.00	0.00	0.16	0.00	0.00	0.00
Mexico(2007)	15.60	45.30	0.00	39.10	2.38	6.91	0.00	5.98
Nicaragua(2002)	44.00	5.00	11.00	40.00	0.56	0.06	0.14	0.51
Panama(2005)	49.00	46.10	4.90	0.00	0.33	0.31	0.03	0.00
Paraguay(2006)	34.10	1.80	10.80	53.30	1.23	0.07	0.39	1.91
Peru(2008)	43.20	48.30	0.00	8.50	2.62	2.92	0.00	0.52

Source: UCLG data collection.

7. MEWA

Annex 7.1: Transfer Characteristics and Allocation Rules in Selected MEWA Countries

	Transfer Characteristics	Source	Allocation Rules
Iran	Transfers to urban LGs appear to be negligible, particularly, in the larger cities. Development transfers: 60% earmarked 30-40% discretionary.	Oil revenues.	No formula. Allocation rules decided annually by the Parliament.
Jordan	Transfers to all municipalities from central government's fuel tax collections	Special legislation fee of 6% on petroleum products produced or imported (except fuel oil) by the Jordan Petroleum Refinery Company 40% of the proceed of Vehicles Licensing fees.	Cities and Villages Development Bank distributes to the municipalities according to a ratio (or transfer formula) based on such general factors as population, proportion of its contribution in overall revenue generation, particular importance of location and non-local responsibilities.
Lebanon	Transfers to all municipalities from the central government (autonomous Municipal fund)	Indirect taxes accumulated into the Autonomous Municipal Fund. 10 % of national public service revenue (water and energy)	The Ministry of Finance (MoF) distributes to the municipalities according to a ratio (or transfer formula) based on such general factors as population, proportion of its contribution in overall revenue generation, particular importance of location and non-local responsibilities. Allocation rules decided annually by the MoIM + MoF with the approval of the central government.
Palestine	Current transfers and grants for transport fees are not earmarked. Discretionary/emergency transfers are channeled to specific projects.	Transport fees and a separate account assigned for discretionary/emergency transfers.	A formula for the pool and distribution of transport fees exists on paper (1997 Local Government Law). Yet, the formula is only partially applied. Discretionary/emergency transfers are ad hoc.
Syria	Two types of transfers. First is unconditional and second is conditional based on expropriation reimbursement	Oil revenues Customs taxes Income taxes Real estate taxes	National amount of the transfer is ad hoc in both types of transfers.
Turkey	System based on unconditional transfers. Specific percentages from the Overall Budget Tax Revenues that is set by the central government are distributed among different local units.	National taxes such as income and consumption taxes.	According to a new law of July 2, 2008: from the overall budget tax revenue 2.85% for Municipalities (other than Metropolitan) 2.50% for District Municipalities of the Metropolitan, 30% of which is to be spared for Metropolitan 1.15% for Special Provincial Administration plus: 5% for Metropolitan Municipalities from the tax revenue collected within the borders of the Metropolitan City extras: 0.1% of the finally decided overall budget tax revenue is handled to the Ministry of Finance as Municipal Balancing Payment (to be distributed through 2 payments in March and July), of which: 60% for Municipalities with a population not exceeding 5,000 40% for Municipalities with a population between 5,001-9,999 No conditions attached, but according to certain decided criteria such as population, acreage, number of villages belonging to the city, rural population, city development index.
Yemen	30% of grants from extra-budgetary funds that are earmarked, others are not.	Shared revenues from 28 taxes, mainly – Zakat.	No formula, but Council of Ministers uses non-binding guidelines – population density, financing gap, degree of deprivation, performance in revenue collection.

Source: Compiled by Mehmet S. Tosun and Serdar Yilmaz based on World Bank and UCLG consultancy missions and UCLG country datasheets.

Annex 7.2: Domestic and Foreign Debt Stock of Turkish Local Administrations

Million TL	2006	2007	2008
Domestic Debt:	16,520	23,577	21,666
Short Term	5,140	7,384	8,375
Long Term	11,379	16,193	13,290
Foreign Debt:	2,298	3,602	4,797
Short Term	167	984	386
Long Term	2,131	2,617	4,410
Total Debt	18,819	27,179	26,463
Domestic Debt (% of GDP)	2.18	2.80	2.28
Foreign Debt (% of GDP)	0.30	0.43	0.50
Total Debt (% of GDP)	2.48	3.22	2.78

Source: Turkish Ministry of Interior, General Directorate for Local Authorities.
http://www.mahalliidareler.gov.tr/Home/Dokumanlar/faaliyet_raporu.pdf

BIBLIOGRAPHY

Africa

African Center for Gender and Social Development. 2009. *African Perspectives on the Global Economic and Financial crisis, including the impact on health.*

Agence Française de Développement, AFD. 2005. *Financer les investissements des villes des pays en développement*. Synthèse des travaux du groupe de travail, Financement des investissement des collectivités locales. Paris, AFD.

Akindele S. T. and Olaopa. 2002. *Fiscal federalism and local government finance in Nigeria*. Republic of Nigeria.

Banque Africaine de Développement (BAD), le Centre de développement de l'Organisation de coopération et de développement économique (OCDE) et la Commission économique des Nations Unies pour l'Afrique. 2008. *Perspectives Économiques en Afrique.* Tunis.

Bird, Richard, and François Vaillancourt. 1998. *Fiscal Decentralization in Developing Countries*. Cambridge University Press, Cambridge, 318 pages.

Boex, Jameson, and Jorge Martínez-Vázquez. 2005. *Local Government Finance Reform in Developing Countries: The Case of Tanzania.* Palgrave MacMillan.

Boex, Jamie, Randson Mwadiwa, R. Kampanje. 2001. *Malawi Intergovernmental Fiscal Transfers Study. Final Report.* Lilongwe and Atlanta, Georgia State University, UNDP.

Boschmann, Niña. 2009. *Fiscal Decentralization and Options for Donor Harmonisation*. Development Partners Working Group on Local Governance and Decentralization. Berlin, Germany.

Boutayeb N. 2007. *Fiscalité: principal levier de mobilisation des ressources locales*. Note présentée au 7° Global Forum on Reinventing Government. Vienne, Autriche.

Brun, Jean-François, Gérard Chambas, Martial Laurent. 2010. *Économie politique de la réforme de transition fiscale: le cas du Maroc*. Document de travail de la série Études et Documents.

Busse, Mathias, Axel Bormann, Simon Mevel. 2004. *The Impact of ACP/EU Economic Partnership Agreements on ECOWAS Countries: An Empirical Analysis of Trade and Budget Effects.* Hamburg Institute of International Economics, Hamburg.

Chambas, Gérard. 2005. *Afrique au Sud du Sahara : Mobiliser des ressources fiscales pour le développement*. Ministère délégué à la Coopération, au Développement et à la Francophonie. Economica.

Champagne, Eric and Ben Mamadou Ouedraogo. 2008. "Decentralization in Burkina Faso: A Policy Reform Process in Slow Motion, Obstacles to Decentralization: Lessons from selected countries, International Studies Program". Andrew Young School of Policy Studies, International Studies Program, Georgia State University, Atlanta, September 23, 2008.

Cités et Gouvernements Locaux Unis. 2008. *Premier Rapport Mondial sur la Décentralisation*. Paris, L'Harmattan.

Commission Économique pour l'Afrique. 2004. *Renforcer la gestion financière locale et la décentralisation fiscale en Afrique : Etat des lieux et proposition d'un plan d'action*. Addis-Abeba.

Dafflon, Bernard, et Thierry Madies. 2009. *Les finances publiques locales des collectivités territoriales au Burkina Faso.* miméo AFD.

Odd-Helge Fjeldstad. 2001. *Fiscal decentralisation in Tanzania: For better or for worse?* Bergen, Chr. Michelsen Institute (CMI Working Paper WP 2001:10) 15 p.

Fonds d'Équipement Communal. 2003. *Note d'information, Émission obligataire réservée aux investisseurs institutionnels*. Royaume du Maroc.

Gagnon, Gérard. 2002. *Le financement du développement local ; Un état des lieux en Afrique de l'Ouest, Éléments de comparaison Ghana-UEMOA.* Contributions issues des ateliers de validation du chapitre Club du Sahel – OCDE, Paris.

Gilbert, Guy, Réjane Hugounenq et Emmanuelle Taugourdeau. 2009. *Le système de financement des collectivités locales au Sénégal*. miméo AFD.

Hinkle, Laurence, Mombert Hoppe and Richard Newfarmer. 2006. "Beyond Cotonou : Economic Partnership Agreements in Africa", *in Trade, Doha, and Development - A Window into the Issues.* Chapter 22, The World Bank, Trade Department, 2006.

Hugounenq, Réjane, Yvon Rocaboy et François Vaillancourt. 2010. *Les finances publiques locales des collectivités territoriales au Kenya*. miméo AFD.

JICA. 2006. *Local Level Service Delivery, Decentralization and Good Governance: A comparative study of Uganda, Kenya and Tanzania : education, health and agriculture sectors*. Synthesis Report, Research Group, Institute for International Cooperation, Tokyo, accessed 08 May 2009.

Martínez-Vázquez, Jorge and Andrey Timofeev. 2008. *Decentralizing Egypt: Not Just Another Economic Reform.* International Studies Program, Andrew Young School of Policy Studies, Georgia State University. Working Paper Series, at AYSPS, GSU, number paper 0833.

Mahjoub, Azzam. 2010. *L'implantation de la zone de libre-échange. Situation en 2010 et perspectives pour 2010-2015.* Université de Tunis El-Manar.

Meddeb, Radhi. 1996. *La zone de libre-échange Tunisie-UE, un modèle et un défi.* Chambre de commerce franco-arabe, Paris.

Minister of Finance of the Republic of South Africa. 2007. *Municipal fiscal powers and functions bill*. Republic of South Africa.

Organisation for Economic Co-operation and Development (OECD), African Development Bank and United Nations Economic Commission for Africa. 2010. *African Economic Outlook 2010 - Public Resource Mobilisation and Aid.*

Oriakhi, D.E. 2006. "Fiscal Decentralization, Public Expenditure and Efficient Service Delivery: An assessment of the performance of sub national levels of governments in Nigeria", in *Workshop on Public expenditures and service delivery in Africa: Managing public expenditures to improve service quality and access*. Lusaka, Zambia, 9-11 october 2006. United Nations Economic Commission for Africa.

Partenariat pour le Développement Municipal (PDM). 2002. *La Decentralisation Financière en Côte d'Ivoire.*

Presentations made during the Seminars on Local Finance in Africa, organized by UCLG in Harare, 3 May 2010, and Rabat, 7 May 2010 :

- Akoete Massan, Emilie, Les Finances locales du Togo.
- Awal, Mouhamadou, Le Financement local au Gabon.
- Ben Akezouh, Chabane, Projet de loi portant code communal déposé à l'A.P.N. : innovations (Algérie).
- Ben Letaieff, Mustapha, La Décentralisation fiscale en Tunisie.
- Djacoto, Victorin, Grands traits des finances des collectivités locales en république du Bénin.
- El Madani, M., Organisation des finances locales au Maroc.
- Kebd, Yahya Ould, Atelier sur le Rapport Mondial (GOLD) : Mauritanie
- Mactar Gaye, Amadou, Le Financement local au Sénégal (Ministère de l'Intérieur, Direction des collectivités locales).
- Itsana, Pacôme, Description du système de financement local au Gabon.
- Kadewere, Felix, Fiscal Decentralization in Malawi.
- Kouassi, Charles Yao, La Décentralisation fiscale en Côte d'Ivoire.
- Maganlal, Mayur, State of Fiscal Decentralization in South Africa.
- Mboga, Hamisi, Comments on the African Chapter GOLD II on Kenya.

San, Olisa Agbakoba, and Hilary Ogbonna. 2004. *Local Government Administration and Development in Nigeria – A Capacity Building Manual for the Human Rights Law Service.* Hurilaws, Lagos, Nigeria.

Schoeman, Niek J. 2005. *Rethinking Fiscal Decentralization in South Africa*. Department of Economics, University of Pretoria, South Africa. ESSA conference held in Durban, 7-9 december 2005.

Steffensen, Jesper, et Svend Trollegaard. 1999. *Sénégal - Décentralisation Fiscale et Finances des Collectivités Locales en relation avec la fourniture d'infrastructures et de services.*

United Nations Population Fund (UNFPA). 2007. State of World Population 2007, *Unleashing the Potential of Urban Growth.*

Vaillancourt, François. 2008. *La décentralisation en Côte d'ivoire; état des lieux en 2007 et observations*. Banque Mondiale. miméo.

Yatta, François. 2009. *La décentralisation fiscale en Afrique ; enjeux et perspectives.* Karthala 324pp.

Yatta, François Paul. 2006. *Villes et Développement économique en Afrique : une approche par les comptes économiques locaux*. Editions Economica, 315 pages. Paris, France.

Asia Pacific

2011 to 2013 Implementation Plan of the National Program for Sub-National Democratic Development, National Committee for Democratic Development, Royal Government of Cambodia, May 2010.

Amornvivat, Sutapa. 2004. *Fiscal Decentralization: The Case of Thailand*. Ministry of Finance. Thailand. Miméo.

An, Jongseok. 2003. *Local Public Finance and Intergovernmental Fiscal Relations*. Korea Institute of Public Finance. Miméo.

Aoki, Ichiro. 2008. *Decentralization and Intergovernmental Finance in Japan*. PRI Discussion Paper Series No. 08A-04. Research Department Policy Research Institute, Ministry of Finance.

Asian Development Bank. 2008. *Philippines: Sources of Local Government Unit Financing*. Sector Study Report, Manila.

Asian Development Bank. 2009. *Decentralization and Devolution in the Philippines: Status, Triumphs, Tests, and Directions*. Manila.

Association of District Development Committees of Nepal. August 2007. *State Restructuring and Issues of Local Self Governance in Nepal*.

Australian Government. *Assessing Local Government Revenue Raising Capacity*. Productivity Commission Research Report, April 2008.

Australian Government. Local Government National Reports, 2005-06 to 2007-08, Department of Infrastructure, Transport, Regional Development and Local Government.

Australian Government. Report on Government Services 2008, Steering Committee for the Review of Government Services.

Azfar, O., S. Kähkönen, and P. Meagher. 2001. *Conditions for effective decentralized governance: A synthesis of research findings*. Working Paper No. 256. IRIS Center, University of Maryland.

Bahl, Roy and Jorge Martínez-Vázquez. 2009. *Fiscal Federalism and Economic Reform in China*. Miméo.

Bahl, Roy and Musharraf Cyan. 2008. *Local Government Taxation in Pakistan. Miméo*.

Bahl, Roy, Eunice Heredia-Ortiz, Jorge Martínez-Vázquez, and Mark Rider. 2005. *India: Fiscal Condition of the States, International Experience, and Options for Reform*. Georgia State University. Andrew Young School of Public Policy. International Studies Program. Working Paper 05-13 (1) May.

Bahl, Roy, Sally Wallace, and Musharraf Cyan. 2008. *Pakistan: Provincial Government Taxation*. Georgia State University. Andrew Young School of Policy Studies. World Bank. Miméo.

Bjornestad, Liv. 2009. *Fiscal Decentralization, Fiscal Incentives, and Pro-Poor Outcomes: Evidence from Viet Nam*. ADB Economics Working Paper Series. No 168. Asian Development Bank, Manila.

Boex, Jamie, Peter Grudgeon, and Roger Shotton. 2002. *Role of UNDP in Promoting Local Governance & Decentralization in Bangladesh*. Mimeo.

Canel, Patrick, Sakon Varanyuwatana, and Francoise Brunet, 2007. *Étude Sur Les Collectivités Locales en Thaïlande*. Agence Française de Développement. Miméo.

Doi, Takero. 2004. *A Missing Link in Decentralization Reform in Japan: Trinity Reform Package*. PRI Discussion Paper Series No. 04A-08. Research Department Policy Research Institute, Ministry of Finance.

Fox, William F. and Balakrishna Menon. 2008. *Decentralization in Bangladesh: Change Has Been Elusive*. Mimeo.

Garcia, Beatriz Carrillo. 2008. *China's Fiscal Decentralization: Consequences for Promotion of Local Development*. Analisis, vol. 11, no. 31.

Hanai, Kiyohito and Bach Thi Minh Huyen. 2008. *Revenue Assignments between Central and Local Budgets in Vietnam*. Miméo.

Hossain Md. Awal. 2006. *Administrative Decentralization: A Framework for Discussion and Its Practices in Bangladesh. Miméo*.

Interim Constitution of Nepal. 2007.

International Monetary Fund. 2002. *Thailand: Selected Issues and Statistical Appendix*. IMF. Washington.

JICA. 2008. *Trends and Developments in Decentralization in Thailand. Miméo*.

Kardar, Shahid. 2006. *Local Government Finance in Pakistan Post 2001. Miméo*.

Keefer, Phillip E., Ambar Narayan, and Tara Vishwanath. 2003. *The Political Economy of Decentralization in Pakistan. Miméo*.

Law on Administrative Management of the Capital, Provinces, Municipalities, Districts and Khans, (The Organic Law on Decentallization and Democratic Development), 2009.

Lee, Yongmo. 2003. *Fiscal Decentralization, Institutional Arrangements, and Economic Performance in Korea*. Ph.D Dissertation. Robert F. Wagner School of Public Service. New York University.

Lee, Yongmo. 2004. "Adequacy of Korea's Tax Assignment: A Fiscal Federalism Approach", International Journal of Public Administration, Vol. 9, No. 2.

Lee, Yongmo. 2006. "Decentralization and Fiscal Disparities in Korea: With Special Reference to Seoul Metropolitan City", Journal of Local Government Studies, Vol. 8, No. 2.

Lewis, Blane. 2002. "Indonesia", in P. Smoke and Y. H. Kim eds., *Intergovernmental Transfers in Asia: Current Practice and Challenges for the Future*. Manila, Asian Development Bank.

Lewis, Blane. 2003a. "Local Government Borrowing and Repayment in Indonesia: Does Fiscal Capacity Matter?" World Development, vol. 31, no. 6.

Lewis, Blane 2003b. "Property Taxation in Indonesia: Measuring and Explaining Administrative (Under-) Performance", Public Administration and Development, vol. 23, no. 3.

Lewis, Blane. 2003c. "Tax and Charge Creation by Regional Governments under Fiscal Decentralization: Estimates and Explanations", Bulletin of Indonesian Economic Studies, vol. 39, no. 2.

Lewis, Blane. 2005. "Indonesian Local Government Spending, Taxing, and Saving: An Explanation of Pre- and Post-Decentralization Fiscal Outcomes", Asian Economic Journal, vol. 19, no. 3.

Lewis, Blane. 2006. "Local Government Taxation: An Analysis of Administrative Cost Inefficiency", Bulletin of Indonesian Economic Studies, vol. 42, no. 2.

Lewis, Blane. 2007a. "On-Lending in Indonesia: Past Performance and Future Prospects", Bulletin of Indonesia Economic Studies, vol. 43, no. 1.

Lewis, Blane. 2007b. "Revisiting the Price of Residential Land in Jakarta", Urban Studies, vol. 44, no. 11.

Lewis, Blane. 2009a. "Fiscal Decentralization in Indonesia: Accountability Deferred". Miméo.

Lewis, Blane. 2009b. "Philippine Local Government Unit Surpluses and Reserves: Facts, Comparative Perspective, Preliminary Questions, and a Research Agenda". Manila. Miméo.

Lewis, Blane and Andre Oosterman. 2009. "The Impact of Decentralization on Sub-National

Government Fiscal Slack in Indonesia", Public Budgeting & Finance, vol. 29, no. 2.

Lewis, Blane and Daan Pattinasarany. 2009a. "Determining Citizen Satisfaction with Local Public Education in Indonesia: The Significance of Actual Service Quality and Governance Conditions", (with Daan Pattinasarany) Growth and Change, vol. 40, no. 1.

Lewis, Blane and Daan Pattinasarany. 2009b. "A Stochastic Cost Frontier Analysis of Primary Education in Indonesia: Do Schools Need More Money?", (December) Education Economics.

Lewis, Blane and Paul Smoke. 2009. "Incorporating Sub-National Performance Incentives in the Indonesian Intergovernmental Framework", National Tax Association Proceedings, 101st Conference on Taxation, November.

Lewis, Blane and David Woodward. 2010. "Debt Restructuring in Indonesia: Reform or Reversion?", Bulletin of Indonesian Economic Studies, vol. 46, no. 1.

Lim, Sung Il. 2010. *Recent Trends in Intergovernmental Fiscal Relations in Korea and the Future Tasks*. (publication pending)

Local Government and Shires Associations of New South Wales. *Independent Inquiry into Financial Sustainability of NSW Local Government: Are Councils Sustainable?* Final Report, May 2006.

Local Government New Zealand. 2006. *Devolution – Fact or Fiction: A Report on the Extent of New Functions and Costs Acquired by Local Government Since Reform in 1989.*

Local Government New Zealand. July 2005. *Local Authority Funding Issues: Report of the Joint Central Government/Local Authority Funding Project Team.*

Local Government Rates Inquiry. Trends in the Level of Local Government Funding and Expenditure, Thomas Consulting, July 2007.

Localcouncils.govt.nz, Statistical reports.

Ma Jun and John Norregaard. 1998. *China's Fiscal Decentralization*. Miméo.

Manasan, Rosario G. 2004. *Local Public Finance in the Philippines: In Search of Autonomy with Accountability*. Philippine Institute for Development Studies. Discussion Paper Series No. 2004-42.

Manning, Nick, Doug Porter, Jackie Charlton, Musharraf Cyan, and Zahid Hasnain. 2003. *Devolution in Pakistan-Preparing for Service Delivery Improvements*. Working Paper. Mimeo.

Martínez-Vázquez, Jorge. 2005. *Making Fiscal Decentralization Work in Vietnam*. Georgia State University. Andrew Young School of Policy Studies. Working Paper Series 05-13.

Martínez-Vázquez, Jorge and Bob Searle. 2007. *Fiscal Equalization: Challenges in the Design of Intergovernmental Transfers*. Springer.

Mathur, Om Prakash and George Peterson. 2006. *State Finance Commissions and Urban Fiscal Decentralization in India*. Miméo.

Meemakshisundaram. 2005. *Delivering Basic Services through Local Governments in Rural India*. Miméo.

Mochida, Nobuki. 2008. *Fiscal Decentralization and Local Public Finance in Japan*. Routledge.

New Zealand Government. *Draft copy of Observations and Trends from the 2009-2019 Long-term Consolidated Council Plans*, Department of Internal Affairs, Received November 2009.

New Zealand Government. *Policy Statement on Land Transport Funding 2009-10 to 2018-19*, Minister of Transport, May 2009.

Oommen, M.A. 2008. *Fiscal Decentralization to Local Governments in India.* Cambridge Scholars Publishing.

Peterson, George. 2002. *Pakistan's Fiscal Decentralization: Issues and Opportunities*. Miméo.

Ping Xin-Qiao and Jie Bai. 2005. *Fiscal Decentralization and Local Public Good Provision in China*. China Center for Economic Research Working Paper Series. No.E2005004.

Pradhan, Hemanta K. 2004. *India: Local Government Finance and Bond Markets*. Miméo.

Rao, M. Govinda. 2000a. "Fiscal Decentralization in Vietnam: Emerging Issues", Hitotsubashi Journal of Economics, Vol. 41, no. 2.

Rao, M. Govinda. 2000b. *Fiscal Decentralization in Indian Federalism*. Miméo.

Rao, M. Govinda. 2003. "Fiscal Decentralization in China and India: A Comparative Perspective", Asia Pacific Development Journal, vol. 10, no. 1.

Rao, M. Govinda and Nirvkiar Singh. 2006. *The Political Economy of India's Fiscal Federal System and its Reform. Miméo.*

Reports on and Analysis of the Operations of the Commune/Sangkat Fund. Provided by the Secretariat of the National Committee for Democratic Development, Royal Government of Cambodia for author research, May 2010. *Reports on and Analysis of the Operations of the Commune/Sangkar fund.*

Saigal, Suraj. 2002. *Literature Review on Service Delivery in India*. Background Reference for World Development Report 2004. Mimeo.

Shen, Chunli and Heng-fu Zou. 2007. *Fiscal Decentralization and Public Service Provision in China*. Miméo.

Shen, Chunli, Jing Jin, and Heng-fu Zou. 2006. *Fiscal Decentralization in China: History, Impact, Challenges, and Next Steps.* World Bank. Miméo.

Shun'ichi Furukawa. 2003. *Decentralization in Japan.* Japan Center for International Exchange. Miméo.

Takero Doi and Shunichiro Bessho. 2003. "Japan's Reform for Decentralization: Trinity Reform Package". International Symposium on the Legislation of Fiscal Transfers, Ministry of Finance, P. R. China.

Weerasak, Krueathep. 2006. *Fiscal Strategies of Thai Local Governments during the Decentralization Movement: A Preliminary Exploration of Characteristics and Causes.* Institute for Local Government Initiatives Working Paper 01-2549.

World Bank. 2004. *India State Fiscal Reforms*. PREM. Report No. 28849-IN. South Asia Region. New Delhi, India.

World Bank. 2006. *Spending for Development: Making the Most of Indonesia's New Opportunities.* World Bank Public Expenditure Review, Jakarta, Indonesia.

World Bank. 2007. *West Bengal: Fiscal Decentralization to Rural Governments: Analysis and Reform Options*. Miméo.

World Bank. 2009. *Background Notes on Fiscal Decentralization*. Miméo, Manila.

World Bank and Asian Development Bank. 2005. *Decentralization in the Philippines: Strengthening Local Government Financing and Resource Management in the Short-Term.* Manila.

Yagi, Kinnosuke. 2004. *Decentralization in Japan.* Policy and Governance Working Paper Series No. 30. Graduate School of Media and Governance, Keio University, Japan.

Yao, Yi and Xiaobo Zhang. 2007. "Race to the Top and Race to the Bottom: Tax Competition in Rural China". International Food and Policy Research Institute. Discussion Paper 00799.

Zaidi, S. Akbar. 2005. *The Political Economy of Decentralization in Pakistan*. NCCR North South Working Paper No. 1. Miméo.

Zhang, Xiaobo. 2006. *Fiscal Decentralization and Political Centralization in China*. United Nations University. World Institute for Development Economics Research. Research Paper No. 2006/93.

Zhang, Xiaobo and Jorge Martínez-Vásquez. 2003. *The System of Equalization Transfers in China*. Miméo.

Eurasia

Alymkulov, Emil and Marat Kulatov. 2001. "Local Government in the Kyrgyz Republic", in Victor Popa and Igor Munteanu ed., *Developing New Rules in the Old Environment: Local Governments in Eastern Europe, Caucasus, and Central Asia.* Budapest: Local Government Initiative of the Open Society Institute.

Asanakunov, Bolotbek and Gulnara Bekbasarova. 2009. *The budgetary process and management of municipal resources*. Toolkit for local governments. Bishkek: The Association of Municipalities of the Kyrgyz Republic (*in Russian*).

Assignments of Responsibilities to Different Levels of Government in Countries of Central Asia: Prospects for Further Development. 2003. Budapest: Fiscal Decentralization Initiative for Central and Eastern Europe.

Bakanova, Marina and Jorge Martínez-Vázquez. 2007. *Taking Stock of Intergovernmental Fiscal Relations: Issues and Challenges*. *Belarus Policy Note*. World Bank, unpublished manuscript.

Caucasian Institute for Economic and Social Research - CIESR. 2009. *Expenditure policy of Local self-governments in Georgia*. Analytical research.

Chiriac, Liubomir, Igor Munteanu, Victor Popa and Victor Mocanu. 2001. "Local Government in Moldova", in Emilia Kandeva, ed., *Stabilization of Local Governments: Local Governments in Central and Eastern Europe*. Budapest: Local Government Initiative of the Open Society Institute.

De Silva, Migara, Galina Kurlyandskaya, Yelena Andreeva and Natalia Golovanova. 2009. *Intergovernmental Reforms in Russian Federation: One Step Forward, Two Steps Back?* Washington, DC: World Bank.

Decentralization and local democracy in the world. First UCLG Global Report. 2008. World Bank and United Cities and Local Governments.

Deryugin, Aleksandr. 2007. "The Kyrgyz Republic — Government Structure and Reform of the Budgetary System" in Toft, David, ed. *The challenges of decentralization in the Kyrgyz Republic.* Budapest: Fiscal Decentralization Initiative for Central and Eastern Europe.

Expert Analysis of the Impact of the Local Governance Reform and the Intergovernmental Fiscal Relations Reform on the Financial Standing of Municipalities in the Russian Federation. 2009. Moscow: The Institute for Urban Economics (*in Russian*).

Expert-Group. 2009. *Impact of the global financial crisis on local communities in Moldova*. UNDP-Moldova.

Government Finance Statistics Yearbook 2009, IMF Statistics Department.

Khachikyan, Sos. 2009. "A Simple Look on Local Self-government System in Armenia" in V. Klimanov, ed.,

Foreign Experience of Intergovernmental Fiscal Innovations. Public Finance Series: Vol. 19, Moscow: IPFR.

Kirn, Tanja and Elguja Khokrishvili. 2008. *Will an Asymmetrical System of Fiscal Decentralisation Resolve the Conflicts in the Republic of Georgia?* Finanzwissenschaftliche Diskussionsbeiträge.

Kurlandskaya, Galina, Yelena Nikolayenko, and Natalia Golovanova. 2001. "Local Governments in the Russian Federation", in Victor Popa and Igor Munteanu ed., *Developing New Rules in the Old Environment: Local Governments in Eastern Europe, Caucasus, and Central Asia*. Budapest: Local Government Initiative of the Open Society Institute.

Kurlandskaya, Galina. 2001. "Budgetary Pluralism of Russian Authorities". *Local Government and Public Service Reform Discussion Paper Series 17*. Budapest: Local Government Initiative of the Open Society Institute.

Kurlyandskaya, Galina, and Natalia Golovanova. 2006. "Decentralization in the Russian Federation", in *Economic Change and Restructuring* 39 (3): 213–33.

Losaberidze, David, Konstantine Kandelaki and Niko Orvelashvili. 2001. "Local government in Georgia", in Victor Popa and Igor Munteanu ed., *Developing New Rules in the Old Environment: Local Governments in Eastern Europe, Caucasus, and Central Asia*. Budapest: Local Government Initiative of the Open Society Institute.

Losaberidze, David. 2007. "Kyrgyzstan and Georgia — Perspectives Based on Georgia's Decentralization Experience" in Toft, David, ed. *The challenges of decentralization in the Kyrgyz Republic.* Budapest: Fiscal Decentralization Initiative for Central and Eastern Europe.

Losaberidze, David. 2009 [2]. *Administrative Structure of Local Self-Government: Civil Sector Perspective*. Caucasus Institute for Peace, Democracy and Development, Policy Brief, March.

Losaberidze, David. 2009. "Local Self-Government in Georgia", in Tumanyan, David, ed., *Local Self-Government in South Caucasus: local finance and services, central-local relations* (in Russian).

Martínez-Vázquez, Jorge, Jamie Boex and Andrey Timofeev. 2005. "Country Report: An Assessment of Fiscal Decentralization Reform in Armenia", in *Fiscal Decentralization in Transition Economies: Case Studies from the Balkans and Caucasus*. UNDP.

Martínez-Vázquez, Jorge, Jamie Boex and Michael Schaeffer. 2005. "Country Report: An Assessment of Fiscal Decentralization Reform in Georgia", in *Fiscal Decentralization in Transition Economies: Case Studies from the Balkans and Caucasus*. UNDP.

Martínez-Vázquez, Jorge and Wayne R.Thirsk. 2008. *Fiscal Decentralization in Ukraine: Accomplishments and Challenges in the Transition*. unpublished manuscript.

Martínez-Vázquez, Jorge, Andrey Timofeev, and Jameson Boex. 2006. *Reforming Regional-Local Finance in Russia.* Washington, DC: World Bank.

Meruert Mahmutova. 2001. "System of Local Government In Kazakhstan", in Victor Popa and Igor Munteanu ed., *Developing New Rules in the Old Environment: Local Governments in Eastern Europe, Caucasus, and Central Asia*. Budapest: Local Government Initiative of the Open Society Institute.

Miroslav Kobasa, Alexander Karamyshev and Valentin Dritz. 2001. "Local Government in Belarus", in Victor Popa and Igor Munteanu ed., *Developing New Rules in the Old Environment: Local Governments in Eastern Europe, Caucasus, and Central Asia*. Budapest: Local Government Initiative of the Open Society Institute.

Morozov, Boris. 2008. *Property Tax in Republic of Moldova – Basis for Local Autonomy?* Unpublished manuscript.

Movsisyan, Vahan. 2007. *The Development of Financial Equalization Mechanism in Armenia.* Communities Finance Officers Association.

Narmania, David. 2007. *Rights of Local Jurisdictions and Tax Revenue Distribution in Georgia*. Finanzwissenschaftliche Diskussionsbeiträge.

Navruzov, Yury. 2001. "Local Government in Ukraine", in Victor Popa and Igor Munteanu ed., *Developing New Rules in the Old Environment: Local Governments in Eastern Europe, Caucasus, and Central Asia*. Budapest: Local Government Initiative of the Open Society Institute.

Popa, Victor. 2007. "The Endless Reform of Local Self-government in the Republic of Moldova" in Toft, David ed., *The challenges of decentralization in the Kyrgyz Republic.* Budapest: Fiscal Decentralization Initiative for Central and Eastern Europe.

Problems of Reforming Local Self-governance: Structural and Financial Aspects. 2005. Consortium for Economic Policy Research and Advice. Moscow: IET.

Regional Peculiarities of the Municipal Reform in the Period of Transition. 2007. Consortium for Economic Policy Research and Advice. Moscow: IET.

Shergelashvili, Tengiz and David Narmania. 2006. "Fiscal Equalization in Georgia", in Natela, Mshvidobadze ed., *Fiscal Equalization in Caucasus*. Budapest: Fiscal Decentralization Initiative for Central and Eastern Europe.

Slavgorodskaya, Margarita, Tatiana Letunova, Alexey Khrustalev. 2008. *Analysis of Financial Aspects of*

Local Self governance Reform Implementation. Moscow: IET. (in Russian)

Slukhai, Sergii and Ihor Tsekhanovskiy. 2011. "Ukrainian local finance under pressure: central and local governments respond" in Lucie Sedmihradska, Nadezhda Babcheva, Mihaly Lagos ed. *Local Government Finance in Times of Crisis: An Early Assessment.* NISPAcee publication.

Tumanyan, David. 2010. "Local Self-government in the Republic of Armenia: Current Developments",in *D+.* Diputació Barcelona.

Tumanyan, David, David Losaberidze and Maise Gyullaliev. 2007. *Local Self-Government in South Caucasus: current situation and Prospects*. GTZ (in Russian).

Tumanyan, David ed. 2007. *Local Self-government Reforms in Armenia (2004-2006). Book 2.* Communities Finance Officers Association.

Tumanyan, David. 2006. "Fiscal Equalization in Armenia" in Natela, Mshvidobadze ed., *Fiscal Equalization in Caucasus*. Budapest: Fiscal Decentralization Initiative for Central and Eastern Europe.

Tumanyan, David, ed. 2009. *Local Self-government Reforms in Armenia (2007 and 2008). Book 3.* Communities Finance Officers Association.

Tumanyan, David. 2009 [2]. "Local Self-Government in Armenia", in Tumanyan, David ed., *Local Self-Governmment in South Caucasus: local finance and services, central-local relations* (in Russian).

Veverita, Eugenia. 2006. "Fiscal Equalization: The Case of the Republic of Moldova", in Gabor Peteri ed., *Fiscal Equalization in South Eastern Europe.* Budapest: Fiscal Decentralization Initiative for Central and Eastern Europe.

World Development Indicators, World Bank, Washington, DC.

Europe

Bergvall, Daniel, Claire Charbit, Dirk-Jan Kraan and Olaf Merk. 2006. *Intergovernmental Transfers and Decentralised Public Spending*. Working Paper, No. 3, OECD Network on Fiscal Relations Across Levels of Government, OECD, Paris.

Bibbee, Alexandra. 2008. *Making Federalism Work in Italy.* Economics Department Working Paper, No. 590, OECD, Paris.

Blöchliger, Hansjörg, Claire Charbit, José Maria Pinero Campos and Camila Vammalle. 2010. *Sub-Central Governments and the Economic Crisis: Impact and Policy Responses.* Economics Department Working Paper, No. 752, OECD, Paris.

Blom-Hansen, Jens. 2003. "Is Private Delivery of Public Services Really Cheaper? Evidence from Public Road Maintenance in Denmark", *Public Choice*, Vol. 115, pp. 419-38.

Buettner, Thiess. 2001. "Local Business Taxation and Competition for Capital: The Choice of the Tax Rate", *Regional Science and Urban Economics*, Vol. 31, pp. 215-45.

Carlsen, Frederik. 1995. "Why Is Central Regulation of Local Spending Decisions so Pervasive? Evidence from a Case Study", *Public Budgeting and Finance*, Vol. 15, pp. 43-57.

CDLR. 2009. "The Impact of the Economic Downturn on Local Government: What is Happening and What Can Be Done about It?" Report to the Council of Europe, *European Committee on Local and Regional Democracy*, Strasbourg.

CEMR. 2009a. "Balancing Democracy, Identity and Efficiency: Changes in Local and Regional Structures in Europe", Council of European Municipalities and Regions.

CEMR. 2009b. "The Economic and Financial Crisis: Impact on Local and Regional Authorities", Council of European Municipalities and Regions.

CEMR. 2009c. "Social Dialogue in the Local and Regional Government Sector: An Overview", Council of European Municipalities and Regions.

Christoffersen, Henrik, Martin Paldam and Allan H. Wurtz. 2007. "Public versus Private Production and Economies of Scale", *Public Choice*, Vol. 130, pp. 311-28.

de Mello, Luiz. 2000. "Fiscal Decentralization and Intergovernmental Fiscal Relations: A Cross-Country Analysis", *World Development*, Vol. 28, pp. 365-80.

de Mello, Luiz. 2008. "Local Government Finances: The link between Intergovernmental Transfers and Net Worth", in G.K. Ingram and Y.H. Hong eds., *Fiscal Decentralization and Land Policies* (Cambridge, MA: Lincoln Institute).

DEXIA 2008. *Sub-National Governments in the European Union: Organisation, Responsibilities and Finance*, DEXIA Editions, Paris.

EUROSTAT. 2009. *February 2009.* European Commission.

Heyndels Bruno and Jeff Vuchelen. 1998. "Tax Mimicking among Belgian Municipalities", *National Tax Journal*, Vol. 51, pp. 89-101.

Hulst, Rudy and André van Montfort. 2007. *Inter-Municipal Cooperation in Europe*. Springer.

Magnussen, J., T.P. Hagen and O.M. Kaarboe . 2007. "Centralized or Decentralized? A Case Study of Norwegian Hospital Reform", *Social Science and Medicine*, Vol. 64, 2129-37.

OECD. 1999. *Decentralising Employment Policy: Trends and Challenges*. OECD, Paris.

OECD. 2003. *OECD Economic Outlook*, Chapter 3, OECD, Paris.

OECD. 2006. *Projecting OECD Health and Long-Term Care Expenditures: What Are the Main Drivers?.* OECD Economics Department Working Papers, No. 477, OECD, Paris.

OECD. 2009a. *OECD Employment Outlook*, OECD, Paris.

OECD. 2009b. *OECD Interim Economic Outlook*, March, OECD, Paris.

OECD. 2009c. *OECD Economic Outlook*, No. 86, December, OECD, Paris.

OECD. 2010. *OECD Economic Outlook,* No. 87, June, OECD, Paris.

Richard, Jean-François, Henry Tolkens and Magali Verdonck. 2002. "Dynamiques des Interactions Fiscales entre les Communes Belges 1984-97", *Économie et Prévisions*, Vol. 156, pp. 1-14.

Solé-Ollé, Albert. 2003. "Electoral Accountability and Tax Mimicking: The Effects of Electoral Margins, Coalition Governments and Ideology", *European Journal of Political Economy*, Vol. 19, pp. 685-713.

Sutherland, Douglas, Robert Price and Isabelle Joumard. 2005. "Sub-Central Government Fiscal Rules", *OECD Economic Studies*, Vol. 41, pp. 141-81.

WHO. 2008. *Decentralized Health Systems in Transition*, World Health Organization. Geneva.

World Bank. 2009. *World Development Indicators 2009.* The World Bank.

Wurzel, Eckhard. 1999. *Towards More Efficient Government: Reforming Federal Fiscal Relations in Germany.* OECD Economics Department Working Paper, No. 209, OECD, Paris.

Latin America

Abers, R. N. 2000. "Inventing Local Democracy. Grassroots Politics in Brazil". Boulder: Lynne Rienner Publishers.

Acosta, Olga Lucía and Richard Bird. 2005. "The Dilemma of Decentralization in Colombia" in Richard Bird, James Porteba and Joel Slemrod ed., *Fiscal Reform in Colombia: Problems and Prospects, 247-286. Cambridge. MA: The MIT Press.*

Afonso, José Roberto. 2006. "Decentralization and Budget Management of local Government in Brazil". http://info.worldbank.org/etools/docs/library /233842/Afonso.pdf

Afonso, José Roberto, Érika Amorim Araújo, and Geraldo Biasoto Jr. 2005. *Fiscal Space and Public Investments in Infrastructure: A Brazil Case Study.* Texto para Discussão n. 1141. Brasília: Institute of Applied Economic Research. http://www.ipea.gov.br /pub/td /2005/td_1141.pdf

Arze, F. y J. Martínez-Vázquez. 2004. "Descentralización en América Latina desde una perspectiva de países pequeños: Bolivia, El Salvador, Ecuador y Nicaragua".*Gestión y Política Pública*, 13, 3: 619-661.

Autonomia Local, Descentralización y Desarrollo Municipal en Latinoamérica. Capitulo Latinoamericano de la Union Internacional de Municipios y Autoridades Locales (IULA). Cuaderno del Centro Latinoamericano de Capacitación y Desarrollo de los Gobiernos Locales, IULA/CELCADEL.

Bahl, Roy, and Johannes Linn. 1992. *Urban Public Finance in Developing Countries*. Washington, D.C. World Bank and Oxford University Press.

Bahl, Roy, and Jorge Martínez-Vázquez. 2006. "Sequencing Fiscal Decentralization Reform" in R. Ebel and G. Peteri eds., *Decentralization Briefing Notes*. Open Society Institute. Budapest.

Bahl, Roy and Jorge Martínez-Vázquez. 2008. "The Determinants of Revenue Performance", in Bahl, Roy, Martínez-Vázquez and Youngman eds., *Making the Property Tax Work: Experiences in Developing and Transitional Countries*. Lincoln Institute of Land Policies, Cambridge, Massachusetts.

Bahl, Roy, Jorge Martínez-Vázquez and Joan Youngman. 2008. *Making the Property Tax Work.* Lincoln Institute of Land Policy, Cambridge, Massachusetts.

Bahl, Roy, Jorge Martínez-Vázquez and Joan Youngman. 2010. *Challenging the Conventional Wisdom on the Property Tax.* Lincoln Institute of Land Policy, Cambridge, Massachusetts.

Banco Central do Brasil.2000 – Focus (February 6), http://www4.bcb.gov.br/Pec/Gci/Ingl/Focus/ F20000605-Tax%20Re form.pdf

Banco Mundial. Abril de 2007. *Paraguay - Impuesto Inmobiliario: Herramienta Clave para la Descentralización Fiscal y el Mejor Uso de la Tierra Volumen I: Informe Principal.* Informe No. 37456-PA. Unidad de Reducción de la Pobreza y Gestión Económica Región de América Latina y el Caribe.

Banco Mundial. 2004. *Perú: Estudio de la Situación de la Deuda Municipal.*

Batista Domínguez, Abel A. Panamá. Régimen Jurídico del Municipio. In *Régimen Jurídico Municipal en Iberoamérica*. Cienfuegos Salgado, David (coordinador). Instituto de investigaciones Jurídicas, Universidad nacional Autónoma de México, 2008. http://www.bibliojuridica.org/libros/ 6/2545/20.pdf

BID, Federacion de Municipios del Istmo Centroamericano (FEMICA), Fondo Suizo de Cooperacion Tecnica/BID. Departamento Regional de Operaciones para el Istmo Centroamericano, México, República Dominicana y Haití. *La modernización de las finanzas municipales un paso esencial para la consolidación institucional.* Editores

Huáscar Eguino y Fabrice Henry. Anales del seminario realizado en la quinta reunión de la Red Centroamericana para la Descentralización y el Fortalecimiento Municipal. Antigua, Guatemala 18-20 de septiembre de 1998.

BID. Agosto, 2007. *Aportes para el Desarrollo del Sistema Financiero Municipal: El papel de los ingresos propios municipales, estudio para los países del cono sur. País: Uruguay*. Proyecto Regional RG-P1186. Estudio preparado por: Daniel Sureda, Consultor Coordinador del Proyecto: Huáscar Eguino Especialista en Desarrollo Urbano y Municipal.

Bird, Richard M. 2003. *Taxation in Latin America: Reflections on Sustainability and the Balance between Equity and Efficiency.* International Tax Program Papers 0306, International Tax Program, Institute for International Business, Joseph L. Rotman School of Management, University of Toronto.

Bird, Richard M. and Enid Slack. *The Role of the Property Tax in Financing Rural Local Governments in Developing Countries*. ITP Paper 0608, http://www.rotman.utoronto.ca /iib/ITP0608.pdf

Cardona Recinos, Rakael. 2006. "Honduras: Debilidad estructural de la autonomía municipal" in *Los Gobiernos Locales y la Decentralización del Estado en Centroamérica.* Diputació Barcelona.

Caribbean Update, June 1, 2002.

Castaneda, Tarsicio. 1986. *Innovations in the Financing of Education: The Case of Chile*. A World Bank Discussion Paper, Education and Training Series. Washington, DC.

CEPAL. David Glejberman. Diciembre del 2005. *El sistema municipal y la superación de la pobreza y precariedad urbana en Uruguay.* División Desarrollo Sostenible y Asentamientos Humanos. Santiago de Chile.

Constitución de la Provincia de Córdoba (Argentina), http://www.mininterior.gov.ar /municipales /regimen/archivos/cordoba.doc

Constitución de la nación Argentina, http://www .argentina.gov.ar/argentina/portal/documentos/con stitucion_nacional.pdf

Constitución de la República (Uruguay), http://www .parlamento.gub.uy/constituciones/const004.htm

Constitución de la República Bolivariana de Venezuela, http://www.venezuela-oas.org/Constitu cion%20de%20Venezuela.htm

Constitución Política de Colombia, http://www.banrep .gov.co/regimen/resoluciones/cp91.pdf

Constitución Política de Nicaragua y sus reformas, http://www.bcn.gob.ni/banco/legislacion/constitucio n.pdf

CSIS. Katherine Bliss Peter DeShazo. Enero de 2009. *El control de la corrupción en los gobiernos locales de América Latina.* Center For Strategic & International Studies. Documentos de Política sobre las Américas. Volumen XX Estudio 1.

Daughters, R. and L. Harper. 2007. "Fiscal and Political Decentralization Reforms", in E. Lora ed., *The State of State Reform in Latin America*. Inter-American Development Bank, Washington, D.C.

De Cesare, Claudia, and José Francisco Lazo Marín. 2008. *Impuestos a los patrimonios en América Latina*. Serie Macroeconomía del Desarrollo No.66, Comisión Económica para América Latina y el Caribe (CEPAL), Naciones Unidas.

Deloitte Touche Tohmatsu. 2010. *International Tax Business Guide Brazil 2010*.

http://www.deloitte.com/assets/DcomGlobal/Local %20Assets/Documents/Tax/Intl%20Tax%20and%2 0Business%20Guides/2010/dtt_tax_guide_2010_Br azil.pdf

Dunin, Lubomir Ficinski. 2000. *Decentralizing City Management: A Successful Experiment.* World Bank, Washington, D.C.

Eaton, Kent. 2004. "Designing Subnational Institutions: Regional and Municipal Reforms in Postauthoritarian Chile". Comparative Political Studies, Vol. 37, No. 2, March 2004, pp. 218-44.

Faguet, Jean-Paul and Fabio Sanchez. 2006. "Decentralization's Effects on Educational Outcomes in Bolivia and Colombia", *STICERD - Development Economics Papers 47*, Suntory and Toyota International Centres for Economics and Related Disciplines, LSE.

Faguet, Jean-Paul. 2004. "Does decentralization increase government responsiveness to local needs?: Evidence from Bolivia". Journal of Public Economics, Elsevier, vol. 88(3-4), 867-893, March.

French Ministry of Foreign Affairs. 2005. *Decentralization Policies in Latin America*.

Gamba Ladino, Julio C. Colombia. 2008. "Régimen municipal", in *Régimen Jurídico Municipal en Iberoamérica*. Cienfuegos Salgado, David (coordinador). Instituto de investigaciones Jurídicas, Universidad nacional Autónoma de México. http://www.bibliojuridica.org /libros/6/2545/9.pdf

Goldfrank, Benjamin. 2006. "Los procesos de presupuesto participativo en América Latina: Exito, fracaso y cambio". *Revista de Ciencia Política* Political Science Journal, Political Science Institute, Catholic University of Chile, 26:2 (December).

Government of Brazil. 2009. *Taxes on Consumption of Goods and Services in Brazil.* https://www.receita .gov.br/publico/estudotributarios/Eventos/Especialis tasPoliticaTributaria/Taxes%20on%20Consumption

%20of%20Goods%20and%20Services%20in%20Brazil%20-%20Raimundo %20Carvalho.pdf

GPC, Grupo Propuesta Ciudadana. Abril de 2007. *Vigilancia del proceso de descentralización.* Reporte Nacional Nro. 11, Balance 2003-2006. Participa Perú, Vigila Perú.

Gustafson, Lowell S.. 1990. "Factionalism, Centralism and Federalism in Argentina". *Publius: The Journal of Federalism,* 20 (Summer): 163-176.

Imansyah, Muhammad Handry and Jorge Martínez-Vázquez. 2010. *Understanding Sub-National Government Fragmentation in Indonesia*. Asian Development Bank and University of Indonesia.

International Budget Partnership. 2005. *The Latin American Index of Budget Transparency.* http://www.internationalbud get.org/themes/BudTrans/LA05.htm

International Monetary Fund. January 2006. *Paraguay: Report on observance of standards and codes—Fiscal Transparency Module.* IMF Country Report No. 06/14.

KPMG. 2006. *International Corporate Tax Brazil #16*, (November). http://www.kpmg.com.br/publicacoes/tax /ITB/KPMG_ITB_16_Recent_Changes.pdf

Letelier, Leonardo. 2003. "La descentralización fiscal en el contexto de los gobiernos regionales chilenos", in *A diez años de la creación de los gobiernos regionales: evaluaciones y proyecciones.* Santiago: Subsecretaría de Desarrollo Regional y Administrativo.

Ley 136 de 1994 (ley municipal). Colombia. http://www.medellin.gov.co/ManualContratacion/Normatividad/LEY 20136 20de 20199 4.doc

Ley No. 40 Ley de los Municipios. Nicaragua. http://www.femica.org/archivos/codigonicaragua.pdf

Ley Orgánica de las Municipalidades. Prov. De Buenos Aires-Argentina. http://www.tribctas.gba.gov.ar/secciones/inf_especifica/informacionlegal/leyOrganicaMunicipales/LEY%20ORGANICA%20DE%20LAS%20MUNICIPALIDADES.doc

Ley Orgánica del Poder Público Municipal. Venezuela. http://www.fides.gob.ve/DOCS /LOPPM.doc

Ley Orgánica Municipal. Prov. De Córdoba-Argentina. http://www.villasantarosa.gov.ar/bajando_legislacion.php?id=ley_8102.pdf

Ley Orgánica Municipal 9515. Uruguay. http://www.parlamento.gub.uy/leyes/AccesoTextoLey.asp?Ley=09515&Anchor

López Ghio, María C. Argentina. "Algunos aspectos del régimen municipal", in *Régimen Jurídico Municipal en Iberoamérica*. Cienfuegos Salgado, David (coordinador). Instituto de Investigaciones Jurídicas, Universidad Nacional Autónoma de México, 2008. http://www .bibliojuridica.org/libros/6 /2545/5.pdf

Martínez-Vázquez, Jorge and Juan Luis Gómez Reino. 2008. "El tamaño importa: la estructura vertical de gobierno y la gestión del gasto público local". Presentado en la conferencia del CAF: "*Las Promesas y las Realidades de la Descentralización Fiscal en América Latina*" Lima 4 de Diciembre 2008.

Martínez-Vázquez, Jorge and Bob Searle eds., 2007. *Fiscal Equalization: Challenges in the Design of Intergovernmental Transfers*. Springer.

Martínez-Vázquez, Jorge and Andrey Timofeev. 2005. "Choosing between Centralized and Decentralized Models of Tax Administration", in N. Bosch and J.M. Duran eds., *Financiación, solidaridad interterritorial y políticas tributarias de las comunidades autónomas*. Edicions i Publicacions de la Universitat de Barcelona : Barcelona (in Spanish) and Internacional Studies Working Paper #05-2, Andrew Young School of Policy Studies, Georgia State University, Atlanta (in English).

Ministerio de Economía y Finanzas – *MEF. Glosario del SIAF – MEF.* Peru.

Ministerio de Economia y Finanzas - MEF. *Boletín de transparencia fiscal - Informe especial procesos de descentralización en Latinoamérica: Colombia, México, Chile y Perú*. Perú.

Ministerio de la Presidencia. Julio 2004. *Ecuador: Los presupuestos de los gobiernos seccionales y la Asamblea Constituyente de 1997-8 Silke Lechner.* Unidad de Coordinación de la Asamblea Constituyente - Componente Descentralización y Administración Pública. La Paz.

Ministry of Finance. n.d. *The Brazilian Tax System*. Ministry of Finance, Brasília. http://www.receita.fazenda.gov.br/principal/Ingles/SistemaTributarioBR/BrazilianTaxSystem/default.htm

Nassuno, M. 2006. *Burocracia e Participao: A Experienca Do Orcamento Participativo Em Porto Alegre*. Tese de doutorado. Universidade de Brasilia.

Nickson, R. Andrew. 1995. *Local Government in Latin America*, Lynne Rienner Publishers, Boulder.

Oxford Analytica. December 2006. *Peru Fiscal Transparency.* Country Report 2006.

Oxford Analytica. December 2006. *Venezuela Fiscal Transparency.* Country Report 2006.

Parry, Taryn Rounds. 1997. "Achieving Balance in Decentralization: A Case Study of Education Decentralization in Chile". *World Development*, Vol. 25, No. 2, pp. 211-25.

Peterson, George. 1996. *Building Local Credit Systems.* UNDP/UNCHS (Habitat) /World.

Porto, Alberto. 2009. *Perfiles del sector público municipal en países del cono sur y de la región andina.* Banco Interamericano de Desarrollo, Washington, D.C.

Purohit, Mahesh C. 1997. "Value Added Tax in a Federal Structure: A Case Study of Brazil". Economic and Political Weekly, Vol. 32, No. 7 (Feb. 15-21, 1997), pp. 357-362, The World Bank, Washington, D.C.

Rezende, Fernando, and José Roberto Afonso. 2006. "The Brazilian Federation: Facts, Challenges, and Prospects", in Jessica Wallack and T. N. Srinivasan ed., *Federalism and Economic Reform: International Perspectives*, 143–88. New York: Cambridge University Press.

Rotondo Tornaría, Felipe. 2008. Uruguay. El municipio. En *Régimen jurídico municipal en Iberoamérica*. Cienfuegos Salgado, David (coordinador). Instituto de Investigaciones Jurídicas, Universidad Nacional Autónoma de México. http://www.bibliojuridica.org /libros/6/2545/23.pdf

Santos, B. (org.). *2004. Democratizar a Democracia. Os Caminhos da Democracia Participativa*. Rio de Janeiro: Civilização Brasileira.

Saravia Aldana, Mario Danilo. 2008. "Nicaragua. Régimen del municipio". In *Régimen Jurídico Municipal en Iberoamérica*, Cienfuegos Salgado, David (coordinador). Instituto de investigaciones Jurídicas, Universidad nacional Autónoma de México. http://www.bibliojuridica.org/libros/6/2545/19.pdf

Sepulveda, Cristian and Jorge Martínez-Vázquez. 2009. *Explaining Property Tax Collections in Developing Countries: The Case of Latin America*. Paper prepared for CEPAL.

Shah, Anwar (editor). 2006. *Public expenditure analysis for citizen-centered governance.* The World Bank Washington D.C.

Shah, Anwar (editor). 2006. *Local public financial management.* The World Bank Washington D.C.

Shah, Anwar (editor). 2006. *Local governance in developing countries.* The World Bank Washington D.C.

Shah, Anwar (editor). 2007. *Participatory Budgeting*. Washington, DC: World Bank Institute, Public Sector Governance and Accountability Series.

Sirtaine, S. 2005. *Financing Sources for Infrastructure Projects in LAC*. World Bank, Washington, D.C.

Smoke, Paul, Eduardo J. Gomez, and George E. Peterson (Editors). 2006. *Decentralization in Asia And Latin America: A Comparative Interdisciplinary Perspective*. Studies in Fiscal Federalism and State-Local Finance, Edgard Elgar.

Subsecretaria de Desarrollo Regional y Administrativo. 2007. *Memoria de la Descentralización*. Gobierno de Chile.

Tulchin, Joseph S. and Andrew Selee. 2004. *Decentralization and Democratic Governance in Latin America*. Woodrow Wilson Center Report on the Americas #12. Washington, D.C.

United Cities and Local Governments. 2008. *Decentralization and Local Democracy in the World: First Global Report.* World Bank and CGLU.

Uribe, Maria C. Bogota's Betterment Levy. Conference on Unlocking Urban Land Values for Infrastructure Finance, Bangalore (India) September 14th, 2009. http://indiausp.org /brookings/Bogota-Betterment-Levy.pdf

Villegas Moreno, José L. Venezuela. 2008. "El municipio. Aproximación a su configuración en el nuevo ordenamiento constitucional y legal", in *Régimen Jurídico Municipal en Iberoamérica*. Cienfuegos Salgado, David (coordinador). Instituto de Investigaciones Jurídicas, Universidad Nacional Autónoma de México. http://www.bibliojuri dica.org /libros/6/2545/24.pdf

Von Haldenwang, Christian, Elke Büsing, Katharina Földi, Tabea Goldboom, Ferdinand Jenrich and Jens Pulkowski. 2009. *Administración tributaria municipal en el contexto del proceso de descentralización en el Perú.* Deutsches Institut für Entwicklungspolitik.

World Bank. 1998. *Impact Evaluation Report, Building Institutions and Financing Local Development: Lessons from Brazil and the Philippines.*

World Bank. 1999. World Development Report 1998/99. *Knowledge for Development. Summary*. Washington: Oxford University Press.

Middle East West Asia

Adib, Mustapha. 2008. "Middle East/ Western Asia", in *Decentralization and Local Democracy in the World, First Global Report*. United Cities and Local Governments: 200-229.

Al-Hajaj, Muaffak. 2010. Director of Follow up and Evaluation, Ministry of Public Sector Development "Local Government Finance in Jordan" Presentation during the UCLG organized workshop in Istanbul 15 march 2010.

Al-Hajjeh, Tamer. 2009. "Development of the Local Administration Structure in Syria", *in Euro Syrian Cities Congress*. Minister of Local Administration.

Arzhagi, Mohammed and J. Vernon Henderson. 2005. "Why Countries are Fiscally Decentralizing", in *Journal of Public Economics*, 89, 1157-1189.

Atallah, Sami. 1999. *The legal and administrative dimensions of municipalities in Lebanon*, Interventions during CERMOC symposium in Beirut 17 April 1999, Cermoc 1999 document nº4, Municipal finance in Lebanon (as referenced by Bassil, Najwa & Karam Karam. 2009)

Barkey, Karen. 2008. *Empire of Difference: The Ottomans in Comparative Perspective*. New York, NY: Cambridge University Press.

Bassil, Najwa & Karam Karam. 2009. *Local Finance in Lebanon*. Study realized for UCLG/BTVL.

Beck, Thorston, George Clarke, Alberto Groff, Phillip Keefer and Patrick Walsh. 2001. "New Tools in Comparative Political Economy: The Database of Political Institutions", *The World Bank Economic Review*, 15 (1): 165-176.

Doherty, Pat. 2005. *Municipal Administration Modernization Project in Syria: Report on Financial Resources Management, Local Taxes / Duties, Evaluation of Current Position, Proposals for interventions.* Municipal Administration Modernization Programme (MAM).

Ebel, Robert D. and Serdar Yilmaz. 2003. "On the Measurement and Impact of Decentralization", in Jorge Martínez-Vázquez and James Alm, *Public Finance in Developing and Transitional Countries: Essays in Honor of Richard Bird.* pp 101-119. Cheltenham, UK: Edward Elgar.

Ecevit, Bulent. 1990. *Mithat Pasa ve Turk Ekonomisinin Tarihsel Sureci – Mithat Pasha and Historical Continuum of the Turkish Economy*, Demokratik Sol Parti. Istanbul: Tekin Yayinevi.

Economic Research Forum (ERF). 2005. *Jordan Country Profile: The Road Ahead for Jordan* (August). Cairo, Egypt: the Economic Research Forum and Institut de la Mediterranee.

Hammond, George and Mehmet S. Tosun. 2011. "The Impact of Local Decentralization on Economic Growth: Evidence from U.S. Counties", *Journal of Regional Science*. 51 (1): 47-64.

Hanna, Nelly. 1995. *The State and its Servants: Administration in Egypt from Ottoman Times to the Present*. Cairo, Egypt: The American University in Cairo Press.

Inalcik, Halil. 1977. "Centralization and Decentralization in Ottoman Administration", in Thomas Naff and Roger Owen ed., *Studies in Eighteenth-Century Islamic History*. Carbondale: Southern Illinois University Press, 27-52.

Jordan Ministry of Municipal Affairs. 2009. *Jordan Resource Transfer Pool and Allocation to Municipalities Bulletin,* No. 01. Regional Planning/Development and International Programs Department, September 15.

Keefer, Philip. 2007. *DPI2006, Database of Political Institutions: Changes and Variable Definitions.* http://siteresources.worldbank .org/INTRES /Resources/469232-1107449512766/dpi2006_vote _share_variable_definitions.pdf

Milton-Edwards, Beverly and Peter Hinchcliffe. 2004. *Conflicts in the Middle East Since 1945*. New York, NY: Routledge.

Municipal Administration Modernization Syria (n.d.). Retrieved from http://www.mam-sy. org/index.php ?p_id=11&lang=en.

OECD. 2004. OECD *Economic Surveys Turkey*. Volume 2004/15-December. OECD.

Saliba, Najib E. 1978. "The Achievements of Midhat Pasha as Governor of the Province of Syria, 1878-1880", *International Journal of Middle East Studies* 9 (3): 307-323.

Tajbakhsh, Kian. 2000. "Political Decentralization and the Creation of Local Governments in Iran: Consolidation or Transformation of the Theocratic State?", *Social Research* 67 (2): 210-222.

Tosun, Mehmet S. and Arzu Sen. 2008. "Preventing Regional Conflicts as a Global Public Good: the Case of the MENA Region". manuscript.

Tosun, Mehmet S. and Serdar Yilmaz. 2010a. "Centralization, Decentralization and Conflict in the Middle East and North Africa", *Middle East Development Journal* 2 (1):1-14.

Tosun, Mehmet S. and Serdar Yilmaz. 2010b. "Decentralization, Economic Development, and Growth in Turkish Provinces", *Emerging Markets Finance and Trade* 46 (4): 23-44.

Tosun, Mehmet S. and Serdar Yilmaz. 2008. *Centralization, Decentralization and Conflict in the Middle East and North Africa*. World Bank Policy Research Working Paper No.4774. Washington, D.C.: The World Bank.

Turkish Ministry of Interior, General Directorate for Local Authorities. 2009. Mahalli Idareler Genel Faaliyet Raporu, 2008. http://www.mahalli-idarele r.gov.tr/Home /Dokumanlar/faaliyet_raporu.pdf.

UCLG. 2007. *UCLG Country Profiles: The Hashemite Kingdom of Jordan.* Retrieved from http://www .cities-localgovernments.org /gold/Upload/country _profile/Jordan.pdf

UNDP Programme on Governance in the Arab Region (POGAR). 2010a. *Country Theme: Local Government: Jordan*. Retrieved from http://www .pogar.org/countries/theme.aspx?t=6&cid=7

UNDP Programme on Governance in the Arab Region (POGAR). 2010b. *Country Theme: Local Government: Lebanon*. Retrieved from http:// www.pogar.org/countries/theme.aspx?t=6&cid=9

UNDP Programme on Governance in the Arab Region (POGAR). 2010c. *Country Theme: Local Government: Saudi Arabia*. Retrieved from http:// www.pogar.org/countries/theme .aspx?t=6&cid=16

World Bank. 2006. *West Bank and Gaza: Intergovernmental Fiscal Relations and Municipal*

Finance Policy Note. Report Number. 36519-WBG, World Bank, Washington, DC.

North America

American Society of Civil Engineers. 2009. 2009 Report Card for America's Infrastructure, March 25.

Anderson, John, 1990. "Tax Increment Financing: Municipal Adoption and Growth", National Tax Journal, 155-164.

Augustine, Nancy Y., Michael E. Bell, David Brunori, and Joan M. Youngman eds., 2009. *Erosion of the Property Tax Base, Trends, Causes, and Consequences.* Cambridge, MA: Lincoln Institute of Land Policy.

Bartik, Timothy J. 1991. *Who Benefits from State and Local Economic Development Policies?* Kalamazoo, MI: W.E. Upjohn Institute.

Benton, J. Edwin. 2009. "Trends in Local Government Revenues: The Old, The New, and The Future", presented at the 2009 Lincoln Institute of Land Policy Conference, *The Changing Landscape of Local Public Revenues.* Cambridge, MA: June 2009.

Besley, Timothy and Harvey Rosen. 1998. "States' Responses to Federal Tax Setting: Evidence from Gasoline and Cigarettes", Journal of Public Economics 73.

Bird, Richard, M. and Enid Slack. 2003. *International Handbook on Land and Property Taxation.* Cheltenham, UK: Edward Elgar.

Bird, Richard M. and Michael Smart, 2002. *Intergovernmental Fiscal Transfers: International lessons for developing countries.* World Development, 30.

Bird, Richard, M. and Almos Tassonyi. 2001. "Constraints on Provincial and Municipal Borrowing in Canada: Markets, Rules, and Norms". Canadian Public Administration, 44.

Bird, Richard M. and Almos Tassonyi. 2003. "Constraining Subnational Fiscal Behavior in Canada: Different Approaches, Similar Results?" in Rodden, Jonathan A., Gunnar S. Eskeland, and Jennie Litvack eds., *Fiscal Decentralization and the Challenge of Hard Budget Constraints.* Cambridge, MA: MIT Press.

Bird, Richard M., and Francois Vaillancourt 1998. "Fiscal Decentralization in Developing Countries: An Overview", in Richard M. Bird and Francois Vaillancourt ed., *Fiscal Decentralization in Developing Countries.* Cambridge, UK: Cambridge University Press.

Bruce, Donald, William F. Fox, and LeAnn Luna. 2009. "State and Local Government Sales Tax Revenue Losses from E-Commerce", State Tax Notes, May 18, 2009.

Brunori, David. 2003. "Local Tax Policy: A Federalist Perspective". Washington, DC: The Urban Institute Press.

Courchene, Thomas J. 2005. *Citistates and the State of Cities: Political-Economy and Fiscal-Federalism Dimensions.* Montreal: Institute for Research on Public Policy.

Courchene, Thomas, J. 2004. "Hourglass Federalism – How the Feds Got the Provinces to Run Out of Money in a Decade of Liberal Budgets". Policy Options, April, 2004.

Esteller-More, Alex and Albert Sole-Olle. 2001. "Vertical Income Tax Externalities and Fiscal Interdependence: Evidence from the U.S"., Regional Science and Urban Economics 31: 247-72.

Federation of Canadian Municipalities. 2008. *Innovative Mechanisms for Fiscal Transfers to Municipalities – The Canadian Experience in Municipal Financing.* Ottawa: FCM.

Gallo, Theresa. 2004. "History and Evaluation of the Unfunded Mandates Reform Act", National Tax Journal, 57.

Garcia-Mila, Teresa, and Therese J. Mc Guire. 2002. *Tax Incentives and the City.* Brookings-Wharton Papers on Urban Affairs.

Gendron, Pierre-Pascal. 2005. "Value Added Treatment of Public Sector Bodies and Non-Profit Organizations: A Developing Country Perspective", Bulletin of International Fiscal Documentation, 59 (12).

Glaeser, Edwin. 2002. Comment on *Tax Incentives and the City*, Brookings-Wharton Papers on Urban Affairs.

Harchaoui, Tarek, M., Faouzi Tarkhani, and Paul Warren. 2004. "Public Infrastructure in Canada, 1961-2002", Canadian Public Policy, 30 (3).

Hoene, Christopher and Michael A. Pagano 2008. *Cities and State Fiscal Structure, Research Report on America's Cities.* Washington, DC: National League of Cities.

Karkalakos, Sotiris and Christos Kotsogiannis. 2007. "A Spatial Analysis of Provincial Corporate Income Tax Responses: Evidence from Canada", Canadian Journal of Economics 40.

Kitchen, Harry, M. 2006. *A State of Disrepair: How to Fix the Financing of Municipal Infrastructure in Canada.* Toronto: C.D. Howe Institute.

Kitchen, Harry M. and Enid Slack, "Special Report: New Finance Options for Municipal Governments". Canadian Tax Journal, Volume 51, Number 6, 2003.

Merriman, David and Mark Skidmore. 2000. "Did Distortionary Sales Taxation Contribute to the Growth of the Service Sector", National Tax Journal, March.

Mikesell, John. 2010. "State Sales Taxes in the Great Recession", State Tax Notes, July 19, 2010.

Mintz, Jack M. and Tom Roberts, 2006. *Running on Empty: A Proposal to Improve City Finances,* Toronto: C.D. Howe Institute.

Mirza, Saeed. 2007. *Danger Ahead: The Coming Collapse of Canada's Municipal Infrastructure.* A report prepared for the Federation of Canadian Municipalities, November 2007.

O'Sullivan, Arthur, Terri A. Sexton, and Steven M. Sheffrin. 1995. *Property Taxes and Tax Revolts: The Legacy of Proposition 13.* New York: Cambridge University Press.

Ring, Raymond. 1999. "Consumer's share and producer's share of the general sales tax" in *National Tax Journal*, 52, 79-90.

Sexton, Terri A. 2009. "Assessment Limits as a Means of Limiting Homeowner Property Taxes", In Augustine, Nancy, Y., Michael E. Bell, David Brunori, and Joan M. Youngman eds., *Erosion of the Property Tax Base, Trends Causes, and Consequences.* Cambridge, Mass.: Lincoln Institute of Land Policy.

Simeon, Richard and Martin Papillon. 2006 "Canada", in Akhtar Majeed, Ronald L. Watts, and Douglas M. Brown eds., *Distribution of Powers and Responsabilities in Federal Countries.* Global Dialogue on Federalism, Vol. 2. Montreal McGill-Queen's University Press. 91-122.

Slack, Enid. 2003. *Municipal Finance and the Pattern of Urban Growth.* Toronto: C.D. Howe Institute.

Slack, Enid. 2005. "Municipal Financing of Capital Infrastructure in North America", Journal of Property Tax Assessment and Administration, 2(1).

TD Economics. 2004. "Mind the Gap: Finding the Money to Upgrade Canada's Aging Infrastructure", Toronto, May.

TD Economics. 2004. "Mind the Gap: Finding the Money to Upgrade Canada's Aging Infrastructure, Toronto", 2004.

Vander Ploeg, Casey. 2004. "No Time to be Timid: Addressing Infrastructure Deficits in the Western Big Six", Western Cities Project Report #30, Calgary: Canada West Foundation, 2004.

Wassmer, Robert W. 2007. *Increasing Use of Property Tax Abatement as a Means of Promoting Sub-National Economic Activity in the United States.* Sacramento, CA: California State University.

Wassmer, Robert. 1990. "Can Local Incentives Alter a Metro City's Economic Development?" Urban Studies, 1994: 1251-1278.

Wasylenko, Michael, J. 1997. "Taxation and Economic Development: The State of the Economic Literature", New England Economic Review, March/April.

Winters, John. 2008. "An Overview of Property Tax Limitations". State Tax Notes.

Youngman, Joan. 1999. "The Hardest Challenge for Value-Based Property Taxes: Part I". State Tax Notes, March 1999.

Yuan, Bing, Joseph Cordes and David Brunori. 2009. "Tax and Expenditure Limitations and Local Public Finances", in Augustine, Nancy Y., Michael E. Bell, David Brunori, and Joan M. Youngman eds., *Erosion of the Property Tax Base, Trends, Causes, and Consequences*. Cambridge, MA: Lincoln Institute of Land Policy.

Financing Metropolitan Areas

Acosta, Olga Lucia and Richard Bird. 2005. "The Dilemma of Decentralization in Colombia" in Richard Bird, James Porterba and Joel Slemrod ed., *Fiscal Reform in Colombia: Problems and Prospects*, 247-286. Cambridge, MA: The MIT Press.

Bahl, Roy. 2010. *Financing Service Delivery in Metropolitan Areas.* International Studies Program, Andrew Young School of Policy Studies, Georgia State University, working paper.

Bahl, Roy and Johannes Linn. 1992. *Urban Public Finance in Developing Countries*. New York: Oxford University Press.

Bahl, Roy and David Solomon. 2003. "The Regional Service Council Levy", in Roy Bahl and Paul Smoke ed., *Restructuring Local Government Finance in Developing Countries: Lessons from South Africa*, 127-172. Cheltenham UK: Edward Elgar.

Bahl, Roy and Richard Bird. 2008. "Subnational Taxes in Developing Countries: The Way Forward" *Public Budgeting & Finance*, 28(4):1-25.

Benjamin, Gerald and Richard P. Nathan. 2001. *Regionalism and Realism: A Study of Governments in the New York Metropolitan Area.* Washington: Brookings Institution Press.

Bird, Richard and Enid Slack. 2004. *Fiscal Aspects of Metropolitan Governance.* Joseph T. Rotman School of Management, ITP Paper 0401, Toronto: University of Toronto.

Bird, Richard and Eric Zolt. 2005. "Redistribution via Taxation: The limited Role of the Personal Income Tax in Developing Countries", *UCLA Law Review,* August, 52 (6): 1627-1695.

Bordignon, Massimo, Silvia Giannini, and Paolo Panteghini. 2001. "Reforming business Taxation: Lessons from Italy?", *International Tax and Public Finance*, March, 8(2): 191-210.

Campbell, Alan K. and Guthrie Birkhead. 1976. "Municipal Reform Revisited: The 1970s Compared with the 1920s", in Alan Campbell and Roy Bahl ed., *State and Local Government: The Political Economy of Reform*, 1-15. New York: The Free Press.

Chernik, Howard and Andrew Reschovsky. 2006. "Local Public Finance: Issues for Metropolitan Regions" in *Competitive Cities in the Global Economy.* Paris: OECD Territorial Reviews, 415-432.

De Cesare, Claudia M. 2004. "General Characteristics of Property Tax Systems in Latin America". Paper presented at 7th International Conference on Optimizing Property Tax Systems in Latin America, Guadalajara, Jalisco, Mexico.

Diaz-Cayeros, Alberto and Charles McLure. 2000. "Tax Assignment", in Marcelo Giugale and Steven Webb ed., *Achievements and Challenges of Fiscal Decentralization*, 177-196. Washington: The World Bank.

Fu, Gao. 2007. "Urban Infrastructure Investment and Financing in Shanghai" in George Peterson and Patricia Annez ed., *Financing Cities: Fiscal Responsibility and Urban Infrastructure in Brazil, China, India, Poland and South Africa*, chapter 6. Los Angeles and Washington DC: Sage Publications and The World Bank.

International Monetary Fund Various Issues. *Government Finance Statistics,* Washington DC: International Monetary Fund.

Jouve, Bernard and Christian Lefevre, eds. 2002. *Local Power, Territory and Institutions in European Metropolitan Regions* London: Frank Cass.

Lotz, Jorgen 2006. "Local Government Organization and Finance: Nordic Countries" in Anwar Shah ed., *Local Governance in Industrial Countries*, 223-264. Washington DC: World Bank.

Martínez-Vázquez, Jorge. 2008. "Revenue Assignments in the practice of Fiscal Decentralization", in Nuria Bosch and Jose Duran, eds. *Fiscal Federalism and Political Decentralization: Lessons from Spain, Germany and Canada.* Edward Elgar Cheltenham, UK and Northampton, M.A.

Mathur, Om, Debdulal Thakur, Nilesh Rajadhyaksha and Roy Bahl. 2009. *Urban Property Tax Potential in India*. New Delhi: National Institute of Public Finance and Policy.

McLure, C.E. 1998. "The Revenue Assignment Problem: Ends, means and constraints". *Public Budgeting, Accounting and Financial Management*. Winter.

Mohanty, P.K., B.M. Misra, Rajan Goyal, and P.D. Jeromi. 2007. "Municipal Finance in India: An Assessment", Study No. 28. Development Research Group, Department of Economic Analysis and Policy, Mumbai: Reserve Bank of India.

Musgrave, Richard A. 1983. "Who Should Tax, Where and What?" in Charles E. McLure, Jr., ed., *Tax Assignment in Federal Countries.* Canberra: Centre for Research on Federal Financial Relations, Australian National University.

Oates, Wallace. 1972. *Fiscal Federalism* New York: Harcourt Brace Jovanovich.

OECD. 2003. "The Metropolitan Region of Melbourne, Australia", OECD Territorial Reviews.

OECD. 2004. "Busan, Korea", OECD Territorial Reviews.

OECD. 2004a "Mexico City", OECD Territorial Reviews.

OECD. 2006. "Competitive Cities in the Global Economy", OECD Territorial Reviews.

OECD. 2006a. "Stockholm, Sweden", OECD Territorial Reviews.

OECD. 2006b. "Milan, Italy", OECD Territorial Reviews.

OECD. 2007. "Madrid, Spain", OECD Territorial Reviews.

OECD. 2007a. "Randstadt Holland, Netherlands", OECD Territorial Reviews.

OECD. 2008. "Cape Town, South Africa", OECD Territorial Reviews.

OECD. 2008a. "Istanbul, Turkey", OECD Territorial Reviews.

OECD. 2009. "Copenhagen, Denmark", OECD Territorial Reviews.

OECD. 2009a. "Toronto, Canada", OECD Territorial Reviews.

Phares, Don. 2009a. "Prologue on Metropolitan Government and Governance" in Don Phares ed., *Governing Metropolitan Regions in the 21st Century*. London: Sharpe, xi-xvii.

Rezende, F. and S. Garson. 2006. "Financing Metropolitan Areas in Brazil", *Revista de economia contemporanea*, 10(1): 5-34.

RTI International. 2005. "Case Study on Mobilization of Private Capital in Bogota, Colombia", Research Triangle Park, North Carolina: RTI.

Slack, Enid. 2000. "A Preliminary Assessment of the New City of Toronto", *Canadian Journal of Regional Science* Spring, 2000 XXIII: 1, 13-29.

Slack, Enid. 2007. *Managing the Coordination of Service Delivery in Metropolitan Cities: The Role of Metropolitan Governance.* Policy Research Working paper 4317 Washington: The World Bank.

Taliercio, Robert. 2005. "Subnational Own-Source Revenue: Getting Policy and Administration Right" in Roland White and Paul Smoke ed., *East Asia Decentralizes: Making Local Government Work*, 107-128. Washington: The World Bank.

Togo, Hisatake. 1995. "The Metropolitan Strategies of Tokyo: Toward the Restoration of Balanced Growth" in L.J. Sharpe ed., *The Government of World Cities: The Future of the Metro Model*, 177-202. Chichester, UK: Wiley.

Tokyo Metropolitan Government: 2006. 2010. http://www.metro.tokyo.jp/ENGLISH/PROFILE/index.htm

United Nations. 2008. *World Urbanization Prospects: The 2007 Revision*, New York: United Nations.

Webster, D. 2000. "Financing City Building: The Bangkok Case Discussion Paper" Asia Pacific Research Center, Institute for International Studies, Stanford University.

World Bank. 2007. *Brazil Sao Paulo: Inputs for a Sustainable Competitive City Strategy.* Report No. 37324-BR Washington: The World Bank.

World Bank. 2009. *Reshaping Economic Geography*, World Development Report Washington: The World Bank.